Lecture Notes in Computer Science 16623

Founding Editors

Gerhard Goos
Juris Hartmanis

Editorial Board Members

Elisa Bertino, *Purdue University, West Lafayette, IN, USA*
Wen Gao, *Peking University, Beijing, China*
Bernhard Steffen, *TU Dortmund University, Dortmund, Germany*
Moti Yung, *Columbia University, New York, NY, USA*

The series Lecture Notes in Computer Science (LNCS), including its subseries Lecture Notes in Artificial Intelligence (LNAI) and Lecture Notes in Bioinformatics (LNBI), has established itself as a medium for the publication of new developments in computer science and information technology research, teaching, and education.

LNCS enjoys close cooperation with the computer science R & D community, the series counts many renowned academics among its volume editors and paper authors, and collaborates with prestigious societies. Its mission is to serve this international community by providing an invaluable service, mainly focused on the publication of conference and workshop proceedings and postproceedings. LNCS commenced publication in 1973.

Vianey Guadalupe Cruz-Sánchez ·
Osslan Osiris Vergara-Villegas ·
Juan Humberto Sossa-Azuela ·
Jesús Ariel Carrasco-Ochoa ·
José Francisco Martínez-Trinidad ·
José Arturo Olvera-López
Editors

Pattern Recognition

18th Mexican Conference, MCPR 2026
Ciudad Juárez, Mexico, June 24–27, 2026
Proceedings

Editors
Vianey Guadalupe Cruz-Sánchez (iD)
Universidad Autónoma de Ciudad Juárez
Ciudad Juárez, Chihuahua, Mexico

Osslan Osiris Vergara-Villegas (iD)
Universidad Autónoma de Ciudad Juárez
Ciudad Juárez, Chihuahua, Mexico

Juan Humberto Sossa-Azuela (iD)
Centro de Investigación en Computación del
Instituto Politécnico Nacional (CIC-IPN)
Mexico, Distrito Federal, Mexico

Jesús Ariel Carrasco-Ochoa (iD)
Instituto Nacional de Astrofísica, Óptica y
Electrónica (INAOE)
Puebla, Mexico

José Francisco Martínez-Trinidad (iD)
Instituto Nacional de Astrofísica, Óptica y
Electrónica (INAOE)
Puebla, Mexico

José Arturo Olvera-López (iD)
Benemérita Universidad Autónoma de Puebla
(BUAP)
Puebla, Mexico

ISSN 0302-9743   ISSN 1611-3349 (electronic)
Lecture Notes in Computer Science
ISBN 978-3-032-28392-4   ISBN 978-3-032-28393-1 (eBook)
https://doi.org/10.1007/978-3-032-28393-1

This Springer imprint is published by the registered company Springer Nature Switzerland AG
The registered company address is: Gewerbestrasse 11, 6330 Cham, Switzerland

If disposing of this product, please recycle the paper.

Preface

The Mexican Conference on Pattern Recognition 2026 (MCPR 2026) was the 18th event in the series, this time organized by the Department of Computer Science of the Instituto Nacional de Astrofísica, Óptica y Electrónica (INAOE) of Mexico and the company Durol. The conference was hosted by the Mexican Association for Pattern Recognition (MexAPR), a member society of the International Association for Pattern Recognition (IAPR). MCPR 2026 took place in Ciudad Juárez, Chihuahua, Mexico, between June 24–27, 2026.

MCPR aims to provide a forum for the exchange of scientific results, practices, and new knowledge, and to promote collaboration among research groups in pattern recognition and related areas in Mexico and worldwide.

In this edition, as in previous years, MCPR 2026 attracted Mexican researchers and participation from all over the world. We received 58 manuscripts from authors in 7 countries: Brazil, Ireland, Japan, Mexico, Spain, the USA, and Vietnam. Each paper was strictly peer-reviewed by at least two members of the Program Committee. All members of the Program Committee are experts in many fields of pattern recognition. As a result of the single-blind peer review, 34 papers were accepted for presentation at the conference and included in these conference proceedings.

We were very honored to have as invited speakers such internationally recognized researchers as

- Erik Rodner, University of Applied Sciences Berlin, Germany.
- Walterio Mayol Cuevas, University of Bristol, UK.
- Salvador Elías Venegas Andaca, Instituto Tecnológico y de Estudios Superiores de Monterrey, Mexico.

The organizers of MCPR 2026 wish to express their profound appreciation to every individual whose dedication and hard work ensured the event's success. We are deeply indebted to the contributing authors for their scholarly input and to our distinguished keynote speakers, who enriched the conference with their specialized insights into pattern recognition. Furthermore, we express our sincere thanks to the Program Committee and our external reviewers; their meticulous evaluation and commitment to excellence were instrumental in upholding the rigorous standards and exceptional quality of this year's program.

We extend our deepest appreciation to Durol for their invaluable financial support, which was fundamental to this event's success. Beyond their generous support, we recognize their commitment to advancing technological development in Mexico and their vital role in bridging the gap between academic research and industrial applications, thereby fostering a collaborative ecosystem.

We are sure that MCPR 2026 provided a fruitful forum for Mexican pattern recognition researchers and the broader international pattern recognition community.

June 2026

Vianey Guadalupe Cruz-Sánchez
Osslan Osiris Vergara-Villegas
Juan Humberto Sossa-Azuela
Jesús Ariel Carrasco-Ochoa
José Francisco Martínez-Trinidad
José Arturo Olvera-López

Organization

General Conference Co-chairs

Vianey Guadalupe Cruz-Sánchez	Universidad Autónoma de Ciudad Juárez, Mexico
Osslan Osiris Vergara-Villegas	Universidad Autónoma de Ciudad Juárez, Mexico
Juan Humberto Sossa-Azuela	CIC-Instituto Politécnico Nacional, Mexico
Jesús Ariel Carrasco-Ochoa	Instituto Nacional de Astrofísica, Óptica y Electrónica, Mexico
José Francisco Martínez-Trinidad	Instituto Nacional de Astrofísica, Óptica y Electrónica, Mexico
José Arturo Olvera-López	Benemérita Universidad Autónoma de Puebla, Mexico

Local Arrangement Committee

Felipe Arias del Campo	Universidad Autónoma de Ciudad Juárez, Mexico
Elizabeth Burrola Meléndez	CIITA-Chihuahua-Instituto Politécnico Nacional, Mexico
Brenda Alicia Cervantes Cuahuey	Instituto Nacional de Astrofísica, Óptica y Electrónica, Mexico
Josué Domínguez Guerrero	Universidad Autónoma de Ciudad Juárez, Mexico
María Cristina Guevara Neri	Universidad Tecnológica Paso del Norte, Mexico
Erick Jair González Rivas	CIITA-Chihuahua-Instituto Politécnico Nacional, Mexico
Alicia Margarita Jiménez Galira	CIITA-Chihuahua-Instituto Politécnico Nacional, Mexico
Manuel de Jesus Nandayapa Alfaro	Universidad Autónoma de Ciudad Juárez, Mexico
René Noriega Armendariz	Universidad Autónoma de Ciudad Juárez, Mexico
Humberto de Jesús Ochoa Domínguez	Universidad Autónoma de Ciudad Juárez, Mexico
José Alfredo Olivas Acosta	Durol, Mexico
Alfredo Olivas Mendoza	Durol, Mexico
Elva Lilia Reynoso Jardón	Universidad Autónoma de Ciudad Juárez, Mexico
Everardo Santiago Ramírez	Universidad Autónoma de Ciudad Juárez, Mexico
Anabel Trejo Tejeda	Durol, Mexico

Program Committee

Antunes, F.	University of Coimbra, Portugal
Bernal, J.	Friedrich-Alexander University of Erlangen–Nuremberg, Germany
Biasotti, S.	IMATI-CNR, Italy
Borges, D. L.	Universidade de Brasília, Brazil
Cabrera, S.	University of Texas at El Paso, USA
Cancela, P.	Universidad de la República, Uruguay
Cimmino, L.	University of Salerno, Italy
Couto, P.	University of Trás-os-Montes and Alto Douro, Portugal
Escalante-Balderas, H. J.	Instituto Nacional de Astrofísica, Óptica y Electrónica, Mexico
Facon, J.	Pontifícia Universidade Católica do Paraná, Brazil
Fumera, G.	University of Cagliari, Italy
García-Borroto, M.	Universidad de La Habana, Cuba
Grau, A.	Universitat Politècnica de Catalunya, Spain
Heutte, L.	Université de Rouen, France
Hurtado-Ramos, J. B.	CICATA-Instituto Politécnico Nacional, Mexico
Ibn-Khedher, M.	IRT-SystemX, France
Jiang, X.	University of Münster, Germany
Kampel, M.	Vienna University of Technology, Austria
Kim, S. W.	Myongji University, South Korea
Lazo-Cortés, M. S.	Instituto Tecnológico de Tlalnepantla, TecNM, Mexico
Levano, M. A.	Universidad Católica de Temuco, Chile
López-Monroy, A. P.	Centro de Investigación en Matemáticas, Mexico
Mandal, B.	Uppsala University, Sweden
Mezura-Montes, E.	Universidad Veracruzana, Mexico
Milián-Núñez, V.	Universidad de las Ciencias Informáticas, Cuba
Mitrea, D.	Technical University of Cluj-Napoca, Romania
Moctezuma, M.	Universidad Nacional Autónoma de México, Mexico
Molina, J. M.	Universidad Carlos III de Madrid, Spain
Montes-Y-Gomez, M.	Instituto Nacional de Astrofísica, Óptica y Electrónica, Mexico
Morales, E.	Instituto Nacional de Astrofísica, Óptica y Electrónica, Mexico
Moreno-Cañadas, A.	National University of Colombia, Colombia
Nalepa, J.	Silesian University of Technology, Poland
Oliveira, J. L.	University of Aveiro, Portugal

Palagyi, K.	University of Szeged, Hungary
Pedrini, H.	University of Campinas, Brazil
Perez-Suay, A.	Universitat de València, Spain
Real, P.	Universidad de Sevilla, Spain
Realpe, M.	Escuela Superior Politécnica del Litoral, Ecuador
Rudrusamy, B.	Heriot-Watt University Malaysia, Malaysia
Ruiz-Shulcloper, J.	Universidad de las Ciencias Informáticas, Cuba
Salas, J.	Instituto Politécnico Nacional, Mexico
Sanchez, J. A.	Universitat Politècnica de València, Spain
Sanchez-Cortes, D.	Groupe Mutuel Holding SA, Switzerland
Sansone, C.	Università di Napoli, Italy
Silva, C.	University of Coimbra, Portugal
Subbarayappa, S.	M. S. Ramaiah University of Applied Sciences, India
Sucar, L. E.	Instituto Nacional de Astrofísica, Óptica y Electrónica, Mexico
Sánchez-Salmerón, A. J.	Universitat Politècnica de València, Spain
Tang, J.	George Mason University, USA
Trujillo, M.	Universidad del Valle, Colombia
Valle, M. E.	Universidade Estadual de Campinas, Brazil
Yanushkevich, S.	University of Calgary, Canada

Additional Reviewers

Altamirano-Robles, L.	Instituto Nacional de Astrofísica, Óptica y Electrónica, Mexico
Barradas-Palmeros, J.A.	Universidad Veracruzana, Mexico
Fuentes-Tomás, J.A.	Universidad Veracruzana, Mexico
Huerta, M.	Instituto Nacional de Astrofísica, Óptica y Electrónica, Mexico
Morales-González, A.	Centro de Aplicaciones de Tecnologias de Avanzada, Cuba
Olachea, C.	Instituto Nacional de Astrofísica, Óptica y Electrónica, Mexico
Peregrina-Barreto, H.	Instituto Nacional de Astrofísica, Óptica y Electrónica, Mexico
Prado-Valderrábano, U.R.	Universidad Veracruzana, Mexico
Ramos-Aguilar, E.	Instituto Politécnico Nacional, Mexico
Sanchis-Juan, S.	Universitat Politècnica de València, Spain

Sponsoring Institutions

Instituto Nacional de Astrofísica, Óptica y Electrónica (INAOE)
DUROL
Mexican Association for Pattern Recognition (MexAPR)
Secretaría de Ciencias, Humanidades, Tecnología e Innovación (SECIHTI)

Contents

Deep Learning and Neural Networks

Computer Vision

Language Processing and Recognition

Medical Applications of Pattern Recognition

Pattern Recognition and Machine Learning Techniques

Evaluation of Clustering and Consensus Models for Classifying Adulterant Levels in Alcoholic Beverages Using Single-Shot Interferograms

Elizabeth López-Meléndez[1] , Ricardo-Iván Álvarez-Tamayo[2,3] ,
Antonio Barcelata-Pinzón[4] , Patricia Prieto-Cortés[4] ,
and Luis-David Lara-Rodríguez[4(✉)]

[1] Technological University of Huejotzingo, Puebla 74169, México
elizabeth.lopez@uth.edu.mx
[2] Autonomous Popular University of the State of Puebla, Puebla 72410, México
ricardoivan.alvarez01@upaep.mx
[3] Secretariat of Science, Humanities, Technology, and Innovation (SECIHTI),
CDMX 03940, México
[4] Technological University of Puebla, Puebla 72300, México
antonio.barcelata@utpuebla.edu.mx, patricia.prieto@correo.buap.mx,
luisdavid.lara@upaep.mx

Abstract. This research evaluates the ability of seven unsupervised clustering models to identify the inherent structure in interferograms of commercial brandy adulterated with isopropyl alcohol (IPA). The models include two partitioning models (K-means and K-medoids), a probabilistic model (GMM), three hypergraph-based clustering models (CSPA, MCLA and HGPA) and a model based on a co-association matrix. Single-shot interferograms captured using a common-path double-aperture interferometer form the basis of the data, with six levels of adulterant concentration being considered. After 200 repetitions across two experimental sets, the models achieved average accuracy values of 0.8915 an adjusted Rand index of 0.7942, and a V-Measure of 0.8348. This demonstrates substantial agreement with the true classes and partitions of high purity and completeness. The consistent agreement between the obtained partitions and the actual classes across multiple algorithms and repetitions confirms that the separability of the data stems from genuine differences in the refractive index induced by the adulterant rather than random artifacts. These results validate the use of common-path interferometry as a viable technique for detecting adulteration in alcoholic beverages.

Keywords: Optical interferometry · Clustering Ensemble · Clustering · Matrix Consensus

1   Introduction

Adulteration of alcoholic beverages is a public health problem of growing concern worldwide. The substitution of ethanol with methanol and other substances is an illegal practice with potentially devastating consequences, including irreversible blindness, permanent neurological damage, and death [1]. This problem is significantly exacerbated by the consumer's inability to detect it through sensory means, as methanol and other adulterants have organoleptic properties that are virtually indistinguishable from those of ethanol [2]. Given this situation, it is imperative to develop rapid, reliable, and affordable detection systems that can be implemented in both specialized laboratories and at points of sale.

Detection of adulterants in alcoholic beverages has been addressed using analytical techniques that can be classified into non-optical and optical methods [3]. Gas chromatography coupled with mass spectrometry (GC-MS) is the gold standard method due to its exceptional detection limits, although its implementation requires expensive equipment, qualified personnel, and lengthy analysis times [4]. Electrochemical methods have emerged as portable alternatives using electrodes modified with nanomaterials, although they face limitations related to electrode stability and variable reproducibility [5]. Among non-destructive optical techniques, Fourier transform infrared spectroscopy (FTIR) generates molecular fingerprints, Raman spectroscopy provides structural specificity, UV-Visible spectroscopy offers operational simplicity, and fluorescence achieves superior sensitivities conditioned by specific physicochemical parameters [6].

Interferometry detects adulterants based on the refractive index, an optical property that depends on chemical composition. By coherently superimposing light beams, interferograms are generated whose morphology encodes information about the composition, achieving resolutions of micrometers (μm) that allow for the generation of unique optical fingerprints to detect adulterants at minimal concentrations [7]. Classic interferometric configurations such as Michelson and Mach-Zehnder offer highly sensitive measurements; however, because they rely on physically separate optical paths, they are vulnerable to mechanical and thermal disturbances. This limitation motivated the development of common-path interferometers, where the interfering beams share substantially the same spatial path and are inherently insensitive to external disturbances [8].

In the initial phase of this line of research, the qualitative detection of adulterants was explored using traditional phase-shifting methods and generalized phase-shifting algorithms, successfully detecting adulteration levels of up to 2%, although this relied on traditional phase extraction and visual interpretation [9]. To overcome the limitations of deterministic methods, the research evolved toward the use of artificial intelligence, proposing an unsupervised machine learning methodology using principal component analysis and Gaussian mixture models that achieved 90.78% accuracy [10]. Subsequently, deep learning techniques were integrated using two-arm convolutional neural networks, achieving accuracy exceeding 99% [11]. Currently, the implementation of dense autoencoders achieves accuracies of up to 99.68% for drugs such as ketamine with low computational cost [7].

Given this methodological development, it is necessary to study the internal patterns captured in the interferograms. This study proposes to analyze the quality of the partitions obtained by a set of unsupervised clustering models against the reference labels of interferograms captured from isopropyl alcohol levels in commercial rum. The selected models represent a variety of approaches, including traditional clustering models, ensemble models, and a hybrid model with a probabilistic consensus function, all of which will be evaluated using various external quality metrics.

2   Methodology

2.1   DACPI Experimental Setup

Interferometric applications require precise and robust experimental setups that ensure reliable measurements. The Double Aperture Common-Path Interferometer (DACPI) offers significant advantages inherent to common-path systems, including the minimization of environmental disturbances, mechanical vibrations, and external fluctuations that typically compromise the stability of conventional setups [10].

The DACPI is a $4f$ telecentric imaging system consisting of two windows positioned in the object plane and a Ronchi ruling that acts as a spatial filter in the Fourier plane, as illustrated in Fig.1. A collimated laser beam with a wavelength of 630 nm passes through windows A and B. Window A functions as the reference arm, allowing beam A to propagate through the reference liquid contained in cell A, while window B constitutes the test arm where beam B passes through the sample contained in cell B; both cells have an optical thickness of 4 mm. The system does not require high-precision optical components and responds exclusively to variations in the refractive index, which simplifies both its implementation and interpretation.

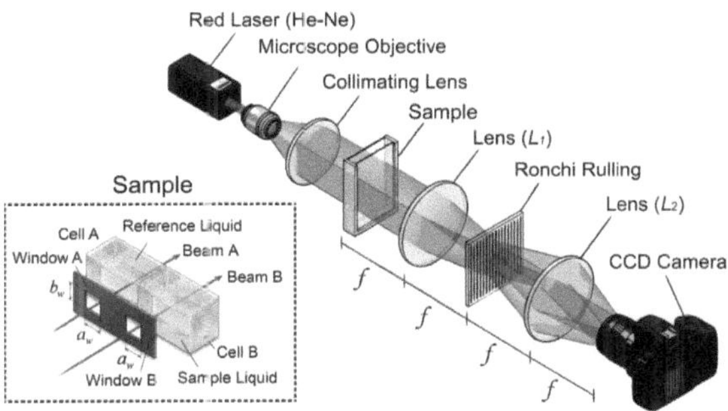

Fig. 1. Experimental setup of the common-path double-aperture interferometer, with the trajectories of the reference containers and the adulterated sample.

The phase difference between the recombined optical paths is determined by the refractive indices of the liquids contained in cells A and B, respectively. Since both beams travel an identical physical distance through the same optical components, the phase difference depends exclusively on the difference in refractive index (Δn) between the solutions, thus allowing the degree of adulteration to be determined by direct comparison between the pure reference liquid and the adulterated sample.

2.2   Capture of the Training Dataset

To implement the partition quality analysis methodology, interferograms were recorded for two datasets corresponding to variations in isopropyl alcohol (IPA) concentration in commercial rum, which served as the base liquid. Both datasets consist of six classes representing increasing levels of IPA adulteration, ranging from 0 to 0.5 ml added in 0.1 ml increments to 2 ml of rum contained in the sample cell. The first dataset (S1) comprises 51 interferograms per class, totaling 306 interferograms, while the second dataset (S2) contains 52 interferograms per class, totaling 312 interferograms. Each dataset was captured under different initial DACPI calibration conditions and different external experimental conditions.

The acquisition protocol consisted of automatically capturing interferograms every 30 s using the CCD camera, with careful replacement of the mixtures between each class. The captures were performed in accordance with general guidelines for interferometric measurements, including a laboratory temperature controlled at $22\,°C$, the use of a vibration-isolated optical bench, the absence of ambient light during capture, and automation of the process to avoid human interaction.

2.3   Clustering Models

Unsupervised clustering algorithms constitute a fundamental branch of machine learning that enables the identification of latent structures in datasets without predefined labels, aiming to partition the data into groups that are homogeneous within themselves and heterogeneous relative to one another [12].

K-means, introduced by MacQueen in 1967 [13], is the most widely used unsupervised learning algorithm. Its fundamental principle involves defining k cluster centers that act as representatives of each cluster. The procedure operates iteratively by assigning each point to the nearest cluster center based on Euclidean distance and recalculating the positions until convergence is reached. The iterative nature seeks to optimize a cost function that quantifies the quality of the clustering by minimizing the sum of squared distances between each point and its assigned cluster center [14].

K-medoids is a variant designed to overcome the limitations of using mean-based centroids. This algorithm selects medoids defined as actual data points that minimize the total dissimilarity with respect to the other elements in the cluster, providing greater interpretability and statistical robustness against outliers [15].

Gaussian mixture models (GMMs) adopt a probabilistic paradigm that models clustering structures using probability distributions [16]. This approach conceptualizes the data as a linear superposition of Gaussian distributions, where each component corresponds to a multivariate normal distribution associated with a specific cluster. Parametric estimation is performed using the Expectation-Maximization algorithm, which iteratively optimizes the assignment probabilities until convergence is reached [17].

2.4   Models of Clustering by Ensemble

Ensemble-based clustering is an unsupervised learning paradigm aimed at combining multiple partitions of a dataset to generate a consolidated solution that improves the robustness and stability of the results [18,19]. The consensus functions based on graph and hypergraph theory proposed by Strehl and Ghosh include the CSPA, HGPA, and MCLA algorithms [20].

The Cluster Similarity Partitioning Algorithm (CSPA) is based on the premise that each partition establishes a proximity relationship between objects assigned to the same group. This scheme constructs a co-occurrence matrix for each partition, where binary entries indicate the co-occurrence of objects in identical clusters. The consensus function averages these matrices to generate a global similarity matrix, which is subsequently processed using graph partitioning algorithms [20].

The Hypergraph Partitioning Algorithm (HGPA) formulates the problem as the direct partitioning of a hypergraph structure via the minimal cutting of hyperedges. The vertices represent objects, and each original cluster is mapped to a hyperedge, seeking a separator that divides the structure into k disconnected components of approximately uniform size [18].

The Meta-Clustering Algorithm (MCLA) treats integration as a cluster matching problem by grouping the ensemble's own clusters. The procedure transforms each cluster into a vertex of a meta-graph where the edges have weights proportional to the binary Jaccard similarity, quantifying the intersection over the union of the sets of objects. Each object is assigned to the group with the highest average association index [19].

3   Results and Discussions

Before combining the interferograms from both datasets, the red channel is extracted, as this channel contains the relevant information following the use of a red laser beam. Subsequently, the single-channel images are normalized and flattened to construct a matrix that integrates all samples from each dataset, enabling their processing using unsupervised models. The resulting matrix is standardized and subjected to dimensionality reduction via principal component analysis (PCA) [21]. The first 100 principal components are selected, which account for over 98% of the explained variance in both datasets.

The joint consensus matrix is a fundamental tool for estimating the areas of overlap between clusters and determining the partition that exhibits the greatest structural similarity [22]. This matrix is characterized by its symmetric structure, where each element (i, j) represents the proportion of times that two observations fall into the same cluster. Unit values indicate maximum consensus, zero values indicate an absence of joint clustering, while intermediate values reveal inconsistent clustering patterns.

The quality of the partitions is evaluated using external metrics that compare the assignments from clustering models against known reference labels. Accuracy represents the proportion of correct assignments relative to the total number of observations [23]. The Adjusted Rand Index (ARI) quantifies the agreement between two partitions by correcting for the expected random effect, where values close to 1 indicate perfect agreement [24]. V-Measure is the harmonic mean of Homogeneity, which measures whether each cluster contains only samples from a single class, and Completeness, which assesses whether all samples from a class belong to the same cluster [25]. The Silhouette coefficient evaluates the structural quality of the clustering by simultaneously considering the internal cohesion of each cluster and the separation between different clusters [26].

The clustering algorithms evaluated on the S1 and S2 datasets demonstrate an effective ability to distinguish the six IPA concentrations in interferometric samples, although there are substantial differences in performance and stability. Tables 1 and 2 present the complete results, including 95% confidence intervals and coefficients of variation for 200 replicates.

Table 1. Results of performance metrics for the first set (S1), with confidence interval (95% CI) and coefficient of variation ($CV = \sigma/\mu \times 100\%$) for 200 repetitions

Model	Accuracy	ARI	Homogeneity	Completeness	V-Measure	Silhouette
K-means	0.8465 ± 0.0080	0.7411 ± 0.0096	0.8061 ± 0.0058	0.8291 ± 0.0042	0.8173 ± 0.0050	0.3933 ± 0.0027
	6.74%	9.30%	5.16%	3.65%	4.36%	4.92%
K-medoids	**0.9075 ± 0.0043**	**0.8070 ± 0.0054**	**0.8345 ± 0.0027**	0.8419 ± 0.0014	**0.8382 ± 0.0021**	0.3946 ± 0.0004
	3.40%	**4.77%**	**2.32%**	**1.23%**	**1.78%**	**0.73%**
GMM	0.8467 ± 0.0080	0.7414 ± 0.0096	0.8067 ± 0.0058	0.8296 ± 0.0042	0.8179 ± 0.0049	0.3934 ± 0.0027
	6.74%	9.30%	5.14%	3.62%	4.34%	4.92%
Consensus	0.8749 ± 0.0073	0.7752 ± 0.0086	0.8204 ± 0.0045	0.8356 ± 0.0030	0.8278 ± 0.0037	**0.3967 ± 0.0016**
	6.01%	7.95%	3.97%	2.53%	3.25%	2.81%
CSPA	0.8891 ± 0.0074	0.7922 ± 0.0080	0.8257 ± 0.0052	**0.8444 ± 0.0021**	0.8347 ± 0.0036	0.3886 ± 0.0027
	6.00%	7.23%	4.54%	1.75%	3.06%	4.95%
MCLA	0.8801 ± 0.0058	0.7669 ± 0.0074	0.8154 ± 0.0043	0.8299 ± 0.0031	0.8225 ± 0.0037	0.3771 ± 0.0031
	4.70%	6.89%	3.78%	2.69%	3.18%	5.88%
HGPA	0.8912 ± 0.0070	0.7927 ± 0.0079	0.8300 ± 0.0044	0.8415 ± 0.0032	0.8357 ± 0.0038	0.3946 ± 0.0014
	5.63%	7.11%	3.80%	2.70%	3.23%	2.61%

K-medoids achieves the best overall performance with an accuracy of 0.9075 ± 0.0043 on S1 and 0.9455 ± 0.0003 on S2, followed by the consensus methods, which achieve values between 0.87 and 0.92 on both datasets. K-Means and GMM consistently rank at the bottom with accuracy close to 0.8465 ± 0.0079

Table 2. Results of performance metrics for the second set (S2), with confidence interval (95% CI) and coefficient of variation (CV%) for 200 repetitions.

Model	Accuracy	ARI	Homogeneity	Completeness	V-Measure	Silhouette
K-means	0.8745 ± 0.0086	0.7628 ± 0.0103	0.7991 ± 0.0062	0.8080 ± 0.0046	0.8034 ± 0.0054	0.3339 ± 0.0025
	7.06%	9.64%	5.56%	4.08%	4.79%	4.72%
K-medoids	**0.9455 ± 0.0003**	**0.8757 ± 0.0002**	**0.8825 ± 0.0001**	**0.8834 ± 0.0002**	**0.8829 ± 0.0003**	**0.4010 ± 0.0003**
	0.23%	**0.16%**	**0.08%**	**0.16%**	**0.24%**	**0.54%**
GMM	0.8776 ± 0.0087	0.7691 ± 0.0104	0.8072 ± 0.0063	0.8162 ± 0.0048	0.8116 ± 0.0055	0.3336 ± 0.0025
	7.08%	9.66%	5.63%	4.18%	4.87%	4.72%
Consensus	0.9210 ± 0.0059	0.8363 ± 0.0076	0.8530 ± 0.0052	0.8578 ± 0.0042	0.8554 ± 0.0047	0.3940 ± 0.0022
	4.56%	6.56%	4.37%	3.49%	3.91%	4.04%
CSPA	0.9117 ± 0.0088	0.8331 ± 0.0103	0.8516 ± 0.0072	0.8649 ± 0.0046	0.8579 ± 0.0057	0.3915 ± 0.0027
	6.92%	8.90%	6.04%	3.85%	4.78%	4.96%
MCLA	0.9162 ± 0.0064	0.8258 ± 0.0097	0.8461 ± 0.0061	0.8515 ± 0.0049	0.8488 ± 0.0055	0.3341 ± 0.0040
	5.05%	8.43%	5.21%	4.16%	4.68%	7.45%
HGPA	0.8991 ± 0.0082	0.8002 ± 0.0099	0.8286 ± 0.0060	0.8372 ± 0.0045	0.8328 ± 0.0053	0.3371 ± 0.0022
	6.51%	8.84%	5.23%	3.83%	4.54%	4.15%

on S1 and 0.8746 ± 0.0086 on S2. The ARI index confirms this performance hierarchy, with KMedoid achieving 0.8070 ± 0.0054 in S1 and 0.8757 ± 0.0002 in S2, validating that the partitions reflect genuine structure in the interferometric data rather than random coincidences. Information theory-based metrics show that K-medoids achieves the best balance between Homogeneity and Completeness with a VMeasure of 0.8382 ± 0.0021 in S1 and 0.8829 ± 0.0003 in S2. The Silhouette coefficient shows moderate values for all models, ranging between 0 38 and 0.40, indicating that adjacent concentrations of IPAs produce interferograms with subtle differences that generate some overlap at the decision boundaries.

The stability of the models, quantified using the coefficient of variation over 200 repetitions, reveals informative patterns regarding the robustness of each algorithm. K-medoids exhibits the lowest variability in S1 with coefficients of variation of 3.40% for Accuracy and 4.77% for ARI, while in S2 it converges deterministically, reaching values close to 0% across all evaluated metrics. Consensus methods show intermediate stability, with Matrix Consensus recording coefficients of variation of 6.01% for Accuracy in S1 and 4.56% in S2, while HGPA shows values of 5.63% and 6.51%, respectively. K-Means and GMM exhibit the highest variability, with coefficients exceeding 6.7% in Accuracy, reaching 9.28% in ARI for S1 and 9.65% for S2, reflecting sensitivity to initial conditions and lower reproducibility.

The consensus matrices (Fig 2) illustrate the agreement among partitions obtained across experimental replicates. In S1, the six diagonal blocks corresponding to each IPA concentration are distinguishable, although they exhibit blurred edges, particularly in samples with low adulterant concentrations where spurious co-associations with other classes are observed. This behavior suggests that the interferometric signal from samples with low IPA content is more ambiguous for clustering algorithms. In S2, the diagonal blocks appear more

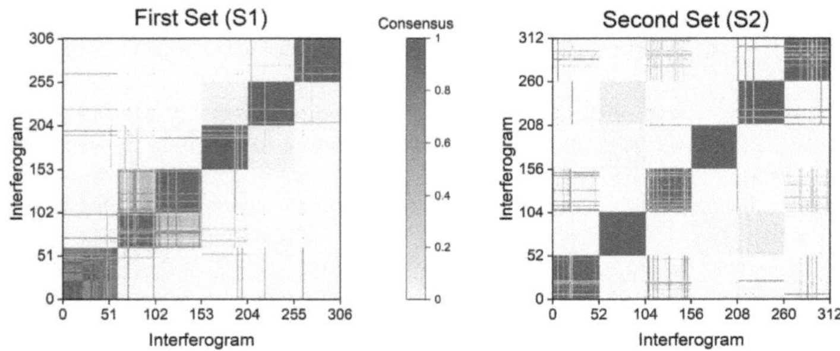

Fig. 2. Consensus matrices, left side of the first set and right side of the second set.

compact with abrupt transitions, confirming greater inherent separability in that set.

The consistent superiority of K-medoids over centroid-based approaches suggests that IPA concentration classes are better characterized by representative samples than by statistical averages. The interferograms corresponding to each concentration exhibit distinctive prototypical patterns rather than symmetric distributions around a centroid, allowing the selection of medoids to more effectively capture the underlying structure of the data. Consensus methods, by integrating multiple base partitions obtained from different algorithms, mitigate the variability inherent in individual methods and constitute robust alternatives when greater interpretability of the decision process is required in interferometric classification applications.

4   Conclusions

The IPA adulteration detection system based on common-path interferometry and dimensionality reduction via PCA demonstrates its ability to distinguish between six levels of adulterant concentration. The clustering algorithms evaluated achieve accuracies ranging from 0.8465 ± 0.0079 to 0.9455 ± 0.0003, with K-medoids being the model that exhibits optimal performance in terms of Accuracy, ARI, Homogeneity, Completeness, VMeasure, and Silhouette in both experimental datasets.

Statistical analysis based on 200 repetitions reveals substantial differences in stability among the models analyzed. K-medoids exhibits coefficients of variation below 5% in S1 and deterministic convergence in S2, in contrast to K-means and GMM, which show CVs exceeding 9% in ARI, indicating high sensitivity to initial conditions. The 95% confidence intervals provide accurate estimates of expected performance and allow for quantifying the uncertainty associated with each algorithm.

The consensus matrices reveal that intermediate IPA concentrations generate more distinctive interferometric patterns than extreme concentrations, thereby identifying the problem areas where future improvements in data acquisition or preprocessing would have the greatest impact. The deterministic convergence of K-medoids in S2 and its high stability in S1 confirm the suitability of this algorithm for quality control applications in alcoholic beverages.

The success achieved by the clustering models confirms the assumption that the discriminatory capability lies in the separability associated with the change in refractive index induced by the presence of the adulterant, which alters the optical path of the sample and is effectively detected by the common-path interferometer. Extending this methodology to other interferometric configurations or different types of adulterants would help establish this approach as a robust alternative in the field of optical metrology applied to beverage quality control.

Acknowledgments. L. D. Lara-Rodríguez and P. Prieto-Cortés would like to express their gratitude to the SECIHTI program, Estancias Posdoctorales por México.

Disclosure of Interests. The authors have no competing interests relevant to the content of this article.

References

1. Rot, T., Gavran, S., Babić, J., Lončarić, A.: Occurrence of pesticides, mycotoxins, and heavy metals in distilled alcoholic beverages: a review of contaminants and health risks. Foods **14**(8), 1303 (2025). https://doi.org/10.3390/foods14081303
2. Alrashed, M., et al.: The perils of methanol exposure: insights into toxicity and clinical management. Toxics **12**(12), 924 (2024). https://doi.org/10.3390/toxics12120924
3. Patra, S., Choudhary, R., Madhuri, R., Sharma, P.K.: Quality control of beverages for health safety: starting from laboratory to the point-of-care detection techniques. In: Quality Control in the Beverage Industry, pp. 39–83. Elsevier (2019). https://doi.org/10.1016/B978-0-12-816681-9.00002-3
4. Kisher, H., Gould, O., Honeychurch, K.C.: Applications of gas chromatography and gas chromatography-mass spectrometry for the determination of illegal drugs used in drink spiking. Chemosensors **13**(6), 205 (2025). https://doi.org/10.3390/chemosensors13060205
5. Kumar, S., Kalkal, A.: Electrochemical detection: cyclic voltammetry/differential pulse voltammetry/impedance spectroscopy. In: Nanotechnology in Cancer Management, pp. 43–71. Elsevier (2021). https://doi.org/10.1016/B978-0-12-818154-6.00008-1
6. Fernando Barrios-Rodriguez, Y., Devia-Rodriguez, Y., Gutierrez Guzmán, N.: Detection of adulterated coffee by Fourier-transform infrared (FTIR) spectroscopy associated with sensory analysis. Coffee Sci. **17**, 1–12 (2022). https://doi.org/10.25186/.v17i.1970
7. Lara-Rodriguez, L.D., Prieto-Cortés, P., López-Meléndez, E., Barcelata-Pinzón, A., Álvarez-Tamayo, R.I.: Autoencoder-based clustering of DACPI interferograms for detection of adulteration levels of two different dopants in alcoholic beverages. Appl. Opt. **65**(2), 607 (2026). https://doi.org/10.1364/AO.574636
8. Alvarez-Tamayo, R.I., Prieto-Cortés, P., Barcelata-Pinzón, A.: Optical interferometry as a solution to detect liquid adulteration. In: North-Morris, M.B., Creath, K., Zhang, S. (eds.) Interferometry and Structured Light 2024, pp. 21. SPIE, San Diego (2024). https://doi.org/10.1117/12.3027088

9. Barcelata-Pinzón, A. et al: Qualitative determination of different amounts of adulterant in a liquid using a double aperture common-path interferometer. In: Wilcox, C.C., Creath, K. (eds.) Applied Optical Metrology VI, pp. 37. SPIE, San Diego (2025). https://doi.org/10.1117/12.3064790

10. Lara-Rodriguez, L.D., Álvarez-Tamayo, R.I., Barcelata-Pinzón, A., López-Meléndez, E., Prieto-Cortés, P.: Classification of adulterant degree in liquid solutions through interferograms with machine learning. Opt. Laser Technol. **180**, 111402 (2025). https://doi.org/10.1016/j.optlastec.2024.111402

11. Prieto-Cortés, P., López-Meléndez, E., Álvarez-Tamayo, R.I., Barcelata-Pinzón, A., Lara-Rodriguez, L.D.: Measurement of adulteration in liquids by optical interferograms analysis and deep learning. Appl. Intell. **55**(7), 654 (2025). https://doi.org/10.1007/s10489-025-06550-x

12. Naeem, S., Ali, A., Anam, S., Ahmed, M.M.: An unsupervised machine learning algorithms: comprehensive review. Int. J. Comput. Digit. Syst **13**(1), 911–921 (2023). https://doi.org/10.12785/ijcds/130172

13. McQueen, J.B.: Some methods of classification and analysis of multivariate observations. In: 5th Berkeley Symposium on Mathematical Statistics and Probability, vol. 5, pp. 281–297 (1967)

14. Ikotun, A.M., Ezugwu, A.E., Abualigah, L., Abuhaija, B., Heming, J.: K-means clustering algorithms: a comprehensive review, variants analysis, and advances in the era of big data. Inf. Sci. **622**, 178–210 (2023). https://doi.org/10.1016/j.ins.2022.11.139

15. Park, H.-S., Jun, C.-H.: A simple and fast algorithm for K-medoids clustering. Expert Syst. Appl. **36**(2), 3336–3341 (2009). https://doi.org/10.1016/j.eswa.2008.01.039

16. Patel, E., Kushwaha, D.S.: Clustering cloud workloads: K-means vs Gaussian mixture model. Procedia Comput. Sci. **171**, 158–167 (2020). https://doi.org/10.1016/j.procs.2020.04.017

17. Gao, C.X., et al.: An overview of clustering methods with guidelines for application in mental health research. Psychiatry Res. **327**, 115265 (2023). https://doi.org/10.1016/j.psychres.2023.115265

18. Iam-On, N., Boongoen, T., Garrett, S., Price, C.: A link-based approach to the cluster ensemble problem. IEEE Trans. Pattern Anal. Mach. Intell. **33**(12), 2396–2409 (2011). https://doi.org/10.1109/TPAMI.2011.84

19. Vega-Pons, S., Ruiz-Shulcloper, J.: A survey of clustering ensemble algorithms. Int. J. Pattern Recognit Artif Intell. **25**(3), 337–372 (2011). https://doi.org/10.1142/S0218001411008683

20. Strehl, A., Ghosh, J.: Cluster ensembles—a knowledge reuse framework for combining multiple partitions. J. Mach. Learn. Res. **3**(Dec), 583–617 (2002)

21. Kurita, T.: Principal component analysis (PCA). In: Computer Vision, pp. 1–4. Springer, Cham (2020). https://doi.org/10.1007/978-3-030-03243-2_649-1

22. Lancichinetti, A., Fortunato, S.: Consensus clustering in complex networks. Sci. Rep. **2**(1), 336 (2012). https://doi.org/10.1038/srep00336

23. Grandini, M., Bagli, E., Visani, G.: Metrics for multi-class classification: an overview, (2020). https://doi.org/10.48550/ARXIV.2008.05756. arXiv:2008.05756 arXiv preprint

24. Chacón, J.E., Rastrojo, A.I.: Minimum adjusted Rand index for two clusterings of a given size. Adv. Data Anal. Classif. **17**(1), 125–133 (2023). https://doi.org/10.1007/s11634-022-00491-w

25. Rosenberg, A., Hirschberg, J.: V-measure: a conditional entropy-based external cluster evaluation measure. In: Joint Conference on Empirical Methods in Natural Language Processing and Computational Natural Language Learning (EMNLP-CoNLL), pp. 410–420. (2007)
26. Shutaywi, M., Kachouie, N.N.: Silhouette analysis for performance evaluation in machine learning with applications to clustering. Entropy **23**(6), 759 (2021). https://doi.org/10.3390/e23060759

Beyond Pareto: A High-Efficiency Approach to Bi-objective Regression Trees

Erick G. G. de Paz[1]([envelope]) [ORCID], Arturo Hernández-Aguirre[1] [ORCID],
and Iván Cruz-Aceves[2] [ORCID]

[1] Centro de Investigación en Matemáticas A.C., Guanajuato, Mexico
{erick.giles,artha}@cimat.mx
[2] SECIHTI-Centro de Investigación en Matemáticas A.C., Guanajuato, Mexico
ivan.cruz@cimat.mx

Abstract. This paper introduces a novel Bi-objective Regression Tree (BORT) for efficiently learning vector-valued functions $f : \mathbb{R}^m \to \mathbb{R}^2$. While existing methods, such as fitting independent trees per objective or a single tree minimising the sum of errors, rely on constructing multiple models or scalarising the problem, BORT integrates the exploration of the Pareto front directly into a single tree's growth process. Guided by a new theorem, BORT selects splits by randomly weighting the two objectives at each step, ensuring a dynamic yet principled trade-off. In comprehensive Monte Carlo experiments on a benchmark of hard-to-predict functions, a single BORT is shown to Pareto dominate an entire Pareto-consistent family of several trees, often requiring only a modest increase in model complexity. Rigorous statistical testing confirms the superiority of this high-efficiency, single-model approach.

Keywords: Multiobjective regression · Decision trees · Machine learning · Pareto optimality · Surrogate modelling

1 Introduction

A multiobjective function, mapping $f : \mathbb{R}^m \to \mathbb{R}^n$, presents a significant challenge for approximation, as it requires balancing error trade-offs across multiple outputs. In machine learning, regression trees offer a transparent, nonparametric approach. For such functions, two primary strategies exist in the literature. Verbeeck et al. [9] propose fitting n independent surrogate trees, one for each objective, effectively decoupling the problem. Conversely, Breiman et al. [1] define a Multiobjective Regression Tree (MORT) fitted by minimising the sum of mean square errors across all objectives, a form of scalarisation. This paper generalises these concepts into a Pareto-consistent family of trees and, more significantly, proposes a new, superior model: the Bi-objective Regression Tree (BORT). BORT's key innovation is a splitting criterion derived from a new theorem for $n = 2$, which allows a single tree to adaptively explore the Pareto front during its construction, outperforming the ensemble approach in both accuracy and memory efficiency.

© The Author(s), under exclusive license to Springer Nature Switzerland AG 2026
V. G. Cruz-Sánchez et al. (Eds.): MCPR 2026, LNCS 16623, pp. 14–24, 2026.
https://doi.org/10.1007/978-3-032-28393-1_2

The remainder of this paper is organised as follows. Section 2 establishes the mathematical framework for multiobjective regression trees, detailing the top-down partitioning approach and introducing the Pareto-consistent family that generalises prior work. Section 3 presents the core theoretical contribution: a theorem for bi-objective problems that underpins the proposed BORT algorithm. Section 4 describes the experimental setup and presents statistical results demonstrating BORT's dominance over the Pareto-consistent family on a standard benchmark suite. Finally, Sect. 5 discusses the implications of these findings and concludes with directions for future work, including extensions to more than two objectives and applications in multiobjective optimisation.

2 Mathematical Framework

This section introduces basic definitions and theorems about the design of a generalised family of top-down multiobjective regression trees.

2.1 Multiobjective Regression Trees

Let us consider the problem of approximating (learning) a function $f : \mathbb{R}^m \to \mathbb{R}^n$, given a finite sample of s paired-vectors denoted $Y_1 = f(X_1), \ldots, Y_s = f(X_s)$. A regression tree is a machine learning model based on partitioning the domain to assign different scalars (local averages of f) as approximation. This principle is restricted to one objective $n = 1$, but conceptually easy to extend to $n \geq 1$.

Definition 1. *A **multiobjective regression tree** $\hat{f}$ is an approximation to a sampled function $f : \mathbb{R}^m \to \mathbb{R}^n$ defined as:*

$$\hat{f}(X) = \sum_{i=1}^{t} \left[\hat{Y}|A_i\right] \mathcal{I}_{A_i}(X) \ , \ where: \tag{1}$$

1. $\mathbb{A} = \{A_i | A_i \subset \mathbb{R}^m, 1 \leq i \leq t\}$ is a mutually exclusive partition of the sampled domain $D \subset \mathbb{R}^m$, i.e. $\bigcup_{i=1}^{t} A_i = D$ and $A_i \cap A_j = \emptyset \, \forall \, i \neq j, 1 \leq i, j \leq t.$

2. $\mathcal{I}_{A_i}$ is the indicator function, i.e. $\mathcal{I}_{A_i}(X) = \begin{cases} 1 \ , \ if \ X \in A_i \\ 0 \ , \ otherwise \end{cases}$

3. $\left[\hat{Y}|A_i\right] = \sum_{j=1}^{s} Y_j \mathcal{I}_{A_i}(X_j) / \left[\sum_{j=1}^{s} \mathcal{I}_{A_i}(X_j)\right]$, which is an unbiased estimator of $E\{Y|X \in A_i\} = \int_{A_i} f(X) d\Pr(X).$

Under the last definition, the fitness of a multiobjective regression tree is remarkably related to the partition $\mathbb{A} = \{A_1, \ldots, A_t\}$. Inside each subset A_i, f should ideally map to close values of $\hat{f}$. In other words, the partition must define subsets which map to similar values in the codomain. To measure the similarity and build up a proper partition, there exist two main approaches in the literature:

1. The **top-down** approach based on recursively splitting the domain by means of axis thresholds [8]. This constitutes a greedy method that maximises similarity scores in each splitting step [7].
2. The approach based on a **likelihood** and a **prior distribution** for trees [2]. This approach has a global vision of tree-fitness by defining a family of trees where a Markov Chain Monte Carlo search is performed [2].

Due to formal restrictions of the second approach, and the facilities for Pareto given by the first one (see Theorem 1), this paper only deals with the top-down approach, which is detailed in Algorithm 1. Initially, the partition just contains the entire sampled domain as a single set (line 1). To compute t additional subsets, the following steps (lines $3-6$) are iterated t times: 1) Select the subset with the largest Lebesgue measure (length, area, volume, etc.) as suggested by [5], 2) Remove the selected subset A_{selected} from $\mathbb{A}$, 3) Split the selected subset into two mutually exclusive subsets $\{A_{\text{left}}, A_{\text{right}}\}$, and 4) Insert the resultant subsets in the collection $\mathbb{A}$. The selection step (line 3) ensures that the largest unexplored parts of the domain be modelled first than others [3,5]. The splitting step (line 5) is the most relevant to produce a proper partition [5]. The decision about how to split a given subset may be efficiently guided by the Mean Squared Error between the resultant model $\hat{f}$ and the observed samples (see Definition 2).

Algorithm 1. Algorithmic schema for top-down partition

Require: A function $f : \mathbb{R}^m \to \mathbb{R}^n$
Ensure: A domain partition $\mathbb{A}$
  1: $\mathbb{A} = \{A_1 = D\}$
  2: **for** $i = 2, \ldots, t$ **do**
  3:     Select the largest subset A_{selected} from the collection $\mathbb{A}$
  4:     Remove A_{selected} from $\mathbb{A}$
  5:     Split A_{selected} into $\{A_{\text{left}}, A_{\text{right}}\}$
  6:     Insert $\{A_{\text{left}}, A_{\text{right}}\}$ into the collection $\mathbb{A}$
  7: **end for**

Definition 2. *The **mean squared error** (MSE) of a multiobjective regression tree $\hat{f}$ based on the partition $\mathbb{A}$ is given by:*

$$MSE\{\mathbb{A}\} = \frac{1}{s}\sum_{i=1}^{s}(Y_i - \hat{f}(X_i))^2 \ , \ where: V^2 = [v_1^2, \ldots, v_n^2]^T \qquad (2)$$

To explain the decision process for splitting, consider that $A_{\text{selected}} \in \mathbb{A}$ is the selected subset to be split, and $s_{\text{selected}} = \sum_{i=1}^{s} \mathcal{I}_{A_{\text{selected}}}(X_i)$ is the number of samples contained in A_{selected}. The most basic form of splitting is a rule based on an axis threshold such as $A_{\text{left}} = \{X \in A_{\text{selected}} \mid x_i < \alpha_i\}$ and $A_{\text{right}} = \{X \in A_{\text{selected}} \mid x_i \geq \alpha_i\}$, which splits A_{selected} into two subsets by defining a threshold α_i in the i-th entry (axis i) of each vector $X \in A_{selected}$. Given a fixed axis $i \in [1, m]$, α_i can only hold values such that the $s_{selected}$-size sample be differently distributed into A_{left} and A_{right}, and neither A_{left} nor A_{right} be empty. Therefore, the number of different splitting rules per axis is $s_{selected} - 1$, and the total number of possible rules is $m \times (s_{selected} - 1)$. This quantity is feasible to be exhaustively computed. By sorting the sample in $A_{selected}$ according to each axis, it is possible to efficiently find each α_i and compute the error measure of every possible candidate partition [5,7]. Formally,

Definition 3. *The **associated mean squared error** (AMSE) of $\hat{f}$ based on a top-down updated version of the partition $\mathbb{A}$ is given by: $AMSE\{\mathbb{A}, i, \alpha_i\} = MSE\{\mathbb{A}'\}$, where*

1. *$\mathbb{A}' = (\mathbb{A} - A_{selected}) \cup \{A_{left}, A_{right}\}$,*
2. *$A_{left} = \{X \in A_{selected} \mid x_i < \alpha_i\}$ and $A_{right} = \{X \in A_{selected} \mid x_i \geq \alpha_i\}$*

In the specific case of $n = 1$, i.e. f maps to a scalar not to a vector, all definitions above lead to the CART (Classification and Regression Tree) [8] model as defined in [5]. Given a subset $A_{selected}$ to split, the optimal axis $i \in [1, m]$ and threshold α_i for splitting are trivially given by:

$$(i^\star, \alpha_i^\star) = \arg\min_{i, \alpha_i} AMSE\{\mathbb{A}, i, \alpha_i\} \tag{3}$$

For $n = 1$, the improvement based on top-down partitions is ensured by:

Theorem 1. *Let $\hat{f}$ be a regression tree for modelling $f : \mathbb{R}^m \to \mathbb{R}$ based on a partition $\mathbb{A}$. Any top-down updated partition based on splitting $A_{selected} \in \mathbb{A}$ by whichever threshold α_i in any axis $i \in [1, m]$ produces a better model than the original. Formally,*

$$AMSE\{\mathbb{A}, i, \alpha_i\} < MSE\{\mathbb{A}\}$$

Proof. To prove, $AMSE\{\mathbb{A}, i, \alpha_i\}$ and $MSE\{\mathbb{A}\}$ are re-written in terms of the sample X_i, Y_i, then some algebraic manipulations lead to the inequality. This is fully proven in de Paz et al. [4] as the Iterative partition theorem.

For $n = 1$, Theorem 1 states that even splitting an arbitrarily selected subset leads to improvements, and Eq. 3 identifies which is the best splitting rule. However if $n > 1$, then f maps to a vector, so MSE and AMSE are n-length vectors and there is no trivial expression such as Eq. 3 for identifying the best splitting rule. Subsection 2.3 and Sect. 3 state two approaches for finding the best partition for $n > 1$. The following subsection introduces relevant concepts of multiobjective optimisation.

2.2   Pareto Dominance and Pareto Front

For scalars $c_1, c_2 \in \mathbb{R}$, order relations such as $c_1 < c_2$ or $c_1 > c_2$ can be stated. In the context of a multiobjective minimisation problem, this notion of order can be partially extended to vectors $V_1 = [v_{1,1}, \ldots, v_{1,n}]^T, V_2 = [v_{2,1}, \ldots, v_{2,n}]^T \in \mathbb{R}^r$,

Definition 4. *It is said that V_1 **Pareto dominates** V_2, denoted $V_1 \prec V_2$, if and only if $v_{1,i} < v_{2,i} \ \forall \ i \in [1, n]$.*

Theorem 1 states that an arbitrarily top-down partition works for $n = 1$, i.e. for modelling a function $f : \mathbb{R}^m \to \mathbb{R}$ whose domain is progressively split into $\mathbb{A}$. Now, let us consider that a function $f : \mathbb{R}^m \to \mathbb{R}^n$, i.e. $[y_1, \ldots, y_n] = f(X)$, is constituted by n mono-objective functions $f_1 : \mathbb{R}^m \to \mathbb{R}, \ldots, f_n : \mathbb{R}^m \to \mathbb{R}$ whose domain is shared and similarly partitioned as $\mathbb{A}$. Then, the top-down iterative schema produces improvement for all mono-objective functions. Formally,

Corollary 1. *From Theorem 1, it follows that, given a multiobjective tree $\hat{f}$ based on the partition $\mathbb{A}$ for modelling $f : \mathbb{R}^m \to \mathbb{R}^n$, the $AMSE\{\mathbb{A}, i, \alpha_i\}$ associated to whichever feasible threshold **Pareto dominates** the $MSE\{\mathbb{A}\}$.*

Corollary 1 enunciates that $AMSE\{\mathbb{A}, i, \alpha_i\} \prec MSE\{\mathbb{A}\}$ for whichever feasible threshold. Therefore, the top-down algorithmic schema remains proper even for $n > 1$. For $n = 1$, Eq. 3 uses scalar order relations to identify the optimal splitting parameters (axis i and threshold α_i). However, the Pareto dominance differs, because it identifies a collection of optimum parameters rather than a single optimum. This collection is constituted by different solutions which achieve different degrees of minimum for different dimensions by making concessions in others. The collection called Pareto front is formally defined as:

Definition 5. *For a given partition $\mathbb{A}$, let $\mathbb{E} = \{AMSE\{\mathbb{A}, i, \alpha_i\} \mid i, \alpha_i$ are feasible threshold parameters$\}$ be the set of vector errors estimated with a finite s-size sample. The Pareto Front is given by $\mathcal{P} = \{V \in \mathbb{E} \mid \nexists U \in \mathbb{E} : U \prec V\}$.*

2.3   A Pareto-Consistent Family of Multiobjective Trees

In the multiobjective literature, a popular approach is reformulating a multiobjective problem as a mono-objective problem easier to optimise than the original. Let us consider the following scalarising technique.

Definition 6. *An associated error vector $AMSE\{\mathbb{A}, i, \alpha_i\}$ can be scalarised as a $c \in \mathbb{R}$ defined by the following dot product:*

$$c = AMSE\{\mathbb{A}, i, \alpha_i\} \cdot [w_1, \ldots, w_n], \text{ where } \sum_{i=1}^{n} w_i = 1, 0 \leq w_i \leq 1 \ \forall \ i \in [1, n]$$

The parameters vector $W = [w_1, \ldots, w_n]$ allows to specify which objectives to favour at the decrement of others. For a fixed W, c is a function of i and α_i to minimise such as Eq. 3 for a mono-objective problem. Although not explicitly as in Definition 6, the literature about multiobjective trees implicitly explores instances of this scalarising technique:

1. Verbeeck et al. [9] suggest an approach based on surrogate trees for multiobjective optimisation. For a problem with n functions, n independent trees

are fitted, one per function. In terms of Definition 6, n trees are computed by minimising c for different vectors W, each vector focuses on one objective at a time: $W = [w_1 = 1, \ldots, w_n = 0]$ for the first tree, and so on until $W = [w_1 = 0, \ldots, w_n = 1]$ for the n-th tree.

2. Breiman et al. [1] defines a data structure called Multiobjective Regression Tree (MORT) which is fitted by minimising the sum of mean square errors between the model and all objectives. Formally, MORT is the result of minimising c with $W = [w_1 = 1/n, \ldots, w_n = 1/n]$.

The scalarising technique commented above has been successfully applied in Multiobjective Evolutionary Algorithms based on Decomposition (MOEA/D) [10], where k vectors W are sampled from a Dirichlet distribution (i.e. uniformly inside a simplex) to define k mono-objective problems. If the Pareto front is convex, then this approach ensures that optimising every k problem leads to a uniform sample over the Pareto front [10]. In MOEA/D, evolutionary algorithms (EAs) collaborate to optimise those k problems. Inspired by the scalarising decomposition approach of MOEA/D, the definition below formalises a family of k trees fitted by the top-down schema instead of EAs. This family creates a collection of trees whose errors are uniformly distributed on the Pareto front under the same conditions of convexity as MOEA/D.

Definition 7. *For a given function $f : \mathbb{R}^m \to \mathbb{R}^n$, a **Pareto-consistent family** of trees $\mathcal{F}(k, t) = \{\hat{f}_1, \ldots, \hat{f}_k\}$ is a collection of k multiobjective regression trees, each one based on different partitions $\mathbb{A}_i = \{A_{i,1}, \ldots, A_{i,t}\}$ constituted by t subsets, i.e. t leaves or terminal nodes. For every $i \in [1, k]$, a set of k parameter vectors are drawn as $W_i \sim Dirichlet(\bar{\alpha} = \bar{1})$. Given a W_i, each corresponding $\hat{f}_i$ is fitted by the top-down approach minimising $c(i, \alpha_i) = AMSE\{\mathbb{A}_i, \cdot, \alpha_i\} \cdot W_i$ as splitting criterion.*

The family above, firstly defined in this paper, embraces the listed instances proposed by Verbeeck et al. [9] and Breiman et al. [1]. Therefore, $\mathcal{F}$ is an excellent comparison point that represents both: 1) two state-of-the-art approaches, and 2) a fully Pareto-consistent approach.

3   An Efficient Bi-objective Regression Tree

This section defines a Bi-objective Regression Tree (BORT) supported by a novel theorem restricted to $n = 2$. Let us consider two vectors $V_1 = AMSE(\mathbb{A}, i, \alpha_i)$ and $V_2 = AMSE(\mathbb{A}, j, \beta_j)$, which are the errors associated to two different options for splitting a selected subset. In a broader sense, $V_1, V_2 \in \mathbb{R}^2$.

Theorem 2. *Let $W = [w, 1 - w]$ be a vector parameterised by $w \in [0\ 1] \subset \mathbb{R}$:*

1. If $V_1 \cdot W < V_2 \cdot W \ \forall \, w \in [0, 1]$, then $V_1 \prec V_2$
2. If $\exists \, w \in [0, 1] : V_1 \cdot W < V_2 \cdot W$, then $V_1 \nprec V_2$ and $V_2 \nprec V_1$

Proof. The assumption $V_1 \cdot W < V_2 \cdot W$ is denoted $v_{1,1}w + v_{1,2}(1 - w) < v_{2,1}w + v_{2,2}(1 - w)$, and re-written as $w(v_{1,1} - v_{2,1} - v_{1,2} + v_{2,2}) < -v_{1,2} + v_{2,2}$.

- If $v_{1,1}-v_{2,1}-v_{1,2}+v_{2,2} < 0 \Rightarrow (-v_{1,2}+v_{2,2})/(v_{1,1}-v_{2,1}-v_{1,2}+v_{2,2}) < w < 1$
  - The interval for w, if $[0,1] \subset [(-v_{1,2}+v_{2,2})/(v_{1,1}-v_{2,1}-v_{1,2}+v_{2,2}),1]$:
    * $(-v_{1,2}+v_{2,2})/(v_{1,1}-v_{2,1}-v_{1,2}+v_{2,2}) < 0 \Rightarrow v_{2,2} > v_{1,2}$
    * $(-v_{1,2}+v_{2,2})/(v_{1,1}-v_{2,1}-v_{1,2}+v_{2,2}) < 1 \Rightarrow v_{2,1} > v_{1,1}$

    Therefore: $V_1 \prec V_2$
  - The interval for w, if $[(-v_{1,2}+v_{2,2})/(v_{1,1}-v_{2,1}-v_{1,2}+v_{2,2}),1] \subset [0,1]$:
    * $(-v_{1,2}+v_{2,2})/(v_{1,1}-v_{2,1}-v_{1,2}+v_{2,2}) > 0 \Rightarrow v_{2,2} < v_{1,2}$
    * $(-v_{1,2}+v_{2,2})/(v_{1,1}-v_{2,1}-v_{1,2}+v_{2,2}) < 1 \Rightarrow v_{2,1} > v_{1,1}$

    Therefore: $V_1 \not\prec V_2$ and $V_2 \not\prec V_1$
- If $v_{1,1}-v_{2,1}-v_{1,2}+v_{2,2} > 0 \Rightarrow 0 < w < (-v_{1,2}+v_{2,2})/(v_{1,1}-v_{2,1}-v_{1,2}+v_{2,2})$
  - The interval for w, if $[0,1] \subset [0,(-v_{1,2}+v_{2,2})/(v_{1,1}-v_{2,1}-v_{1,2}+v_{2,2})]$, following analogous steps $V_1 \prec V_2$
  - The interval for w, if $[0,(-v_{1,2}+v_{2,2})/(v_{1,1}-v_{2,1}-v_{1,2}+v_{2,2})] \subset [0,1]$, following analogous steps $V_1 \not\prec V_2$ and $V_2 \not\prec V_1$

Corollary 2. *Given a function $f : \mathbb{R}^m \to \mathbb{R}^2$, let $\hat{f}$ be a Bi-objective Regression Tree (BORT) fitted by a top-down schema that minimises the function $c(i,\alpha_i) = AMSE\{\mathbb{A},i,\alpha_i\} \cdot W$, where $W = [w, 1-w]$ with $w \sim Uniform(0,1)$ drawn randomly at each iteration. From the statements of Theorem 2, it is possible to conclude that: 1) An AMSE can only be selected if it belongs to the Pareto front (it is not dominated); 2) During each iteration, one of at least two mutually not dominated AMSE is randomly selected. These mutually not dominated AMSE favour opposite objectives.*

In contrast to a tree from a Pareto-consistent family $\mathcal{F}$, that consistently focuses on the same region of the Pareto Front, a BORT model progressively explores different parts of the Pareto Front. For a BORT model, the track of the MSE is a random walk that depends on the geometry of the Pareto Front. A Pareto-consistent family creates a collection of trees, such that each one achieves different degrees of fitness and error for the objectives. Conversely, BORT explores these different degrees during its training process. A highly desirable behaviour of a BORT is to outperform an entire family $\mathcal{F}$; this will be illustrated by Fig. 1 in Sect. 4, but for the moment it is defined as follows:

Definition 8. *It is said that a BORT model based on a partition $\mathbb{A}$ **fully dominates a Pareto-consistent family** of trees $\mathcal{F}(k,t) = \{\hat{f}_1,\ldots,\hat{f}_k\}$ based on partitions $\{\mathbb{A}_1,\ldots,\mathbb{A}_k\}$ respectively, if $MSE\{\mathbb{A}\} \prec MSE\{\mathbb{A}_i\} \,\forall\, i = 1,\ldots,k$.*

4   Experimental Results

To contrast the proposed BORT vs the generalised Pareto-consistent family, whose instances are applied in [1,9], a Monte Carlo experiment is performed. For different bi-objective functions and configurations of Pareto-consistent families, a BORT is fitted until being fully dominant. Formally, given a bi-objective function f with real domain in dimension d, and a Pareto-consistent family with fixed parameters t (subsets or terminal nodes) and k (number of trees), let $L(f,d,t,k)$ be a random variable computed as following:

1. Draw a sample $(Y_i = f(X_i), X_i)$ with $X_i \sim \text{Uniform}([0,1]^d)$, for $i = [1, 1000]$
2. Compute the Pareto-consistent family $\mathcal{F}(k,t)$ based on the sample. The family $\mathcal{F}$ is constituted by k different trees, each one based on a different partition $\mathbb{A}$ with t subsets (i.e. t terminal nodes or leaves).
3. Fit a BORT $\hat{f}$ by defining new subsets in its partition $\mathbb{A}$ until fully dominating $\mathcal{F}$. L is defined as the number of needed subsets $L(f,d,t,k) = |\mathbb{A}|$.

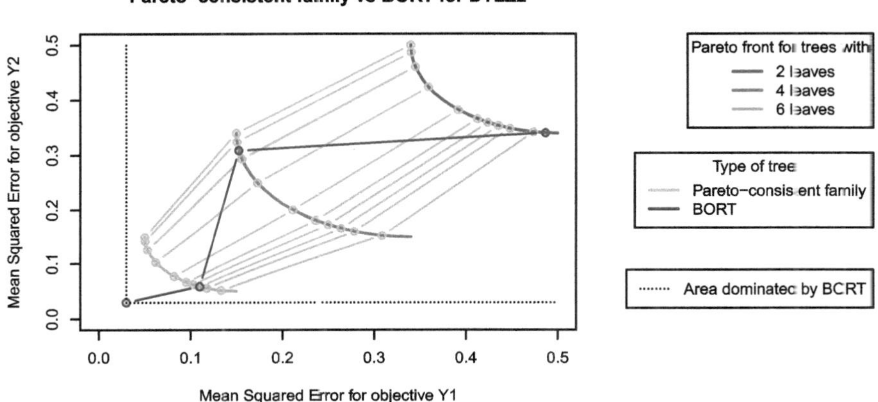

Fig. 1. Testing function DTLZ-2 modelled by: 1) a Pareto-consistent family $\mathcal{F}(10,6)$ (10 trees, each one with 6 terminal nodes) and, 2) a single BORT with 7 terminal nodes

To visualise the Monte Carlo experiment associated to compute each L, Fig. 1 illustrates the Pareto-consistent family $\mathcal{F}(10,6)$ for the testing function DTLZ-2, and a single BORT that dominates this family $\mathcal{F}$.

The testing set $\mathbb{F}$ embraces 7 functions $f : [0,1]^d \rightarrow \mathbb{R}^2$ from the Deb-Thiele-Laumanns-Zitzler (DTLZ) benchmark suite [6], which is selected because of constituting a hard-to-predict and well-documented collection. The tested combinations of parameters for computing L are: function dimension $d \in D = \{4, 8\}$, number of subsets (terminal nodes) $t \in T = \{10, 20\}$, and size of families $k \in K = \{10, 20\}$. For each experimental setup in $\mathbb{F} \times D \times T \times K$, the random variable $L(f,d,t,k)$ is computed 30 times to get statistics that appeal to the central limit theorem. Statistics of each setup are arranged in Table 1. The p-value reported is associated to a t-Student statistical test for the hypothesis $H_0 : E\{L(f,d,t,k)\} > 2t$, i.e. the mean number of terminal nodes for BORT is greater than double the nodes per tree of the dominated family. This hypothesis was carefully stated to support a statement about the topology of the contrasted trees. Let us consider that for a binary tree with any topology (balanced or unbalanced), if each terminal node is split into two, then the average depth (distance from the root to terminal nodes) increases by one and the number of terminal nodes is duplicated. *Therefore, if H_0 is rejected, then the Pareto-consistent family of trees with t terminal nodes is fully dominated by a single BORT model that has less than one additional depth-level on average.*

The Pareto-consistent family and BORT were implemented in the C programming language as a dynamic library for the R statistical environment 4.3.3. The scripts for running and statistically analysing these experiments were also written in R language. Running the entire experiment took 16:41 h on a computer with Intel(R) Core(TM) i5-2435M CPU 2.40GHz and Linux Mint 22.1.

Table 1. Statistics of the needed subsets by BORT to fully outperform a Pareto-consistent family. All p-values are associated to the hypothesis $H_0 : E\{L(f,d,t,k)\} > 2t$, and are highlighted if H_0 is not rejected with $\alpha = .05$

		$d=$ 4	4	4	4	8	8	8	8
		$k=$ 10	10	20	20	10	10	20	20
		$t=$ 10	20	10	20	10	20	10	20
DTLZ1	Mean	12.233	24.100	14.733	28.567	14.700	30.267	19.967	43.867
	Std Dev	0.679	1.768	1.230	2.635	0.702	3.523	2.141	11.557
	P-value	0.000	0.000	0.000	0.003	0.000	0.024	0.008	**0.334**
DTLZ2	Mean	10.700	22.167	13.433	26.500	13.400	26.267	17.833	32.900
	Std Dev	1.088	1.367	2.161	3.608	0.621	3.903	1.663	7.689
	P-value	0.000	0.000	0.000	0.015	0.000	0.020	0.000	**0.197**
DTLZ3	Mean	11.000	21.700	13.233	27.633	13.333	27.067	18.067	36.900
	Std Dev	0.983	1.343	1.073	4.514	0.661	3.226	1.617	2.006
	P-value	0.000	0.000	0.000	0.045	0.000	0.009	0.000	0.003
DTLZ4	Mean	11.100	21.367	14.233	26.633	13.300	25.800	17.867	35.700
	Std Dev	0.662	1.217	2.254	2.798	1.119	1.648	1.502	13.365
	P-value	0.000	0.000	0.001	0.003	0.000	0.000	0.000	**0.325**
DTLZ5	Mean	11.200	21.967	13.233	26.833	13.467	26.900	19.433	34.633
	Std Dev	0.887	2.042	1.194	3.206	0.860	3.736	2.825	8.495
	P-value	0.000	0.000	0.000	0.008	0.000	0.019	0.028	**0.231**
DTLZ6	Mean	13.200	26.500	16.167	31.233	15.900	32.200	21.567	43.233
	Std Dev	0.714	1.253	0.913	3.655	0.803	1.730	3.339	8.529
	P-value	0.000	0.000	0.000	0.032	0.000	0.000	**0.069**	**0.278**
DTLZ7	Mean	13.100	26.167	16.133	31.033	15.900	31.900	21.467	44.933
	Std Dev	0.481	1.020	1.613	2.593	0.995	2.510	1.814	7.922
	P-value	0.000	0.000	0.000	0.005	0.000	0.005	0.004	**0.271**

5   Discussion and Conclusion

The experimental results support the efficacy of the proposed BORT. The null hypothesis $H_0 : E\{L(f, d, t, k)\} > 2t$ is mostly rejected, with some exceptions in the last columns of Table 1 for dense families in high dimensions. In the vast majority of tested scenarios, a single BORT with less than $2t$ terminal nodes Pareto dominates an entire family of several t-nodes trees. In terms of computational efficiency, a BORT with $2t$ terminal nodes needs $2t - 2$ internal nodes, the total number of nodes $4t - 2$ is the same as the terminal and non-teminal nodes needed by two members of the dominated family $2(2t - 1)$.

BORT offers a more parsimonious and interpretable model without sacrificing performance for bi-objective regression. A key advantage of BORT is its unification of the modelling process. By design, it avoids the post-hoc decision of selecting which tree from a family to interpret, as it produces a single, coherent model for the multiobjective problem. This integrated approach allows BORT to capture relevant interactions between objectives during its construction, a feature that is lost when objectives are modelled independently or rigidly scalarised. The random weighting at each split, guided by Theorem 2, ensures an adaptive exploration of trade-offs, leading to a model that is robust and representative of the Pareto front's geometry.

In conclusion, this work has demonstrated that the proposed BORT can outperform Pareto-consistent family of trees, a generalisation of existing state-of-the-art methods. The theoretical foundation provides an efficient splitting criterion that enables a single tree to dynamically balance multiple objectives. This result is significant for applications requiring interpretable, efficient surrogate models, such as in multiobjective optimisation. Future work should focus on applying BORT in practical optimisation frameworks, building upon the surrogate-based approaches suggested in related literature [4].

Acknowledgments. The authors thank SECIHTI and CIMAT A.C.

Disclosure of Interests. The authors do not have competing interests to declare.

References

1. Breiman, L., et al.: Classification and Regression Trees. Routledge, Boca Raton (2017). https://doi.org/10.1201/9781315139470
2. Chipman, H., George, E.I., McCulloch, R.E.: A Bayesian approach to CART. In: Madigan, D., Smyth, P. (eds.) Proceedings of the Sixth International Workshop on Artificial Intelligence and Statistics. Proceedings of Machine Learning Research, vol. R1, pp. 91–102. PMLR (1997)
3. de Paz, E.G., et al.: A regression tree as acquisition function for low-dimensional optimisation. In: Pattern Recognition, pp. 23–33. Springer, Cham (2024). https://doi.org/10.1007/978-3-031-62836-8_3
4. de Paz, E.G., et al.: Convex partition: a bayesian regression tree for black-box optimisation. Pattern Recogn. Lett. **196**, 344–350 (2025). https://doi.org/10.1016/j.patrec.2025.03.009

5. de Paz, E.G., et al.: A splitting criterion for cart models based on bayesian optimisation. In: Statistics, Society and Environment. pp. 19–35. Springer, Cham (2025). https://doi.org/10.1007/978-3-031-78401-9_2
6. Deb, K., et al.: Scalable multi-objective optimization test problems. In: Proceedings of the 2002 Congress on Evolutionary Computation (CEC'02), vol. 1, pp. 825–830. IEEE (2002). https://doi.org/10.1109/CEC.2002.1006939
7. Hastie, T., Tibshirani, R., Friedman, J.: The Elements of Statistical Learning: Data Mining, Inference, and Prediction. Springer Series in Statistics, 2nd edn. Springer, New York (2009). https://doi.org/10.1007/978-0-387-84858-7
8. Loh, W.Y.: Fifty years of classification and regression trees. Int. Stat. Rev. **82**(3), 329–348 (2014). https://doi.org/10.1111/insr.12016
9. Verbeeck, D., et al.: Multi-objective optimization with surrogate trees. In: Proceedings of the 15th Annual Conference on Genetic and Evolutionary Computation, GECCO '13, pp. 679–686. Association for Computing Machinery, New York (2013). https://doi.org/10.1145/2463372.2463455
10. Zhang, Q., Li, H.: MOEA/D: a multiobjective evolutionary algorithm based on decomposition. IEEE Trans. Evol. Comput. **11**(6), 712–731 (2007). https://doi.org/10.1109/TEVC.2007.892759

Ensembles of Manifold Learners for Supervised and Unsupervised Learning

Fabiola Muñoz Vera[✉], Juan Manuel Pérez Ortega, Eduardo F. Morales, and Hugo Jair Escalante

Instituto Nacional de Astrofísica, Óptica y Electrónica, Puebla, Mexico
{fabiola.munoz,jmanuel.perez,emorales,hugojair}@inaoep.mx

Abstract. Dimensionality reduction and manifold learning methods have been widely used to expose the most relevant information from high-dimensional datasets. Leading to improved efficiency and performance while, to some extent, avoiding the *curse of dimensionality*. Although different techniques have properties that make them suitable for different types of data, an open question in this context is whether a combination of models could result in improved performance. We propose ensembles of manifold learning methods to exploit the complementarity of different techniques for obtaining better results in supervised and unsupervised learning tasks. Extensive experimental evaluations in clustering and classification domains were performed, considering several variants of our ensemble models. Our results show that ensembles are beneficial for unsupervised learning, while remaining competitive for supervised learning tasks.

Keywords: Manifold learning · Dimensionality reduction · Ensembles

1 Introduction

Dimensionality reduction transforms the original representation of a dataset into a lower-dimensional one so that the relevant information is preserved [3]. A number of solutions to this problem have been proposed ranging from linear to non-linear techniques, the latter often referred to as *manifold learners*.

Numerous methods for manifold learning have been proposed (see [3]), each based on specific assumptions in the data and adopting different learning processes. Although these methods have obtained satisfactory performance on supervised and unsupervised learning tasks [2–4,9], choosing a method for a specific dataset is a daunting task. This is mainly because, in a realistic scenario, one does not know anything about the structure of the data. Likewise, the properties of different methods can be redundant and complementary to each other.

This paper explores the combination of multiple dimensionality reduction techniques. Our hypothesis is that by combining different techniques the resulting manifold will simplify the learning process for clustering and classification

V. G. Cruz-Sánchez et al. (Eds.): MCPR 2026, LNCS 16623, pp. 25–36, 2026.
https://doi.org/10.1007/978-3-032-28393-1_3

methods. For ensembling manifold learning methods, we consider several strategies, from plain concatenation to serial and alignment-based variants. Experimental results show that the selection of manifold learning techniques is critical for the performance of the ensemble.

The contributions of this paper are as follows: a novel serial ensemble strategy for manifold learning method with strong competitive performance; an extensive evaluation of ensemble variants in the mentioned tasks, considering up to seven reduction techniques (to the best of our knowledge, this is the largest number of techniques considered so far); also, our study motivates further research on the active selection of manifold learning methods for building ensembles.

2   Background and Related Work

2.1   Methods for Dimensionality Reduction

The manifold hypothesis states that, since each feature of the data does not carry an equal amount of information, the most important features lie on a specific lower-dimensional structure in the space. In this context, many methods have been proposed, often classified as either global (geodesic or long-range structures) or local (neighborhood relationships). More fine-grained taxonomies classify methods according to the geometric or statistical principles they rely on (e.g., spectral, geodesic-based, neighborhood-based, topological, or latent-variable models). In this work, we adopt the latter categorization and consider for our study the methods presented in Table 1. These methods were chosen because they are representative of the wide variety of available techniques, and are among the most used ones in pattern recognition.

2.2   Related Methods for Ensemble Manifold Learning

The idea of combining manifold learning techniques is not new; there are a few works that have studied this problem. Chahooki et al. proposed an application specific fusion of manifold learners [2]. However, they only considered variants of the same manifold learning technique (Isomap) for building the ensemble. Most notably, Zhang et al. [12] introduced a manifold learning ensemble that relies on *ASIM (Anisotropic Scaling Independent Measure)* to align two manifold learning techniques. ASIM is a measure that compares the similarity between two configurations under grid motion and anisotropic coordinate scaling (see [13] for a detailed description). While effective, this methodology only combined two methods and limited the fusion to one global and one local technique. Furthermore, their method was not evaluated in clustering or classification. In this work, we reproduced a variant of this methodology and used ASIM in one of our introduced ensemble variants.

3   Ensembles of Manifold Learners

Two variants for building ensembles are evaluated, where we consider the dimensionality reduction techniques presented in Table 1 as potential learners to build

Table 1. Manifold learning and related dimensionality reduction methods considered in this study. In column **Type**, G, Lo, H,/L and N stand for Global, Local, Hybrid/Linear and NonLinear, respectively.

Method	Type	Category	Key characteristics
PCA	G/L	Spectral	Maximizes variance along orthogonal directions; yields a linear subspace; fast, deterministic; sensitive to global covariance structure [6]
Kernel PCA	G/N	Spectral	Applies PCA in a high-dimensional feature space using a kernel; can capture nonlinear manifolds; depends on kernel choice (RBF, poly, sigmoid) [3]
LLE	L/N	Neighborhood	Preserves local linear relationships; reconstructs each point from neighbors; sensitive to noise and neighborhood size; good for unfolding smooth manifolds [10]
LTSA	L/N	Neighborhood	Estimates and aligns local tangent spaces, preserving local geometry. Due to its greater robustness its computational cost is higher [10]
Isomap	G/ N	Geodesic-based	Preserves global geodesic distances on the manifold using shortest paths; good for unrolling curved manifolds; sensitive to graph connectivity [11]
t-SNE	L/N	Probabilistic	Preserves local similarities using probability distributions; excellent for cluster visualization; non-metric, stochastic, not suitable for out-of-sample extension [7]
UMAP	H/N	Topological	Preserves local and some global structure using fuzzy simplistic sets; faster and more scalable than t-SNE; supports out-of-sample embedding; captures manifold topology [8]
Factor Analysis (FA)	G/L	Latent-variable	Identifies latent variables explaining correlations among observed variables; separates common variance from noise; suitable when variables share hidden structure; interpretable factors, linear mapping. [5]

ensembles. Critical for our proposal is the selection of methods to be considered in the fusion. We based our choice of methods on preliminary experimentation, but mostly on the desirable properties that an ensemble manifold learner should have. In the following, we describe the fusion variants we considered.

3.1 Concatenation of Learned Manifolds

A first variant for building ensembles is by a simple concatenation of the manifolds learned by a selection of individual methods. The final fused embedding is constructed by concatenating all resulting sub-embeddings into a joint space as shown in Fig. 1, left. The expectation is that the merged representation will carry richer and more balanced information than any individual method or the original space alone.

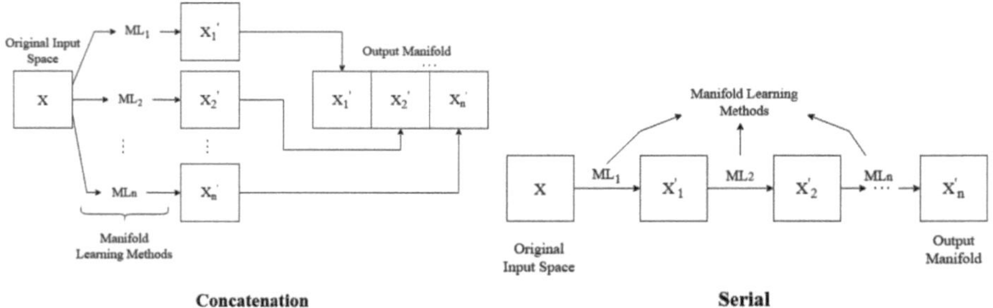

Fig. 1. Left: concatenation-based strategy. Right: serial fusion variant.

Although we could perform the fusion of an arbitrary number of methods (even the same technique with different hyperparameters), for this work we decided to build ensembles of size three[1]. Specifically, the concatenated ensemble includes the Isomap, PCA and UMAP techniques. Isomap was included to preserve the global geometric structure of the data manifold; PCA was considered to emphasize dominant linear correlations; finally, UMAP focuses on capturing local neighborhood relationships, thereby maintaining both global and local characteristics of the dataset.

Aligned Concatenation. We evaluated a concatenation variant in which the same methods and fusion strategy are considered. Fusion is preceded by an alignment of methods based on procrustes analysis [1], which finds an optimal linear transformation (translation, rotation, and scaling) to align the embeddings into a common coordinate system. Specifically, the embeddings obtained from UMAP and PCA are aligned to the Isomap embedding, which is selected as the reference space due to its ability to preserve the global manifold structure of the data. The alignment preserves their internal geometric relationships. Afterward, the embeddings are concatenated to create a unified representation.

ASIM Based Aligment. We evaluated two variants implementing ASIM. First, we evaluated the alignment and concatenation of UMAP, LLE and LTSA. The underlying hypothesis was to integrate complementary global and local geometric information. To ensure compatibility among independently learned embeddings, ASIM aligns the LLE and LTSA embeddings to the UMAP reference space, removing arbitrary rotational and reflective discrepancies while preserving intrinsic geometric relationships. This alignment enables a meaningful comparison and subsequent concatenation of the embeddings. A second ASIM variant combines FA, KernelPCA, and PCA methods. This formulation integrates complementary representations of the data, capturing latent factors, linear structure, and mild nonlinear relationships respectively. PCA is used as the

---

[1] Initial experiments with larger number of elements were not as promising as the results with our choices.

reference embedding due to its stable global structure and deterministic nature, whereas FA and KernelPCA provide alternative views of the underlying data organization. The inclusion of ASIM ensures consistency among independently learned coordinate systems and removes arbitrary rotational differences prior to concatenation.

3.2 Serial Fusion

We introduce a novel fusion method that applies manifold learning techniques in series. In this case, the output embedding of a manifold learner is the input of another technique (see Fig. 1, right). Intuitively, we wanted to explore whether applying each method sequentially allowed us to leverage the main advantages of each method, and hence produce better quality embeddings. Under this variant the order in which methods are applied is crucial.

After extensive experimental evaluation, we arrived to a competitive serial fusion configuration: UMAP(local version) $\to$ LLE $\to$ UMAP(local version). Intuitively, this configuration first preserves local relations, then refines neighborhood structures, and stabilizes the embedding with a second UMAP projection. We used default parameters for LLE, and for UMAP we set the neighbors to 15 (local version, see [8]), and the Euclidean distance was considered.

Serial Fusion + ASIM. A variant of the previous formulation enhanced with ASIM (see Sect. 2) was also evaluated. The sequence is similar to the previous one, but an additional step is applied between the local UMAP-LLE embedding and the local UMAP embedding.

4 Experimental Settings

4.1 Datasets

We tested each resulting manifold for both classification and clustering tasks using the datasets described in Table 2. Due to resource constraints, we took a stratified sample for each dataset and considered subsets of size 2,500 and 5000 samples for clustering and classification, respectively. For the classification task, we generated (stratified) random partitions for training (80%) and testing (20%). The training partition was used to learn the embeddings and then applied to the test data. For clustering, no partitioning was performed prior to experimentation.

Table 2. Summary of considered datasets.

Name	Dimensions	Examples	Classes
Fashion MNIST	784	70,000	10
COIL100	3,072	7,200	100
ISOLET	617	7,797	26
HAR	561	12,000	15

Each dataset was reduced to 30% and 6% of their original size using the different configurations detailed above. Dimensions were proportionally reduced in each stage of the serial method. For concatenation, dimensions were proportionally reduced for each method for the resulting manifold to match the reduction rates. It is important to note that before applying any dimensionality reduction method, the data were standardized.

4.2 Supervised and Unsupervised Learning Techniques

We assess the effectiveness of manifold learning techniques by evaluating the performance of clustering and classification methods using the reduced input spaces. All algorithms were implemented using the scikit-learn library with default parameter settings.

Clustering. Five clustering methods were used: Agglomerative Clustering, Birch, DBSCAN, KMeans, and OPTICS. For each ensemble variant and dataset, the ensemble technique was first applied to reduce the original input space; the clustering algorithms were then applied, and their performance was evaluated using the silhouette coefficient.

Classification. Six classifiers were considered: Gaussian Naive Bayes, KNN, Logistic Regression, MLP, Random Forest, and SVM. Each classifier was trained using an 80%–20% stratified train-test split. For each variant and dataset, the ensemble technique was first applied to the training set; then, the test data were projected onto the learned manifold. Finally, classifiers were trained and evaluated, in the corresponding partitions, with the macro F_1 score.

5 Experimental Results

5.1 Clustering

Table 3 summarizes the performance of the ensemble variants for unsupervised tasks, while Fig. 2 presents detailed results for agglomerative and K-means clustering. The best results were consistently achieved by the proposed serial variants, particularly those including ASIM. This is partially due to the fact that both methods preserving local relationships, which forms dense regions where clusters can be identified. UMAP attracts nearby points and repels distant ones; LLE compacts local neighborhoods; finally, a second UMAP refines local and global relationships. Although the Serial-Local-ASIM method achieves better average performance than the Serial-Local variant, the boxplots in Fig. 2 indicate that the latter is more stable.

Overall, the worst performers are our implementations of the ensemble methods introduced in [12]: `ASIM_FA_KPCA_PCA` and `ASIM_LLE_LTSA_UMAP`. The performance of the concatenation formulations was also limited, possibly due to

Table 3. Average and standard deviation performance (Silhouette) for the methods across the datasets. The best result is in **bold**. The − symbol indicates experiments in which DBSCAN only found a single cluster. Note that UMAPg is for the global configuration while UMAP stands for the local.

Clustering	Fusion Method	Silhouette 6%		Silhouette 30%	
		mean	std	mean	std
	Concatenated	0.268	0.072	0.178	0.068
	Concatenated Precrustes	0.268	0.072	0.178	0.068
	Serial Local	0.68	0.056	0.44	0.184
Agglomerative	Serial Local ASIM	**0.788**	**0.146**	**0.616**	**0.238**
	ASIM_LLE_LTSA_UMAP	0.504	0.122	0.404	0.156
	ASIM_FA_KPCA_PCA	0.234	0.085	0.167	0.074
	Best individual method: UMAP	0.505	0.076	0.505	0.088
	Original space	0.1275	0.0837	0.1275	0.0837
	Concatenated	0.268	0.072	0.178	0.068
	Concatenated Precrustes	0.268	0.072	0.178	0.068
	Serial Local	0.673	0.053	0.444	0.168
Birch	Serial Local ASIM	**0.734**	**0.208**	**0.586**	**0.226**
	ASIM_LLE_LTSA_UMAP	0.501	0.125	0.403	0.153
	ASIM_FA_KPCA_PCA	0.233	0.085	0.167	0.074
	Best individual method: UMAP	0.511	0.099	0.509	0.09
	Original space	0.1275	0.0837	0.1275	0.0837
	Concatenated	−	−	−	−
	Concatenated Precrustes	−	−	−	−
	Serial Local	0.561	0.098	0.098	0.304
DBSCAN	Serial Local ASIM	0.335	0.289	0.512	0.042
	ASIM_LLE_LTSA_UMAP	−0.401	0.160	−0.402	0.222
	ASIM_FA_KPCA_PCA	−	−	−	−
	Best individual method: UMAPg	**0.844**	−	**0.836**	−
	Original space	−	−	−	−
	Concatenated	0.294	0.054	0.175	0.064
	Concatenated Precrustes	0.294	0.054	0.175	0.064
	Serial Local	0.672	0.052	0.428	0.167
K-means	Serial Local ASIM	**0.790**	**0.147**	**0.551**	**0.173**
	ASIM_LLE_LTSA_UMAP	0.511	0.115	0.42	0.13
	ASIM_FA_KPCA_PCA	0.256	0.071	0.167	0.068
	Best individual method: UMAP	0.518	0.075	0.513	0.068
	Original space	0.1297	0.074	0.1297	0.074
	Concatenated	−0.367	0.216	−0.326	0.149
	Concatenated Precrustes	−0.369	0.215	−0.327	0.146
	Serial Local	**0.261**	**0.011**	**0.031**	**0.343**
OPTICS	Serial Local ASIM	−0.059	0.131	−0.189	0.153
	ASIM_LLE_LTSA_UMAP	−0.33	0.21	−0.381	0.238
	ASIM_FA_KPCA_PCA	−0.357	0.257	−0.253	0.174
	Best individual method: LLE	−0.034	0.011	−0.075	0.065
	Original space	−0.2411	0.1418	−0.2411	0.1418

the simplicity of the fusion methodology. Calculating similarities for the clustering process seems to be complicated with the manifolds resulting from the fusion. Neither of the aforementioned methods was able to outperform the best individual solution.

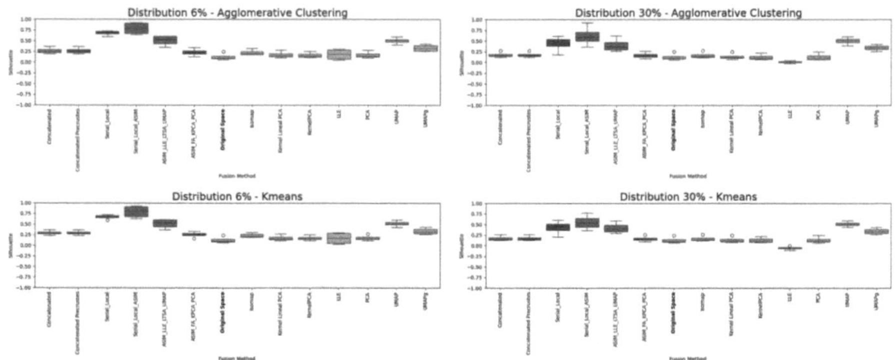

Fig. 2. Clustering performance for the considered ensemble methods. Top: agglomerative clustering; bottom: K-means. Reductions of 6% (left) and 30% (right) of the original dimensionality were considered.

5.2   Classification

Table 4 and Fig. 3 present the classification results. Concatenation-based ensemble variants performed best overall, surpassing other ensemble approaches across classifiers. Unlike clustering, classification models learn to weight over the assembled manifold to define a decision surface. Although no ensemble consistently outperformed the best individual model, their performance was comparable when dimensionality reduction was moderate, as shown in Fig. 3.

Concatenation-based approaches often outperform alignment-based methods, such as ASIM-based ones (Table 4). This is not due to ineffective alignment, but because enforcing a shared geometric frame can remove informative variability between embeddings. In contrast, concatenation preserves the heterogeneity of the original methods, allowing each to contribute directly to the classifier. As a result, concatenated embeddings often achieve higher F1-scores, particularly in datasets where both local and global structures influence class separation.

Table 4. Average and standard deviation performance (f_1 measure) for the fusion methods.

Classifier	Fusion Method	F1-score 6%		F1-score 30%	
		mean	std	mean	std
Gaussian Naive Bayes	Concatenated	0.825	0.099	0.855	0.099
	Concatenated Precrustes	0.822	0.101	**0.864**	**0.093**
	Serial Local	0.771	0.056	0.618	0.359
	Serial Local ASIM	0.260	0.297	0.054	0.073
	ASIM_LLE_LTSA_UMAP	0.504	0.222	0.169	0.142
	ASIM_FA_KPCA_PCA	0.571	0.314	0.226	0.298
	Best individual method: KernelPCA	**0.877**	**0.087**	0.857	0.105
	Original space	0.7276	0.1329	0.7276	0.1329
KNN	Concatenated	0.835	0.078	0.849	0.070
	Concatenated Precrustes	0.835	0.078	0.849	0.070
	Serial Local	0.804	0.062	0.645	0.313
	Serial Local ASIM	0.699	0.147	0.510	0.324
	ASIM_LLE_LTSA_UMAP	0.798	0.090	0.715	0.107
	ASIM_FA_KPCA_PCA	0.842	0.100	0.854	0.104
	Best individual method: KernelPCA	**0.894**	**0.062**	**0.892**	**0.064**
	Original space	0.8928	0.0723	0.8928	0.0723
Logistic Regression	Concatenated	0.890	0.082	0.904	0.083
	Concatenated Precrustes	0.890	0.081	0.905	0.083
	Serial Local	0.804	0.062	0.618	0.368
	Serial Local ASIM	0.495	0.267	0.429	0.301
	ASIM_LLE_LTSA_UMAP	0.800	0.098	0.679	0.082
	ASIM_FA_KPCA_PCA	0.799	0.123	0.696	0.359
	Best individual method: PCA	**0.913**	**0.076**	**0.926**	**0.089**
	Original space	0.9264	0.0952	0.9264	0.0952
MLP	Concatenated	0.876	0.056	0.891	0.062
	Concatenated Precrustes	0.876	0.057	0.895	0.059
	Serial Local	0.793	0.085	0.600	0.403
	Serial Local ASIM	0.388	0.304	0.429	0.378
	ASIM_LLE_LTSA_UMAP	0.757	0.116	0.644	0.064
	ASIM_FA_KPCA_PCA	0.735	0.187	0.604	0.359
	Best individual method: KernelPCA	**0.930**	**0.062**	**0.933**	**0.078**
	Original space	0.6933	0.4659	0.6933	0.4659
Random Forest	Concatenated	**0.886**	**0.073**	0.887	0.061
	Concatenated Precrustes	0.884	0.077	0.887	0.069
	Serial Local	0.801	0.065	0.651	0.300
	Serial Local ASIM	0.354	0.378	0.219	0.275
	ASIM_LLE_LTSA_UMAP	0.861	0.083	0.759	0.104
	ASIM_FA_KPCA_PCA	0.859	0.090	0.773	0.153
	Best individual method: LLE	0.883	0.088	**0.902**	**0.077**
	Original space	0.9315	0.0709	0.9315	0.0709
SVM	Concatenated	0.858	0.069	0.896	0.072
	Concatenated Precrustes	0.858	0.070	0.895	0.073
	Serial Local	0.797	0.077	0.617	0.369
	Serial Local ASIM	0.364	0.428	0.017	0.022
	ASIM_LLE_LTSA_UMAP	0.722	0.092	0.635	0.162
	ASIM_FA_KPCA_PCA	0.827	0.062	0.439	0.497
	Best individual method: KernelPCA	**0.931**	**0.073**	**0.944**	**0.064**
	Original space	0.9411	0.0673	0.9411	0.0673

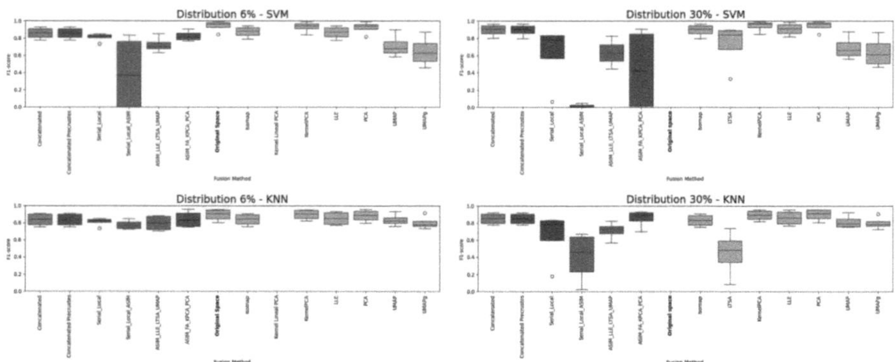

Fig. 3. Classification performance for the considered ensemble methods. Top: SVM; bottom: K-NN. Reductions of 6% (left) and 30% (right) of the original dimensionality were considered.

5.3   Visualization of Learned Manifolds

Figure 4 shows 2D visualizations of the learned manifolds for all methods and datasets (the classification scenario was considered). Although interpreting these plots is subjective, some methods (e.g., concatenation-based and best individual ones, columns 1, 2, 6, and 7) tend to spread samples across the 2D plane, potentially facilitating the identification of a decision surface. In contrast, serial variants (columns 3–4) form compact and well-defined groups, which may explain their strong performance in clustering tasks.

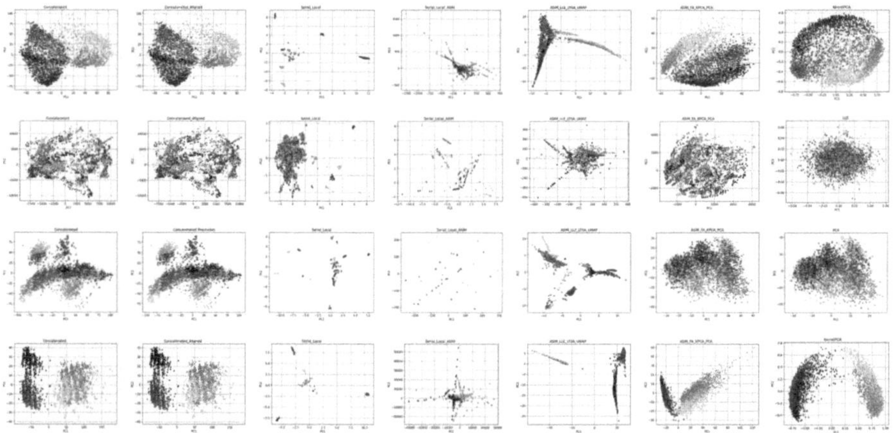

Fig. 4. 2D visualizations of the manifolds obtained by the considered methods. PCA was applied to the embedding reduced to 30% of the original size. From top to bottom: results for FashionMNIST, COIL100, ISOLET and HAR datasets.

6   Conclusions and Future Work

This paper studies the feasibility of building ensembles of manifold learning techniques for supervised and unsupervised tasks. Two ensemble variants were considered, including a novel serial fusion approach. We showed through an extensive experimental study that committee-based models are a promising direction for obtaining higher-quality manifolds.

From our study we can conclude the following: (i) By combining dimensionality reduction techniques, it is possible to obtain manifolds that outperform each of the individual methods in the context of supervised and unsupervised learning. The study of ensembles in this context is promising. (ii) The proposed serial ensemble variants result in combined manifolds that are well suited for unsupervised learning, presumably because this form of fusion implicitly groups instances in the learned manifold. (iii) For classification, concatenated fusion was mostly beneficial for non-drastic reductions with a performance close to the best individual model. As future work, we will explore alternative strategies for selecting and combining manifold learning methods, inspired by the ensemble learning theory [14]. We will also conduct ablation studies on dimensionality levels and hyperparameter variations of individual methods.

References

1. Browne, M.W.: On oblique procrustes rotation. Psychometrika **32**(2), 125–132 (1967)
2. Chahooki, M.A., Charkari, N.M.: Unsupervised manifold learning based on multiple feature spaces. Mach. Vision Appl. **25**(4), 1053–1065 (2014)
3. Ghojogh, B., Crowley, M., Karray, F., Ghodsi, A.: Elements of Dimensionality Reduction and Manifold Learning. Springer, Cham (2023)
4. Guyon, I., Nikravesh, M., Gunn, S., Zadeh, L.A. (eds.): Feature Extraction Foundations and Applications. Springer, Heidelberg (2006)
5. Harman, H.H.: Modern Factor Analysis, 3rd edn. University of Chicago Press, Chicago (1976)
6. Jolliffe, I.T., Cadima, J.: Principal component analysis: a review and recent developments. Phil. Trans. R. Soc. A **374**(2065), 20150202 (2016)
7. van der Maaten, L., Hinton, G.: Visualizing data using t-sne. J. Mach. Learn. Res. **9**, 2579–2605 (2008)
8. McInnes, L., Healy, J., Melville, J.: Umap: uniform manifold approximation and projection for dimension reduction. arXiv preprint arXiv:1802.03426 (2020)
9. Olson, C., Judd, K., Nichols, J.: Manifold learning techniques for unsupervised anomaly detection. Expert Syst. Appl. **91**(C), 374–385 (2018)
10. Roweis, S., Saul, L.: Nonlinear dimensionality reduction by locally linear embedding. Science **290**(5500), 2323–2326 (2000)
11. Tenenbaum, J.B., de Silva, V., Langford, J.C.: A global geometric framework for nonlinear dimensionality reduction. Science **290**(5500), 2319–2323 (2000)

12. Zhang, P., Fan, C., Ren, Y., Zhang, N.: Manifold learner ensemble. In: Emerging Intelligent Computing Technology and Applications, vol. 9, pp. 94–99 (2013)
13. Zhang, P., Ren, Y., Zhang, B.: A new embedding quality assessment method for manifold learning. Neurocomputing **97**, 251–266 (2012)
14. Zhou, Z.H.: Ensemble Methods: Foundations and Algorithms. Chapman & Hall CRC (2012)

Application of Unsupervised Pattern Recognition Techniques for The Structural Characterization of Masonry Walls

Miguel Angel Tlatzimatzi Flores[1]($\boxtimes$), María Guadalupe Medina Barrera[1], and Eduardo Ismael Hernández[2]

[1] Instituto Tecnológico de Apizaco, Tecnológico Nacional de México, Av. Instituto Tecnológico s/n Conurbado Tzompantepec, 90300 Cd. de Apizaco, Tlaxcala, Mexico
`{miguel.tf,guadalupe.mb}@apizaco.tecnm.mx`
[2] Universidad Popular Autónoma del Estado de Puebla, 21 Sur 1103, Barrio de Santiago, 72410 Puebla, Mexico
`eduardo.ismael@upaep.mx`

Abstract. In the performance of masonry buildings, it is required to understand the behavior of walls capable of supporting combined vertical and lateral loads up to critical levels of deformation. Assessing damage to masonry walls requires identifying structural patterns related to geometry, strength, and mechanical properties. This study uses unsupervised artificial intelligence techniques, based on self-organizing maps (SOM) of MiniSom, K-means and K-medoids, to classify confined masonry walls according to their geometric and mechanical characteristics, with three limit states: first cracking, strength and ultimate deformation, associated with strength degradation. A database was compiled from experimental studies carried out over the last 20 years in Mexico, Peru, Chile, Argentina and Venezuela. There is a database of 89 masonry walls. The objective is to generate consistent groupings that support the interpretation of building codes in Mexico and some Latin American countries, defining five levels of damage (Insignificant, Mild, Moderate, Severe, Very Severe), and also allowing the behavior of new walls to be predicted based on geometric and mechanical characterization data. Among the evaluated techniques, the K-Means method obtained the highest value of the silhouette index (0.341), indicating well-defined and consistent groupings. These results demonstrate that K-Means is effective in identifying general changes in structural behavior, although its performance can be influenced by the presence of outliers.

Keywords: masonry · Damage level · validation indices

1 Introduction

Confined masonry is a predominant structural system in Mexico, Latin American countries, and worldwide. According to the Complementary Technical Standards

V. G. Cruz-Sánchez et al. (Eds.): MCPR 2026, LNCS 16623, pp. 37–46, 2026.
https://doi.org/10.1007/978-3-032-28393-1_4

for the Structural Evaluation and Rehabilitation of Existing Buildings (Government of Mexico City, Official Gazette 2023, November 6), the magnitude of damage to structural elements is classified into five levels: a) Insignificant, b) Minor, c) Moderate, d) Severe, e) Very severe. Among the proposed models are those based on bilinear and trilinear representations of the wall's load-lateral displacement response. [1–3], adopted by Zúñiga and Terán [4] in their proposal to modify the wide column model; that of Tomazevic [5]; that of Ruiz and Miranda [6]; and more recently the model of Riahi [7].

In particular, unsupervised clustering methods allow cluster analysis without prior labeling; the importance of developing RVS methods based on machine learning has been highlighted in the literature [19,22–25], but these studies did not take structural characteristics into account. Compared to the RVS method developed in this study, which achieved an accuracy of 73.65%, the machine learning-based building damage classification models developed by Chen and Zhang and Adi showed higher accuracy (74.42% and 78.3%). Chen and Zhang (2022) attribute the high accuracy to the use of less data from a single city, which reduces the variability of the building screening data used for model development, while the number of data points used for model development and the location of the data remain unspecified by Adi et al. Furthermore, the data used in these studies were also used in the Kaggle [26,27] analyses.

This article presents the application of pattern recognition techniques to characterize damage in confined masonry walls, based on K-Means and K-Medoid self-organizing maps (SOMs) to assess the level of damage in walls subjected to lateral loads. Current regulations for the construction of masonry structures stipulate that the type and magnitude of damage must be classified. The behavior of the damage will depend on the relative resistance of the element to the different mechanical forces acting upon it. The article is structured as follows: Sect. 2 presents a review of the relevant literature. Section 3 describes the methodology applied and the self-organizing map models used to develop the dataset and algorithms. Sections 4 and 5 present the results and discussions derived from the proposed network. Finally, Sect. 6 presents the conclusions of this research.

2   Background

The structural behavior of masonry walls under lateral load has been a significant topic in structural engineering. The characterization of mechanical parameters has been based on empirical correlations, experimental tests, and analytical models Meli & Sánchez, [8]; Scrivener, [9]. However, in the analysis of structural databases and their inherent complexity of the mechanisms of damage, they have motivated the use of advanced data analysis techniques. Within these tools, the Self-Organizing Maps (SOM) neural networks developed by Kohonen (1982, 2001) [10], have established themselves as one of the most effective unsupervised methods for the projection of multidimensional data in smaller spaces, preserving essential topological relationships. Applications such as MiniSom, proposed by Vettigli (2019), have facilitated the adoption of SOMs in applied research settings. MiniSom has enabled reproducible training, flexible parameter tuning, and the generation of topological maps with a lower computational load, which is useful in exploration and classification processes. Clustering methods, such as K-means, formally introduced by MacQueen (1967), are a widely used technique for partitioning datasets into homogeneous groups or clusters by minimizing the distance between groups. K-means has proven to be useful for characterizing element typologies, recognizing damage patterns, classifying geometric configurations, and obtaining representative centroids of similar groups [11,12]. Several studies have shown that the combination of SOM and K-means produces robust hybrid systems. SOM allows topological analysis of data, while K-means refines quantitative partitioning, obtaining well-defined clusters [13,14]. The rapid advancement of information processing and the emergence of different artificial intelligence approaches have led to the development of diverse applications. According to Jasmine et al. (2021) and Thai (2022), machine learning (ML) is an important subfield of artificial intelligence (AI) that deals with the study, design, and development of algorithms that can learn from data and make predictions using that learned data. Different types of machine learning algorithms have been adopted in engineering-related applications, such as artificial neural networks (ANNs), support vector machines, nearest neighbors, and random forests. Friaa et al. (2020) used ANNs to predict the elastic membrane and bending constants of the Love-Kirchhoff plate equivalent of a hollow concrete block masonry wall. Drosopoulos and Stavroulakis (2020) employed the machine learning approach in multiscale computational homogenization to obtain the nonlinear response of the masonry wall. In Cascardi et al. (2016), propose an analytical model to predict the shear strength of fiber-reinforced mortar masonry using the RNA approach. Zhang et al. (2010) adopted ANN techniques to predict cracking patterns of masonry cavities subjected to vertical loads. Studies by Zhou et al. (2010) focused on the use of ANN to predict the failure of a wall panel subjected to lateral loads using laboratory data. All these techniques provide solid tools for a better understanding of the behavior of masonry walls, allowing for the generation of more accurate design models and thus strengthening the professional practice of damage assessment in masonry structures.

3   Methodology

The methodology employs unsupervised learning techniques, Self-Organizing Maps (SOMs), K-Means, and K-Medoids to classify walls with structural characteristics, extract patterns, and predict mechanical properties of masonry walls.

3.1   Formulation of the Damage Index

According to performance-based seismic assessment approaches [15,16] the damage index is defined as:

$$D = \frac{X - X_{\min}}{X_{\max} - X_{\min}} \tag{1}$$

where X represents a structural response parameter, while $X_{\min}$ and $X_{\max}$ correspond to the minimum and maximum values observed in the dataset.

3.2 Data Normalization

Input variables were normalized to avoid biases associated with scale differences. [17,18]. Min–max normalization was applied according to:

$$x_i^* = \frac{x_i - \min(x)}{\max(x) - \min(x)} \tag{2}$$

where x_i is the original value of the variable and x_i^* is the normalized value.

3.3 Formulation of the K-Means Algorithm

The K-Means algorithm partitions the dataset into k clusters by minimizing the sum of squared intracluster distances, defined as:

$$J = \sum_{j=1}^{k} \sum_{i \in C_j} \|x_i - \mu_j\|^2 \tag{3}$$

where x_i denotes the feature vector of observation i, and μ_j represents the centroid of cluster C_j.

3.4 Formulation of the K-Medoids Algorithm

In this method, the cluster centers correspond to the actual observations (medoids). The objective function is expressed as:

$$J = \sum_{j=1}^{k} \sum_{i \in C_j} d(x_i, m_j) \tag{4}$$

where m_j is the medoid of cluster C_j, and $d(\cdot)$ represents the distance metric, herein taken as the Euclidean distance.

3.5 Formulation of Self-Organizing Maps (SOM)

Self-Organizing Maps (SOMs) were incorporated to preserve the topological structure of the data. The SOM learning rule is given by:

$$w_i(t + 1) = w_i(t) + \alpha(t)\, h_{ci}(t)\, [x(t) - w_i(t)] \tag{5}$$

where $w_i(t)$ is the weight vector of neuron i, $\alpha(t)$ is the learning rate, and $h_{ci}(t)$ is the neighborhood function centered on the winning neuron c.

3.6   Clustering Validation Metrics

To assess the quality of the clustering results, the Silhouette index was adopted, defined as:

$$S(i) = \frac{b(i) - a(i)}{\max\{a(i), b(i)\}} \tag{6}$$

where $a(i)$ is the average distance between observation i and all other points within the same cluster, and $b(i)$ is the minimum average distance between observation i and points belonging to other clusters.

The global Silhouette index is obtained by averaging $S(i)$ over all observations. Additionally, the statistical stability of the results was evaluated using the coefficient of variation (CV):

$$CV = \frac{\sigma}{\mu} \tag{7}$$

where σ and μ denote the standard deviation and mean of the performance metrics obtained from multiple executions of the clustering algorithms.

3.7   Database and Damage Variables

The experimental database contains 89 confined masonry partition walls, of which 80 were used for training (see Tables 1, 2, and 3) and 9 for prediction, developed by different authors [28–30]. For each wall, the following wall data were collected: length, height, thickness, gross and net cross-sectional area, slenderness ratio, compressive strength, shear strength, maximum and ultimate cracking shear forces, and associated displacements.

Table 1. Extract from the training wall database: Test performed, length, height, and thickness of masonry walls

Test	ID	Length L (cm)	Height H (cm)	Thickness (cm)
Sepúlveda (2003)	M36	99.00	193.00	14.00

Table 2. Excerpt from the training wall database: Gross and net area, force ratio, compressive strength, and shear strength of masonry specimens

ID	Gross area (cm^2)	Net area (cm^2)	Ratio	F'_m (MPa)	V_m (MPa)
M1	1,445.60	841.68	1.05	3.93	0.20

For damage analysis, the following were used: crack shear (Vagr), crack displacement (dagr), maximum shear (Vmax), maximum displacement (dmax), ultimate shear (Vult), ultimate displacement (dult).

Table 3. Excerpt from the training wall database: Force–displacement parameters of masonry specimens

ID	V_{agr} (kN)	d_{agr} (mm)	V_{max} (kN)	d_{max} (mm)	V_{ult} (kN)	d_{ult} (mm)
M1	21.80	0.12	40.70	0.37	34.900	0.608

3.8 Self-Organizing Map (SOM) Setup and Training

SOM Architecture. A 10×10 neural map was used. Self-organizing maps (SOMs) were used to project the multidimensional damage space onto a one-dimensional topology of five neurons, preserving topological neighborhoods.

Clustering Using K-Means. The algorithm converges by iteratively adjusting the centroids to minimize intracluster variance. Each cluster represents a wall type, with centroids that capture the geometry, strength, and damage behavior.

K-Medoids (PAM). As a robust alternative, the Partitioning Around Medoids (PAM) algorithm was implemented, in which centroids are replaced by actual observations (medoids).

4 Results

The comparison between the methods was carried out using internal validation metrics, with the objective of evaluating the quality, stability and consistency of the clusters obtained from the structural characteristics identified in the experimental tests.

The evaluation considers the silhouette index, as well as the coefficient of variation (CV) as an indicator of the statistical consistency of the results (Table 4).

Table 4. Internal validation metrics for the clustering methods

Method	Silhouette Index	Mean CV
K-Means	0.34123	0.34019
K-Medoids	0.32374	0.32269
SOM	0.31246	0.28166

The K-Means algorithm showed the best overall performance, achieving a silhouette index of 0.341, accompanied by an average coefficient of variation of 0.34. This behavior demonstrates that the structural damage patterns identified by K-Means are stable and representative of the analyzed dataset (Fig. 1). Regarding the K-Medoids method, it recorded a silhouette index of 0.324 and a mean coefficient of variation of 0.323, values slightly lower than those obtained with

K-Means. However, these results indicate acceptable clustering quality, with a coherent internal structure (Fig. 2). Self-organizing maps showed the lowest silhouette index (0.312) and the highest mean coefficient of variation (0.282) among the methods evaluated. These results reflect a less explicit separation between clusters.

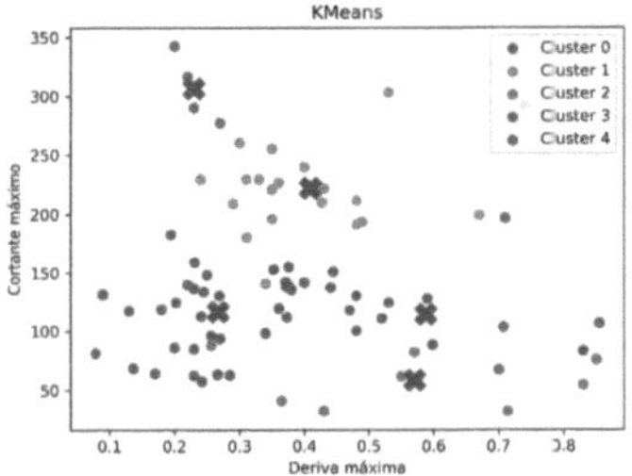

Fig. 1. K-Means clustering classification

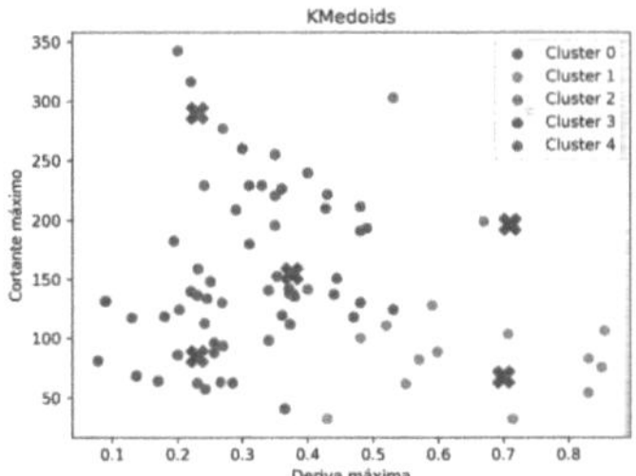

Fig. 2. K-Medoids clustering classification

Table 5, show the main grouping vectors of the k-Means algorithm, and Figs. 3, 4, and 5 show their corresponding graphical representation, visualizing points of interest such as displacement and its resistance to lateral forces. It can be observed that the k-Means method provided better localization. Future work could continue analyzing the deformation and load limit states to distinguish the possible displacement trajectories.

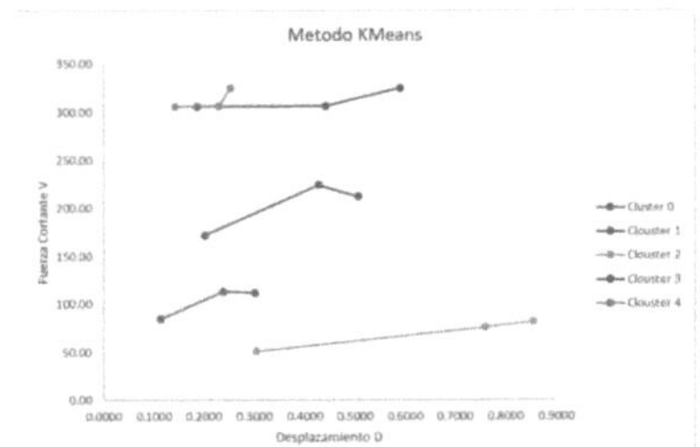

Fig. 3. Graphical representation of K-Means vectors

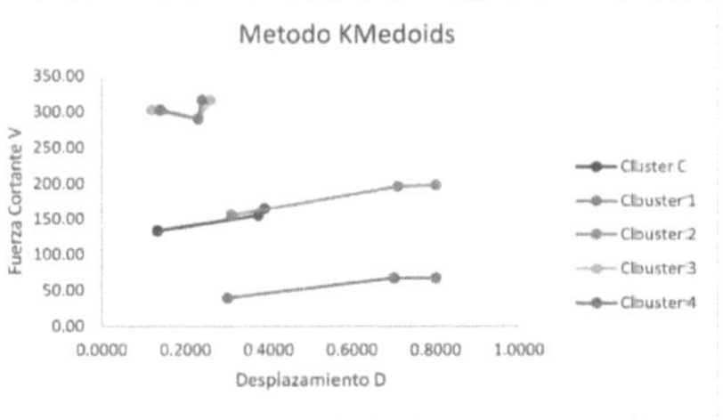

Fig. 4. Graphical representation of K-Medoids vectors

Table 5. Force-displacement parameters obtained through grouping

V_{agr}	d_{agr}	V_{max}	d_{max}	V_{ult}	d_{ult}	Method
84.52	0.1136	113.48	0.2380	112.04	0.3011	K-Means
172.29	0.2017	224.77	0.4274	212.47	0.5059	K-Means
51.29	0.3036	76.29	0.7605	81.96	0.8551	K-Means
80.24	0.1869	108.82	0.4423	109.99	0.5901	K-Means
305.95	0.1425	306.53	0.2300	325.28	0.2525	K-Means[a]
133.70	0.1340	154.90	0.3760	164.80	0.3910	K-Medoids
39.30	0.3000	67.30	0.7000	67.30	0.8000	K-Medoids
156.00	0.3100	196.50	0.7100	198.50	0.8000	K-Medoids
78.60	0.1200	84.60	0.2300	102.80	0.2600	K-Medoids
302.90	0.1400	290.10	0.2300	316.30	0.2400	K-Medoids[a]
305.95	0.1425	306.53	0.2300	325.28	0.2525	SOM
204.10	0.1800	255.20	0.3500	239.80	0.3600	SOM
232.50	0.2700	297.30	0.6350	295.90	0.7200	SOM
136.55	0.2265	192.40	0.4850	201.85	0.5330	SOM
154.55	0.2100	197.75	0.6900	188.55	0.7800	SOM[a]

[a] Results corresponding to representative wall typologies obtained from K-Means clustering.

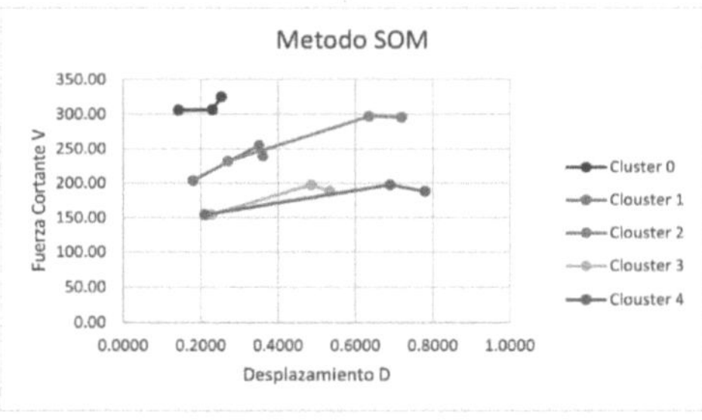

Fig. 5. Graphical representation of SOM vectors

5   Discussion

The recent literature agrees that the most robust approaches to assessment are based on the combination of multiple machine learning techniques, rather than relying on a single algorithm [19,20]. The results of this study support this perspective, showing that each method has specific strengths: K-Means offers efficiency and clarity in classification; K-Medoids provide robustness in the face of uncertainties; and SOMs facilitate the physical interpretation of the level of damage. Recent research aimed at the development of intelligent decision support systems in engineering recommends the use of hybrid approaches [20,21]. The consistency of the results with previous studies validates the applicability of these methodologies in the evaluation of confined masonry buildings, reinforcing their integration into advanced seismic performance evaluation schemes.

6   Conclusion

Based on the results obtained through the combined application of self-organizing maps (SOM) and the K-Means clustering algorithm, relevant conclusions are reached for the structural characterization of brick masonry walls, as well as for the development of methodologies based on artificial intelligence applied to structural engineering. Unsupervised grouping methods allow consistent patterns of structural damage in masonry walls to be identified without the need for pre-labeling, K-Medoids and SOM have greater stability than K-Means, being more suitable for structural databases with dispersion and possible outliers, Stability-based cross-validation is a robust and methodologically correct tool to evaluate unsupervised clustering.

Acknowledgments. The authors gratefully acknowledge the contributions of the National Center for Disaster Prevention (CENAPRED). The first author also expresses gratitude to the Secretariat of Science, Humanities, Technology and Innovation (SECIHTI) and the National Technological Institute of Mexico (TecNM) for their support and funding for the research presented in this work.

Disclosure of Interests. The authors have no competing interests to declare that are relevant to the content of this article.

References

1. Meli, R.: Behavior of masonry walls under lateral loads. Institute of Engineering, UNAM (1979)
2. Astroza, M., Blondet, M., Lagos, R.: Seismic behavior of masonry walls. Earthquake Engineering Research Institute (1991)
3. Flores, L., Alcocer, S.M.: Seismic behavior of confined masonry walls. J. Struct. Eng. (1996)
4. Zú: Seismic behavior and analytical modeling of masonry walls subjected to lateral loads. Earthq. Eng. Struct. Dyn. (2008)
5. Tomazevic, M.: Earthquake-Resistant Design of Masonry Buildings. Imperial College Press (1999)
6. Ruiz, A., Miranda, E.: Evaluation of seismic performance of masonry structures using displacement-based approaches. Earthq. Eng. Struct. Dyn. (2003)
7. Riahi, Z., Elwood, K.J., Brzev, S.: Analytical modeling of masonry walls subjected to lateral loading. Eng. Struct. (2008)
8. Meli, R., Sá: Structural behavior of masonry walls. Institute of Engineering, UNAM (1968)
9. Scrivener, J.: Mechanical Behavior of Masonry Walls. Wiley (1967)
10. Kohonen, T.: Self-organized formation of topologically correct feature maps. Biol. Cybern. (1982)

11. Jain, A.K.: Data clustering: 50 years beyond K-means. Pattern Recogn. Lett. (2010)
12. Xu, D., Tian, Y.: A comprehensive survey of clustering algorithms. Ann. Data Sci. (2015)
13. Kohonen, T.: Self-Organizing Maps. Springer (2001)
14. Vesanto, J., Alhoniemi, E.: Clustering of the self-organizing map. IEEE Trans. Neural Netw. (2000)
15. Park, Y.J., Ang, A.H.: Mechanistic seismic damage model for reinforced concrete. J. Struct. Eng. (1985)
16. Lourenç, P.B.: Simplified indexes for the seismic vulnerability of ancient masonry buildings. Construct. Build. Mater. (2006)
17. Sohn, H., Farrar, C.R., Hemez, F.M., Czarnecki, J.J., Shunk, D.D.: A review of structural health monitoring literature: 1996–2001 (2004)
18. Masciotta, M.G., Figueiredo, E., Lourenç, P.B.: A data-driven approach for damage diagnosis in masonry structures. Struct. Control Health Monit. (2016)
19. Ghahramani, Z.: Probabilistic machine learning and artificial intelligence. Nature (2015)
20. Farrar, C.R., Worden, K., Park, G.: Structural Health Monitoring: A Machine Learning Perspective. Wiley (2019)
21. Worden, K., Farrar, C.R., Haywood, J., Todd, M.: A review of nonlinear dynamics applications to structural health monitoring. Struct. Control Health Monit. (2011)
22. Ghimire, S., Guéguen, P., Schorlemmer, D.: Earthquake damage prediction of buildings in Nepal using machine learning tools. Nat. Hazards (2021)
23. Chen, Y., Zhang, X.: Machine learning–based seismic damage prediction using post-earthquake screening data. Bull. Earthq. Eng. (2022)
24. Chaurasia, J.K., Ghimirey, V., Poudel, B.: Building damage assessment and rapid visual screening after seismic events. In: Proceedings of the 7th International Conference on Structural Safety and Reliability (2019)
25. Adi, A., Pradhan, B., Paudel, D.: Machine learning classification of building damage grades following seismic events. Nat. Hazards (2020)
26. Kaggle Dataset Contributors. Earthquake magnitude, damage and impact (2024)
27. Kaggle Dataset/Code Contributors. Modelo para los daños causados por el terremoto de Nepal 2024 (2024)
28. Ramírez, P.: Experimental study on in-plane cyclic response of partially grouted reinforced concrete masonry shear walls. Eng. Struct. (2016)
29. Calderón Díaz, S.A.: Experimental and numerical study of partially grouted reinforced masonry shear walls subjected to in-plane loading (2017)
30. Flores, L.E., Alcocer, S.M.: Estudio analítico de estructuras de mampostería confinada. Technical report, Coordinación de Investigación, Área de Ingeniería Estructural, México (2014)

Dynamic Assessment of Landslide Susceptibility at Pico De Orizaba Using Ensemble Classifiers and Multitemporal Analysis

Adhara Alejandra Avendaño Barajas⬤, Leopoldo Altamirano Robles(✉)⬤,
Raquel Díaz Hernández⬤, and Saúl Zapotecas Martínez⬤

Instituto Nacional de Astrofísica, Óptica y Electrónica, Luis Enrique Erro #1, Sta. María Tonantzintla, 72840 San Andrés Cholula, Puebla, Mexico
`robles@inaoep.mx`

Abstract. Landslide Susceptibility Modeling (LSM) in active volcanic regions is often hampered by a lack of comprehensive historical inventories, limiting its applicability to data-driven models. Traditional approaches generally treat susceptibility as a static property, ignoring the temporal variability of risk due to climatic or terrain factors. This work proposes a dynamic supervised learning framework that integrates time series from Landsat-8 and ensemble classifiers to model mass movement risk on the Pico de Orizaba volcano (Mexico). To compensate for the significant lack of reference data, we propose a case-control sampling strategy with pseudo-labeling based on spectral and topographic rules. We evaluate three architectures: Random Forest, k-Nearest Neighbors, and Boosted Trees (AdaBoost) using 10-fold cross-validation. The results reveal a critical difference between numerical metrics and spatial visualization: although k-Nearest Neighbors achieved the highest Area Under the Receiver Operating Characteristic Curve (ROC-AUC) of 0.915 and the highest precision (83.4%), it resulted in spatially inconsistent predictions for land management. In contrast, AdaBoost demonstrated superior geomorphological consistency and achieved the highest sensitivity or Recall (83.6%) minimizing false negatives, which is crucial for early warning systems. In addition, multitemporal analysis of 49 scenarios (2022–2025) successfully identified a significant contraction in susceptibility areas during 2023, when a drought occurred, validating the model's sensitivity to environmental changes beyond static topographic factors.

Keywords: Landslide Susceptibility Modeling · Ensemble Classifiers · Label Scarcity

1 Introduction

The study of landslide susceptibility, defined as the spatial probability of a slope failure occurring under a given set of geo-environmental conditions, is a fun-

V. G. Cruz-Sánchez et al. (Eds.): MCPR 2026, LNCS 16623, pp. 47–57, 2026.
https://doi.org/10.1007/978-3-032-28393-1_5

damental challenge for risk management. This is especially critical in the Pico de Orizaba (Mexico), where vulnerable rural communities, agricultural zones, and critical hydrological infrastructure are constantly exposed to these hazards. Although previous geomorphological studies have been conducted in the area, these tend to be based on static approaches that fail to capture the temporal variability of triggering factors or the terrain dynamics that influence mass movements [1]. Currently, the dominant paradigm has shifted toward the use of machine learning algorithms, which offer superior abilities to model nonlinear relationships in this type of problem. However, the application of supervised models is subject to a fundamental limitation: critical dependence on complete and spatially accurate historical landslide inventories. The specialized literature indicates that inventory quality is the most determining factor in model performance, and the absence of such inventories in underdeveloped or hard-to-reach regions prevents the effective use of standard algorithms, often resulting in overfitting or severe spatial biases [2]. To overcome this limitation, this work proposes a dynamic assessment methodology that integrates multitemporal spectral variables with a case-control sampling and pseudo-labeling strategy. Specifically, we evaluate the performance of ensemble classifiers, highlighting the use of AdaBoost for its ability to identify difficult cases and improve spatial consistency over traditional methods [3].

Despite recent advances in Landslide Susceptibility Modeling (LSM) utilizing ensemble learning techniques [13], the vast majority of current literature continues to treat susceptibility as a fixed spatial property governed purely by static topographic features. While emerging dynamic assessments have begun to incorporate rainfall or InSAR data [14], they often overlook the complex terrain instability induced by prolonged environmental anomalies, such as severe droughts. The primary novelty of this work resides in the formulation of a dynamic assessment framework driven by multitemporal Landsat-8 spectral variables. By analyzing a timeline of anomalous climatic events—specifically the 2023 drought at Pico de Orizaba—this study moves beyond traditional static hazard maps to successfully identify slopes with transient, environmentally-driven instability. This provides a highly accurate, dynamic tool for early warning systems in regions lacking comprehensive historical data.

2   Background

2.1   Geological and Geographical Context

The study area focuses on the Citlaltépetl volcano (Pico de Orizaba), which is surrounded by high mountain environments and is a critical hydrological region. In the context of the Pico de Orizaba, previous efforts have established a foundational understanding of geohazards but remain constrained by static methodologies. For instance, Quesada et al. [1] applied Multiple Logistic Regression (MLR) using LOGISNET to map landslide susceptibility relying on algebraic operations that fail to capture the high-frequency temporal variability of the terrain. Similarly, Huggel et al. [4] focused on lahar modeling using empirical (LAHARZ) and probabilistic (MSF) model, highlighting a critical dependency on Digital Elevation Models (DEM). These studies represent the current state of the art in the country, treating susceptibility as a fixed property, overlooking the dynamic role of hydrometeorological drivers which can alter risk levels within months. These areas act as flow channels where material is readily mobilized. Unlike general regional studies, our evaluation specifically targets these geomorphologically active areas to assess how their stability fluctuates with environmental changes.

2.2   Remote Sensing and Spectral Indices

To overcome the limitations of in situ data scarcity, remote sensing provides essential tools for monitoring surface changes. The Landsat 8 mission allows the derivation of spectral indices that characterize vegetation and moisture conditions [15].

NDVI (Normalized Difference Vegetation Index). The integration of NDVI has been shown to significantly improve the performance of statistical models for landslide susceptibility analysis [5,9].

NDWI and NBR (Normalized Difference Water/Burn Index). Different vegetation and moisture indices have been shown to be sufficient for analyzing areas prone to or sensitive to landslides [6]. Specifically, NBR is effective in identifying the severity of burns and sudden changes in land cover [16].

2.3   Machine Learning in Landslide Susceptibility

Recent studies have highlighted the ability of these algorithms to identify and prevent landslides, emphasizing their capacity for generalization even in complex terrain [3,9]. However, traditional statistical models prioritize static factors like lithology and slope [2], modern ML approaches allow for the integration of dynamic variables. Precipitation is often cited as a trigger, but commonly treated it as a static annual average. In contrast, our approach models precipitation as a dynamic state variable competing with topographic factors. As noted by Ma et al. [8], the challenge in modern LSM is integrating temporal datasets. However, we extend this by testing their sensitivity to precipitation anomalies (droughts vs. intense rain), a capability that standard static ML implementations [9] often lack.

3   Methodology

The proposed methodology implements a supervised learning workflow for susceptibility modeling, which is structured in three phases: data acquisition, feature selection, and classifier evaluation. The study area covers approximately 1,200 km^2 around the Pico de Orizaba volcano (Fig. 1), an area characterized by high climatic and geomorphological variability [12].

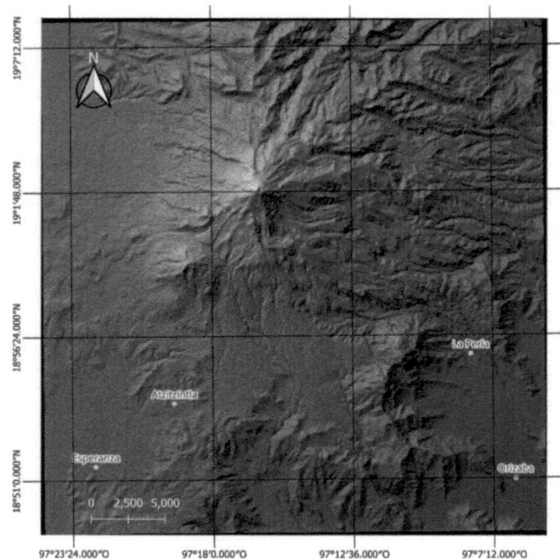

Fig. 1. Geographic location of the Pico de Orizaba National Park (Mexico). The map displays the DEM derived from SRTM data, the spatial distribution of the 744 landslide and control events used for model training and validation.

3.1   Data Acquisition

To construct the multitemporal model, a series of images from the Landsat 8 OLI/TIRS sensor, with a spatial resolution of 30 meters/pixel were acquired through Google Earth Engine, covering the period 2022–2025. This sensor was selected due to the consistency of its historical archive and its radiometric capability for long-term monitoring [15]. Preprocessing included atmospheric correction to convert digital numbers (DN) to Top of Atmosphere (TOA) reflectance. While Surface Reflectance (SR) is often preferred for vegetation analysis, TOA was utilized here to ensure consistency across the historical time series without the artifacts sometimes introduced by automated SR atmospheric correction algorithms in high-altitude, highly reflective volcanic environments. Also, the generation of cloud and shadow masks using the quality assurance (QA) band to ensure the integrity of the time series. A Shuttle Radar Topography Mission (SRTM) digital elevation model (DEM) was also used to derive topographic variables [4]. The images from this stage will be used for the validation and testing of the classification models.

3.2   Feature Selection

Dynamic spectral variables were generated in GEE, serving as indicators of terrain stability. These were calculated using the Normalized Difference Vegetation Index (NDVI), commonly used to monitor the health and density of vegetation cover [5], the Normalized Difference Water Index (NDWI), used to estimate surface water content [6], and the Normalized Burn Ratio (NBR), which is sensitive to abrupt changes in biomass and water stress [16]. In the absence of a dense historical inventory, a pseudo-labeling strategy with case-control sampling was implemented. Positive cases (y = 1) were validated from the National Inventory of Geological Phenomena [11]. While global satellite-based landslide catalogs exist, this national inventory was strictly preferred to guarantee field-validated ground truth and high spatial fidelity specific to the complex volcanic topography. Controls (y = 0) were randomly computer-based generated (GEE) by applying a 5 km spatial exclusion buffer to avoid bias and/or noise during training. Using these points, a training dataset was constructed with 744 points, including positive cases and controls (Table 1).

Table 1. Table of dynamic spectral variables.

Index	Abbreviation	Geophysics Utility
Vegetation	NDVI	Vegetation health and density indicator
Humidity	NDWI	Water content in foliage and water bodies
Burn Index	NBR	Detection of bare soil and water stress
Short Wave InfraRed	SWIR	Sensitivity to soil moisture
Moisture Index	-	Indirect indicator of moisture in soil

3.3   Classifier Evaluation

Tree-based ensemble architectures were explicitly selected over kernel methods or deep neural networks due to their proven robustness against overfitting on moderately-sized datasets and their ability to provide interpretable feature importance metrics, which is essential for geomorphological analysis. The performance of three ensemble classification models was compared: Random Forest (RF), used as a baseline due to its robustness in reducing overfitting in noisy data [7]; AdaBoost, a model that sequentially optimizes the weights of misclassified instances, improving predictive accuracy [3]; k-nearest neighbors (k-NN) used to contrast performance based on distances [7,8]. For validation, the traditional static split (70/30) was discarded in favor of k-fold cross-validation with k = 10. This strategy ensures that all samples (N = 744) are used for both training and validation, reducing variance in error estimation and conforming to recent standards in geomorphology [9].

4   Experiments and Results

The results obtained demonstrate that the risk of landslides on Pico de Orizaba is a fluctuating phenomenon, which is modulated by the nonlinear interaction between static factors (topography) and dynamic forces (precipitation and humidity).

4.1 Performance and Model Selection

To ensure generalization and avoid overfitting, the models were evaluated using a k-fold cross-validation scheme ($k = 10$). Table 2 summarizes the quantitative performance of the three evaluated architectures: Random Forest (RF), AdaBoost, and k-Nearest Neighbors (k-NN).

Table 2. Cross-validation performance metrics for the evaluated models. Accuracy includes the standard deviation ($\pm$) representing the variability across the 10 folds.

Model	Accuracy	Precision	Recall	F1 Score
AdaBoost	**83.5 $\pm$ 3.3 %**	80.5%	**83.6%**	**82.0%**
Random Forest	82.7 $\pm$ 5.0 %	80.8%	80.6%	80.7%
k-NN	83.1 $\pm$ 4.2 %	**83.4%**	77.9%	80.6%

To assess the statistical significance of the performance differences among the models, a paired t-test was conducted on the accuracy scores obtained from the cross-validation. The analysis revealed no statistically significant differences between AdaBoost and Random Forest ($p = 0.839$), nor between AdaBoost and k-NN ($p = 0.991$). This parity indicates that the selected predictors are robust enough to yield high predictive performance regardless of the specific classification algorithm. Nevertheless, the ensemble methods (AdaBoost and Random Forest) remain the preferred approach for this study, as they inherently provide feature importance metrics—a critical capability for interpreting the physical drivers of geomorphological dynamics.

Furthermore, the Receiver Operating Characteristic (ROC) curve analysis (Fig. 2) confirms the competitive and robust diagnostic ability of the models, where the ROC-AUC metric reinforces the stable behavior of AdaBoost in distinguishing between stable and susceptible terrain at a standard 0.5 threshold. Internal feature selection analysis derived from the AdaBoost architecture confirmed that precipitation and slope were the dominant predictors, contributing to over 60% of the model's decision criteria, validating the physical principles of slope instability (Fig. 3).

The comparative analysis reveals critical patterns for risk management:

Superiority of AdaBoost: This model achieved the highest sensitivity (recall) in the study (83.6%). In the context of geological risks, this metric is crucial, as it indicates the algorithm's ability to correctly identify unstable pixels (true positives), minimizing dangerous omissions. Moreover, it achieved the best overall balance with an F1 score of 82.0%.

Limitations of K-NN: Despite showing the highest precision (83.4%), which implies a low false alarm rate, the k-NN model had the lowest performance

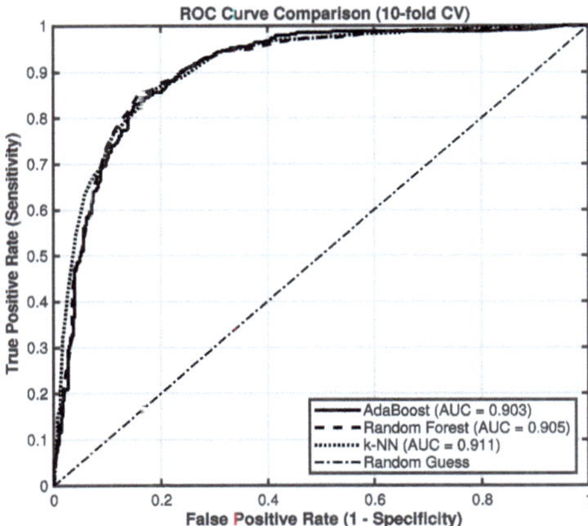

Fig. 2. Receiver Operating Characteristic (ROC) curves for AdaBoost, Random Forest, and k-NN. The Area Under the Curve (ROC-AUC) demonstrates the robust diagnostic ability of the models across the 10-fold cross-validation sets.

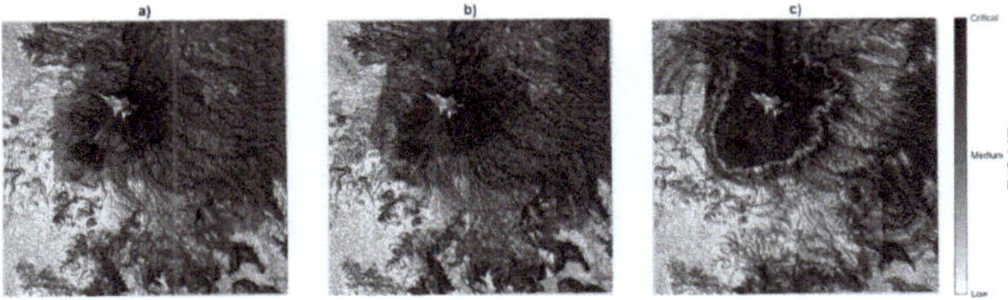

Fig. 3. Visual comparison of landslide susceptibility maps generated by the three evaluated models: a) AdaBoost, b) Random Forest, c) k-NN, for the target date of March 6, 2023. The models demonstrate different spatial clustering behaviors and boundary definitions.

in sensitivity (77.9%). This suggests an excessively conservative behavior, as it omits almost 23% of the actual risk areas. Visually, this model generated a kind of concentric bands or "terrain curves" due to its rigidity in the feature space, which is unacceptable when mapping the area.

Spatial Consistency: From a visual perspective, AdaBoost managed to define the high-probability zones around the volcano with greater structural continuity. While Random Forest exhibited a scattered distribution of risk pixels across the study area, AdaBoost produced sharp boundaries that differentiate critical slopes from stable plains.

4.2   Analysis of the Conditioning Factors

To validate the physical consistency of the predictions, a frequency ratio (FR) analysis (Table 3) was conducted. The FR defines the probabilistic relationship between the spatial distribution of landslide events and the classes of each conditioning factor. The results confirm that the model correctly learned the geomorphological relationships in the area: Precipitation, which showed a clear threshold behavior was observed, where $FR > 1$ values (strong association with landslides) only occur in the highest precipitation ranges ($1466 - 2504$ mm); Slope, where moderate-high slope ranges showed significantly high FR values, in accordance with soil mechanics, where gravity acts as the driving force and Spectral variables, where the variable response of NDVI and NDWI confirmed their role as seasonal modulators of susceptibility.

Table 3. Frequency Ratio (FR) of Conditioning Factors.

Factor	Class	Pixels	LS (%)	FR	Factor	Class	Pixels	LS (%)	FR
Slope	$0.00 - 12.95$	344	19.70%	0.43	**Water**	-0.81 − -0.67	325	36.12%	0.83
(Âř)	$12.95 - 25.89$	207	37.61%	1.35	(NDWI)	-0.67 − -0.54	189	33.43%	1.32
	$25.89 - 38.84$	132	28.96%	1.63		-0.54 − -0.40	92	17.91%	1.45
	$38.84 - 51.78$	50	10.75%	1.60		-0.40 − -0.27	108	7.46%	0.51
	$51.78 - 64.73$	11	2.99%	2.02		-0.27 − -0.13	30	5.07%	1.26
Precip.	$428 - 947$	158	14.93%	0.70	**Humidity**	-0.31 − -0.17	6	1.79%	2.22
(mm)	$947 - 1466$	123	21.79%	1.32	(M.I.)	-0.17 − -0.02	84	7.76%	0.69
	$1466 - 1985$	261	39.10%	1.11		-0.02 − 0.13	163	25.67%	1.17
	$1985 - 2504$	180	24.18%	1.00		0.13 − 0.28	206	36.42%	1.32
	> 2504	180	24.18%	1.00		0.28 − 0.43	285	28.36%	0.74
Veget.	$0.02 - 0.19$	39	4.78%	0.91	**Burn**	-0.21 − -0.02	20	3.28%	1.22
(NDVI)	$0.19 - 0.37$	119	10.75%	0.67	(NBR)	-0.02 − 0.17	140	11.34%	0.60
	$0.37 - 0.55$	78	17.01%	1.62		0.17 − 0.35	95	20.60%	1.61
	$0.55 - 0.72$	170	31.34%	1.37		0.35 − 0.54	187	36.12%	1.44
	$0.72 - 0.90$	338	36.12%	0.80		0.54 − 0.73	302	28.66%	0.71
SWIR	$0.05 - 0.12$	53	7.46%	1.05					
	$0.12 - 0.19$	498	69.55%	1.04					
	$0.19 - 0.27$	175	19.40%	0.82					
	$0.27 - 0.34$	17	3.28%	1.44					
	$0.34 - 0.42$	1	0.30%	2.22					

4.3　Spatio-Temporal Dynamics of Susceptibility

Using AdaBoost, a time series of 49 susceptibility maps was generated for the period 2022–2025. The analysis of the maximum annual susceptibility maps revealed a remarkable spatial consistency in the identification of critical structural areas (gullies and volcanic cone slopes). However, significant interannual variations driven by hydrometeorology were detected. When comparing the year 2023 with 2024 (Fig. 4a), an expansion of medium-risk areas in the foothill zones was observed during 2024, correlated with an increase in the accumulated annual precipitation. This demonstrates the model's ability to reduce the probability in dry years and not statistically overestimate the risk if moisture was not an important factor that year.

Finally, the temporal variability map (Fig. 4b) distinguishes between stable zones (invariant susceptibility) and zones of high variability, where the susceptibility index fluctuates significantly depending on conditioning factors, identifying slopes where stability is transient and highly sensitive to seasonal rainfall or changes in vegetation and soil moisture. This confirms that instability in these slopes is transient and environmentally driven, identifying them as priority targets for dynamic monitoring

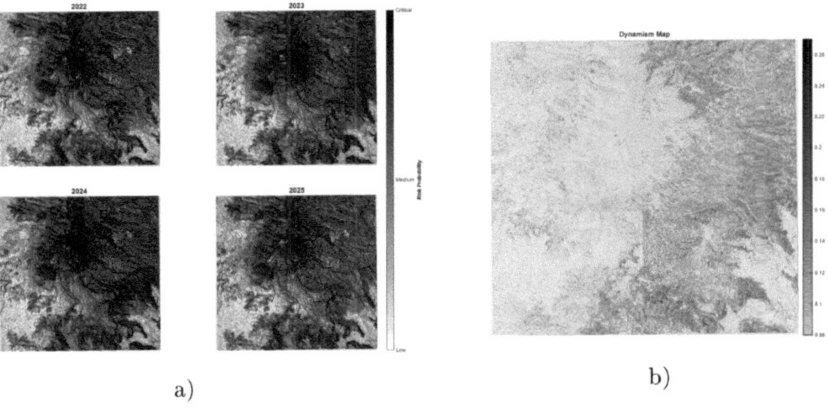

Fig. 4. Spatio-temporal dynamics of landslide susceptibility. a) Maximum annual susceptibility maps (2022–2025) derived from the AdaBoost model, highlighting the inter-annual expansion and contraction of risk zones in response to cumulative precipitation. b) Temporal variability map (standard deviation), where darker areas indicate high dynamic behavior, representing slopes whose stability is transient and highly sensitive to environmental factors.

5   Conclusions

This study addressed the challenge of modeling landslide susceptibility in regions with scarce data by proposing an assessment methodology that integrates multitemporal spectral variables with a case-control sampling strategy. The results validate the effectiveness of this approach in overcoming the limitations of static inventories and capturing the temporal variability of risk factors on the Pico de Orizaba volcano. From the comparative analysis, AdaBoost was positioned as the most robust algorithm, achieving a sensitivity (Recall) of 83.6% and an F1-Score of 82.0%. Unlike k-NN, which showed significant omissions, and Random Forest, which introduced spatial noise into the analysis, AdaBoost demonstrated a superior ability to identify unstable pixels and maintain spatial consistency around the volcanic edifice. Frequency Ratio (FR) analysis confirmed the model's ability to interpret the physics of the phenomenon, identifying slope angles greater than $12.95°$ and precipitation levels greater than $1466\,mm$ as the primary conditioning factors. In addition, the temporal integration of spectral indices (NDVI, NDWI, NBR) allowed for the modeling of susceptibility based on seasonal changes. This was evidenced by the expansion of risk areas in 2024 compared to 2023, which was directly correlated with hydrological variations. Finally, the generation of a Dynamism Map is a key contribution to risk management. By distinguishing between "Stable" and "Dynamic" domains, this methodology provides a practical tool that prioritizes near real-time monitoring in areas where stability is transient and critically dependent on hydrometeorological events.

This work demonstrates that susceptibility to landslides is a fluctuating phenomenon and that machine learning models, when trained with validated, high-quality temporal data, can effectively bridge the gap in regions that lack historical inventories.

Acknowledgments. The author acknowledges the support provided by SECIHTI and INAOE for her postgraduate studies with a scholarship in the Master's Program in Space Sciences and Technologies.

Data Availibility Statement. To support the principles of open science and ensure the reproducibility of this research, the MATLAB scripts used for the training and evaluation of the ensemble classifiers, along with the cross-validation splits and the processed training dataset, are publicly available in the following GitHub repository: https://github.com/arteemiz11/LSM-Pico-Orizaba-Ensemble/tree/main.

Disclosure of Interests. The authors declare no conflicts of interest.

References

1. Quesada, J.F.A., Gabrie, L.P., Hubp, J.L., Romero, J.U., Cuevas, H.A.L.: GIS and geomorphological mapping applied to landslide inventory and susceptibility mapping in the El Estado River basin, Pico de Ori-zaba. Mexico. J. Geogr. Cartography **5**(1), 100–109 (2022)
2. Reichenbach, P., Rossi, M., Malamud, B.D., Guzzetti, F.: A review of statistically based landslide susceptibility models. Earth Sci. Rev. **180**, 60–91 (2018)
3. Wang, H., Zhang, L., Yin, K., Luo, H., Li, J.: Landslide identification using machine learning. Geosci. Front. **12**(1) (2021)
4. Huggel, C., Schneider, D., Miranda, P.J., Delgado Granados, H., Kääb, A.: Evaluation of ASTER and SRTM DEM data for lahar modeling: A case study on lahars from Popocatépetl Volcano. Mexico. J. Volcanol. Geoth. Res. **170**(1), 99–110 (2008)
5. Niraj, K.C., Singh, A., Dericks, P.S.: Effect of the normalized difference vegetation index (NDVI) on GIS-enabled bivariate and multivariate statistical models for landslide susceptibility mapping. J. Indian Soc. Remote Sens. **51**(8), 1739–1756 (2023)

6. Giordano, L.D.C., Marques, M.L., Reis, F.A., Gomes, V., Corrêa, C.V.D.S., Riedel, P.S.: The suitability of different vegetation indices to analyses area with landslide propensity using Sentinel -2 Image. Boletim de Ciências Geodésicas (2023)
7. Merghadi, A.: Machine learning methods for landslide susceptibility studies: a comparative overview of algorithm performance. Earth Sci. Rev. **207** (2020)
8. Ma, Z., Mei, G., Piccialli, F.: Machine learning for landslides prevention a survey. Neural Comput. Appl. **33** (2021)
9. Chang, Z., et al.: Landslide susceptibility prediction based on remote sensing images and GIS: comparisons of supervised and unsupervised machine learning models. Remote Sens. **12**(3), 502 (2020)
10. Avendaño, A., Altamiranc, L.: Evaluación Dinámica de la Suscept bilidad a Deslizamientos en el Pico de Orizaba mediante Clasificadores de Ensamb e y Análisis Multitemporal (2026). Master thesis. INAOE
11. Geografía e Informática: Inventario Nacional de Fenómenos Geológicos Instituto Nacional de Estadística (2024)
12. Secretaría de Medio Ambiente y Recursos Naturales: El Parque Nacional Pico de Orizaba protege ambientes de alta montaña. https://www.gob.mx/semarnat/es/articulos/parque-nacional-pico-de-orizaba-protege-ambientes-de-alta-montana?idiom=es. Accessed 29 Nov 2025
13. Xu, Q., Yordanov, V., Amici, L., Brovelli, M.A.: Landslide susceptibility mapping using ensemble machine learning methods: a case study in Lombardy, Northern Italy (2024)
14. Wei, Y., et al.: Refined and dynamic susceptibility assessment of landslides using InSAR and machine learning models. Geosci. Front. **15**(6), 101890 (2024)
15. U.S. Geological Survey Landsat 8. https://www.usgs.gov/landsat-missions/landsat-8. Accessed 23 Nov 2025
16. UN-SPIDER Normalized Burn Ratio (NBR). https://un-spider.org/advisory support/recommended-practices/recommended-practice-burn-severity/in-detail/normalized-burn-ratio. Accessed 23 Nov 2025

Customer Preferences Recognition in Neuromarketing: Improving Accuracy with Autoregressive Modeling, Genetic Algorithms, and Naive Bayes

Christian Ruiz-Ugalde$^{(\boxtimes)}$, René Arnulfo García-Hernández ,
Jonathan Rojas-Simón , Yulia Ledeneva , and Marco Antonio Ramos-Corchado

Universidad Autónoma de Estado de México, Instituto Literario 100, 50000 Toluca,
State of México, México
`{cruizu,reagarciah,jrojass,ynledeneva,maramosc}@uaemex.mx`

Abstract. Understanding consumer preferences has been commonly addressed by big companies, which rely on surveys and interviews to comprehend customer needs. However, these methods cannot capture some critical aspects of decision-making. Neuromarketing addresses this limitation by capturing subconscious processes through electroencephalography (EEG) devices, which monitor brain activity in response to marketing stimuli. However, the high dimensionality of that can produce EEG data poses challenges for efficient analysis and classification. In this study, we used EEG data on consumer preferences obtained from a previous study, from which we extracted relevant information using Autoregressive Modeling (AR). Subsequently, these features were introduced into a wrapper selection scheme that employs Genetic Algorithms (GA) to identify the most relevant features. The results showed that the use of AR, GA, and a Gaussian Naive Bayes (GNB) model improved classification accuracy from 70.33% to 77.99%. The selected features highlighted the importance of specific EEG channels associated with decision-making and emotional regulation according to the 10–20 system. This study demonstrates the effectiveness of the proposed method for EEG signal classification, revealing the neural mechanisms underlying consumer preferences.

Keywords: Neuromarketing · Autoregressive Modeling · Genetic Algorithm · Gaussian Naive Bayes · Feature Engineering

1 Introduction

Traditionally, consumer preference studies have relied on surveys, interviews, and focus groups to identify which product attributes are valued by customers. Although these approaches are useful, they do not always capture the unconscious processes involved in decision-making. For this reason, neuromarketing has emerged as an interdisciplinary field that seeks to understand consumer behavior through physiological and neural responses, providing complementary evidence beyond self-reported data [16, 25].

V. G. Cruz-Sánchez et al. (Eds.): MCPR 2026, LNCS 16623, pp. 58–67, 2026.
https://doi.org/10.1007/978-3-032-28393-1_6

Among the techniques used in neuromarketing, electroencephalography (EEG) has attracted considerable attention because it enables the analysis of brain activity during exposure to marketing stimuli [25]. However, EEG-based preference recognition remains challenging due to the high dimensionality, variability, and noise that characterize these signals. As a result, the design of suitable preprocessing, feature extraction, and feature selection strategies is critical for improving classification performance [7, 23].

Feature engineering has therefore become a central stage in EEG analysis. In this context, transformation methods help reduce noise, feature extraction methods generate compact signal representations, and feature selection methods identify the variables that contribute most to classification [7, 23]. Recent studies have shown that autoregressive (AR) modeling is effective for representing temporal dynamics in EEG signals [6, 10], while genetic algorithms (GA) are useful for selecting informative subsets of features in high-dimensional search spaces [8, 14, 22]. This combination is especially attractive in neuromarketing scenarios, where the objective is not only to improve predictive performance but also to identify brain regions associated with consumer responses [25].

In this study, we evaluate whether the combination of AR modeling, GA-based feature selection, and Gaussian Naive Bayes (GNB) can improve EEG-based recognition of customer preferences on the dataset reported by Yadava et al. (2017). Unlike the original study, which reported the best accuracy of 70.33% using Hidden Markov Models, our approach first compares several feature extraction strategies and identifies AR modeling as the most effective baseline representation. Then, a wrapper feature selection scheme based on GA is applied to refine the AR coefficient set and maximize classification accuracy.

The proposed method achieved an accuracy of 77.99%, outperforming the best result reported in the original study. In addition, the GA reduced the feature space from 280 to 118 coefficients, indicating that a more compact representation can also improve predictive performance. The selected coefficients were concentrated mainly in channels AF3, P8, and T8, suggesting that prefrontal, parietal, and temporal brain activity contains relevant information for discriminating between Like and Dislike responses.

The main contribution of this work is twofold. First, it shows that AR modeling is a competitive feature extraction method for EEG-based neuromarketing classification when compared with other time-, frequency-, and decomposition-domain alternatives. Second, it demonstrates that GA-based wrapper selection can substantially improve classification efficiency by identifying a reduced subset of discriminative features. These findings support the use of temporal modeling and evolutionary optimization as a practical strategy for preference recognition from EEG signals.

The remainder of this paper is organized as follows. Section 2 presents the related work on transformation, feature extraction, and feature selection for EEG analysis. Section 3 describes the dataset and the proposed methodology. Section 4 reports the experiments and obtained results. Section 5 discusses the main findings and their interpretation. Finally, Sect. 6 presents the conclusions and future work.

2 Related Work

2.1 The Savitzky-Golay Filter as a Method for the Transformation Phase.

During the transformation phase, EEG signals are filtered to reduce noise and improve data quality before feature extraction. In this study, the Savitzky-Golay (SG) filter was adopted because it smooths biosignals while preserving waveform morphology, which is especially desirable in EEG analysis [3, 13]. Since the mathematical formulation and signal-processing properties of the SG filter have been extensively described in the literature, a detailed derivation was omitted and refer the reader to the original work of Savitzky and Golay (1964). Recent studies have also reported its usefulness in EEG and biosignal preprocessing, particularly for reducing artifacts while retaining relevant diagnostic and frequency-related information [2, 21]. For these reasons, the SG filter was selected as the transformation method in our preprocessing stage.

2.2 Autoregressive Modeling as a Method for the Feature Extraction Phase

The autoregressive modeling (AR) is a feature extraction technique belonging to the time-domain set of methods, as it considers the signal's values at different time points to predict a future value. The mathematical definition of an AR model of order p [24] can be expressed by the following equation:

$$x(n) = \sum_{i=1}^{p} a_p(i)x(n-1) + \varepsilon(n), \tag{1}$$

where $x(n)$ is the signal value at sample point n, $a_p(i)$ are the coefficients of the AR model, and $\varepsilon(n)$ is white noise with zero mean. In practice, the values of the AR model coefficients are estimated from a finite data sample [24]. The model order selection is critical, as it determines the ability to capture the signal dynamics. Thus, if the order is very low, the model fails to represent the signal. On the contrary, whether the order is excessively high, it overfits the model to the noise naturally present in the data [17].

In the state-of-the-art, several studies have used AR models to extract significant features from EEG signals. Fryz et al. [6] demonstrated that features derived from AR model coefficients enhance the performance of classical machine learning classifiers compared to raw EEG data. Haderlein et al. [10] applied linear and nonlinear AR models to improve brain activity detection in BCI interfaces, showing potential for prosthesis control and brain dynamics analysis. Acharya et al. [1] used linear and bilinear models to predict intracranial EEG responses in epilepsy patients, accurately capturing interaction patterns in brain networks. Additionally, in [4] enhanced EEG-based BCI classification by integrating spatial and temporal signal information through AR models, outperforming conventional methods.

2.3 Genetic Algorithms as a Method for the Feature Selection Phase

Genetic algorithms (GA) are optimization techniques inspired by biological evolution processes such as natural selection and genetics. They utilize operators like selection, crossover, and mutation to explore optimal solutions for complex problems. In the context of EEG signal processing, GAs is employed to reduce data dimensionality by selecting relevant features, eliminating redundancies, and improving classification model accuracy. These techniques enable efficient optimization of complex systems [8, 14].

Therefore, several studies have utilized genetic algorithms to select relevant features. Ghorbanzadeh et al. [8] proposed the Deep GA Fitness Formation (DGAFF), combining GA with sequential search to enhance motor imagery BCI channel selection, improving real-time EEG dimensionality reduction. Luo et al. [14] introduced a parallel GA using MapReduce (MRPGA) for CSP-based feature selection, optimizing multichannel EEG recognition. Pijackova et al. [20] applied GA to optimize neural network architectures for intracranial EEG (iEEG) analysis, improving F1-score with preprocessing techniques like STFT and Wavelet Transform. Finally, Saibene & Gasparini [22] developed a GA for heterogeneous EEG data feature selection, effectively integrating time, frequency, and time-frequency domains to reduce dimensionality and enhance classification performance.

2.4 EEG Signals and Dataset Used for This Paper

EEG records electrical brain activity through scalp electrodes and has been widely used in neuromarketing to analyze neural responses to marketing stimuli [16, 25]. In this study, we used the dataset reported by Yadava et al. (2017), acquired with a 14-channel Emotiv EPOC + headset arranged according to the 10–20 system, as shown in Fig. 1. The dataset includes EEG recordings from 25 participants who evaluated 42 products, each presented for 4 s, after which they indicated whether they liked or disliked the item [25]. As EEG signals are high-dimensional and require processing before classification, feature engineering methods are commonly applied through transformation, feature extraction, and feature selection stages [7, 23]. In the original study, the best reported result was 70.33% accuracy using Hidden Markov Models.

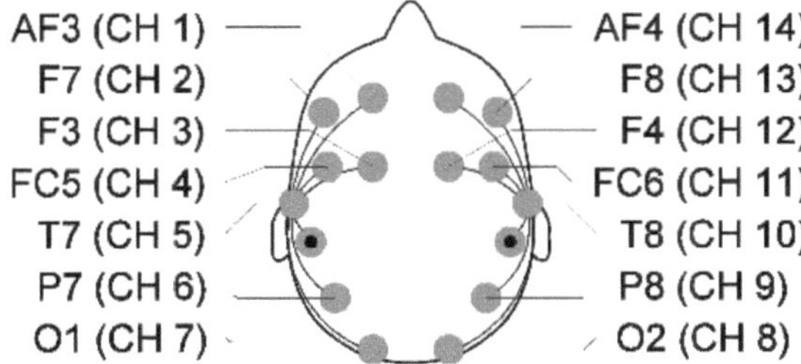

Fig. 1. A 10–20 system for electrode positioning for Emotiv EPOC + headset

3 Proposed Method

In this section, we present our proposal to improve the classification accuracy of the signals from the original study. Our approach consists of using Autoregressive Modeling (AR) combined with the Gaussian Naive Bayes (GNB) model for feature extraction and Genetic Algorithms (GA) for feature selection, aiming to reduce computational complexity and enhance classification accuracy.

3.1 Transform and Feature Extraction

For the transformation phase, we propose applying the SG filter, as in the previous study, since, as discussed, this type of filtering significantly preserves the shape of the signals.

Based on the comprehensive review of FE techniques presented in [23] we will test various methods from the time, frequency, and decomposition domains. In this study, a wrapper-based approach is introduced, ensuring that the selected features optimize classification performance through an iterative evaluation of their impact on the model's accuracy.

To determine the optimal order of the AR, the Akaike Information Criterion (AIC) and Bayesian Information Criterion (BIC) will be applied and compared with the results of empirical tests. The optimal model will then be evaluated using different classifiers to compare their accuracy results.

3.2 Feature Selection

To refine feature selection and improve classification accuracy, a GA was implemented. Below, we describe the genetic operators proposed for this phase.

Solution Representation: Each solution or individual i in generation g is represented by a binary chromosome of length equal to the number of extracted features. A value of 1 at position i indicates the corresponding feature is selected, while 0 indicates the opposite. These values are organized in a vector of N genes:

$$X_i(g) = \left[X_{i,1}(g), X_{i,2}(g), \ldots, X_{i,n}(g) \right], X_{i,k}(g) \in \{0,1\}, \tag{2}$$

Initial Population: The initial population is generated randomly, ensuring diversity in the possible feature combinations. Each chromosome contains randomly assigned binary values are.

Fitness Function: The fitness function evaluates the accuracy obtained using the GNB classifier with only the features selected by a given chromosome. Performance is measured by the model's accuracy in predicting labels on a test set. Mathematically, the fitness function is expressed as:

$$f(X_i(g)) = \max\left(\frac{TP + TN}{TP + TN + FP + FN} \right), \tag{3}$$

where TP, TN, FP, and FN are the evaluation of the classifier's outputs: TP and TN are correctly classified positives and negatives, respectively, while FP and FN are incorrectly classified positives and negatives.

Chromosome Selection: *Tournament selection* is used, where subsets of k random individuals are selected, and the individual with the highest fitness in each tournament is chosen as a parent. This approach promotes the selection of high-fitness solutions while preserving genetic diversity [5, 19].

Crossover: The uniform crossover operator was applied, that combines the genes from two selected parents. The random cutting points are generated with a defined probability, dividing chromosomes into segments. Alternating segments from the parents are combined to create a new offspring chromosome. The proposed crossover method can be understood as follows. First, a Crossover Probability value is established. Then, a logical condition is evaluated, where for each gene, a random value is generated. If this value is greater than or equal to the Crossover Probability, the gene undergoes crossover in the offspring; otherwise, the gene remains unchanged.

Mutation: *Inversion mutation* is applied with a predetermined probability to the chromosomes obtained from the crossover operator. This operator flips the value of a randomly selected gene, changing a 0 to a 1 or vice versa.

Termination Criteria: The algorithm terminates after completing a fixed number of generations G. During each generation, the best, average, and worst fitness values are recorded, along with metrics like the number of selected features.

4 Experiments and Obtained Results

4.1 Transformation and Feature Extraction

For data smoothing, we applied the SG to significantly preserve the signal shape. Subsequently, we tested various feature extraction methods, as shown in Table 1. Based on these results, we hypothesized that using AR for feature extraction could achieve better results than those reported in by [25]. To prevent the AR model from experiencing underfitting or overfitting, we initially implemented the AIC and BIC Criteria. These methods penalize model complexity to mitigate these issues. However, due to the complexity of EEG signals, the AR model tends to adjust to the highest values within the analyzed range, which contradicts the objective. Given this situation, we conducted empirical tests to measure classification accuracy using GNB with AR models of orders ranging from 0 to 99. The results indicated that increasing the model order did not necessarily improve classification efficiency. The highest accuracy within this range was achieved with an AR model of order 19.

The selected model generated a set of coefficients equal to the model order plus one per channel; that is, for the AR model of order 19, 20 coefficients per channel were produced. Since the headset used in the study has 14 channels, the proposed AR model includes 280 features.

With the AR model order set to 19, we also evaluated the performance of the HMM, Decision Tree (DT), Artificial Neural Networks (ANN), Random Forest (RF), and GNB classifiers, obtaining accuracy values of 53.11%, 56.93%, 58.37%, 62.68%, and 63.11%, respectively. The best performance was observed with GNB, possibly because AR is a time-domain technique that assumes the data follows a normal distribution, making the GNB classifier align well with this assumption.

Table 1. Experimentation with different feature extraction techniques presented in [23].

Technique	Features and Hyperparameters considered	Accuracy
Statistical Features	Mean, standard deviation, first and second absolute differences (raw & normalized signals	53%
Autoregressive Model	Lags = 10, generating 11 AR coefficients per channel	61%
Fractal Dimension	Higuchi algorithm (k = 10), one coefficient per channel	55%
Fast Fourier Transform	Delta, Theta, Alpha, Beta, Gamma power features per channel	47%
Power Spectral Density		46%
Continuous Wavelet Transform	Wavelet = "morl", scale spectrum 0–30, 30 energy features per channel	47%
Discrete Wavelet Transform	Daubechies 4 (db4), mean, standard deviation, energy coefficients, level 4 decomposition	47%
Short-Time Fourier Transform	nperseg = 128 (short windows), mean magnitude, standard deviation, total energy per channel	53%
S Transform	Combines Fourier & Wavelet Transforms, extracts mean magnitude, standard deviation, total energy	54%

4.2 Adjustment of Parameters for the Proposed GA

To identify the subset of AR coefficients that maximized classification accuracy, several GA configurations were evaluated by varying the selection strategy, crossover operator, elitism, population size, number of generations, and mutation rate. The tested versions included random, roulette, and tournament selection, as well as uniform and multipoint crossover. In general, the configurations based on tournament selection produced better results than those using random or roulette selection, and the best overall performance was obtained when tournament selection was combined with multipoint crossover.

The best result was achieved with the fourth GA configuration, which used elitism of 2, tournament selection with 5 individuals, and multipoint crossover. For this version, the search space was extended by varying the number of individuals from 560 to 840, the number of generations from 700 to 1400, and the mutation rate from 0.05 to 0.11. Among the 256 executions performed, the highest accuracy obtained was 77.99%, achieved with 680 individuals, 1100 generations, and a mutation rate of 0.09. In addition to improving classification performance, this configuration reduced the number of coefficients from 280 to 118, indicating that the GA was effective not only for optimization but also for dimensionality reduction.

5 Discussion

The proposed AR-GA-GNB pipeline improved classification accuracy to 77.99%, reducing the feature space from 280 to 118 coefficients. According to Table 2, the coefficients most frequently selected by the GA were concentrated mainly in channels 1, 9, and 10, which correspond to electrodes AF3, P8, and T8 in the 10–20 system. In addition, the average signals for the Like and Dislike classes showed visible differences in these channels, reinforcing their relevance for preference discrimination.

Table 2. The number of selected features in each channel (out of the total 20 features per channel) by the GA in the best solution.

Channel	**1**	2	3	4	5	6	7	8	**9**	**10**	11	12	13	14
Number of coefficients	**14**	6	7	10	9	6	7	8	**13**	**13**	9	3	9	4

The AF3 electrode is located in the left prefrontal cortex, a region associated with decision-making and attention [12]. This may explain why features from this channel were repeatedly selected by the genetic algorithm. The P8 electrode is positioned in the right parietal region, which has been associated with visuospatial integration, attention, and spatial orientation [15]. This may be related to the visual processing and attentional focus involved while participants observed product images. Finally, the T8 electrode is located in the right temporal region, which has been linked to emotional regulation and decision-related neural dynamics [9]. This finding suggests that emotional processes may have played an important role in product preference formation.

Another relevant finding is that time-domain feature extraction methods outperformed frequency-domain and decomposition-domain alternatives. A plausible explanation is that EEG signals are highly non-stationary and exhibit rapid temporal fluctuations, which are more directly captured by time-domain representations [11]. In this context, AR modeling appears to provide a compact and informative representation of the temporal dynamics associated with immediate consumer responses.

The Gaussian Naive Bayes classifier also yielded the best performance among the evaluated classifiers when using AR-based features. This may be because GNB assumes that features are approximately normally distributed and conditionally independent, assumptions that may be better satisfied by AR coefficients than by other feature representations [18]. Overall, these results support the use of temporal modeling and evolutionary feature selection as an effective strategy for EEG-based preference recognition in neuromarketing.

6 Conclusions and Future Work

In this study, it was demonstrated that the combination of AR and GA is an effective strategy to improve EEG signal classification in neuromarketing applications, emphasizing that GA, as a metaheuristic, allowed us to increase accuracy to 77.99%, surpassing the value reported in the original study.

The results highlight the significance of EEG signals originating from brain activity in the left prefrontal cortex, the right parietal region, and the right temporal lobe, as these areas may provide valuable information to enhance the understanding of the decision-making process in product selection.

For future work, it is suggested to experiment with different genetic operators and hyperparameters in GA, explore alternative feature selection methods, apply the proposed methodology to other neuromarketing studies, and further investigate, from a physiological and psychological perspective, the influence of these brain regions on consumer behavior.

Acknowledgments. This study was fully funded by the Secretaría de Ciencia, Humanidades, Tecnología e Innovación (Secithi) of Mexico.

Disclosure of Interests. The authors have no competing interests to declare that are relevant to the content of this article.

References

1. Acharya, G., et al.: Predictive modeling of evoked intracranial EEG response to medial temporal lobe stimulation in patients with epilepsy. Commun, Biol. **7**(1), 1–11 (2024). https://doi.org/10.1038/s42003-024-06859-2
2. Alzahrani, S.I., Alsaleh, M.M.: The influence of smoothing filtering methods on the performance of an EEG-based brain-computer interface. IEEE Access **11**, 60171–60180 (2023). https://doi.org/10.1109/ACCESS.2023.3285660
3. Browarska, N., et al.: Comparison of smoothing filters' influence on quality of data recorded with the emotiv EPOC flex brain–computer interface headset during audio stimulation. Brain Sci. **11**(1), 98 (2021). https://doi.org/10.3390/brainsci11010098
4. Carrara, I., Papadopoulo, T.: Classification of BCI-EEG based on the augmented covariance matrix. IEEE Trans. Biomed. Eng. **71**(9), 2651–2662 (2024). https://doi.org/10.1109/TBME.2024.3386219
5. Felix-Saul, J.C.,et al.: Extending genetic algorithms with biological life-cycle dynamics. Biomimetics **9**(8), 476 (2024). https://doi.org/10.3390/biomimetics9080476
6. Fryz, M., et al.: Linear random process model-based EEG classification using machine learning techniques. In: Presented at the Congreso Internacional de Tecnologías e Innovación (2023)
7. García-Ponsoda, S., et al.: Feature engineering of EEG applied to mental disorders: a systematic mapping study. Appl. Intell. **53**(20), 23203–23243 (2023). https://doi.org/10.1007/s10489-023-04702-5
8. Ghorbanzadeh, G., et al.: DGAFF: deep genetic algorithm fitness Formation for EEG Bio-Signal channel selection. Biomed. Signal Process. Control **79**, 104119 (2023). https://doi.org/10.1016/j.bspc.2022.104119
9. Guitart-Masip, M., et al.: Synchronization of medial temporal lobe and prefrontal rhythms in human decision making. J. Neurosci. **33**(2), 442–451 (2013). https://doi.org/10.1523/JNEUROSCI.2573-12.2013
10. Haderlein, J.F. et al.: Autoregressive models for biomedical signal processing. In: 2023 45th Annual International Conference of the IEEE Engineering in Medicine & Biology Society (EMBC), pp. 1–6 (2023). https://doi.org/10.1109/EMBC40787.2023.10340714
11. Hjorth, B.: EEG analysis based on time domain properties. Electroencephalogr. Clin. Neurophysiol. **29**(3), 306–310 (1970). https://doi.org/10.1016/0013-4694(70)90143-4

12. Jobson, D.D., et al.: The role of the medial prefrontal cortex in cognition, ageing and dementia. Brain Commun. **3**(3), fcab125 (2021). https://doi.org/10.1093/braincomms/fcab125

13. Kyriaki, K., et al.: A comprehensive survey of EEG preprocessing methods for cognitive load assessment. IEEE Access. **12**, 23466–23489 (2024). https://doi.org/10.1109/ACCESS.2024.3360328

14. Luo, T.: Parallel genetic algorithm based common spatial patterns selection on time–frequency decomposed EEG signals for motor imagery brain-computer interface. Biomed. Signal Process. Control **80**, 104397 (2023). https://doi.org/10.1016/j.bspc.2022.104397

15. Mazzi, C., et al.: Coherent activity within and between hemispheres: cortico-cortical connectivity revealed by rTMS of the right posterior parietal cortex. Front. Hum. Neurosci. **18** (2024). https://doi.org/10.3389/fnhum.2024.1362742

16. Morin, C.: Neuromarketing: the new science of consumer behavior. Soc. **48**(2), 131–135 (2011). https://doi.org/10.1007/s12115-010-9408-1

17. Muthuswamy, J., Thakor, N.V.: Spectral analysis methods for neurological signals. J. Neurosci. Methods **83**(1), 1–14 (1998). https://doi.org/10.1016/S0165-0270(98)00065-X

18. Najmusseher et al.: Impact of multi-domain features for EEG based epileptic seizures classification. In: Hassanien, A.E.. et al. (eds.) Proceedings of the 10th International Conference on Advanced Intelligent Systems and Informatics 2024, pp. 317–329 Springer, Cham (2024). https://doi.org/10.1007/978-3-031-71619-5_27

19. Nebro, A.J. et al.: Is NSGA-II Ready for Large-Scale Multi-Objective Optimization? Mathematical and Computational Applications. 27, 6, 103 (2022). https://doi.org/10.3390/mca27060103

20. Pijackova, K. et al.: Genetic algorithm designed for optimization of neural network architectures for intracranial EEG recordings analysis. J. Neural Eng. **20**(3), 036034 (2023). https://doi.org/10.1088/1741-2552/acdc54

21. Rawash, Y. et al.: Advanced low-pass filters for signal processing: a comparative study on gaussian, mittag-leffler, and savitzky-golay filters. Math. Model. Eng. Prob. **11**, 1841–1850 (2024). https://doi.org/10.18280/mmep.110713

22. Saibene, A., Gasparini, F.: Genetic algorithm for feature selection of EEG heterogeneous data. Expert Syst. Appl. **217**, 119488 (2023). https://doi.org/10.1016/j.eswa.2022.119488

23. Singh, A.K., Krishnan, S.: Trends in EEG signal feature extraction applications. Front. Artif. Intell. **5** (2023). https://doi.org/10.3389/frai.2022.1072801

24. Xu, B., et al.: Algorithm of imagined left-right hand movement classification based on wavelet transform and AR parameter model. In: 2007 1st International Conference on Bioinformatics and Biomedical Engineering, pp. 539–542 (2007). https://doi.org/10.1109/ICBBE.2007.141

25. Yadava, M., et al.: Analysis of EEG signals and its application to neuromarketing. Multimed Tools Appl. **76**(18), 19087–19111 (2017). https://doi.org/10.1007/s11042-017-4580-6

Clustering Algorithms for Density Variations: An Empirical Comparison

Adrián J. Ramírez-Díaz$^{(\boxtimes)}$ (iD), José Fco. Martínez-Trinidad (iD),
and J. Ariel Carrasco-Ochoa (iD)

Instituto Nacional de Astrofísica, Óptica y Electrónica Luis Enrique Erro # 1,
Luis Enrique Erro # 1, 72840 Tonantzintla, Puebla, Mexico
{aramirez,fmartine,ariel}@inaoep.mx

Abstract. Density-based clustering algorithms identify clusters with
arbitrary shapes and manage noise. Nevertheless, they face limitations
when datasets exhibit density variations. Traditional separation criteria rely on identifying low-density regions, which often fail to distinguish density-separated clusters. While several algorithms have been
developed to detect density variations, they have been evaluated independently. This study presents an empirical comparison, within a unified evaluation framework, of six clustering algorithms—DVBSCAN,
RNN-DBSCAN, IDDC, AMD-DBSCAN, EDBSCAN, and ADBSCAN—
specifically designed to identify density variations. The study integrates a
parameter tuning process to identify the parameters' values that yield the
highest clustering quality and runtime performance. Our results show the
algorithms' performance across a collection of public standard datasets
selected for their diverse challenges regarding density variations. The
study not only determines the algorithms that have the best quality-
runtime trade-offs but also analyzes the number of parameters and how
they affect overall performance. These findings provide insights for selecting the most suitable clustering algorithm to address density variations.

Keywords: Clustering · Density-Based Clustering · Density Variations

1   Introduction

Clustering algorithms partition unlabeled datasets into subsets of similar objects,
relying on their characteristics or similarity metrics that quantify their relationships [1,11]. Depending on the strategy used to build clusters, clustering algorithms can be classified into partition-based, hierarchical, density-based, model-
based, and grid-based approaches [7].

Density-based clustering algorithms are widely used due to their ability
to identify clusters of arbitrary shapes, handle noise, and eliminate the need
for prior specification of the number of clusters [6,10]. These algorithms typically build clusters by identifying high-density regions separated by low-density

V. G. Cruz-Sánchez et al. (Eds.): MCPR 2026, LNCS 16623, pp. 68–78, 2026.
https://doi.org/10.1007/978-3-032-28393-1_7

regions [9]. However, the reliance on low-density regions as a separation criterion can limit their applicability in scenarios where datasets exhibit density variations.

In this context, Zhong et al. [17] distinguish three types of cluster structures: well-separated clusters, density-separated clusters, and touching clusters. Well-separated clusters are divided by a low-density region between their boundaries. Density-separated clusters, in contrast, are not separated by low-density regions but can be distinguished by changes in data density. Finally, touching clusters correspond to groups of objects connected by a region whose removal would result in well-separated clusters. Consistent with this characterization, Yao and Zeng [16] identify the detection of density variations in cluster separations as one of the main challenges in density-based clustering.

Although several density-based clustering algorithms have been proposed to address density variations, existing studies have evaluated them independently. This gap motivates an empirical comparison of six state-of-the-art density-based clustering algorithms that aim to separate clusters by identifying both low-density regions and density variations. The algorithms under consideration include DVBSCAN [8], RNN-DBSCAN [3], IDDC [13], AMD-DBSCAN [14], EDBSCAN [4], and ADBSCAN [5]. To the best of our knowledge, no study has analyzed the characteristics and performance of this kind of algorithms within a unified comparative framework.

The remainder of this article is organized as follows. Section 2 describes the density-based clustering algorithms that address the density variations compared in this study. Section 3 presents the evaluation framework employed for the empirical comparison of the clustering algorithms for density variations studied in this work. Section 4 reports and discusses the obtained results, covering clustering quality and runtime performance. Finally, Sect. 5 concludes the paper and outlines directions for future work.

2 Clustering Algorithms Under Study

The selected density-based algorithms are designed to address datasets that exhibit density variations, either by adapting neighborhood definitions, modifying cluster expansion criteria, or introducing additional density comparison mechanisms. In this section, the evaluated algorithms are described at the level of their operational principles, focusing on how density is estimated, how clusters are constructed, and how density variations are handled, including cases where clusters are not separated by low-density regions.

DVBSCAN [8] was proposed as an extension of DBSCAN to address datasets with density variations. As in DBSCAN, DVBSCAN examines, for each object in the dataset, the number of neighbors located within a distance ε. If this number is at least *MinPts*, the object is treated as a core point and used to initiate or expand a cluster by recursively visiting neighboring objects. The difference introduced by DVBSCAN appears during this recursive expansion. In addition to satisfying the *MinPts* condition, a candidate object must meet two additional criteria based on the Cluster Density Variance (CDV) and the Cluster Similarity Index (CSI). The candidate object is added to the expanding cluster only if both CDV and CSI are less than or equal to their respective thresholds, α and δ; otherwise, it is used to start a new cluster. As a result, DVBSCAN requires four parameters: ε and $MinPts$, inherited from DBSCAN, and α and δ, which set the admissible density variation between clusters.

RNN-DBSCAN [3] is a density-based clustering algorithm that identifies density variations between clusters using a single input parameter, k, rather than relying on the ε and $MinPts$ parameters required by the DBSCAN algorithm. For each object o_i, its k-nearest neighbors are determined. Following this, the reverse k-nearest neighbor (RkNN) set is computed for each object o_i, this set comprises all objects that include o_i within their kNN sets. The clustering process is executed in two phases. In the first phase, unvisited objects whose RkNN set satisfies $|RkNN| \geq k$ (the core condition) initiate new clusters, which are expanded through a recursive density-connectivity procedure, similar to DBSCAN but by traversing their RkNN sets. Objects that do not satisfy the core condition are temporarily labeled as noise. In the second phase, these noise objects are reconsidered and assigned to the near cluster if their k-nearest neighbors include core objects from that cluster.

IDDC [13] is a density-based clustering algorithm that identifies clusters with varying densities using a single parameter, k. For each object, the k-distance, defined as the distance to its kth nearest neighbor, is computed to determine its neighborhood. These neighborhoods are used to calculate reachability and the relative density of each object. The clustering process is performed in three stages. First, a mutual k-nearest neighbor graph is constructed, allowing for a graph-based expansion procedure to group core objects with a small relative density value into clusters. Second, unassigned objects are iteratively assigned to clusters if their distance to the nearest cluster member is less than or equal to the average k-distance of that cluster. Finally, the remaining objects are assigned to the nearest existing cluster based on minimum distance.

AMD-DBSCAN [14] extends the DBSCAN to identify clusters with varying densities by leveraging k-nearest neighbors (kNN). The algorithm determines multiple density thresholds by applying K-means clustering to the set of distances between each point and its k-th nearest neighbor. Each resulting centroid represents a distance that serves as a specific ε threshold. These ε values are sorted in ascending order to prioritize the extraction of high-density regions first, since a smaller ε identifies denser regions. Consequently, AMD-DBSCAN iteratively applies DBSCAN using this sequence of thresholds while keeping $MinPts$ fixed at k. At each iteration, the extracted clusters are removed from the dataset, and the points labeled as noise serve as the input to the next execution with the next (larger) ε value.

EDBSCAN [4] is an algorithm that extends DBSCAN to address density variations by relying on density similarity rather than a distance threshold ε. EDBSCAN requires three parameters: the neighborhood size k, the minimum number of points $MinPts$ ($< k$), and a similarity level $SL \in [0, 1]$. For each object, a density value is computed as the total of lengths to its $MinPts$-nearest neighbors. The clustering process identifies core objects by evaluating density similarity between an object and its k-nearest neighbors. Two objects are considered similar if their density values satisfy the specified similarity level. An object is classified as a core point if it has at least $MinPts$ similar neighbors within its k-nearest neighbor set. Clusters are expanded recursively by incorporating similar neighbors that also satisfy the core condition, following a density-connectivity procedure similar to DBSCAN. Objects that do not satisfy these criteria are labeled as noise.

ADBSCAN [5] is a density-based clustering algorithm that uses k-nearest neighbor to estimate local densities and relies on DBSCAN for cluster construction. ADBSCAN initially computes a single ε value as the average distance between each point in the dataset and its kth nearest neighbor. This estimated ε is used to perform an initial DBSCAN execution, producing a preliminary set of clusters. A subsequent stage merges nearby clusters with similar densities. If 0.6% of the dataset remains labeled as noise, the algorithm enters an iterative phase in which DBSCAN is reapplied exclusively to the noise points. During this phase, ε is progressively increased based on the average distance between noise points, and the merging process is applied to the newly formed clusters. This iterative process enables the analysis of multiple density levels, progressing from denser to sparser regions. Finally, the remaining points are assigned to the nearest cluster, provided that the distance satisfies a predefined proximity criterion.

All the algorithms described above serve as the basis for the empirical comparison study presented in this paper, within the same evaluation framework.

3 Evaluation Framework for Density Variation Clustering Algorithms

The empirical comparison of clustering algorithms for density variations follows a unified evaluation framework to assess clustering quality and runtime across the compared algorithms, while mitigating implementation-specific biases.

To ensure a fair comparison, all algorithms are implemented within a single environment using the same programming language, data structures, distance functions, and neighborhood query methods. This way, our evaluation framework seeks to guarantee that performance differences are attributable to algorithmic design rather than implementation decisions.

Since the behavior and clustering results of the evaluated algorithms depend on their input parameters, it is necessary to identify the parameter settings that yield the best results for each algorithm on all datasets. To this end, our framework includes a hyperparameter tuning strategy. For algorithms that rely on a single density parameter k (RNN-DBSCAN, IDDC, AMD-DBSCAN, and ADBSCAN), an exhaustive search is conducted for $k \in [2, 30]$, a range consistent with the authors' recommendations and suitable for the density variations in the evaluated datasets. For algorithms requiring two or more parameters (DVBSCAN and E-DBSCAN), hyperparameter selection is performed using a Differential Evolution optimizer to explore the search space, maximizing the NMI metric. The optimization process was configured with a population of 15 over 30 iterations as suggested in the literature [18].

This parameter-setting strategy not only identifies the parameter values that yield the highest clustering quality but also enables an analysis of parameter sensitivity. This analysis reveals whether an algorithm consistently produces stable results across a range of values or requires precise fine-tuning to achieve good performance. Once the parameter values are determined, clustering quality and runtime are evaluated using the best parameter values for each dataset.

To assess clustering algorithms, our evaluation framework uses an external validation approach, leveraging datasets with known ground-truth labels to directly evaluate clustering quality. We use external validation metrics— specifically the Adjusted Rand Index (ARI), Adjusted Mutual Information (AMI), and Normalized Mutual Information (NMI) [12]—because density-based algorithms often discover clusters with arbitrary shapes and heterogeneous densitie, which internal metrics cannot adequately evaluate [15]. Finally, clustering runtime is measured, excluding data loading and result storage.

4 Experiments and Results

To perform the empirical comparison of clustering algorithms for density variations, we followed the evaluation framework presented in the previous section. Thus, in Subsect. 4.1, we first present experiments to determine the parameter values to use in the algorithms under study via parameter sensitivity analysis. Once the parameter values for the algorithms are determined, as described in the evaluation framework, we report the clustering quality and runtime of the algorithms under study in Subsect. 4.2.

The experiments were conducted using 14 synthetic datasets obtained from Tomas Barton's repository [2]. These benchmarks are widely used in the literature to evaluate density-based clustering algorithms and their ability to detect density variations [3–5,13,14]. The selected datasets incorporate diverse challenges, including clusters with arbitrary shapes, varying sizes, and heterogeneous densities. Furthermore, they feature complex scenarios such as high-density regions connected by low-density bridges, clusters with gradual density gradients, and noise. Classical distributions, such as Gaussian, concentric, and uniform clusters, are also represented to ensure a comprehensive assessment. The datasets were processed using their raw feature values without additional normalization, employing the Euclidean distance as the similarity metric across all experiments. Table 1 summarizes the characteristics of these datasets, including their size, the number of clusters, and the presence of noise.

To ensure a fair comparison, all experiments were conducted on an Intel Core i7-12700H processor (4.70 GHz) with 16 GB of RAM, running Fedora Linux 39. The algorithms were implemented in Python 3.12, using NumPy for data structures and SciPy for distance calculations and neighborhood queries.

Table 1. Datasets used to evaluate clustering algorithms for density variations

Dataset	Size	Clusters	Noise	Dataset	Size	Clusters	Noise
Flame	240	2	No	Wingnut	1016	2	No
Pathbased	300	3	No	D31	3100	31	No
Jain	373	2	No	Impossible	3673	8	No
Compound	399	6	No	Cluto-t4-8k	8000	7	No
R15	600	15	No	Cluto-t5-8k	8000	6	Yes
Aggregation	788	7	No	Cluto-t8-8k	8000	8	Yes
Rings	1000	3	No	Cluto-t7-10k	10000	9	Yes

4.1 Parameter Search and Sensitivity Analysis

For algorithms relying solely on the k-nearest neighbors parameter, clustering quality (ARI, AMI, NMI) and runtime were evaluated across the range $k \in [2, 30]$. This procedure identifies the best k values for each algorithm and provides details on parameter sensitivity. Figure 1 shows the mean performance and runtime for these algorithms. In all subfigures, the y-axis corresponds to quality, while the secondary y-axis (on the right side of the figure) represents the runtime in seconds. The x-axis shows the k value used as a parameter. Reporting the mean across datasets serves to evaluate algorithmic robustness relative to parameter selection.

As shown in Fig. 1a, RNN-DBSCAN exhibits consistent behavior across all quality metrics. Performance improves as k increases, reaching the highest quality at $k \approx 19$, followed by a marginal decay of approximately 0.1 before stabilizing. However, the runtime grows quadratically with k, suggesting that high values for this parameter should be avoided.

In contrast, Fig. 1b shows the results for IDDC; the runtime decreases at a quadratic rate. The quality initially increases, reaching its highest value at $k \approx 11$, then it decreases as k continues to increase. This behavior indicates that IDDC is highly sensitive to the choice of k and requires precise tuning to maintain its effectiveness.

The results for AMD-DBSCAN are shown in Fig. 1c, where the quality improves when k grows, reaching its highest values at $k \approx 17$, and it remains stable for further increases in k. On the other hand, the runtime increases slowly with k.

Finally, Fig. 1d shows that ADBSCAN achieves its highest quality values at $k \approx 5$, after which performance decreases continuously as k increases. The runtime is high for $k < 5$ but decreases rapidly, showing only slight variations for larger values of k.

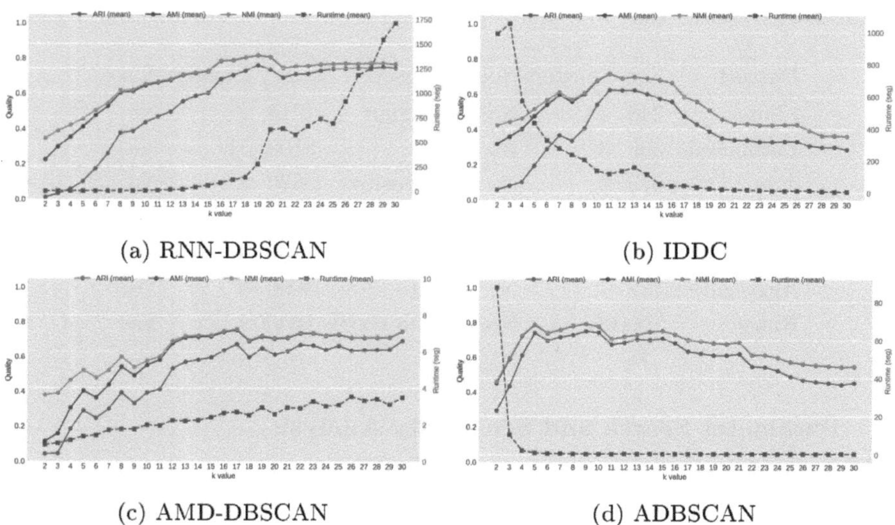

(a) RNN-DBSCAN

(b) IDDC

(c) AMD-DBSCAN

(d) ADBSCAN

Fig. 1. Mean clustering quality and runtime performance for single-parameter algorithms varying k values

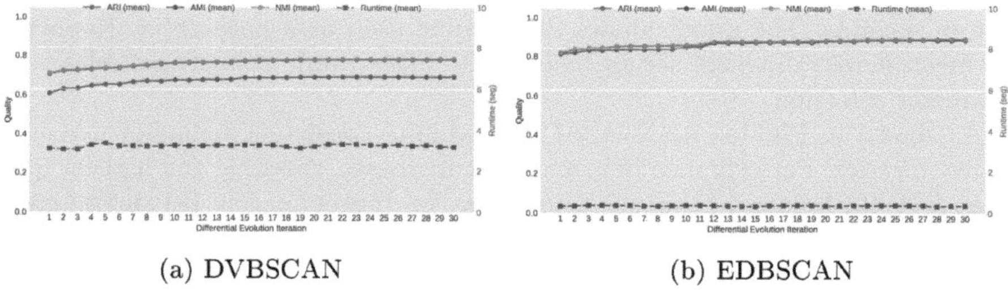

(a) DVBSCAN

(b) EDBSCAN

Fig. 2. Mean performance convergence and runtime for algorithms with more than one parameter during the parameter search process

For algorithms requiring more than one parameter, a heuristic search using Differential Evolution was performed to identify the parameter settings that yield the highest clustering results, maximizing the NMI metric. Figure 2 presents the convergence curves over 30 iterations, where the x-axis represents the iteration number and the y-axis shows the mean of the best quality values found per dataset, along with the corresponding mean runtime averaged across datasets.

Figure 2a shows the search process for DVBSCAN. The quality metrics exhibit a similar upward trend, increasing slightly in each iteration. The runtime remained short across iterations, indicating a stable computational cost during the search. Lastly, Fig. 2b shows the results for EDBSCAN. The convergence behavior resembles that of DVBSCAN, though it achieves higher average quality. Similar to DVBSCAN, the runtime remained short throughout the iterations.

Table 2. Best parameter configurations identified for each algorithm across the evaluated datasets

Dataset	RNNDBSCAN k	IDDC k	AMDDBSCAN k	ADBSCAN k	DVBSCAN eps, alpha, minPts, delta	EDBSCAN k, minPts, SL
Flame	18	7	12	4	1.5, 62, 14, 158	14, 3, 0.8
Pathbased	9	10	13	7	3.1, 170, 28, 114	7, 3, 0.5
Jain	19	30	30	16	6.7, 291, 22, 206	10, 6, 0.4
Compound	11	6	16	6	2.8, 172, 21, 230	4, 3, 0.5
R15	28	12	28	11	0.7, 201, 30, 324	21, 20, 0.4
Aggregation	14	30	19	8	13.6, 356, 22, 438	23, 21, 0.7
Rings	28	11	14	15	1.9, 74, 29, 500	18, 16, 0.6
Wingnut	19	17	22	21	0.4, 218, 13, 177	9, 8, 0.5
D31	15	11	29	5	3.0, 4, 5, 27	16, 12, 0.6
Impossible	30	26	15	15	1.7, 2305, 28, 192	44, 15, 0.6
Cluto-t4-8k	29	13	30	12	67.7, 5100, 19, 5361	33, 30, 0.7
Cluto-t5-8k	26	14	23	6	76.5, 4021, 10, 2775	32, 30, 0.6
Cluto-t8-8k	30	14	26	11	88.6, 3094, 8, 4757	28, 23, 0.7
Cluto-t7-10k	29	12	27	12	67.7, 790, 14, 5294	31, 27, 0.7

4.2 Clustering Quality and Runtime Evaluation

The parameter search process described in the previous section determined the configurations that produce the highest clustering quality for each algorithm across the evaluated datasets, which are summarized in Table 2.

Figure 3 presents the AMI, ARI, and NMI results obtained using the best parameter configuration on each dataset. Each subfigure displays six boxplots, one for each algorithm, where the boxes represent the interquartile range (IQR), the whiskers extend to the minimum and maximum values, the central line indicates the median, and points denote outliers.

The evaluation using the AMI metric (Fig. 3a) shows that ADBSCAN achieved the highest median, followed by EDBSCAN, which, despite having a slightly lower median, exhibits lower dispersion, reflecting more consistent results. These are followed by RNN-DBSCAN, AMD-DBSCAN, and IDDC, all of which rely on the k-nearest neighbors parameter. Conversely, DVBSCAN presents greater dispersion and the lowest median.

A similar trend is observed for the ARI metric (Fig. 3b); however, RNN-DBSCAN outperforms EDBSCAN in median quality. Nevertheless, EDBSCAN maintains lower dispersion, reflecting higher consistency in its results, despite the slightly lower median values. The NMI results (Fig. 3c) are similar, positioning ADBSCAN as the top-performing algorithm. Its superior performance across all metrics can be attributed to its cluster construction strategy, which estimates multiple density levels by approximating different ε values using k-nearest neighbors.

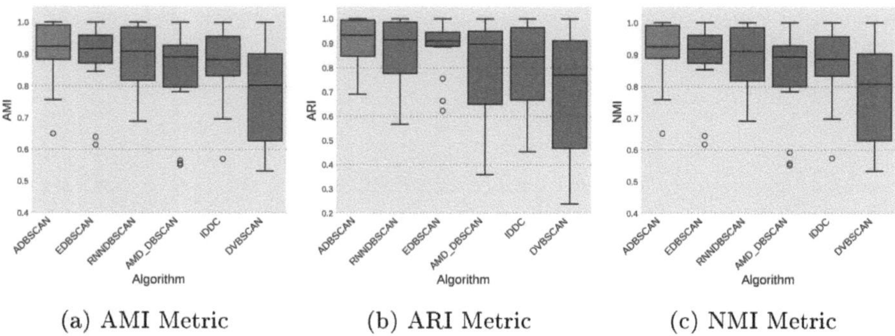

(a) AMI Metric   (b) ARI Metric   (c) NMI Metric

Fig. 3. Distribution of clustering quality metrics (AMI, ARI, and NMI) for each algorithm across all datasets using best parameter settings

Regarding runtime, Fig. 4 shows the distribution of runtimes across the 14 datasets on a logarithmic scale. The longest runtimes were recorded by RNN-DBSCAN, which, despite ranking third in clustering quality, requires high k values to achieve such results, significantly increasing its computational overhead. In contrast, EDBSCAN and ADBSCAN achieved the lowest runtimes while maintaining high quality, identifying them as the most balanced algorithms in the quality-runtime trade-off.

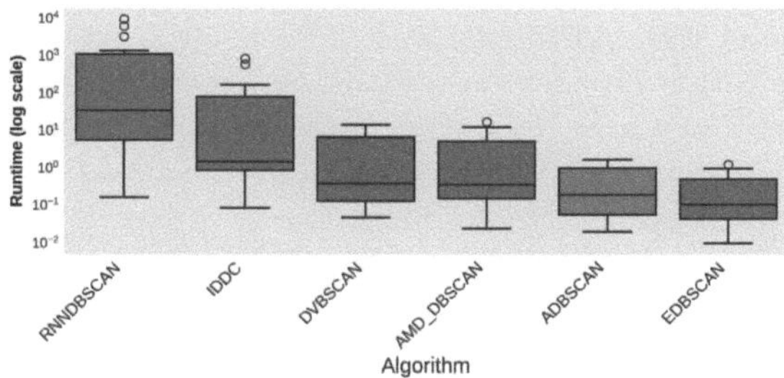

Fig. 4. Distribution of runtime (logarithmic scale) across all datasets, illustrating the computational cost associated with each algorithm's best performance

5   Conclusion and Future Work

This study evaluated several clustering algorithms for density variations, focusing on their clustering quality, runtime, and parameter sensitivity. Given their ability to handle complex data structures, these algorithms are relevant for applications in fields such as anomaly detection, image processing, and bioinformatics, where data often lacks a uniform structure. This work addresses the need for a comparative study under a unified framework to provide a standardized assessment of their performance.

From our experiments, we conclude that density variations can be identified using k-NN without the need for additional thresholds. Although thresholds may offer greater control over density-based partitioning in specific clustering problems, they do not consistently outperform techniques based on the direct analysis of dense regions. Furthermore, we observed a distinction in algorithmic stability: some algorithms preserve quality as k increases, while others exhibit a decay. Real-world applications may limit the feasibility of exhaustive parameter tuning, making this a key factor.

Among the analyzed algorithms, ADBSCAN shows the best trade-off, achieving the highest clustering quality with low runtime while requiring only the k parameter. However, its performance is sensitive to the choice of k, requiring careful selection to achieve good results. EDBSCAN ranked second-best, offering high quality and fast execution, though tuning it is more complex because it requires three parameters: k, $minPts$, and a dissimilarity threshold. RNN-DBSCAN has low sensitivity to parameter changes; nevertheless, its runtimes were higher than those of ADBSCAN and EDBSCAN.

Our results indicate that while density can be estimated using fixed-radius ($\varepsilon, minPts$) or k-nearest neighbours (k-NN) techniques, the latter is often more practical. Algorithms that use k-NN require fewer parameters, simplifying parameter tuning while still effectively identifying density variations. Future work will focus on developing techniques for identifying density variations that further automate the parameter selection process of density-based clustering algorithms and evaluating the impact of noise and high dimensionality on performance across density variations. Aiming to create algorithms that are not only strong in terms of clustering quality but also have as low a runtime as possible across a wide range of parameters.

Acknowledgments. This research was financially supported by the Secretaría de Ciencia, Humanidades, Tecnología e Innovación (SECIHTI) through the scholarship grant 778974.

References

1. Alasalı, T., Ortakcı, Y.: Clustering techniques in data mining: a survey of methods, challenges, and applications. Comput. Sci0 **9**(Issue:1), 32–50 (2024). https://doi.org/10.53070/bbd.1421527
2. Barton, T.: clustering benchmark (2015). https://github.com/deric/clustering-benchmark
3. Bryant, A., Cios, K.: RNN-DBSCAN: a density-based clustering algorithm using reverse nearest neighbor density estimates. IEEE Trans. Knowl. Data Eng. **30**(6), 1109–1121 (2018). https://doi.org/10.1109/TKDE.2017.2787640
4. Fahim, A.: An extended DBSCAN clustering algorithm. Int. J. Adv. Comput. Sci. Appl. **13**(3) (2022).https://doi.org/10.14569/IJACSA.2022.0130331

5. Fahim, A.: Adaptive density-based spatial clustering of applications with noise (ADBSCAN) for clusters of different densities. Comput. Mater. Continua **75**(2), 3695–3712 (2023). https://doi.org/10.32604/cmc.2023.036820, http://www.techscience.com/cmc/v75n2/52099

6. Kulkarni, O., Burhanpurwala, A.: A survey of advancements in DBSCAN clustering algorithms for big data. In: 2024 3rd International conference on Power Electronics and IoT Applications in Renewable Energy and its Control (PARC), pp. 106–111. (2024). https://doi.org/10.1109/PARC59193.2024.10486339

7. Oyewole, G.J., Thopil, G.A.: Data clustering: application and trends. Artif. Intell. Rev. **56**(7), 6439–6475 (2023)

8. Ram, A., Jalal, S., Jalal, A.S., Kumar, M.: A density based algorithm for discovering density varied clusters in large spatial databases. Int. J. Comput. Appl. **3**(6), 1–4 (2010). https://doi.org/10.5120/739-1038. https://ijcaonline.org/archives/volume3/number6/739-1038/

9. Shafi, I., et al.: A review of approaches for rapid data clustering: challenges, opportunities, and future directions. IEEE Access **12**, 138086–138120 (2024)

10. Singh, H.V., Girdhar, A., Dahiya, S.: A literature survey based on DBSCAN algorithms. In: 2022 6th International Conference on Intelligent Computing and Control Systems (ICICCS), pp. 751–758 (2022). https://doi.org/10.1109/ICICCS53718.2022.9788440

11. Singh, J., Singh, D.: A comprehensive review of clustering techniques in artificial intelligence for knowledge discovery: taxonomy, challenges, applications and future prospects. Adv. Eng. Inform. **62**, 102799 (2024). https://doi.org/10.1016/j.aei.2024.102799. https://www.sciencedirect.com/science/article/pii/S1474034624004476

12. Spalenza, M.A., Pirovani, J.P.C., de Oliveira, E.: Structures discovering for optimizing external clustering validation metrics. In: Abraham, A., Siarry, P., Ma, K., Kaklauskas, A. (eds.) Intelligent Systems Design and Applications, pp. 150–161. Springer, Cham (2021)

13. Wang, Y., Yang, Y.: Relative density-based clustering algorithm for identifying diverse density clusters effectively. Neural Comput. Appl. **33**(16), 10141–10157 (2021). https://doi.org/10.1007/s00521-021-05777-2

14. Wang, Z., et al.: AMD-DBSCAN: an adaptive multi-density DBSCAN for datasets of extremely variable density. In: Huang, J.Z., Pan, Y., Hammer, B., Khan, M.K., Xie, X., Cui, L., He, Y. (eds.) 9th IEEE International Conference on Data Science and Advanced Analytics, DSAA 2022, Shenzhen, China, October 13-16, 2022, pp. 1–10. IEEE (2022). https://doi.org/10.1109/DSAA54385.2022.10032412

15. Warrens, M.J., van der Hoef, H.: Understanding the adjusted rand index and other partition comparison indices based on counting object pairs. J. Classif. **39**(3), 487–509 (2022). https://doi.org/10.1007/s00357-022-09413-z

16. Yao, J., Zeng, Y.: Clustering criteria: what defines a good cluster? Pattern Recogn. Lett. (2026). https://doi.org/10.1016/j.patrec.2026.01.011. https://www.sciencedirect.com/science/article/pii/S0167865526000152

17. Zhong, C., Miao, D., Wang, R.: A graph-theoretical clustering method based on two rounds of minimum spanning trees. Pattern Recogn. **43**(3), 752–766 (2010). https://doi.org/10.1016/j.patcog.2009.07.010. www.sciencedirect.com/science/article/pii/S0031320309002945

18. Zielinski, K., Weitkemper, P., Laur, R., Kammeyer, K.D.: Parameter study for differential evolution using a power allocation problem including interference cancellation. In: 2006 IEEE International Conference on Evolutionary Computation, pp. 1857–1864 (2006). https://doi.org/10.1109/CEC.2006.1688533

Dissimilarity-Based Graph Embedding via Local and Global Approximate Graph Patterns

Daybelis Jaramillo-Olivares[(✉)] , J. Ariel Carrasco-Ochoa
and José Fco. Martínez-Trinidad

Instituto Nacional de Astrofísica, Óptica y Electrónica, Luis Enrique Erro # 1,
Tonantzintla, 72840 Puebla, Mexico
{daybelis,ariel,fmartine}@inaoep.mx

Abstract. Pattern-based representations are widely utilized for tasks
such as supervised classification. Approximate graph patterns can also be
used in this context, but it remains unclear how the patterns mined from
a single graph (Local Approximate Graph Patterns) influence the quality of embeddings compared to those mined from a collection of graphs
(Global Approximate Graph Patterns). This paper assesses Dissimilarity-
based Graph Embedding for supervised classification by comparing both
kinds of approximate graph pattern embeddings. We introduce a unified
evaluation framework that assesses embeddings derived from both graph
pattern sets, enabling us to evaluate them using traditional machine
learning methods. Our experiments, conducted on seven datasets, show
which embedding produces better results in supervised classification
regarding accuracy and F1-score.

Keywords: Dissimilarity-based Graph Embedding · Approximate
Graph patterns · Supervised classification

1 Introduction

Data mining for graph-structured data is known as graph mining [1]. Graph
mining aims to identify graph patterns, and it is commonly known as frequent
subgraph mining (FSM) [2,3]. Graph patterns are subgraphs that appear at
least a user-specified number of times [4–6]. There are two types of graph patterns: approximate patterns, which allow flexibility in the subgraphs' structure
or labeling, and exact patterns, which seek a perfect match of subgraphs with
one-to-one correspondence (isomorphism). Mining approximate patterns can be
helpful when dealing with noisy data or where it is difficult to find a strict
one-to-one correspondence.

FSM can be addressed either in a single graph or in a collection of graphs.
In the case of a single graph, patterns are defined by the number of occurrences
within the same graph. In contrast, mining patterns in a collection of graphs
focuses on identifying patterns that appear repeatedly across different graphs

V. G. Cruz-Sánchez et al. (Eds.): MCPR 2026, LNCS 16623, pp. 79–90, 2026.
https://doi.org/10.1007/978-3-032-28393-1_8

within the collection [7]. The literature reports that algorithms designed to mine graph patterns within a single graph can also be applied to collections of graphs; however, the resulting sets of graph patterns in both cases differ. Both sets can be used for supervised classification via graph embedding, but it is not clear which embedding would be better.

In the literature, Dissimilarity-based Graph Embedding has been applied in supervised classification [8–11]. In this paper, we evaluate the Dissimilarity-based Graph Embeddings built from approximate graph patterns mined from a single graph (Local Approximate Graph Patterns) against those mined from a collection of graphs (Global Approximate Graph Patterns). We introduce a unified evaluation framework that assesses Dissimilarity-based Graph Embeddings derived from both graph pattern sets, enabling us to evaluate them utilizing traditional machine learning methods.

The remainder of this paper is organized as follows: Sect. 2 provides basic concepts. Section 3 describes the methodology used in our experimental comparison. Section 4 details the experiments and analyzes our findings. Finally, Sect. 5 presents the conclusions and outlines future work.

2   Basic Concepts

This section defines approximate graph patterns in either a single graph (Local Approximate Graph Patterns) or in a collection of graphs (Global Approximate Graph Patterns). As well as their use for building Dissimilarity-based Graph Embeddings.

First, we consider a collection of graphs $\mathcal{C}$ containing n labeled graphs, denoted as $\mathcal{C} = \{G_1, G_2, \ldots, G_n\}$. Each graph $G = (V, E, L)$ consists of a set of vertices V, a set of edges E, and a function L, which assigns labels to vertices and edges. A subgraph $g = (V', E', L')$ of a graph G is a subset of vertices and edges of G, along with its labels.

Frequent approximate subgraph mining aims to identify subgraphs whose occurrences satisfy a minimum support threshold $\sigma_{\min}$ (patterns). For local patterns, support is based on the number of occurrences within a single graph, whereas for global patterns, it is based on the number of graphs that contain the pattern.

A subgraph's occurrence can be either exact or approximate. Exact matching is based on isomorphism, while approximate matching allows variations in structure or labels, provided they remain below a specified user-defined maximum dissimilarity threshold δ_{max}.

Definition 1 (Support of Local Approximate Graph Patterns). *The support of a pattern p in a single graph G is defined as the number of approximate occurrences of p within a single graph G.*

$$supp(p, G) = |\{h \subseteq G \mid\mid d(p, h) \leq \delta_{max}\}|,$$

where $h \subseteq G$ denotes a subgraph of G, $d(p, h)$ is a graph dissimilarity function, and δ_{max} is a user-defined dissimilarity threshold.

Definition 2 (Support of Global Approximate Graph Patterns). *The support of a pattern p in a collection of graphs $\mathcal{C} = \{G_1, \ldots, G_n\}$ is defined as the number of graphs in the collection $\mathcal{C}$ in which p has at least one approximate occurrence h.*

$$supp(p, \mathcal{C}) = |\{G_i \in \mathcal{C} \mid \exists h \subseteq G_i \mid d(p, h) \leq \delta_{max}\}|.$$

where h denotes a subgraph of G_i, $d(h, G_i)$ is a graph dissimilarity function, and δ_{max} is a user-defined maximum dissimilarity threshold.

These concepts allow us to formally define the frequent approximate subgraph mining problem.

Definition 3 (Frequent Approximate Subgraph Mining in a Single Graph). *The frequent approximate subgraph mining in a single graph problem is to find the set of all approximate graph patterns $\mathcal{P}$ (Local Approximate Graph Patterns), such that each graph pattern $p \in \mathcal{P}$ satisfies the minimum support threshold $\sigma_{\min}$.*

$$\mathcal{P} = \{p | supp(p, G) \geq \sigma_{\min}\}.$$

where $supp(p, G)$ refers to the Support of Local Approximate Graph Patterns (Definition 1).

Definition 4 (Frequent Approximate Subgraph Mining in a Collection of Graphs). *The frequent approximate subgraph mining in a collection of graphs $\mathcal{C}$ is to find the set of all approximate graph patterns $\mathcal{P}$ (Global Approximate Graph Patterns), such that the occurrences of each graph pattern $p \in \mathcal{P}$ satisfy the minimum support threshold $\sigma_{\min}$.*

$$\mathcal{P} = \{p | supp(p, \mathcal{C}) \geq \sigma_{\min}\}.$$

where $supp(p, \mathcal{C})$ refers to the Support of Global Approximate Graph Patterns (Definition 2).

The resulting set of frequent approximate subgraph patterns $\mathcal{P}$ can be used for supervised classification through graph embedding [10–12]. Graph embedding converts graphs into a vector representation [13]. In this paper, we apply the Dissimilarity-based Graph Embedding method, as detailed in [11], using the mined patterns. For the embedding process, a dissimilarity function is required. In this paper, we use the next dissimilarity function, which is based on graph edit distance [14].

Definition 5 (Dissimilarity function). *The dissimilarity function between two graphs G_1 and G_2 measures the number of operations (insertion, deletion, and label substitution) required for transforming a graph G_1 into a graph G_2.*

$$d(G_1, G_2) = \sum_{i=1}^{k} c_V(v_i) + \sum_{j=1}^{m} c_E(e_j)$$

where $c_V(v_i)$ and $c_E(e_j)$ refer to the costs associated with k modifications on vertices and m modifications on edges, respectively, required for transforming G_1 into G_2, where k and m may be zero.

The Dissimilarity-based Graph Embedding represents a graph as a vector, where each entry corresponds to the distance of the graph to a set of graphs (in this paper, the set of local or global approximate graph patterns). The dissimilarity function described above is used to calculate the distance between a graph in the collection and each pattern.

Definition 6 (Dissimilarity-based Graph Embedding using Patterns).
The Dissimilarity-based Graph Embedding using Patterns represents each graph G_i in a collection of graphs $\mathcal{C} = \{G_1, G_2, \cdots, G_n\}$ as a vector of distances to the patterns in the set of mined patterns $P = \{p_1, p_2, \cdots, p_{|\mathcal{P}|}\}$.

$$z_i = [d_{min}(G_i, p_1), \cdots, d_{min}(G_i, p_{|\mathcal{P}|})].$$

where, $d_{min}(G_i, p_j)$ denotes the minimum dissimilarity between pattern p_j and a subgraph $h \subseteq G_i$.

$$d_{\min}(G_i, p_j) = \min_{h \subseteq G_i} d(p_j, h).$$

where $d(h, G_i)$ is the dissimilarity function of Definition 5.

3   Experimental Framework

Given a collection of graphs $\mathcal{C} = \{G_1, G_2, \cdots, G_n\}$, we propose a unified framework for building dissimilarity-based graph embeddings using local and global approximate graph patterns for supervised classification. We consider two pattern mining strategies: Frequent Approximate Subgraph Mining in a Single Graph and Frequent Approximate Subgraph Mining in a Collection of Graphs. Both types of mining generate patterns (Frequent Approximate Subgraphs) that are then used to embed the graphs of $\mathcal{C}$ in a vector space. This framework is organized into three stages: pattern mining, dissimilarity-based graph embedding using both global and local approximate graph patterns, and evaluation of the embedding through supervised classification.

In the first stage, patterns are mined from the collection of graphs, obtaining a set of frequent approximate patterns $\mathcal{P}$. In the second stage, the mined patterns $\mathcal{P}$ are embedded using a Dissimilarity-based Graph Embedding, yielding vector representations of the graphs in the collection of graphs. Finally, the third stage evaluates the resulting embeddings through supervised classification employing supervised classifiers. Classification performance is assessed using accuracy and F1-score, and since the only thing that changes in this framework is the embedding employed, this performance can be interpreted as a measure of the embedding's quality.

For both mining strategies, the final pattern set (either $\mathcal{P}_G$ or $\mathcal{P}_L$) defines a feature space in which graphs in a dataset will be represented by means of Dissimilarity-based Graph Embedding (Definition 6).

The characteristics of the embeddings depend directly on the mined pattern sets. The global and local mining strategies can produce representations that differ in dimensionality, sparsity, and structural diversity.

To evaluate the resulting embeddings, they are assessed through supervised classification. The same classifiers using k-fold cross-validation evaluate both embeddings, ensuring that any performance differences are due to the mined pattern sets used for building the embeddings.

The k-fold cross-validation involves randomly dividing the dataset into k folds. In each iteration, 80% of the dataset is used for training, and the remaining 20% for testing.

Finally, the performance is evaluated using accuracy and F1-score. This framework enables a comparison of how global and local graph patterns influence the quality of the resulting embeddings.

4   Experiments

This section assesses the quality of Dissimilarity-based Graph Embeddings constructed using local and global approximate graph patterns with supervised classification within the framework proposed in the previous section.

For our experiments, we used seven datasets: three synthetic datasets (Coenen) obtained from artificial images generated by the Coenen image generator and transformed into collections of graphs by the method proposed in [15] and four real-world datasets (PTC), which are four collections of graphs that contain compounds labeled according to carcinogenicity obtained from the Network Repository [16]. Table 1 summarizes the properties of the datasets, including the size of the collection of graphs $|\mathcal{C}|$, the average of vertices $|\bar{V}|$ and edges $|\bar{E}|$, the number of labels for vertices $|L_V|$ and edges $|L_E|$, the class distribution denoted by $|C_1|$ and $|C_2|$, and the imbalance ratio (IR).

Table 1. Description of graph datasets used in the experiments

Dataset	$|\mathcal{C}|$	$|\bar{V}|$	$|\bar{E}|$	$|L_V|$	$|L_E|$	$|C_1|$	$|C_2|$	IR
Coenen-100	100	9.04	13.08	12	6	61	39	1.56
Coenen-200	200	9.04	13.08	14	6	103	97	1.06
Coenen-300	300	8.91	12.86	14	6	162	138	1.17
PTC-MM	336	13.97	14.32	18	4	207	129	1.60
PTC-MR	344	14.29	14.69	20	4	192	152	1.26
PTC-FM	349	14.11	14.18	18	4	206	143	1.44
PTC-FR	351	14.56	15	19	4	230	121	1.90

Graph patterns are mined using two distinct strategies: Frequent Approximate Subgraph Mining in a Single Graph and Frequent Approximate Subgraph Mining in a Collection of Graphs, each evaluated across four configuration parameters. In the former, patterns are mined independently from each graph, then merged into a unified graph pattern set after removing duplicates. We use the AGRAP algorithm [17] to mine Frequent Approximate Subgraphs in a Single Graph (Local Approximate Graph Patterns). AGRAP mines approximate graph patterns within a single graph, accounting for structural and label variations. In contrast, in the Frequent Approximate Subgraph Mining in a Collection of Graphs strategy, graph patterns are mined directly from the entire collection of graphs. We use AGCM-SLV [18] to mine Frequent Approximate Subgraphs in a Collection of Graphs. AGCM-SLV mines approximate graph patterns from a collection of graphs with structural and label variations (Global Approximate Graph Patterns).

Table 2 summarizes, for each dataset, mining strategy, and parameter configuration (dissimilarity threshold δ_{max} and support threshold $\sigma_{\min}$), the average number of mined patterns ($|\mathcal{P}_L|$ or $|\mathcal{P}_G|$) over the five folds and the average and maximum number of nodes in a pattern, $\bar{V}$ and Max(V), respectively.

Table 2. Average number of Local Approximate Graph Patterns (LAGP) and Global Approximate Graph Patterns (GAGP) mined over the 5-fold cross-validation.

Dataset	δ_{max}	LAGP				GAGP			
		$\sigma_{\min}$	$|\mathcal{P}_L|$	$\bar{V}$	Max(V)	$\sigma_{\min}$	$|\mathcal{P}_G|$	$\bar{V}$	Max(V)
Coenen-100	1	2	7	1	1	80%	65.6	2.33	4
		3	5.8	1	1	90%	48.8	2.12	3
	2	2	72.8	1.90	2	80%	379.8	3.35	6
		3	5.8	1	1	90%	249.2	3.03	4
Coenen-200	1	2	7.8	1	1	80%	71.8	2.30	4
		3	6.6	1	1	90%	55.6	2.14	3
	2	2	93.08	1.92	2	80%	484.6	3.28	5
		3	6.6	1	1	90%	268.2	2.85	4
Coenen-300	1	2	8	1	1	80%	70.2	2.28	3
		3	6.8	1	1	90%	55.2	2.12	3
	2	2	101.4	1.92	2	80%	476.2	3.22	5
		3	6.8	1	1	90%	251.2	2.72	4
PTC-MM	1	2	10.6	1	1	80%	17.6	2.18	3
		3	8.8	1	1	90%	11.8	1.92	2
	2	2	45.8	1.77	2	80%	101	2.98	4
		3	8.8	1	1	90%	55.2	2.64	4
PTC-MR	1	2	10.6	1	1	80%	18.4	2.22	3
		3	8.8	1	1	90%	12.4	1.95	3
	2	2	46.4	1.77	2	80%	114.2	3.09	5
		3	8.8	1	1	90%	65.2	2.79	4
PTC-FM	1	2	10.6	1	1	80%	21	2.23	3
		3	8.8	1	1	90%	13.2	1.92	2
	2	2	47.2	1.78	2	80%	118.4	3.10	6
		3	8.8	1	1	90%	73.8	2.77	4
PTC-FR	1	2	10.6	1	1	80%	19.6	2.21	3
		3	8.8	1	1	90%	13.8	1.95	3
	2	2	47.4	1.78	2	80%	104.6	2.10	4
		3	8.8	1	1	90%	58.4	2.66	4

The results show that for all datasets and parameter configurations, Frequent Approximate Subgraph Mining in a Collection of Graphs yields more and larger patterns ($\bar{V}$ and Max(V)). In contrast, Frequent Approximate Subgraph Mining in a Single Graph often produces single-vertex patterns. Increasing the maximum dissimilarity threshold δ_{max} from 1 to 2 increases the number of mined patterns for both strategies, while increasing the minimum support threshold σ_{min} reduces the number of patterns. The number of patterns directly affects the resulting embedding dimensionality.

The mined patterns are used to build Dissimilarity-based Graph Embeddings, which are evaluated using six classifiers: decision trees (DT), random forests (RF), gradient boosting (GBM), k-nearest neighbors (KNN), linear support vector machines (LinearSVM), and multilayer perceptrons (MLP). All are implemented in the scikit-learn library in Python using the default hyperparameters. Performance is measured using accuracy and F1-score. All experiments were conducted on a computer running Ubuntu 22, equipped with two Intel Xeon E5-2620 processors at 2.40 GHz and 256 GB of RAM.

Table 3 reports the classification accuracy and F1-scores of the Dissimilarity-based Graph Embeddings built from the Local Approximate Graph Patterns (LAGP) and Global Approximate Graph Patterns (GAGP) for all configuration parameters. For each dataset, results are presented as the mean and standard deviation over 5-fold cross-validation. Performance values are averaged across all evaluated classifiers.

Table 3. Classification performance (mean $\pm$ std over 5-fold cross-validation) averaged across all evaluated classifiers.

Dataset	δ_{max}	σ_{min}		Accuracy		F1	
		LAGP	GAGP	LAGP	GAGP	LAGP	GAGP
Coenen-100	1	2	80%	0.596 ± 0.09	$\mathbf{0.978 \pm 0.03}$	0.683 ± 0.14	$\mathbf{0.983 \pm 0.03}$
		3	90%	0.601 ± 0.09	$\mathbf{0.981 \pm 0.03}$	0.694 ± 0.10	$\mathbf{0.985 \pm 0.03}$
	2	2	80%	0.570 ± 0.10	$\mathbf{0.976 \pm 0.04}$	0.621 ± 0.19	$\mathbf{0.981 \pm 0.03}$
		3	90%	0.594 ± 0.10	$\mathbf{0.981 \pm 0.04}$	0.686 ± 0.12	$\mathbf{0.986 \pm 0.03}$
Coenen-200	1	2	80%	0.544 ± 0.09	$\mathbf{0.988 \pm 0.02}$	0.535 ± 0.20	$\mathbf{0.989 \pm 0.02}$
		3	90%	0.540 ± 0.09	$\mathbf{0.990 \pm 0.02}$	0.567 ± 0.17	$\mathbf{0.985 \pm 0.03}$
	2	2	80%	0.537 ± 0.09	$\mathbf{0.978 \pm 0.04}$	0.554 ± 0.19	$\mathbf{0.980 \pm 0.04}$
		3	90%	0.540 ± 0.09	$\mathbf{0.986 \pm 0.03}$	0.552 ± 0.18	$\mathbf{0.987 \pm 0.03}$
Coenen-300	1	2	80%	0.535 ± 0.06	$\mathbf{0.987 \pm 0.02}$	0.534 ± 0.21	$\mathbf{0.989 \pm 0.02}$
		3	90%	0.531 ± 0.06	$\mathbf{0.990 \pm 0.02}$	0.544 ± 0.19	$\mathbf{0.991 \pm 0.02}$
	2	2	80%	0.535 ± 0.05	$\mathbf{0.984 \pm 0.03}$	0.548 ± 0.20	$\mathbf{0.986 \pm 0.02}$
		3	90%	0.537 ± 0.05	$\mathbf{0.990 \pm 0.02}$	0.566 ± 0.18	$\mathbf{0.991 \pm 0.02}$
PTC-MM	1	2	80%	0.617 ± 0.07	$\mathbf{0.639 \pm 0.11}$	0.298 ± 0.22	$\mathbf{0.458 \pm 0.16}$
		3	90%	0.617 ± 0.07	$\mathbf{0.636 \pm 0.10}$	0.287 ± 0.22	$\mathbf{0.401 \pm 0.22}$
	2	2	80%	0.617 ± 0.07	$\mathbf{0.674 \pm 0.13}$	0.312 ± 0.22	$\mathbf{0.538 \pm 0.17}$
		3	90%	0.618 ± 0.07	$\mathbf{0.631 \pm 0.12}$	0.288 ± 0.23	$\mathbf{0.486 \pm 0.18}$
PTC-MR	1	2	80%	0.567 ± 0.07	$\mathbf{0.602 \pm 0.11}$	0.314 ± 0.21	$\mathbf{0.524 \pm 0.17}$
		3	90%	0.564 ± 0.07	$\mathbf{0.558 \pm 0.08}$	0.308 ± 0.21	$\mathbf{0.429 \pm 0.21}$
	2	2	80%	0.567 ± 0.07	$\mathbf{0.667 \pm 0.11}$	0.290 ± 0.21	$\mathbf{0.593 \pm 0.15}$
		3	90%	0.568 ± 0.07	$\mathbf{0.646 \pm 0.10}$	0.299 ± 0.22	$\mathbf{0.542 \pm 0.16}$
PTC-FM	1	2	80%	0.609 ± 0.07	$\mathbf{0.658 \pm 0.09}$	0.380 ± 0.21	$\mathbf{0.464 \pm 0.22}$
		3	90%	0.613 ± 0.07	$\mathbf{0.618 \pm 0.07}$	0.356 ± 0.23	$\mathbf{0.354 \pm 0.21}$
	2	2	80%	0.605 ± 0.08	$\mathbf{0.703 \pm 0.11}$	0.376 ± 0.21	$\mathbf{0.586 \pm 0.15}$
		3	90%	0.612 ± 0.07	$\mathbf{0.684 \pm 0.10}$	0.354 ± 0.23	$\mathbf{0.554 \pm 0.16}$
PTC-FR	1	2	80%	0.644 ± 0.07	$\mathbf{0.687 \pm 0.08}$	0.201 ± 0.21	$\mathbf{0.367 \pm 0.21}$
		3	90%	0.645 ± 0.07	$\mathbf{0.666 \pm 0.07}$	0.193 ± 0.21	$\mathbf{0.268 \pm 0.21}$
	2	2	80%	0.636 ± 0.08	$\mathbf{0.696 \pm 0.12}$	0.191 ± 0.21	$\mathbf{0.491 \pm 0.20}$
		3	90%	0.644 ± 0.07	$\mathbf{0.671 \pm 0.13}$	0.184 ± 0.21	$\mathbf{0.440 \pm 0.23}$

Across all datasets, Dissimilarity-based Graph Embedding using Global Patterns outperforms Dissimilarity-based Graph Embedding using Local Patterns in both accuracy and F1-score. This suggests that Global Approximate Graph Patterns (GAGP) better capture regularities across the whole dataset, whereas Local Approximate Graph Patterns (LAGP) do not capture this information because some of the patterns may not appear repeated inside the individual graphs.

The largest performance gaps observed with the Coenen datasets coincide with variations in the number of patterns and in the average number of nodes per pattern. The Local Approximate Graph Pattern (LAGP) sets mined are small, resulting in accuracies between 0.53 and 0.60 and F1-scores between 0.53 and 0.69, while the Global Approximate Graph Patterns (GAGP) set builds Dissimilarity-based Graph Embeddings that obtain an accuracy and F1-score of approximately 0.98. In contrast, for the PTC datasets, the differences in both the number of graph patterns and the number of nodes in mined patterns between the two strategies are smaller than those in the Coenen datasets, resulting in a smaller gap in accuracy.

To further analyze the quality of the Dissimilarity-based Graph Embeddings built from the two different strategies, we also show the evaluation of the six supervised classifiers used. By evaluating performance across this set of classifiers, we analyze how well the Dissimilarity-based Graph Embeddings behave in different learning models.

Figure 1 presents boxplots showing the distributions of accuracy and F1-scores across the six classifiers for both strategies, evaluated over the five folds, all datasets, and all configuration parameters.

Figure 1 confirms that Dissimilarity-based Graph Embeddings built from Global Approximate Graph Patterns (GAGP) achieve higher accuracy and F1-score across all classifiers. In Fig. 1a, the accuracies achieved by the embeddings built from Local Approximate Graph Patterns (LAGP) are around 0.6, with a compact distribution. The difference among the results from the different classifiers is small. In contrast, Fig. 1b shows that the accuracies achieved by embeddings built from Global Approximate Graph Patterns (GAGP) are higher, with KNN achieving the best performance. However, the boxplots are more widely distributed, indicating greater variation in accuracy between the highest and lowest value per classifier. Figures 1c and 1d show a similar behavior, with the Global Approximate Graph Patterns (GAGP) achieving a higher performance for the F1-score.

We also analyze parameter variations across four different mining configurations for each strategy. For both mining strategies, the maximum dissimilarity threshold δ_{max} ranged from 1 to 2. This range allows for variations between patterns and detects approximate matches; a value of zero (0) would lead to only detecting exact matches, and higher values would introduce excessive variability given the small size of the graphs used. For the Frequent Approximate Subgraph Mining in a Single Graph mining strategy, the minimum support threshold σ_{min} ranged from 2 to 3, and for the Frequent Approximate Subgraph Mining in a

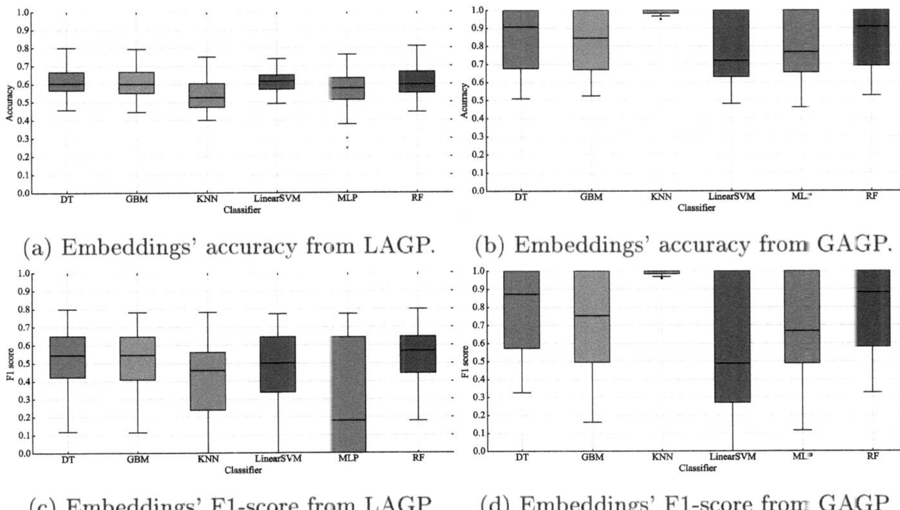

(a) Embeddings' accuracy from LAGP.

(b) Embeddings' accuracy from GAGP.

(c) Embeddings' F1-score from LAGP

(d) Embeddings' F1-score from GAGP

Fig. 1. Average accuracy and F1-score of the Dissimilarity-based Graph Embedding built from global and local approximate graph patterns across all evaluated classifiers.

Collection of Graphs mining strategy, the support varied between 80% and 90%. The support threshold differs for both strategies due to the nature of the mining process. In a collection of graphs, requiring 80% support means the pattern must appear in most graphs within the collection, but within a single graph, it's not the same. An 80% support threshold would require nearly all nodes to have an approximate match to the mined graph patterns. For Frequent Approximate Subgraph Mining in a Single Graph, small thresholds of 2 and 3 are employed to ensure that patterns appear without being overly restrictive. Higher thresholds would lead to discarding most patterns due to their low frequency. Conversely, for Frequent Approximate Subgraph Mining in a Collection of Graphs we used thresholds of 80% and 90% to prevent the generation of an excessive number of patterns.

Figure 2 presents boxplots showing the distributions of accuracy and F1-score for each parameter configuration across the five folds, across all datasets, and for all evaluated classifiers under the Dissimilarity-based Graph Embedding built from local and global approximate graph patterns.

The figures show that Dissimilarity-based Graph Embeddings built from Global Approximate Graph Patterns (GAGP) achieve higher accuracy and F1-scores across all parameter configurations. In Fig. 2a, the Dissimilarity-based Graph Embeddings built from Local Approximate Graph Patterns show little variation in accuracy across the different parameter configurations. In contrast, Fig. 2b shows the accuracies achieved from the Dissimilarity-based Graph Embeddings built from Global Approximate Graph Patterns (GAGP), which are higher. However, the boxplots are more widely distributed. The best config-

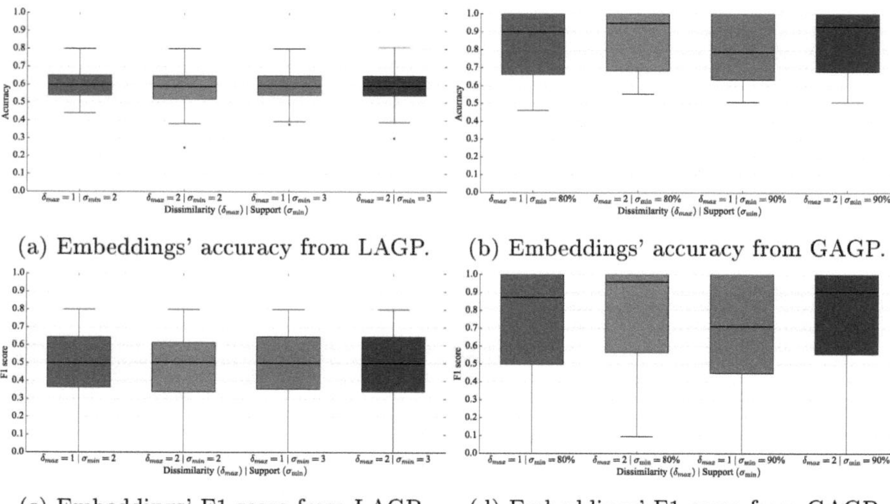

(a) Embeddings' accuracy from LAGP.   (b) Embeddings' accuracy from GAGP.

(c) Embeddings' F1-score from LAGP.   (d) Embeddings' F1-score from GAGP.

Fig. 2. Average accuracy and F1-score of the Dissimilarity-based Graph Embedding built from local and global approximate graph patterns mined under different parameter configurations.

uration in terms of performance is $\delta_{max} = 2$ and $\sigma_{\min} = 80\%$, and the worst is $\delta_{max} = 1$ and $\sigma_{\min} = 90\%$. Figures 2c and 2d show a similar behavior, with the Dissimilarity-based Graph Embeddings built from the Global Approximate Graph Patterns (GAGP) achieving higher performance for F1-score.

Overall, the experimental results demonstrate that the mined set of Global Approximate Graph Patterns (GAGP) is larger than that of Local Approximate Graph Patterns (LAGP). Furthermore, Dissimilarity-based Graph Embeddings built from the set of Global Approximate Graph Patterns achieve higher accuracy and F1-scores for supervised graph classification.

5   Conclusion and Future Work

In this paper, we present a study of Dissimilarity-based Graph Embeddings built from two different graph pattern sets: Global Approximate Graph Patterns (GAGP) and Local Approximate Graph Patterns (LAGP). Both embeddings were evaluated in a supervised classification task using six classifiers, and performance was measured by accuracy and F1-score averaged over five-fold cross-validation.

In our experiments, we analyzed the number of mined patterns and their average and maximum number of nodes. Global Approximate Graph Patterns (GAGP) were more numerous and larger in size, yielding higher-dimensional embeddings and improved performance. Conversely, Local Approximate Graph Patterns (LAGP) were fewer in number and smaller in size, leading to lower-dimensional embeddings, producing lower classification results.

The experimental results showed that Dissimilarity-based Graph Embeddings built from Global Approximate Graph Patterns (GAGP) achieved higher average classification results across all experiments in both accuracy and F1-scores. In contrast, Dissimilarity-based Graph Embeddings built from Local Approximate Graph Patterns (LAGP) achieved lower classification results but more compact distributions in both accuracy and F1-score.

This work constitutes a first step toward the study of Dissimilarity-Based Graph Embedding built using Global Approximate Graph Patterns (GAGP) and Local Approximate Graph Patterns (LAGP) within the same framework. Based on our study in this paper, we highlight the challenges in selecting parameters for mining patterns useful for Dissimilarity-Based Graph Embedding. In particular, our results show that selecting a good parameter configuration is not easy, as the values depend heavily on the characteristics of the data and the mining stage. Future work will therefore focus on a more detailed analysis of these parameters. Additionally, we aim to use larger collections of graphs.

Acknowledgments. This research was financially supported by the Secretaría de Ciencia, Humanidades, Tecnología e Innovación (SECIHTI) through the scholarship grant 778343.

Disclosure of Interests. The authors have no competing interests to declare that are relevant to the content of this article.

References

1. You, Y., Liu, Z., Wen, X., Zhang, Y., Ai, W.: Large language models meet graph neural networks: a perspective of graph mining. Mathematics **13**(7) (2025). https://doi.org/10.3390/math13071147, https://www.mdpi.com/2227-7390/13/7/1147
2. Ergenç Bostanoğlu, B., Abuzayed, N.: Dynamic frequent subgraph mining algorithms over evolving graphs: a survey. PeerJ Comput. Sci. **10**, e2361 (2024)
3. Bhowmick, S., Bell, P., Taufer, M.: A survey of graph comparison methods with applications to nondeterminism in high-performance computing. Int. J. High Perform. Comput. Appl. **37**(3–4), 306–327 (2023). https://doi.org/10.1177/10943420231166610
4. Jiang, C., Coenen, F., Zito, M.: A survey of frequent subgraph mining algorithms. Knowl. Eng. Rev. **28**(1), 75–105 (2013). https://doi.org/10.1017/S0269888912000331
5. Ramraj, T., Prabhakar, R.: Frequent subgraph mining algorithms – a survey. Procedia Comput. Sci. **47**, 197–204 (2015). https://doi.org/10.1016/j.procs.2015.03.198. Graph Algorithms, High Performance Implementations and Its Applications (ICGHIA 2014)
6. Mrzic, A., et al.: Grasping frequent subgraph mining for bioinformatics applications. BioData Min. **11**(1), 1–24 (2018)
7. Cook, D.J., Holder, L.B. (eds.): Mining Graph Data. Wiley-Interscience, New York (2006)

8. Bunke, H., Riesen, K.: Graph classification based on dissimilarity space embedding. In: da Vitoria Lobo, N., Kasparis, T., Roli, F., Kwok, J.T., Georgiopoulos, M., Anagnostopoulos, G.C., Loog, M. (eds.) SSPR /SPR 2008. LNCS, vol. 5342, pp. 996–1007. Springer, Heidelberg (2008). https://doi.org/10.1007/978-3-540-89689-0_103

9. Fuchs, M., Riesen, K.: Graph embedding in vector spaces using matching-graphs. In: Reyes, N., Connor, R., Kriege, N., Kazempour, D., Bartolini, I., Schubert, E., Chen, J.-J. (eds.) SISAP 2021. LNCS, vol. 13058, pp. 352–363. Springer, Cham (2021). https://doi.org/10.1007/978-3-030-89657-7_26

10. Leonardi, F., Riesen, K.: Dissimilarity-based graph embedding: an efficient gat-based approach. In: Antonacopoulos, A., Chaudhuri, S., Chellappa, R., Liu, C.-L., Bhattacharya, S., Pal, U. (eds.) ICPR 2024. LNCS, vol. 15310, pp. 361–374. Springer Nature Switzerland, Cham (2025). https://doi.org/10.1007/978-3-031-78192-6_24

11. Jaramillo-Olivares, D., Carrasco-Ochoa, J.A., Martínez-Trinidad, J.F.: Exact versus approximate patterns in dissimilarity-based graph embedding for supervised classification. In: López-Monroy, A.P., Rosales-Pérez, A., Carrasco-Ochoa, J.A., Martínez-Trinidad, J.F., Olvera-López, J.A. (eds.) MCPR 2025. LNCS, vol. 15715, pp. 56–67. Springer, Cham (2025). https://doi.org/10.1007/978-3-031-96255-4_6

12. Noori, A., Balafar, M.A., Bouyer, A., Salmani, K.: Review of heterogeneous graph embedding methods based on deep learning techniques and comparing their efficiency in node classification. Soc. Netw. Anal. Min. **14**(1), 17 (2024). https://doi.org/10.1007/s13278-023-01178-6

13. Bunke, H., Riesen, K.: Improving vector space embedding of graphs through feature selection algorithms. Pattern Recogn. **44**(9), 1928–1940 (2011). https://doi.org/10.1016/j.patcog.2010.05.016, https://www.sciencedirect.com/science/article/pii/S0031320310002360. Computer Analysis of Images and Patterns

14. Sanfeliu, A., Fu, K.-S.: A distance measure between attributed relational graphs for pattern recognition. IEEE Trans. Syst. Man Cybern. SMC **13**(3), 353–362 (1983)

15. Acosta-Mendoza, N., Gago-Alonso, A., Medina-Pagola, J.E.: Frequent approximate subgraphs as features for graph-based image classification. Knowl.-Based Syst. **27**, 381–392 (2012)

16. Rossi, R.A., Ahmed, N.K.: The network data repository with interactive graph analytics and visualization. In: AAAI (2015). https://networkrepository.com

17. Flores-Garrido, M., Carrasco-Ochoa, J.-A., Martínez-Trinidad, J.F.: AGraP: an algorithm for mining frequent patterns in a single graph using inexact matching. Knowl. Inf. Syst. **44**(2), 385–406 (2015). https://doi.org/10.1007/s10115-014-0747-x

18. Jaramillo-Olivares, D., Carrasco-Ochoa, J.A., Martínez-Trinidad, J.F.: An algorithm for mining frequent approximate subgraphs with structural and label variations in graph collections. Appl. Sci. **15**(14) (2025). https://doi.org/10.3390/app15147880, https://www.mdpi.com/2076-3417/15/14/7880

Comprehensive Validation of BREX Sequential Classifier Model for Robust Pattern Recognition

Gerardo Acevedo-Sánchez[1] (iD), Jorge Pacheco-Senard[1] (iD),
Antonio Alarcón-Paredes[1] (iD), Óscar Camacho-Nieto[2] (iD),
and Cornelio Yáñez-Márquez[1 (✉)] (iD)

[1] Centro de Investigación en Computación, Instituto Politécnico Nacional, Ciudad de México, México
{gacevedos2024,jpachecos2024,aalarcon,cyanez}@cic.ipn.mx
[2] Centro de Innovación y Desarrollo Tecnológico en Cómputo, Instituto Politécnico Nacional, Ciudad de México, México
oscarc@cic.ipn.mx

Abstract. The objective of this work was to validate the BREX model (Blend of Ranked-sequential Algorithms Executed for boosting-based classification) and compared with standalone classifiers of machine learning. For these purposes, 18 public datasets selected spanning diverse domains, imbalance ratios (1.0 to 639), cardinalities (28 to 45,211 instances), dimensionalities (3 to 1,070 attributes), and classes (2 to 28). Results showed a consistent trend: initial stages (i.e., Euclidean, kNN, IBk) classified most easily separable patterns, while later stages (i.e., trees, SVM, ensembles) progressively refined the remaining complex patterns. In 12 datasets, BREX achieved higher performance (≥ 0.99). On the most challenging datasets, BREX delivered significant improvements, with Balanced Accuracy increasing by up to 42% (e.g., *Student performance*: 0.52 to 0.79; *Abalone*: 0.55 to 0.87; or *White wine*: 0.56 to 0.98). The final classifier achieving maximum performance varied by dataset: XGBoost was the most frequent (12), followed by C5.0 (3), with simpler algorithms sufficing in specific cases. Comparison with standalone classifiers confirmed BREX's outperformance. For instance, on *Student performance*, the best independent model (XGBoost) achieved BA = 0.53 *versus* BREX's 0.79; on *Abalone* (CART) reached BA = 0.57 *versus* BREX's 0.87. Computational efficiency analysis showed BREX exceeded the patterns-per-second rate of the best standalone classifier in 14/18 datasets, e.g., *White wine*: 27.9 *vs.* 0.088 patterns/sec (317 × faster); *Dropout*: 26.1 *vs.* 0.193 (135 × faster); *Obesity*: 30.7 *vs.* 0.148 (207 × faster). These gains stem from BREX's hierarchical design. This validation establishes BREX as a robust, generalizable model with high performance and efficiency, well-suited for resource-constrained environments and standard computing.

Keywords: Pattern classification · Boosting · LOOCV · Data complexity · Computational efficiency

V. G. Cruz-Sánchez et al. (Eds.): MCPR 2026, LNCS 16623, pp. 91–102, 2026.
https://doi.org/10.1007/978-3-032-28393-1_9

1 Introduction

The No Free Lunch theorem underscores that no single algorithm excels universally, making data complexity and computational efficiency critical in resource-limited settings [1–3]. Hybrid strategies such as boosting, cascades, and stacking integrate multiple models to improve classification, often via progressive refinement of misclassified instances [4–7]. However, these approaches differ fundamentally from BREX in architecture and objective [8, 9]. Stacking aggregates base-model outputs via a meta-learner without instance filtering; voting combines decisions in parallel without sequential correction; cascading relies on fixed confidence thresholds rather than deterministic ranking. In contrast, BREX employs: i) a strictly sequential cascade processing only prior-stage residual errors; ii) a fixed complexity-based algorithm ordering (Euclidean to XGBoost) validated across domains; and iii) per-stage leave-one-out cross-validation (LOOCV) for unbiased, partition-free evaluation. BREX is thus proposed not as a direct competitor to stacking or voting, but as a complementary architecture for scenarios where sequential refinement of hard instances proves advantageous. A full empirical comparison lies beyond the present scope.

In this respect, the Blend of Ranked-sequential Algorithms Executed for boosting-based classification (BREX) was recently introduced as a hybrid hierarchical model combining machine learning techniques with deterministic Leave-One-Out validation [9]. In the initial *proof-of-concept* on the *white wine* dataset, characterized by extreme class imbalance ($n = 4898$, $m = 12$, 7 classes, IR $= 439.6$), BREX demonstrated remarkable performance. Fifteen classifiers were ranked and executed according to increasing algorithmic complexity. The performance measures achieving near-optimal values (e.g., BA $= 0.98$, F1-score $= 0.98$) outperforming top standalone algorithms such as Random Forest (BA $= 0.77$) or XGBoost (BA $= 0.72$). Computationally, BREX completed classification 13.6-fold faster, demonstrating a dual advantage in predictive accuracy and efficiency [9].

Despite these promising results, the initial validation was limited to a single dataset, which raises questions about the model's generalization capability across different domains and data complexities. As noted in previous work [9], addressing performance in other domains with high imbalance or other complexity indicators is essential for future research. The feasibility of LOOCV, the behavior of early versus late stages, and the comparative performance against standalone classifiers needed to be tested on a broader collection of datasets to establish BREX as a robust and generalizable framework. Therefore, the objective of this work was to perform a comprehensive validation of the BREX model across datasets from several domains with varying data complexity, including different imbalance ratios, cardinalities, dimensionalities, and class structures, and systematically comparing its performance against standalone classifiers of machine learning. This multi-dataset validation seeks to confirm whether the sequential, hierarchically ranked architecture of BREX consistently confers advantages in both performance and computational efficiency.

2   Materials and Methods

This section details the experimental setup for evaluating the BREX model, covering dataset characteristics, validation strategy, classifier selection/ranking, performance measures, computational resources, and implementation settings.

2.1   Data Collection

The BREX model's efficacy in scenarios involving extreme imbalance, high dimensionality, and varied cardinalities was tested by analyzing a collection of 18 datasets from the public UCI Machine Learning Repository (https://archive.ics.uci.edu/). These datasets were selected to cover contrasting domains and a wide range of classification challenges. A total of 18 datasets encompasses scenarios of complexity data from binary and multiclass problems, low to extremely high imbalance ratios (IR ranging from 1.0 to 689), low to very high dimensionality (from 3 to 1,070 attributes), and varying cardinalities (from 28 to 45,211 instances) [3, 10]. This diversity ensures a rigorous and comprehensive evaluation of the BREX model's generalizability, scalability, and robustness under heterogeneous real-world conditions.

2.2   Brex Model Description

The Blend of Ranked-sequential Algorithms Executed for Boosting-based classification (BREX) is a hybrid hierarchical model designed for extreme class imbalance, high cardinality, and multi-class complexity. It combines boosting principles with deterministic validation via a sequential architecture of classifiers ranked by increasing algorithmic complexity. At each stage, a classifier trains and tests exclusively on instances misclassified by the preceding stage, systematically forwarding errors to more sophisticated models while maintaining a rigid, predefined hierarchy [9].

The BREX sequential process applies LOOCV at each stage, starting with the simplest classifier and removing correctly classified instances. Misclassified ones advance to more complex algorithms until exhaustion or perfect classification. The architecture comprises: i) a complexity-ranked hierarchy (Euclidean to XGBoost); ii) progressive forwarding of residual errors; and iii) deterministic LOOCV validation, eliminating stochastic bias [9]. Fifteen classifiers were selected and ranked by computational cost, interpretability, and nonlinear capacity: simple models (Euclidean, kNN, I3k, Naive Bayes, LDA) handle separable instances early; decision trees (CART, C5.0) and SVM address moderate complexity; ensembles (Random Forest, GBM, XGBoost) resolve intricate patterns last, optimizing resources by concentrating costly algorithms on the hardest data subset.

LOOCV is applied only to the current misclassified subset per stage, ensuring computational feasibility (full data early with simple algorithms, reduced subsets later with complex models) and statistically rigorous, partition-free results [9]. Removing correct instances yields three advantages: 1) efficiency, simple classifiers reduce complex-model load; 2) performance, powerful algorithms target hard patterns under extreme imbalance; and 3) deterministic rigor progressive cardinality reduction enables unbiased LOOCV evaluation [9].

2.3 Hyperparameter Configuration and Stopping Criterion

All classifiers in the BREX model were executed with default hyperparameters as implemented in the R environment (e.g., for k-NN and IBk with $k = 1,3$ and 5; for CART $cp = 0.01$, *minsplit* $= 20$, and *maxdepth* $= 30$; for C5.0 *trials* $= 1$ and *rules* $=$ FALSE (tree); for SVM *kernel* $=$ radial and *cost* $= 1$; for Random Forest *ntree* $= 500$ and mtry $=$ sqrt(ncol(x)); for GBM with *n.trees* $= 100$ and *interaction.depth* $= 3$; for XGBoost *nrounds* $= 50$ and *eta* $= 0.3$). No dataset-specific tuning was performed to preserve generalizability. The stopping criterion of BREX was when all instances are correctly classified or the classifier sequence is exhausted by a deterministic rule eliminating model-selection bias.

2.4 Performance Measures

The confusion matrix (CM) was maintained for evaluating the performance of classifiers in BREX model comparison. The CM cells (i.e., True Positives (TP), True Negatives (TN), False Positives (FP), and False Negatives (FN)) were used for obtaining key measures including Recall, Specificity, Balanced Accuracy, Precision, F1-score, and Matthews Correlation Coefficient (MCC) [11]. The one-versus-all approach and weighted-average measure was computed for multi-class scenarios [12].

2.5 Computer Resources, Analyses and Software

The analyses were performed using an 8-core, 16-thread AMD Ryzen™ 7 7730U processor with integrated AMD Radeon™ GPUs and 40 GB of RAM (8 GB soldered DDR4–3200 and 32 GB SO-DIMM DDR4–3200). The BREX model implementation and comparison with single classifiers by dataset were performed in R-Studio following the original six structured phases [9, 13].

3 Results and Discussion

This section presents the results obtained from executing the BREX model on a total of 18 collection datasets It includes a comparison of predictions at each stage by dataset, as well as the performance when the same algorithms are executed independently.

3.1 BREX Model Results

The BREX model was successfully evaluated on 18 datasets spanning diverse imbalance ratios and dimensionalities, with final-stage improvements observed across all performance measures (Fig. 1, 2; Table 1). In the biological domain, the challenging Abalone dataset (28 classes, IR $= 689$) improved from Euclidean (BA $= 0.55$) to XGBoost (BA $= 0.87$, 75.6% correctly classified, 36.67 min), outperforming prior neural network results (BA $= 0.88$) [14]. Agaricus lepiota (balanced, IR $= 1.07$) was perfectly classified at stage 1 by Euclidean (BA $= 1.0$, 1.05 min), consistent with reported accuracy > 0.99. Iris (IR $= 1.0$) reached high final performance (BA $= 0.99$) after 15 stages (0.68 min), though five boundary instances remained unclassified; recent quantum CNN architectures report up to 100% [15] (Fig. 1, 2; Table 1). For Red wine (IR = 68.1), XGBoost at stage 15 improved BA from 0.58 to 0.97 (81.6% classified, 0.93 min). White wine (IR = 439.6), the proof-of-concept dataset, saw BA rise from 0.56 to 0.98 (78.8% classified, 2.31 min). Both confirm BREX's efficacy under extreme imbalance, surpassing prior neuronal network results [16] (Fig. 1, 2; Table 1).

Table 1. Performance results of the BREX model per dataset, including the final stage (last classifier executed), total processing time (min), and the initial (*Ini*) and final (*Fin*) values of the main performance measures.

Dataset	Final Stage	Predicted	Time (min)	Recall		Balanced Accuracy		F1-score		Precision	
				Ini	*Fin*	*Ini*	*Fin*	*Ini*	*Fin*	*Ini*	*Fin*
Abalone	XGB	3159	36.67	0.20	0.76	0.55	0.87	0.20	0.75	0.20	0.75
Agaricus	Euclidean	8124	1.05	1.00	1.00	1.00	1.00	1.00	1.00	1.00	1.00
Car	5NN	1728	0.57	0.76	1.00	0.69	1.00	0.71	1.00	0.67	1.00
Cleveland	XGB	285	0.79	0.41	0.94	0.54	0.95	0.40	0.94	0.40	0.94
Credit approval	C5.0	690	0.62	0.74	1.00	0.67	1.00	0.72	1.00	0.70	1.00
Diabetes	C5.0	768	0.54	0.76	1.00	0.65	1.00	0.75	1.00	0.75	1.00
Dropout	XGB	4393	2.80	0.57	0.99	0.66	0.99	0.57	0.99	0.58	0.99
Electricity	XGB	2397	0.77	0.85	1.00	0.82	1.00	0.85	1.00	0.85	1.00
German	CART	1000	0.58	0.73	1.00	0.54	1.00	0.73	1.00	0.72	1.00
Haberman	XGB	277	0.63	0.86	0.99	0.60	0.97	0.82	0.99	0.79	0.99
Iris	XGB	145	0.68	0.96	0.99	0.97	0.99	0.96	0.99	0.96	0.99
Newthyroid	RF	215	0.81	0.95	1.00	0.94	1.00	0.95	1.00	0.95	1.00
Nutt	1NN	28	0.26	0.36	1.00	0.68	1.00	0.53	1.00	1.00	1.00
Obesity	XGB	2078	1.13	0.91	1.00	0.95	1.00	0.91	1.00	0.91	1.00
Red wine	XGB	1305	0.93	0.46	0.96	0.58	0.97	0.46	0.96	0.46	0.96
Student perform	XGB	599	7.36	0.13	0.62	0.52	0.79	0.13	0.62	0.13	0.62
White wine	XGB	3858	2.31	0.42	0.97	0.56	0.98	0.41	0.97	0.41	0.97
wdbc	XGB	568	0.52	0.95	1.00	0.90	1.00	0.93	1.00	0.92	1.00

In the medical domain, Cleveland (5 classes, IR = 12.6) improved from BA = 0.54 to 0.95 with XGBoost (94.1% classified, 0.79 min), outperforming prior reports by 4–6% [17]. Diabetes (binary, IR = 1.87) reached correct classification at stage 11 via C5.0 (0.54 min), exceeding recurrent neural network results by > 6% [18]. Haberman (IR = 2.88) achieved BA = 0.97 with XGBoost (97.9% classified, 0.63 min), surpassing classical classifiers [19]. Newthyroid (IR = 5.0) was perfectly classified by Random

Forest at stage 13 (0.81 min) [20]. Nutt (high-dimensional, 28 instances, 1070 features) reached 100% accuracy with 1NN at stage 2 (0.26 min), aligning with minimalist ML approaches [21]. Obesity (7 classes, IR = 1.29) reached high final performance via XGBoost (98.4% classified, 1.13 min) [22]. WDBC (binary, IR = 1.68) left only one instance unclassified with XGBoost (99.8%, 0.52 min), matching with reports [23].

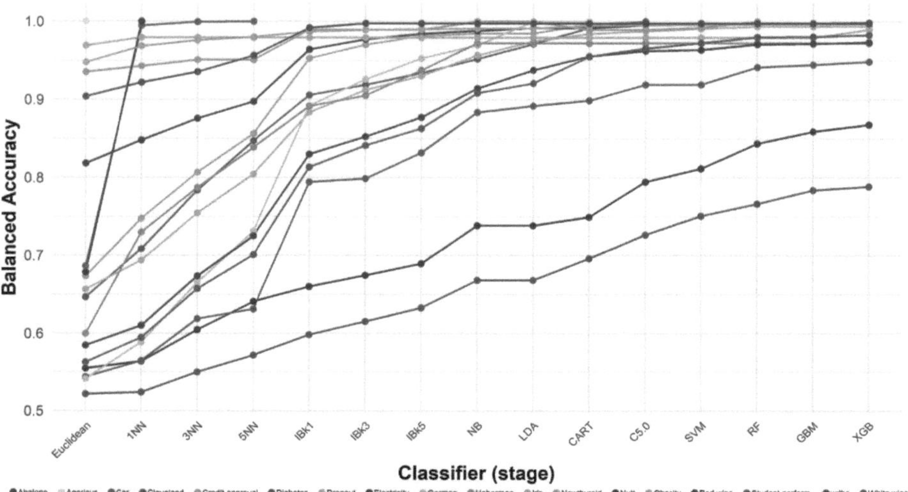

Fig. 1. Comparative analysis of the sequential progression of *Balanced Accuracy* in the BREX model applied to 18 datasets from diverse domains. Each line corresponds to an individual dataset, while the horizontal axis represents the successive BREX classification stages.

In the financial domain, Credit Approval (IR = 1.25) and German Credit (IR = 2.33) both achieved perfect classification using decision trees (C5.0 and CART) at stages 10–11 (0.58–0.62 min), demonstrating that simple models suffice when data align with splitting criteria (Fig. 1, 2; Table 1). In the educational domain, Student Dropout (3 classes, IR = 2.78) improved from BA = 0.66 to 0.99 with XGBoost at stage 15 (99.3% classified, 2.8 min), surpassing boosting and metaheuristic methods [24]. Student Performance (19 classes, IR = 153), despite extreme imbalance, saw BA rise from 0.52 to 0.79 (57.4% classified, 7.36 min) [25]. In other domains, Car (4 classes, IR = 18.6) was perfectly classified by 5NN at stage 4 (0.57 min), outperforming prior results [26]. Electricity (binary, IR = 1.47) reached 100% accuracy with XGBoost at stage 15 (0.77 min) (Fig. 1, 2; Table 1).

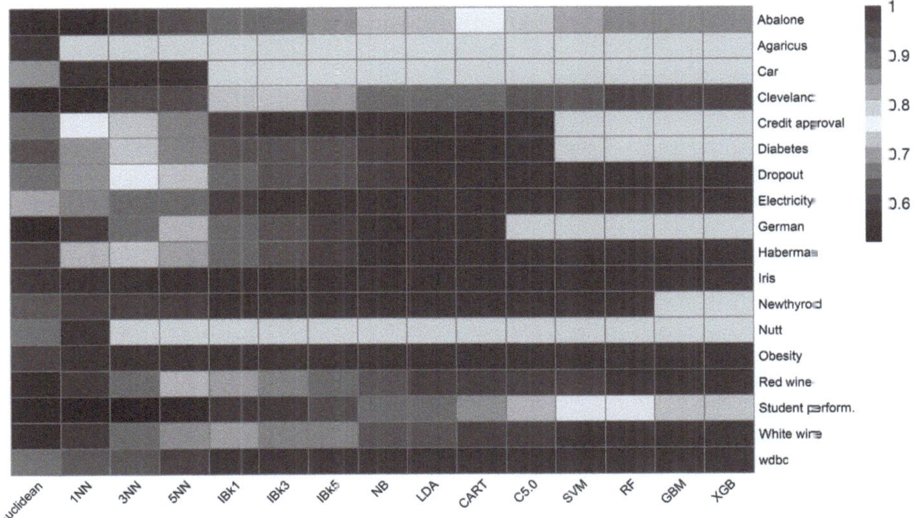

Fig. 2. Heatmap representation of *Balanced Accuracy* values across the sequential classification stages of the BREX model for 18 datasets. Rows correspond to individual datasets, while columns represent successive classifiers. Color intensity reflects performance magnitude, with warmer tones indicating higher accuracy and gray tone indicating stages not executed.

3.2 BREX Model Results Comparison *Versus* Independently Executed Classifiers

BREX consistently outperformed the best standalone classifiers across all 18 datasets. For instance, in White wine, BREX achieved BA = 0.98 vs. 0.77 for the best independent model. On Abalone (IR = 689), BREX correctly classified 2.9 × more instances than CART (3159 vs. 1093), improving BA from 0.57 to 0.87 and F1 from 0.18 to 0.75 [14]. On Student Performance (19 classes, IR = 153), BREX correctly predicted 4 × more instances than standalone XGBoost (599 vs. 153), raising BA from 0.53 to 0.79 and F1 from 0.15 to 0.62 [25] (Fig. 2; Table 1,2).

For Red wine (IR = 68.1), BREX elevated correct predictions from 835 (Random Forest, BA = 0.69) to 1305 instances (BA = 0.97), mirroring the White wine gains (BA: 0.65 to 0.98) [16] (Fig. 2; Table 1,2). Even on strong standalone baselines, BREX achieved very high performance. Car achieved 100% with 5NN (vs. XGBoost's 99.5%), stopping early and saving computation [26]. Agaricus finished at stage-1 with Euclidean alone, an adaptive behavior absent when preselecting models blindly (Fig. 2; Table 2). The best standalone classifier varied across datasets, underscoring the lack of a universal optimum: XGBoost led in 6/18 datasets, Random Forest in 4/18, while simpler models (e.g., Euclidean, LDA, Naive Bayes) sufficed in others. Notably, on high-dimensional Nutt (1070 features, 28 instances), Random Forest attained BA = 0.89 (25 correct), yet BREX's stage-2 1NN classified all 28, demonstrating that sequential refinement can leverage simpler algorithms after initial filtering (Fig. 2; Table 1,2).

Notable contrasts highlight BREX's advantage. For instance, Cleveland had a 58% increase in correct predictions (180 to 285, BA: 0.71 to 0.95) [17]; Dropout achieved 27% more predictions with a 10 × time reduction (2.80 vs. 29.87 min) [23]; German

Credit reached 100% vs. 771 correct [34]; Newthyroid attained perfect classification (215 vs. 209) [20]; and WDBC had only one instance unclassified (568 vs. 554) [22] (Fig. 2; Table 1,2).

Table 2. Performance results of independent classifier across 18 datasets and comparison of best classifier versus others, including predicted patterns, total processing time (min), and the values of performance measures.

Dataset	Best Classifier	Predicted	Time	Recall	Balanced Accuracy	F1-score	Precision
Abalone	CART	1093	2.47	0.26	0.57	0.18	0.14
	Others	0–1075	0.1–181.5	0.2–0.26	0.55–0.58	0.17–0.25	0.19–0.24
Agaricus	Euclidean	8124	1.19	1.00	1.00	1.00	1.00
	Others	0–8124	0.29–116.85	1–1	0.98–1	0.99–1	0.97–1
Car	XGB	1720	5.82	1.00	1.00	1.00	1.00
	Others	1181–1674	0.03–3.34	0.68–0.97	0.58–0.98	0.64–0.97	0.61–0.97
Cleveland	LDA	180	0.02	0.59	0.71	0.58	0.57
	Others	125–177	0.02–1.17	0.41–0.58	0.54–0.7	0.4–0.56	0.38–0.56
Credit approval	RF	608	0.87	0.89	0.88	0.89	0.89
	Others	463–600	0.05–2.7	0.74–0.9	0.66–0.87	0.72–0.88	0.68–0.93
Diabetes	CART	597	0.10	0.86	0.74	0.83	0.81
	Others	522–595	0.04–3.07	0.76–0.93	0.65–0.73	0.75–0.84	0.74–0.8
Dropout	XGB	3460	29.87	0.78	0.82	0.77	0.77
	Others	2541–3437	0.19–58.18	0.57–0.78	0.66–0.81	0.57–0.76	0.58–0.76
Electricity	XGB	2336	5.33	0.98	0.97	0.98	0.98
	Others	1695–2323	0.04–5.69	0.85–0.98	0.65–0.97	0.79–0.97	0.69–0.97
German	XGB	771	2.51	0.88	0.70	0.84	0.81
	Others	613–769	0.03–1.57	0.72–0.93	0.52–0.69	0.72–0.85	0.71–0.83
Haberman	NB	214	0.02	0.95	0.58	0.85	0.77
	Others	192–213	0.02–0.51	0.81–1	0.49–0.61	0.79–0.85	0.74–0.79
Iris	LDA	144	0.02	0.98	0.98	0.98	0.98
	Others	135–142	0.02–0.17	0.92–0.97	0.94–0.97	0.92–0.97	0.93–0.97
Newthyroid	IBk1	209	0.04	0.97	0.97	0.97	0.97
	Others	190–208	0.02–0.25	0.88–0.97	0.85–0.96	0.88–0.97	0.88–0.97
Nutt	RF	25	0.10	0.86	0.89	0.89	0.92
	Others	0–24	0.03–0.29	0.14–1	0.57–0.86	0.25–0.85	0.73–1
Obesity	XGB	2029	22.84	0.97	0.98	0.97	0.97
	Others	1255–1999	0.06–9.87	0.6–0.96	0.77–0.98	0.57–0.96	0.61–0.96
Red wine	RF	835	3.11	0.61	0.69	0.59	0.58
	Others	628–799	0.03–8.45	0.46–0.59	0.57–0.67	0.45–0.57	0.44–0.56
Student	XGB	153	15.98	0.16	0.53	0.15	0.15

(continued)

Table 2. (*continued*)

Dataset	Best Classifier	Predicted	Time	Recall	Balanced Accuracy	F1-score	Precision
perform	Others	0–134	0.02–3.96	0.05–0.14	0.5–0.52	0.05–0.13	0.05–0.13
wdbc	GBM	554	0.20	0.98	0.97	0.98	0.98
	Others	515–553	0.03–0.81	0.95–1	0.87–0.97	0.93–0.98	0.87–0.97
White	RF	2281	43.17	0.58	0.65	0.55	0.57
wine	Others	1626–2173	0.07–47.99	0.41–0.55	0.55–0.64	0.4–0.53	0.4–0.53

3.3 Computational Efficiency Analysis

BREX's computational efficiency is equally notable: on White wine, BREX was 13.6 × faster than standalone Random Forest (2.31 vs. 43.17 min) while improving BA from 0.65 to 0.98. On Abalone, BREX took only 23% longer yet classified nearly triple the instances (3159 vs. 1093). On Obesity, BREX achieved a 20 × speedup (1.13 vs. 22.84 min) with equivalent BA. Gains stem from simple algorithms resolving most instances early, reserving costly ensembles for a reduced hard subset (Fig. 3, Table 1,2).

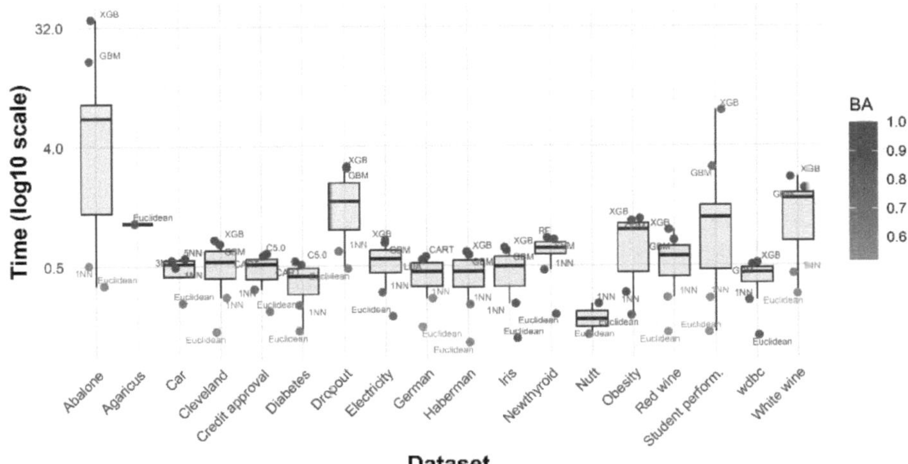

Fig. 3. Boxplot of computational time ($\log_{10}$ scale) across 18 datasets for the BREX classification. Boxes summarize the distribution of execution times per dataset, while overlaid points correspond to the initial and final classification stages of the BREX model. Point color encodes the associated *Balanced Accuracy* (BA) values.

Computational efficiency was evaluated via patterns classified per second. BREX surpassed the best standalone classifier in 14/18 datasets (Fig. 3; Table 1,2). This gain arises from progressive filtering where simple early algorithms handle most instances, leaving only hard patterns for costly ensembles. Striking efficiency gains emerged on high-cardinality or imbalanced datasets. White wine (IR $= 440$) was a $317 \times$ faster (27.9 vs. 0.088 patterns/sec); Dropout achieved $135 \times$ (26.1 vs. 0.193); Obesity reached $207 \times$ (30.7 vs. 0.148) (Fig. 3 Table 1,2). BREX's hierarchical design focuses costly ensembles on hard patterns only, avoiding wasteful computation on easily separable instances.

Exceptional performance was also observed on high-cardinality and high-dimensional specific datasets occurred. On Car, BREX's stage-4 5NN classified all 1728 instances at 50.5 patterns/sec, $102 \times$ faster than standalone XGBoost (0.49 patterns/sec). On high-dimensional Nutt, stage-2 1NN reached 1.8 patterns/sec, $4.2 \times$ faster than Random Forest (Fig. 3; Table 2). Simple algorithms, when well-positioned, thus outperform costly ensembles in both accuracy and speed. In specific cases, standalone classifiers achieved higher patterns/sec: Cleveland (LDA: 13.5 vs. BREX: 6.1), Haberman (Naive Bayes: 16.4 vs. 7.31), and Iris (LDA: 13.1 vs. 3.55) (Fig. 3; Table 1,2). However, BREX correctly classified 58% more instances on Cleveland and reached near-perfect totals on all three, trading modest runtime for substantially improved predictive completeness, a valuable trade-off in performance applications.

4 Conclusions

In summary, BREX offers a robust framework for imbalanced multiclass classification. Initial stages (Euclidean, kNN, IBk) resolved most separable instances, while later stages (trees, SVM, ensembles) refined complex patterns. Across 18 datasets, 12 achieved near-perfect performance (≥ 0.99); the most challenging (Abalone, Student, wine) had BA improves up to 42%. XGBoost was the most frequent final stage (12/18), followed by C5.0 (3), with simpler algorithms sufficing in isolated cases.

Multi-dataset validation confirms BREX decisively outperforms standalone classifiers, matching or exceeding the best independent model across all datasets with an order-of-magnitude gain in efficiency per correct instance. This dual advantage rests on three principles: 1) progressive filtering reduces later-stage complexity; 2) deterministic LOOCV eliminates partition bias; and 3) complexity-ranked sequencing aligns algorithms with pattern difficulty. Potential information leakage is prevented by applying LOOCV solely to the residual set, guaranteeing each instance is predicted by a model trained without it. Indirect dependence, inherent to any sequential algorithm, is mitigated by a fixed, dataset-independent ranking, ensuring active-set evolution reflects only empirical pattern difficulty against a predetermined order.

BREX's architecture also reduces runtime, for instance, times remained modest (0.26–36.67 min) even under high dimensionality and extreme imbalance. Simple algorithms handle most instances, limiting costly ensembles to a shrinking hard subset and yielding pattern-per-second rates an order of magnitude above the fastest standalone classifiers. This efficiency makes BREX well-suited for resource-constrained and standard computing environments.

5 Limitations and Future Work

Although empirical comparison with stacking, voting, or cascade classifiers remains pending, such comparison lies outside the current scope and does not diminish BREX's demonstrated superiority over all standalone classifiers across 18 datasets, establishing a strong baseline for future comparative work. Thus, for full reproducibility would require access to pipeline, including hyperparameter defaults and random seed settings. To address this limitation, the complete source code will be made available upon publication at an institutional repository (e.g., GitHub).

Acknowledgments. This work was supported by a scholarship from Mexico's Secretariat of Science, Humanities, Technology and Innovation (SECIHTI). The authors additionally acknowledge the Centro de Investigación en Computación of the Instituto Politécnico Nacional (CIC-IPN) for the institutional support throughout this research.

Declaration of Interest. The authors declare no conflict of interest.

References

1. Wolpert, D.H., Macready, W.G.: No free lunch theorems for optimization. IEEE Trans. Evol. Comput. **1**(1), 67–82 (1997). https://doi.org/10.1109/4235.585893
2. Chen, T, Guestrin, C: XGBoost: a scalable tree boosting system. Proceedings of the 22nd ACM SIGKDD International Conference on Knowledge Discovery and Data Mining (2016). https://doi.org/10.1145/2939672.2939785
3. Eberlein, J., et al.: The effect of data complexity on classifier performance. Empir. Softw. Eng. **30**, 16 (2025). https://doi.org/10.1007/s10664-024-10554-5
4. Ahmad, S., Khan, M.A., Al-Jumeily, D.: Dynamic weighted stacking for medical diagnostic systems under high-dimensional imbalance. Expert Syst. Appl. **207**, 117947 (2022). https://doi.org/10.1016/j.eswa.2022.117947
5. Al-Sai, Z., Abdullah, R., Husin, M.H.: Optimizing industrial process efficiency through ensemble learning: a comparative study of bagging and random forest approaches. J. Ind. Inf. Integr. **35**, 100542 (2023). https://doi.org/10.1016/j.jii.2023.100542
6. Zhou, L., Xu, B., Tang, W.: Sequential classification model for software defect prediction using hybrid feature spaces. Electronics **12**(15), 3354 (2023). https://doi.org/10.3390/electronics12153354
7. Sami, N.M., Naeini, M.: Machine learning applications in cascading failure analysis in power systems: a review. Electric Power Syst. Res. **232**, 110415 (2024). https://doi.org/10.1016/j.epsr.2024.110415
8. Sławiński, T., et al. Artificial Intelligence in the diagnosis of laryngeal cancer based on endoscopic images: a comprehensive narrative review. Int. J. Innov. Technol. Social Sci. (2025). https://doi.org/10.31435/ijitss.3(47).2025.3838
9. Gerardo, AS., et al. BREX: blend of ranked-sequential algorithms executed for boosting-based classification applied to wine dataset. In: Palma-Preciado, C., et al. (eds,) Advances in Computing, AI, and ICT for Innovation, Sustainability, and Environmental Stewardship. CORE 2025. Advances in Computer Science Applications and Research, 3. Springer, Cham (2026). https://doi.org/10.1007/978-3-032-08894-9_15
10. Acevedo-Sanchez, G., et al.: Effect of agriculture-related dataset complexity on classical machine learning and deep learning classifiers performance. Comput. Electron. Agric. **239** (2025). https://doi.org/10.1016/j.compag.2025.110941
11. Amin, F., Mahmoud, M.: Confusion matrix in binary classification problems: a step-by-step tutorial. J. Eng. Res. **6**(5), 1–12 (2022). https://digitalcommons.aaru.edu.jo/erjeng/vol6/iss5/1
12. Cheng, Z., Zhang, X.Y., Liu, C.L.: Unified classification and rejection: a one-versus-all framework. Mach. Intell. Res. **21**, 870–887 (2024). https://doi.org/10.1007/s11633-024-1514-4

13. RStudio Team: RStudio: Integrated Development Environment for R (2024.09.1+394). Posit Software (2024). https://posit.co/download/rstudio/

14. Guney, S., et al.: Abalone age prediction using machine learning. In: Djeddi, C., Siddiqi, I., Jamil, A., Ali Hameed, A., Kucuk, İ. (eds.) Pattern Recognition and Artificial Intelligence. MedPRAI 2021. Communications in Computer and Information Science, vol. 1543 (2022). Springer, Cham. https://doi.org/10.1007/978-3-031-04112-9_25

15. Tomal, S.Y.I., et al.: Quantum convolutional neural network: a hybrid quantum-classical approach for iris dataset classification. J. Future Artif. Intell. Technol. **1**(3), 284–295 (2024). https://doi.org/10.62411/faith.3048-3719-48

16. Jana, D.K., et al.: Analyzing of salient features and classification of wine type based on quality through various neural network and support vector machine classifiers. Res. Control Optim. **11**, 100219 (2023). https://doi.org/10.1016/j.rico.2023.100219

17. Shrestha, D.: Advanced machine learning techniques for predicting heart disease: a comparative analysis using the cleveland heart disease dataset. Appl. Med. Inf. **46**(3) (2024). Retrieved from https://ami.info.umfcluj.ro/index.php/AMI/article/view/1060

18. Shams, M.Y., et al.: A novel RFE-GRU model for diabetes classification using PIMA Indian dataset. Sci. Rep. **15**, 982 (2025). https://doi.org/10.1038/s41598-024-82420-9

19. Das, S., et al.: A differential evolution-based optimized ensemble for balanced and imbalanced medical datasets. F1000Research **14**, 1003 (2026). https://doi.org/10.12688/f1000research.169456.2

20. Abbad Ur Rehman, H., Lin, C.-Y., Mushtaq, Z., Su, S.-F.: Performance analysis of machine learning algorithms for thyroid disease. Arab. J. Sci. Eng. **46**(10), 9437–9449 (2021). https://doi.org/10.1007/s13369-020-05206-x

21. Solorio-Ramírez, J., et al.: Minimalist machine learning: binary classification of medical datasets with matrix transformations. J. Adv. Comput. Intell. Intell. Inf. **29**(2), 277–286 (2025). https://doi.org/10.20965/jaciii.2025.p0277

22. Citak, A.C., et al.: Classification of obesity levels using machine learning algorithms. In: Intelligent Methods in Engineering Sciences, vol. 4, no. 3, pp. 100–113 (2025). https://doi.org/10.58190/imiens.2025.157

23. Singh, L.K., Khanna, M., Singh, R.: An enhanced soft-computing based strategy for efficient feature selection for timely breast cancer prediction: Wisconsin Diagnostic Breast Cancer dataset case. Multimedia Tools Appl. **83**, 76607–76672 (2024). https://doi.org/10.1007/s11042-024-18473-9

24. Goran, R., et al.: Identifying and understanding student dropouts using metaheuristic optimized classifiers and explainable artificial intelligence techniques. IEEE Access **12**, 122377–122400 (2024). https://doi.org/10.1109/ACCESS.2024.3446653

25. Pallathadka, H., et al.: Classification and prediction of student performance data using various machine learning algorithms. Mater. Today: Proc. **80**, 3782–3785 (2021). https://doi.org/10.1016/j.matpr.2021.07.382

26. Ramya, V., RK, P.: Evaluation of vehicle quality performance using logistic regression in comparison with RBF SVM to measure the accuracy, recall and precision. In: Proceedings of the 2022 4th International Conference on Advances in Computing, Communication Control and Networking (ICAC3N), pp. 642–646. IEEE (2022). https://doi.org/10.1109/ICAC3N56670.2022.10074487

A Machine Learning Framework for High-Performance Electrolyte Classification in Lithium Metal Batteries

Sergio Rubén Ocampo-Pérez[1]($\boxtimes$) , Noureddine Lakouari[2,3] ,
and Outmane Oubram[4]

[1] Maestría en Optimización y Cómputo Aplicado, Facultad de Contaduría,
Administración e Informática (FCAeI), Universidad Autónoma del Estado de
Morelos, 62200 Cuernavaca, Morelos, Mexico
sergio.ocampo@fcaei.uaem.edu.mx
[2] Secretaría de Ciencia, Humanidades, Tecnología e Innovación (SECIHTI),
Insurgentes Sur 1582, 03940 Ciudad de México, Mexico
[3] Instituto Nacional de Astrofísica, Óptica y Electrónica (INAOE), 72840 Puebla,
Mexico
n.lakouari@inaoep.mx
[4] Facultad de Ciencias Químicas e Ingeniería, Universidad Autónoma del Estado de
Morelos (UAEM), 62210 Cuernavaca, Morelos, Mexico
oubram@uaem.mx

Abstract. The development of high-performance electrolytes for lithium
metal batteries remains a key challenge for enabling next-generation
energy storage technologies. In this study, we present a machine learning based framework designed to classify electrolytes according to their
Coulombic Efficiency (CE), using a critical threshold of $CE \geq 99\%$ to
distinguish high-performance systems. A consolidated dataset of 283 electrolytes for LMBs was constructed by integrating two specialized sources
(initially comprising 292 samples). During data curation, 9 records were
identified as outliers and removed due to Coulombic Efficiency values
below 80%, ensuring the exclusion of unrepresentative operational data.
Feature engineering included second-degree polynomial expansion and
Lasso-based regularization, reducing the feature space from 104 to 20 key
predictive variables. Four classification algorithms (XGBoost, Random
Forest, K-NN, and Logistic Regression) were optimized using Bayesian
optimization through the Optuna framework. XGBoost demonstrated the
highest robustness, achieving a test AUC of 0.9537 and a recall of 94%
for high-performance electrolyte detection. SHAP interpretability analysis revealed that oxygen-rich interactions act as performance inhibitors,
while dual fluorination in both solvent and anion promotes cycling stability. These findings validate the proposed framework as an effective virtual screening tool to accelerate electrolyte discovery and rational design
in lithium metal battery research.

Keywords: Lithium metal batteries · Coulombic efficiency · Machine
learning · XGBoost · SHAP interpretability · Electrolyte design

V. G. Cruz-Sánchez et al. (Eds.): MCPR 2026, LNCS 16623, pp. 103–113, 2026.
https://doi.org/10.1007/978-3-032-28393-1_10

1   Introduction

Coulombic efficiency (CE) is a critical indicator of electrochemical reversibility in batteries, defined as the ratio between the discharge capacity and the charge capacity in a given cycle:

$$CE = \frac{Q_{discharge}}{Q_{charge}} \tag{1}$$

CE values close to 100% are imperative to mitigate the formation of irreversible lithium and electrolyte degradation, factors that severely limit cycle life in lithium metal systems. However, modeling CE represents a complex challenge due to its multivariable nature and the lack of standardized databases [1]. To address this challenge, Machine Learning (ML) has emerged as a transformative tool to predict electrochemical performance without resorting to costly experimental testing.

Recently, researchers have created new methods that use linear regression and interpretability tools to pinpoint important chemical characteristics—like solvents with low oxygen content. By modeling the logarithm of Coulombic efficiency, these methods can make highly accurate predictions, with an average error (MSE) of just 0.343. This makes it possible to discover the most important factors influencing how well materials can be cycled [2].Similarly, by combining Bayesian Optimization with Pareto frontier analysis, researchers have been able to maximize both Coulombic efficiency and ionic conductivity at the same time. Using these computational methods, they identified promising localized high-concentration electrolytes (LHCEs), which were then confirmed through experiments to achieve impressive average efficiencies of 99.4%. This is important because the machine learning system acts as a virtual screening tool, helping scientists find the most promising electrolyte formulas before actually making them in the lab. [3].

Beyond traditional transport metrics, current research suggests that variations in CE for high-performance electrolytes are primarily governed by galvanic corrosion phenomena [4]. These findings validate the use of molecular descriptors and classification models to segment electrolyte performance, enabling the identification of the underlying physical factors that determine high stability.

2   Methodology

2.1   Dataset

The dataset used in this study is the result of the integration of two primary sources specialized in electrolytes for lithium metal batteries, aiming to construct a robust database that correlates chemical composition with Coulombic Efficiency. To address potential inconsistencies between these distinct sources, a systematic harmonization protocol was implemented.

The first source corresponds to the dataset curated by [2], composed of 150 electrolyte records that include conventional, high-concentration, fluorinated, and additive-containing formulations. This subset, experiments were

Table 1. Descriptor variables used for electrolyte modeling.

Abbreviation	Description
O% / C% / F%	Molar fraction of Oxygen, Carbon, and Fluorine
sO / sC / sF	Molar fraction of O, C, and F in solvents
aO / aC / aF	Molar fraction of O, C, and F in anions
F/O, F/C, O/C	Elemental ratios
InOr	Inorganic/Organic ratio

only included if they used a current density between 0.4–1.0 mA cm^{-2} and an areal capacity from 0.5–1.0 mAh cm^{-2}. By limiting these testing conditions, the researchers were able to minimize differences that might come from anything other than the chemical makeup of the electrolytes

The second source was obtained from [1], from which 142 records were extracted. To ensure consistency, we strictly followed the feature engineering framework established by [2]. For the entries in [1], which were originally reported in Simplified Molecular Input Line Entry System (SMILES) notation, 13 key descriptor variables were calculated using a volumetric-atomic method. This meant figuring out the molar fraction of each element by dividing the number of atoms of each element by the total number of atoms in one liter of solution, assuming weighted average densities for solvent mixtures.

These 13 descriptor variables, detailed in Table 1, focus on elemental composition and the molar relationships between the solvent and the anion, which are critical factors influencing the solvation structure and the formation of the Solid Electrolyte Interphase (SEI). The Inorganic-Organic ratio ($InOr$) was standardized across both datasets; organic content was defined exclusively as carbon, while inorganic content encompassed all elements except hydrogen, lithium, and carbon. Furthermore, although both sources provided performance metrics in both linear percentage and logarithmic transformation, the linear percentage was selected to maintain a uniform scale. This consistency allowed for the application of a single classification threshold across the final consolidated dataset of 283 records.

To ensure the integrity of the dataset, an outlier detection filter was applied. Records with $CE < 80\%$ were removed, as they were located more than three standard deviations away from the mean of the global dataset, being classified as measurement noise or digitization errors. A total of 9 records were excluded through this process, resulting in a final consolidated dataset of 283 records.

2.2 Class Definition

For binary classification, shown in Fig. 1, electrolytes with $CE \geq 99\%$ were defined as Class 1 (high performance). The definition of the high-performance threshold strictly aligns with the electrochemical reversibility requirements for real-world applications. As stated by Attias et al. [5], for a rechargeable metal

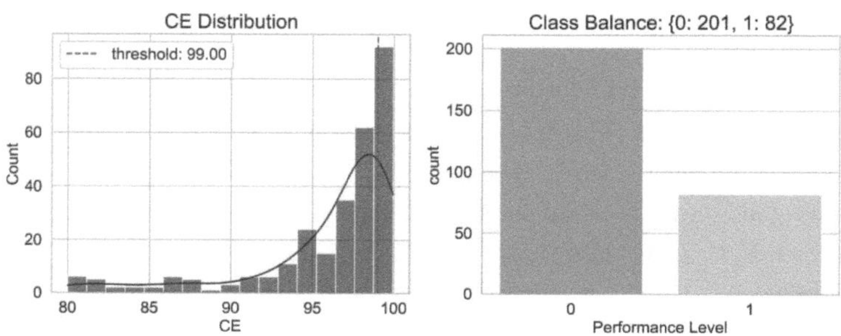

Fig. 1. Distribution of the CE variable and the resulting class balance.

battery to be viable in practical applications and withstand hundreds of stable charge–discharge cycles, its coulombic efficiency must exceed 99%. [6] indicate that in practical applications, the protected lithium metal anode must operate at high current densities, where uncontrolled lithium growth and significant volume changes may occur. To preserve high energy density and ensure long cycle life, it is essential that the coulombic efficiency of protected lithium remains above 99%.

For experimental applications, [7] highlight that a coulombic efficiency of 99% constitutes a high value, achieved and sustained over 230 cycles, evidencing strong electrochemical reversibility. Establishing a threshold of $CE \geq 99\%$ guides research toward practical scenarios while simultaneously laying the groundwork for achieving more stringent future targets, such as those proposed by [8], who indicate that electric vehicle applications will require efficiencies exceeding 99.9%–99.95%.

In contrast, those with $CE < 99\%$ were assigned to Class 0 (low performance), as they imply a significant cumulative loss of active lithium per cycle, incompatible with real-world standards.

To ensure model robustness and prevent biases derived from class imbalance, the dataset was divided into training (80%) and testing (20%) subsets using a stratified sampling strategy, as shown in Fig. 2.

This technique ensures that the original proportion of high- and low-performance electrolytes is preserved in both the training and evaluation sets, allowing the model to learn representative features from both categories without neglecting the minority class.

2.3   Feature Engineering

Since processes such as solvation and SEI formation exhibit nonlinear behavior, exclusive use of the 13 original descriptor variables could limit the predictive capacity of the model. To address this limitation, a two-stage strategy was implemented: polynomial expansion and regularized selection.

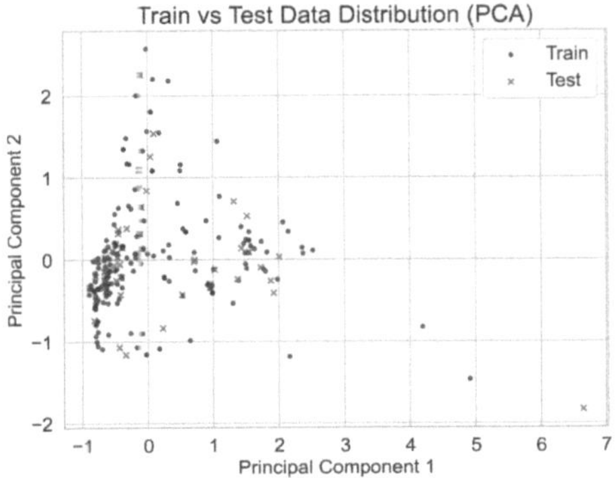

Fig. 2. Stratified sampling using PCA.

Table 2. Variables resulting from the Lasso selection process.

Type of Variable	Selected Variables	Interpretation
Interactions $(x_i \cdot x_j)$	$sO \cdot C$, $F/O \cdot sC$, $aO \cdot aC$, $aF \cdot C$, $F/O \cdot aO$, $F/O \cdot C$, $sF \cdot aF$, $F/C \cdot O/C$, $F/C \cdot InOr$, $F/C \cdot sF$, $F/C \cdot aF$	Synergistic effects between components
Quadratic (x_i^2)	$(O/C)^2$, $(F/C)^2$	Nonlinear saturation effects
Linear (x_i)	C, O, aO, sO, aC, sC, aF	Direct effects of elemental composition.

Generation of Nonlinear Interactions. A second-degree polynomial transformation was applied to the original feature space, incorporating interaction
terms $(x_i x_j)$ and quadratic terms (x_i^2). This allows the modeling of combined
effects between variables and individual nonlinear relationships, including potential optimal behaviors. As a result, the dimensionality increased from 13 to 104
candidate features.

Variable Selection Through Lasso Regularization. The increase in dimensionality raises the risk of overfitting, particularly due to the limited size of the
dataset. To control this effect and select only the most relevant descriptors, a
Lasso-based feature selection was implemented using a Logistic Regression model
with an $L1$ penalty. To ensure uniform penalization, the features were standardized using the StandardScaler algorithm. To prevent data leakage, the scaler
was fitted exclusively on the training data, and the resulting parameters were
subsequently applied to the test set. The regularization strength was controlled
by an inverse parameter $C = 0.5$ using the liblinear solver. This process forced
the coefficients associated with irrelevant variables to zero. As a result, the input
space was reduced from 104 to 20 predictive variables, eliminating approximately
80% of the generated features. The 20 selected variables, which constitute the
final input vector, are those listed in Table 2.

2.4 Models and Training

To address the prediction of electrolyte performance, four complementary algorithms were selected to evaluate the classification problem. XGBoost, based on Gradient Boosting, was included for its high predictive capability and efficient handling of class imbalance through weighting. Random Forest, a parallel ensemble method, was used for its robustness against overfitting and its ability to model nonlinear relationships. K-Nearest Neighbors was included to assess whether the polynomial feature space induces sufficient class separability, as its instance-based classification relies on local proximity rather than learned decision boundaries. Finally, Logistic Regression was employed as a linear baseline model to determine whether the problem can be solved with a simple decision boundary or requires greater nonlinear complexity.

Hyperparameter Optimization and Cross-Validation. Since the performance of these algorithms critically depends on their configuration (hyperparameters), an automated search strategy was implemented using the Optuna framework [9], which employs a Tree-structured Parzen Estimator (TPE) [10] to perform Bayesian optimization. This approach efficiently explores the hyperparameter space by focusing on promising regions. The final optimized parameters for the primary model (XGBoost) are summarized in Table 3. To address the inherent class imbalance (201 samples in Class 0 vs. 82 in Class 1), a cost-sensitive learning approach was implemented. Specifically, for the XGBoost model, the *scale_pos_weight* parameter was set to 2.45, as shown in Table 3. This value represents the ratio between the majority and minority classes, ensuring the model prioritizes the detection of high-performance electrolytes. The training process was conducted under a 10-Fold Stratified Cross-Validation scheme ($k = 10$). The objective function for optimization primarily focused on maximizing the Area Under the ROC Curve (AUC-ROC), due to its ability to evaluate classifier quality independently of the decision threshold. Additionally, the F1-Score was incorporated as a secondary control metric. By representing the harmonic mean between Precision and Recall, the F1-Score ensures that the selected models maintain a practical balance in predicting the minority class, penalizing those that excessively favor the majority class.

3 Results

To evaluate the robustness of the models, the metrics Area Under the ROC Curve (AUC), Accuracy, and F1-Score were compared for both the training and testing sets.

3.1 Global Performance Comparison of the Models

The predictive performance of the implemented architectures is summarized in Table 4. Ensemble-based models, specifically XGBoost and Random Forest,

Table 3. Final optimized hyperparameters for the XGBoost model via Optuna.

Hyperparameter	Value	Description
n_estimators	1276	Number of boosting rounds
max_depth	3	Maximum tree depth for complexity control
learning_rate	0.0116	Step size shrinkage to prevent overfitting
subsample	0.9357	Fraction of samples used per tree
colsample_bytree	0.5591	Fraction of features used per tree
gamma	4.7139	Minimum loss reduction for a split
scale_pos_weight	2.45	Weighting factor to address class imbalance (201/82)

Table 4. Comparison of global metrics (Training vs. Test).

Model	AUC (Train)	AUC (Test)	Accuracy (Test)	F1-Score (Test)
XGBoost	0.9411	**0.9537**	**0.9123**	**0.8649**
Random Forest	0.9486	0.9346	0.8596	0.7895
KNN	0.8652	0.8993	0.8421	0.7273
Logistic Regression	0.8937	0.8978	0.8246	0.7368

exhibited a clear superiority in classifying electrolyte performance compared to the baseline models (k-NN and Logistic Regression). Among these, XGBoost achieved the highest overall metrics, reaching a test AUC of 0.9537 and an F1-Score of 0.8649 (Fig. 3).

The high consistency between the training AUC 0.9411 and the test AUC 0.9537 indicates a robust generalization capability. This suggests that the model effectively captured the underlying patterns of the dataset without overfitting, despite the high dimensionality introduced by the second-degree polynomial expansion. The significant performance gap between the ensemble methods and the linear baseline (Logistic Regression, AUC 0.8978) confirms that the mapping between electrolyte chemical composition and Coulombic Efficiency is governed by nonlinear, synergistic relationships. Such complexity justifies the use of gradient boosting algorithms to model the chemical interactions within the electrolyte-anode interface.

3.2   High-Performance Electrolyte Detection Capability

While global metrics provide a comprehensive overview of model quality, the efficacy of the proposed framework for virtual screening depends specifically on its performance regarding the minority class ($CE \geq 99\%$). In materials discovery, the priority is often shifted from overall accuracy toward the minimization of False Negatives (Type II errors). Missing a high-performance candidate represents a significant cost in terms of lost innovation, whereas a False Positive merely results in a standard laboratory validation of a suboptimal formulation.

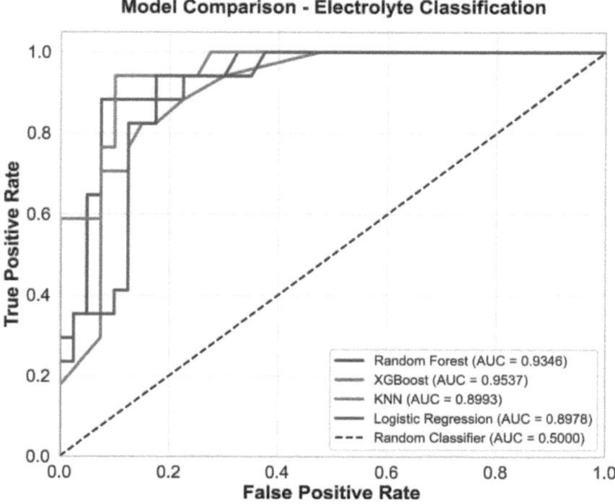

Fig. 3. Comparison of electrolyte classification models.

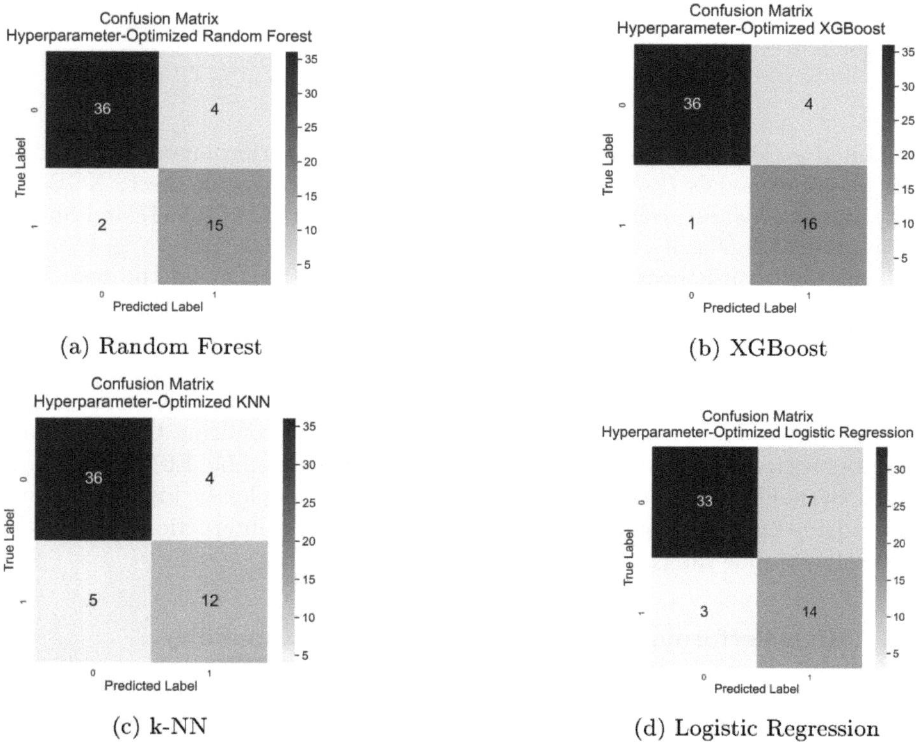

(a) Random Forest

(b) XGBoost

(c) k-NN

(d) Logistic Regression

Fig. 4. Confusion matrices for the hyperparameter-optimized models.

Table 5. Performance in Class 1 classification ($CE \geq 99\%$).

Model	Precision	Recall	F1-Score (Class 1)
XGBoost	**0.80**	**0.94**	**0.86**
Random Forest	0.71	0.88	0.79
KNN	0.75	0.71	0.73
Logistic Regression	0.67	0.82	0.74

Table 5 details the specific performance for the positive class.

Consequently, Sensitivity (Recall) for Class 1 is the primary performance indicator for this study. As detailed in Table 5, the XGBoost model correctly identified 94% of the high-performance electrolytes in the test set ($Recall = 0.94$).

This high sensitivity is achieved alongside a Precision of 0.80, indicating a favorable trade-off for experimental workflows. In a practical pipeline, this model ensures that the vast majority of promising electrolytes are captured while maintaining an 80% success rate in the candidates proposed for synthesis, thereby drastically reducing the search space and resource allocation in experimental design. The confusion matrices shown in Fig. 4 further illustrate this behavior, where XGBoost displays the lowest rate of misclassified high-performance samples compared to the other architectures.

3.3 Physicochemical Interpretation of the Model (SHAP)

To evaluate the model's consistency with electrochemical principles, we employed the SHAP (SHapley Additive exPlanations) framework, a game-theoretic approach introduced by [11], to interpret the XGBoost predictions. The results underscore that the most influential variables are polynomial interactions, confirming that electrolyte design is inherently nonlinear and synergistic. Specifically, the interaction ($sO \cdot C$) emerged as the primary performance inhibitor according to the model, where high values markedly decreased the predicted probability of achieving a high CE. This observation aligns with the known reactivity of oxygen-rich solvents, which tend to facilitate the formation of unstable SEI layers in systems with high organic content. Furthermore, the global oxygen fraction (O) exhibited a consistent negative effect when elevated, reinforcing the preference for oxygen-poor formulations to achieve superior cycling stability. Conversely, the interaction ($sF \cdot aF$) acts as a promoter, suggesting that simultaneous fluorination of both the solvent and the anion facilitates the formation of a LiF-rich SEI, which is typically more stable and ionically conductive. Additional synergistic effects were observed in interactions such as ($FO \cdot aO$), which indicate stability in fluorinated environments containing modern oxygenated anions. However, the ($aF \cdot C$) interaction exhibited limiting behavior, in which extreme combinations of these features led to performance degradation. These findings demonstrate that the XGBoost model not only achieves high predictive accuracy

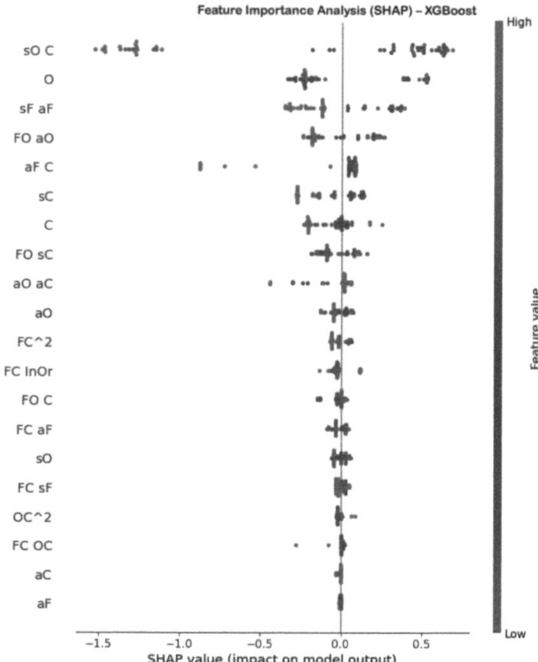

Fig. 5. XGBoost SHAP values.

but also captures the complex interfacial dynamics required for the discovery of high-performance electrolytes. However, one should note that SHAP values reflect learned model association instead of confirmed mechanism, and experimental validation would be required to establish definitive structure performance relationships (Fig. 5).

4   Conclusions

This research establishes a robust machine learning framework for the accelerated discovery of high-performance electrolytes for lithium metal batteries. By integrating specialized datasets and implementing a second-degree polynomial expansion, the model effectively captured the nonlinear synergies governing SEI stability. The results demonstrate that the XGBoost architecture, optimized via Bayesian search, provides superior predictive performance, achieving a Test AUC of 0.9537 and identifying 94% of high-performance candidates ($CE \geq 99\%$). This high sensitivity, coupled with a precision of 0.80, validates the model as an effective virtual screening tool capable of significantly reducing the experimental search space and resource allocation in material synthesis. Furthermore, the interpretability analysis using SHAP values provided critical mechanistic insights that align with electrochemical theory, specifically highlighting the inhibitory role of oxygen-rich interactions and the promoting effect of dual fluorination in both solvents and anions. The transition from 13 original descriptors to 20 regularized predictive variables, of which 11 are interaction terms, and 2 are quadratic, suggests that synergistic effects between components play a more significant role than isolated elemental properties in determining electrolyte performance. However, the specific subset of selected features is dependent on the regulation strength ($C = 0.5$), and an alternative configuration may yield partially different feature sets while preserving the overall dominance of interaction terms. Ultimately, this data-driven approach not only achieves high accuracy in performance classification but also offers a scalable methodology to guide the rational design of next-generation energy storage systems, bridging the gap between computational screening and experimental validation.

Acknowledgments. S.R.O.-P. acknowledges support from SECIHTI (Mexico) through a graduate studies fellowship.

Disclosure of Interests. The authors have no competing interests to declare that are relevant to the content of this article.

References

1. Kumar, R., Vu, M.C., Ma, P., Amanchukwu, C.V.: Electrolytomics: a unified big data approach for electrolyte design and discovery. Chem. Mater. **37**(8), 2720–2734 (2025)
2. Kim, S.C., et al.: Data-driven electrolyte design for lithium metal anodes. Proc. Natl. Acad. Sci. U.S.A. **120**(10), e2214357120 (2023)
3. Zhang, J., Sarker, D., Matthew Beltran, Yu., Xiang, C.T., Laisuo, S.: Dual-objective optimization of lithium metal battery electrolytes via machine learning. Mater. Today Energy **51**, 101909 (2025)
4. Oyakhire, S.T., Kim, S.C., Zhang, W., Shuchi, S.B., Cui, Y., Bent, S.F.: Galvanic corrosion underlies coulombic efficiency differences. Energy Environ. Sci. **18**, 4347 (2025)
5. Attias, R., et al.: Determination of average coulombic efficiency for rechargeable magnesium metal anodes. ACS Appl. Mater. Interfaces **14**(27), 30952–30961 (2022)
6. Rui, X., et al.: Artificial interphases for highly stable lithium metal anode. Matter **1**(2), 317–344 (2019)
7. Yang, J., et al.: Multi-dimensional hybrid flexible films promote uniform lithium deposition. J. Energy Chem. **65**, 583–591 (2022)
8. Hobold, G.M., et al.: Moving beyond 99.9% coulombic efficiency for lithium anodes in liquid electrolytes. Nat. Energy **6**(10), 951–960 (2021)
9. Akiba, T., Sano, S., Yanase, T., Ohta, T., Koyama, M.: Optuna: a next-generation hyperparameter optimization framework. In: Proceedings of the 25th ACM SIGKDD International Conference on Knowledge Discovery and Data Mining, pp. 2623–2631, 2019
10. Bergstra, J., Rémi, B., Bengio, Y., Kégl, B.: Algorithms for hyper-parameter optimization. Adv. Neural Inf. Process. Syst. **24** (2011)
11. Lundberg, S.M., Lee, S.-I.: A unified approach to interpreting model predictions. arXiv:1705.07874, 2017

Deep Learning and Neural Networks

Banking Fraud Detection Using Neural Network Models

Ostin Uriel Martínez Campos[ID], Andrés Ferreyra-Ramírez[ID],
Eduardo Rodríguez-Martínez[(✉)][ID], and Carlos Avilés-Cruz[ID]

Universidad Autónoma Metropolitana, Av. San Pablo No. 420 Col. Nueva e. Rosario,
Ciudad de México, Mexico
{al2173037924,fra,erm,caviles}@azc.uam.mx

Abstract. Detecting banking fraud remains a persistent and complex challenge in digital financial systems, primarily due to rising transaction volumes and the ongoing evolution of fraudulent techniques. The central thesis of this article is that an empirically validated neural network–based system that leverages both supervised and unsupervised learning can significantly enhance banking fraud detection by analyzing real transaction data. By comparatively evaluating multiple neural architectures, including multilayer perceptrons, recurrent networks, and autoencoders, this study seeks to offer practical guidance on model selection aligned with specific operational requirements.

Keywords: Banking fraud detection · Neural networks · Imbalanced datasets · Anomaly detection · Siamese neural networks · Recall · F1-score

1 Introduction

The sustained growth of digital financial services has markedly increased banks' exposure to fraud, as demonstrated in [5,13]. Modern financial systems process millions of electronic transactions, making manual detection of suspicious activities impractical. As a result, institutions must develop automated mechanisms capable of analyzing large data volumes with reduced response times [3,5]. Effective banking fraud detection is therefore essential for maintaining financial security and trust in electronic payment systems [5].

Historically, banks have addressed fraud detection using systems based on heuristic rules and traditional statistical models [5,13]. Although these approaches provide interpretability and have been used in production environments for extended periods, they are limited in their ability to address dynamic, highly nonlinear, and evolving fraudulent patterns [2,16].The necessity to adapt detection systems to changing behaviors has prompted the adoption of machine learning techniques that learn directly from historical transaction data.

Neural networks have emerged as a robust alternative for detecting banking fraud because they can model complex relationships and capture subtle patterns

V. G. Cruz-Sánchez et al. (Eds.): MCPR 2026, LNCS 16623, pp. 117–129, 2026.
https://doi.org/10.1007/978-3-032-28393-1_11

that conventional methods often miss [8,11]. Multiple studies have shown that architectures such as multilayer neural networks, recurrent models, and autoencoders can substantially improve performance, especially in scenarios characterized by a pronounced imbalance between legitimate and fraudulent transactions [7].

Despite advances reported in the literature, significant challenges persist in selecting suitable architectures, ensuring training stability, managing computational costs, and generalizing models to unseen data [5,10]. Furthermore, much of the existing research evaluates only a single family of models, which complicates objective comparisons under consistent experimental conditions and limits the applicability of results to practical contexts [5].

This study demonstrates measurable improvements in fraud detection. It details the design, implementation, and empirical evaluation of a neural network-based system deployed on two authentic financial transaction datasets. The results indicate that neural networks can address diverse operational requirements for fraud detection.

This work directly compares families of neural architectures, including multilayer networks, recurrent models, autoencoders, and Siamese networks. All architectures are evaluated using a standardized protocol [8] to assess performance, accuracy, training stability, and computational cost. This approach provides clear criteria for selecting models in bank fraud detection systems.

The principal contributions of this study are as follows:

1. The design of a modular architecture for bank fraud detection that integrates and evaluates different families of neural networks within a uniform experimental framework.
2. A comparative evaluation of supervised and unsupervised models, including autoencoders and Siamese architectures, utilizing real transactional data.
3. An analysis of the trade-off between predictive accuracy and computational complexity, providing decision-makers with actionable criteria for selecting optimal architectures and improving fraud detection outcomes in practical settings.
4. Empirical validation of anomaly-detection-based approaches as effective alternatives for banking fraud detection in financial environments.

The remainder of this article is organized as follows. Section 2 reviews the state of the art in computational methods for bank fraud detection, with an emphasis on machine learning and neural networks. Section 3 describes the proposed system's general architecture, modular structure, and processing flow. Section 4 outlines the experimental methodology, including dataset descriptions, processing stages, neural architectures, and the validation protocol. Section 5 presents experimental results and comparative analysis. Section 6 discusses the key findings and their practical implications. Section 7 concludes and suggests directions for future research.

2 State of the Art

Numerous studies have addressed the problem of detecting bank fraud using computational methods, resulting in a wide variety of solutions [3]. Early research in this field relied on rule-based systems and statistical models, such as logistic regression and Bayesian methods, which provide high interpretability [5,13]. However, these techniques are limited in handling the complex nonlinear relationships and dynamic patterns characteristic of real transactional data.

The adoption of machine learning techniques introduced more flexible models, including decision trees, support vector machines, and ensemble methods such as *Random Forest* and *Gradient Boosting* [2,11,16]. Multiple studies have shown that these approaches outperform traditional statistical methods in terms of accuracy. However, their performance is often affected by class imbalance and the challenge of capturing temporal dependencies inherent in financial behavior [1,11].

In recent years, deep neural networks have emerged as highly promising alternatives for detecting banking fraud [4]. Architectures based on multilayer neural networks and recurrent models, such as *Long Short-Term Memory* (LSTM) and *Gated Recurrent Units* (GRU), have demonstrated superior ability to learn complex representations and temporal dependencies from transaction sequences [8,10,14]. Additionally, approaches based on *autoencoders* and unsupervised learning have been explored for anomaly detection, particularly in scenarios with limited labeled data [6,7,12].

Recent research highlights the importance of using evaluation metrics beyond overall accuracy, such as *recall*, *F1-score*, and the area under the *ROC* curve. It also emphasizes the need for strategies to address class imbalance and reduce model overfitting [9,11,16]. Despite these advances, significant challenges persist regarding model stability in the presence of concept drift and the need for solutions that balance predictive performance and computational complexity [5].

In this context, our work contributes to the ongoing research on neural network-based fraud detection by designing and implementing a system architecture oriented toward transactional analysis. Unlike studies that focus exclusively on evaluating a single model, we propose a modular architecture that enables integrating different families of neural networks and evaluating their performance within a common processing flow. Furthermore, empirical validation is prioritized using real transactional data, with systematic analysis of model behavior in controlled scenarios to assess generalization capacity and practical viability for financial applications.

3 Proposed System Architecture

The proposed system employs a modular architecture to automate the analysis of banking transactions. The primary objective is to estimate the risk level associated with each transaction. The processing workflow consists of three stages: preprocessing transactional data, classifying transactions using neural network-based models, and generating a final fraud determination.

Input variables for the system encompass transaction characteristics such as amounts, frequencies, temporal patterns, and user behavior attributes. These variables facilitate modeling of individual customer transactions and form the basis for inference. The neural model is trained to differentiate between legitimate and fraudulent transactions, capturing complex nonlinear relationships that are often overlooked by traditional methods.

The system design prioritizes structural simplicity and computational efficiency to facilitate implementation, reproducibility, and experimental evaluation. This approach is especially critical in contexts where large volumes of transactions must be analyzed under limited computational resources.

Figure 1 provides an overview of the proposed system's functional architecture. The process includes the following stages: (i) intake of transactional data, (ii) preprocessing, which involves cleaning, normalization, and transformation, (iii) inference, where the neural model analyzes data patterns to classify each transaction, and (iv) final fraud or non-fraud decision-making. In siamese architectures, the decision relies on comparing similarities and applying an optimal threshold.

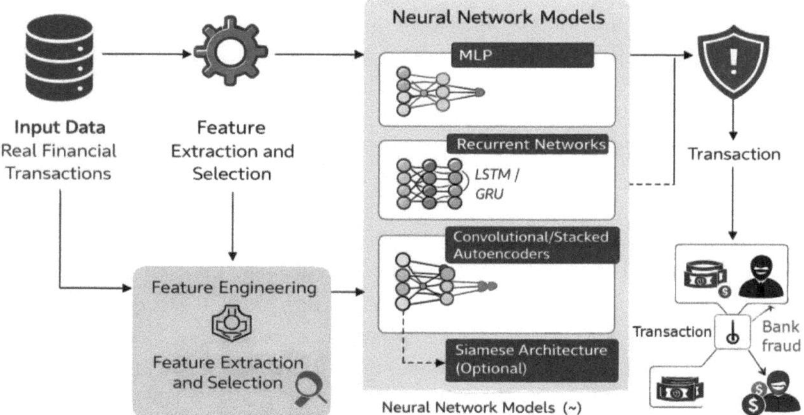

Fig. 1. The general architecture of the neural network-based bank fraud system integrates processing stages, feature engineering, and supervised and unsupervised neural models to produce the final decision.

4   Methodology

The proposed methodology systematically evaluates various neural network architectures for bank fraud detection. The experimental process is designed to be reproducible and controlled, aligning with the study's objectives. The approach involves preparing real transactional data, designing diverse neural models, and comparing their performance using robust evaluation metrics.

4.1   Data Sets and Ethical Considerations

To experimentally validate the proposed system, two sets of real transactional data were utilized. These datasets represent scenarios with varying information volumes and operational complexities. Each record corresponds to a single financial transaction, labeled as either legitimate or fraudulent, resulting in a binary classification problem with significant class imbalance.

The first dataset comprises 802 transactions from a single bank account, including 126 fraudulent and 676 legitimate transactions. This dataset facilitates analysis of system performance in a controlled, limited-data scenario with a relatively homogeneous transactional pattern.

The second dataset contains 2,941 transactions from multiple bank accounts, with 1,208 fraudulent and 1,733 legitimate transactions. This dataset exhibits greater diversity in transactional behavior patterns and enables evaluation of the generalization capacity of neural architectures in conditions similar to a real operating environment.

Both datasets include transactional and behavioral variables related to financial operations and user history. Additionally, a public Kaggle database was used as a structural reference, with its attributes adjusted to enhance data representativeness and facilitate comparisons with previous studies.

Due to confidentiality restrictions, all sensitive information was anonymized. The research was conducted in accordance with ethical principles to ensure that neither customers or financial institutions could be identified.

4.2   Data Preprocessing and Preparation

Data preprocessing is a critical step in ensuring the quality of neural model training. First, the datasets were cleaned to eliminate inconsistent records and outliers that could affect the learning process. Then, normalization and scaling techniques were applied using schemes such as *MinMaxScaler* and *Standard-Scaler* according to each architecture's specific requirements.

The *MinMaxScaler* scheme performs a linear transformation of numerical variables to rescale them within the interval $[0, 1]$. Rescaling is performed dimension-wise by subtracting the maximum value and divided by the range. This type of normalization is suitable for architectures sensitive to the absolute magnitude of inputs, such as multilayer perceptrons and other deep neural networks.

Conversely, the *StandardScaler* scheme standardizes the variables so that they have zero mean and standard deviation equal to one. This approach favors more stable training of models that assume centered distributions, such as recurrent neural networks.

For recurrent architectures and the Siamese neural network, the data were transformed into three-dimensional representations to allow modeling of temporal dependencies and sequential relationships between consecutive transactions. In this context, each input example is constructed from an ordered sequence of consecutive transactions associated with the same bank account. Given a set of T consecutive transactions, each represented by an 8-dimensional feature vector $d = 8$, the input to the model is a 2-dimensional representation corresponding to the sequence $\mathbf{X} \in \mathbb{R}^{(T,d)}$.

For example, a sequence of five consecutive transactions ($T{=}5$) is represented as a 5×8 matrix, where each row corresponds to a transaction and each column corresponds to an attribute described in Table 1. When considering multiple sequences during training, the data is ultimately organized as a tensor of dimension $\mathbb{R}^{(N,T,d)}$, where N denotes the total number of sequences used. For *Database 1*, $N = 798$ sequences were used; for *Database 2*, $N = 2,927$ sequences were used. In both cases, the sequence length was fixed at $T = 5$ transactions per sample, and the dimensionality was fixed at $d = 8$, corresponding to the number of features per transaction. Thus, the input tensor X belongs to the spaces $X \in \mathbb{R}^{(798,5,8)}$ and $X \in \mathbb{R}^{(2927,5,8)}$ for *Database 1* and *2*, respectively. This representation enables recurrent and Siamese architectures to capture temporal dependencies and sequential patterns in users' transactional behavior.

For experimental evaluation, each dataset was divided into 80% training records and 20% testing records to ensure that model performance was measured on data not seen during learning.

Additionally, each financial transaction was represented by a fixed set of attributes describing temporal, financial, and operational information about the account. Each example is defined by a total of eight input attributes, and an additional attribute corresponds to the classification label. Table 1 presents the order, type, and description of the considered attributes, explicitly identifying the dimensionality of each transaction used in the experiments.

4.3   Architecture, Design, and Training Strategy

The methodology involved implementing and evaluating multiple families of neural models within a common system architecture. We considered multilayer neural networks (MLP), recurrent networks (LSTMs, GRUs, and dense variants), autoencoders (convolutional and stacked), and Siamese neural networks (both recurrent and autoencoder-based).

Each model was configured with specific hyperparameters, including the number of layers and neurons, activation functions, batch size, number of epochs, and optimization algorithms. The detailed configuration of these hyperparameters is presented in Table 2. These hyperparameter values were determined through an empirical adjustment process that considered configurations commonly reported in the literature and selected those that offered an adequate compromise between training stability and performance in the validation set. We used optimizers such as *Adam*, *RMSprop*, and *Adagrad*, as well as L1 and L2 regularization techniques

Table 1. Features considered for the representation of each financial transaction.

ID	Attribute	Type	Description
1	Account No	Categorical	Identifier of the bank account associated with the transaction
2	Date	Temporal	Date on which the transaction was made
3	Transaction Details	Categorical	Type or description of the operation performed
4	Chq.No.	Categorical	Check number associated with the transaction, when applicable
5	Value Date	Temporal	Effective date of the transaction value
6	Withdrawal Amt	Numeric	Amount withdrawn from the account in the transaction
7	Deposit Amt	Numeric	Amount deposited into the account in the transaction
8	Balance Amt	Numeric	Balance of the account after the transaction

and early stopping mechanisms to mitigate overfitting and improve generalization capacity.

For autoencoders and Siamese architectures, optimal thresholds were determined using cross-validation and performance metrics to allow for more accurate classification of anomalous transactions in unbalanced contexts.

Table 2. The architectural configuration and hyperparameters of neural network models.

Network type	Architecture/ layers	Number of neurons	Activation function	Loss function	Optimizer	Batch size	Regularization
MLP (Multilayer)	2 hidden layers + output	64, 32	ReLU (hidden), Sigmoid (output)	Binary cross entropy	Adam RMSprop Adagrad	32	No
MLP + Regularization	2 hidden layers + output	64, 64	ReLU (hidden), Sigmoid (output)	Binary cross entropy	Adam RMSprop Adagrad	32	L1 y L2
RNN LSTM	1 LSTM layer + output	64	tanh/ Sigmoid	Binary cross entropy	Adam	32	No
RNN GRU	1 GRU layer + output	64	tanh/ Sigmoid	Binary cross entropy	Adam	64	No
Convolutional Autoencoder	Convolutional + MaxPooling+ UpSampling	195	ReLU	MSE	Adam	128	No
Stacked Autoencoder	Dense symmetric layers	224	ReLU	MSE	Adam	32	No
Recurrent siamese network	LSTM + Dropout + Dense layer	1153	tanh/ Sigmoid	Contrastive loss	Adam	128	Dropout

The architectures were trained on normalized and scaled data according to the procedure described in Sect. 4.2 to promote stability and convergence of the learning process.

4.4 Experimental Protocol and Performance Evaluation

The experimental protocol involved running multiple experiments for each architecture and evaluating how the models behaved with different numbers of epochs (10, 25, 50, 75, and 100). There were at least five runs for each configuration. This approach enabled us to analyze training stability and model sensitivity to weight initialization and the variability inherent to the learning process.

We evaluated model performance using metrics appropriate for imbalanced classification problems, including accuracy, loss, *Recall*, *F1-score*, and *AUC-ROC*. Additionally, we analyzed confusion matrices and ROC curves to understand how classifiers behave under different decision thresholds. Results were compared between architectures under a uniform processing flow to ensure consistent experimental conditions and allow for an objective evaluation of each approach's advantages and limitations.

4.5 Validation Strategy and Threshold Determination

To ensure an objective evaluation of model performance and reduce the risk of overfitting, the datasets were strictly separated into training and test subsets. The test set was used exclusively for the final performance evaluation and did not interfere with the selection of hyperparameters or the optimization of decision thresholds.

For models based on autoencoders and Siamese architectures, classification thresholds were determined using statistical analyses of reconstruction errors or similarity measures from the training set, respectively. Descriptive statistics of these distributions, including mean, standard deviation, and percentiles, were analyzed as initial criteria for defining candidate thresholds. These values were then refined using ROC curve analysis and by optimizing minority-class-oriented metrics such as *recall* and *F1-score*.

This process selected thresholds that offered the best compromise between detection capability and false positive control in the training set. Additionally, each experimental configuration was run multiple times independently. This allowed us to analyze performance stability and report average metrics, thus reducing the influence of random fluctuations in the results.

5 Results

This section presents experimental results from evaluating various neural architectures for bank fraud detection using two real-world transactional datasets of 802 and 2,941 records, enabling analysis under varying data volumes and complexities. Table 3 summarizes peak performance for each model family. The table lists test-set accuracy, associated loss, the epochs to peak performance, and execution time.

The results reveal distinct performance differences among the architectures. Multilayer neural networks achieved test-set accuracy near 90% in early training. As epochs increased, performance declined due to overfitting. Applying regularization mitigated overfitting, stabilized learning, and raised accuracy to about 94%, with a steady reduction in loss.

Recurrent architectures—GRU and LSTM—showed consistent performance when modeling transaction sequences using the temporal representation described in Sect. 4.2. Compared to LSTM networks, GRU networks achieved higher accuracy (near 90%), required less computational cost, and had shorter training times, demonstrating robust training dynamics across configurations. In contrast, LSTM networks demonstrated marginally lower accuracy, greater computational cost, and longer training times. These results show that on these datasets, LSTM networks present a less favorable trade-off between predictive performance and computational efficiency than GRU networks.

Autoencoder-based architectures achieved the highest overall results. Specifically, the convolutional autoencoder achieved high recall in detecting fraudulent transactions, indicating its strong performance in identifying anomalies compared to the other supervised architectures tested in highly unbalanced scenarios. Under the experimental protocol, this model performed near the maximum on the test set among all supervised architectures evaluated, confirming its effectiveness for banking fraud detection with these datasets.

These results require cautious interpretation. Small dataset sizes and high model complexity pose a substantial risk of overfitting, especially when optimizing classification thresholds. Thus, the analysis focuses on the consistency of relative performance across architectures.

The stacked autoencoder also performed competitively, achieving test-set accuracy above 90%, though this accuracy was still lower than that of the convolutional autoencoder. These findings indicate that convolutional layers contribute more significantly to the extraction of discriminative representations in transaction analysis than the stacked autoencoder approach.

Siamese neural networks offered an alternative by comparing transaction patterns. Though their overall accuracy was lower than that of autoencoder-based models, these networks achieved high recall. This trait is especially valuable for prioritizing fraudulent transaction detection, despite the increased number of false positives.

5.1   Evaluation Using Metrics for Unbalanced Classification

Following the protocol described in Sect. 4.2, independent runs were averaged and metrics for unbalanced classification were used to evaluate each architecture's performance. Because bank fraud detection is inherently imbalanced, accuracy alone is insufficient for evaluating model performance. Table 4 presents a comparison of metrics for the minority class, including *recall*, *F1-score*, and the

Table 3. A summary of the best performance obtained by each evaluated neural architecture, considering test set accuracy, associated loss, the number of epochs required to achieve that performance, and the corresponding execution time.

Model	Epochs (best)	Accuracy (%)	Loss	Time (s)
MLP	25	90.2	0.35	12.4
MLP + Regularization	50	93.8	0.28	18.7
GRU	50	89.5	0.41	25.3
LSTM	75	81.7	0.52	38.9
Convolutional Autoencoder	25	99.8	0.001	22.1
Stacked Autoencoder	50	91.2	0.19	31.6
Recurrent Siamese Network	50	84.3	0.44	29.4

ROC curve. These metrics were averaged across independent runs for each architecture.

The results indicate that anomaly detection-based models, particularly autoencoders, prioritize sensitivity. The convolutional autoencoder achieved the highest average *recall* (1.00), followed by the stacked autoencoder (0.90). These findings demonstrate that the models effectively identify fraudulent transactions. However, this prioritization results in a lower *F1-score* (0.42 and 0.38), indicating a higher false-positive rate. This pattern aligns with expectations for thresholds that maximize rare-event detection.

In contrast, the Siamese neural network balances sensitivity and accuracy. Its average *recall* (0.77) is lower than that of autoencoders (0.80), but its *F1-score* is higher (0.62 compared to 0.58), indicating that it detects more fraud with fewer false alerts. The area under the *ROC* curve is 0.82, demonstrating strong discrimination across thresholds.

Traditional supervised models, such as k-NN, Random Forest, MLP with regularization, and recurrent architectures (GRU and LSTM), demonstrate intermediate performance. These models achieve moderate *recall* and *F1-score* in some cases, but their final averages are more sensitive to execution-to-execution variability. As a result, their average values are more moderate than those of the Siamese network. This pattern reflects the influence of supervised training and class imbalance on learning outcomes.

The results indicate that no architecture consistently outperforms others across all metrics. Autoencoders maximize fraud detection but generate more alerts, while the Siamese network offers a balanced trade-off between detection and accuracy. The choice of architecture should be guided by specific operational requirements.

6   Discussion

The results underscore the necessity of analyzing fraud detection models using metrics beyond accuracy, particularly in the context of class imbalance. Employ-

Table 4. The average performance of the neural architectures was evaluated using metrics suitable for imbalanced classification. Two base-line classifiers are also shown for comparison.

Model	Recall	F1-score	AUC-ROC
MLP	0.53	0.56	0.84
MLP + Regularization	0.46	0.44	0.75
GRU	0.41	0.47	0.70
LSTM	0.49	0.50	0.73
Convolutional Autoencoder	1.00	0.42	0.65
Stacked Autoencoder	0.90	0.38	0.61
Recurrent Siamese Network	0.77	0.62	0.82
Random Forest	0.66	0.74	0.95
k-NN	0.69	0.74	0.94

ing minority-class metrics revealed differences between models that would remain undetected if only average accuracy were considered.

Anomaly-based methods, such as convolutional and stacked autoencoders, demonstrated high sensitivity. Elevated *recall* values indicate effective identification of fraudulent transactions, thereby reducing false negatives. However, their precision decreases, as reflected in moderate *F1 scores*. This outcome is consistent with the approach of anomaly detection methods, which prioritize identifying rare events even at the expense of increased false alarms.

The Siamese neural network demonstrated a balance between sensitivity and accuracy. Although its *recall* is lower than that of autoencoders, the higher *F1-score* suggests a more favorable ratio of fraud detection to false alerts. The area under the *ROC* curve also indicates stable discrimination as thresholds change, which is important when alert criteria may vary.

Traditional supervised models, including k-NN, Random Foret, MLP, MLP with regularization, GRU, and LSTM, performed at an intermediate level. While these models occasionally achieved high *recall* and *F1 scores*, they were, on average, more sensitive to experimental variability. This sensitivity is attributable to the supervised process and the effects of class imbalance on decision-making.

No single architecture is optimal for detecting bank fraud. Performance reflects a trade-off between sensitivity and precision, depending on operational requirements. Autoencoders are preferable when maximizing fraud detection is critical, whereas Siamese models are advantageous for managing a great number of alerts without compromising detection.

7 Conclusions

This study compared neural network architectures for bank fraud detection using metrics appropriate for severe class imbalance. The results indicate that, while accuracy is a useful starting point, it is insufficient. Metrics such as recall, F1-score, and area under the ROC curve provide a more comprehensive assessment of detection performance.

Anomaly detection-based models effectively identified fraudulent transactions, achieving recall values near 1. This supports their use when minimizing missed fraud is a priority. However, these models also produced more false positives, resulting in lower F1 scores. The Siamese network balanced sensitivity and precision, making it a strong option for managing both detection and alert volume.

Traditional supervised models, including k-NN, Random Forest, MLPs, MLPs with regularization, and recurrent models, exhibited moderate performance and high variability between runs. Their effectiveness depends more on stable training and data quality. The results suggest that there is no single optimal architecture for bank fraud detection.

Model selection should address operational requirements and balance sensitivity with accuracy. Future research should explore hybrid supervised and unsupervised approaches, as well as dynamic threshold adjustments for evolving scenarios and risks [15].

Disclosure of Interests. The authors have no competing interests to declare that are relevant to the content of this article.

References

1. Afriyie, J.K., et al.: A supervised machine learning algorithm for detecting and predicting fraud in credit card transactions. Decis. Anal. J. **6**, 100163 (2023). https://doi.org/10.1016/j.dajour.2023.100163
2. Bagga, S., Goyal, A., Gupta, N., Goyal, A.: Credit card fraud detection using pipelining and ensemble learning. Procedia Comput. Sci. **173**, 104–112 (2020). https://doi.org/10.1016/j.procs.2020.06.014
3. Carcillo, F., Dal Pozzolo, A., Borgne, Y.A.L., Caelen, O., Mazzer, Y., Bontempi, G.: SCARFF: a scalable framework for streaming credit card fraud detection with spark. Inf. Fusion **41**, 182–194 (2018). https://doi.org/10.1016/j.inffus.2017.09.005
4. Chen, J., Chen, Q., Jiang, F., Guo, X., Sha, K., Wang, Y.: SCN_GNN: a GNN-based fraud detection algorithm combining strong node and graph topology information. Expert Syst. Appl. **237**, 121643 (2024). https://doi.org/10.1016/j.eswa.2023.121643
5. Cherif, A., Badhib, A., Ammar, H., Alshehri, S., Kalkatawi, M., Imine, A.: Credit card fraud detection in the era of disruptive technologies: a systematic review. J. King Saud Univ. - Comput. Inf. Sci. **35**(1), 145–174 (2023). https://doi.org/10.1016/j.jksuci.2022.11.008
6. Ding, L., Liu, L., Wang, Y., Shi, P., Yu, J.: An autoencoder-enhanced light gradient boosting machine method for credit card fraud detection. PeerJ Comput. Sci. **10**, e2323 (2024). https://doi.org/10.7717/peerj-cs.2323
7. Du, H., Lv, L., Guo, A., Wang, H.: Autoencoder and LightGBM for credit card fraud detection problems. Symmetry **15**(4), 870 (2023). https://doi.org/10.3390/sym15040870

8. Forough, J., Momtazi, S.: Ensemble of deep sequential models for credit card fraud detection. Appl. Soft Comput. **99**, 106883 (2021). https://doi.org/10.1016/j.asoc.2020.106883
9. Huang, M., et al.: AUC-oriented graph neural network for fraud detection. In: Proceedings of the Web Conference (WWW), pp. 1311–1321 (2022). https://doi.org/10.1145/3485447.3512178
10. Lei, Y.T., Ma, C.Q., Ren, Y.S., Chen, X.Q., Narayan, S., Huynh, A.N.Q.: A distributed deep neural network model for credit card fraud detection. Financ. Res. Lett. **58**, 104547 (2023). https://doi.org/10.1016/j.frl.2023.104547
11. Li, Z., Huang, M., Liu, G., Jiang, C.: A hybrid method with dynamic weighted entropy for handling the problem of class imbalance with overlap in credit card fraud detection. Expert Syst. Appl. **175**, 114750 (2021). https://doi.org/10.1016/j.eswa.2021.114750
12. Ma, S., Hargreaves, C.A.: Addressing credit card fraud detection challenges with adversarial autoencoders. Big Data Cogn. Comput. **9**(7), 168 (2025). https://doi.org/10.3390/bdcc9070168
13. Rtayli, N., Enneya, N.: Enhanced credit card fraud detection based on SVM-recursive feature elimination and hyper-parameters optimization. J. Inf. Secur. Appl. **55**, 102596 (2020). https://doi.org/10.1016/j.jisa.2020.102596
14. Wu, Y., Wang, L., Li, H., Liu, J.: A deep learning method of credit card fraud detection based on continuous-coupled neural networks. Mathematics **13**(5), 819 (2025). https://doi.org/10.3390/math13050819
15. Yang, Y., Xu, C., Tian, G.: Lightweight financial fraud detection using a symmetrical GAN-CNN fusion architecture. Symmetry **17**(8), 1366 (2025). https://doi.org/10.3390/sym17081366
16. Zhu, H., Liu, G., Zhou, M., Xie, Y., Abusorrah, A., Kang, Q.: Optimizing weighted extreme learning machines for imbalanced classification and application to credit card fraud detection. Neurocomputing **407**, 50–62 (2020). https://doi.org/10.1016/j.neucom.2020.04.078

Variational Standard Simplex Hierarchical Encoder for Clustering

Ulises Rodríguez-Domínguez[(✉)]

National Autonomous University of Mexico, Mexico City, Mexico
ulises.rodriguez.dominguez@ciencias.unam.mx

Abstract. The unsupervised task of data clustering continues to benefit from deep learning based approaches. Generative deep learning models in particular allow not only to obtain improved clustering results but also to capture the underlying distributions involved in the model, potentially allowing other applications beyond clustering with a single model. In this work we propose a new variational hierarchical encoder model tailored for the clustering task, which extends a previous deep clustering neural network to the deep generative scheme. The latent space of the model has support in the standard $K - 1$ dimensional simplex, where K is the number of clusters. The population mean parameter of the standard simplex samples considers a Dirichlet prior distribution, and this parameter is automatically learned from the data based on posterior updates during the training of the variational model. The model remains competitive with state-of-the-art deep clustering methods and can be used for applications beyond clustering such as generation of new samples in the data space belonging to specific or to hybrid categories due to the structured latent space. Furthermore, instead of being limited to specific encoder networks, the model can take advantage of transfer learning to either obtain improved results or to adapt to specific data domains based on previously trained deep networks.

Keywords: Clustering · Variational encoder · Standard simplex · Dirichlet prior

1 Introduction

The fundamental task of data clustering, whose goal is to discover the natural groupings of a set of data points [9], has recently benefited from deep learning based approaches. Data clustering continues to be important in various pre-processing or preliminary analysis tasks such as: image analysis [2], customer segmentation [13], weather anomaly detection [14], etc. Hence a wide variety of data processing pipelines benefit from improved clustering methods.

Different clustering methods have recently been recategorized due to the continual success of deep learning based approaches. Many classic clustering approaches are now known as shallow clustering [18], where each data point is

V. G. Cruz-Sánchez et al. (Eds.): MCPR 2026, LNCS 16623, pp. 130–140, 2026.
https://doi.org/10.1007/978-3-032-28393-1_12

represented in some feature vector space, by a linear or a nonlinear transformation, and then a clustering model finds groups in such space. On the other hand, approaches based on deep learning representations are categorized depending on their usage of [18]: an auto encoder, a deep generative model, mutual information maximization, contrastive learning, friendly clustering, subspace learning or data type specific learning. An important distinction is whether or not the representation learned with a deep model interacts with the clustering task, because this has shown to be beneficial [18].

Improving on previous deep autoencoders for the clustering task, in [6] a deep convolutional autoencoder was devised for the clustering task, improving over previous image clustering methods. Recently a state-of-the-art clustering method [19] was proposed combining the reconstruction loss from deep autoencoders with the fuzzy C-Means clustering loss, achieving improved results and learned representations. Among deep generative models, proposals from the variational autoencoder (VAE) scheme have been employed for clustering. Examples of the later include a VAE clustering model using a Gaussian mixture for the prior combined with the idea of graph embedding, improving results over previous deep models based on Gaussian mixtures [17]. A different VAE was proposed very recently [5], modeling the prior based on a hierarchical Gamma mixture model, instead of a Gaussian mixture model, obtaining improved clustering results.

Our proposed deep learning based clustering method falls into the deep generative model category. The deep representations learned in the model are coupled to the clustering task. The contributions in this work can be summarized as follows:

- We extend a previously proposed deep clustering model [12] to the deep generative setting, specifically a deep hierarchical variational encoder.
- A population distribution parameter of our structured latent space, with support in the standard simplex, is now automatically learned from data, based on posterior updates.
- Our model can be combined with a properly designed decoder network to obtain new samples in the latent space, where hard cluster categories are located only at the corners of the simplex latent space. Hence samples from hybrid categories can be generated.
- Different encoder networks can be used for the model and hence transfer learning can be considered from task-specific deep networks.
- We experimentally demonstrate clustering performance improvement over our previous account, which remains competitive with state-of-the-art deep learning approaches.

The rest of the paper is organized as follows. In Sect. 2 we present our proposed variational encoder model for clustering, which extends a previous deep clustering network to the deep generative model scheme. Then in Sect. 3 we present clustering results evaluated in a benchmark image dataset together with an empirical parameter analysis relevant to the model extension.

2 Variational Standard Simplex Hierarchical Encoder

Here we describe the proposed variational encoder model, which is an extension of a deep clustering model previously proposed in [12]. The model considers a batch of n_s output vectors from a deep neural network, namely $\hat{\mathbf{Y}}_\Theta \equiv h(\mathbf{X}; \Theta)$, with weight and bias parameters Θ. The batch is such that $\hat{\mathbf{Y}} = \left[\hat{\mathbf{y}}^{(1)}, \hat{\mathbf{y}}^{(2)}, ..., \hat{\mathbf{y}}^{(n_s)}\right]$, with $\hat{\mathbf{y}}^{(j)} \in [0,1]^K$ and where K is the number of clusters ($K > 1$). The capacity of the model for improved clustering is demonstrated in the experiments section. However, the extension to the generative setting, has additional advantages for unsupervised latent space regularization because it imposes structured posterior samples over the $K - 1$ dimensional simplex, which can be the input to another decoder network.

We consider the following generative model over the batch-dependent transformations $v\left(\hat{Y}_\theta\right)$ and $u\left(\hat{Y}_\theta\right)$, which are population statistics, and over the prior parameter $\tilde{\pi}$. Its joint distribution is

$$
\mathcal{P}\left(v\left(\hat{Y}_\theta\right), u\left(\hat{Y}_\theta\right), \tilde{\pi}\right) = \mathcal{P}_{\lambda_B}\left(v\left(\hat{Y}_\theta\right)\right) \mathcal{P}_\theta\left(u\left(\hat{Y}_\theta\right) \mid \tilde{\pi}\right) \mathcal{P}_{\lambda_D}\left(\tilde{\pi}\right) \tag{1}
$$

with the following distributions that promote properties over the standard simplex population samples contained in $\hat{Y}_\theta$

$$
\mathcal{P}_{\lambda_B}\left(v\left(\hat{Y}_\theta\right)\right) \sim \mathcal{N}\left(1,1\right), \qquad \mathcal{P}_\theta\left(u\left(\hat{Y}_\theta\right) \mid \tilde{\pi}\right) \sim \mathcal{N}\left(\tilde{\pi}, \frac{1}{\gamma}\right), \tag{2}
$$

with γ a precision parameter. We highlight that the Gaussian distributions for $v\left(\hat{Y}_\theta\right)$ and for $u\left(\hat{Y}_\theta\right)$ model the distribution of population properties (over a batch). In particular the value

$$
u\left(\hat{Y}_\theta\right) = \frac{1}{n_s} \sum_{j=1}^{n_s} \hat{\mathbf{y}}_\theta^{(j)}, \tag{3}
$$

models the average over the network output vector samples, where $\hat{\mathbf{y}}_\theta^{(j)} \in \mathbb{P}$, with $\mathbb{P}$ the set for the $K - 1$ dimensional standard simplex. Note that the mean is chosen as the vector parameter $\tilde{\pi}$, with its own prior distribution. On the other hand the value for $v\left(\hat{Y}_\theta\right)$ models the average norm over the standard simplex samples

$$
v\left(\hat{Y}_\theta\right) = \frac{1}{n_s} \sum_{j=1}^{n_s} ||\hat{\mathbf{y}}_\theta^{(j)}||_2. \tag{4}
$$

Hence both Gaussian distributions impose a parametric model over these batch-wise properties.

On the other hand, the prior distribution for the $\tilde{\pi}$ parameter is chosen with support in the standard simplex. In particular we consider the Dirichlet prior

$$\mathcal{P}_{\lambda_D}\left(\tilde{\pi}\right) \sim \operatorname{Dir}\left(K, \alpha_0\right). \tag{5}$$

The Dirichlet prior for the mean parameter of the simplex average has its own meta-parameter vector α_0 which needs to be specified. However, once specified, $\tilde{\pi}$ is generated by the variational model during training, and hence it is learned from data. Assuming a single value α for all the entries in the vector parameter α_0 we can consider three cases: if $\alpha > 1$ the distribution gets concentrated if $\alpha = 1$ we have a uniform (or ignorant) prior and if $\alpha < 1$ we have a sparse prior (specially for smaller values). The sparse regime is particularly suitable for the clustering task because we have concentrated modes on each corner of the standard simplex. For our model we focus on $0 \leq \alpha \leq 1$.

Instead of the exact posterior $\mathcal{P}\left(\tilde{\pi}|\mathbf{X}\right)$ we consider an approximated model $q_\phi\left(\tilde{\pi}|\mathbf{X}\right)$ as is usual in the variational encoder setting. This is the model for our encoder network

$$q_\phi\left(\tilde{\pi}|\mathbf{X}\right) \sim \operatorname{Dir}\left(K, \alpha_\phi\left(\mathbf{X}\right)\right), \tag{6}$$

where $\alpha_\phi\left(\mathbf{X}\right)$ is the network encoder output, i.e., the encoder estimates the posterior Dirichlet vector parameter. Despite the fact that it is not possible to apply the reparameterization trick for a Dirichlet encoder, the work by [4] made this possible by using implicit reparameterization, after which backpropagation can be applied in the usual manner.

With the previous generative model we obtain the evidence lower bound (ELBO) based on the following marginal distribution, where $\tilde{\pi}$ is the latent vector random variable

$$\mathcal{P}\left(v\left(\hat{Y}_\theta\right), u\left(\hat{Y}_\theta\right)\right) = \int \mathcal{P}_{\lambda_B}\left(v\left(\hat{Y}_\theta\right)\right) \mathcal{P}_\theta\left(u\left(\hat{Y}_\theta\right)|\tilde{\pi}\right) \mathcal{P}_{\lambda_D}\left(\tilde{\pi}\right) \mathrm{d}\tilde{\pi}. \tag{7}$$

We arrive at the following ELBO (see the supplementary material for the details)

$$\mathcal{L}^B\left(\theta, \phi; \mathbf{X}\right)$$
$$= \log \mathcal{P}_{\lambda_B}\left(v\left(\hat{Y}_\theta\right)\right) + \mathbb{E}_{q_\phi\left(\tilde{\pi}|\mathbf{X}\right)}\left[\log \mathcal{P}_\theta\left(u\left(\hat{Y}_\theta\right)|\tilde{\pi}\right)\right] - \mathcal{D}_{KL}\left(q_\phi\left(\tilde{\pi}|\mathbf{X}\right)||\mathcal{P}_{\lambda_D}\left(\tilde{\pi}\right)\right)$$
$$\tag{8}$$

From which we obtain the following loss function by taking the negative value of the ELBO and considering an approximation of the true expectation by a simple average

$$\mathcal{L}\left(\theta, \phi; \mathbf{X}\right)$$
$$= \left(1 - v\left(\hat{Y}_\theta\right)\right)^2 + \frac{\gamma}{n_s} \sum_{\tilde{\pi} \in S_{\pi|\mathbf{X}}} ||u\left(\hat{Y}_\theta\right) - \tilde{\pi}||_2^2 + \lambda_{KL}\mathcal{D}_{KL}\left(q_\phi\left(\tilde{\pi}|\mathbf{X}\right)||\mathcal{P}_{\lambda_D}\left(\tilde{\pi}\right)\right),$$
$$\tag{9}$$

where $S_{\pi|\mathbf{X}}$ is a set with n_s samples from the posterior model $q_\phi\left(\tilde{\pi}|\mathbf{X}\right)$. Note that in (9) we ignored the logarithm of the Gaussian normalization constants (since they do not depend on learnable parameters), and we additionally introduced a regularization parameter λ_{KL} to weigh the relevance of the Kullback-Leibler prior-posterior regularization. The first and second terms in (9) promote population properties in the batch of standard simplex samples, which appeared in a previous deep clustering model [12]. However, in [12] the underlying distribution was unknown and the $\tilde{\pi}$ vector parameter was fixed without any prior distribution. Now in this extension of the previous model to the variational encoder setting, we have the following advantages:

- The $\tilde{\pi}$ parameter is now learned from the data by the posterior model updates during the training stage. This can be appreciated in Fig. 1, where for $K = 3$ clusters we show batch population posterior samples of $\tilde{\pi}$ over the 2 dimensional simplex as the training epochs vary.
- When coupled with a properly designed decoder network, we can generate new samples in the original space after training the model. This can be carried out by sampling from the latent space over the $K - 1$ dimensional simplex. The obtained samples can vary from being very specific to a particular cluster at a standard simplex corner, to hybrid-like samples for the in-between regions. Then the decoder can generate the samples in the data space using the latent space samples as input.
- The model can work with different network encoders to produce the batch-wise samples $\hat{Y}_\theta$. This allows the usage of transfer learning from previously trained deep encoders.

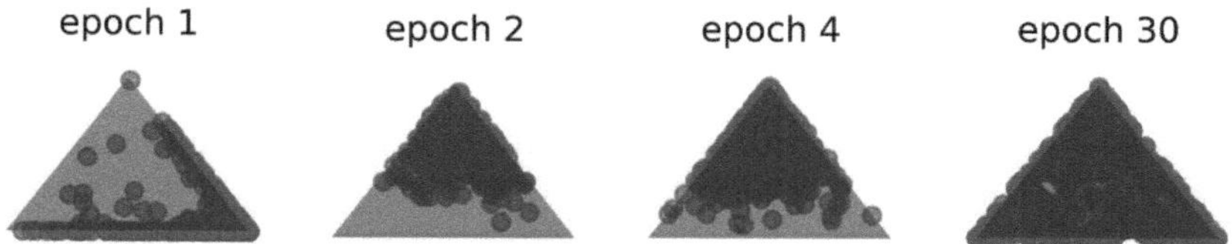

Fig. 1. Evolution of $\tilde{\pi}$ population samples during the training of the variational encoder. For illustration purposes, the number of clusters considered is $K = 3$ for the fashion MNIST dataset (see Sect. 3 for the dataset description). Initially the samples get biased towards a specific corner, i.e., a single cluster, but as the posterior model is updated based on observed data, samples are obtained from the whole range of the 2 dimensional standard simplex.

2.1   Optimization Objective

To learn the model parameters, we target the following maximization problem, to maximize the average ELBO over N_B batches, equivalent to minimizing the average loss over such batches

$$\boldsymbol{\theta}^*, \boldsymbol{\phi}^* = \underset{\boldsymbol{\theta},\boldsymbol{\phi}}{\operatorname{argmax}} \frac{1}{N_B} \sum_{b=1}^{N_B} \mathcal{L}^3 \left(\boldsymbol{\theta}, \boldsymbol{\phi}; \mathbf{X}^{(b)} \right) = \underset{\boldsymbol{\theta},\boldsymbol{\phi}}{\operatorname{argmin}} \frac{1}{N_B} \sum_{b=1}^{N_B} \mathcal{L} \left(\boldsymbol{\theta}, \boldsymbol{\phi}; \mathbf{X}^{(b)} \right).$$

$$(10)$$

3   Experiments and Results

We evaluated our clustering model on the following datasets, described as follows:

- **Fashion MNIST** [15]: it contains 60,000 28×28 item images (with 10 balanced classes) for training and 10,000 item images for testing. The items are mostly clothes and the database is intended to replace the original MNIST database. For our clustering experiments we scaled the dynamic range of the images to $[0, 1]$ and we used the full 70,000 item images.
- **USPS** [8]: it contains 7,291 16×16 digit images (with 10 approximately balanced classes) for training and 2,007 digit images for testing. For our clustering experiments we scaled the dynamic range of the images to $[0, 1]$ and we used the full 9,298 digit images.

We report both the clustering accuracy (CA) and the normalized mutual information (NMI) for our method and for the compared methods. The CA refers to the percentage of correctly predicted cluster labels. Since we are in an unsupervised setting, we first compute the maximum bipartite matching between the obtained cluster labels and the dataset ground-truth labels by employing the Kuhn-Munkres algorithm [10]. The results are shown in Table 1 for our model and for other clustering methods, mainly based on deep models. It can be seen that we achieve the highest results in both CA and NMI in both datasets, but we note that our improvement in Fashion MNIST is only marginal compared to the extended model SSICHDDL [12].

Since the main extension of the model is related to the Dirichlet prior distribution and the Kullback-Leibler prior-posterior regularization we also report how the model performs as the parameters related to these terms vary. This is shown in Fig. 2 where the CA is reported as the α Dirichlet prior parameter varies. We evaluated α over a discrete grid to impose either the uniform $\alpha = 1$ or the sparse regime $\alpha \in \{0.4, 0.5, 0.6, 0.7, 0.8, 0.9\}$ for the Dirichlet prior over the standard simplex support. Although the curves in Fig. 2 show variation as λ_{KL} varies a bimodal tendency over the sparse regime can be appreciated in all the curves, with maximum values approximately around $\alpha = 0.6$ and $\alpha = 0.9$. Furthermore, in all the curves the CA consistently gets smaller for the uniform regime ($\alpha = 1$). This means that the best results are achieved by an informative prior, contrary to the ignorant uniform prior, specifically in the sparse regime (with modes at the simplex corners).

For the Kullback-Leibler regularization term Fig. 3 shows the CA as the λ_{KL} regularization parameter varies. Unlike the previous case, the curves in Fig. 3

show an unimodal tendency, with a maximum approximately around $\lambda_{KL} = 1$. Although this suggests that the λ_{KL} parameter may not be needed for practical purposes, further evaluation is required in a wider variety of datasets.

Table 1. Clustering accuracy (CA) and normalized mutual information (NMI) across methods. The number of clusters is $K = 10$.

Method	Fashion MNIST		USPS	
	CA	NMI	CA	NMI
K-means	0.5107	0.5164	0.6679	0.6256
SEC [11]	0.5424	0.5580	0.6519	0.6488
DEC [16]	0.5781	0.6283	0.7278	0.7352
IDEC [6]	0.5764	0.6013	0.7513	0.7595
DNFCS [3]	0.6250	0.6567	0.7580	0.7696
GrDNFCS [3]	0.6351	**0.6609**	0.7652	0.7761
SSICHDDL [12]	0.6821	0.5867	0.7639	0.6619
VESSHC	**0.6824**	0.5908	**0.7807**	**0.7142**

4   Discussion

We proposed a new deep generative model tailored for the clustering task by extending a previous deep clustering network [12] to a variational encoder model. This extension has the advantages discussed below, which go beyond achieving a specific clustering result in a dataset.

The previous deep clustering model from [12] showed that hierarchical deep dictionary layers coupled with an unsupervised loss over standard simplex network outputs is able to improve deep clustering results. This previous model also demonstrated that regularization is even more important in the unsupervised case compared to supervised classification. The underlying statistical model in this previous proposal was unknown. We now show the underlying hierarchical generative model, which considers Gaussian distributions for population properties over standard simplex samples (the final encoder outputs), which comprise the likelihood model. One of these Gaussian distributions considers a mean parameter for the standard simplex samples. This parameter in turn has a Dirichlet prior distribution, whose support is the standard simplex, also called the probability simplex. By the deep variational scheme we approximate the posterior based on a network encoder model and thus learn this parameter from data by posterior updates in a self contained manner during the training of the model. The reparameterization trick commonly employed in variational encoders cannot be used with a Dirichlet prior, but previous work extended this to an implicit reparameterization trick [4], which we employ.

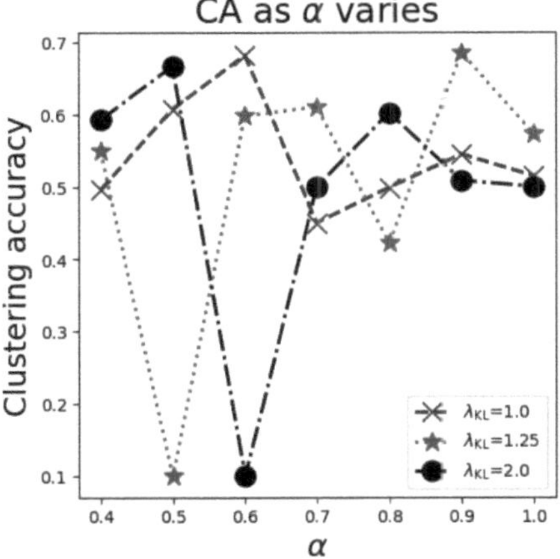

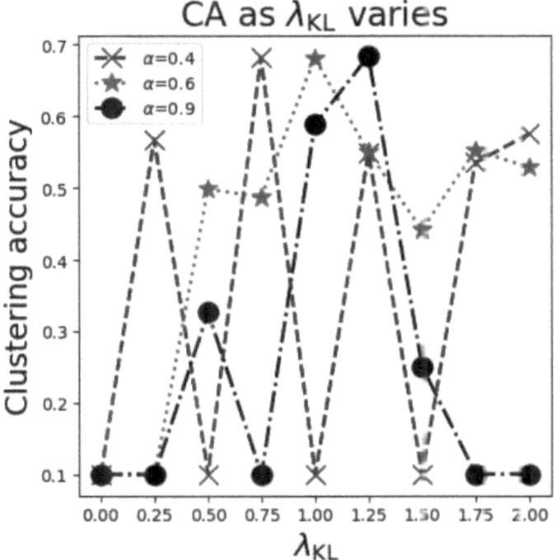

Fig. 2. Clustering accuracy (CA) over the full FASHION MNIST data set as the α sparsity prior parameter varies. Three curves are shown for different λ_{KL} regularization parameters. See the supplementary material for other parameters/metaparameters used.

Fig. 3. Clustering accuracy (CA) over the full FASHION MNIST data set as the λ_{KL} regularization parameter for the Kullback-Leibler divergence varies. Three curves are shown for different α sparsity prior parameter values. See the supplementary material for other parameters/metaparameters used.

The structured latent space over the $K - 1$ dimensional standard simplex we employ coupled with the generative model scheme allows two things. On one hand regularization over this support is facilitated due to its specific structure, where we can conceptually and also for practical purposes move the population statistics between the center and the simplex corners. A sample located at a specific corner represents membership to a specific cluster group while on the other extreme, as this sample moves away from all corners, towards the center, equal membership to all clusters is achieved (latent space region of highest membership overlap). Since we now have a generative model, once the model is trained we can also obtain new samples from this structured latent space. These latent space samples can be the input to a properly designed decoder network, which means we can generate new unseen samples in the original data space (as with any standard VAE). However, with our new model we can sample from the whole range of cluster categories, from samples clearly belonging to a specific category to the whole range of hibrid-like samples for in-between categories.

Our model is not limited to the specific encoder network employed in our experiments for the estimation of standard simplex samples. We can potentially use transfer learning from a very deep encoder, using for instance a backbone network from the ResNet family of architectures [1,7] to either improve the quality of the samples or to adapt our model for other domain specific data. This is also the case for the decoding step mentioned previously.

Beyond clustering, the most evident application of the proposed model is the generation of new data samples from a variety of domains, e.g., image, audio or text domain, with hybrid category membership in each corresponding domain. Transfer learning is appropriate for such application both for the encoder and the decoder. In addition of this application opportunity of our model, we also highlight a limitation related to the Dirichlet prior parameter. We empirically showed that the clustering task benefits from the sparse regime, but we found evidence of bimodality for appropriately selecting the prior parameter value. As a future work we expect to address both the application opportunity and the problem with the selection of the prior distribution parameter.

5   Supplementary Material

5.1   Evidence Lower Bound

Here we derive the evidence lower bound (ELBO) starting from the marginal distribution

$$
\begin{aligned}
\mathcal{P}&\left(v\left(\hat{Y}_{\theta}\right), u\left(\hat{Y}_{\theta}\right)\right) \\
&= \int \mathcal{P}_{\lambda_B}\left(v\left(\hat{Y}_{\theta}\right)\right) \mathcal{P}_{\theta}\left(u\left(\hat{Y}_{\theta}\right)|\tilde{\pi}\right) \mathcal{P}_{\lambda_D}(\tilde{\pi})\, \mathrm{d}\tilde{\pi} \\
&= \mathcal{P}_{\lambda_B}\left(v\left(\hat{Y}_{\theta}\right)\right) \int \mathcal{P}_{\theta}\left(u\left(\hat{Y}_{\theta}\right)|\tilde{\pi}\right) \mathcal{P}_{\lambda_D}(\tilde{\pi})\, \mathrm{d}\tilde{\pi} \\
&= \mathcal{P}_{\lambda_B}\left(v\left(\hat{Y}_{\theta}\right)\right) \int q_{\phi}(\tilde{\pi}|\mathbf{X}) \frac{\mathcal{P}_{\theta}\left(u\left(\hat{Y}_{\theta}\right)|\tilde{\pi}\right) \mathcal{P}_{\lambda_D}(\tilde{\pi})}{q_{\phi}(\tilde{\pi}|\mathbf{X})}\, \mathrm{d}\tilde{\pi}
\end{aligned}
\tag{11}
$$

then we take the logarithm on both sides and by concavity of the logarithm we obtain the lower bound

$$
\begin{aligned}
\log \mathcal{P}&\left(v\left(\hat{Y}_{\theta}\right), u\left(\hat{Y}_{\theta}\right)\right) \\
&= \log \mathcal{P}_{\lambda_B}\left(v\left(\hat{Y}_{\theta}\right)\right) + \log \left(\int q_{\phi}(\tilde{\pi}|\mathbf{X}) \frac{\mathcal{P}_{\theta}\left(u\left(\hat{Y}_{\theta}\right)|\tilde{\pi}\right) \mathcal{P}_{\lambda_D}(\tilde{\pi})}{q_{\phi}(\tilde{\pi}|\mathbf{X})}\, \mathrm{d}\tilde{\pi} \right) \\
&\geq \log \mathcal{P}_{\lambda_B}\left(v\left(\hat{Y}_{\theta}\right)\right) + \mathbb{E}_{q_{\phi}(\tilde{\pi}|\mathbf{X})}\left[\log \left(\frac{\mathcal{P}_{\theta}\left(u\left(\hat{Y}_{\theta}\right)|\tilde{\pi}\right) \mathcal{P}_{\lambda_D}(\tilde{\pi})}{q_{\phi}(\tilde{\pi}|\mathbf{X})} \right) \right] \\
&= \log \mathcal{P}_{\lambda_B}\left(v\left(\hat{Y}_{\theta}\right)\right) + \mathbb{E}_{q_{\phi}(\tilde{\pi}|\mathbf{X})}\left[\log \mathcal{P}_{\theta}\left(u\left(\hat{Y}_{\theta}\right)|\tilde{\pi}\right) \right] - \mathcal{D}_{KL}\left(q_{\phi}(\tilde{\pi}|\mathbf{X})\,||\,\mathcal{P}_{\lambda_D}(\tilde{\pi})\right) \\
&= \mathcal{L}^{B}(\boldsymbol{\theta}, \boldsymbol{\phi}; \mathbf{X}).
\end{aligned}
\tag{12}
$$

5.2 Model Parameter Values

The following are the parameter values used to obtain the results in Table 1 in the main text:

	Fashion MNIST	USPS
Epochs	66	189
Learning rate	0.001	0.001
Batch size	500	700
α (Dirichlet prior)	0.4	0.4
λ_{KL}	0.75	1.5

References

1. Bhogal, R.K., Singh, A.: A comprehensive review of ResNet-18: architecture and applications. In: Bansal, J.C., Saha, S., Coello, C.A.C., Rathore, H. (eds.) ADCIS 2024. LNNS, vol. 1333, pp. 595–607. Springer, Singapore (2025). https://doi.org/10.1007/978-981-96-4536-7_42
2. Caron, M., Bojanowski, P., Joulin, A., Douze, M.: Deep clustering for unsupervised learning of visual features. In: Proceedings of the European Conference on Computer Vision (ECCV). (2018)
3. Feng, Q., Chen, L., Chen, C.L.P., Guo, L.: Deep fuzzy clustering–a representation learning approach. IEEE Trans. Fuzzy Syst. **28**(7), 1420–1433 (2020)
4. Figurnov, M., Mohamed, S., Mnih, A.: Implicit reparameterization gradients. In: Proceedings of the 32nd International Conference on Neural Information Processing Systems, NIPS 2018, pp. 439–450. Curran Associates Inc., Red Hook (2018)
5. Guo, J., Fan, W., Amayri, M., Bouguila, N.: Deep clustering analysis via variational autoencoder with gamma mixture latent embeddings. Neural Netw. **133**, 106979 (2025). https://doi.org/10.1016/j.neunet.2024.106979
6. Guo, X., Gao, L., Liu, X., Yin, J.: Improved deep embedded clustering with local structure preservation. In: Proceedings of the 26th International Joint Conference on Artificial Intelligence, IJCAI 2017, pp. 1753–1759. AAAI Press (2017)
7. He, K., Zhang, X., Ren, S., Sun, J.: Deep residual learning for image recognition. In: Proceedings of the IEEE Conference on Computer Vision and Pattern Recognition (CVPR) (2016)
8. Hull, J.J.: A database for handwritten text recognition research. IEEE Trans. Pattern Anal. Mach. Intell. **16**(5), 550–554 (1994)
9. Jain, A.K.: Data clustering: 50 years beyond k-means. Pattern Recogn. Lett. **31**(8), 651–666 (2010). https://doi.org/10.1016/j.patrec.2009.09.011
10. Lovász, L., Plummer, M.: Matching Theory, vol. 367. AMS Chelsea Publishing (2009)
11. Nie, F., Xu, D., Tsang, I.W., Zhang, C.: Spectral embedded clustering. In: IJCAI, pp. 1181–1186 (2009)
12. Rodríguez-Domínguez, U., Dalmau, O.: Standard simplex induced clustering with hierarchical deep dictionary learning. Signal Process.: Image Commun. **112**, 116918 (2023). https://doi.org/10.1016/j.image.2022.116918

13. Sehgal, N., Vij, S., Virmani, D., Ansari, M.Y.: An approach of deep clustering applied for customer segmentation to escalate businesses. In: Tiwari, R., Saraswat, M., Pavone, M. (eds.) ICCI 2023. Algorithms for Intelligent Systems, pp. 141–152. Springer, Singapore (2024). https://doi.org/10.1007/978-981-97-3526-6_12
14. Wibisono, S., Anwar, M.T., Supriyanto, A., Amin, I.H.A.: Multivariate weather anomaly detection using DBSCAN clustering algorithm. J. Phys.: Conf. Ser. **1869**(1), 012077 (2021). https://doi.org/10.1088/1742-6596/1869/1/012077
15. Xiao, H., Rasul, K., Vollgraf, R.: Fashion-MNIST: a novel image dataset for benchmarking machine learning algorithms (2017)
16. Xie, J., Girshick, R., Farhadi, A.: Unsupervised deep embedding for clustering analysis. In: Proceedings of the 33rd International Conference on International Conference on Machine Learning, ICML 2016, vol. 48, pp. 478–487. JMLR.org (2016)
17. Yang, L., Cheung, N.M., Li, J., Fang, J.: Deep clustering by gaussian mixture variational autoencoders with graph embedding. In: 2019 IEEE/CVF International Conference on Computer Vision (ICCV), pp. 6439–6448 (2019). https://doi.org/10.1109/ICCV.2019.00654
18. Zhou, S., et al.: A comprehensive survey on deep clustering: taxonomy, challenges, and future directions. ACM Comput. Surv. **57**(3) (2024). https://doi.org/10.1145/3689036
19. Zhu, L., Liu, Z., Liu, G.: A deep multiple self-supervised clustering model based on autoencoder networks. Sci. Rep. **15**(1) (2025). https://doi.org/10.1038/s41598-025-00349-z

Chest CT Gender Domain Translation: Comparative Evaluation of CycleGAN and cVAE in Radiometric and Volumetric Coherence

Irlein Delgado Navarro[(✉)] [iD], Gabriela Judith Alvarado Flores[iD],
Leopoldo Altamirano Robles[iD], Raquel Díaz Hernández[iD],
and Saúl Zapotecas Martínez[iD]

Instituto Nacional de Astrofísica, Óptica y Electrónica (INAOE), Puebla, Mexico
delgadoirlein@gmail.com

Abstract. Surgical planning for gender-affirming mastectomies faces significant challenges due to the scarcity of representative anatomical datasets, as most medical imaging tools are trained on cisgender cohorts. This technological gap often leads to sub-optimal surgical outcomes and a lack of specialized 3D planning resources for the transgender population. This study proposes a deep learning pipeline for gender domain translation in chest computed tomography (CT) scans. We evaluate and compare two generative architectures: a Conditional Variational Autoencoder (cVAE) and a robust CycleGAN. Our results demonstrate that CycleGAN significantly outperforms cVAE in structural preservation and radiometric fidelity, achieving a Structural Similarity Index (SSIM) of 0.889 and preserving densities of up to 825 Hounsfield Units (HU), while cVAE is limited to 413 HU. Furthermore, manual 3D morphometric validation in the 3D Slicer confirms a consistent redistribution of pectoral soft tissue, with an average reduction of 25.8% in transmasculine synthesis and a 101.5% increase in transfeminine synthesis. Although limitations in the synthesis of large breast volumes and 3D continuity persist, this study establishes a solid technical foundation for gender-diverse surgical planning tools, aiming to improve anatomical precision and surgical safety for the transgender community.

Keywords: Synthetic CT · CycleGAN · cVAE · Transgender Healthcare · Hounsfield Units · 3D Reconstruction

1 Introduction

Gender-affirming surgery, such as masculinizing mastectomy, is essential for transgender health, yet technical literature and planning tools remain limited compared to those for cisgender patients [2]. This lack of representation in medical datasets introduces critical biases; as demonstrated by Larrazabal et al.,

© The Author(s), under exclusive license to Springer Nature Switzerland AG 2026
V. G. Cruz-Sánchez et al. (Eds.): MCPR 2026, LNCS 16623, pp. 141–151, 2026.
https://doi.org/10.1007/978-3-032-28393-1_13

gender imbalance in diagnostic imaging produces biased classifiers, necessitating synthetic data strategies [8]. Currently, a significant "data gap" exists where anatomical variations of gender-diverse bodies are often overlooked or pathologized in standard training sets.

Precise planning is vital given the higher complication rates reported in transgender patients [3], often arising from a lack of preoperative 3D visualizations that account for specific chest wall morphology. In Mexico, where 34.8% of the LGBTI+ population identifies as transgender, this technological gap is a priority challenge [1]. In response, this work proposes a synthetic data generation *pipeline* through gender domain translation in chest CT scans.

By leveraging generative architectures, we aim to synthesize "virtual twins" for precise mastectomy planning. We evaluate and compare a Conditional Variational Autoencoder (cVAE) and a CycleGAN, focusing on their ability to preserve Hounsfield Unit (HU) integrity and volumetric coherence. Our contributions include: (i) a specialized preprocessing workflow for gender-balanced CT data, (ii) a comparative analysis of radiometric fidelity between adversarial and variational spaces, and (iii) a 3D morphometric validation using clinical software.

The paper is organized as follows: Sect. 2 discusses related work; Sect. 3 details the methodology; Sect. 4 presents the results; and Sect. 5 summarizes the conclusions.

2   Related Work

The use of Generative Adversarial Networks (GAN), introduced by Goodfellow et al. [4], has gained significant relevance in medical image synthesis. A consolidated application is the generation of synthetic computed tomography (sCT) from MRI for radiotherapy planning (*MRI-only radiotherapy planning*). Works such as Han [7] and Wolterink et al. [6] demonstrated that GANs can accurately map electron densities, reducing the need for real CT acquisition. Recent reviews [11,14] and technical proposals [12,13] confirm the validity of this approach and highlight improvements in structural fidelity and preservation of diagnostic textures. However, these methods primarily focus on the translation between different imaging modalities (cross-modality) rather than the morphological translation within the same modality (intra-modality) required for gender-specific anatomical changes.

Most of these developments have focused on specific organs such as the brain or pelvis and rely on paired MRI–CT data from the same patient to guide the learning process. This represents a significant research gap, as paired datasets for gender-affirming pre- and post-operative states are virtually non-existent, and standard supervised models cannot account for the large-scale volumetric redistributions of soft tissue needed for masculinization or feminization planning. To date, no studies have reported the integration of CT synthesis with gender domain translation for surgical planning.

Our proposal stands out by employing a CycleGAN inspired by Zhu et al. [5], which enables the translation of anatomical gender domains without the need for paired data. By utilizing an unpaired learning strategy, we overcome the data scarcity constraint inherent in transgender healthcare. This approach is critical to addressing gender bias in medical AI, as highlighted by Larrazabal et al. [8], allowing the creation of "virtual twins" for surgical planning in transgender healthcare, an area that Cuccolo et al. [3] have identified as technologically underserved.

3   Methodology

3.1   Data Acquisition and Preparation

Volumes from the public NSCLC-Radiomics collection (v4) of the Cancer Imaging Archive (TCIA) were used [9,10]. The original cohort consists of 422 patients with Non-Small Cell Lung Cancer (NSCLC), featuring CT scans with a slice thickness ranging from 3.0 to 5.0 mm and an in-plane resolution of approximately 0.97×0.97 mm^2. From this population, 262 volumes were selected according to the following criteria:

1. **Class Balancing:** An equal set of 131 male and 131 female patients was formed to mitigate gender bias in the generative process.
2. **Preprocessing:** Conversion from DICOM to NIfTI format was performed to preserve spatial metadata and facilitate volumetric handling.
3. **2D Sampling Strategy:** To optimize computational load while ensuring anatomical relevance, 12 to 15 axial slices were extracted per patient from the central third (30% to 70%) of the total volume. This region consistently captures the pectoral muscle and breast tissue distribution necessary for gender translation. Slices were rescaled to a fixed resolution of 128×128 pixels.
4. **Normalization:** Radiometric truncation was applied in the range $[-1000, 1000]$ HU to focus on soft tissue and bone densities, followed by linear normalization to $[-1, 1]$ to facilitate network convergence (Fig. 1).

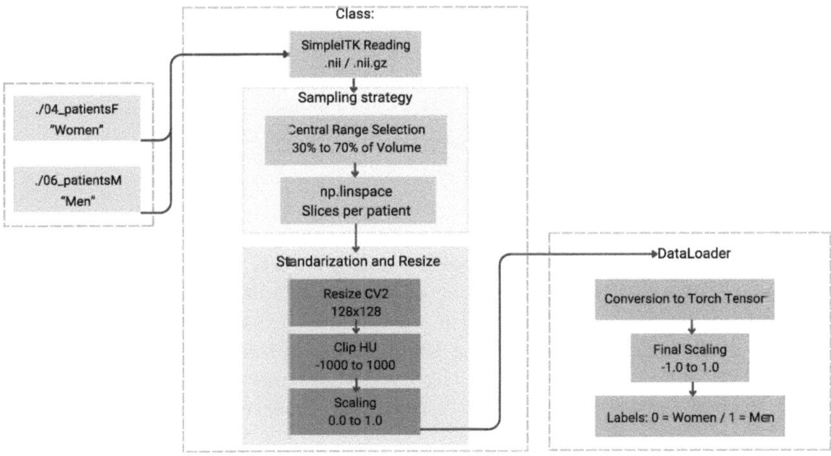

Fig. 1. EnhancedAnatomyDataset preprocessing workflow. Steps include: (1) volume loading, (2) 30%–70% central sampling, (3) 128×128 rescaling, and (4) intensity normalization. Output data is gender-labeled for discriminator training.

3.2   Domain Translation Using cVAE

The Conditional Variational Autoencoder (cVAE) model was implemented to learn a compact representation of thoracic anatomy in a latent space of dimension $z = 128$. The main objective is to decouple the intrinsic anatomical variance of the patient from gender information, enabling the synthesis of alternative versions by manipulating the conditioning variable c in the decoder.

Architecture and Configuration:

- **Encoder and Decoder:** The network consists of a compression stage with four convolutional layers (filters from 64 to 512) using *Instance Normalization* to stabilize learning against contrast variations in CT scans. The decoder performs the inverse process, projecting the latent vector into a feature volume of $512 \times 8 \times 8$. Through transposed convolutional layers and a final Tanh activation, the image is reconstructed while ensuring that output values remain within the normalized Hounsfield Unit (HU) range.
- **Optimization Strategy:** The model was trained for 150 epochs using the AdamW optimizer ($lr = 2 \times 10^{-4}$ and *weight decay* $= 1 \times 10^{-5}$), whose decoupled weight regularization helps mitigate overfitting in small medical datasets. A *Cosine Annealing* scheduler was applied to smoothly decrease the learning rate.
- **Loss Function:** The multi-objective function minimized was

$$\mathcal{L}_{\text{total}} = \mathcal{L}_{\text{MSE}} + \beta \cdot \mathcal{L}_{\text{KLD}}$$

where $\mathcal{L}_{\text{MSE}}$ ensures fidelity of anatomical details (such as rib cage and lungs), while $\mathcal{L}_{\text{KLD}}$ acts as a regularizer approximating the latent distribution to a unit Gaussian. A weighting factor $\beta = 0.1$ was applied to prevent latent space collapse and preserve visual sharpness (Fig. 2).

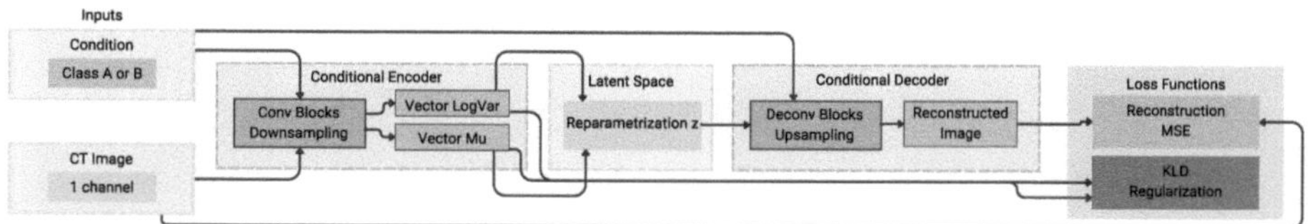

Fig. 2. Conditional generation pipeline using cVAE. The proposed architecture enables the synthesis of CT images controlled by a conditioning variable (class A or B). Unlike a conventional VAE, both the encoding and decoding processes are conditioned on class information, facilitating the learning of latent representations specific to each domain. The figure illustrates the transition from the single-channel input to the reconstructed image under latent regularization constraints imposed by the KLD loss.

3.3   Robust Domain Translation Using CycleGAN

To address the translation of sex-related features without requiring paired identical images, a CycleGAN architecture was implemented. This model enables
learning the mapping between the female domain (X) and the male domain
(Y), prioritizing the preservation of the patient's anatomical integrity during
radiological style transfer.

Generator and Discriminator Architecture: An *Encoder-Decoder* generator with skip connections based on the U-Net architecture was used. The encoder
employs four convolutional layers with instance normalization, while the decoder
uses transposed convolutions to recover the original resolution of 128×128 pixels, mitigating the loss of spatial details. On the other hand, the patch-based
discriminator (*PatchGAN*) evaluates the local authenticity of the image, favor-
ing the reconstruction of realistic tissue densities and fine textures.

Loss Functions and Training: Optimization was based on a multi-objective
function balancing visual realism with physical accuracy:

- **Cycle-consistency ($\lambda = 10$):** Ensures that the translated and reverted volume matches the original, preserving critical structures such as the rib cage.
- **Identity ($\lambda = 5$):** Preserves contrast and color mapping when the input
  already belongs to the target domain.
- **Perceptual VGG ($\lambda = 0.1$):** Uses a pre-trained VGG-16 network to refine
  the sharpness of organ boundaries.

The model was trained for 300 epochs with a batch size of 8 using the Adam
optimizer ($lr = 2 \times 10^{-4}$), applying mixed precision (*autocast*) to optimize GPU
memory usage (Fig. 3).

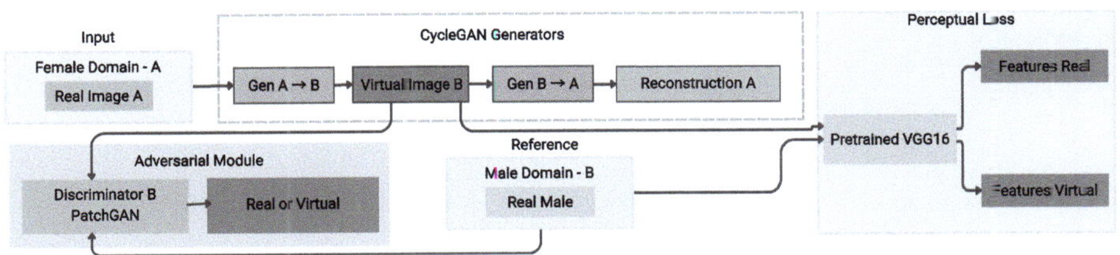

Fig. 3. Training workflow and loss functions of the generative network. The
pipeline integrates three critical components: (1) U-Net based generators for gender
domain transfer, (2) a PatchGAN discriminator that evaluates the local authenticity
of the virtual image against the real reference, and (3) a perceptual VGG16 block.
The latter ensures that the patient's anatomical structure is preserved by comparing
feature maps of the real and virtual images, minimizing semantic information loss
during domain translation.

3.4 Inference and Validation Protocol

After training, volumes were synthesized through sequential axial inference, rescaling each slice to the Hounsfield Unit (HU) domain while preserving the original spatial metadata. Model integrity was quantified at three levels: (1) **Image Quality**, using SSIM to assess structural similarity and PSNR to evaluate fidelity against noise; (2) **Radiometric Fidelity**, analyzing HU histograms to verify the persistence of bone densities ($\approx$825 HU); and (3) **Morphometric Validation**, manually measuring pectoral thickness in *3D Slicer* to validate the redistribution of breast tissue in gender-affirming surgery planning.

4 Results and Discussion

4.1 Image Quality Metrics

Structural fidelity was evaluated using SSIM and PSNR (Table 1). CycleGAN consistently outperformed cVAE, achieving a higher SSIM (0.889) that confirms optimal preservation of anatomical edges, essential for surgical planning. Conversely, cVAE (SSIM=0.792) exhibits a *blurring* effect derived from KL divergence, degrading the sharpness of the thoracic cage (Fig. 4).

An independent two-tailed t-test ($N = 80$) yielded a t-statistic of 11.1769 and a p-value of 5×10^{-18} ($p < 0.001$), confirming that the performance gap is statistically significant. This suggests that cycle-consistency and adversarial losses are more effective at preserving high-frequency anatomical details and bone densities than the variational latent space, which is prone to smoothing effects.

Table 1. Comparison of image quality metrics. **Bold** values indicate the best performance for each metric. Arrows ($\uparrow, \downarrow$) denote that higher or lower values are preferred, respectively.

Model	SSIM ($\uparrow$)	PSNR ($\uparrow$)	MSE ($\downarrow$)
cVAE	0.7921 $\pm$ 0.0007	24.86 $\pm$ 0.03	0.0033 $\pm$ 0.0000
CycleGAN	**0.8898 $\pm$ 0.0042**	**29.10 $\pm$ 0.13**	**0.0012 $\pm$ 0.0001**

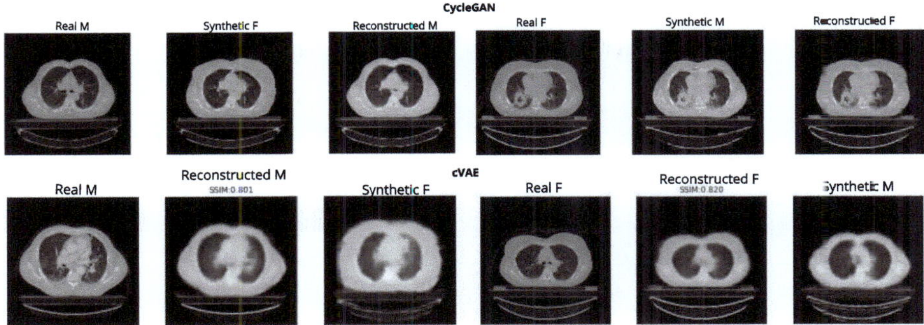

Fig. 4. 2D samples: CycleGAN vs. cVAE. First row: CycleGAN; second row: cVAE. Left columns: Male→Female translation ($M \rightarrow F$) and cycle reconstruction. Right columns: Female→Male ($F \rightarrow M$) and reconstruction. CycleGAN preserves bone edges and lung texture, while cVAE exhibits blurring and loss of fine anatomical details.

4.2   Convergence and Stability Analysis

The evolution of the loss functions during training served as an indicator of model stability and convergence. Both CycleGAN and cVAE reached stable convergence states, with losses progressively decreasing and plateauing after a sufficient number of epochs.

For CycleGAN, the adversarial and cycle-consistency losses exhibited smooth oscillations that gradually stabilized around epoch 200, reflecting the balance between generator and discriminator. This behavior suggests stable adversarial training while preserving anatomical consistency across domains. The inclusion of the perceptual VGG loss further supported the preservation of fine structural details, particularly in rib cage boundaries.

In contrast, the cVAE demonstrated faster convergence of the reconstruction loss, reaching stability around epoch 100. However, the KL divergence term introduced fluctuations associated with a smoothing effect in the synthesized volumes. Although the model achieved numerical convergence, the latent regularization imposed by the KLD loss limited its ability to preserve high-frequency anatomical details.

4.3   Radiometric Fidelity

Radiometric fidelity ensures that the synthesized densities correspond to real physical values in Hounsfield Units (HU). Table 2 details this analysis for the critical cases of transmasculine translation ($F \rightarrow M$) and transfeminine translation ($M \rightarrow F$) (Fig. 5).

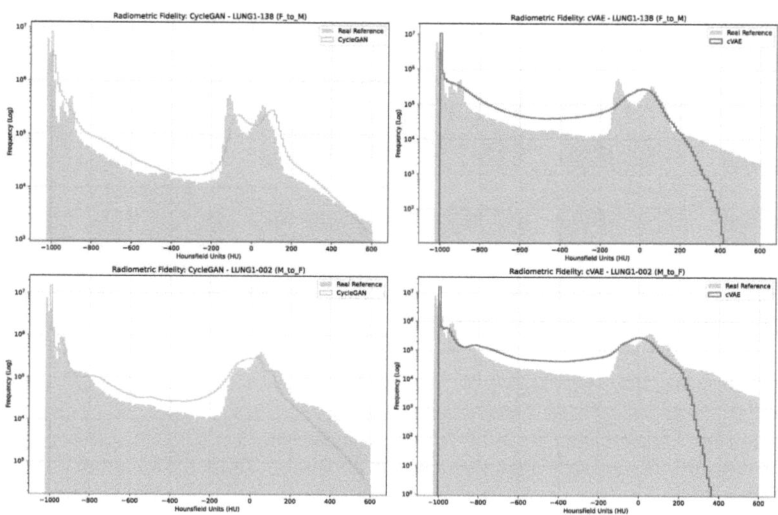

Fig. 5. Radiometric density distribution (HU). Left: CycleGAN (cyan) closely matches the real volume distribution (gray). Right: cVAE (magenta) fails to capture densities above 400 HU.

Table 2. HU density distribution and radiometric fidelity. **Bold** values indicate best radiometric preservation.

Model / Patient	Min	Max (↑)	Mean	Std. Dev.
LUNG1-002 (Real M)	−1024	3071	−755.27	431.23
cVAE (Synth. F)	−1000	357	−762.37	381.83
CycleGAN (Synth. F)	**−1000**	**778**	**−753.29**	**399.75**
LUNG1-138 (Real F)	−1024	3071	−731.39	431.90
cVAE (Synth. M)	−1000	413	−716.40	399.37
CycleGAN (Synth. M)	**−1000**	**825**	**−711.91**	**427.78**

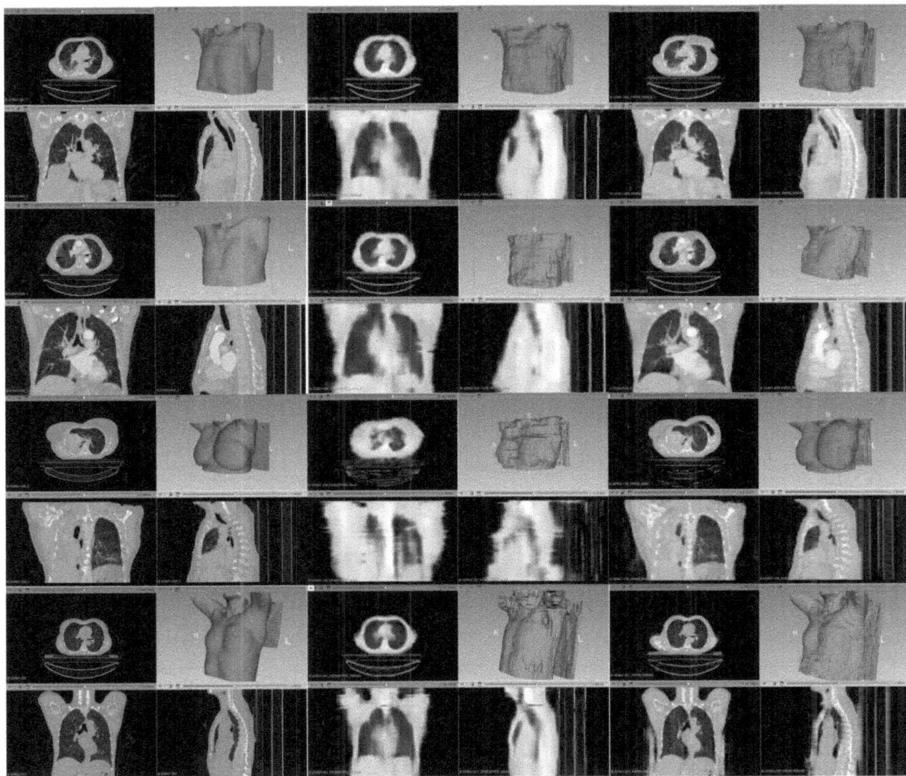

Fig. 6. 3D volumetric reconstruction comparison. Rows 1–2: $M \rightarrow F$; Rows 3–4: $F \rightarrow M$. Col 1: Real. Col 2: cVAE (edge smoothing, bone loss). Col 3: CycleGAN (radiometric fidelity, rib morphology).

The results confirm the superiority of CycleGAN in preserving the original radiometric signature. While cVAE exhibits a reduced standard deviation due to texture smoothing (*blurring*), CycleGAN maintains variability ($\sigma \approx 427$) very close to the real case ($\sigma \approx 431$). Furthermore, CycleGAN's ability to recover densities up to 825 HU, compared to 413 HU with cVAE, is decisive for surgical planning, ensuring that high-density bone structures are not omitted in the 3D reconstruction (Fig. 6).

4.4   Morphometric Validation

The results confirm that CycleGAN provides greater anatomical fidelity by synthesizing volumes aligned with the averages of the target population. As shown in Table 3, the adversarial model was more consistent in the redistribution of pectoral tissue, particularly in transfeminine translation, where cVAE exhibited a significantly higher standard deviation (15.60 mm vs 6.63 mm for CycleGAN).

This volumetric precision is fundamental for successful segmentation and surgical planning in *3D Slicer* (Fig. 7)

Table 3. Morphometric validation comparison (mm). **Bold** values represent the synthesis closest to the original anatomical reference.

Scenario	Original (Real)	CycleGAN	cVAE
Transmasculine ($F \rightarrow M$)	38.32 ± 19.83	**28.45 ± 16.29**	33.15 ± 17.50
Transfeminine ($M \rightarrow F$)	15.11 ± 3.19	**30.45 ± 6.63**	36.94 ± 15.60

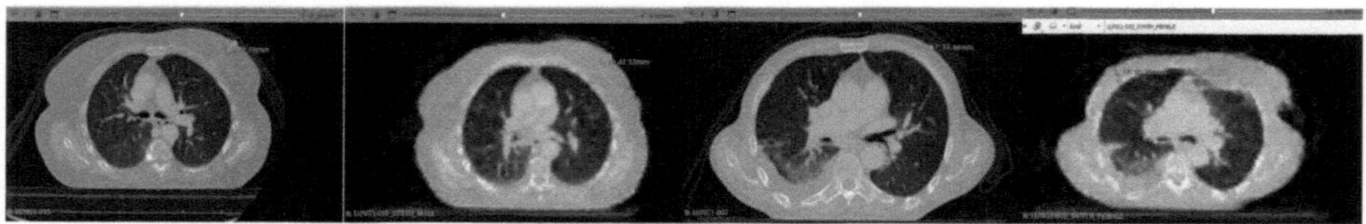

Fig. 7. Morphometric validation in 3D Slicer. First pair ($F \rightarrow M$): reduction of pectoral tissue (47.19 to 41.37 mm). Second pair ($M \rightarrow F$): increase of soft tissue (11.46 to 20.92 mm). Red lines delimit the measurement from the skin to the muscular fascia.

5   Conclusions and Future Work

This study validates the use of adversarial learning for thoracic CT synthesis in transgender healthcare. The results demonstrate that CycleGAN preserves the radiometric coherence required for surgical planning, maintaining essential bone densities (825 HU) that the cVAE model fails to reconstruct. Morphometric validation confirms that the redistribution of pectoral tissue achieves sufficient diagnostic precision for multiplanar navigation in *3D Slicer*.

As future work, three main areas of opportunity are identified: addressing challenges in breast morphology translation, improving structural quality affected by sub-sampling, and enhancing volumetric coherence to reduce discontinuities across sagittal and coronal planes.

Data Availibility Statement. The source code for the architectures and evaluation pipeline is available from the corresponding author upon reasonable request. The CT volumes are part of the public *NSCLC-Radiomics* collection available via TCIA. [9,10].

References

1. INEGI: Encuesta Nacional sobre Diversidad Sexual y de Género (ENDISEG) (2021). https://www.inegi.org.mx/contenidos/saladeprensa/boletines/2022/endiseg/Resul_Endiseg21.pdf, último acceso 15 Nov 2025
2. Calderon, T., et al.: Mastectomy reconstruction techniques for gender diverse breast cancer and high risk patients: a case series and literature overview. J. Clin. Med. **15**(2), 441 (2024). https://doi.org/10.3390/jcm15020441
3. Cuccolo, N.G., et al.: Mastectomy in transgender and cisgender patients: a comparative analysis of epidemiology and postoperative outcomes. Plast. Reconstr. Surg. **144**(3), 531–541 (2019). https://doi.org/10.1097/GOX.0000000000002316
4. Goodfellow, I., et al.: Generative adversarial networks. In: Proceedings of the Advances in Neural Information Processing Systems (NeurIPS), pp. 2672–2680 (2014).https://doi.org/10.48550/arXiv.1406.2661
5. Zhu, J.Y., Park, T., Isola, P., Efros, A.A.: Unpaired image-to-image translation using cycle-consistent adversarial networks. In: Proceedings of the IEEE International Conference on Computer Vision (ICCV), pp. 2242–2251 (2017).https://doi.org/10.1109/ICCV.2017.244
6. Wolterink, J.M., et al.: Deep MR to CT synthesis using unpaired data. In: Tsaftaris, S.A., Gooya, A., Frangi, A.F., Prince, J.L. (eds.) SASHIMI 2017. LNCS, vol. 10557, pp. 14–23. Springer, Cham (2017). https://doi.org/10.1007/978-3-319-68127-6_2
7. Han, X.: MR-based synthetic CT generation using a deep convolutional neural network method. Med. Phys. **44**(4), 1408–1419 (2017). https://doi.org/10.1002/mp.12155
8. Larrazabal, A.J., Nieto, N., Peterson, V., Ferrante, E.: Gender imbalance in medical imaging datasets produces biased classifiers for computer-aided diagnosis. Proc. Nat. Acad. Sci. (PNAS) **117**(23), 12592–12594 (2020). https://doi.org/10.1073/pnas.1919012117
9. Clark, K., et al.: The Cancer Imaging Archive (TCIA): maintaining and operating a public information repository. J. Digit. Imaging **26**(6), 1045–1057 (2013). https://doi.org/10.1007/s10278-013-9622-7
10. Aerts, H.J.W.L., et al.: Data from NSCLC-Radiomics (v4) [Data set]. Cancer Imaging Archive (2015). https://doi.org/10.7937/K9/TCIA.2015.PF0M9REI
11. Guo, Y., et al.: Deep learning for CT synthesis in radiotherapy. J. Pers. Med. **14**(3), 254 (2024). https://www.doi.org/2306-5354/12/12/1297
12. Li, Y., Xu, S., Lu, Y., Qi, Z.: CT synthesis from MRI with an improved multi-scale learning network. Fronti. Phys. **11**, 1088899 (2023). https://doi.org/10.3389/fphy.2023.1088899
13. Li, Y., Xu, S., Qi, Z.: CT synthesis from MRI using generative adversarial network with frequency-aware discriminator. J. Electr. Eng. Technol. **19**, 763–771 (2024). https://doi.org/10.1007/s42835-023-01602-z
14. Spadea, M.F., Maspero, M , Zaffino, P., Seco, J.: Deep learning-based synthetic-CT generation in radiotherapy and PET: a review. arXiv preprint arXiv:2102.02734 (2021). https://arxiv.org/abs/2102.02734. Accessed 29 Jan 2026

Detection of Dangerous Wildlife in a Dynamic Environment Using Deep Learning

David Cruz-Villavicencio(✉)🆔 and Jesús Alberto Martínez-Castro🆔

Centro de Investigación en Computación, Instituto Politécnico Nacional,
Mexico City, Mexico
{dcruzv2024,macj}@cic.ipn.mx
https://www.cic.ipn.mx/

Abstract. Detection algorithms must be capable of automatic recognition of any object, regardless of its size in relation to the image. This work focuses on studying a proposal of detection using mathematical morphology, Laplacian filter and convolutional neural networks (CNN) to detect potentially dangerous animals. Our results were compared to those of YOLO and Faster RCNN. Considering that scorpion and spider stings represent a National health problem in Mexico, we focused our attention on searching this kind of dangerous fauna with the aid of the cameras provided by mobile gadgets. The dataset used for training and validation was carefully curated to include diverse lighting conditions, backgrounds, and object scales, ensuring robust generalization across real-world scenarios. The mobile application has been developed and deployed, and is currently available for use in rural areas, enabling communities to identify potentially dangerous fauna in real time. To assess model performance, several evaluation metrics were used, including precision-recall curves, F1 score, mean average precision (mAP), and ROC curves.

Keywords: Object detection · Deep learning · Dangerous fauna detection · Computer vision · Mobile applications

1 Justification

In Mexico, more than 250,000 cases of scorpion stings are reported each year, making it one of the countries with the highest incidence; most accidents occur in rural areas, at home, and at night [4]. Among the main causes of infant mortality in the state of Guerrero, Mexico are scorpion stings, children being the most vulnerable to the venom compared to other ages. With the current development of digital image processing and advances in automatic tracking of moving objects [1], developing a computer application that alerts users of nearby dangerous animals becomes evident.

This work focuses on the detection of dangerous fauna such as scorpions and spiders as a preventive measure [15]. The system must be low-cost and capable of running on equipment with limited resources, since in states such as Nayarit, San Luis Potosí, and Zacatecas—which also have high scorpion sting incidence—over 40% of the population lacks social security and poverty rates exceed 50% [5].

V. G. Cruz-Sánchez et al. (Eds.): MCPR 2026, LNCS 16623, pp. 152–161, 2026.
https://doi.org/10.1007/978-3-032-28393-1_14

2   Similar Works

There are several works on insect and arachnid detection. One [10] detects bees using morphological operators in a controlled, fixed-camera environment without neural networks. Another [2] detects insects with YOLOv3 [13] and tracking algorithms using a Jetson Nano GPU and a fixed webcam, achieving high accuracy on a fully custom dataset. A recent approach [16] uses YOLO combined with YOLito to study mosquito swarm collective flight in natural environments.

For scorpions, a work from Argentina [7] applies YOLOv4 for detection and MobileNet for species classification, developing a mobile application; however, it only evaluates large scorpions relative to the image and does not specify training image content. Giambelluca et al. [6] proposed an automatic system combining UV fluorescence detection and Haar cascade classifiers with VGG-16-based transfer learning on 132 images, achieving 89% recall for distinguishing dangerous (*Tityus*) from harmless (*Bothriurus*) scorpions, and 76% accuracy for species-level differentiation. For spiders, Luong et al. [12] developed SpiderID APP using YOLOv7 trained on 24,000 images across 120 genera, reaching an F1-score of 0.885 and demonstrating performance comparable to citizen science tools, while noting that species-level identification still requires complementary methods such as DNA barcoding.

3   Proposed Algorithm

The proposed algorithm is inspired by Edge Boxes [18], which uses Structured Edge Detection (SED) and Canny [3] to produce an edge map with magnitude and orientation, distinguishing internal edges (within an object) from external edges (at boundaries). In our method, we use morphological image analysis to extract edges, apply a Laplacian filter to enhance edge definition, and determine bounding boxes via a Depth-First Search (DFS) algorithm that yields better closed contours (See Algorithm 1).

Insects typically form a closed connected component—a set of pixels connected by adjacency corresponding to the object's silhouette—that contrasts with the background. We define a binary image as:

$$I : \Omega \subset \mathbb{Z}^2 \to \{0,1\}, \tag{1}$$

where Ω is the set of all pixel positions and $I(x,y) = 1$ if the pixel belongs to an edge, 0 otherwise. The edge set is $B = \{(x,y) \in \Omega \mid I(x,y) = 1\}$. Connectivity is determined via an 8-connected neighborhood:

$$\mathcal{N}_8(p) = \{q \in \Omega \mid \|p - q\|_\infty = 1\}, \quad \|(a,b)\|_\infty = \max(|a|, |b|). \tag{2}$$

3.1   Image Represented as a Graph

An image is represented as a graph $G = (V, E)$, where vertices correspond to edge pixels ($V = B$) and two vertices $p, q \in V$ are connected by an edge $(p, q) \in E$ if $q \in \mathcal{N}_8(p)$ and $I(q) = 1$. Starting from an initial pixel $p_0 \in B$, the contour is:

$$C(p_0) = \text{DFS}(p_0), \tag{3}$$

Algorithm 1: Region of Interest Detection Algorithm

Input: Image I (RGB or grayscale)
Output: Region proposals sent to CNN EfficientNet classifier

   // Preprocessing
1   Convert I to grayscale $\rightarrow I_g$
2   Equalize histogram of $I_g \rightarrow I_{prep}$

   // Edge extraction
3   $M_{lap}, M_{morph} \leftarrow$ Apply Laplacian filter and morphological operators on I_{prep}
4   $M_{edges} \leftarrow M_{lap}$ **OR** M_{morph} // Edge map fusion

   // Cleaning
5   $B \leftarrow$ Morphological opening, and afterward closing(M_{edges})

   // Connected component detection
6   $C \leftarrow$ DFS to obtain connected components of B
7   $\mathcal{R} \leftarrow$ Compute bounding box for each $C_i \in C$

   // Proposal filtering
8   $\mathcal{P} \leftarrow \emptyset$
9   **foreach** $R_i \in \mathcal{R}$ **do**
10   **if** R_i *meets area criteria* **then**
11        $\mathcal{P} \leftarrow \mathcal{P} \cup \{R_i\}$ // Keep proposal
12   **else**
13   Discard R_i // Noise or component too small
14   **end**
15   **end**

   // Post-processing
16   $\mathcal{P} \leftarrow$ Non-maximum suppression$(\mathcal{P})$ // Remove overlapping boxes
17   Send $\mathcal{P}$ to CNN EfficientNet classifier

---

collecting all pixels connected to p_0. The full set of contours is:

$$\mathcal{C} = \{C(p) \mid p \in B \text{ and } p \text{ has not been visited}\}, \tag{4}$$

with a new DFS traversal started for each unvisited edge pixel. After obtaining all contours, bounding boxes are computed and classified by EfficientNet [17]. Proposals with area smaller than 30 pixels are discarded, as a mobile camera cannot clearly resolve objects at that resolution.

The stages of the proposed method are illustrated in Fig. 1.

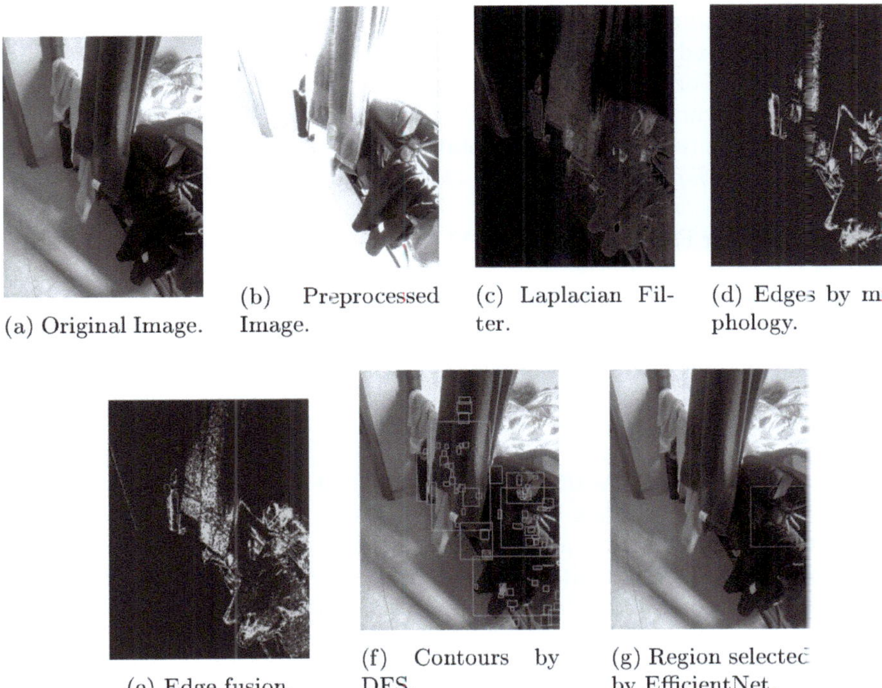

(a) Original Image.

(b) Preprocessed Image.

(c) Laplacian Filter.

(d) Edges by morphology.

(e) Edge fusion.

(f) Contours by DFS.

(g) Region selected by EfficientNet.

Fig. 1. Steps of the edge detection process on a sample image.

4 Dataset (Scorpions and Spiders)

To ensure cross-validation, two different datasets were used: one for the proposed algorithm and another for Faster R-CNN and YOLOv11, as illustrated in Fig. 2. The dataset for the proposed algorithm consists of foreground images of arachnids from public internet sources.

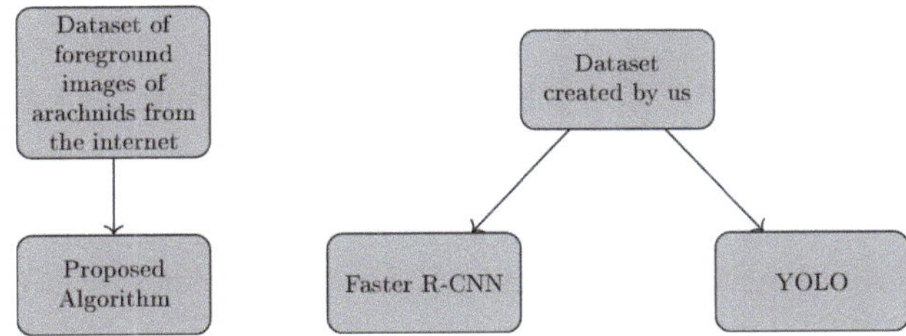

Fig. 2. Diagram of datasets used by the algorithms.

To recognize different types of arachnids we used the EfficientNet architecture, which achieved better performance than AlexNet [11] and is a more modern architecture. For training, 1,500 images per class (scorpions, spiders, background) from iNaturalist were used, totaling 4,500 images. The dataset was balanced and augmented with random rotations (0–360°) and brightness/contrast adjustments (±10%). It was split into 4,000 training / 300 validation / 200 test images.

The dataset for Faster R-CNN and YOLOv11 was fully created for this work[1] and consists of spider and scorpion photographs taken in varied indoor and outdoor locations (Fig. 3). It includes 1,000 training images from one indoor environment and 200 test images from a different indoor environment, enabling evaluation of the models' ability to generalize to unseen scenarios.

5   Experiments

In Mexico, regulation NOM-059-SEMARNAT-2010 protects several vulnerable species of spiders, tarantulas, and scorpions, making capture for research purposes without SEMARNAT authorization illegal. Therefore, plastic arachnid models were used throughout. Although toys, their morphology—silhouette, proportions, and coloration—faithfully represents real specimens, allowing controlled dataset creation with well-defined lighting, size, and background conditions, while reducing costs, ethical concerns, and risks.

Experiments were conducted under varied conditions: daytime and nighttime, partial occlusion, surfaces with different colors and textures, complex backgrounds without guaranteed contrast, and varying illumination. Two biologically relevant traits were considered: the nocturnal behavior of both spiders and scorpions, and the UV fluorescence of scorpions (Fig. 3). The dataset was supplemented with iNaturalist images under Creative Commons licenses, including nighttime and UV-light captures.

A detection is considered positive when the model confidence exceeds 0.5[2]. By varying this threshold, precision-recall, F1-score, and ROC curves are constructed for each model. In object detection, evaluation must jointly account for class prediction and bounding box localization accuracy.

6   Results

Bounding Box Generation. The selective search algorithm [9] produces a very large number of candidate regions, a known bottleneck [8,14]. The Region Proposal Network (RPN) [14] was introduced to overcome this by generating bounding boxes directly from the image. Table 1 and Figs. 4–5 compare the number of proposals generated over 246 test images (from the test set only). Our algorithm produces on average 66.88 boxes per image versus 4,553 for Selective Search—a 68× reduction—substantially lowering the computational cost of the classification stage, see Fig. 4 and 5 for histograms.

---

[1] Available at: https://universe.roboflow.com/spider-man-xhhtx/spoder-man.

[2] This threshold is a standard criterion enabling fair comparison with prior studies.

(a) Indoor: spider on a table, partially occluded by a suitcase, good lighting.

(b) Indoor: spider under low-light conditions with strong shadows.

(c) Scorpion under UV light, showing fluorescence and high background contrast.

Fig. 3. Representative experimental conditions: partial occlusion with good lighting (a), low illumination (b), and UV fluorescence (c).

Table 1. Average, minimum, and maximum number of bounding boxes generated per image.

Algorithm	Average	Minimum	Maximum
Proposed Algorithm	66.88	7	233
Selective Search	4553	1773	8220

Detection Performance. EfficientNet was trained for 14 epochs using transfer learning. YOLOv11 required 35 epochs (from 50, with early stopping at patience 6). Faster R-CNN also used pre-trained weights.

Confusion matrices for all models are shown in Table 2. Quantitative comparisons at a fixed threshold of 0.5 are in Table 3, and mAP values in Table 4.

Among the evaluated models, YOLOv11 nano achieved the best overall performance (mAP@0.5 = 0.933, mAP@0.5:0.95 = 0.699) while maintaining realtime inference on CPU (approx. 1s/image). Faster R-CNN attained competitive accuracy but at significantly higher computational cost. The proposed algorithm exhibits low precision (Precision = 0.0967) and moderate recall (0.545) indicating a high false-positive rate and poor bounding box localization (average IoU = 0.064). These differences are reflected in the Precision–Recall curves in Fig. 6, where YOLOv11 and Faster R-CNN maintain a more stable trade-off between precision and recall, whereas the proposed method exhibits a sharp precision decline. Similarly, the ROC curves in Fig. 7 highlight the superior discriminative capability of YOLOv11 and Faster R-CNN compared with the proposed algorithm.

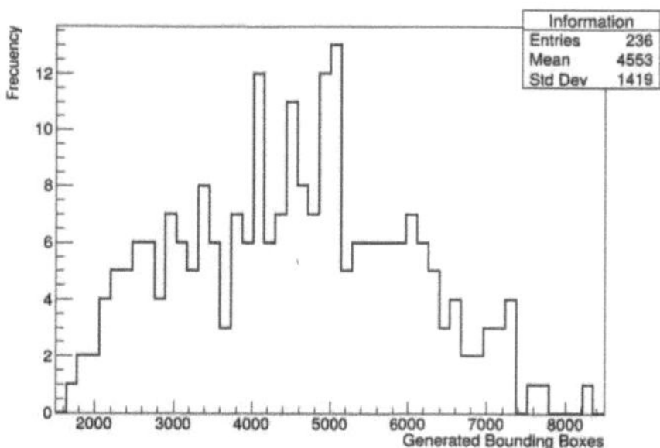

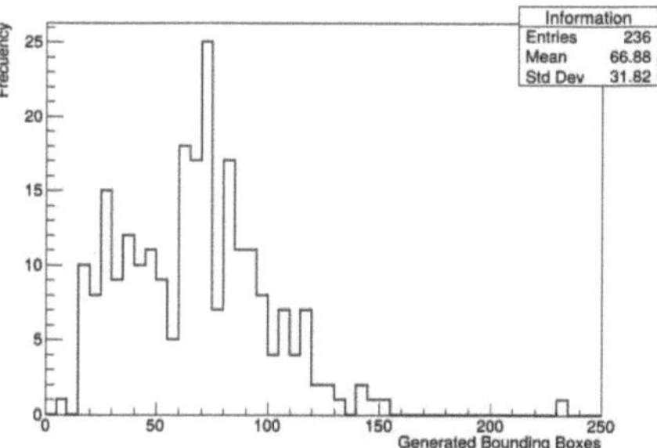

Fig. 4. Bounding boxes generated by Selective Search for 236 test images.

Fig. 5. Bounding boxes generated by our algorithm; note the reduction vs. Selective Search.

Table 2. Confusion matrices for the three evaluated models.

Proposed Algorithm

	Predicted	
Actual	Scorp.	Spider
Scorpion	547	6
Spider	31	388

YOLOv11

	Predicted	
Actual	Scorp.	Spider
Scorpion	12	3
Spider	-	67

Faster R-CNN

	Predicted	
Actual	Scorp.	Spider
Scorpion	13	-
Spider	4	72

Table 3. Comparison of detection model metrics at confidence threshold 0.5.

Model	Precision	Recall	AP	F1
Proposed Algorithm	0.0967	0.5454	0.1051	0.163
Faster R-CNN	0.88	0.85	0.869	0.8647
YOLOv11	0.9285	0.8242	0.9063	0.8762

Table 4. Comparison of detection model performance in terms of mAP.

Model	mAP@0.5	mAP@0.5:0.95
Proposed Algorithm	0.1201	0.1201
Faster R-CNN	0.9165	0.5914
YOLOv11	0.933	0.699

UV-Illuminated Scorpion Detection. When restricted to UV-illuminated scorpion images, the proposed method achieves precision 0.652, recall 0.967, and AP 0.900 (Table 5, Fig. 8). These results demonstrate that the algorithm benefits significantly from high-contrast conditions and that its primary limitations are associated with low-contrast natural environments rather than with the underlying detection approach itself.

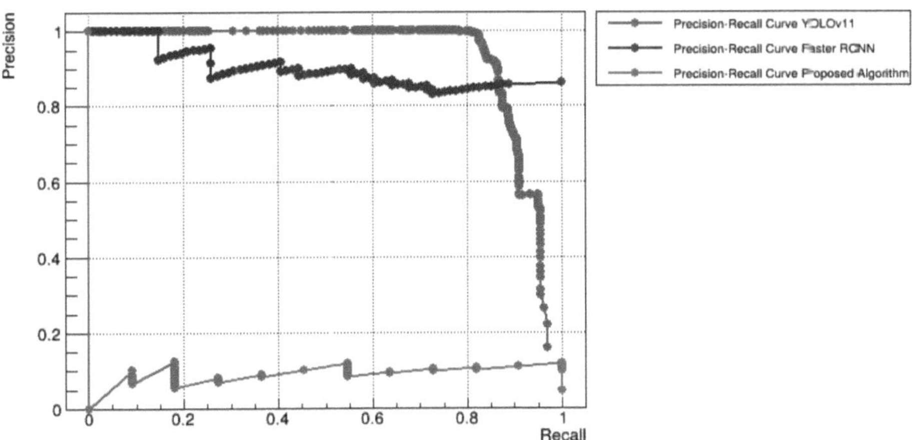

Fig. 6. Precision-Recall curves for YOLO, Faster R-CNN, and the proposed algorithm.

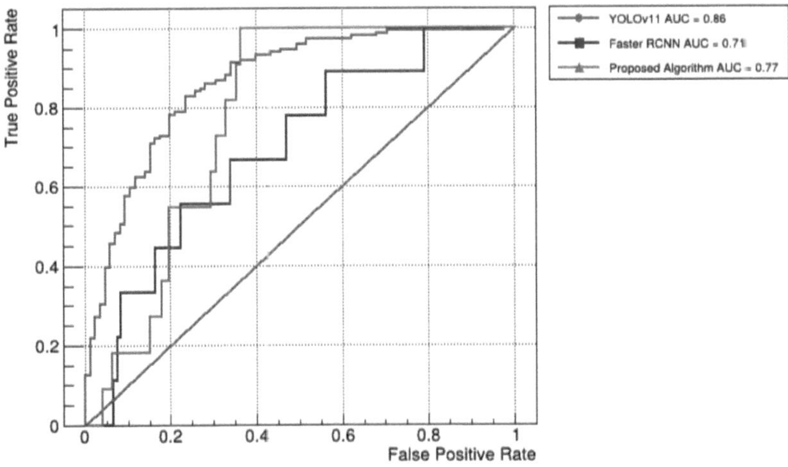

Fig. 7. ROC curves for YOLO, Faster R-CNN, and the proposed algorithm.

Table 5. Proposed algorithm metrics using only UV-illuminated scorpion images (threshold 0.5).

Model	Precision	Recall	AP	F1
Proposed Algorithm	0.6522	0.9666	0.9001	0.7936

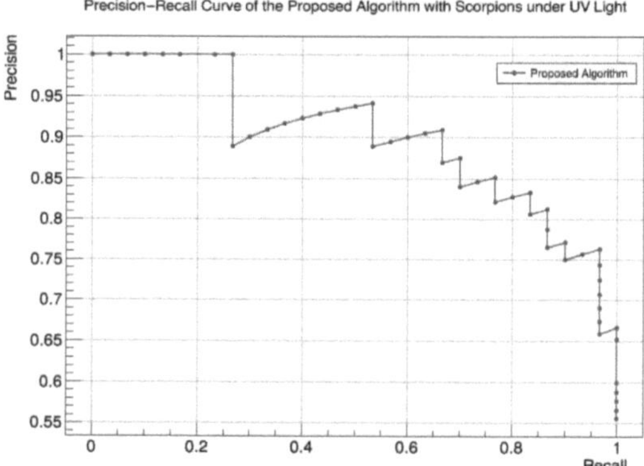

Fig. 8. Precision-Recall curve of the proposed algorithm on UV-illuminated scorpions only.

7   Conclusions

Methods such as Selective Search provide accurate region proposals but are too computationally expensive for real-time use. Approaches such as Faster R-CNN with RPN and YOLO significantly improve inference speed, though they may struggle to detect very small objects.

The proposed algorithm leverages edge information and a DFS strategy to generate region proposals, achieving a 68× reduction in candidate regions compared to Selective Search. Its main limitation is inaccurate bounding box localization in low-contrast environments; however, in high-contrast conditions such as UV-illuminated scorpions, performance improves substantially (AP = 0.900).

YOLOv11 achieves the best accuracy-speed trade-off. ROC analysis shows YOLOv11 attains the highest AUC (0.86), followed by the proposed method (0.77) and Faster R-CNN (0.71); all models perform well above random chance. Regarding runtime on CPU, YOLOv11 is fastest, the proposed approach is intermediate, and Faster R-CNN is slowest.

A mobile application integrating YOLOv11, Faster R-CNN, and the proposed algorithm was developed in Unity, which executes models in ONNX format—files that describe the network architecture, enabling inference similar to PyTorch. The application captures video from any connected camera and allows the user to select the video source and detection model. Upon detecting an arachnid, it displays a bounding box. Source code is available at https://github.com/ibtr54/Deteccion-aracnidos.

Acknowledgment. This study was funded by Instituto Politécnico Nacional and Secretaría de Ciencia, Humanidades, Tecnología e Innovación.

Disclosure of Interests. The authors have no competing interests to declare that are relevant to the content of this article.

References

1. Amit, Y., Felzenszwalb, P., Girshick, R.: Object detection. In: Proceedings of the Computer vision: A reference guide, pp. 875–883. Springer (2021)
2. Bjerge, K., Mann, H.M., Høye, T.T.: Real-time insect tracking and monitoring with computer vision and deep learning. Remote Sens. Ecol. Conserv. 8(3), 315–327 (2022)
3. Canny, J.: A computational approach to edge detection. IEEE Trans. Pattern Anal. Mach. Intell. 6, 679–698 (2009)
4. Chávez-Haro, A.L., Ortiz, E.: Scorpionism and dangerous species of Mexico. Scorpion venoms, pp. 201–213 (2015)
5. Consejo Nacional de Evaluación de la Política de Desarrollo Social (CONEVAL): Medición de la pobreza 2022 (2023). https://www.coneval.org.mx/Medicion/MP/Paginas/Pobreza_2022.aspx. Accessed 03 Apr 2026
6. Giambelluca, F.L., Cappelletti, M.A., Osio, J.R., Giambelluca, L.A.: Novel automatic scorpion-detection and-recognition system based on machine-learning techniques. Mach. Learn. Sci. Technol. 2(2), 025018 (2021)
7. Giambelluca, F.L., Cappelletti, M.A., Osio, J., Giambelluca, L.A.: Scorpion detection and classification systems based on computer vision and deep learning for health security purposes. arXiv preprint arXiv:2105.15041 (2021)
8. Girshick, R.: Fast R-CNN. In: Proceedings of the IEEE International Conference on Computer Vision (ICCV), pp. 1440–1448 (2015)
9. Girshick, R., Donahue, J., Darrell, T., Malik, J.: Rich feature hierarchies for accurate object detection. In: Proceedings of the IEEE Conference on Computer Vision and Pattern Recognition (CVPR), pp. 580–587. IEEE (2014)
10. Karahan, M., Inal, M., Yetik, I.S.: Detection of the flying bees using morphological image processing. Int. J. Eng. Res. Dev. 19(6), 100–106 (2023)
11. Krizhevsky, A., Sutskever, I., Hinton, G.: ImageNet classification with deep convolutional neural networks. In: Proceedings of the Advances in Neural Information Processing Systems, vol. 25, pp. 1097–1105 (2012)
12. Luong, C.T., et al.: Spiderid_app: a user-friendly app for spider identification in Taiwan using yolo-based deep learning models. Inventions 8(6), 153 (2023)
13. Redmon, J., Divvala, S., Girshick, R., Farhadi, A.: You only look once: unified, real-time object detection. In: Proceedings of the IEEE Conference on Computer Vision and Pattern Recognition, pp. 779–788 (2016)
14. Ren, S., He, K., Girshick, R., Sun, J.: Faster R-CNN: towards real-time object detection with region proposal networks (2015)
15. Rodríguez Soto, C., Roque Vilchis, L.F., Cadena Vargas, E.G., Gómez Albores, M.A.: Anthropogenic risk to poisonous species in Mexico. Sustainability 15(17), 13214 (2023)
16. Sar-Shalom, E., et al.: Yolito: a generalizable model for automated mosquito detection. bioRxiv (2025)
17. Tan, M., Le, Q.V.: EfficientNet: rethinking model scaling for convolutional neural networks. In: Proceedings of the 36th International Conference on Machine Learning (ICML), vol. 97, pp. 6105–6114 (2019)
18. Zitnick, C.L., Dollár, P.: Edge boxes: locating object proposals from edges. In: Fleet, D., Pajdla, T., Schiele, B., Tuytelaars, T. (eds.) ECCV 2014. LNCS, vol. 8693, pp. 391–405. Springer, Cham (2014). https://doi.org/10.1007/978-3-319-10602-1_26

Spatiotemporal Prediction of Wildfires Spread Using Deep Learning

Ángel Itzcoatl Huizar Bretado, Raquel Díaz Hernández[✉],
Kelsey Alejandra Ramírez Gutiérrez, and Leopoldo Altamirano Robles

Instituto Nacional de Astrofísica, Óptica y Electrónica,
Luis Enrique Erro #1, Sta. MaríaTonantzintla, 72840 San Andrés Cholula, Puebla, México
raqueld@inaoep.mx, kramirez@inaoe.mx

Abstract. The increase in wildfires presents a global challenge due to the ecological and socioeconomic damages they cause. Predicting the progression of a wildfire is of paramount importance for formulating effective mitigation and response strategies. The application of satellite imagery, enhanced by advanced deep learning models, functions as a powerful tool toward this purpose.

This article delineates the implementation of four deep learning architectures—MobileNetV2, U-Net, ConvLSTM, and xLSTM—for the purpose of predicting wildfire spread on the subsequent day, utilizing the Next Day Wildfire Spread database. All models were evaluated under standardized experimental conditions to ensure a fair comparison. The performance assessment was conducted using quantitative metrics such as Intersection over Union (IoU), precision, recall, and F1-score.

The results indicate that the U-Net architecture demonstrated the highest overall performance, with an Intersection over Union (IoU) score of 0.6345 and an F1-score of 0.4627. The ConvLSTM model also exhibited competitive performance, attaining an IoU of 0.6049. Although the model incorporating xLSTM temporal modeling exhibited lower average metrics, it achieved superior results for smaller fires, with an IoU of 0.588 and an F1-score of 0.741, indicating enhanced detection capabilities for smaller fires.

Keywords: Deep learning · wildfires spread · remote sensing

1 Introduction

Wildfires are among the natural disasters that frequently occur across various regions of the planet and can exert detrimental effects on ecosystems and socioeconomic activities. A fire may be ignited by natural factors, such as lightning strikes, or by human actions, including campfires or uncontrolled agricultural burning. Nonetheless, certain regions are more susceptible to ignition owing to their climatic and vegetation conditions. These causes result in environmental damage, such as air pollution and ecosystem destruction, and may also lead to socioeconomic issues, particularly when they impact areas surrounding human settlements or cultivated lands.

© The Author(s), under exclusive license to Springer Nature Switzerland AG 2026
V. G. Cruz-Sánchez et al. (Eds.): MCPR 2026, LNCS 16623, pp. 162–171, 2026.
https://doi.org/10.1007/978-3-032-28393-1_15

The incidence of wildfires in regions of North America, particularly between Mexico and the United States, has markedly increased annually. For instance, in the United States during 2023, a total of 56,580 fires were documented, affecting an area of 1,090,000 hectares; in 2024, the number of fires rose to 64,897, impacting an area of 3,613,000 hectares [2], constituting a 14% rise in fire occurrences. The most affected states include Oregon, Texas, California, Idaho, and Washington. Conversely, in Mexico, the year 2024 saw 8,002 fires with a total of 1,672,215.70 hectares affected, reflecting a 13% increase from the previous year, which recorded 7,080 fires and 1,470,439 hectares. The states with the largest burnt areas are Guerrero, Chiapas, Oaxaca, Michoacán, Quintana Roo, Chihuahua, Jalisco, Nayarit, Durango, and Sinaloa [3]. The latter five states constitute the Sierra Madre Occidental, an area characterized by climatic, vegetative, and topographical conditions conducive to the spread of fire. Under these circumstances, there exists a critical need to develop tools capable of predicting the spread and progression of fires, thereby enabling the formulation of effective prevention and response strategies.

Satellite remote sensing has been instrumental in the surveillance of Wildfires, offering regular large-scale observations of active fires, vegetation health, and surface temperature measurements [4, 5]. Derivatives obtained from sensors such as MODIS (Moderate Resolution Imaging Spectroradometer) and VIIRS (Visible infrared Imaging Radiometer Suite) facilitate the creation of daily fire masks and environmental variable mappings that support predictive modeling efforts. Nonetheless, translating these observations into precise forecasts of wildfire progression continues to be a challenging endeavor owing to the inherently unpredictable behavior of the involved elements.

The integration of remote sensing data and deep learning models provides a comprehensive framework for analyzing wildfire dynamics and the meteorological factors that influence their progression. This integration facilitates the creation of predictive models and decision-support systems aimed at optimizing mitigation strategies and minimizing related damages [1]. Consequently, the development of dependable short-term wildfire prediction systems has emerged as a vital research challenge in disaster mitigation and emergency response planning. Numerous studies have proposed architectures for estimating fire spread by examining correlations between current environmental conditions and subsequent fire masks [6].

The utilization of public datasets enables an objective assessment of the performance of various architectures and supports their future adaptation to regional contexts characterized by specific spatio-temporal features. This approach aims to enhance wildfire propagation prediction over a one-day horizon, surpassing methods that primarily focus on spatial representation. A comparative analysis was conducted involving four deep learning architectures: MobileNetV2, serving as a baseline for prior methodologies [7]; a U-Net architecture for spatial segmentation [8]; a ConvLSTM model designed to capture short-term spatiotemporal dependencies [9]; and an xLSTM model intended to augment temporal memory capacity and sequence modeling [10].

To ensure a rigorous comparison, all architectures were trained and evaluated under identical experimental conditions, including the same satellite dataset, preprocessing, and evaluation metrics. The results obtained provide a starting point for adapting and validating the most effective models in regions with high wildfire incidence.

The primary contribution of this research is a comparative assessment of the MobileNetV2, U-Net, ConvLSTM, and xLSTM architectures for predicting the next day's wildfires, along with an analysis of their ability to model the spatial and temporal dynamics of fire propagation.

2 Related Work

The prediction of forest fires has advanced through the integration of remote sensing technologies and deep learning methodologies, thereby partially superseding traditional physical model-based approaches [11].

Although these models simulate fire behavior, they possess limitations in fully capturing the intricate and highly variable environmental dynamics. The use of satellite imagery has enabled the development of deep learning models to predict fire spread. Notably, the creation of datasets for spatiotemporal analysis has been fundamental to recent research. These studies facilitate the assessment of the efficacy of deep neural network architectures for short-term forecasting; for instance, a benchmark for daily predictions was established [12], and convolutional and hybrid models were also explored to optimize performance [13, 14].

Architectures such as U-Net have demonstrated resilience in segmenting burned areas and forecasting short-term spread using satellite time-series data. However, their predominantly spatial approach limits the capture of temporal dependencies. Spatio-temporal models such as ConvLSTM address this gap [15]; other studies show that temporal sequences significantly improve the accuracy of daily forecasts [16]. Likewise, hybrid approaches integrating physical models with deep learning techniques have shown promising outcomes through data fusion [17, 18].

In contrast, this study systematically compares four architectures—MobileNetV2, U-Net, ConvLSTM, and xLSTM—within a unified experimental framework, employing identical inputs, preprocessing protocols, and evaluation metrics. This methodological approach ensures equitable comparison and elucidates the specific strengths and limitations of these models in short-term wildfire spread prediction.

This work incorporates the xLSTM architecture, which has been minimally examined for predicting wildfire spread, thereby enabling an assessment of its capacity to model complex temporal dependencies in this domain.

3 Materials

The effectiveness of deep learning models in predicting the spread of wildfires depends both on the quality and availability of data and on the model used, so it is essential to analyze different models to assess their reliability. This requires a large number of satellite images; another way to obtain this data is through simulations. This study uses a dataset widely used in the literature, allowing for the comparative evaluation of different models under controlled conditions and with real data.

3.1 Data Set

This study employed the Next Day Wildfire Spread dataset, as referenced in [12], which is extensively utilized for the prediction of wildfire propagation. The study area encompasses a compilation of fires occurring within the United States, with data collected in regions measuring 64 km × 64 km and a spatial resolution of 1 km per pixel. Each sample comprises information regarding environmental conditions at time t and the fire mask observed at time t + 1, facilitating the training of predictive spread models for the subsequent day.

The dataset comprises meteorological and topographical data, vegetation indices, and fire history, all obtained from multiple satellite sources.

1. **Fire history:** The MOD14A1, offering information on fires with a daily temporal resolution and 1000 m of spatial resolution. [4]
2. **Digital elevation:** The data were acquired from the Shuttle Radar Topography Mission (SRTM), with a spatial resolution of 30 m [19].
3. **Vegetation data:** From the VIIRS (VNP13A1) dataset, utilizing the NDVI (Normalized Difference Vegetation Index) band, which provides a spatial resolution of 500 m and a temporal resolution of 8 days [5].
4. **Population density data:** Was obtained from the Gridded Population of the World Version 4 (GPWv4) dataset, with a temporal resolution of five years [20].
5. **Soil moisture**: From the Global Land Data Assimilation System Version 2 (GLDAS-2) with a temporal resolution of three hours [21].
6. **Temperature and precipitation:** These data were obtained from the ECMWF/ERA5/DAILY dataset. [22]

The input variables in the dataset comprise essential characteristics necessary for modeling wildfires. Among these, the NDVI offers insights into vegetation conditions; temperature, humidity, and precipitation represent environmental factors that influence the propagation of fires, while elevation encapsulates terrain features. Furthermore, the fire history provides temporal masks of antecedent events, thereby enabling the evaluation of fire evolution. Collectively, these variables are employed to train models that discern spatiotemporal relationships pertinent to predicting fire spread.

It is crucial to acknowledge that the dataset demonstrates a significant class imbalance, as the quantity of pixels devoid of fire substantially exceeds that of pixels affected by fire.

4 Methodology

The proposed methodology encompasses data preparation and processing, the implementation of the selected deep learning architectures, and subsequent training and evaluation of the employed models.

4.1 Data Processing

Data processing was conducted utilizing the TensorFlow framework via the tf.data API, facilitating efficient file loading in TFRecord format, which includes mixing, batch processing, and pre-reading operations designed to enhance computational efficiency during training.

The dataset was partitioned into training (70%), validation (15%), and test (15%) subsets according to a temporal criterion to prevent information leakage between consecutive periods. The input variables were pre-normalized, and the fire masks were addressed as a binary segmentation task, wherein each pixel indicates the presence or absence of fire at time t + 1 (Fig. 1).

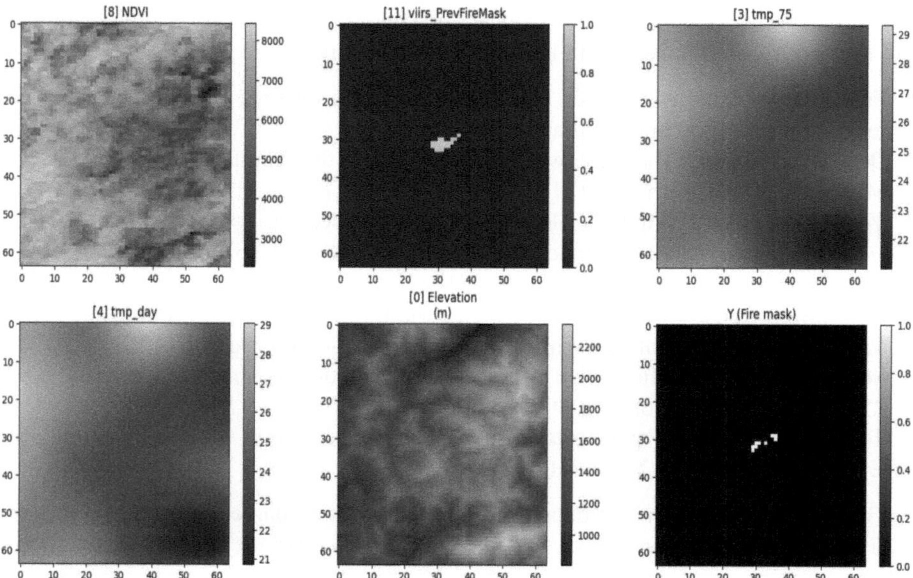

Fig. 1. Examples of input layers from the satellite dataset.

4.2 Implementation of Deep Learning Models

Four deep learning architectures were employed to compare their performance in daily wildfire spread prediction. The architectures evaluated included MobileNetV2 [7], U-Net [8], ConvLSTM [9], and xLSTM [10], to assess their effectiveness in spatiotemporal modeling for the predictive task.

The models were trained under a consistent experimental setup to ensure a fair comparison. An Adam optimizer was employed alongside a combined loss function consisting of binary cross-entropy and the Dice coefficient, as this loss function is appropriate in scenarios involving class imbalance within the dataset, such as in the case of wildfires, where the proportion of fire pixels is lower than that of non-fire pixels. The mathematical equations.

Let y_i be the value of pixel i and $\hat{y}_i$ the probability predicted by the model.

Binary cross-entropy is defined as:

$$\mathcal{L}_{BCE} = -\frac{1}{N} \sum_{i=1}^{N} \left[y_i \log(\hat{y}_i) + (1 - y_i) \log(1 - \hat{y}_i) \right] \tag{1}$$

where N is the total number of pixels

The Dice coefficient is defined as:

$$Dice = \frac{2\sum_{i=1}^{N} y_i \hat{y}_i + \epsilon}{\sum_{i=1}^{N} y_i + \sum_{i=1}^{N} \hat{y}_i + \epsilon} \tag{2}$$

where ϵ is a small term to avoid division by zero.

The loss based on Dice is expressed as:

$$\mathcal{L}_{\text{Dice}} = 1 - Dice \tag{3}$$

The total loss function used during training is defined as:

$$L = \alpha \mathcal{L}_{BCE} + (1 - \alpha)\mathcal{L}_{\text{Dice}} \tag{4}$$

where α controls the balance between both contributions.

The training process employed the Adam optimizer, commencing with an initial learning rate of 0.001 and implementing a gradient normalization of 1.0 to enhance numerical stability. All models were trained for 100 epochs with a batch size of 8 samples, using a consistent hyperparameter configuration to ensure uniform conditions across architectures and to isolate the impact of each model on predictive performance.

Model 1: MobileNetV2

A MobileNetV2-based encoder was employed as a spatial feature extractor, followed by a convolutional decoder that reconstructed the fire mask at time t + 1. This model functions as a compact spatial baseline devoid of explicit skip connections or temporal memory. [7].

Model 2: U-Net

The U-Net architecture was implemented utilizing an encoder-decoder configuration with skip connections, thereby enabling the preservation of high-resolution spatial information throughout the segmentation process. [8].

Model 3: ConvLSTM

The ConvLSTM model incorporates temporal memory through convolutional recurrent units, thereby enabling the simultaneous modeling of spatial dependencies and the temporal progression of the fire. Time-series data were used to predict the mask for the following day. [9].

Model 4: Model xLSTM

xLSTM constitutes an advanced variant of Long Short-Term Memory (LSTM) networks, meticulously designed to augment the modeling capacity of long-range temporal dependencies and to ensure enhanced training stability. This architecture incorporates sophisticated memory mechanisms that facilitate the capture of more complex temporal patterns relative to traditional recurrent architectures [10], thereby potentially advancing the prediction of fire progression.

The performance of the models was evaluated employing quantitative segmentation metrics, including Intersection over Union (IoU), precision, recall, and F1-score. These metrics were computed through pixel-by-pixel comparison between the actual fire mask and the predictions generated by each model.

To acquire the binary mask from each model's predictions, a threshold of 0.5 was employed, whereby pixels exceeding the threshold were designated as fire.

5 Results

Table 1 illustrates the findings of a comparative analysis of four architectures evaluated using the comprehensive test dataset. The mean metrics demonstrate that the U-Net architecture surpasses others in performance across various indicators, including Intersection over Union, precision, recall, and F1-score. The ConvLSTM model ranks as the second most effective, exhibiting marginally lower performance than U-Net overall. The MobileNetV2 model shows comparatively diminished values, especially in recall, indicating a decreased capacity for detecting fire regions. Lastly, the xLSTM model recorded the lowest average performance among the architectures under consideration.

Table 1. Total assessment data metrics.

Model	IoU	Accuracy	Recall	F1
MobileNetv2	0.5742	0.3927	0.2610	0.3136
U-Net	**0.6345**	**0.4658**	**0.4595**	**0.4627**
ConvLSTM	0.6049	0.3919	0.4073	0.3994
xLSTM	0.1839	0.3748	0.3065	0.3479

Comparative Analysis of Representative Images for Each Model
To evaluate the performance of the four architectures and enable a comparison within a consistent practical context, representative images were selected from the test set corresponding to the same fire area, as illustrated in Fig. 2.

In this single-image test, the xLSTM and U-net models demonstrate superior results according to the metrics presented in Table 2. However, an analysis of the overlap between predicted and actual pixels indicates that the xLSTM model more accurately aligns the predicted pixels with the actual fire mask. It exhibits superior performance in spatial representation compared to the other architectures, accurately detecting the majority of fire pixels.

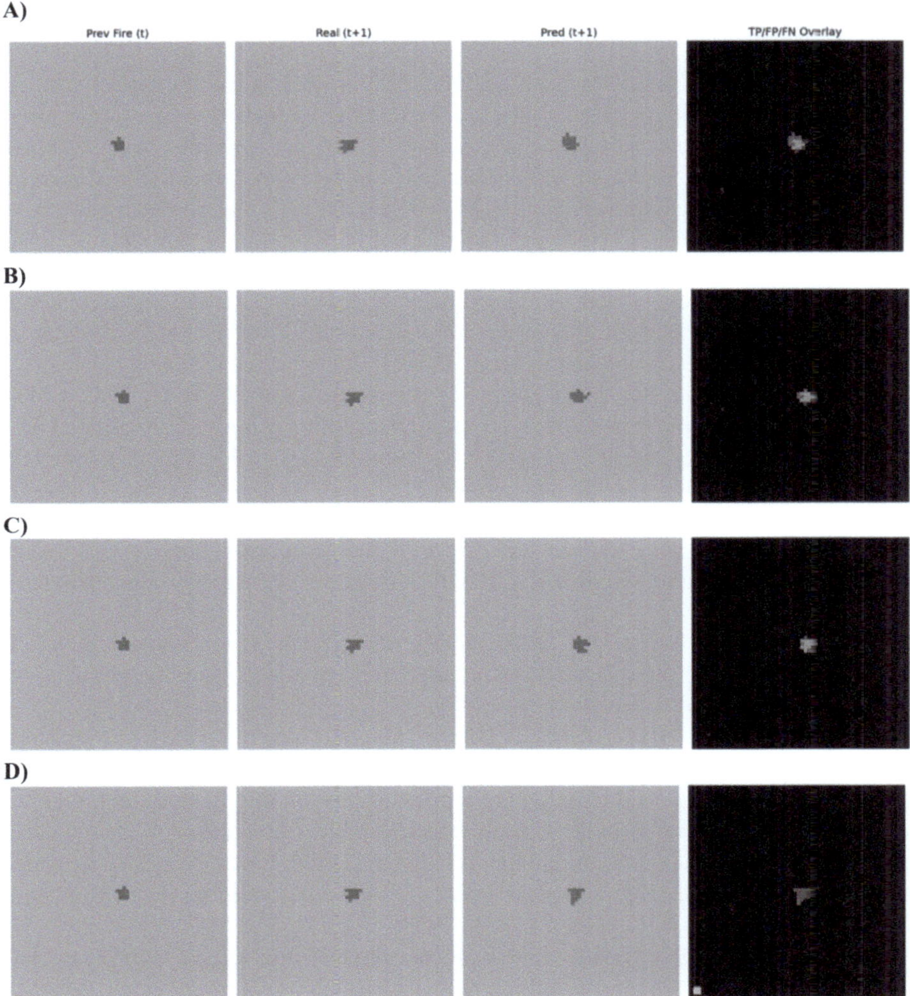

Fig. 2. Comparative analysis of models within specified regions: (A) MobileNet, (B) U-Net, (C) ConvLSTM, (D) xLSTM.

Table 2. Performance metrics of models in a specific region by model

Model	IoU	Accuracy	Recall	F1	True pixel fire	Predict pixel fire
MobileNetv2	0.429	0.529	0.692	0.600	13	17
U-Net	**0.588**	**0.714**	**0.769**	**0.741**	**13**	14
ConvLSTM	0.687	0.687	0.562	0.846	13	16
xLSTM	**0.588**	**0.714**	**0.769**	**0.741**	**13**	14

6 Discussion

The analysis of results indicates that the U-Net architecture exhibits the highest average performance across all evaluated metrics, achieving an Intersection over Union (IoU) of 0.6345, an F1-score of 0.4627, an accuracy of 0.4658, and a recall of 0.4595. These values for the entire test dataset demonstrate its capability to capture spatial patterns in the propagation of wildfires. ConvLSTM underperforms U-Net, achieving an IoU of 0.6049, which is close to U-Net's results, whereas xLSTM shows significantly lower average performance, with an IoU of 0.1839.

The spot analysis conducted via imaging demonstrates that the xLSTM architecture exhibits more stable behavior and, when combined with U-Net, yields results that are very similar in the metrics, as illustrated in Table 2.

Upon analyzing the fire image alongside the predicted-pixel overlay, it is evident that the xLSTM architecture exhibits a spatial distribution more closely aligned with the actual fire spread. Notably, a superior correspondence is observed in fragmented or smaller regions. This observation implies that the integration of temporal memory can offer advantages in detecting emerging or expanding fires. Likewise, ConvLSTM demonstrates an intermediate behavior, indicating that temporal modeling aids in capturing progressive spatial dynamics, although it does not necessarily enhance overall average performance.

Conversely, both U-Net and MobileNetV2 demonstrate superior performance in larger fires, where the consolidated spatial structure seems adequate for modeling the spread on the subsequent day.

This study acknowledges several limitations, notably concerning the input variables, as no individual analysis has been performed to ascertain each variable's contribution to the model's efficacy. Additionally, the availability of satellite imagery at the necessary spatial and temporal resolutions presents a constraint. Furthermore, data imbalance during the model training process remains a challenge. Ultimately, the capacity for generalization across diverse geographic regions is constrained by variations in environmental and terrain features.

As future work, we suggest the development of hybrid models that incorporate both physical and deep learning methodologies.

7 Conclusions

This study demonstrates that various deep learning architectures have distinct applications in wildfire prediction, owing to the spatiotemporal propagation characteristics of wildfires and the timing of fire detection. The findings indicate that model performance is influenced by factors such as fire magnitude and the complexity of its spatial configuration. Notably, the xLSTM architecture exhibited superior capacity and accuracy in detecting small fires. Furthermore, it is evident that utilizing a standardized dataset facilitated a reliable evaluation and comparison of different models, which can serve as a foundational basis for analyzing datasets from diverse geographic regions in future research.

References

1. Jain, P., et al.: Machine learning for wildfire science and management: a review. Environ. Rev. **28**(4), 478–505 (2020). https://doi.org/10.1139/er-2020-0019
2. National Interagency Fire Center (NIFC): Wildland fire summary and statistics annual report 2024. Boise, ID (2024)
3. Gobierno de México: Cierre de la temporada de incendios forestales (2024). https://www.gob.mx
4. Giglio, L., Justice, C.: MODIS thermal anomalies/fire products. NASA (2015). https://doi.org/10.5067/MODIS/MOD14A1.006
5. Didan, K., Barreto, A.: VIIRS vegetation indices product. NASA (2018). https://doi.org/10.5067/VIIRS/VNP13A1.001
6. Marjani, M., et al.: CNN-BiLSTM: a novel deep learning model for near-real-time daily wildfire spread prediction. Remote Sens. **16**(8), 1467 (2024). https://doi.org/10.3390/rs16081467
7. Sandler, M., et al.: MobileNetV2: inverted residuals and linear bottlenecks. In: Proceedings of the IEEE Conference on Computer Vision and Pattern Recognition (CVPR), pp. 4510–4520 (2018). https://doi.org/10.1109/CVPR.2018.00474
8. Ronneberger, O., Fischer, P., Brox, T.: U-Net: convolutional networks for biomedical image segmentation. In: Medical Image Computing and Computer-Assisted Intervention (MICCAI), pp. 234–241 (2015). https://doi.org/10.1007/978-3-319-24574-4_28
9. Shi, X. et al.: Convolutional LSTM network: a machine learning approach for precipitation nowcasting. In: Advances in Neural Information Processing Systems (NeurIPS) (2015)
10. Beck, M. et al.: xLSTM: extended long short-term memory. In: Advances in Neural Information Processing Systems (NeurIPS) (2024)
11. Rothermel, R.C.: A mathematical model for predicting fire spread in wildland fuels. USDA Forest Service, Research Paper INT-115 (1972)
12. Huot, F., et al.: Next day wildfire spread: a machine learning dataset to predict wildfire spreading from remote-sensing data. IEEE Trans. Geosci. Remote Sens. (2023) https://doi.org/10.1109/TGRS.2023.3242346
13. Radke, M. et al.: A deep learning approach for wildfire spread prediction using remote sensing data. Remote Sens. **13**(5) (2021)
14. Kumar, A., et al.: Wildfire prediction using deep learning and remote sensing data. IEEE Access **10**, 123456–123467 (2022)
15. Gao, Y., et al.: Spatiotemporal wildfire prediction using ConvLSTM and remote sensing data. Remote Sens. **14**(3) (2022)
16. Zhao, H., et al.: Deep learning-based wildfire spread prediction using spatiotemporal data. IEEE J. Sel. Topics Appl. Earth Observat. Remote Sens. **16** (2023)
17. Jain, P., et al.: Combining physics-based and machine learning models for wildfire prediction. Environ. Model. Softw. **132** (2020)
18. Xie, Y., et al.: Hybrid deep learning and physical modeling for wildfire spread prediction. Remote Sens. Environ. **300** (2024)
19. Farr, T.G., et al.: The shuttle radar topography mission. Rev. Geophys. **45**(2), RG2004 (2007)
20. Center for International Earth Science Information Network (CIESIN), Columbia University: Gridded population of the world, version 4 (GPWv4): Population density, revision 11. NASA SEDAC, Palisades, NY (2018)
21. Rodell, M., et al.: The global land data assimilation system. Bull. Am. Meteor. Soc **85**(3), 381–394 (2004)
22. Muñoz-Sabater, J.: ERA5-Land monthly averaged data from 1981 to present. Copernicus Climate Change Service (C3S) Climate Data Store (CDS) (2019)

A Safety-Aware Approach for Automated Urine Culture Screening Using Calibrated Deep Learning

Gabriela Judith Alvarado Flores[(✉)], Irlein Delgado Navarro,
Raquel Díaz Hernández, Leopoldo Altamirano Robles,
and Saúl Zapotecas Martínez

Instituto Nacional de Astrofísica, Óptica y Electrónica (INAOE), Puebla, Mexico
`alvaradodegaby@gmail.com`

Abstract. Urinary Tract Infections (UTIs) represent a massive clinical workload, with approximately 80% of urine cultures yielding negative results. While deep learning can automate screening, model overconfidence risks false negatives potentially leaving severe infections untreated. To address this, a safety-aware clinical decision-support pipeline is proposed, rather than a diagnostic replacement, designed to auto-validate negative samples under a strict zero-risk constraint. Three distinct architectures (ResNet-18, ViT-B/16, and KAN-C-MLP) were benchmarked to evaluate their suitability for calibrated screening.

Prioritizing clinical reliability over peak accuracy, the model selection strategy emphasizes Macro-F1 stability. The optimized ResNet-18 achieved an accuracy of 0.880 and a Macro-F1 of 0.879. By applying Temperature Scaling, model overconfidence was successfully mitigated, reducing the Expected Calibration Error (ECE) to 0.062.

Importantly, this decision-support framework achieved a 33.333% safe automation rate. By exclusively auto-validating high-confidence negative samples, it maintained a perfect Recall (1.000) for the Negative class, strictly enforcing a zero-false-negative operating point. Ultimately, the proposed pipeline demonstrates that one-third of routine urocultures can be safely automated, deferring all ambiguous cases to expert microbiologists without compromising patient safety.

Keywords: Urine Culture Screening · Deep Learning · Uncertainty Calibration · Clinical Decision-Support · Medical Image Analysis

1 Introduction

1.1 Clinical Burden and Current Diagnostic Challenges

Urinary Tract Infections (UTIs) represent a massive global health burden, with an estimated incidence of 400 million cases annually and over 200,000 associated deaths. They are among the most common bacterial infections, frequently progressing to severe complications such as pyelonephritis or life-threatening sepsis

© The Author(s), under exclusive license to Springer Nature Switzerland AG 2026
V. G. Cruz-Sánchez et al. (Eds.): MCPR 2026, LNCS 16623, pp. 172–182, 2026.
https://doi.org/10.1007/978-3-032-28393-1_16

if not accurately diagnosed [3,13]. Due to this high prevalence, urine culture remains the gold standard for both diagnosis and antimicrobial susceptibility testing [4]. Consequently, it constitutes one of the most significant workloads in clinical microbiology laboratories, often representing the highest volume of diagnostic requests [1].

However, this standard procedure creates a critical operational bottleneck. The protocol requires an incubation period of 18 to 24 h, a significant time investment applied indiscriminately to all samples. Epidemiological data indicate that between 60% and 80% of these cultures yield negative or non-significant growth [2,13], implying that the majority of specialized laboratory resources are exhausted on samples that require no clinical intervention.

This inefficiency is compounded by the increasing complexity of modern microbiology, driven by a rise in immunocompromised patients and the emergence of multidrug-resistant pathogens, which necessitate rigorous quality control measures [1]. Therefore, there is a clear imperative for automation in laboratory protocols. Automating the screening of negative cultures offers a strategic opportunity to reallocate expert attention toward complex diagnostic dilemmas, thereby preventing unnecessary treatment and supporting antimicrobial stewardship efforts [4].

1.2   The Evolution Toward Total Laboratory Automation

To develop and validate the proposed model, we utilized the public repository "Image Dataset of Clinical Urine Test Results on Petri Dishes," developed by da Silva et al. [6]. The dataset consists of 1,500 high-resolution images (3024×3024 pixels) of urine cultures performed on chromogenic agar plates (CPS Elite, bioMérieux), incubated at $35°C$ for 24 h. The ground truth labels were established by experienced microbiologists, classifying samples into three distinct categories: Positive, Negative, and Uncertain, as detailed in Table 1 [5].

Table 1. Dataset class definitions and distribution [5].

Class	Result	Microbiological Criteria	Count
Negative	No Growth	Absence of bacterial colonies	500
Positive	Infection	Growth of 2 to 99,000 CFU/mL or >100,000 CFU/mL	498
Uncertain	Ambiguous	Growth of 1 CFU/mL or mixed polymicrobial growth	502
Total Images			1500

In the field of automated Petri dish analysis, the literature has evolved from basic computer vision toward deep learning. Early systems relied on explicit preprocessing to isolate regions of interest [7]. Subsequently, the adoption of

Convolutional Neural Networks (CNNs), particularly architectures with residual connections such as ResNet-18 [17], improved robustness by enabling deeper feature extraction via local receptive fields.

In contrast, the Vision Transformer (ViT) [16] shifted the paradigm by applying self-attention mechanisms to image patches, capturing global dependencies across the entire plate.

More recently, Kolmogorov–Arnold Networks (KANs) [18] have been proposed as an alternative to traditional Multi-Layer Perceptrons, replacing fixed linear weights with learnable activation functions on the edges. Using the same dataset, Dutta et al. [8] demonstrated that KAN-based models could achieve validation accuracies near 87%.

However, the predominant focus remains on optimizing algorithmic performance metrics. As highlighted by Guo et al. [11], modern architectures often suffer from *miscalibration*, assigning high confidence scores even to incorrect predictions. In clinical screening, this overconfidence poses a severe risk. Unlike previous works that prioritize global accuracy, this study proposes a paradigm shift toward clinical safety.

2   Proposed Methodology

To evaluate the feasibility of the automated screening system, we designed a comprehensive workflow that prioritizes clinical safety. Before analyzing quantitative outcomes, we define the operational structure of the proposed protocol.

2.1   Proposed Safety-Aware Screening Pipeline

Unlike standard classification approaches that prioritize global accuracy over clinical reliability, this work proposes a safety-aware automation pipeline specifically designed to auto-validate negative samples under a strict zero-risk constraint. The overall logic of our clinical decision-support system is illustrated in Fig. 1. Rather than producing deterministic predictions, the pipeline is engineered to distinguish between high-certainty negative cultures and ambiguous cases that require human intervention.

To achieve this, the proposed framework executes three critical stages in its workflow:

Stage 1: Feature Extraction and Classification. Images are standardized and processed through a deep convolutional or transformer-based backbone. Rather than producing a final clinical diagnosis, this stage maps the visual features into uncalibrated raw predictions (logits) across three distinct classes, serving as the foundation for the subsequent safety mechanisms (architecture and training details are discussed in Sect. 2.2).

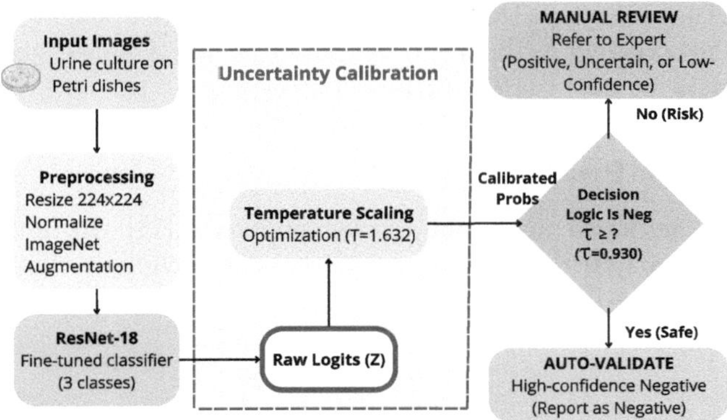

Fig. 1. Safety-aware automation pipeline. The system processes urine culture images through a deep learning architecture. By optimizing a temperature parameter (T) and applying a strict decision threshold (τ), the protocol ensures zero-risk automation of negative results while deferring all other samples to manual review.

Stage 2: Uncertainty Calibration. Standard deep learning models are inherently prone to overconfidence, making their raw outputs unsafe for direct clinical automation. To address this, this stage computationally transforms the raw logits into true empirical likelihoods, ensuring that the predicted probabilities accurately reflect the model's true uncertainty (mathematical formulation detailed in Sect. 2.3).

Stage 3: Risk-Controlled Decision. Operating strictly on the calibrated probabilities, a selective decision logic is applied. The system auto-validates only high-certainty negative samples while systematically deferring any ambiguous or non-negative cases to an expert microbiologist, thereby guaranteeing a zero-risk automation process (threshold optimization is detailed in Sect. 2.4).

2.2 Experimental Setup and Model Selection Criterion

We evaluated the classification performance of the ResNet-18, ViT-B/16, and KAN-C-MLP architectures, with final evaluation performed on the held-out test set. All models were fine-tuned for **20 epochs** using the AdamW optimizer. To ensure stable learning, we applied a learning rate of 10^{-4} for the ResNet-18 model and a more conservative 10^{-5} for the ViT and KAN-based models.

Following the experimental setup, the dataset was stratified into **training (70%)**, **validation (15%)**, and **testing (15%)** sets. In addition, after benchmark comparison, a stratified 5-fold cross-validation was conducted on the selected final model architecture, **ResNet-18**, to assess internal statistical stability. While Dutta et al. [8] emphasized peak validation accuracy on the same dataset and a KAN-based backbone, our approach selects the model state for each architecture based on the highest **Macro-F1 score** achieved on the validation set. This strategy promotes balanced class performance, which is particularly important in safety-critical medical screening.

2.3   Calibration Procedure

Modern neural networks are prone to overconfidence [11]. To mitigate this, we applied **Temperature Scaling**, a post-processing technique that re-scales raw logits (z) by a learned parameter $(T > 0)$:

$$\hat{q}_i = \frac{\exp(z_i/T)}{\sum_j \exp(z_j/T)} \tag{1}$$

This **rank-preserving** post-hoc strategy optimizes a single scalar parameter, effectively reducing the risk of overfitting typical of more complex calibrators (e.g., Isotonic Regression) on limited validation cohorts [11, 19]. Additionally, because it does not require retraining and has a minimal computational footprint, it is well suited for real-time Total Laboratory Automation (TLA) environments.

Optimal T values were obtained by minimizing the Negative Log Likelihood (NLL) via L-BFGS, with final calibration evaluated using the Expected Calibration Error (ECE).

2.4   Risk-Controlled Screening Operating Point

Although the underlying backbones act as 3-class classifiers, the clinical priority of the proposed system is to safely rule out healthy patients. Therefore, we simulated a screening workflow focused exclusively on the probability of the *Negative* class. Samples where the calibrated negative probability exceeds a strict threshold $(\hat{q}_{neg} \geq \tau)$ are automatically validated. To ensure clinical safety, the optimal threshold τ was selected to strictly enforce a constraint of **zero false negatives** (Recall $= 1.000$ for the *Negative* class). All samples failing to meet this high-confidence criterion are systematically referred for manual microbiologist review.

3   Results

3.1   Classification Performance and Benchmarking

As shown in Table 2, ResNet-18 and ViT-B/16 reached a top overall accuracy of **0.880**, while KAN-C-MLP achieved **0.836**. Notably, all three architectures maintained a perfect Recall (**1.000**) for the *Negative* class, providing a robust baseline for the subsequent decision logic. This behavior is further illustrated in the confusion matrices shown in Fig. 2 (a, b, and c), where all models preserve a Recall of 1.000 for the *Negative* class.

Importantly, stratified 5-fold cross-validation on the ResNet-18 architecture confirmed stable classification performance (Accuracy: 0.8987 ± 0.0139, Macro-F1: 0.8978 ± 0.0145, Recall$_{Neg}$: 0.9900 ± 0.0100), indicating that the observed results were not solely dependent on a single data split. Nevertheless, external multi-center validation remains necessary.

Calibration was assessed using reliability diagrams after Temperature Scaling. As shown in Fig. 3, ResNet-18 exhibits the lowest miscalibration (ECE: **0.062**), supporting its use for threshold-based risk-controlled decisions.

Table 2. Classification performance comparison. Model selection was based on optimal Macro-F1 scores over 20 epochs.

Architecture	Accuracy	Macro F1	ECE (Test)	Recall (Neg)
ResNet-18	**0.880**	**0.879**	**0.062**	**1.000**
ViT-B/16	0.880	0.878	0.076	1.000
KAN-C-MLP	0.836	0.833	0.077	1.000

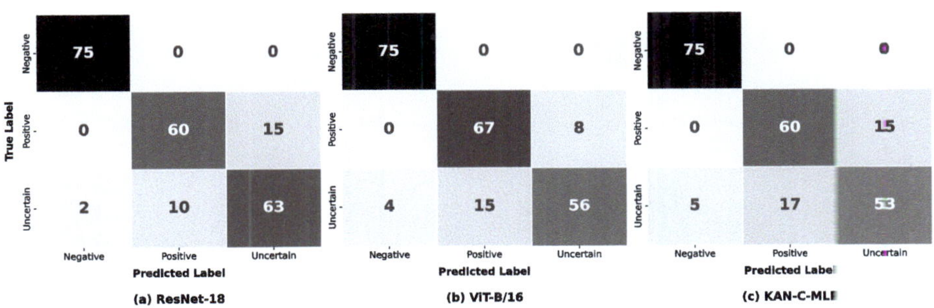

Fig. 2. Confusion matrices for (a) ResNet-18, (b) ViT-B/16, and (c) KAN-C-MLP. All models achieved perfect recall (1.000) for the Negative class, with no missed infections.

3.2   Risk-Coverage Screening Analysis

Table 3 summarizes the results at the 0% false negative operating point. The **ResNet-18** model achieved the highest safe automation coverage at **33.333%**, demonstrating that superior calibration directly translates into higher operational utility by enabling one-third of urocultures to be safely automated. The selected operating point ($\tau = 0.930$) represents the maximum achievable workload reduction under a strict zero-risk constraint (Fig. 4). Although this coverage may appear modest, it reflects a deliberately conservative screening strategy in which avoiding false negatives remains the overriding clinical priority.

Table 3. Screening system performance at the 0% False Negative operating point.

Model	Threshold (τ)	Temperature (T)	Safe Coverage
ResNet-18	**0.930**	**1.632**	**33.333%**
ViT-B/16	0.984	1.527	30.667%
KAN-C-MLP	0.972	1.461	30.222%

3.3 Qualitative Screening Assessment

To visualize the practical implication, Fig. 5 presents representative samples. Panels 1 and 2 illustrate *Negative* samples where the calibrated confidence fell below the safety threshold $\tau = 0.930$. Although the model correctly predicted the class, the uncertainty triggered a "Refer to Expert" action. Panel 3 demonstrates a high-confidence *Negative* sample safely automated, while Panel 4 confirms the system's safety on a *True Positive* case, correctly routing the infected sample to the microbiologist.

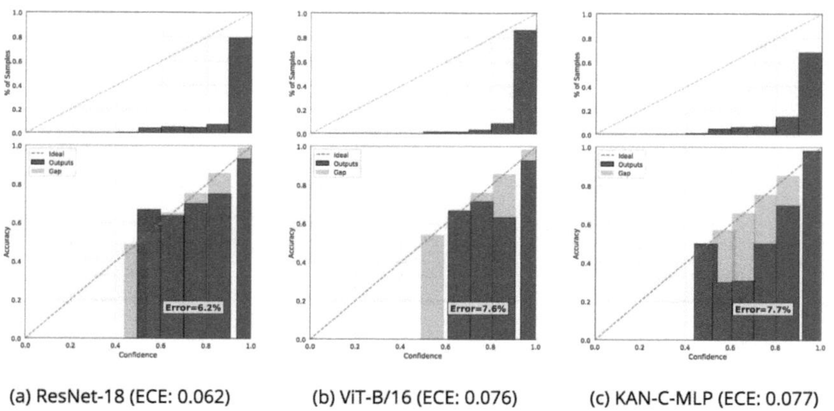

(a) ResNet-18 (ECE: 0.062)   (b) ViT-B/16 (ECE: 0.076)   (c) KAN-C-MLP (ECE: 0.077)

Fig. 3. Reliability diagrams for the evaluated architectures after Temperature Scaling.

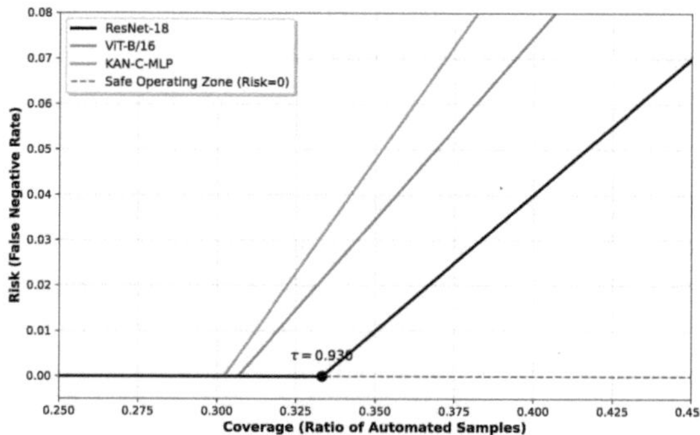

Fig. 4. Comparative Risk-Coverage. The dashed red line marks the safe zone (Risk=0). ResNet-18 (black) achieves the highest safe coverage of 33.333%. (Color figure online)

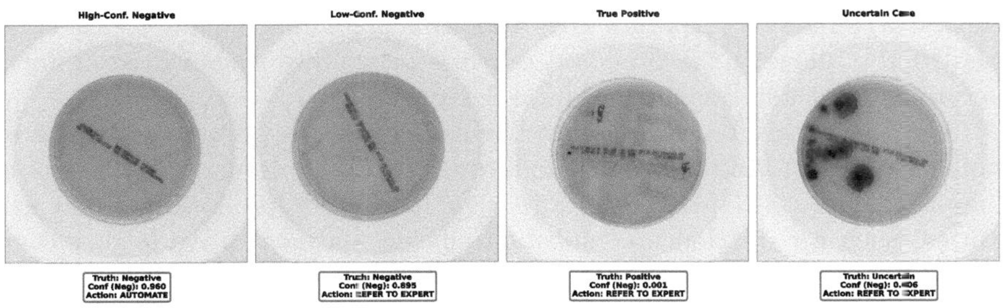

Fig. 5. Decision logic evaluation. Green boxes: safe automation ($\hat{q}(Color figure online)_{neg} \geq 0.930$). Red boxes: manual referral.

4 Discussion

4.1 Performance, Calibration, and Clinical Safety

In medical screening tasks, the clinical cost of a false negative is substantially higher than a false positive, as undetected uropathogens may lead to severe complications such as pyelonephritis or sepsis [13]. While recent studies have emphasized architectural novelty and peak accuracy [8], systems intended for real-world deployment must also ensure reliable confidence estimation.

In this study, a calibrated ResNet-18 achieved **0.880** accuracy and **0.879** Macro-F1, outperforming recent reports on this dataset. Importantly, its superior calibration (**ECE = 0.062**) translated into improved clinical utility under strict safety-aware screening constraints.

Although ResNet-18 and ViT-B/16 reached identical accuracy, their clinical behavior diverged after calibration. ResNet-18 operated with a safety threshold of $\tau = 0.930$, whereas ViT-B/16 required a more conservative $\tau = 0.984$ due to higher overconfidence, resulting in lower safe automation coverage. This suggests that, for specialized medical datasets of limited size, convolutional inductive biases may yield more stable confidence estimates than global attention mechanisms.

These findings reinforce that accuracy alone is insufficient to characterize a screening system; calibration quality ultimately determines how much workload can be safely automated under a fixed risk constraint. By selecting checkpoints based on Macro-F1 rather than peak validation accuracy, we promoted balanced class performance and reduced overfitting, explaining minor discrepancies with previously reported KAN-C-MLP values (0.836 in this implementation).

The resulting fail-safe behavior—perfect Recall (1.000) for the *Negative* class on the test set—ensures that no infected samples were automatically discharged, while ambiguous cases were conservatively deferred to expert review.

4.2 Operational Impact Within Total Laboratory Automation

A common concern regarding image-based screening is acquisition latency. However, modern Total Laboratory Automation (TLA) ecosystems (e.g., WASPLab,

BD Kiestra) already incorporate high-resolution plate imaging into routine work-flows [14,15], allowing the proposed pipeline to operate within existing infrastructure without additional procedural delay.

Under the enforced zero-false-negative constraint, the system achieved a safe automation rate of **33.333%**. Although conservative by design, this corresponds to approximately 333 plates per day in a laboratory processing 1,000 urine cultures. Such a reduction may substantially decrease cognitive load, mitigate fatigue-related errors, and enable microbiologists to focus on complex or clinically significant cases.

4.3   Limitations and Future Directions

Although stratified 5-fold cross-validation supported the classification stability of the selected final model, our 1,500-image dataset still lacks multi-center external validation to confirm the generalizability of the calibrated zero-risk operating point across diverse laboratory settings. While Temperature Scaling was chosen as a post-hoc, low-complexity strategy suited to limited validation data and real-time TLA compatibility, more expressive methods (e.g., Dirichlet calibration, Bayesian networks, or ensembles) could further improve the safety-coverage trade-off. Finally, multimodal integration with patient-level clinical or biochemical data could help resolve ambiguous cases and increase the **33.333%** safe automation rate without compromising strict safety guarantees.

5   Conclusion

This work presented a safety-aware deep learning pipeline for the automated screening of urine cultures. By prioritizing reliability through temperature scaling calibration and implementing a risk-coverage decision protocol, we demonstrated that it is possible to automate the exclusion of negative samples without compromising patient safety.

Our system achieved a safe automation rate of **33.333%** with a **0% false-negative rate** on the held-out test set. This reduces the manual workload for microbiologists by one-third, allowing expert attention to be focused on complex positive cases while minimizing the risk of fatigue-related diagnostic errors.

The calibrated ResNet-18 achieved an accuracy of **0.880** and a Macro-F1 score of **0.879**, performance directly comparable to recent state-of-the-art studies that use more complex architectures, such as Kolmogorov-Arnold Networks (KANs) [8]. Notably, these results were obtained using a model selection strategy based on Macro-F1 stability rather than peak validation accuracy, highlighting the importance of balanced class performance in safety-critical screening.

Beyond raw classification accuracy, this study emphasizes calibrated uncertainty estimation as a necessary component for real-world clinical deployment. By enforcing a strict zero-false-negative operating point, our framework provides a clinically grounded pathway toward trustworthy AI integration in microbiological workflows. Future work will focus on multi-center validation and the incorporation of additional uncertainty modeling strategies to further improve robustness in ambiguous or contaminated samples.

References

1. Kritikos, A., Prod'hom, G., Jacot, D., Croxatto, A., Greub, G.: The impact of laboratory automation on the time to urine microbiological results: a five-year retrospective study. Diagnostics. **14**(13), 1392 (2024). https://doi.org/10.3390/diagnostics14131392
2. Porte, L., Alfaro, M.J., Varela, C., Reyes, J., Weitzel, T.: Automated urine culture system with reduced turnaround time: a prospective real-world evaluation. Diagn. Microbiol. Infect. Dis. **112**(3), 116826 (2025). https://doi.org/10.1016/j.diagmicrobio.2025.116826
3. Bermudez, T., Schmitz, J.E., Boswell, M., Humphries, R.: Novel technologies for the diagnosis of urinary tract infections. J. Clin. Microbiol. **63**(2), e00306-24 (2025). https://doi.org/10.1128/jcm.00306-24
4. Boerman, A.W. et al.: Predicting urine culture outcomes in adult patients using machine learning with the aim of reducing unnecessary urine cultures J. Appl. Lab. Med. **10**(6), 1439–1452 (2025). https://doi.org/10.1093/jalm/jfaf131
5. da Silva, G.R., et al.: Image dataset of urine test results on petri dishes for deep learning classification. Data Brief **47**, 109034 (2023). https://doi.org/10.1016/j.dib.2023.109034
6. da Silva, G.R., et al.: Image dataset of clinical urine test results on petri dishes, Mendeley Data, V3 (2023). https://doi.org/10.17632/xrbtd74pfj.3
7. Bonechi, S., Bianchini, M., Mecocci, A., Scarselli, F., Andreini, P.: Segmentation of petri plate images for automatic reporting of urine culture tests. In: Lim, C.-P., Vaidya, A., Jain, K., Mahorkar, V.U., Jain, L.C. (eds.) Handbook of Artificial Intelligence in Healthcare. ISRL, vol. 211, pp. 127–151. Springer, Cham (2022). https://doi.org/10.1007/978-3-030-79161-2_5
8. Dutta, A., Ramamoorthy, A., Lakshmi, M.G., Kumar, P.K.: Kolmogorov-Arnold Networks for automated diagnosis of urinary tract infections. J. Mol. Pathol. **6**(1), 6 (2025). https://doi.org/10.3390/jmp6010006
9. Deng, J., Dong, W., Socher, R., Li, L.-J., Li, K., Fei-Fei, L.: ImageNet: A large-scale hierarchical image database. In: 2009 IEEE Conference on Computer Vision and Pattern Recognition (CVPR), pp. 248–255 (2009). https://doi.org/10.1109/CVPR.2009.5206848
10. Loshchilov, I., Hutter, F.: Decoupled weight decay regularization. In: International Conference on Learning Representations (ICLR) (2019)
11. Guo, C., Pleiss, G., Sun, Y., Weinberger, K.Q.: On calibration of modern neural networks. In: Precup, D., Teh, Y.W. (eds.) Proceedings of the 34th International Conference on Machine Learning (ICML). Proceedings of Machine Learning Research, vol. 70, pp. 1321–1330. PMLR (2017)
12. Geifman, Y., El-Yaniv, R.: Selective classification for deep neural networks. In: Advances in Neural Information Processing Systems. vol. 30. Curran Associates, Inc. (2017)
13. Flores-Mireles, A.L., Walker, J.N., Caparon, M., Hultgren, S.J.: Urinary tract infections: epidemiology, mechanisms of infection and treatment options. Nat. Rev. Microbiol. **13**(5), 269–284 (2015). https://doi.org/10.1038/nrmicro3432

14. Faron, M.L., Buchan, B.W., Relich, R.F., Clark, J., Ledeboer, N.A.: Evaluation of the WASPLab Segregation Software To Automatically Analyze Urine Cultures Using Routine Blood and MacConkey Agars. J. Clin. Microbiol. **58**(4), e01683-19 (2020). https://doi.org/10.1128/jcm.01683-19
15. Peisach, N., Krotkov, N., Shaye, R., Cárdenas, A.M., Powers, R.L.: Automation of plate inoculation and reading reduces process time in the clinical microbiology laboratory, compared to a manual workflow. medRxiv (2022). https://doi.org/10.1101/2022.03.16.22272483
16. Dosovitskiy, A., et al.: An image is worth 16x16 words: transformers for image recognition at scale. In: International Conference on Learning Representations (ICLR) (2021)
17. He, K., Zhang, X., Ren, S., Sun, J.: Deep residual learning for image recognition. In: Proceedings of the IEEE Conference on Computer Vision and Pattern Recognition (CVPR), pp. 770–778 (2016). https://doi.org/10.1109/CVPR.2016.90
18. Liu, Z., et al.: KAN: Kolmogorov-arnold networks. In: International Conference on Learning Representations (ICLR) (2025)
19. Zadrozny, B., Elkan, C.: Transforming classifier scores into accurate multiclass probability estimates. In: Proceedings of the Eighth ACM SIGKDD International Conference on Knowledge Discovery and Data Mining, pp. 694–699. ACM (2002). https://doi.org/10.1145/775047.775151

Modeling Tumor Progression in Mammography with Conditional Generative Adversarial Networks

Alfonso Rojas-Domínguez[(✉)] [iD] and Jesús Yaljá Montiel Pérez [iD]

Centro de Investigación en Computación-IPN, 07738 Ciudad de México, México
`alfonso.rojas@gmail.com`

Abstract. Modeling tumor progression from mammographic images remains a challenging and inherently ill-posed problem (because multiple valid outcomes or plausible futures exist), particularly in the absence of longitudinal datasets. In this work, we propose a conditional Generative Adversarial Network (cGAN) framework to model statistically plausible tumor progression patterns directly in the image domain, without assuming an explicit temporal horizon. Given a region of interest (ROI) containing a tumor, the model is trained to generate a corresponding future-appearance ROI, conditioned on the input image. Because true longitudinal pairs are unavailable in the Curated Breast Imaging Subset of the Digital Database for Screening Mammography (CBIS-DDSM), we construct clinically consistent pseudo-pairs by matching lesions according to radiological attributes and requiring a minimum size increase criterion. We validate this pairing strategy through expert radiological review. Our training objective combines adversarial loss with reconstruction-based terms, along with stabilization techniques such as instance noise and label smoothing. Quantitative evaluation using LPIPS and SSIM metrics demonstrates structural and perceptual coherence between generated projections and the reference targets, while qualitative assessment by a licensed radiologist indicates that the majority of generated samples are clinically plausible. Although preliminary, and based on pseudo-longitudinal data, these results suggest that cGANs provide a viable data-driven alternative to explicit tumor growth modeling, opening new directions for longitudinal analysis and decision support in mammographic imaging.

Keywords: Tumor Progression · Conditional GANs · Medical Imaging · Image-to-Image Translation · Deep Learning

1 Introduction

Cancer progression is dynamic, yet most CADx systems analyze mammographic images independently. Forecasting tumor evolution could assist treatment planning and risk assessment, but modeling growth remains difficult due to inter-patient variability and limited longitudinal data. Classical biomechanical models often require strong assumptions and patient-specific tuning [16].

© The Author(s), under exclusive license to Springer Nature Switzerland AG 2026
V. G. Cruz-Sánchez et al. (Eds.): MCPR 2026, LNCS 16623, pp. 183–194, 2026.
https://doi.org/10.1007/978-3-032-28393-1_17

Deep generative models offer a data-driven alternative: instead of estimating growth parameters, one may directly synthesize plausible future images conditioned on current observations. We investigate conditional Generative Adversarial Networks (cGANs) [5] for tumor forecasting in mammography using the CBIS-DDSM dataset. The central question is whether a cGAN can generate a plausible future state of a breast mass given its present appearance.

1.1 Problem Formulation

Let m_t denote a mammogram at time t. The objective is to learn a mapping $m_{t+k} = G(m_t, c)$, where G is a generative model and c represents conditional information. The task is not to predict a single deterministic future but to model a distribution of plausible outcomes.

The proposed framework uses a cGAN where the generator maps an input image x to a projected future $\hat{y}$, and the discriminator distinguishes real pairs (x, y) from generated pairs $(x, \hat{y})$ (Fig. 1).

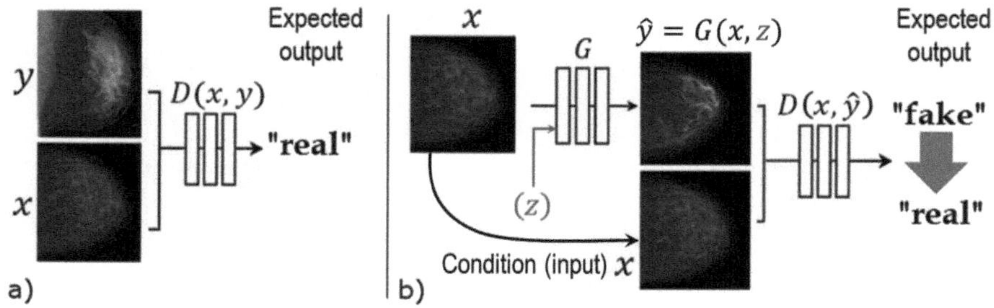

Fig. 1. The cGAN should learn to distinguish between a) *"real"* pseudopairs (x, y), representing real images that are paired together for the purpose of training the cGAN, and b) the *"fake"* pseudopairs $(x, \hat{y} = G(x))$; initially, D will easily classify these pseudopairs as *"fake"*, but as training progresses, G should be able to deceive D into classifying them as *"real"*. Notice z is optional random noise.

2   Related Work

Conditional GANs introduced by Mirza and Osindero [10] enabled controlled generation, later consolidated by the pix2pix framework [5], which demonstrated effective image-to-image translation using adversarial and reconstruction losses. These approaches have been adopted in medical imaging.

In mammography, adversarial learning has mainly addressed data scarcity and class imbalance. Wu et al. [18] inserted or removed lesions within mammographic patches using contextual GANs, improving classifier performance under controlled augmentation ratios [7]. Shen et al. [13] synthesized context-aware masses, achieving improved detection rates while noting fidelity limitations [2].

Other works explored full mammogram synthesis via class-conditional GANs [6,14] to balance pathology classes. Unlike these augmentation-focused approaches, our work investigates temporally coherent tumor forecasting conditioned on a specific input lesion.

3 Loss Functions in GANs and cGANs

The behavior and effectiveness of GANs depend critically on the design of the loss functions used to train the generator G and discriminator D. In the original formulation of [4], training is posed as a two-player zero-sum minimax game:

$$\min_{G} \max_{D} V(D, G) = \mathbb{E}_x[\log D(x)] + \mathbb{E}_z[\log(1 - D(G(z)))] \tag{1}$$

where D seeks to correctly classify real samples x and generated samples $G(z)$, while G aims to produce synthetic outputs that D cannot distinguish from real data. In practice, the networks are optimized alternately via gradient-based updates.

From (1), separate losses are defined for each player. The discriminator minimizes

$$\mathcal{L}_D = -\Big(\mathbb{E}_x[\log D(x)] + \mathbb{E}_z[\log(1 - D(G(z)))]\Big), \tag{2}$$

thus encouraging $D(x) \to 1$, and $D(G(z)) \to 0$. The generator minimizes:

$$\mathcal{L}_G = \mathbb{E}_z[\log(1 - D(G(z)))]. \tag{3}$$

However, as discussed in [4], this formulation may lead to gradient saturation when $D(G(z))$ is close to zero during early training. To mitigate this, a non-saturating alternative is commonly used:

$$\mathcal{L}_G^{\text{NS}} = -\mathbb{E}_z[\log(D(G(z)))]. \tag{4}$$

This variant of the generator loss provides stronger gradients when the discriminator confidently rejects generated samples, improving convergence dynamics. For this reason, it is widely used in modern GAN implementations.

3.1 Conditional Loss Function in cGANs

Conditional GANs (cGANs) extend this framework by incorporating ancillary information into both G and D. Following the image-to-image translation paradigm [5], the model is conditioned on an input image x. The discriminator should classify pairs (x, y) as real and $(x, \hat{y})$, with $\hat{y} = G(x, z)$, as fake. The adversarial objective becomes

$$\mathcal{L}_{cGAN}(G, D) = \mathbb{E}_{x,y}[\log D(x, y)] + \mathbb{E}_{x,z}[\log(1 - D(x, \hat{y}))], \tag{5}$$

which enforces that $\hat{y}$ be both *realistic* and *consistent* with the conditioning input x.

In this supervised conditional setting, it is common to incorporate an explicit reconstruction term to further constrain the solution. A typical choice is the pixel-wise $\mathcal{L}_1$ loss:

$$\mathcal{L}_{L1}(G) = \mathbb{E}_{x,y,z}[\|y - \hat{y}\|_1], \tag{6}$$

which promotes structural fidelity between $\hat{y}$ and y. The complete optimization problem is

$$G^* = \arg \min_G \max_D \mathcal{L}_{cGAN}(G, D) + \lambda \mathcal{L}_{L1}(G), \tag{7}$$

where λ adjusts the importance of reconstruction accuracy. This objective encourages outputs that are not only plausible (appear like real data) but are also aligned with the introduced condition.

4   Proposed Methodology

4.1   Formation of Pseudopairs to Train the cGAN

At inference time, our model receives a region of interest (ROI) from a mammogram A containing a breast tumor and generates a corresponding ROI that simulates the temporal evolution of the lesion. Training such a conditional model requires paired examples of the form $(A_1 \rightarrow B_1), (A_2 \rightarrow B_2), \ldots$, where each pair represents a "before" image (type A) and an "after" image (type B) of the same tumor acquired at different times, ideally from the same patient, and preserving laterality and view.

Since no database with true longitudinal mammographic pairs was available, we constructed *pseudopairs* $(A_i \rightarrow B_i)$ from CBIS-DDSM. Only cases containing masses were considered, excluding other abnormalities. For each mammogram A, we searched CBIS-DDSM for a mammogram B exhibiting consistent attributes: mammographic view, tumor margin type, tissue density, BI-RADS category, tumor pathology, and shape. These metadata are provided for each lesion in the database.

To emulate tumor progression, we added a quantitative constraint: the lesion in B_i must be $\geq 20\%$ larger than that in A_i (in pixels, according to the corresponding ground-truth masks available). This criterion ensures that the pair reflects a plausible growth scenario. Applying this procedure to all eligible tumors in CBIS-DDSM yielded 2,504 pseudopairs $(A_1 \rightarrow B_1), \ldots, (A_{2504} \rightarrow B_{2504})$. Notice that a given tumor may appear as type A in some pairs and as type B in others.

Because CBIS-DDSM does not contain true longitudinal studies of the same lesion, no explicit temporal horizon can be defined. Instead, the proposed framework models a distribution of plausible growth transformations between lesions that satisfy clinically consistent radiological attributes and a minimum size-increase criterion. Therefore, the generated output should be interpreted as a statistically plausible progression pattern rather than a time-calibrated prediction.

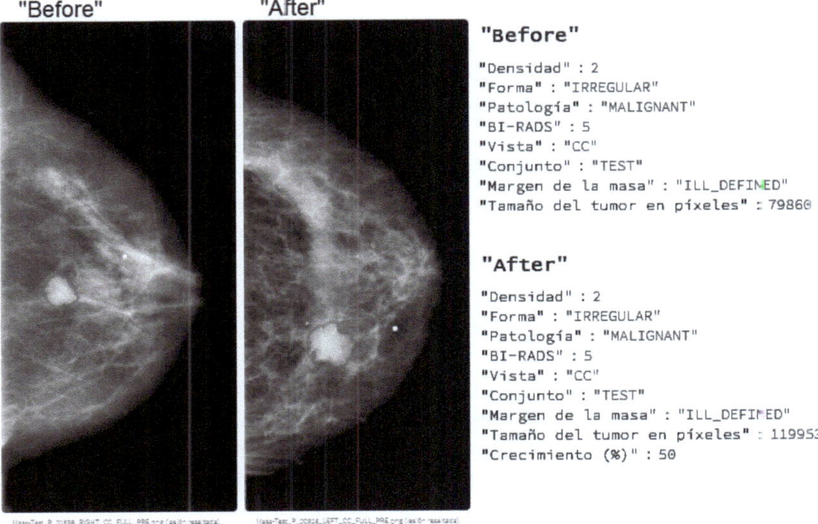

Fig. 2. Left.- Example of two mammograms with "before" and "after" masses (contours shown in red) in a pseudopair (A_i, B_i). Although our model works with ROIs only, whole mammograms were shown to human experts for review. Right.- Features used for pairing masses: tissue density, mass shape, pathology, view, margin type, etc. as well as image set (either *training* or *test*) and size.

4.2 Validation of Pseudopairs

The construction of pseudopairs relies on the assumption that matching lesions across patients, based on radiological attributes and pathology, can approximate the information contained in true longitudinal studies. This is a strong assumption that, even if statistically valid, required independent validation from an experienced radiologist. While data-driven models may capture spurious correlations, our pseudopair construction imposes clinically meaningful constraints and a minimum lesion growth criterion, reducing the risk of learning arbitrary transformations. Expert radiological evaluation further supports the coherence of the generated progression patterns.

For human review, a graphical interface was developed to display a statistically representative subset of pseudopairs to an expert radiologist (see Fig. 2). Each pair was reviewed and classified as acceptable or not from a medical standpoint. The expert feedback and associated comments were subsequently incorporated to refine the pairing criteria and improve methodological consistency. More details are publicly available at https://github.com/ArielXL/review-results.

4.3 Training Strategy

The model is trained using an alternating optimization scheme in which generator and discriminator updates are carefully balanced to promote stable convergence. Given the absence of genuine longitudinal data, data augmentation and intensity normalization are applied to enhance robustness and mitigate overfitting. This strategy aims to preserve anatomical coherence while enabling the generator to learn plausible temporal transformations conditioned on the input ROI.

The main training hyperparameters are summarized in Table 1. These include the weights of the generator loss, the initial and final levels of instance noise, number of filters in the generator, *ngf*, and discriminator, *ndf*, and the adversarial training schedule defined by *n_critic_strong* and *alt_critic_period*. Label smoothing and decaying instance noise were applied to stabilize training by preventing an excessively strong discriminator, while dropout was used to prevent overfitting.

The relatively large weights of the L1 and SSIM losses promote precise reconstruction of target images, whereas increased discriminator capacity ($ndf = 160$) coupled with reduced learning rates promote stable convergence. Cosine annealing learning rate schedule with restarts was implemented with T_{max} adjusted to the number of epochs. Although multiple configurations were evaluated, due to space limitations only the best results are reported in Sect. 6.

5   Experimental Setup

In this work we employed the mammographic images from the publicly available CBIS-DDSM dataset [12]. The dataset comprises 1,566 subjects, most of which include four images (two views per breast). Some cases contain multiple masses, whereas others do not present any lesion. These characteristics were explicitly considered in the construction of pseudo-pairs for training and, independently, for evaluation, as described in Sect. 4.1. Of the 2,504 pseudo-pairs obtained, approx. 90% were used in training and the other 10% were reserved for testing the model.

Quantitative evaluation was based on similarity measures described below, while qualitative assessment by human experts emphasized visual plausibility and clinical coherence.

Learned Perceptual Image Patch Similarity (LPIPS)

Learned Perceptual Image Patch Similarity (LPIPS) measures the perceptual distance between two images ($\mathbf{x}$ and $\hat{\mathbf{x}}$) using deep feature representations extracted from a pretrained CNN (e.g., AlexNet or VGG) [19]. By operating in a feature space that captures high-level structures such as textures and edges, LPIPS approximates human perception of similarity and is therefore suitable for evaluating images generated by cGAN-based models. Formally, LPIPS is computed as a weighted aggregation of normalized feature map differences across layers:

$$\text{LPIPS}(\mathbf{x}, \hat{\mathbf{x}}) = \sum_l \frac{1}{H_l W_l} \sum_{h=1}^{H_l} \sum_{w=1}^{W_l} \left\| \mathbf{w}_l \odot \left(\hat{\phi}_l(\mathbf{x})_{h,w} - \hat{\phi}_l(\hat{\mathbf{x}})_{h,w} \right) \right\|_2^2, \quad (8)$$

Table 1. Main hyperparameters corresponding to the reported results.

Hyperparameter	Value	Hyperparameter	Value
epochs	260	*learning rate: D*	0.00025
batch size	20	*learning rate: G*	0.000125
λ_{TV}	0.03	*cosine_Tmax*	52
λ_{L1_img}	84	*alt_critic_period*	6
L1*loss*	170	*n_critic_strong*	5
SSIM *loss*	24	*noise (initial $\rightarrow$ final)*	$0.05 \rightarrow 0.004$
ngf/ndf	120/160		

where H_l and W_l denote the spatial dimensions of the feature maps at layer l, and $\mathbf{w}_l$ are learned channel-wise weights. $\text{LPIPS}(\mathbf{x}, \hat{\mathbf{x}}) \geq 0$, with lower values corresponding to higher perceptual similarity. In image-to-image translation and mammographic synthesis tasks, LPIPS is commonly reported alongside complementary metrics to provide a more comprehensive evaluation [3]. Low LPIPS values suggest perceptually coherent and anatomically plausible reconstructions [15].

Structural Similarity Index (SSIM)

The Structural Similarity Index (SSIM) evaluates perceptual similarity by comparing structural information between two images [11,17]. SSIM is bounded in $[0, 1]$, with higher values indicating better preservation of structural information; SSIM measures similarity through luminance L, contrast C, and structural S components, computed over local windows [1,8,9]:

$$\text{SSIM}(x, y) = L(x, y)\, C(x, y)\, S(x, y), \tag{9}$$

Letting, μ and σ denote local means and standard deviations, σ_{xy} denote the covariance between windows, and $C_1 = (0.01L)^2$, $C_2 = (0.03L)^2$, $C_3 = C_2/2$ as stability constants, we have:

$$L(x,y) = \frac{2\mu_x\mu_y + C_1}{\mu_x^2 + \mu_y^2 + C_1}, \qquad C(x,y) = \frac{2\sigma_x\sigma_y + C_2}{\sigma_x^2 + \sigma_y^2 + C_2}, \qquad S(x,y) = \frac{\sigma_{xy} + C_3}{\sigma_x\sigma_y + C_3} \tag{10}$$

6   Results and Discussion

We present results under qualitative and quantitative assessments. First, visual examples are given in Fig. 5. These suggest that the proposed cGAN can generate future tumor instances with visually plausible characteristics. A quantitative and expert-based justification is presented below.

Secondly, Fig. 4 shows the distribution of the qualitative assessment made by an expert radiologist who classified a sample of 100 generated images into five categories. Expressed as percentages, 57% of the examined cases were judged *very good* (18%) or *good* (39%), whereas approximately one third (33%) of the instances were assessed as *fair*, meaning that these images presented mild perceptual inconsistencies. Only 10% of the examined images received a negative assessment (*bad* or *very bad*), indicating that the model did not adequately reproduce the expected features, such as the correct density of the mass, or the presence of spiculated mass margins. These qualitative assessment supports our conclusion that the model generates images with sufficient realism and plausibility in most cases, although the challenge of precisely reproducing complex patterns remains.

Finally, Fig. 3 contains a scatter plot of the Structural-Perceptual contrast space based on the LPIPS and SSIM metrics described in Sect. 5. The horizontal axis shows $\Delta_{\text{LPIPS}} = \text{LPIPS}(A, \hat{y}) - \text{LPIPS}(B, \hat{y})$, and the vertical axis presents $\Delta_{\text{SSIM}} = \text{SSIM}(B, \hat{y}) - \text{SSIM}(A, \hat{y})$. Recalling that LPIPS is a distance measure and SSIM is a similarity measure, when both Δ_{LPIPS} and Δ_{SSIM} take positive values, this indicates that the generated image, $\hat{y}$, is consistently (structurally and perceptually) more similar to the "after" reference image than to the "before" image. Other combinations of values can be interpreted and grouped analogously; Fig. 3 shows these clusters labeled accordingly. With average values of SSIM = 0.750807 (closer to 1 is better) and LPIPS=0.235203 (smaller is better), it can be observed that the model is successful under both structural and perceptual criteria. Furthermore, a Pearson correlation coefficient of 0.7301 indicates significant agreement between the two metrics, constituting a positive quantitative outcome.

Our results suggest that GAN-based forecasting can represent complex progression patterns of tumors observed in mammography without explicit growth modeling. For training, we did not know or define the time period that would separate the sets of "before" and "after" reference mammograms. The assumption we made is that all tumors follow arbitrary growth rates. This allowed us to form pseudopairs of tumors under a single size criterion, although this implies that the time separating a tumor A_i from its pair B_i is also arbitrary. Alternatively, a fixed time period (e.g., 6 months) could be defined, but this would require multiple criteria to form pseudopairs of tumors according to their expected growth, depending, for example, on each tumor type. At this initial stage our objective was to verify that we can train a generative model in the manner proposed, and obtain preliminary results that allow us to make adjustments, both to the model itself and to the training process.

In other words, in our first prototype, we included the smallest possible number of variables in order to facilitate the subsequent analysis of the results.

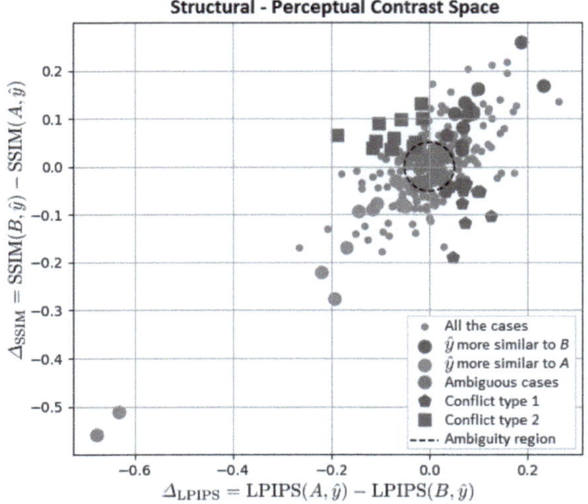

Fig. 3. Structural-Perceptual contrast space based on LPIPS and SSIM metrics. Subsets of results are shown in different shapes/colors according to what these represent (see inlaid legend).

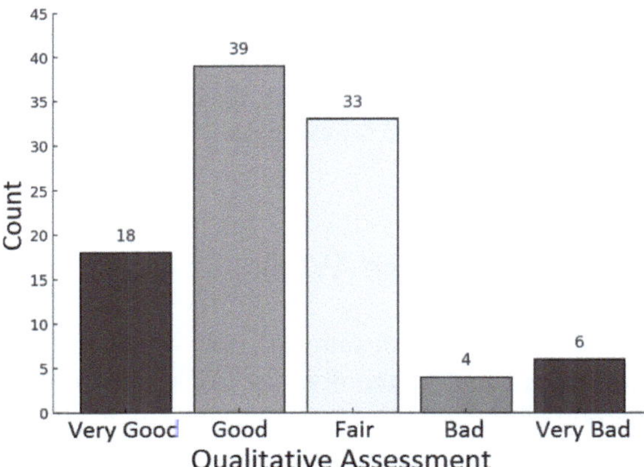

Fig. 4. Qualitative assessment offered by an expert radiologist on a sample of 100 output instances.

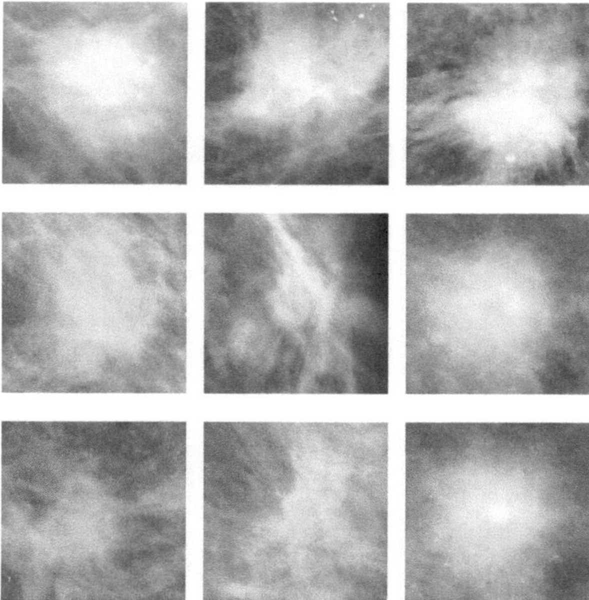

Fig. 5. Example results obtained by the cGAN. From left to right: the input images, x; the target images, y; and the generated images, $\hat{y}$. During training, pairs (x, y) were provided to the cGAN, so that it learned to produce the corresponding $\hat{y}$ images. However, this figure shows examples from the test set, meaning that the cGAN received only x to produce $\hat{y}$, while target y was used for evaluation of the results, both quantitatively and in perceptual assessment.

7   Conclusions and Future Work

We presented a conditional GAN framework for forecasting tumor progression directly in the mammographic image domain. Although preliminary, and based on pseudo-longitudinal data, our results suggest that cGANs provide a viable data-driven alternative to explicit tumor growth modeling, opening new directions for longitudinal analysis and decision support in mammographic imaging.

A key limitation of the present study is the absence of true longitudinal mammographic datasets; validating the proposed framework on patient-specific longitudinal data remains an important direction for future research. We also consider conditioning the generated images on specific features corresponding to clinical phases pertaining to breast cancer progression, and exploring the use of different adversarial models trained on paired or unpaired data.

Acknowledgement. Experiments were conducted by Ariel Plasencia Díaz in partial fulfillment of the requirements for the M.Sc. degree. Dr. Alejandro Becerril Mondragón, M.D., licensed radiologist (License No. 7730085), performed the qualitative assessment of the results and provided valuable guidance throughout the study. This work was supported by the Secretariat of Science, Humanities, Technology and Innovation (SECIHTI) of Mexico through Research Grant IIxM-7012 (A. Rojas).

References

1. Bakurov, I., Buzzelli, M., Schettini, R., Castelli, M., Vanneschi, L.: Structural similarity index (SSIM) revisited: a data-driven approach. Expert Syst. Appl. **189** (2022)
2. Cheng, K.H., Li, W., Lee, F.K.H., Li, T., Cai, J.: Pixelwise gradient model with GAN for virtual contrast enhancement in MRI imaging. Cancers **16**(5), 999 (2024)
3. Ghazanfari, S., Garg, S., Krishnamurthy, P., Khorrami, F., Araujo, A.: R-LPIPS: an adversarially robust perceptual similarity metric. arXiv:2307.15157 (2023)
4. Goodfellow, I.J. et al.: Generative adversarial nets. Adv. Neural. Info. Proc. Syst. **27** (2014)
5. Isola, P., Zhu, J.Y., Zhou, T., Efros, A.A.: Image-to-image translation with conditional adversarial networks. In: Proceedings of the IEEE conference on computer vision and pattern recognition. pp. 1125–1134 (2017)
6. Joseph, A.J., et al.: Prior-guided generative adversarial network for mammogram synthesis. Biomed. Signal Process. Control **87**, 105456 (2024)
7. Kim, E., Cho, H.H., Kwon, J., Oh, Y.T., Ko, E.S., Park, H.: Tumor-attentive segmentation-guided GAN for synthesizing breast contrast-enhanced MRI without contrast agents. IEEE J. Transl. Eng. Health Med. **11**, 32–43 (2022)
8. Lee, S.H., Leeghim, H.: Synthetic infra-red image evaluation methods by structural similarity index measures. Electronics **11**(20), 3360 (2022)
9. Milovic, C., Tejos, C., Silva, J., Shmueli, K., Irarrazaval, P.: Xsim: a structural similarity index measure optimized for MRI QSI. Magn. Reson. Med. **93**(1), 411–421 (2025)
10. Mirza, M., Osindero, S.: Conditional generative adversarial nets. arXiv:1411.1784 (2014)
11. Mudeng, V., Kim, M., Choe, S.W.: Prospects of structural similarity index for medical image analysis. Appl. Sci. **12**(8), 3754 (2022)
12. Sawyer-Lee, R., Gimenez, F., Hoogi, A., Rubin, D.: Curated breast imaging subset of digital database for screening mammography (CBIS-DDSM) [data set] (2016). https://doi.org/10.7937/K9/TCIA.2016.7O02S9CY
13. Shen, T., Hao, K., Gou, C., Wang, F.Y.: Mass image synthesis in mammogram with contextual information based on GANs. Comput. Methods Programs Biomed. **202** (2021)
14. Shodiev, D., Ushakov, E., Litvinov, A., Markin, Y.: Privacy-preserving synthetic mammograms: a generative model approach to privacy-preserving breast imaging datasets. Informatics **12**(4), 112 (2025)
15. Snell, J., Ridgeway, K., Liao, R., Roads, B.D., Mozer, M.C., Zemel, R.S.: Learning to generate images with perceptual similarity metrics. In: 2017 IEEE International Conference on Image Processing (ICIP), pp. 4277–4281. IEEE (2017)
16. Swanson, K.R., Bridge, C., Murray, J.D., Alvord, E.C.: Virtual and real brain tumors: using mathematical modeling to quantify glioma growth and invasion. J. Neurol. Sci. **216**(1), 1–10 (2003). https://doi.org/10.1016/S0022-510X(03)00155-8
17. Wang, Z., Bovik, A.C., Sheikh, H.R., Simoncelli, E.P.: Image quality assessment: from error visibility to structural similarity. IEEE Trans. Image Process. **13**(4), 600–612 (2004)

18. Wu, E., Wu, K., Lotter, W.: Synthesizing lesions using contextual GANs improves breast cancer classification on mammograms. arXiv:2006.00086 (2020)
19. Zhang, R., Isola, P., Efros, A.A., Shechtman, E., Wang, O.: The unreasonable effectiveness of deep features as a perceptual metric. In: Proceedings of the IEEE Conference on Computer Vision and Pattern Recognition, pp. 586–595 (2018)

Computer Vision

UAV Pose Estimation in Low-Light Conditions Using Visual–LiDAR Fusion

Esteban Tlelo–Coyotecatl[✉], Alejandro Gutierrez–Giles,
and José Martínez–Carranza

Instituto Nacional de Astrofísica, Óptica y Electrónica, Puebla, Mexico
esteban.tlelo@inaoep.mx

Abstract. Accurate six-degree-of-freedom (6-DoF) pose estimation is essential for autonomous unmanned aerial vehicles (UAVs) operating in unknown environments, yet remains challenging under low-light conditions where visual information is severely degraded. This work presents a lightweight multimodal pose estimation framework that extends a PoseNet-based architecture by integrating distance measurements from low-cost LiDAR sensors. The proposed approach is designed to operate in real time while satisfying the strict payload, power, and computational constraints of small UAV platforms.

To characterize visual degradation, an entropy-based analysis of the RGB input is introduced, providing a quantitative measure of visual information content beyond illumination levels. Experimental results under low-light and well-lit conditions show that, although visual entropy decreases significantly in degraded environments, multimodal fusion maintains stable and accurate pose estimates. When visual information is sufficient, the framework adapts naturally without performance degradation. These results demonstrate that low-cost LiDAR sensors can effectively enhance robustness for UAV navigation across varying illumination conditions.

Keywords: Low-light · Autonomous vehicles · Pose estimation

1 Introduction

Unmanned aerial vehicles (UAVs) operating in unknown indoor and outdoor environments require accurate, high-frequency six-degree-of-freedom (6-DoF) pose estimation to enable agile, safe, and autonomous flight. Achieving robust pose estimation remains a fundamental challenge when UAVs are deployed in real-world scenarios characterized by uncertainty and environmental degradation.

This challenge becomes significant under degraded visual conditions. Conventional vision-based odometry and SLAM pipelines, while effective in well-lit and structured environments, tend to fail or suffer from drift when visual information is scarce or unreliable. In practice, UAVs operating in real environments must often contend with low illumination, dynamic scenes, and external disturbances, conditions under which purely visual approaches struggle to maintain consistent and accurate pose estimates.

In this work, we focus on UAV operation under the following constraints: (i) low-light conditions, typically below 100 lux [17]; (ii) unexpected environmental changes, such as moving objects or reconfigured layouts; and (iii) external disturbances, including wind gusts or minor impacts that induce abrupt motion. These factors jointly exacerbate estimation errors and limit the applicability of standard visual navigation pipelines.

To mitigate these challenges, many existing solutions rely on external infrastructure—such as motion capture systems, GNSS, or artificial markers—or incorporate large and heavy sensors to compensate for the lack of visual information. Although effective in controlled settings, such approaches significantly increase system cost, payload, energy consumption, and computational requirements, rendering them impractical for small UAVs with strict size, weight, and power constraints. As a result, autonomous inspection and navigation missions are often executed using slow, conservative trajectories or require human supervision, leading to reduced autonomy and prolonged mission times.

The problem addressed in this work is therefore the development of a high-frequency drone pose estimation method capable of operating in low-light conditions without reliance on external infrastructure or heavy sensing modalities. The proposed approach is designed to remain compatible with the payload, power, and computational constraints of small aerial platforms, this work aims to bridge the gap between laboratory-grade localization systems and practical autonomous flight in challenging real-world environments.

The main contributions of this work can be summarized as follows:

- We propose a lightweight learning-based pose estimation framework that extends a PoseNet-based architecture by integrating LiDAR depth measurements as a complementary sensing modality, improving robustness under low-light conditions.
- We introduce a computationally efficient feature-level fusion strategy that combines visual embeddings with LiDAR depth information.
- We experimentally validate the proposed approach under degraded visual conditions and external disturbances, demonstrating improved pose estimation stability compared to vision-only baselines, while remaining compatible with the payload, power, and computational constraints of small UAVs.

Unlike traditional works that aim to outperform state-of-the-art methods on public benchmarks, this work focuses on analyzing the contribution of low-cost LiDAR measurements under controlled low-light conditions.

The objective is to isolate the effect of multimodal fusion within a learning-based pose estimation framework, rather than competing directly with full visual-inertial odometry systems.

2   Related Work

Robust state estimation and navigation for UAVs in degraded visual conditions has been addressed through a variety of approaches. Visual and visual-inertial odometry methods have demonstrated strong performance in well-lit environments, but their reliability degrades significantly under low illumination or dynamic scene changes [5,9,10]. While inertial sensing can partially compensate for visual degradation, long-term drift and sensitivity to abrupt motion remain challenging.

To improve robustness, several works have explored advanced sensor fusion strategies that combine complementary modalities [4,15]. LiDAR-based systems, in particular, provide accurate geometric information and have been successfully applied to UAV navigation in challenging environments [1,18]. However, these approaches often rely on high-resolution sensors or complex processing pipelines that increase payload, power consumption, and computational requirements, limiting their applicability to small aerial platforms.

Another line of research focuses on enhancing visual perception through image preprocessing and neural network-based illumination enhancement [3,12, 14,19,25–27]. While these methods can improve image quality under low-light conditions, they introduce additional computational overhead and may struggle to generalize across varying illumination and scene dynamics.

More recently, learning-based navigation, control, and obstacle detection methods have shown promising results in complex environments [13,20,21]. Despite their potential, such approaches often require extensive training data, specialized sensors, or high-performance computing resources, which can hinder real-time deployment on embedded UAV platforms.

Overall, existing methods reveal inherent trade-offs between robustness and computational efficiency, sensing richness and system portability, and performance and real-time feasibility. While multimodal sensing and learning-based techniques are widely recognized as promising directions, there remains a lack of lightweight, integrated solutions that enable robust pose estimation under low-light conditions while respecting the strict payload, power, and computational constraints of small UAVs. This gap motivates the approach proposed in this work.

3   Methodology

3.1   System Overview

The proposed system extends a learning-based pose estimation framework by integrating LiDAR depth measurements as an auxiliary sensing modality. Visual information is processed using a PoseNet-based architecture, while LiDAR data is incorporated through a lightweight fusion strategy designed to preserve real-time performance on resource-constrained platforms.

The overall pipeline estimates the six-degree-of-freedom (6-DoF) pose of the UAV at high frequency by combining visual features with complementary depth information, improving robustness under degraded visual conditions.

3.2   Visual Feature Extraction

Visual pose estimation is performed using a convolutional neural network based on PoseNet. To enable real-time inference on embedded hardware, the visual processing pipeline is optimized through:

- Input image resolution reduction.
- Lightweight network architectures.
- Input normalization.
- Removal of non-critical operations.

These optimizations significantly reduce computational load while maintaining sufficient representational capacity for pose regression.

3.3   LiDAR-Based Depth Integration

Depth measurements from multiple LiDAR sensors are used as auxiliary inputs to the pose estimation network. Each LiDAR sensor provides distance measurements that capture local geometric information from different viewing angles.

The LiDAR measurements are aggregated into a compact depth vector, which is concatenated with the visual feature embedding extracted by the PoseNet backbone. This feature-level integration enables the network to jointly exploit visual and geometric cues while introducing minimal computational overhead.

3.4   Sensor Fusion Strategy

Information fusion is performed at the feature level by concatenating the LiDAR depth vector with the visual feature embedding prior to pose regression. This early fusion strategy avoids complex geometric preprocessing and additional network branches, ensuring a lightweight and efficient implementation.

The fusion module does not significantly affect end-to-end pipeline latency, allowing the system to operate in real time.

3.5   LiDAR Sensor Configuration

The physical placement of the LiDAR sensors directly influences estimation stability. In the proposed setup, multiple LiDAR sensors are arranged in a triangular configuration covering frontal regions of the UAV. This configuration provides depth redundancy and improves robustness against partial occlusions or missing measurements.

3.6   Embedded Implementation Considerations

All experiments are conducted on a Raspberry Pi platform, selected for its low cost, wide availability, active development ecosystem, and ease of deployment for deep learning inference. While hardware accelerators such as FPGAs can offer performance benefits, they are not considered in this work due to increased implementation complexity, reliance on proprietary toolchains, and higher prototyping costs.

For the scope of this research, the Raspberry Pi enables rapid iteration, flexible experimentation, and reproducibility. Migration to specialized hardware accelerators may be explored in future work targeting commercialization.

3.7   Network Architecture and Training Details

The visual backbone is based on a PoseNet architecture derived from GoogLeNet. The final fully connected layers are adapted to regress 6-DoF pose.

Input images are resized to [224 × 224], and the network produces a feature embedding of dimension N.

LiDAR measurements are represented as a 3-dimensional vector corresponding to the distances measured by three sensors mounted on the UAV.

Fusion is performed by concatenating the LiDAR vector with the visual embedding before the regression head.

The network is trained using the following loss function:

$$L = \|\hat{p} - p\|_2 + \beta\|\hat{q} - q\|_2 \tag{1}$$

where p and q represent position and orientation respectively.

Training is performed using the Adam optimizer with a learning rate of 0.00007, batch size of 32, and for 100 epochs.

4   Experimental Setup

4.1   Experimental Design

The experiments are conducted on a custom dataset designed to evaluate multimodal fusion under controlled low-light conditions.

Public datasets commonly used in visual odometry research do not include synchronized low-cost LiDAR measurements aligned with RGB images in the configuration used in this work. As a result, direct comparison with existing methods would require modifying either the dataset or the sensing pipeline, introducing additional variables.

Instead, we adopt a controlled experimental design where all conditions remain fixed, and only the sensing modality is varied. This allows for a direct and fair comparison between visual-only and visualâĂŞLiDAR configurations.

To evaluate the performance of the proposed multimodal pose estimation framework, a dedicated sensing module and dataset were developed. The dataset was designed to enable fair comparison between different sensing configurations under controlled illumination conditions.

4.2　Sensing Module

A custom sensing module was constructed to collect synchronized visual, depth, and inertial data. The complete module weighs approximately 325 g, making it suitable for integration on small UAV platforms.

The sensing module comprises the following components:

- **Raspberry Pi 5**, used as the onboard computing unit for sensor acquisition and data synchronization (approximately 46 g).
- **Three TF-Luna LiDAR sensors**, arranged in a triangular configuration to capture local geometric information from multiple viewing angles (approximately 5 g each).
- **Logitech webcam** operating at 60 FPS to provide RGB visual input (approximately 200 g).
- **Inertial Measurement Unit (IMU)**, used to measure linear acceleration and angular velocity (approximately 5 g).

An overview of the sensing module, including the system diagram and assembled hardware, is shown in Fig. 1.

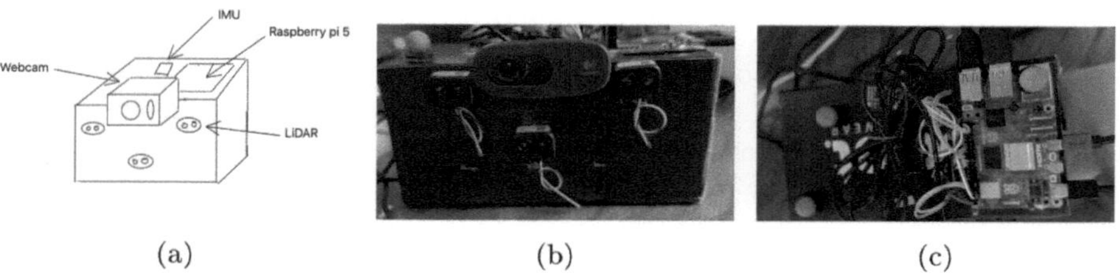

(a)　　　　　　　　　　　(b)　　　　　　　　　　　(c)

Fig. 1. Overview of the sensing module: (a) system diagram, (b) assembled module (front view), and (c) assembled module (upper view).

4.3　Data Collection and Preprocessing

To ensure consistency across sensing modalities, all recorded data were temporally aligned using frame timestamp synchronization. RGB images were normalized prior to processing, and LiDAR distance measurements were scaled to a common numerical range. These preprocessing steps enabled direct comparison between vision-only and multimodal model variants.

Two datasets were collected under controlled illumination conditions to analyze the effect of lighting degradation on pose estimation performance. The first dataset was recorded in a moderately illuminated indoor environment with an average illumination of approximately 124 lux. To extend the range of evaluated lighting conditions, this dataset was further modified through synthetic illumination degradation, producing frames with illumination levels ranging from 20 lux to 90 lux.

The second dataset was acquired in a low-light environment with an average illumination of approximately 36 lux, where visual features are significantly degraded. This dataset represents a challenging scenario for vision-based pose estimation and serves to evaluate the robustness of the proposed multimodal approach.

Representative frames from both datasets are shown in Fig. 2 Together, these datasets enable a systematic evaluation of the impact of illumination on RGB-based pose estimation and the benefits of incorporating complementary LiDAR and IMU measurements under reduced visibility.

(a) Dataset under better illumination conditions. 124 lux

(b) Dataset under low-light conditions. 36 lux

Fig. 2. Comparison between two collected datasets: (a) scenes with adequate illumination, and (b) scenes recorded under low-light conditions.

5   Results

5.1   Experimental Evaluation Under Multiple Sensing Configurations

To assess the contribution of each sensing modality, the proposed model was evaluated under four distinct configurations:

1. PoseNet with artificial illumination only.
2. PoseNet with artificial illumination and added Gaussian noise.
3. PoseNet augmented with LiDAR measurements under artificial illumination.
4. PoseNet augmented with LiDAR measurements and Gaussian noise.

All configurations were trained and evaluated using identical dataset splits and hyperparameters to ensure a fair comparison. Performance was assessed using root mean square error (RMSE) and trajectory error metrics.

To isolate the contribution of LiDAR measurements, we evaluate:

- Visual-only PoseNet
- PoseNet under degraded visual conditions
- Proposed Visualâ ÁŞLiDAR fusion method

All configurations are trained and evaluated under identical conditions.

5.2   Performance Under Extreme Illumination Conditions

Given the large number of experiments conducted under varying illumination levels, the analysis focuses on two representative cases: 22 lux, corresponding to severely degraded visual conditions, and 92 lux, representing moderately illuminated environments.

Figures 3, 4, 5 and 6 present the position estimation errors along the x, y, and z axes for the eight evaluated experimental conditions, obtained by combining the two illumination levels with the four sensing configurations.

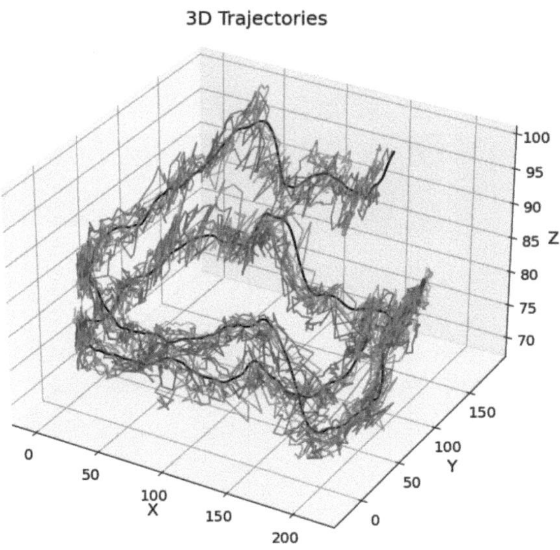

Fig. 3. Position estimation error in 22 lux and 92 lux: ground truth (–), 22 lux (–), 22 lux + noise (–), 22 lux + LiDAR (–), 22 lux + noise + LiDAR (–), 96 lux (–), 96 lux + noise (–), 96 lux + LiDAR (–), 96 lux + noise + LiDAR (–).

5.3   Quantitative Error Analysis

Table 1 summarizes the RMSE values obtained under low-light conditions (22 lux), while Table 2 reports the results under moderate illumination (92 lux).

5.4   Entropy-Based Analysis of Visual Degradation

To further characterize the impact of illumination on visual information quality and its influence on pose estimation, an entropy-based analysis of the RGB input images was conducted under two representative illumination regimes: low-light and well-lit conditions. Image entropy is used as a proxy for visual information

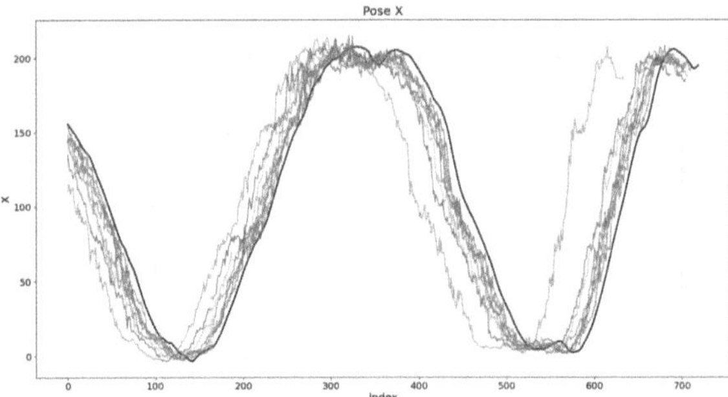

Fig. 4. Position estimation error in the x axis for the eight experimental conditions: ground truth (−), 22 lux (−), 22 lux + noise (−), 22 lux + LiDAR (−), 22 lux + noise + LiDAR (−), 96 lux (−), 96 lux + noise (−), 96 lux + LiDAR (−), 96 lux + noise + LiDAR (−).

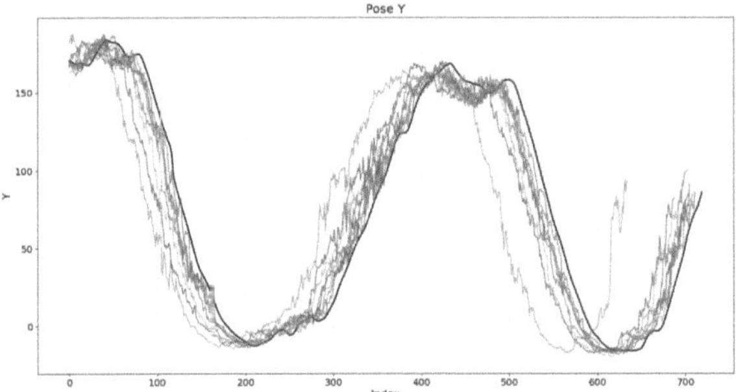

Fig. 5. Position estimation error in the y axis for the eight experimental conditions: ground truth (−), 22 lux (−), 22 lux + noise (−), 22 lux + LiDAR (−), 22 lux + noise + LiDAR (−), 96 lux (−), 96 lux + noise (−), 96 lux + LiDAR (−), 96 lux + noise + LiDAR (−).

Table 1. RMSE results for the four experimental configurations at 22 lux.

Configuration	LiDAR	Gaussian Noise	RMSE (mm)
PoseNet	No	No	12.776
PoseNet + Gaussian noise	No	Yes	49.946
PoseNet + LiDAR	Yes	No	11.105
PoseNet + LiDAR + Gaussian noise	Yes	Yes	7.920

content, capturing variations in texture richness and contrast that are critical for learning-based visual estimation.

Under low illumination, the image entropy exhibits significant fluctuations and pronounced drops, indicating a substantial reduction in usable visual information. While decreases in approximate luminance are often accompanied by

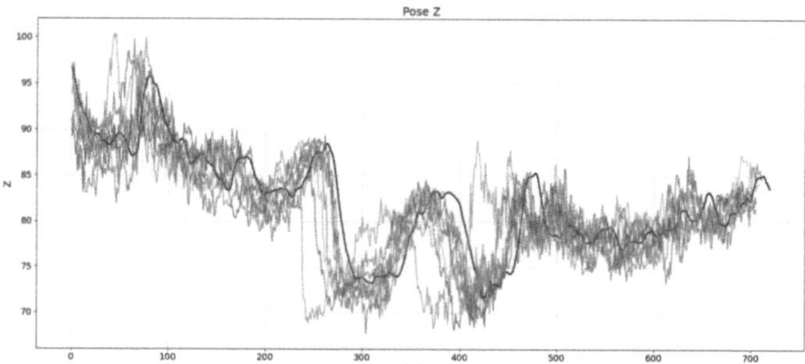

Fig. 6. Position estimation error in the z axis for the eight experimental conditions: ground truth (–), 22 lux (–), 22 lux + noise (–), 22 lux + LiDAR (–), 22 lux + noise + LiDAR (–), 96 lux (–), 96 lux + noise (–), 96 lux + LiDAR (–), 96 lux + noise + LiDAR (–).

Table 2. RMSE results for the four experimental configurations at 92 lux.

Configuration	LiDAR	Gaussian Noise	RMSE (mm)
PoseNet	No	No	27.461
PoseNet + Gaussian noise	No	Yes	16.685
PoseNet + LiDAR	Yes	No	22.345
PoseNet + LiDAR + Gaussian noise	Yes	Yes	11.145

entropy reductions, the relationship is not strictly linear, revealing that illumination alone is insufficient to describe visual degradation. Importantly, despite these entropy drops, the estimated UAV trajectory remains smooth and continuous across the X, Y, and Z axes. This observation suggests that the proposed multimodal fusion framework effectively decouples pose estimation stability from visual quality by leveraging complementary geometric information. In visually challenging segments, LiDAR measurements provide a stabilizing constraint that mitigates the impact of reduced RGB information, enabling robust pose estimation even when visual cues are unreliable.

In contrast, under better illumination the visual input maintains consistently higher entropy values with reduced variability across the sequence, reflecting richer texture and more reliable visual features. In this regime, entropy remains relatively stable even during localized illumination drops, and the estimated trajectories along all spatial axes exhibit increased smoothness and reduced noise. This behavior indicates that, when sufficient visual information is available, the pose estimation pipeline benefits primarily from the RGB modality, while LiDAR acts as a complementary stabilizing factor rather than a dominant constraint.

Taken together, these results demonstrate that image entropy provides a meaningful quantitative characterization of visual degradation beyond raw luminance measurements. The analysis highlights how multimodal fusion adapts naturally to the availability of visual information: LiDAR compensates for reduced entropy in low-light scenarios, while remaining non-intrusive when visual cues are reliable. This adaptive behavior supports the robustness and generality of the proposed approach across varying illumination conditions (Fig. 7).

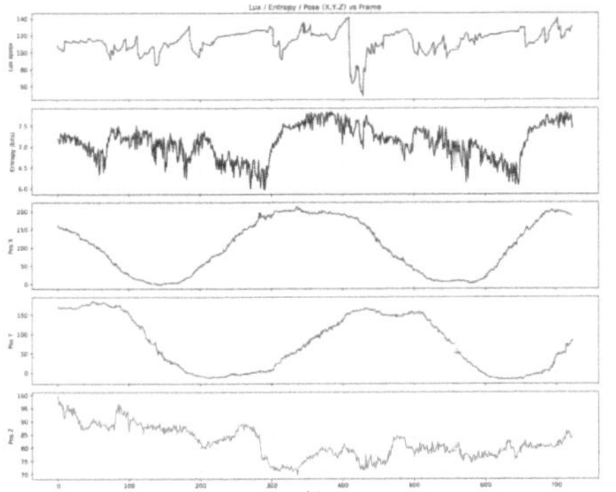 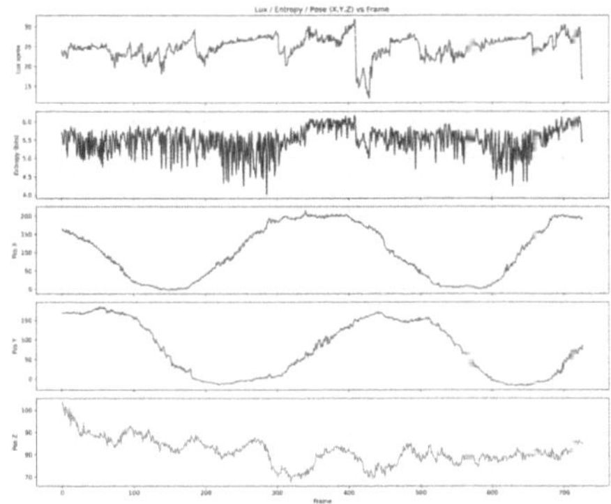

(a) Entropy analysis under better illumi-   (b) Entropy analysis under low-light con-
nation conditions. 124 lux   ditions. 36 lux

Fig. 7. Comparison between two entropy analysis: (a) adequate illumination, and (b) low-light conditions.

The results indicate that the integration of LiDAR measurements significantly reduces positional error under degraded illumination conditions.

Furthermore, the performance gap between visual-only and multimodal approaches increases as illumination decreases, highlighting the robustness of the proposed method in low-light environments.

These results validate the hypothesis that multimodal fusion is beneficial in scenarios where individual sensing modalities are unreliable.

6   Discussion

The results obtained at 22 lux reveal a clear advantage of incorporating LiDAR measurements into the pose estimation pipeline. While the RGB-only PoseNet configuration exhibits significant performance degradation when Gaussian noise is introduced, the multimodal configurations remain stable and achieve lower RMSE values.

Interestingly, under moderate illumination (92 lux), the introduction of Gaussian noise leads to improved performance in both RGB-only and multimodal configurations. This behavior suggests that controlled visual perturbations may act as a regularization mechanism, preventing over-reliance on specific visual features and improving generalization.

The comparative results across illumination levels indicate that the relative contribution of LiDAR measurements is strongly dependent on visual quality.

Under severely degraded conditions, LiDAR provides critical geometric stability, whereas under higher illumination its contribution is complementary but less dominant.

Overall, the results confirm that lightweight multimodal fusion enables robust pose estimation without compromising embedded feasibility, supporting the deployment of small UAVs in visually challenging environments.

The use of a custom dataset enables precise control over illumination conditions and sensor synchronization, which is essential for evaluating the robustness of multimodal fusion under low-light scenarios.

While comparisons with large-scale benchmarks are common, such datasets do not provide the specific sensor configuration required for this study. Therefore, the chosen experimental setup allows for a more controlled and interpretable evaluation.

7   Limitations and Future Work

While the proposed approach demonstrates promising results for multimodal pose estimation under low-light conditions, several limitations remain. First, the current evaluation focuses on pose estimation performance and does not yet include closed-loop autonomous flight experiments. Although the estimated poses are suitable for navigation purposes, their integration into a full control pipeline is left for future work.

Additionally, the use of low-cost LiDAR sensors introduces inherent limitations in range, resolution, and susceptibility to environmental factors. While the results indicate that such sensors can effectively complement visual information under degraded illumination, their reliability under more extreme conditions or highly dynamic environments requires further investigation.

Another limitation of the present study is the partial characterization of visual degradation. While illumination levels are controlled and quantified in terms of lux, a deeper analysis of visual information content is still ongoing. Future work will incorporate an entropy-based analysis of the RGB input to quantitatively assess the relationship between image information content, illumination conditions, and pose estimation performance.

Also the absence of evaluation on standard public benchmarks remains a limitation of this work. However, this is due to the lack of datasets that include synchronized RGB and low-cost LiDAR measurements under controlled illumination conditions.

Future work will explore extending the proposed approach to public datasets through simulated LiDAR inputs or alternative sensor configurations.

Future research will also consider the extension of the evaluation to additional challenging scenarios, such as indoor environments with abrupt lighting changes, smoke, or partial occlusions, in order to further assess the robustness and generality of the proposed approach.

8   Conclusion

This work addressed the problem of robust UAV pose estimation in low-light environments under strict payload, power, and computational constraints. A lightweight multimodal framework was proposed, extending a PoseNet-based architecture through the integration of low-cost LiDAR measurements to complement visual information.

Experimental results under varying illumination conditions demonstrated that the incorporation of LiDAR significantly improves pose estimation stability and accuracy, particularly in severely degraded visual scenarios. The proposed fusion strategy enables robust performance while remaining compatible with embedded platforms and affordable sensing hardware.

Overall, the results suggest that low-cost LiDAR sensors, when properly integrated with learning-based visual estimation, constitute a viable alternative to more expensive sensing solutions for small UAVs operating in challenging environments. This work contributes toward bridging the gap between laboratory-scale localization systems and practical, real-world autonomous navigation under degraded visual conditions.

References

1. Petrlík, M., Krajník, T., Saska, M.: LiDAR-based stabilization, navigation and localization for UAVs operating in dark indoor environments. In: Proceedings of the EEE International Conference on Unmanned Aircraft Systems (ICUAS), pp. 243–251 (2021)
2. Jiang, Y., et al.: EnlightenGAN: deep light enhancement without paired supervision. IEEE Trans. Image Process. **30**, 2340–2349 (2021)
3. Fu, C., Dong, H., Ye, J., Zheng, G., Li, S., Zhao, J.: HighlightNet: highlighting low-light potential features for real-time UAV tracking. In: Proceedings of the IEEE/RSJ International Conference on Intelligent Robots and Systems (IRCS), pp. 12146–12153 (2022)
4. Vidal, A.R., Rebecq, H., Horstschaefer, T., Scaramuzza, D.: Ultimate SLAM? Combining events, images, and IMU for robust visual SLAM in HDR and high-speed scenarios. IEEE Robot. Autom. Lett. **3**(2), 994–1001 (2018)
5. Cioffi, G., Bauersfeld, L., Kaufmann, E., Scaramuzza, D.: Learned inertial odometry for autonomous drone racing. IEEE Robot. Autom. Lett. **8**(5), 2684–2691 (2023)
6. Torrente, G., Kaufmann, E., Föhn, P., Scaramuzza, D.: Data-driven MPC for quadrotors. IEEE Robot. Autom. Lett. **6**(2), 3769–3776 (2021)
7. Youn, W., Ko, H., Choi, H., Choi, I., Baek, J.-H., Myung, H.: Collision-free autonomous navigation of a small UAV using low-cost sensors in GPS-denied environments. Int. J. Control Autom. Syst. **19**(2), 953–968 (2021)
8. Chang, Y., Cheng, Y., Manzoor, U., Murray, J.: A review of UAV autonomous navigation in GPS-denied environments. Robot. Auton. Syst. 104533 (2023)
9. Delmerico, J., Cieslewski, T., Rebecq, H., Faessler, M., Scaramuzza, D.: Are we ready for autonomous drone racing? The UZH-FPV drone racing dataset. In: Proceedings of the IEEE International Conference on Robotics and Automation (ICRA), pp. 6713–6719 (2019)

10. Foehn, P., et al.: AlphaPilot: autonomous drone racing. Auton. Robot. **46**(1), 307–320 (2022)
11. Faessler, M., Mueggler, E., Schwabe, K., Scaramuzza, D.: A monocular pose estimation system based on infrared LEDs. In: Proceedings of the IEEE International Conference on Robotics and Automation (ICRA), pp. 907–913 (2014)
12. Ye, J., Fu, C., Zheng, G., Cao, Z., Li, B.: DarkLighter: light up the darkness for UAV tracking. In: Proceedings of the IEEE/RSJ International Conference on Intelligent Robots and Systems (IROS), pp. 3079–3085 (2021)
13. Kaufmann, E., Bauersfeld, L., Loquercio, A., Müller, M., Koltun, V., Scaramuzza, D.: Champion-level drone racing using deep reinforcement learning. Nature **620**(7976), 982–987 (2023)
14. Fu, C., Yao, L., Zuo, H., Zheng, G., Pan, J.: SAM-DA: UAV tracks anything at night with SAM-powered domain adaptation. In: Proceedings of the International Conference on Advanced Robotics and Mechatronics (ICARM), pp. 31–38 (2024)
15. Sun, S., Cioffi, G., De Visser, C., Scaramuzza, D.: Autonomous quadrotor flight despite rotor failure with onboard vision sensors: Frames vs. events. *IEEE Robotics and Automation Letters***6**(2), 580–587 (2021)
16. Tian, Z., et al.: A survey of deep learning-based low-light image enhancement. Sensors **23**(18), 7763 (2023)
17. Wueller, D.: Low light performance of digital still cameras. In: Proceedings of the SPIE Multimedia Content and Mobile Devices, vol. 8667, pp. 434–442 (2013)
18. Gehrig, D., Scaramuzza, D.: Low-latency automotive vision with event cameras. Nature **629**(8014), 1034–1040 (2024)
19. Messikommer, N., Cioffi, G., Gehrig, M., Scaramuzza, D.: Reinforcement learning meets visual odometry. In: Proceedings of the European Conference on Computer Vision (ECCV), pp. 76–92 (2024)
20. Geles, I., Bauersfeld, L., Romero, A., Xing, J., Scaramuzza, D.: Demonstrating agile flight from pixels without state estimation. arXiv preprint arXiv:2406.12505 (2024)
21. Raju, G.R.G., Zubić, N., Cannici, M., Scaramuzza, D.: Perturbed state space feature encoders for optical flow with event cameras. arXiv preprint arXiv:2504.10669 (2025)
22. Kruber, F., Morales, E.S., Chakraborty, S., Botsch, M.: Vehicle position estimation with aerial imagery from unmanned aerial vehicles. In: Proceedings of the IEEE Intelligent Vehicles Symposium, pp. 2089–2096 (2020)
23. Nguyen, A., Nguyen, N., Tran, K., Tjiputra, E., Tran, Q.D.: Autonomous navigation in complex environments with deep multimodal fusion network. In: Proceedings of the IEEE/RSJ International Conference on Intelligent Robots and Systems (IROS), pp. 5824–5830 (2020)
24. Burdziakowski, P., Bobkowska, K.: UAV photogrammetry under poor lighting conditions–accuracy considerations. Sensors **21**(10), 3531 (2021)
25. Zhang, Y., Li, Y., Lin, Q.: Low-light enhancer for UAV night tracking based on Zero-DCE++. J. Comput. Commun. **11**(4), 1–11 (2023)
26. Singh, A., Chougule, A., Narang, P., Chamola, V., Yu, F.R.: Low-light image enhancement for UAVs with multi-feature fusion deep neural networks. IEEE Geosci. Remote Sens. Lett. **19**, 1–5 (2022)
27. Hai, J., Hao, Y., Zou, F., Lin, F., Han, S.: A visual navigation system for UAV under diverse illumination conditions. Appl. Artif. Intell. **35**(15), 1529–1549 (2021)
28. Klenk, S., Koestler, L., Scaramuzza, D., Cremers, D.: E-NeRF: neural radiance fields from a moving event camera. IEEE Robot. Autom. Lett. **8**(3), 1587–1594 (2023)

29. Eirale, A., Martini, M., Chiaberge, M.: Human following and guidance by autonomous mobile robots: a comprehensive review. IEEE Access (2025)
30. Qu, R., Wang, Z., Liu, Y., Li, C., Jiang, H., Fang, C.: LumiLoc: a low-light-optimized visual localization framework for autonomous drones. Aerospace **12**(6), 454 (2025)

VAR Based on Knowledge Transfer
from VLMs and Video Descriptions

Emilio Vera-Cordero[1] , David Mata-Mendoza[1] , Gibran Benitez-Garcia[2] ,
Hiroki Takahashi[2] , and Mariko Nakano[1(✉)]

[1] Instituto Politécnico Nacional - ESIME Culhuacán, 04440 Mexico City, Mexico
mnakano@ipn.mx
[2] The University of Electro-Communications, Tokyo 182-8585, Japan

Abstract. Video Anomaly Recognition (VAR) is crucial for public
safety, yet it remains challenging due to the coarse labels in existing
datasets that hinder the learning of rich patterns. Unlike standard detection, VAR requires precise classification of complex events. In this paper,
we address instance-level VAR in temporally localized events using a
pre-trained Vision-Language Model (VLM). We propose a classification
framework that transfers visual and textual knowledge by constructing a
classification matrix based on centroids of offline description embeddings.
This matrix, constructed with the VLM text encoder, is used to fine-
tune the VLM visual encoder for more accurate anomaly categorization.
Our video classification experiments on the UCF-Crime dataset demonstrate significant improvements over video-level training and baselines.
The code is publicly available at https://github.com/jemveco/clip4var.

Keywords: Anomaly Classification · Anomalous Event · VAR

1 Introduction

Anomalous events in public places are defined as situations that deviate from
normal patterns, being less frequent than normal situations and potentially dangerous for the people involved, such as traffic accidents, assaults, fights, etc. [4].
An accurate detection and classification of these anomalous events is essential
to improve public safety. While traditionally video surveillance has focused on
Video Anomaly Detection (VAD) to identify when an anomalous event occurs,
the emerging task of Video Anomaly Recognition (VAR) seeks to classify the
specific nature of the event to provide more actionable insights [9].

Developing accurate VAR models remains challenging due to three primary
factors. First, the time-consuming annotation of each video frame or segment.
Second, the prevalence of video-level labels in popular public datasets such as
UCF-Crime [4], which omit temporal localization of anomalous events for its
training samples. And finally, the same anomaly type can be manifested through
diverse behaviors and durations.

To address these limitations, we propose a VAR framework that leverages a pre-trained Vision-Language Model (VLM), specifically Contrastive Language-Image Pretraining (CLIP) [3], to transfer rich visual and textual knowledge into the classification process. To achieve this, the linear classification head of a transformer-based video recognition model is replaced with an offline-generated classification matrix [7] based on CLIP. This matrix encodes deep semantic knowledge by representing each anomaly class as the centroid of text embeddings derived from anomalous events descriptions. By using this matrix, a CLIP-based video encoder can be fine-tuned to align temporally localized video instances with their corresponding textual concepts.

To implement this approach, the UCF-Crime dataset was expanded by generating temporal annotations through a VAD framework [10] and manual verification. It is worth noting that context is added to these descriptive sentences to generate more class-defined centroids, which are then dimensionally reduced using Principal Component Analysis (PCA). This strategy allows our model to learn more discriminative patterns for anomaly categorization, outperforming video-level training and video classification baselines. In our experiments, we achieved 46.79% Top-1 accuracy on the UCF-Crime dataset, demonstrating a significant improvement over previous methods [4,5].

The main contributions of our paper are summarized as follows:

- UCF-Crime fine-grained temporal annotations were generated for anomalous event instances located in training videos, overcoming the limitations of coarse video-level labels. This UCF-Crime add-on is publicly available in our repository.
- We present a novel approach to compute a classification matrix constructed from rich textual descriptions for VAR tasks, without modifying the rest of the model architecture. This allows the model to leverage the latent space of VLMs pre-trained with large datasets, such as CLIP, resulting in an anomaly representations aligned with semantic knowledge, thus improving the performance of the proposed model and reducing training time.
- Extensive experiments were conducted on the UCF-Crime dataset, including performance evaluation of the proposed method against the state-of-the-art, as well as ablation studies demonstrating the impact of the proposed components.

2   Related Work

2.1   Video Anomaly Detection

VAD focuses on the detection of anomalous events in video surveillance and has been extensively studied using approaches such as semi-supervised [2] which train exclusively on normal data, defining anomalies as deviations from a learned "normality" model. Weakly supervised [4,6,10] which utilize video-level labels without frame-level timestamps. And open-set [5] which leverage pre-trained knowledge to detect categories not seen during training. Weakly supervised methods have gained popularity because they produce good results while limiting the effort and time required for datasets annotation. Sultani *et al.* [4] were the first to formulate weakly supervised VAD by introducing a Multiple-Instance Learning (MIL) ranking model and the UCF-Crime dataset, treating each long video as a "bag" of segments with a single anomaly/normal label.

2.2 Video Anomaly Recognition

Sultani *et al.* [4] proposed a basic VAR classifier, but its performance is hindered by the use of coarse video-level labels during training, leading to a poor association between visual features and specific anomaly patterns. Zanella *et al.* [9] introduced AnomalyCLIP, which uses learnable text prompts to define anomaly directions in the CLIP latent space. A key limitation is that these prompts are learned from a limited set of labels, potentially failing to capture the rich semantic nuances of complex scenes. Furthermore, their dependence on a "normality prototype" adds complexity to the optimization process. Regarding Open-Vocabulary frameworks, Wu *et al.* [5] utilize LLMs to inject semantic knowledge. However, their approach primarily yields video-level scores. This lack of temporal localization makes it less effective for real-time surveillance, where identifying the exact moment and type of an instance is critical.

In contrast, our model avoids the instability of learnable prompts by using static semantic centroids derived from detailed event descriptions. By focusing on instance-level classification with a frozen classification matrix, the model achieves a more direct and robust video-text alignment.

2.3 Anomaly Description

New multimodal datasets highlight the benefit of language in surveillance. Yuan *et al.* [8] introduced UCA, a large "surveillance video-and-language" dataset with fine-grained sentence-level annotations for all normal and anomalous events in the UCF-Crime dataset samples. They show that incorporating textual event descriptions into multimodal models can improve anomaly detection performance.

3   Methodology

Figure 1 shows the overall fine-tuning pipeline of our proposed VAR model which leverages knowledge from a pre-trained CLIP model and performs instance-level classification. The fine-tuning consists of two stages:

Stage 1. Offline construction of the classification matrix from the descriptions of anomalous events.

Stage 2. Fine-tuning of the transformer-based video encoder with anomalous event instances.

During both fine-tuning and inference, the input to the video encoder consists of anomalous event segment instances detected by an external VAD model, *e.g.*, [1, 10].

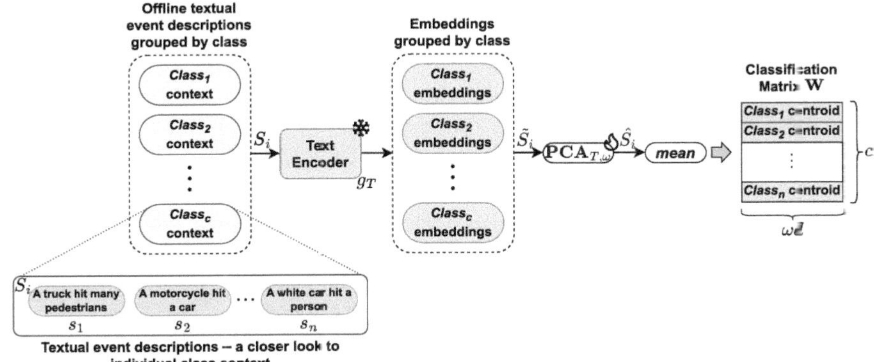

(a) **Stage 1**: Process to obtain the classification matrix from offline events descriptions.

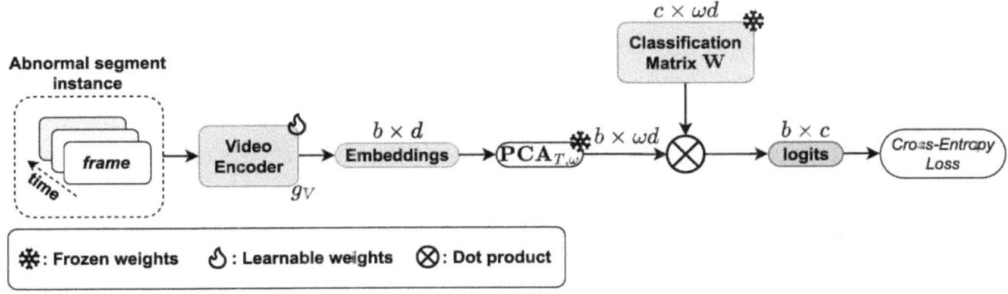

(b) **Stage 2**: Fine-tuning of the video encoder with the classification matrix.

Fig. 1. Overall pipeline of the proposed approach for the VAR task.

3.1 Offline Construction of the Classification Matrix

Inspired by Wu *et al.* [7], we replace the learnable linear classification head of a transformer-based video classification method with a static, offline pre-computed classification matrix $\mathbf{W}$. Similar to their work, the latent space of a pre-trained VLM (CLIP) is used to initialize the classifier. However, while Wu *et al.* construct this matrix using embeddings from simple class labels, our framework utilizes detailed textual descriptions of anomalous events to compute centroids for each class. As shown in Fig. 1a, this allows $\mathbf{W}$ to capture a richer semantic background, specifically tailored to represent the complex and diverse manifestations of anomalies in public spaces. To refine the centroids of the classification matrix, the descriptions of the segments were concatenated with their class labels, *e.g.*, *"Fight: a man hits someone . . . "*, thus creating a common point for the descriptions of each class.

Given a set of anomalous events descriptions defined as Eq. (1):

$$S_i = \{s_1, s_2, \ldots, s_{n_i}\}; \quad i = 1, 2, \ldots, c. \tag{1}$$

where c denotes the number of anomaly classes, and n_i is the number of descriptions of the i-th anomaly class. Each set S_i is encoded using the text encoder

$g_T(\cdot)$ of a pre-trained VLM (CLIP), producing a set of d-dimensional text embeddings as expressed in Eq. (2):

$$\tilde{S}_i = g_T(S_i); \quad i = 1, 2, \ldots, c. \tag{2}$$

where $\tilde{S}_i = \{\tilde{\mathbf{s}}_1, \tilde{\mathbf{s}}_2, \ldots, \tilde{\mathbf{s}}_{n_i}\}$ is the set of textual embeddings of the i-th anomaly class.

To mitigate redundancy and noise within the embeddings, a dimensionality reduction step was implemented using the $\text{PCA}_{T,\omega}$ block as shown in Fig. 1a. Here, the subscript T indicates that the PCA is computed specifically using the text embeddings, while ω denotes the reduction factor. The component matrix is first fitted on the complete collection of text embedding sets $\{\tilde{S}_i\}_{i=1}^c$ and subsequently applied to each $\tilde{S}_i$ to yield a reduced set, as shown in (3):

$$\hat{S}_i = \text{PCA}_{T,\omega}(\tilde{S}_i); \quad i = 1, 2, \ldots, c. \tag{3}$$

This reduction process is controlled by the factor ω, where $0.1 < \omega < 0.9$. The choice of PCA for dimensionality reduction, is motivated by the need to preserve the semantic structure of the pre-trained VLM (CLIP) latent space. PCA reduces dimensions by maximizing variance, effectively filtering out noise and redundancy in the textual embeddings while maintaining the rich knowledge of the VLM, this ensures that the classification matrix $\mathbf{W}$ provides more generalized and robust insights for the fine-tuning of the video encoder.

Finally, a centroid embedding $\mathbf{W}_i$ is computed by averaging each $\hat{S}_i$ embeddings set, expressed by Eq. (4):

$$\mathbf{W}_i = \frac{1}{n_i} \sum_{j=1}^{n_i} \hat{S}_{i,j}. \tag{4}$$

Thus, each $\mathbf{W}_i \in \mathbb{R}^{\omega d}$ centroid vector is a row of the classification matrix $\mathbf{W} \in \mathbb{R}^{c \times \omega d}$.

3.2   Video Encoder Fine-Tuning

The video encoder $g_V(\cdot)$ is fine-tuned to increase the similarity between the visual features and the corresponding class row of the frozen classification matrix $\mathbf{W}$. As illustrated in Fig. 1b, for each anomalous event segment, the encoder generates a d-dimensional embedding, which is subsequently reduced to ωd dimension using the pre-computed $\text{PCA}_{T,\omega}$ transformation.

Let $\mathbf{V} \in \mathbb{R}^{b \times \omega d}$ represent a batch of b reduced video embeddings, and let $\mathbf{Y} \in [0, c)^{b \times c}$ denote the corresponding ground-truth labels in the set . The optimization objective is to minimize the cross-entropy loss between the predicted class distributions and the ground-truth labels. The optimal parameters Θ_V^* for the video encoder are obtained with Eq. (5):

$$\Theta_V^* = \arg\min_{\Theta_V} \mathbb{E}_{(\mathbf{V},\mathbf{Y}) \sim \mathcal{D}} \left[H\left(\mathbf{Y}, \sigma(\mathbf{V}\mathbf{W}^\top)\right) \right]. \tag{5}$$

where $\sigma(\cdot)$ denotes the *softmax* activation applied to the similarity scores, and $H(\cdot)$ represents the *Cross-Entropy* function.

During this stage, only the parameters of the video encoder $g_V(\cdot)$ are updated, while both, the $\text{PCA}_{T,\omega}$ projection and the semantic classification matrix $\mathbf{W}$ remain frozen.

3.3   Generation of the VAR Dataset

To facilitate instance-level VAR, we curated a refined version of the UCF-Crime dataset by establishing precise temporal boundaries for training instances. Since the original training set only provides video-level labels, the state-of-the-art VAD framework proposed by Zhou *et al.* [10] was employed to generate initial frame-level detections. Subsequently, we conducted a manual review of these detections to define accurate temporal segments for each anomalous event.

In parallel, descriptive sentences from the UCA dataset [8] corresponding to the selected segments were extracted. This process ensured a balanced alignment between video instances and textual descriptions, where each annotated segment is paired with a specific description to compute the semantic centroids for the classification matrix $\mathbf{W}$. For the test set, the original temporal ground truth provided by UCF-Crime was utilized to ensure standard evaluation conditions. The final distribution of our instance-level dataset, comprising $1,186$ training segments and 171 testing segments across 13 classes.

4   Experimental Results

4.1   Experiments Setup

Dataset. The performance of our instance-level VAR approach was evaluated using the extended version of the UCF-Crime dataset previously mentioned, which consists of 13 classes and whose sample distribution is shown in Table 1.

Evaluation Metrics. For VAR, the accuracy metric defined in Eq. (6) was used to evaluate the classification performance, as done in previous works [4,5].

$$\text{Accuracy} = \frac{\text{TP} + \text{TN}}{\text{TP} + \text{TN} + \text{FP} + \text{FN}}. \tag{6}$$

Implementation Details. Our model was implemented in PyTorch and trained it on a single NVIDIA RTX 3090 GPU. The AdamW optimizer with a learning rate of 5×10^{-5} and a batch size of 8 was used. Due to the use of a pre-trained VLM, the model was trained for only 30 epochs.

Table 1. Dataset temporal-event instances distribution.

Class	Training	Testing
Abuse	167	2
Arrest	89	5
Arson	52	10
Assault	96	4
Burglary	40	15
Explosion	34	22
Fighting	123	5
Road Accidents	127	23
Robbery	160	5
Shooting	37	25
Shoplifting	25	25
Stealing	103	7
Vandalism	45	8

Training and Inference. The CLIP ViT-L/14 architecture [3] was implemented as the backbone for both visual and textual feature extraction.

For each anomalous event segment, 16 frames were uniformly sampled. These frames were resized to 224×224 pixels before being processed by the visual encoder. To model temporal dependencies, the transformer-based architecture proposed by Wu *et al.* [7] was adapted, which aggregates individual frame embeddings into a cohesive video representation.

The original 768-dimensional embeddings from the CLIP encoders were reduced using a PCA factor of $\omega = 0.5$ determined by an ablation study shown in Table 3. This resulted in a latent space of 384 dimensions for both the textual classification matrix $\mathbf{W}$ and the video embeddings $\mathbf{V}$.

As a baseline for comparison, the same CLIP ViT-L/14 model from Wu *et al.* [7] was implemented using a single Fully Connected (FC) layer as the classification head. Unlike our proposed method, the baseline does not utilize PCA reduction or the context semantic matrix, relying instead on traditional supervised learning of the FC weights.

4.2 Comparison with Previous Works Methods

In order to evaluate the performance of the proposed method, Table 2 presents a comparison of the accuracy values with respect to a baseline and with previous works [4,5]. Our model shows an improvement of 5.36%, demonstrating that the proposed approach has superior performance compared to the previous methods. It is important to point out that our model performs VAR at the level of anomalous event instances in segments of a few frames, unlike the previous works, which uses complete videos to perform VAR.

Table 2. Performance comparison of the proposed method with respect to the state-of-the-art in the VAR task, in terms of accuracy.

Method	Top-1 (%)
Sultani *et al.* (C3D) [4]	23.00
Sultani *et al.* (TCNN) [4]	23.40
Wu *et al.* [5]	41.43
Baseline (ViT–L/14 + FC)	41.66
Ours	**46.79**

4.3   Qualitative Results

In addition, the confusion matrix of the test samples for the 13 classes defined by UCF-Crime is presented as Fig. 2. As can be seen, the correlation between concepts inherent in VLMs facilitates the classification of anomalies. By leveraging the shared latent space of CLIP, the model classifies events based on context; this means that the semantic meaning of an action has more influence than visual similarity between actions when assigning classes. However, this causes the model to confuse the categories of videos that present similar concepts.

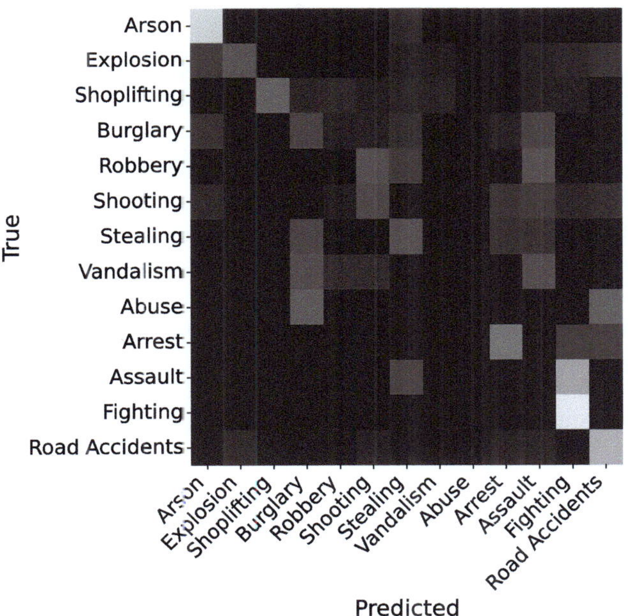

Fig. 2. Confusion matrix of VAR on UCF-Crime test split.

4.4   Ablation Studies

The impact on the discriminatory capacity of the model was also compared when applying dimensionality reduction using PCA. Table 3 shows the effect of varying the dimensionality reduction factor for the embeddings, demonstrating that the best value is 0.5 since as ω continues to decrease the reduction value increases, the results begin to decrease. It is interesting to note that without adding PCA reduction, the results worsen considerably compared to the baseline shown in Table 2.

Table 3. Effect of varying PCA dimensionality reduction (ω).

Method	Top-1 (%)	Top-3 (%)
ViT–L/14 (*without* PCA)	35.89	66.02
ViT–L/14 (PCA$_{\omega=0.75}$)	41.02	66.02
ViT–L/14 (PCA$_{\omega=0.5}$)	**46.79**	**70.51**
ViT–L/14 (PCA$_{\omega=0.25}$)	43.59	66.02

Conclusions

In this paper, we present a novel classification framework for VAR that performs classification at the instance level. By leveraging textual events descriptions through a pre-trained CLIP text encoder, we transfer semantic knowledge from the text encoder of a pre-trained VLM into the visual recognition process via an offline-constructed classification matrix.

Ultimately, our approach achieved a Top-1 accuracy of 46.79% on the UCF-Crime dataset, representing a 5.36% improvement over the previous works and significantly outperforming video-level and classification baselines. Furthermore, because the classification matrix is computed offline, our model maintains high inference efficiency, requiring no textual input or processing during real-time deployment. This work underscores the potential of VLMs to provide more informative and semantically rich solutions for enhancing public safety in surveillance environments.

References

1. Flores-Monroy, J., Benitez-Garcia, G., Nakano-Miyatake, M., Takahashi, H.: An online modular framework for anomaly detection and multiclass classification in video surveillance **15**(17), 9249. https://doi.org/10.3390/app15179249, https://www.mdpi.com/2076-3417/15/17/9249

2. Georgescu, M.I., Barbalau, A., Ionescu, R.T., Shahbaz Khan, F., Popescu, M., Shah, M.: Anomaly detection in video via self-supervised and multi-task learning. In: 2021 IEEE/CVF Conference on Computer Vision and Pattern Recognition (CVPR), pp. 12737–12747. IEEE. https://doi.org/10.1109/CVPR46437.2021.01255, https://ieeexplore.ieee.org/document/9578240/

3. Radford, A., et al.: Learning transferable visual models from natural language supervision. In: Proceedings of the 38th International Conference on Machine Learning, pp. 8748–8763. PMLR. https://proceedings.mlr.press/v139/radford21a.html

4. Sultani, W., Chen, C., Shah, M.: Real-world anomaly detection in surveillance videos. In: 2018 IEEE/CVF Conference on Computer Vision and Pattern Recognition, pp. 6479–6488. https://doi.org/10.1109/CVPR.2018.00678, https://ieeexplore.ieee.org/document/8578776

5. Wu, P., et al.: Open-vocabulary video anomaly detection. In: 2024 IEEE/CVF Conference on Computer Vision and Pattern Recognition (CVPR), pp. 18297–18307. https://doi.org/10.1109/CVPR52733.2024.01732, https://ieeexplore.ieee.org/document/10654921

6. Wu, P., et al.: VadCLIP: adapting vision-language models for weakly supervised video anomaly detection 38(6), 6074–6082. https://doi.org/10.1609/aaai.v38i6.28423, https://ojs.aaai.org/index.php/AAAI/article/view/28423

7. Wu, W., Sun, Z., Ouyang, W.: Revisiting classifier: transferring vision-language models for video recognition. In: Proceedings of the Thirty-Seventh AAAI Conference on Artificial Intelligence and Thirty-Fifth Conference on Innovative Applications of Artificial Intelligence and Thirteenth Symposium on Educational Advances in Artificial Intelligence. AAAI'23/IAAI'23/EAAI'23, vol. 37, pp. 2847–2855. AAAI Press. https://doi.org/10.1609/aaai.v37i3.25386

8. Yuan, T., et al.: Towards surveillance video-and-language understanding new dataset, baselines, and challenges. In: 2024 IEEE/CVF Conference on Computer Vision and Pattern Recognition (CVPR), pp. 22052–22061. https://doi.org/10.1109/CVPR52733.2024.02082, https://ieeexplore.ieee.org/document/10356129

9. Zanella, L., Liberatori, B., Menapace, W., Poiesi, F., Wang, Y., Ricci, E.: Delving into CLIP latent space for video anomaly recognition 249, 104163. https://doi.org/10.1016/j.cviu.2024.104163, https://www.sciencedirect.com/science/article/pii/S1077314224002443

10. Zhou, Y., Qu, Y., Xu, X., Shen, F., Song, J., Tao Shen, H.: BatchNorm-based weakly supervised video anomaly detection 34(12), 13642–13654. https://doi.org/10.1109/TCSVT.2024.3450734, https://ieeexplore.ieee.org/document/10649595

Upsampling of Sparse Three-Dimensional Point Clouds Using iFactor-KDTree with Adaptive Interpolation

Dora-Luz Almanza-Ojeda[1] , Mario-Alberto Ibarra-Manzano[1] ,
Carlos A. Perez-Ramirez[2] , and Yair A. Andrade-Ambriz[2(✉)]

[1] Departamento de ingeniería electrónica, DICIS, Universidad de Guanajuato,
Carretera Salamanca - Valle de Santiago Km. 3.5 + 1.8, 36885
Salamanca, Gto, Mexico
`{dora.almanza,ibarram}@ugto.mx`
[2] Facultad de Ingeniería, Universidad Autónoma de Querétaro, Campus Aeropuerto,
Carretera a Chichimequillas S/N, Ejido BolaÃśos, 76140
Santiago de Queretaro, Qro, Mexico
`carlos.perez@uaq.mx, yandradea@icloud.com`

Abstract. Three-dimensional point cloud processing is fundamental to applications such as autonomous driving, object reconstruction, and urban modeling. The complexity of point clouds requires considerable computational resources for analysis, especially when machine learning or deep models are used. While learning-based upsampling methods can achieve high geometric accuracy, they typically necessitate substantial annotated datasets, extensive training procedures, and GPU-accelerated hardware. These requirements limit their applicability in scenarios with limited resources or in real-time. Therefore, this paper introduces a lightweight, deterministic framework for upsampling sparse, real-world point clouds. The framework combines an iFactor-KDTree structure with density-aware, adaptive interpolation. The proposed method selectively densifies low-density regions without requiring prior training. Using spatial neighborhood analysis, the algorithm preserves the geometric structure of the original object while maintaining low computational complexity. Experimental evaluation on the PU1K dataset shows that the method can perform 4x upsampling in 25 milliseconds on a CPU. These characteristics make the proposed framework suitable for real-time processing and deployment in environments with limited computational resources or scarce annotated data.

Keywords: Point cloud · Object upsampling · iFactor-KDTree

1 Introduction

Currently, point clouds are widely used in applications ranging from autonomous driving, to augmented reality, and urban modeling, among others. A point cloud is a collection of disordered points, where each point represents its position in the three-dimensional coordinates X, Y, and Z. Point clouds are created using sensors such as LIDAR (Light Detection and Ranging) and RGB-D cameras (such as Azure Kinect, and Intel RealSense, among others), which provide information such as coordinates, intensity, color, and normals [1].

Sampling three-dimensional point clouds poses a fundamental challenge in many scientific and technological disciplines, including computer graphics, computer vision, geomatics, and complex systems modeling. Discrete representations of spatial information are fragmented and random, making them difficult to analyze, process, and accurately represent. Additionally, sensors that capture point clouds often introduce noise and missing patches due to lighting conditions, sensor vibrations, and other factors.

Due to the sparse, and unstructured nature of point cloud data, their processing is an active research topic with many challenges to overcome [2], and when using deep models, a large amount of data is required for training [3]. The current approach to point cloud sampling is based on random or uniform subsampling techniques, which have significant limitations in their ability to preserve the intrinsic structure and original geometric characteristics of the data. Conventional approaches suffer from several critical problems: loss of structural information, non-optimal distribution, density sensitivity, and computational limitations.

Many existing models can detect, classify, and segment objects within point clouds [2,4–7], processing data from raw points to voxels. However, these models tend to perform poorly on unknown scenes due to differences in object shapes, lighting conditions, and limited generalization during training. Moreover, deep models require large annotated datasets with adequate point density per object [8]; a condition that is rarely met in real-world scenarios, where 3D data is expensive and time-consuming to capture. This has driven the need for techniques that preserve geometric structure while remaining computationally efficient and independent of large training sets.

These constraints have prompted the search for methodologies that preserve geometric structure while remaining computationally efficient. To address these limitations, this paper presents a training-free algorithm for upsampling sparse point cloud objects by constructing a KDTree from the original points. The *iFactor* variable enables the algorithm to identify nearest neighbors and generate N new points per original point via adaptive interpolation, which uses local and global densities to focus densification in sparse regions. The resulting point cloud retains the original shape with a larger number of points, without requiring a training phase.

The remainder of this paper is organized as follows: Sect. 2 reviews related work, Sect. 3 describes the methodology, Sect. 4 presents the results, and Sect. 5 concludes.

2   Related Work

In recent years, point cloud processing and upsampling have emerged as a fundamental area of research, with numerous advances focusing on the use of deep learning techniques. These methods have shown promising results but generally share the need for large volumes of training data. In the following, we review the most significant contributions in this field, emphasizing their methodological approaches and results.

Several deep learning methods have been proposed for point cloud upsampling by learning geometric features from large datasets. Yu *et al.* [9] introduced PU-Net, which extracts point patches and maps them to a feature space to reconstruct a denser point cloud. Building on this idea, Wang *et al.* [10] trained cascaded networks inspired by image super-resolution, focusing on different levels of detail. Li *et al.* [11] proposed PU-GAN, which learns point distributions from a latent space using a GAN topology with a composed loss function to improve point distribution. Later, Li *et al.* [12] refined this line of work with Dis-PU, using two cascading subnetworks, a dense generator and a spatial refiner, to produce and reorganize output points more accurately.

You and Kim [13] proposed a deep model that converts point clouds into 2D range images and fills gaps via nearest-neighbor interpolation, achieving mAP improvements of up to 9.2% on the KITTI dataset for 3D object detection.

Other approaches focus on point cloud completion under partial observations. Wu *et al.* [14] presented SCNet, which combines multiscale features and a coarse-to-fine strategy with graph convolution to generate complete point clouds. Zhu *et al.* [15] proposed RD-Net, which captures both local and global information through iterative sampling and a two-stage reconstruction process, reducing CD error by 2% on the ShapeNet-part dataset. Similarly, Cai *et al.* [16] introduced EINet, combining feature extrapolation and interpolation to recover missing shapes, achieving competitive performance against prior methods.

Huang *et al.* [17] introduced the Learnable Chamfer Distance (LCD), a loss function that dynamically weights point correspondences via learnable networks, improving reconstruction accuracy and convergence over static CD-based approaches. Han *et al.* [18] proposed SR-MDPC-PCU, which combines multiscale local feature extraction and multi-view shape fusion to generate dense point clouds, achieving an average CD improvement of 32.93% over methods such as PU-Net and PU-GCN.

However, methods based on deep neural networks require a high volume of data for training. Real-world scenarios rarely provide the necessary features to train these models. Therefore, this paper introduces an approach for upsampling point cloud objects without requiring a training phase. This work was tested on a public dataset (PU1K dataset [19]) to measure the quantitative and qualitative performance of the proposed methodology. Furthermore, the proposed methodology was tested in a real-world scenario using the LiSurveying dataset [20]. LiSurveying dataset contains a large number of low-point objects, making it difficult to train a classifier.

3   Methodology

This paper presents a point cloud upsampling technique, which does not require a model training phase. This methodology is founded upon the concept of k-dimensional tree (KDTree), which employs an adaptive interpolation to generate new points.

A KDTree is a spatial data structure that organizes points in a k-dimensional space. It is a type of binary search tree where each node represents a point in the k-dimensional space [21]. This type of tree allows us to find nearest neighbors or search for points within a given range. This approach enables the upsampling of point clouds while preserving the original shape of the object, and reducing the computational cost.

The steps of the proposed methodology are illustrated in Fig. 1a. First, the *iFactor* is calculated. This is the ratio of the number of points by which we want to increase the point cloud and the total number of points the object currently has. The *iFactor* affects the processing time required to upsample the point cloud. Next, a KDTree is computed with the original object and used for adaptive interpolation to upsample the point cloud.

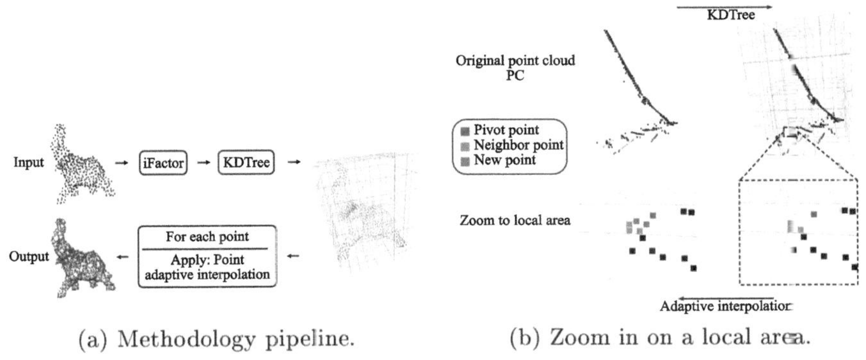

(a) Methodology pipeline.   (b) Zoom in on a local area.

Fig. 1. Proposed methodology: pipeline (left) and local interpolation detail (right).

To interpolate new points it is necessary to find the nearest neighbors of each point within the 3D object. At each point, adaptive interpolation is performed to generate new interpolated points, as shown in Fig. 1b. The first row in Fig. 1b shows the point cloud, the creation of the KDTree, and a section within the point cloud for zooming in and better visualization. The second row shows the selection of a pivot point and the creation of new interpolated points from the pivot point, using the adaptive interpolation.

In this process, as described in Algorithm 1, the variable PC is the original point cloud, and the variable N represents the desired number of additional points within the point cloud for upsampling. Therefore, the algorithm receives

---

Algorithm 1. Upsampling of sparse point clouds using KDTrees with adaptive interpolation.

Input: $N \leftarrow Number\ of\ points\ to\ upsample$
Input: $PC \leftarrow 3D\ Object$
Output: oPC
  1: $points \leftarrow PC.points$
  2: $nPoints \leftarrow Length(points)$
  3: $iFactor \leftarrow Ceil(N/nPoints)$
  4: $newPoints \leftarrow []$
  5: $avgDimension \leftarrow PC$
  6: $searchRadius \leftarrow avgDimension * 0.05$
  7: $tree = KDTree(PC)$
  8: $densities \leftarrow computeDensities(PC, tree, searchRadius)$
  9: **for** $point : points$ **do**
 10:     $distances, indices = tree.neighbors(point, k = iFactor)$
 11:     **for** $i \leftarrow 1 : Length(indices)$ **do**
 12:         $neighbor \leftarrow points[indices[i]]$
 13:         $newPoints \leftarrow AdaptiveInterpolation(neighbor)$
 14:     **end for**
 15: **end for**
 16: $oPC \leftarrow PC + newPoints$
 17: **return** oPC

---

the original point cloud and the desired number of points to which the point cloud should be upsampled.

The target number of points, denoted by N, is a parameter defined by the user and dependent on specific application requirements. N enables the calculation of an $iFactor$ by dividing N by the original number of points. A k-dimensional binary search tree (KDTree) [22] is constructed from the original object, wherein the points are organized in a k-dimensional Euclidean space. Subsequently, a k-nearest neighbor search is conducted for each point within the point cloud. The size of the point cloud is important for upsampling, consequently the average dimension ($avgDimension$) of the objects are calculated. Additionally, empirical tests determined that a search radius of 5% provides an optimal trade-off between capturing local density variations and avoiding excessive computational overhead. Together with the $avgDimension$, this radius enables the upsampling of point clouds of different sizes using adaptive interpolation.

At each iteration, an adaptive interpolation is performed to obtain $iFactor$ percentage of new points. Therefore, to perform adaptive interpolation, the first step is to identify the nearest neighbors of each point within the point cloud. In this first step, we also quantify the local density, ρ_{local}, at each point and then compare it to the maximum density, ρ_{max}, of the entire point cloud. This comparison yields a density factor ρ:

$$\rho = \frac{\rho_{local}}{\rho_{max}} \tag{1}$$

This density factor ρ enables the algorithm to selectively interpolate new points in regions with a lower accumulation of existing points, preventing over-densification in dense areas and achieving a more uniform distribution. The number of points to be interpolated in a given region is dynamically determined:

$$n = max(1, \lfloor 2(1 - \rho) \rfloor) \tag{2}$$

Finally, by traversing the entirety of the point cloud, identifying all adjacent points, and conducting an adaptive interpolation for each neighbor, a comprehensive list of new points is generated. The addition of the aforementioned list of new points to the list of original points results in the formation of a new point cloud oPC comprising N target points.

The $iFactor$ parameter controls how many new points are added per iteration, each defined by its X, Y, and Z coordinates. These points are accumulated into a growing list that, combined with the original cloud, forms the final upsampled output oPC.

A critical aspect of the neighborhood search is the optimal search radius. This radius directly impacts the local density calculation. If the search radius is too small, the algorithm may perceive many areas as sparse. This can lead to excessive interpolation of points, potentially introducing noise or artificial structures. Conversely, if the search radius is too large, it could average out local density variations. This could cause the algorithm to miss genuinely sparse regions and fail to densify them adequately, thus compromising the preservation of fine details. Therefore, selecting an optimal search radius is crucial for balancing densification and shape preservation.

The result is a denser point cloud that preserves the original geometry, achieved without labeled data or GPU hardware; a meaningful advantage in real-world scenarios where such resources are often unavailable.

4   Results

This section presents qualitative and quantitative results on both datasets. Performance tests were conducted on an Apple M2 Pro chip with 16GB of RAM.

We tested our method with the PU1K dataset [19], which is a point cloud upsampling dataset. PU1K is notable for its size and diversity, containing 1,147 models covering 50 different object categories. These models are strategically divided into a training set of 1,020 samples and a test set of 127 samples, allowing for rigorous training and evaluation of upsampling algorithms. In Fig. 2a some point clouds of the PU1K dataset are shown, these objects have 2,048 points each. The LiSurveying dataset [20] is a LIDAR dataset specifically designed for surveying and topography applications, as we can see in Fig. 2b.

(a) Visualization of some point clouds of the PU1K dataset. (b) Visualization of some point clouds of the LiSurveying dataset.

Fig. 2. Visualization of point clouds from both datasets.

The LiSurveying dataset contains 3D point clouds that capture detailed information about terrain, structures and street view objects useful for urban surveys. This type of data is critical for applications such as construction, infrastructure management, mining and urban planning, as it provides real-world information and 3D models of the environment. The LiSurveying dataset consists of three scenes: New Westminster, Nanaimo, and Marine Way in British Columbia, Canada. Within these scenes there are a total of 1,574 objects, divided into 6 main classes: "hydro.tel", "roadworks", "signs", "sto.san.water.misc", "utilities", "vegetation". The database contains a total of 56 subclasses.

On the other hand, there are several metrics to evaluate the quality of object point upsampling [23]. In general, these metrics focus on two aspects, the deviation and the uniformity between the original object and the upsampled object. Some of these metrics could be the Chamfer Distance (CD), Hausdorff Distance (HD), among others. The CD is the sum of the positive distances [19]. HD computes the distance between proper subsets in space [24]. A proper subset is a finite set of points, where HD is the maximum value of the shortest distance from one set of points to another.

As shown in the Table 1, CD and HD metrics are calculated for the PU1K dataset. These values are obtained by performing a 4x upsampling, starting from a point cloud of 512 points. It is essential to note that state-of-the-art learning-based methods achieve lower CD and HD values due to supervised training over large-scale annotated datasets and GPU-accelerated architectures. In contrast, the proposed method operates without prior training and executes in 25 ms on standard CPU hardware. Although the geometric error is higher than that of deep learning approaches, our framework offers a deterministic and lightweight alternative, making it suitable for real-time deployment, edge computing environments, and scenarios where annotated data or high-performance hardware are unavailable. It is worth noting that the CD gap between the proposed method and deep learning approaches reflects the inherent trade-off between geometric precision and computational cost; for applications such as data augmentation or edge deployment, a CD of 0.0249 is geometrically consistent with the original shape, as evidenced qualitatively in Fig. 3.

Table 1. Average time taken to process each point cloud in the test PU1K dataset, as well as the CD and HD averages, when performing a 4x increment from 512 points.

Work	Time (ms)	CD	HD
PU-NET [9]	–	0.0029	0.0361
Dis-PU [12]	–	0.0036	0.0371
SPU-Net [25]	–	0.0028	0.0630
SPU-PMD [26]	–	0.0016	0.0135
Ours	25 ±1	0.0249	0.0461

Finally, Fig. 3 shows the results of a x4 increment, going from 512 points to 2,048 per object. It is important to note that the upsampled objects in Fig. 3a maintain the shape of the target object. Similarly, Fig. 3b shows objects from the LiSurveying database that have been upsampled to four times their original point count. As can be seen, the proposed algorithm is capable of upsampling the point cloud without the need for ground truth.

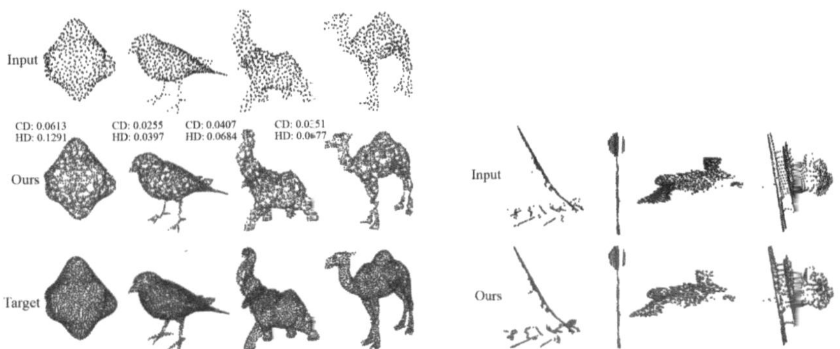

(a) Upsampling from 512 points to 2048 points (x4) using objects from the PU1K dataset.

(b) Upsampling from 512 points to 2048 points (x4) using objects from the LiSurveying dataset.

Fig. 3. Upsampling from low resolution point cloud to a higher resolution point cloud (x4).

5 Conclusions

This paper introduces a lightweight, deterministic framework for upsampling three-dimensional point clouds, combining an iFactor-KDTree structure with density-aware adaptive interpolation. The method performs selective densification in low-density regions without requiring training data or GPU hardware, making it suitable for real-time and resource-constrained environments. While deep learning approaches achieve lower geometric error, they depend on large annotated datasets and intensive training procedures that are often unavailable in practice. Our framework offers a practical and efficient alternative, consistently balancing reconstruction accuracy with computational cost.

Acknowledgements. We acknowledge the University of Guanajuato and the Autonomous University of Querétaro.

References

1. Guo, Y., Wang, H., Qingyong, H., Liu, H., Liu, L., Bennamoun, M.: Deep learning for 3D point clouds: a survey. IEEE Trans. Pattern Anal. Mach. Intell. **43**(12), 4338–4364 (2021)
2. Qi, C.R., Su, H., Mo, K., Guibas, L.J.: Pointnet: deep learning on point sets for 3d classification and segmentation, 2017
3. Boulch, A.: Convpoint: continuous convolutions for point cloud processing. Comput. Graph. **88**, 24–34 (2020)
4. Qi, C.R., Su, H., Mo, K., Guibas, L.J.: Pointnet++: deep hierarchical feature learning on point sets in a metric space (2017)
5. Zhou, Y., Tuzel, O.: Voxelnet: end-to-end learning for point cloud based 3d object detection, 2017
6. Pon, A.D., Ku, J., Li, C., Waslander, S.L.: Object-centric stereo matching for 3D object detection. In: 2020 IEEE International Conference on Robotics and Automation (ICRA), pp. 8383–8389, 2020
7. Engel, N., Belagiannis, V., Dietmayer, K.: Point transformer. IEEE Access **9**, 134826–134840 (2021)
8. Zeng, C., Wang, W., Nguyen, A., Xiao, J., Yue, Y.: Self-supervised learning for point cloud data: a survey. Expert Syst. Appl. **237**, 121354 (2024)
9. Yu, L., Li, X., Fu, C.W., Cohen-Or, D., Heng, P.A.: Pu-net: point cloud upsampling network. In: Proceedings of the IEEE Conference on Computer Vision and Pattern Recognition (CVPR), 2018

10. Yifan, W., Wu, S., Huang. H., Cohen-Or, D., Sorkine-Hornung, O.: Patch-based progressive 3d point set upsampling. CoRR, abs/1811.11286, 2018
11. Li, R., Li, X., Fu, C.W., Cohen-Or, D., Heng, P.A.: Pu-gan: a point cloud upsampling adversarial network. In: Proceedings of the IEEE/CVF International Conference on Computer Vision (ICCV), 2019
12. Li, R., Li, X., Heng, P.A.. Fu, C.-W.: Point cloud upsampling via disentangled refinement. In: Proceedings of the IEEE/CVF Conference on Computer Vision and Pattern Recognition (CVPR), pp. 344–353, 2021
13. You, J., Kim, Y.K.: Up-sampling method for low-resolution lidar point cloud to enhance 3d object detection in an autonomous driving environment. Sensors **23**(1) (2023)
14. Wu, X., Lu, Z., Qu, C., Zhou, H., Miao, Y.: Scnet: shape-aware convolution with kfnn for point clouds completion. Int. J. Mach. Learn. Cybern. (2024)
15. Zhu, L., Yang, Y., Liu, K., Silin, W., Wang, B., Chang, X.: Regional dynamic point cloud completion network. Pattern Recogn. Lett. **186**, 322–329 (2024)
16. Cai, P., Zhang, C., Shi, L., Wang, L., Imanpour, N., Wang, S.: EINet: point cloud completion via extrapolation and interpolation. In: Leonardis, A., Ricci, E., Roth, S., Russakovsky, O., Sattler, T., Varol, G. (eds.) Computer Vision – ECCV 2024. ECCV 2024. LNCS, vol. 15098, pp. 377–393. Springer, Cham (2025). https://doi.org/10.1007/978-3-031-73661-2_21
17. Huang, T., Liu, Q., Zhao, X., Chen, J., Liu, Y.: Learnable chamfer distance for point cloud reconstruction. Pattern Recogn. Lett. **178**, 43–48 (2024)
18. Han, X., Wang, X., Sun, Z., Yang, H.: Point cloud upsampling using multi-density prediction consistency based on surface regularization. Measurement **251**, 117223 (2025)
19. Qian, G., Abualshour, A., Li, G., Thabet, A., Ghanem, B.: Pu-gcn: point cloud upsampling using graph convolutional networks. In: Proceedings of the IEEE/CVF Conference on Computer Vision and Pattern Recognition (CVPR), pp. 11683–11692, 2021
20. Lugo, G., et al.: Lisurveying: a high-resolution tls-lidar benchmark Comput. Graph. **107**, 116–130 (2022)
21. Men, Z., Shen, Z., Gu, Y., Sun, Y.: Parallel kd-tree with batch updates. Proc. ACM Manag. Data **3**(1) (2025)
22. Bentley, J.L.: K-d trees for semidynamic point sets. In: Proceedings of the Sixth Annual Symposium on Computational Geometry, SCG '90, pp. 187–197, New York, NY, USA, 1990. Association for Computing Machinery
23. Zhang, Y., Zhao, W., Sun, B., Zhang, Y., Wen, W.: Point cloud upsampling algorithm: a systematic review. Algorithms **15**(4) (2022)
24. Berger, M., Levine, J.A., Nonato, L.G., Taubin, G., Silva, C.T.: A benchmark for surface reconstruction. ACM Trans. Graph. **32**(2) (2013)

25. Liu, X., Liu, X., Liu, Y.-S., Han, Z.: Spu-net: self-supervised point cloud upsampling by coarse-to-fine reconstruction with self-projection optimization. IEEE Trans. Image Process. **31**, 4213–4226 (2022)
26. Liu, Y., Chen, R., Li, Y., Li, Y., Tan, X.: Spu-pmd: self-supervised point cloud upsampling via progressive mesh deformation. In: 2024 IEEE/CVF Conference on Computer Vision and Pattern Recognition (CVPR), pp. 5188–5197, 2024

Tree Crown Segmentation in UAV RGB Images via Monocular Depth Estimation

Sergio Adán-Juárez[ID], Andrea Magadán-Salazar[✉][ID],
Jorge Fuentes-Pacheco[ID], Raúl Pinto-Elías[ID],
and Jonathan Tavira-Villanueva[ID]

Tecnológico Nacional de Mexico/CENIDET, Internado Palmira, Cuernavaca,
Morelos, Mexico
{d24ce039,andrea.ms,jorge.fp,raul.pe,jonathan.vt}@cenidet.tecnm.mx

Abstract. This paper presents a depth-aware instance segmentation framework for individual tree crown delineation in high-resolution UAV RGB imagery. The method integrates monocular depth estimation, object detection and foundation segmentation model within a unified pipeline. Depth maps are generated using Depth Anything V2 to enhance structural representation from RGB images. These depth-enhanced images are processed by YOLO12 for object detection, and the resulting bounding boxes are used as geometric prompts for SAM 2 (Segment Anything Model), enabling accurate instance-level segmentation. Experimental evaluation on a real-world avocado orchard dataset demonstrates strong performance, achieving an F1-score of 0.929, mAP50 of 0.925, and mAP50–95 of 0.634. The pipeline maintains a computational cost of 5.4 GFLOPs and a model size of 5.3 GB. The results demonstrate that depth-guided prompting enhances segmentation accuracy in structurally complex agricultural environments, particularly under conditions that validate the effectiveness of depth-aware prompting for complex environmental monitoring.

Keywords: Instance Segmentation · Object Detection · YOLO12 · Depth Anything V2 · SAM 2 · Aerial Imagery · Tree Crown

1 Introduction

Precision agriculture has undergone rapid transformation in recent years, driven by advances in UAV-based sensors, high-resolution imaging, and artificial intelligence. These technologies have enabled scalable monitoring and analysis of agricultural systems, supporting applications such as crop health assessment, yield estimation, and forest inventory. These capabilities provide critical information for decision-making, enabling precise and timely interventions in specific production environments, particularly for estimating key parameters such as tree density, spatial distribution, biomass, and phytosanitary conditions. However, traditional field-based inventory methods remain labor-intensive, time-consuming,

© The Author(s), under exclusive license to Springer Nature Switzerland AG 2026
V. G. Cruz-Sánchez et al. (Eds.): MCPR 2026, LNCS 16623, pp. 233–246, 2026.
https://doi.org/10.1007/978-3-032-28393-1_21

and difficult to scale over large areas. Although UAV-acquired RGB imagery is a promising alternative for automating forest inventories, accurate segmentation of individual tree crowns remains technically challenging due to canopy overlap, illumination variability, understory presence, and the complex three-dimensional structure of forest ecosystems. Traditional methods (such as watershed segmentation, morphological operations, and region-growing techniques) exhibit limited robustness in complex environments [2,5,8]. While deep learning approaches such as U-Net, Mask R-CNN, and semantic segmentation models offer improvements [4,9,11], significant challenges persist: (1) dependence on large annotated datasets; (2) difficulty distinguishing individual crowns in high-density areas; (3) sensitivity to illumination and background variability; and (4) lack of depth information, which limits the resolution of ambiguities in overlapping canopies. The integration of depth information extracted from monocular RGB imagery with advanced detection and segmentation techniques represents an unexplored opportunity to improve the precision of individual crown delineation, particularly in scenarios of high structural complexity. This work proposes a methodology integrating three neural network models for precise crown segmentation in monocular RGB images acquired via UAV: (1) Depth Anything V2 for monocular depth estimation and region-of-interest enhancement; (2) YOLO12 for efficient crown detection using depth-enriched imagery; and (3) SAM 2 (Segment Anything Model) for universal segmentation guided by said detections. The main contributions of this work are: (1) a segmentation pipeline integrating monocular depth estimation, object detection, and prompt-based segmentation; (2) a depth-guided prompting strategy that enhances spatial discrimination in RGB imagery; (3) an efficient framework that performs well under limited data conditions; and (4) a real-world UAV dataset for crown detection and segmentation. The system achieves an F1 score of 0.929 under real-world avocado cultivation conditions, outperforming existing methods in the presence of understory vegetation and variations in scale and illumination. Additionally, a fully labeled dataset with data augmentation is made publicly available to support future research. The remainder of this article is organized as follows: Sect. 2 describes the proposed methodology and model integration; Sect. 3 presents the experiments conducted with three YOLO architectures; Sect. 4 analyzes the results; and Sect. 5 presents the conclusions and future work.

2   Materials and Methods

2.1   Problem Definition

Given an RGB aerial image:

$$I \in R^{H \times W \times 3} \tag{1}$$

the objetive is to estimate a set of instance masks:

$$M = \{M_i\}_{i=1}^{N} \ where \ each \ M_i \in \{0,1\}^{H \times W} \tag{2}$$

Each mask corresponds to an individual tree crown.

Monocular depth estimation is defined as:

$$f_{depth} : R^{H \times W \times 3} \rightarrow R^{H \times W} \tag{3}$$

and produces:

$$D = f_{depth}(I) \tag{4}$$

The detection model is given by:

$$f_{det} : R^{H \times W \times 3} \rightarrow B \tag{5}$$

where:

$$B = \{b_i\}_{i=1}^N, \quad b_i = (x_i, y_i, w_i, h_i) \tag{6}$$

(x_i, y_i) is the top left corner of the bounding box. (w_i, h_i) are the standardized width and height of the bounding box.

The complete applied pipeline is defined as:

$$M = f_{SAM}(I, f_{det}(g(I, D))) \tag{7}$$

where $g(I, D)$ represents depth-enhanced image fusion.

The methodology (pipeline) of this work is structured into three fundamental stages: 1) Image acquisition and construction of Ground Truth as a dataset necessary to train the YOLO model in tree crown detection using depth images; 2) training and evaluation of three different versions of YOLO; and, finally, 3) evaluation of the selected model in combination with SAM using geometric prompting and the Dice coefficient to validate the segmentation.

2.2   Ground Truth Generation

The construction of the ground truth consists of the following stages.

Image Acquisition. Data were collected from an avocado orchard (*Persea americana*) located in Buenavista del Monte, Morelos, Mexico, at coordinates $18°56'45.2''$ N and $99°18'11.6''$ W, at an altitude of $1,948$ meters above sea level. The study area covers 2.61 hectares, under representative agro-climatic conditions of the south-central region of Mexico for avocado cultivation. The orchard URL is: https://maps.app.goo.gl/7nucWkNCmZ7mtvps9. Figure 1 shows an aerial view of the site.

Fig. 1. Aerial view of the avocado orchard. Source: Google Maps.

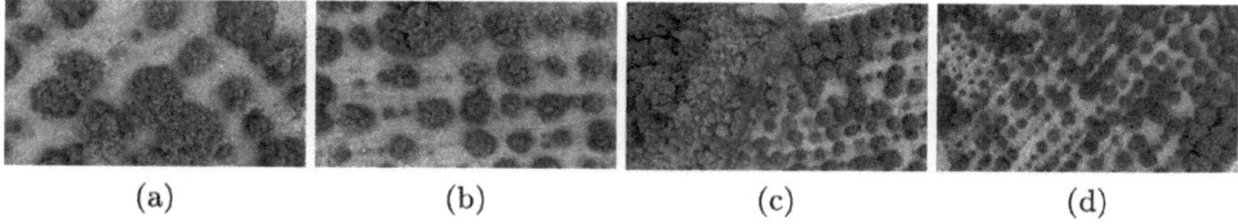

(a)   (b)   (c)   (d)

Fig. 2. Sample images captured at different flight altitudes: (a) 20 m, (b) 50 m, (c) 70 m, and (d) 100 m. All images maintain a resolution of 4000 × 2250 pixels.

Image acquisition was done at midday under overcast conditions to ensure diffuse illumination and minimize shadow artifacts. A total of 157 RGB images were acquired using a UAV at 20, 50, 70, and 100 meters. Each image has a resolution of 4000 × 2250 pixels with the camera in a nadir orientation (90°) relative to the horizontal plane, ensuring a constant zenith perspective.

This methodology allowed for images encompassing different tree densities and morphological variations in the avocado tree crowns. A DJI Mini 3 drone was utilized for data collection. The technical specifications of the UAV are available on its website [1]. Figure 2 presents sample images from the dataset captured using the aforementioned drone.

Monocular Depth Estimation. Before the dataset was annotated for the detection task, depth maps were generated using Depth AnythingV2. This model was selected based on evaluation against alternative methods (including Depth Pro, MiDaS and Depth AnythingV1) demonstrating superior structural detail, inference efficiency and faster inference speeds [10]. Depth maps were normalized to the interval $[0, 1]$ to ensure numerical stability:

$$\hat{D} = \frac{D - min(D)}{max(D) - min(D)} \tag{8}$$

Depth maps are a key step in the differentiation between tree crowns and lower vegetation, facilitating improved detection. Depth information is crucial for effective discrimination between target vegetation and undesirable environmental elements. These include lower-level vegetation (e.g. shrubs), herbaceous cover, various weeds and shadow artefacts cast by the arboreal structure itself, as illustrated in Fig. 3.

A significant advantage of the selected model lies in its ability to process high-resolution images without requiring prior resizing. This capability allowed for maintaining the original resolution of 4000×2250 pixels throughout the depth extraction process, this ensured the spatial integrity of the data and optimizing the computational efficiency of the workflow.

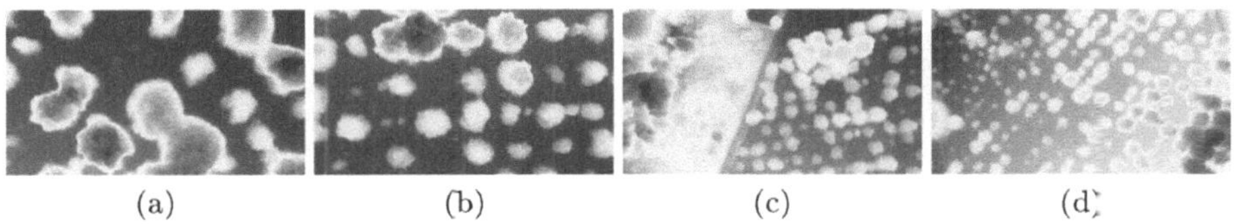

(a)   (b)   (c)   (d)

Fig. 3. Examples of depth maps extracted with Depth Anything V2.

Annotation Process. Manual annotations were performed using bounding boxes for each tree crown instance. All images were labeled using the Roboflow web platform [9], a specialized tool for the management and annotation of computer vision datasets. Each identified tree crown instance within the imagery was delineated using bounding boxes and uniformly labeled under the class *crown-Tree*. The annotations are formatted in the YOLO format [6]. Each annotation file contains the normalized coordinates of the bounding box center, along with its corresponding width and height dimensions.

Data Augmentation. Given the inherent limitations of the available dataset size, a data augmentation strategy was implemented to increase training set diversity and mitigate *overfitting* effects, and to improve generalization under limited data conditions. The following transformations were applied: *i)* Horizontal and vertical flips, *ii)* Rotation ($\pm15°$), *iii)* Grayscale: applied to 15% of the images, *iv)* Brightness adjustment ($\pm15\%$) *v)* Blur: up to 4.5%, *vi)* Noise: up to 1% of pixels. The dataset was expanded from 157 to 377 images, generating 220 new samples.

2.3   Object Detection Model

Object detection was performed using YOLOv8, YOLO11 and YOLO12 for comparative analysis.

$$D \in \{f_{depth}\}(I) \tag{9}$$

$$B = \{b_i\}_{i=1}^{N}$$

Bounding boxes are defined as: $b_i = (x_i, y_i, w_i, h_i)$.

YOLO12 incorporates advanced mechanisms such as Area Attention (A2) and Residual Efficient Layer Aggregation Networks (R-ELAN), improving feature representation [7].

The detection training phase generates inference files in *.txt* format as output, containing precise coordinates and confidence scores for all bounding boxes corresponding to the detected tree crowns in each image. These output files include structured information regarding: *i)* Normalized width and height dimensions, *ii)* Detection confidence levels, *iii)* Class identifier (*crownTree*).

The geometric information that has been extracted is essential for the next stage of the processing pipeline. This stage involves the implementation of segmentation algorithms, which are used to accurately define the boundaries of tree canopies and estimate the structural parameters of the vegetative cover.

2.4   Segmentation with SAM 2

For each bounding box, the segmentation model generates a binary mask:

$$M_i = f_{SAM}(I, b_i) \tag{10}$$

SAM 2 (Segment Anything Model 2) [3] is distinguished by its ability to perform universal segmentation with exceptional precision, operating under a zero-shot learning paradigm without task-specific training. The model's performance is significantly enhanced when a priori information regarding the spatial detection of the objects of interest is provided. Bounding boxes serve as geometric prompts guiding the segmentation process. This feature is especially beneficial for applications in specialized domains, such as precision agriculture, where the availability of labeled data may be limited.

The implemented methodology enables the precise segmentation of individual tree crowns, generating binary masks that accurately delineate the contours of each canopy. This hybrid approach, which combines supervised detection (YOLO12) with universal segmentation (SAM 2), is a robust strategy for the automated analysis of vegetative cover in aerial imagery.

The Dice similarity coefficient (DSC) is used to validate the accuracy of the segmentation performed using the SAM 2 model. This metric is intended to validate the overlap between two datasets: the area segmented in the prediction and the manually annotated (ground truth).

$$Dice = \frac{2|A \cap B|}{|A| + |B|} \tag{11}$$

where, A is the area/pixels of the prediction and B is the area/pixels of the ground truth.

3   Experimentation

Two experimental scenarios were evaluated: The objective of the first case is to compare the performance of three YOLO architectures without and with depth information. A comparison of YOLOv8, YOLO11, and YOLO12 is conducted, with consideration given to the *nano, small, medium, large* and *extra-large* variants for each. The evaluation of detection involved the use of various performance metrics, including Precision, Recall, F1-score, mAP50, and mAP50 − 95. The evaluation was first performed using original images and then using images with depth estimation.

The second case evaluates the performance of the fine segmentation achieved using SAM 2.

The training of the YOLO networks was performed using the *ground truth* consisting of 377 labeled images. The dataset was partitioned into an 88% split for training, 8% for validation, and 4% for testing.

The computational hardware and software environment utilized for the training process are detailed in Table 1. The number of layers for each model evaluated is shown in Table 2.

Table 1. Hardware and Software specifications of the experimental setup

Component	Specification
Processor	AMD Ryzen 9 5900X (12 cores)
RAM	2 × 16 GB Kingston Fury
Storage	2 × 240 GB SSD
Graphics Card	MSI GeForce RTX 4080 Ventus 3X
Motherboard	Gigabyte B550 AX V2 Aorus Elite
Operating System	Ubuntu 24.04 LTS
CUDA Version	12.3.2

Table 2. Number of layers per YOLO model.

Architecture	nano	small	medium	large	xlarge
YOLOv8	72	72	92	112	112
YOLO11	100	100	125	190	190
YOLO12	159	159	169	283	283

4 Results

As shown in Table 3, the results for three YOLO architectures (v8, 11, and 12) and their corresponding models (*nano, small, medium, large, and extra-large*) are presented. It is evident that the larger models, ranging from *extra-large* to *large*, consistently outperform the smaller models across all parameters. In terms of training time, there is a significant discrepancy between the *nano* and *extra-large* models across all three architectures. The models with fewer layers (*nano* and *small*) demonstrated the strongest performance across all three YOLO versions in overall metrics. As illustrated in Table 3, the *nano* and *small* variants of YOLOv8 exhibited the highest performance metrics. However, it is important to note that the performance difference compared to YOLO11 and YOLO12 is minimal. Therefore, the subsequent experiment will concentrate on YOLO11 or YOLO12, as these architectures are more recent and generate trained models with a smaller memory footprint. As shown in Fig. 4, the three previously mentioned YOLO versions are presented in comparative training plots. It is important to note that the *nano* models demonstrate minimal variation across the four metrics presented.

Table 3. Performance metrics were calculated during YOLO validation using two different sets of images. The first set was composed of original images without depth information, and the second set was a custom dataset with depth map information. P: Precision, R: Recall, F1: F1-score.

Arch.	Model	Original images					Images with depth				
		P	R	F1	$mAP50$	$mAP50-95$	P	R	F1	$mAP50$	$mAP50-95$
YOLOv8	nano	0.913	0.874	0.893	0.934	0.597	0.917	0.941	**0.929**	**0.963**	**0.693**
	small	0.902	0.896	0.899	0.930	0.609	0.896	**0.946**	0.920	0.957	0.691
	medium	0.882	**0.906**	0.894	0.927	**0.616**	**0.926**	0.906	0.916	0.957	0.681
	large	0.880	0.894	0.887	0.928	0.596	0.876	0.825	0.850	0.906	0.584
	xlarge	**0.920**	0.898	**0.909**	**0.939**	0.610	0.900	0.815	0.855	0.920	0.611
YOLO11	nano	0.885	0.880	0.883	0.922	0.569	0.918	**0.931**	**0.924**	**0.963**	0.683
	small	**0.893**	0.881	0.887	0.927	0.589	**0.922**	0.900	0.911	0.954	**0.685**
	medium	0.893	0.885	0.889	0.933	0.622	0.907	0.925	0.916	0.962	0.679
	large	0.899	0.890	0.895	**0.942**	**0.623**	0.907	0.847	0.876	0.935	0.631
	xlarge	0.893	**0.886**	**0.890**	0.929	0.602	0.908	0.844	0.875	0.929	0.611
YOLO12	nano	0.904	0.897	0.901	0.938	0.618	**0.921**	0.904	0.912	0.960	0.687
	small	0.893	0.876	0.884	0.923	0.598	**0.921**	**0.920**	**0.920**	**0.961**	**0.689**
	medium	**0.905**	0.853	0.878	0.921	0.596	0.913	0.888	0.900	0.952	0.659
	large	0.895	**0.883**	**0.889**	**0.941**	**0.650**	0.900	0.847	0.873	0.935	0.632
	xlarge	0.893	0.877	0.885	0.936	0.616	**0.921**	0.820	0.868	0.937	0.620

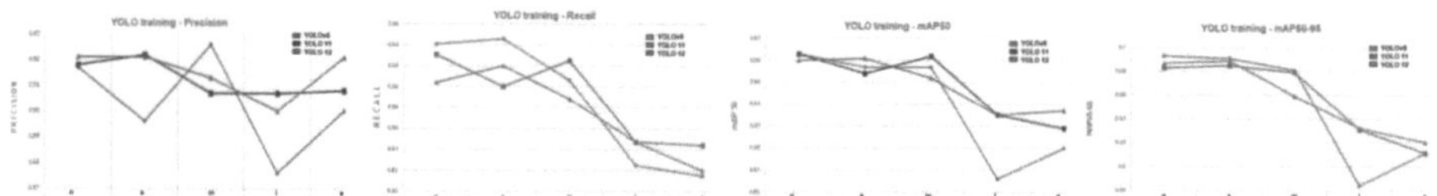

Fig. 4. Training metrics for YOLOv8, YOLO11, and YOLO12.

As a reminder, the initial process involves depth estimation, and the resulting depth map is what serves as input for the YOLO models for detection. Detection results across the YOLOv8, YOLO11, and YOLO12 *nano* variants consistently demonstrate that depth-enhanced inputs significantly improve object localization and subsequent segmentation performance. In all cases, the integration of monocular depth estimation enables accurate delineation of tree crowns, particularly for small instances and in scenarios with structural complexity. The YOLOv8 *nano* model achieves highly satisfactory detection performance, effectively distinguishing trees from surrounding vegetation such as shrubs. Similarly, YOLO11 benefits from its enhanced backbone and neck architecture improving feature extraction and yielding robust detection in complex environments. YOLO12 produces comparable results, confirming that depth information consistently supports precise bounding box generation. Overall, the incorporation of depth maps contributes to more reliable geometric prompts, which in turn enhance the accuracy and stability of SAM 2-based instance segmentation. As illustrated in Fig. 5, the following elements are presented: (a, c, e) the detections, and (b, d, f) the final segmentation. The detection results are highly satisfactory. The models effectively localize small trees and accurately differentiate between them and shrubs.

4.1   Inference Testing

For the testing phase, 10% of the dataset (16 images) was used. These images were captured at various altitudes and contain a varying number of tree crowns each. A series of detection tests were carried out on the YOLOv8, YOLO11, and YOLO12 models. All architectures were evaluated across the *nano, small, medium, large, and extra-large* model variants.

Tables 4 and 5 summarize the quantitative evaluation of tree crown detection across all model variants. Table 4 reports the number of manually annotated tree crowns (ground truth) alongside the detections produced by each YOLO12 variant, while Table 5 presents the corresponding error metrics, including Mean Absolute Error (MAE), Mean Squared Error (MSE), and Root Mean Squared Error (RMSE) for YOLOv8, YOLO11, and YOLO12.

Among the YOLO12 variants, the *medium* model achieved the lowest detection error, with an RMSE of 3.482. However, during training and validation, the *small* variant obtained the highest F1-score (0.920), followed by the *nano* model (0.912). This discrepancy suggests that while the *medium* model minimizes counting error, smaller models provide a better balance between precision and recall. Notably, *nano* and *small* variants consistently outperformed *large* and *extra-large* models, indicating that increased architectural complexity may lead to overfitting or reduced generalization in high-resolution imagery with repetitive structural patterns, such as tree crowns.

A similar trend is observed for YOLO11 and YOLOv8. In the YOLO11 architecture, the *nano* variant achieved the highest F1-score and showed strong alignment with target metrics such as Recall and mAP50, while the *small* variant obtained the lowest RMSE (3.1334), followed by the *nano* model (3.6055). For YOLOv8, the *nano* model delivered the best overall performance in terms of mAP50, mAP50–95, and F1-score (0.929), whereas the small and *medium* variants achieved the highest Recall (0.947) and Precision (0.927), respectively.

In terms of error minimization, the *medium* YOLOv8 model recorded the lowest RMSE (3.691). However, YOLOv8 exhibited greater variability compared to YOLO11 and YOLO12, suggesting less stable performance across different configurations. Overall, these results reinforce the effectiveness of lightweight models (*nano* and *small*) in achieving robust detection performance under limited data conditions, particularly when combined with depth-enhanced inputs.

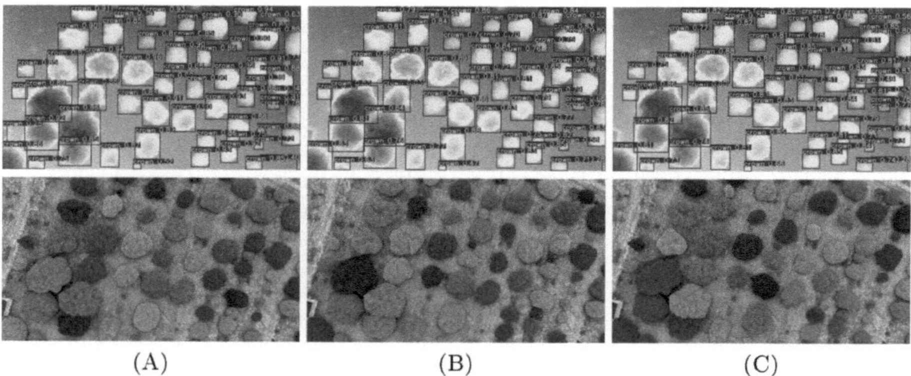

(A)   (B)   (C)

Fig. 5. Detection and segmentation results for YOLOv8 (column A), YOLO11 (column B), and YOLO12 (column C) using the *nano* model.

Table 4. Tree crown detection results using YOLO12 variants. Gt=Ground truth

Item	Image	Gt	12n	12s	12m	12l	12x	Item	Image	Gt	12n	12s	12m	12l	12x
1	41	19	18	21	19	22	19	9	162	25	25	27	25	25	20
2	47	11	11	11	11	12	10	10	167	35	36	37	34	35	31
3	48	8	7	9	8	8	7	11	179	76	76	77	75	63	70
4	120	77	70	72	71	67	66	12	186	36	40	43	38	39	37
5	122	35	41	46	42	37	37	13	205	64	60	63	55	54	55
6	132	35	36	37	35	34	32	14	210	92	90	92	92	77	78
7	145	63	71	74	67	60	62	15	218	77	78	84	78	71	78
8	155	44	43	46	46	41	43	16	223	153	157	169	152	116	131

Table 5. Error metrics for the variants of YOLOv8, YOLO11, and YOLO12.

YOLOv8	nano	small	medium	large	extra-large
MAE	3.250	3.438	2.875	6.813	5.813
MSE	22.000	23.188	13.625	113.688	62.313
RMSE	4.690	4.815	**3.691**	10.662	7.894
YOLO11	nano	small	medium	large	extra-large
MAE	2.75	2.1875	2.3125	5.125	8.3125
MSE	13.00	9.8125	10.1875	44.125	139.9375
RMSE	3.6055	**3.5324**	3.1918	6.6427	11.8295
YOLO12	nano	small	medium	large	extra-large
MAE	2.5625	4.375	2.125	6.6875	5.125
MSE	12.9375	40.25	12.125	127.5625	61.125
RMSE	3.596	6.344	**3.482**	11.294	7.818

4.2   Segmentation Test

Table 6 shows the results of the Dice coefficient calculation. Sixteen images from the test set were used to create the ground truth; these images were manually labeled by outlining each tree crown with polygons. The trained YOLO12 medium model was used for inference. Figure 6 shows two examples of binary masks for the ground truth and the prediction, as well as the original image.

Table 6. Calculation of the Dice coefficient using ground-truth binary masks versus predicted masks. ImNum = image number in the dataset, Gt = *Ground truth*, NPredictions = number of predictions in the inference.

Item	ImNum	Gt	NPredictions	Dice	Item	ImNum	Gt	NPredictions	Dice
1	41	19	21	0.9315	9	162	25	27	0.7575
2	47	11	14	0.9318	10	167	35	39	0.8962
3	48	8	10	0.9328	11	179	76	71	0.8240
4	120	77	75	0.9029	12	186	36	47	0.6167
5	122	35	41	0.8335	13	205	64	61	0.8611
6	132	35	36	0.9054	14	210	92	69	0.8855
7	145	63	67	0.9175	15	218	77	70	0.8385
8	155	44	46	0.8953	16	223	153	124	0.8529
								Average	0.8427

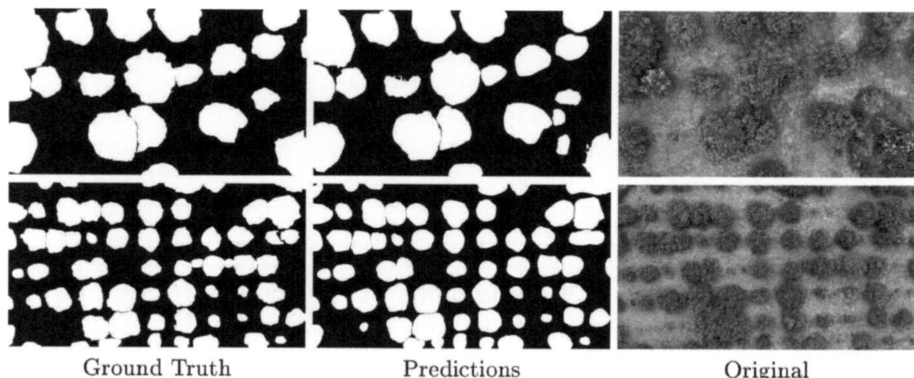

<table>
<tr><td>Ground Truth</td><td>Predictions</td><td>Original</td></tr>
</table>

Fig. 6. Binary masks to calculate Dice coefficients.

5   Discutions

a) **Overlapping and merged crowns:**   *i)* The detection network occasionally identifies multiple adjacent crowns as a single instance. *ii)* Touching or overlapping tree crowns present significant separation challenges, a common occurrence in dense forests or orchards with younger, smaller trees. *iii)* Smaller trees may fail to reach the confidence threshold required by the detection model. *iv)* Visual features in these cases are less distinctive, which can lead to potential confusion with background noise or understory furthermore, Depth Anything V2 may inadvertently filter these small features during depth estimation.

b) **Illumination and contrast variations:**   *i)* Crowns obscured by shadows exhibit reduced visibility, which can misguide the detection model. *ii)* High-contrast variations may cause certain crowns to "disappear" from the feature map. *iii)* Lighting conditions during image acquisition significantly impact overall detection stability.

c) **Hyperparameter configuration and model constraints:**   *i)* If the detection threshold is overly conservative, the model prioritizes the avoidance of false positives over exhaustive detection, indicating a bias toward precision at the expense of recall. *ii)* The algorithm responsible for eliminating duplicate detections may be too stringent, occasionally discarding valid closely-spaced crowns.

d) **Training dataset and labeling constraints:**   *i)* Potential biases in the training data may affect the model's ability to generalize across all orchard conditions. *ii)* If the training set contains missing or inconsistent manual annotations, the model may inherit these errors during the learning process. *iii)* While the training and test sets share similar characteristics in this study, ensuring representative diversity remains a critical factor for robustness.

e) **Morphological and phenological factors:**   *i)* Some trees exhibit less distinct canopy boundaries, complicating the detection of clear geometric features. *ii)* Non-spherical or irregular tree crown shapes increase the complexity of the detection task. *iii)* Factors such as flowering stages or variations in leaf size and pigmentation due to phenological changes can alter the spectral and spatial signature of the trees.

Conclusions and Future Work: This study demonstrates that integrating monocular depth estimation with detection and prompt-based segmentation significantly improves tree crown delineation in UAV RGB imagery. The proposed framework is efficient, scalable, and robust under challenging environmental conditions. In order to enhance the precision of the proposed pipeline, the following strategies will be explored: *i)* Fine- tuning the confidence thresholds to balance precision and recall. *ii)* Adjusting Non-Maximum Suppression (IoU) parameters to better handle high-density clusters of tree crowns. *iii)* Re-training the models with an emphasis on "difficult" cases, such as highly overlapping or small-scale crowns. *iv)* Implementing K-Fold cross-validation techniques to maximize the utility of limited datasets. *v)* Per- forming ablation studies on the YOLO12 architecture to identify and optimize the components most critical for aerial forest inventory tasks.

Acknowledgements. This research has been made possible thanks to generous support from the Secretaría de Ciencia, Humanidades, Tecnología e Innovación (Secihti), Mexico.

Disclosure of Interests. The authors declare no competing interests.

References

1. DJI: DJI Mini 3 Specs (2026). https://www.dji.com/mini-3/specs. Accessed 09 Apr 2026
2. Gomes, M.F., Maillard, P., Deng, H.: Individual tree crown detection in sub-meter satellite imagery using marked point processes and a geometrical-optical model. Remote Sens. Environ. **211**, 184–195 (2018). https://doi.org/10.1016/j.rse.2018.04.002
3. Kirillov, A., et al.: Segment anything (2023)
4. Martins, J.A.C., et al.: Semantic segmentation of tree-canopy in urban environment with pixel-wise deep learning. Remote Sens. **13**(16), 3054 (2021). https://doi.org/10.3390/rs13163054
5. Maschler, J., Atzberger, C., Immitzer, M.: Individual tree crown segmentation and classification of tree species using airborne hyperspectral data. Remote Sens. **10**(8), 1218 (2018). https://doi.org/10.3390/rs10081218
6. Roboflow: Yolov8 pytorch txt (2025). https://roboflow.com/formats/yolov8-pytorch-txt. Accessed 10 Aug 2025
7. Ultralytics: YOLO12: Detección de objetos centrada en la atención (2026). https://docs.ultralytics.com/es/models/yolo12. Accessed 06 Feb 2026
8. Wagner, F.H., et al.: Individual tree crown delineation in a highly diverse tropical forest using very high resolution satellite images. ISPRS J. Photogramm. Remote. Sens. **145**, 362–377 (2018). https://doi.org/10.1016/j.isprsjprs.2018.08.013

9. Weinstein, B.G., Marconi, S., Bohlman, S.A., Zare, A., White, E.P.: Cross-site learning in deep learning RGB tree crown detection. Ecol. Inform. **56**, 101061 (2020). https://doi.org/10.1016/j.ecoinf.2020.101061
10. Yang, L., et al.: Depth anything v2 (2024)
11. Yang, M., et al.: Detecting and mapping tree crowns based on convolutional neural network and google earth images. Int. J. Appl. Earth Obs. Geoinf. **108**, 102764 (2022). https://doi.org/10.1016/j.jag.2022.102764

Embedded System for Vehicle Environment Perception and License Plate Recognition (LPR) Using Computer Vision and Deep Learning

Rogelio Leonardo Mendez-Macias[1], Juan Villegas-Cortez[2(✉)],
Andrés Ferreyra Ramírez[1], Arturo Zúñiga-López[1],
and Salomón Cordero-Sánchez[3]

[1] Unidad Azcapotzalco, Departamento de Electrónica, Universidad Autónoma
Metropolitana, Av. San Pablo 420, Col. Nueva El Rosario, Alc. Azcapotzalco,
02128 Cd. de México, Mexico
{al2183041127,fra,azl}@azc.uam.mx

[2] Unidad Azcapotzalco, Departamento de Sistemas, Universidad Autónoma
Metropolitana, Cd. de México, Mexico
juanvc@azc.uam.mx

[3] Unidad Iztapalapa, Departamento de Química, Universidad Autónoma
Metropolitana, San Rafael Atlixco 186, Col. Vicentina, 09340 Cd. de México, Mexico
scs@xanum.uam.mx

Abstract. The integration of multi-stage vehicle perception pipelines such as object detection and license plate recognition (LPR) into low-cost embedded systems poses significant challenges in software optimization and computational efficiency. This paper presents a distributed edge-assisted architecture for an Advanced Driver Assistance System (ADAS), targeting deployment on a Raspberry Pi 5 equipped with a Hailo-8 AI accelerator. The system interconnects three specialized nodes via MQTT: an edge perception node, a central processing node for LPR and OCR, and a cognitive node integrating a Large Language Model for natural language scene description. The perception pipeline employs a coarse-to-fine strategy, where a general-purpose detector first identifies vehicle regions of interest, narrowing the search space for a specialized high-precision license plate detector. Model optimization via a PyTorch-ONNX-TFLite-HEF conversion pipeline yielded an 88% footprint reduction, enabling real-time inference at 30–58 FPS. The system was experimentally validated in a controlled laboratory environment, achieving over 93% OCR precision and a total Edge-to-Host latency of 230 ms, confirming the effectiveness of the distributed cascade detection strategy for accessible road safety applications.

Keywords: Advanced Driver Assistance Systems (ADAS) · Computer Vision · Deep Learning · Embedded Systems · License Plate Recognition

1 Introduction

The evolution of intelligent systems has repositioned computer vision from a mere image processing tool to the primary sensory mechanism for autonomous interpretation, shifting the focus towards the extraction of quantitative descriptors that facilitate automated decision-making [10,23]. Within the mobility domain, this paradigm shift—integrated with Deep Learning (DL)—has established Advanced Driver Assistance Systems (ADAS) as the cornerstone of active safety strategies [8]. To overcome historical hardware constraints, the field has gravitated toward distributed edge-assisted architectures, leveraging single-stage detection architectures like the YOLO family to optimize the precision-speed trade-off on compact embedded platforms such as the Raspberry Pi, while offloading computationally intensive tasks to dedicated processing nodes [6,7,9]. This technological transition addresses a critical public health urgency in the Mexican context, where national statistics attribute approximately 96% of over 402,000 annual road incidents to human factors, underscoring the imperative for automated systems that function as a "second pair of eyes" to mitigate risks associated with distraction and fatigue.

To address the functional gap in user interaction, where generic acoustic warnings often exacerbate cognitive load, this research proposes a "Cognitive ADAS" framework capable of semantic scene comprehension and natural language risk communication [4]. The presented solution implements a distributed, low-latency architecture that executes optimized DL models (YOLOv8) on specialized embedded hardware (Raspberry Pi 5 with Hailo-8 accelerator) for vehicle detection and Automatic License Plate Recognition (LPR). By decoupling perception from contextual processing via lightweight protocols like MQTT, the system facilitates the integration of Large Language Models (LLM) to provide qualitative environmental descriptions rather than simple alarms. This work documents the complete engineering lifecycle—from curating datasets like BDD100K and model quantization into efficient formats (HEF) to overcoming thermal constraints—ultimately validating a scalable, real-time solution that contributes to the state of the art in accessible road safety technologies.

The primary contribution of this work is a system-level engineering integration demonstrating hardware-software co-design on low-cost embedded hardware, bridging the gap between theoretical deep learning models and real-world, resource-constrained deployment.

2 State of the Art

ADAS have emerged as a priority research vector, defined as cyber-physical systems that integrate sensors and perception algorithms to mitigate road accidents through early threat detection [8,12]. While early perception systems relied on classical computer vision techniques susceptible to environmental noise, the transition toward DL has enabled the learning of hierarchical representations directly from data, significantly increasing robustness in dynamic scenarios [10,23]. In

Table 1. Qualitative comparison of embedded platforms for real-time computer vision inference.

Platform	AI Accel.	Cost	Power/Thermal	Compatibility and Deployment
Raspberry Pi 5 + Hailo-8 (AI HAT+)	NPU (INT8)	Medium	Low–Medium (∼7 W; <60 °C)	High for deployment with HEF/HailoRT; requires conversion pipeline
NVIDIA Jetson (Nano/Xavier, depending on version)	GPU (CUDA/TensorRT)	High	Medium–High (30–50 W; high load)	High with NVIDIA ecosystem; dependency on CUDA/TensorRT versions
Raspberry Pi + Coral TPU (USB/PCIe)	TPU (INT8)	Medium	Low (2–4 W; <55 °C)	Good for supported models; limitations depending on toolchain/models
CPU (PC/RPi without accelerator)	No acceleration	Low (if existing)	Medium–High (>5 W; up to 91.7 °C)	Simple deployment; limited performance for real-time intensive loads

this context, single-stage detectors, particularly the YOLO family, have become a transversal component for tasks such as vehicle detection due to their balance between precision and latency, a critical factor for computationally constrained applications [7,14,19]. This evolution aligns with research precedents within the Mexican institutional framework, which have validated the viability of computer vision as a primary sensor for navigation and safety in robotic and automotive systems [2,5,16,25] (Table 1).

Complementary to general object detection, LPR constitutes a relevant subproblem often addressed through two-stage pipelines: Region-of-Interest (ROI) localization followed by character recognition [13,15,18]. To facilitate real-time operation on low-power hardware, the *Edge AI* paradigm proposes shifting inference loads to local embedded devices, necessitating strict optimization of models and software architectures to manage energy and thermal constraints [3,9]. A critical challenge in LPR is domain dependence; specifically in the Mexican context, the variability of plate formats and capture conditions requires the adaptation of datasets and validation strategies to ensure performance under local operational constraints rather than relying on generic pipelines [11,17]. Table 1 summarizes the trade-offs regarding cost and compatibility for these embedded implementations.

Furthermore, a significant trend toward "Cognitive ADAS" has been observed, aiming to transcend simple detection by utilizing Large Language Models to provide contextual situational awareness and natural language alerts, thereby reducing driver cognitive load [1,20,26]. Despite these advancements, practical gaps persist regarding the seamless integration of multi-stage pipelines that satisfy real-world computation, energy, and communication constraints while delivering semantic information. Consequently, it is pertinent to investigate modular architectures oriented toward embedded deployment that integrate vehicle detection and LPR, maintaining experimental traceability and enabling more informative cognitive interactions [9,11].

3   Methodology

The implemented methodology adopts an iterative design approach, evolving from a monolithic proposal to a distributed architecture to guarantee real-time performance, experimental traceability, and dependency compatibility. The final system comprises three physical nodes interconnected via an asynchronous messaging bus (MQTT): an edge perception node for low-latency visual detection, a central node for intensive processing (LPR/OCR and persistence), and a cognitive node dedicated to auditory interaction. As illustrated in Fig. 1, the prototype deployment features a Raspberry Pi 5 accelerated by a Hailo-8 via PCIe acting as the perception node, a central server responsible for image acquisition and data management, and a Raspberry Pi 4 integrating a WM8960 codec via I2S serving as the cognitive node for speech synthesis.

To decouple responsibilities and mitigate thermal load at the edge, the logical architecture is structured into functional layers: a perception layer executing high-frequency visual inference, a central processing layer handling computationally intensive tasks such as ROI generation and OCR, and a cognitive layer transforming events into auditory alerts. This decomposition, summarized in Fig. 2, supports a deterministic operational pipeline presented in Fig. 4. In this flow, the perception node publishes MQTT metadata upon triggering a condition, prompting the central server to acquire the local frame, persist raw evidence, and execute the license plate detector and specialized preprocessing to obtain recognized text.

Ensuring reproducibility, an event-driven domain model associates each timestamped detection with persisted evidence (raw frames, ROIs) and confidence metadata (Fig. 3). Vehicle detection was trained on BDD100K [27] (100,000 diverse driving sequences), while the plate detector was fine-tuned on the *Vehicle Registration Plates* dataset [22] (8,823 images, CC BY 4.0); cross-domain transfer is feasible as detection targets region localization, not character recognition. Models were quantized to INT8 for embedded execution, with LPR and OCR running as decoupled components on the central server; their outputs subsequently feed the LLaVA-based cognitive module [26], which generates natural language scene descriptions within the same processing node.

4   Results

The experimental validation of the distributed ADAS demonstrates robust pattern recognition capabilities. The BDD100K vehicle model converged steadily through epoch 15; subsequent oscillations reflect learning rate decay rather than overfitting, as the model achieved reliable bounding box localization in deployment (Fig. 5).

The YOLOv8n plate detector reached $mAP_{50}{=}0.986$ and precision of 0.97 (Fig. 6), confirming its reliability as the ROI extraction stage of the pipeline.

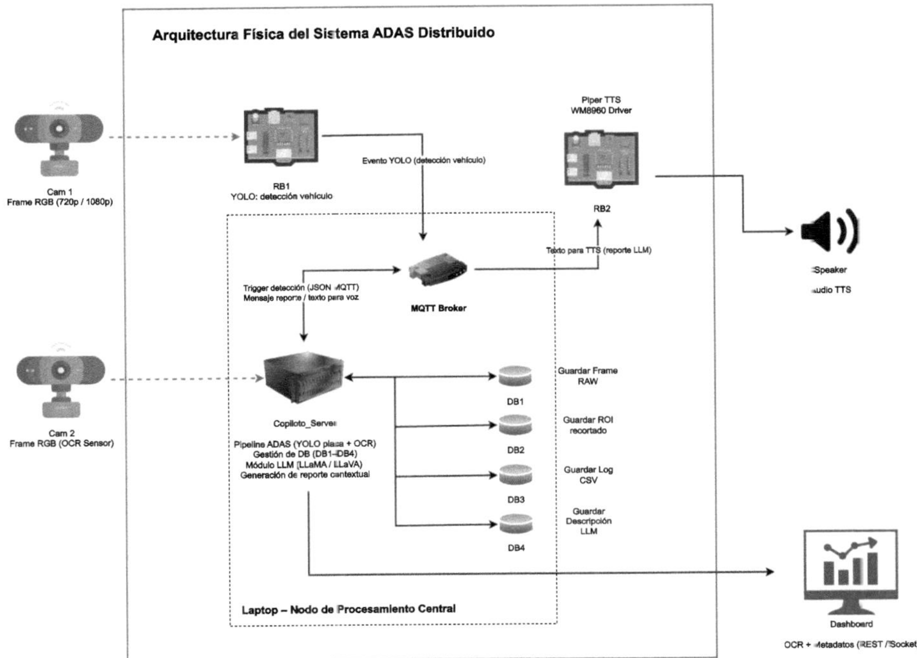

Fig. 1. Distributed system physical architecture: perception node (RPi 5 + Hailo-8), central node (server), and cognitive node (RPi 4 + WM8960) interconnected via MQTT.

To enable edge deployment, model optimization via a PyTorch-ONNX-TFLite-HEF conversion pipeline yielded an 88% footprint reduction. When executed on a Hailo-8 NPU, this quantization allowed for real-time spatial feature extraction at 30–58 FPS with a minimal inference latency of 17–33 ms (Table 2). These optimized perception models were successfully integrated into the physical hardware assembly, ensuring reliable bounding box localization and detection across varying environmental scenarios.

Following localized object detection, the central Host pipeline effectively processes the extracted Regions of Interest (ROIs) through an Optical Character Recognition (OCR) module. Experimental conditions were simulated in a controlled laboratory environment using a camera positioned at 40–50 cm from a monitor at a perpendicular angle, with reduced ambient lighting to minimize screen glare; ideal scenes used static dataset images while degraded scenes introduced dashcam video sequences with motion blur and variable illumination. This OCR subsystem achieved a 93–96% character recognition precision under ideal conditions with an average event latency of 85 ms (Table 3). Telemetry metrics from the distributed Copilot Server confirmed seamless sequential activation, recording a total Edge-to-Host pipeline latency of 230 ms with stable continuous operation (Table 4). Furthermore, the system's asynchronous cognitive

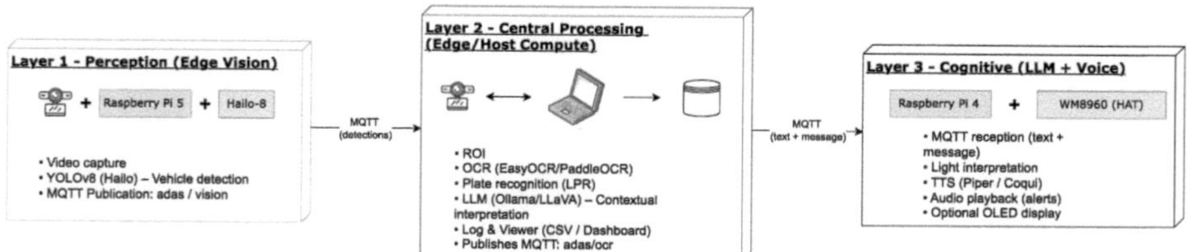

Fig. 2. Layered logical architecture: edge perception, central processing, and cognitive layer using asynchronous MQTT messaging.

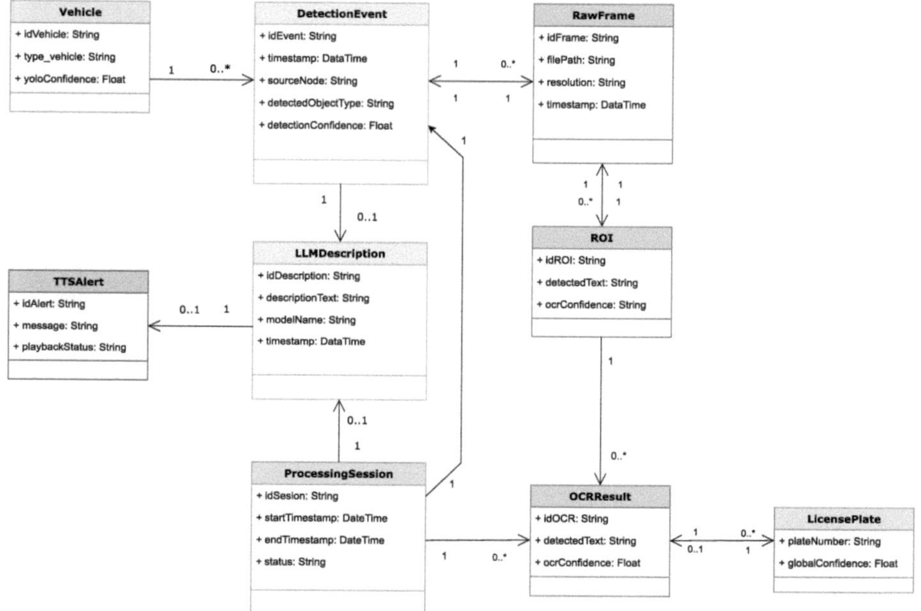

Fig. 3. Event-driven domain model: association between detection, raw evidence, ROI, OCR result, and metadata, enabling end-to-end traceability.

layer, integrating a Large Language Model (LLM) and a Text-to-Speech (TTS) module, successfully validated its multimodal interaction capabilities with an average end-to-end processing time of 240 s consistent with locally embedded LLM benchmarks on low-cost hardware [21,24] and a 100% trigger success rate (Table 5).

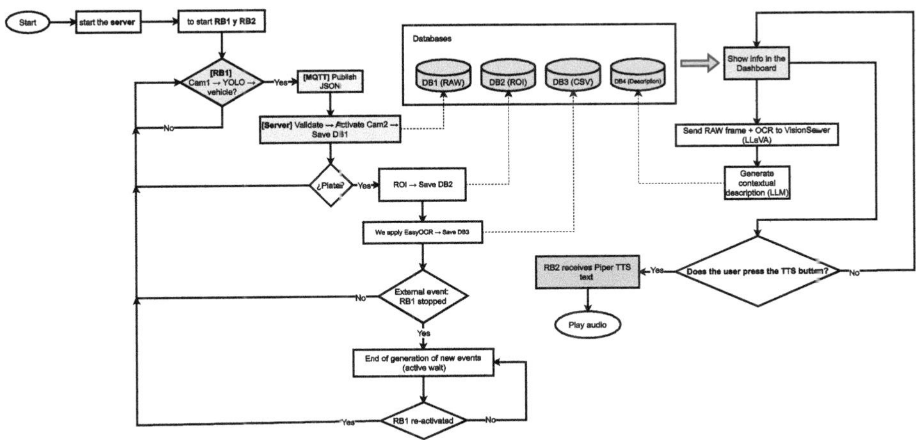

Fig. 4. Reproducible operational flowchart: edge event triggering, evidence acquisition/persistence, central server LPR/OCR, and output distribution to dashboard/DB and cognitive layer (TTS).

Table 2. Vehicle detector performance comparison post-optimization and deployment.

Model/Format	Platform	Size	FPS	Latency
YOLOv8n (.onnx)	CPU (PC/RPi)	158 MB	2	500 ms
YOLOv8n (.tflite)	TFLite	42.8 MB	6–8	120 ms
YOLOv8n (.hef)	Hailo-8 (NPU)	19 MB	30–58	17–33 ms

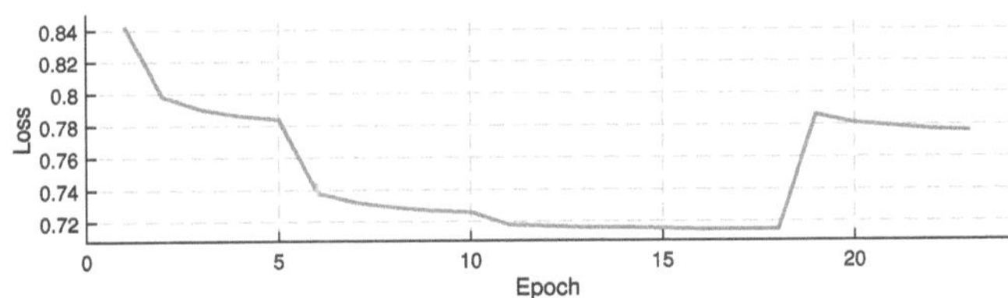

Fig. 5. Training loss curve for YOLOv8n on BDD100K.

Table 3. Representative OCR metrics observed during testing.

Condition	Precision	Latency per event
Ideal scenes	93–96%	55–90 ms
Degraded scenes	82–87%	55–90 ms (avg. 85 ms)

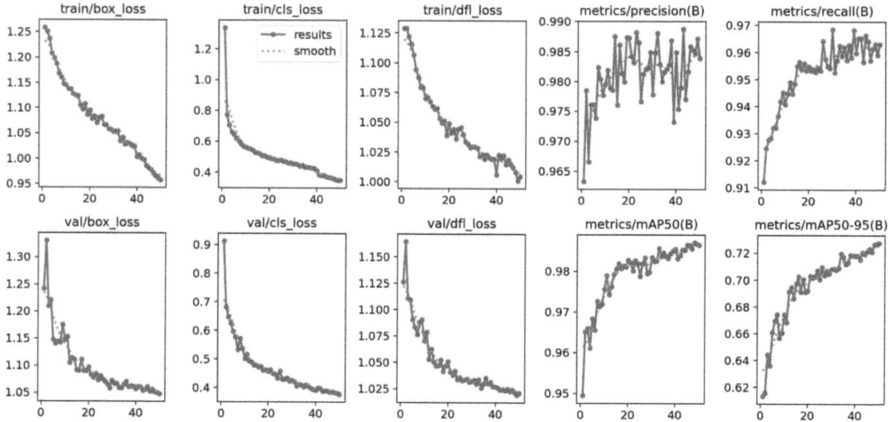

Fig. 6. Training and validation curves for the YOLOv8n plate detection model.

Table 4. Copilot Server experimental metrics summary.

Component	Metric	Observed Result
MQTT	Reception latency	50 ms
Central pipeline	Activation	100 ms
OCR	Latency per event	85 ms
Total pipeline	Edge Host	230 ms
Persistence	Write per event	50 ms
Dashboard	Visual latency	200 ms
Stability	Observed failures	None

Table 5. Cognitive layer (LLM + TTS) performance metrics in distributed operation.

Metric	Result	Interpretation
Avg. response time (text)	70 s	LLM in embedded execution with context
Avg. total time (event audio)	240 s	End-to-end cognitive flow latency
TTS time (Piper)	1.5 s	Fast conversion for short phrases
Trigger success rate	100%	No failures during tests

5   Discussion

This work demonstrates that successful embedded ADAS deployment requires rigorous hardware-software co-engineering beyond isolated pattern recognition metrics. As a system-level engineering contribution, the distributed architecture (Edge, Host, and Cognition layers) proved essential to protect safety-critical perception paths from computational bottlenecks introduced by secondary subsystems such as OCR. Quantitatively, the distributed approach achieved a total Edge→Host latency of 230 ms with zero observed failures (Table 4), a result that would be unattainable in a centralized deployment given the thermal throttling and resource contention documented at the edge node under full load. It is important to note that the reported performance metrics including the mAP_{50} of 0.986 and OCR precision of 93–96% were obtained under controlled laboratory conditions; generalization to uncontrolled real-world scenarios remains a subject for future validation.

This architectural decoupling ensures that the temporal urgency of the primary pattern recognition models is preserved, allowing for advanced post-event analysis and enhanced user interaction without compromising the operational safety margins of the ADAS. While end-to-end latencies in the hundreds of milliseconds are acceptable for assistance-oriented applications, the system's current reliance on a central Host for localized OCR processing introduces portability constraints that limit full edge autonomy. Furthermore, since the current operational validation was primarily constrained to controlled laboratory conditions, the system's robustness under real-world perturbations—including extreme lighting, adverse weather, motion blur, and partial occlusions—remains an open challenge. Future iterations will prioritize domain adaptation and field validation to fully characterize performance limits beyond the laboratory setting.

6   Conclusions and Future Work

This work implemented and experimentally validated a distributed ADAS prototype focused on real-time vehicular perception using low-cost embedded hardware. The evaluation confirmed that dedicated acceleration enables visual detection as a safety-critical task on a Raspberry Pi 5, maintaining stable operation near 30 FPS, which supports the feasibility of this approach for driver assistance scenarios. Regarding deployment, quantitative verification demonstrated that model optimization and compilation into HEF format, coupled with INT8 quantization, are effective steps for enabling edge inference. This conversion chain reduced the detector size from 158 MB to 19 MB (an 88% reduction) and increased performance by approximately 15× compared to CPU execution, achieving per-frame latencies in the tens of milliseconds range without compromising the detection functionality required by the prototype.

The distributed architecture, interconnected via MQTT, demonstrated operational effectiveness in sustaining end-to-end performance without resource saturation. A total Edge→Host pipeline latency of 230 ms was measured, with MQTT reception latency under 50 ms and central pipeline activation under 100 ms, confirming that decoupling perception from heavy processing maintains viable response times for assistance systems. Additionally, the technical feasibility of integrating a cognitive subsystem based on LLM and speech synthesis (TTS) without obstructing the critical perception path was demonstrated. The cognitive layer operated as an asynchronous flow, providing contextualization and an enriched human-machine interface for non-critical analysis.

This research highlights the engineering rigor applied at the undergraduate level within a Mexican public university context. The primary strength of this work lies in solving the complex integration challenges inherent to embedded systems—specifically the hardware-software co-design required to bridge the gap between theoretical deep learning models and functional, resource-constrained deployment. By successfully orchestrating a distributed pipeline that balances thermal constraints, real-time latency, and "dependency hell" management, this project delivers a cost-effective, accessible solution for road safety, empirically validated through rigorous experimental protocols in a laboratory setting.

Future engineering efforts will focus on increasing the system's Technological Readiness Level (TRL). A priority is the migration of the Optical Character Recognition (OCR) module towards accelerated execution directly at the edge, aiming to eliminate the dependency on the central Host/PC. Furthermore, validation will be expanded to encompass uncontrolled stochastic conditions—such as heavy rain, extreme low-light environments, and sustained mechanical vibrations—to fully characterize the system's robustness and performance limits in real-world field scenarios.

References

1. Al-Safi, H., Ibrahim, H., Steenson, P.: Vega: LLM-driven intelligent chatbot platform for IoT control. Sensors **25** (2025)
2. Abdulkareem, A.Q., Humod, A.T., Ahmed, O.A.: Robust pattern recognition based fault detection and isolation method for ABS speed sensor. Int. J. Automot. Technol. **23**(6), 1747–1754 (2022). https://doi.org/10.1007/s12239-022-0152-5
3. Abraham, G., Nithya, M.: Multi-functional personal assistant robot using raspberry pi and coral accelerator. In: 2021 5th International Conference on Computing Methodologies and Communication (ICCMC), pp. 638–643 (2021). https://doi.org/10.1109/ICCMC51019.2021.9418299
4. Aggarwal, C.C.: Neural Networks and Deep Learning: A Textbook. Springer International Publishing, Cham (2023). https://doi.org/10.1007/978-3-031-29642-0
5. Ali, W., Tian, W., Din, S.U., Iradukunda, D., Khan, A.A.: Classical and modern face recognition approaches: a complete review. Multimed. Tools Appl. **80**(3), 4825–4880 (2021). https://doi.org/10.1007/s11042-020-09850-1
6. Bishop, C.M.: Pattern Recognition and Machine Learning. Information Science and Statistics. Springer, New York (2006)
7. Diwan, T., Anirudh, G., Tembhurne, J.V.: Object detection using YOLO: challenges, architectural successors, datasets and applications. Multimed. Tools Appl. **82**(6), 9243–9275 (2023). https://doi.org/10.1007/s11042-022-13644-y
8. Eskandarian, A.: Handbook of Intelligent Vehicles. Springer Reference. Springer, New York (2012)
9. García-Martín, E., Rodrigues, C.F., Riley, G., Grahn, H.: Estimation of energy consumption in machine learning. J. Parallel Distrib. Comput. **134**, 75–88 (2019). https://doi.org/10.1016/j.jpdc.2019.07.007, https://www.sciencedirect.com/science/article/pii/S0743731518308773
10. Gonzalez, R.C., Woods, R.E.: Digital Image Processing, 4th global edn. Pearson Education, New York (2018)

11. Görgülü, E., Özcan, A.R.: Deep learning-based Turkish license plate recognition system on low-power microcontroller systems. In: 2024 8th International Artificial Intelligence and Data Processing Symposium (IDAP), pp. 1–6 (2024). https://doi.org/10.1109/IDAP64064.2024.10710693
12. Horgan, J., Hughes, C., McDonald, J., Yogamani, S.: Vision-based driver assistance systems: survey, taxonomy and advances. In: 2015 IEEE 18th International Conference on Intelligent Transportation Systems, pp. 2032–2039 (2015). https://doi.org/10.1109/ITSC.2015.329
13. Kharina, N., Chernyadyev, S.: Software for car license plates recognition with minimal computing resources. In: 2022 24th International Conference on Digital Signal Processing and its Applications (DSPA), pp. 1–4 (2022). https://doi.org/10.1109/DSPA53304.2022.9790745
14. Liu, J.: Survey of the image recognition based on deep learning network for autonomous driving car. In: 2020 5th International Conference on Information Science, Computer Technology and Transportation (ISCTT), pp. 1–6 (2020). https://doi.org/10.1109/ISCTT51595.2020.00007
15. Mala, S., Vidyashree, H.R., Chanda, K.: YOLO model-based license plate extraction and toll generation for smart parking systems. In: 2024 2nd International Conference on Networking, Embedded and Wireless Systems (ICNEWS), pp. 1–7 (2024). https://doi.org/10.1109/ICNEWS60873.2024.10730931
16. Matieş, G., Fosalau, C.: Detection of ABS events in electronic brake systems using machine learning algorithms. In: 2023 13th International Symposium on Advanced Topics in Electrical Engineering (ATEE), pp. 1–6 (2023). https://doi.org/10.1109/ATEE58038.2023.10108131
17. Moreno, C.H., Trejo, N., Soto, M.: License plates recognition of Mexican private vehicles. Comput. Tools **2018**, 19 (2018)
18. Nareddy, N.S., et al.: Autonomous number plate detection system for vehicle identification and tracking. In: 2024 2nd International Conference on Recent Trends in Microelectronics, Automation, Computing and Communications Systems (ICMACC), pp. 315–320 (2024). https://doi.org/10.1109/ICMACC62921.2024.10894466
19. Phatangare, S., Sakpal, R.A., Kasurde, S.N., Punde, S.S., Khan, S.S.: Real-time traffic management using deep learning and object detection using YOLOv8. In: 2024 15th International Conference on Computing Communication and Networking Technologies (ICCCNT), pp. 1–5 (2024). https://doi.org/10.1109/ICCCNT61001.2024.10725412
20. Sandhya Devi, R.S., Varshni, S.D.: Embedded large language models for enhanced human-machine interface in autonomous vehicles. In: 2025 International Conference on Multi-Agent Systems for Collaborative Intelligence (ICMSCI), pp. 1143–1150 (2025). https://doi.org/10.1109/ICMSCI62561.2025.10894287
21. Sakai, T., Uehara, Y., Kashihara, S.: Implementation and evaluation of LLM-based conversational systems on low-cost devices. J. Embed. Artif. Intell. (2025)
22. Startups, A.: Vehicle registration plates dataset (2022). https://universe.roboflow.com/augmented-startups/vehicle-registration-plates-trudk. Roboflow Universe, CC BY 4.0
23. Szeliski, R.: Computer Vision: Algorithms and Applications. Springer, Cham (2011)
24. Taveekitworachai, P., Suntichaikul, P., Nukoolkit, C., Thawonmas, R.: Speed up! Cost-effective large language model for ADAS via knowledge distillation. In: Proceedings of the IEEE International Conference on Intelligent Vehicles. Ritsumeikan University (2024)

25. Villanueva-Escudero, C., Villegas-Cortez, J., Zúñiga-López, A., Avilés-Cruz, C.: Monocular visual odometry based navigation for a differential mobile robot with android OS. In: Gelbukh, A., Espinoza, F.C., Galicia-Haro, S.N. (eds.) MICAI 2014. LNCS (LNAI), vol. 8856, pp. 281–292. Springer, Cham (2014). https://doi.org/10.1007/978-3-319-13647-9_26
26. Wang, S., Zhu, Y., Li, Z., Wang, Y., Wang, L., He, Z.: ChatGPT as your vehicle co-pilot: an initial attempt. IEEE Trans. Intell. Veh. (2023)
27. Yu, F.: BDD100K: a large-scale diverse driving video database (2018). https://bair.berkeley.edu/blog/2018/05/30/bdd/. Berkeley Artificial Intelligence Research Blog

Interpretable Human Activity Recognition for Subtle Robbery Detection in Surveillance Videos

Bryan Jhoan Cazáres Leyva[1], Ulises Gachuz Davila[1],
José Juan González Fonseca[1], Juan Irving Vasquez[2]($\boxtimes$) (iD),
Vanessa A. Camacho-Vázquez[1] (iD), and Sergio Isahí Garrido-Castañeda[2] (iD)

[1] Escuela Superior de Cómputo, Instituto Politécnico Nacional, México City, Mexico
[2] Centro de Innovación y Desarollo Tecnológico en Cómputo, Instituto Politécnico
Nacional, México City, Mexico
jvasquezg@ipn.mx

Abstract. Non-violent street robberies (snatch-and-run) are difficult to detect automatically because they are brief, subtle, and often indistinguishable from benign human interactions in unconstrained surveillance footage. This paper presents a hybrid, pose-driven approach for detecting snatch-and-run events that combines real-time perception with an interpretable classification stage suitable for edge deployment. The system uses a YOLO-based pose estimator to extract body keypoints for each tracked person and computes kinematic and interaction features describing hand speed, arm extension, proximity, and relative motion between an aggressor-victim pair. A Random Forest classifier is trained on these descriptors, and a temporal hysteresis filter is applied to stabilize frame-level predictions and reduce spurious alarms. We evaluate the method on a staged dataset and on a disjoint test set collected from internet videos, demonstrating promising generalization across different scenes and camera viewpoints. Finally, we implement the complete pipeline on an NVIDIA Jetson Nano and report real-time performance, supporting the feasibility of proactive, on-device robbery detection.

Keywords: Human activity recognition · surveillance · explainable AI

1 Introduction

Public safety, particularly in regard to non-violent street robbery, remains a critical challenge for urban security [1]. Despite the global expansion of video surveillance infrastructure, its effectiveness is often hindered by heavy reliance on real-time human interpretation.

B. J. Cazáres Leyva, U. Gachuz Davila and J. J. González Fonseca—These authors contributed equally to this work.

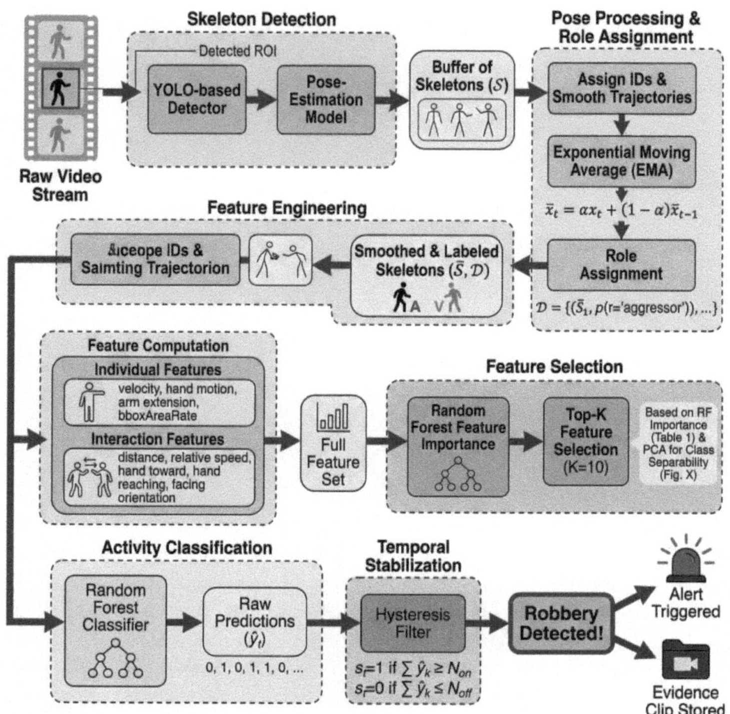

Fig. 1. General flow of the proposed method for the recognition of robbery in surveillance videos.

Traditionally, action recognition relied on computationally intensive modalities like RGB image sequences or depth videos [2]. However, 3-dimensional (3D) skeleton-based action recognition (SAR) has emerged as a more robust alternative, providing detailed topological representations of the human body through joints and bones [3]. Early methods primarily utilized handcrafted features to capture relative 3D rotations and translations among body parts [4]. Recent advancements have shifted toward deep learning architectures, specifically Recurrent Neural Networks (RNNs) and Long Short-Term Memory (LSTM) networks, which excel at capturing temporal dependencies in joint movements [5] [6]. Despite their temporal proficiency, standard RNNs often lack spatial modeling capabilities [7]. To address this, Convolutional Neural Networks (CNNs) are frequently employed to identify spatial features and local patterns by transforming skeleton sequences into pseudo-image formats [8]. Furthermore, Graph Convolutional Networks (GCNs) have gained prominence by treating the human skeleton as a natural graph structure, effectively modeling the interdependence between joints and bones [9]. For high-stakes interactions like robbery, modern approaches increasingly leverage Transformer-based architectures and hybrid models to capture long-range dependencies and global relationships within the data [3,10]. These methodologies are typically evaluated on large-scale datasets such as NTU-RGB+D and NTU-RGB+D 120, which offer challenging cross-subject and cross-view evaluation protocols [2]. While existing studies explore violent behavior detection using pose estimation and neural networks, these models target broad categories of aggression. Consequently, there remains a lack of specialized systems focusing on the specific subtle kinematics of non-violent robbery incidents between two individuals.

Although AI-driven video analytics have significantly reduced false alarms and improved detection of defined actions such as shoplifting or explicit violent behaviors [11], research and technical deployments indicate substantial gaps remain in automating the recognition of subtle, non-violent behavioral signatures (e.g., rapid snatching followed by immediate flight), which are harder to characterize and detect using current models. Furthermore, end-to-end methods based on deep learning lack of explainability.

This paper addresses the detection of non-violent robbery (snatch-and-run) by proposing a method that combines neural-network-based perception with an explainable, feature-based classifier. The system uses the YOLO architecture to detect individuals and estimate their body keypoints. Next, an interpretable feature-extraction stage computes kinematic and interaction descriptors from the skeleton trajectories; a formally ranked subset of the most relevant features is then used to detect the event using a Random Forest classifier. The main contribution of this work is the proposed explainable classification pipeline for pose-driven robbery recognition.

The implemented system is evaluated in controlled environments designed to replicate real-world theft dynamics. We report accuracy and response time to establish a baseline for proactive surveillance efficiency relative to traditional manual monitoring. In addition, the experiments show that the method can run on the NVIDIA Jetson Nano, supporting its suitability for edge deployment.

2   Robbery Recognition Methodology

Overall, the proposed method takes a raw video stream as input. First, a YOLO-based detector identifies people in each frame; then, for each detected ROI, a pose-estimation model computes the corresponding skeleton. Next, we assign consistent IDs to the detected individuals and smooth the resulting pose trajectories over time. For each person, we refine the pose sequence by computing relative features and then retain only a subset of the most informative ones. These selected features are fed into a previously trained Random Forest classifier to predict the activity class. Because the classifier may produce sporadic misclassifications, we apply a hysteresis-based decision rule to stabilize predictions over time. Finally, when a robbery is detected, the system triggers an alert and stores the corresponding evidence. A general flow diagram is presented in Fig. 1, and the details are provided next.

2.1 Skeleton Detection

The raw video is split into a frame buffer. Skeletons are then extracted in two stages: first, the YOLO detector identifies the people in the scene; next, for each detected bounding box, a pose-estimation model predicts the corresponding skeleton. This produces a buffer of skeletons over time, denoted as $\mathcal{S} = \{S_1, \ldots, S_n\}$, where n is the number of people in the scene. Each skeleton consists of 17 body keypoints: the nose (0), eyes (1,2), ears(3, 4), shoulders (5, 6), elbows (7, 8), wrists (9, 10), hips (11, 12), knees (13, 14), and ankles (15,16).

2.2 Pose Estimation

To reduce noise in the skeleton measurements over time, $\mathcal{S}$, we smooth each joint trajectory using an Exponential Moving Average (EMA). For a joint coordinate x_t at time t, the EMA is defined as shown in Eq. (1):

$$\bar{x}t = \alpha x_t + (1 - \alpha)\bar{x}t - 1, \qquad 0 < \alpha < 1, \tag{1}$$

with initialization $\bar{x}_0 = x_0$. Applying this update to every joint and coordinate yields the smoothed skeleton sequence $\bar{\mathcal{S}}$.

In this human-to-human interaction scenario, there are two possible roles: victim and aggressor. Because we have no prior knowledge of each person's intent, we evaluate both role assignments and attach a probability to each one. Thus, we augment the set of detected and filtered skeletons with an aggressor label, represented by the set $\mathcal{D}$ in Eq. (2).

$$\mathcal{D} = (\bar{S}_1, p(r = \text{'aggressor'})), \ldots, (\bar{S}_n, p(r = \text{'aggressor'})), \tag{2}$$

where the probability of being an aggressor is estimated from the mean translation of the skeleton over time and converted into a normalized score using a softmax function. This heuristic assumes that the aggressor (or thief) exhibits more abrupt movements.

2.3 Explainable Feature Extraction

This section describes the interpretable kinematic and interaction features computed from the smoothed skeleton sequences. All distances and velocities are normalized by the torso height to reduce sensitivity to scale changes caused by subject–camera distance. We group the features into two categories:

Individual Features Per Track. They characterize the motion and posture of each person independently. They are divided in four groups:

– **Body-center kinematics features.** `velocity`: normalized velocity of the person center. `acceleration`: normalized acceleration of the person center.

– **Hand motion features.** `handVelocity`: normalized wrist speed. High values suggest rapid hand movement (e.g., a slap, grab, or snatch attempt). `fastHandPct`: percentage of frames for which the wrist speed exceeds a fixed threshold. It measures the duration of fast hand motion. `timeToPeakHandVel`: number of frames required to reach the maximum wrist speed within the segment (timing of the fastest motion). `handAcceleration`:('aggressor') wrist acceleration. `handJerkMin`:('aggressor') minimum wrist jerk (derivative of acceleration).
– **Arm extension and posture features.** `armExtension`: normalized arm extension (wrist-shoulder distance). `timeToPeakArmExt`('aggressor'): frames until it reaches the max. arm extension. `armRetractionOp2s`('aggressor'): drop in aggressor's arm extension 0.2 s after its peak. This "retraction" metric captures whether the aggressor quickly withdraws the arm after reaching maximum reach. `elbowFlexPct`[L/R]: percentage of frames in which the elbow angle is below a threshold indicating a tendency to keep the arms flexed. `elbowAngle`[L/R]: Estimation of the elbow angle.
– **Bounding-box features.** `bboxAreaRate`: relative derivative of the bounding-box area. Positive values may indicate motion toward the camera.

Interaction Features. Characterize the joint movement. Subjects A and B.

– **Distance and contact features:** `distance`: normalized distance between the centers of subjects. `distanceRate`: distance change rate (approach/separation speed). `iou`: IoU between their bounding boxes (physical contact or crowding). `iouPeak`: maximum IoU within the segment. `iouDropOp2s`: IoU drop 0.2 s after the peak, measuring how quickly they separate after maximum overlap.
– **Relative movement features.** `relativeSpeed`: relative speed between the centers of subjects. `handTowardCos`: cosine similarity between A's hand velocity vector and the vector from A to B's torso. Values close to 1 indicate that A's hand moves directly toward B, serving as an intent cue. `handTowardPct`: percentage of frames with high directionality, measuring the duration of "attack intent."
– **Hand reaching features.** `handToTorsoMin`: minimum normalized distance from A's wrist to B's torso center. `closeHandPct`: percentage of frames in which agrressor's hand is very close to victims's torso. `handToHipMin`: minimum normalized distance from aggressors's wrist to victims's hips, which can help detect interactions directed to the lower torso (e.g., pockets). `fastAndClosePct`: percentage overlap of "fast hand" and "close hand" conditions, combining rapid action with close interaction. `fastAndCloseLongest`: longest consecutive run (frames) satisfying the "fast and close" condition. `postContactSepMean`: mean center distance in a 0.4 s window after A's hand reaches its closest point to B's torso, capturing immediate withdrawal/separation.

- **Relative face orientation features.** `BfacingToA`: cosine similarity between B's facing direction and the vector from B to A. Values close to -1 indicate that B is facing A, while values close to 1 indicate that B is turned away. `AfacingToB`: cosine similarity between A's facing direction and the vector from A to B. Values close to 1 indicate that A is facing B. `facingRate`: derivative of the facing direction.

2.4 Feature Selection Analysis

To select a compact and informative subset of variables, we first trained a Random Forest model using the full set of available features. We then used the model's feature importances attribute to estimate the contribution of each feature to the classifier's decision process. Based on this ranking, we retained the 10 most important features, which helps reduce noise and redundancy while preserving discriminative power. The choice of 10 features was made empirically.

Table 1 lists the selected features in descending order of importance. Among the top-10, `AB_dist_p95` provides the highest contribution to classification, whereas `AB_handTowardGtO7Pct` has the lowest contribution within the selected subset.

Table 1. Top 10 features ranked by Random Forest importance (Two columns).

Rank	Feature	Imp. (10^{-2})	Rank	Feature	Imp. (10^{-2})
1	`dist_p95`	5.236	6	`distancet_max`	4.188
2	`handToHip_max`	4.802	7	`handToTorso_median`	3.340
3	`handToTorso_mean`	4.781	8	`handToHip_p95`	2.763
4	`handToTorso_p95`	4.297	9	`distance_mean`	2.459
5	`handToTorso_max`	4.239	10	`closeHandPct`	2.352

Finally, to analyze class separability using the selected 10 features, we applied Principal Component Analysis (PCA) and visualized the projected samples as shown in Fig. 2.

2.5 Hysteresis Filtering

Frame-by-frame predictions produced by the activity classifier may be unstable due to pose-estimation noise, partial occlusions, and short-term ambiguous motion. To avoid raising spurious alarms, we apply a temporal hysteresis filter that enforces different activation and deactivation conditions.

Let $\hat{y}_t \in \{0, 1\}$ be the raw prediction at time t, where $\hat{y}_t = 1$ denotes "robbery". We define an internal alarm state $s_t \in \{0, 1\}$ updated as shown in Eq.

(3). The alarm is activated only if the classifier predicts robbery for at least N_{on} frames within a sliding window of length W.

$$s_t = 1 \quad \text{if} \quad \sum_{k=t-W+1}^{t} \hat{y}_k \geq N_{\text{on}} \tag{3}$$

Once activated, the alarm remains on until the robbery prediction has been absent for at least N_{off} frames in the same window (with $N_{\text{off}} < N_{\text{on}}$), a condition expressed by Eq. (4).

$$s_t = 0 \quad \text{if} \quad \sum_{k=t-W+1}^{t} \hat{y}k \leq N\text{off}. \tag{4}$$

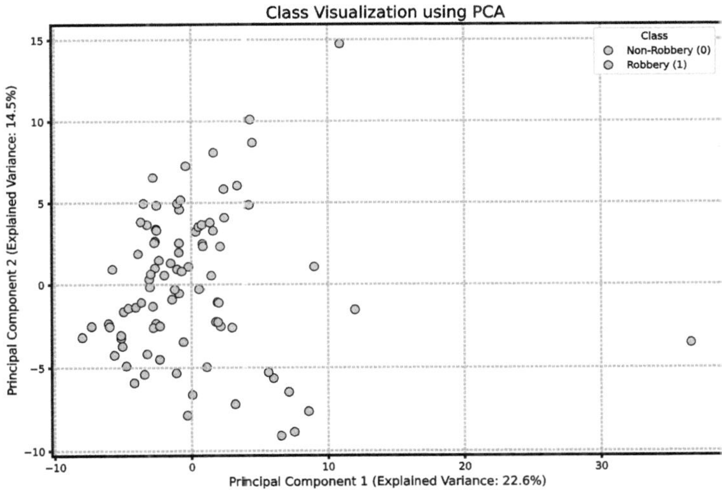

Fig. 2. Class visualization using PCA. As we can observe, the projected samples are in a general way distinguishable. This graph is only a projection of the feature vectors of 10 elements.

Otherwise, the previous state is preserved ($s_t = s_{t-1}$). This two-threshold mechanism prevents rapid state switching and attenuates short bursts of false positives/negatives.

In practice, W is chosen according to the frame rate (e.g., $W \approx 0.4\,$s of video), and N_{on} and N_{off} are tuned to trade off detection latency against robustness. When s_t transitions from 0 to 1, the system triggers an alert and stores the corresponding evidence clip.

3   Experiments

The experimentation is divided into two phases: the performance analysis of the behavioral classifier and the functional validation of the integrated prototype.

The proposed method was implemented in Python 3.12 using isolated virtual environments to ensure reproducibility. Communication between the embedded device and the desktop application is mediated by a RESTful API built with Flask, where both the NVIDIA Jetson Nano and the desktop client run independent Flask instances with complementary roles. The data flow follows the sequence Jetson Nano (detection and upload) client Flask server (storage and REST API) Electron interface (visualization and control), enabling a decoupled design.

For train and validation, we created a dataset focused on non-violent robbery. We recorded staged snatching events across different days, times, viewpoints, and locations to increase contextual diversity while keeping the target action consistent. The resulting dataset was labeled into two classes and then split into training and validation subsets. In total, it contains 90 examples: 29 robbery samples (positive class) and 61 non-robbery samples (negative class). Representative frames from the training/validation dataset are shown in Fig. 3.

Fig. 3. Representative frames from the training/validation video dataset recorded for this work. Faces were deliberately blurred for this paper.

Fig. 4. Representative frames from the test video dataset. These videos are publicly available on YouTube. Faces were deliberately blurred for this paper.

For testing, we collected a disjoint dataset from various sources on the internet. To better assess robustness, these clips include substantial contextual variability (e.g., different camera angles, different subjects, and variations in how the snatching event is executed). The labeled test set contains 47 examples: 17 robbery samples and 30 non-robbery samples. Representative frames from the test dataset are shown in Fig. 4.

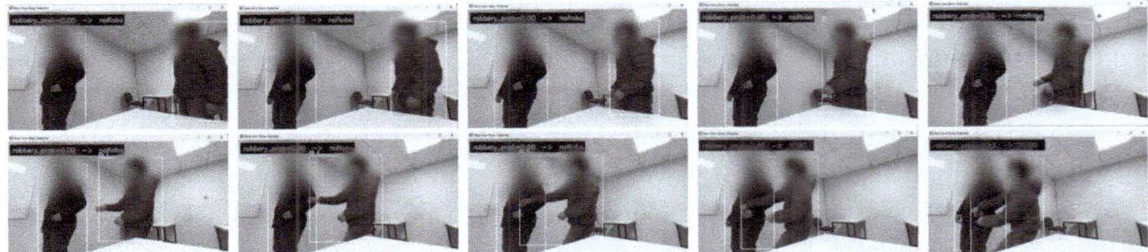

Fig. 5. Example sequence of the functioning of the implemented method. The sequence shows the detection of a robbery.

Classification was performed with a Random Forest model. To mitigate class imbalance, we used $n\_estimators = 500$, $random\_state = 42$, and $class_weight = $ 'balanced'. The validation results are reported in Table 2.

The proposed method achieves an overall validation accuracy of 0.83. For the non-robbery class, the model attains a precision of 0.91 and an F1-score of 0.87. Importantly, for the robbery class—the target event of interest—the model reaches a recall of 0.83 and an F1-score of 0.77, reflecting a favorable sensitivity to snatch-and-run behaviors while maintaining acceptable precision (0.71). These results support the capacity of the proposed pipeline to address the target task under realistic variability and limited data, providing a robust basis for proactive surveillance. Figure 5 shows a sequence of frames of the implemented systems working on real time.

Table 2. Classification results for validation stage.

Class	Acc.	Prec.	Recall	F1-Score	Support
Non-Robbery	0.83	0.91	0.83	0.87	12
Robbery	0.83	0.71	0.83	0.77	6

Table 3. Classification results for the test experiment.

Class	Acc.	Precision	Recall	F1-Score	Support
Non-Robbery	73.3	0.78	0.83	0.81	30
Robbery	58.8	0.67	0.59	0.62	17

The model was further evaluated on a held-out test set to assess generalization under higher contextual variability. As summarized in Table 3, the method achieves a class accuracy of 73.3% for *Non-Robbery* samples, with precision, recall and F1-score of 0.78, 0.83 and 0.81.

For the target *Robbery* class, the system obtains a precision of 0.67, recall of 0.59 and F1-score of 0.62. While these values reflect the increased difficulty of recognizing subtle snatch-and-run events in unconstrained internet videos, the results still demonstrate that the pose-driven, feature-based methodology can detect a substantial portion of robberies while maintaining moderate precision.

The experimental data reveals that the system performs adequately even for the test set that uses quite different scenes. The occasional misclassifications observed in the test phase can be attributed to camera angles, lighting variations, and the inherent diversity of "snatch-and-run" movements in low-resolution internet footage. Nevertheless, the results on the internet-based test set provide a benchmark for this variability. This performance reflects a deliberate design trade-off that prioritizes interpretability and real-time execution. The current effectiveness of the method is centered on rapid interactions between two individuals in scenarios with adequate visibility and lighting. Additionally, the focus on binary interactions is consistent with the nature of snatching events, where the interaction typically involves two individuals in close proximity. Despite these challenges, the use of a lightweight YOLO model combined with a Random Forest classifier allowed for an adequate response time on the NVIDIA Jetson Nano, validating the feasibility of the proposed architecture for real-time proactive surveillance.

4   Conclusions

This study presented a method for detecting non-violent robbery (snatch-and-run) in surveillance videos. Starting from raw video, the pipeline combines pose keypoints and an interpretable, feature-based classifier to recognize suspicious interactions. To improve temporal robustness, we incorporated a hysteresis filtering stage that reduces sporadic false positives in frame-level predictions. While the current findings are based on a limited dataset, the experimental results show promising performance across videos captured in different contexts. These results suggest the potential of the proposed approach for real-world surveillance. Finally, we validated the implementation on an NVIDIA Jetson device, demonstrating that the method can run on edge hardware. Future work will focus on addressing class imbalance and extending the model to additional behaviors.

References

1. Tykesson, M., Se, M.T.: Effects of CCTV on fear of crime: a systematic literature review. Eur. J. Crim. Policy Res. **2025**, 1–29 (2025)
2. Liu, J., Shahroudy, A., Perez, M., Wang, G., Duan, L.Y., Kot, A.C.: Ntu rgb+ d 120: a large-scale benchmark for 3d human activity understanding. IEEE Trans. Pattern Anal. Mach. Intell. **42**(10), 2684–2701 (2019)
3. Liu, Y., et al.: Transtm: a device-free method based on time-streaming multiscale transformer for human activity recognition. Defence Technol. **32**, 619–628 (2024)
4. Poppe, R.: A survey on vision-based human action recognition. Image Vis. Comput. **28**(6), 976–990 (2010)

5. Shu, X., Zhang, L., Sun, Y., Tang, J.: Host-parasite: graph LSTM-in-LSTM for group activity recognition. IEEE Trans. Neural Netw. Learn. Syst. **32**(2), 663–674 (2020)
6. Balakrishnan, T.S., Jayalakshmi, D., Geetha, P., Saju Raj, T., Hemavathi, R.: Accurate recognition of human abnormal behaviours using adaptive 3d residual attention network with gated recurrent units (GRU) in the video sequences. Comput. Methods Biomech. Biomed. Eng. Imaging Visual. **12**(1), 2429402 (2024)
7. Wang, C., Yan, J.: A comprehensive survey of rgb-based and skeleton-based human action recognition. IEEE Access **11**, 53880–53898 (2023)
8. Ko, K.E., Sim, K.B.: Deep convolutional framework for abnormal behavior detection in a smart surveillance system. Eng. Appl. Artif. Intell. **67**, 226–234 (2018)
9. Liu, Z., Zhang, H., Chen, Z., Wang, Z., Ouyang, W.: Disentangling and unifying graph convolutions for skeleton-based action recognition. In: Proceedings of the IEEE/CVF Conference on Computer Vision and Pattern Recognition. pp. 143–152 (2020)
10. Wang, L., Koniusz, P.: 3mformer: multi-order multi-mode transformer for skeletal action recognition. In: Proceedings of the IEEE/CVF Conference on Computer Vision and Pattern Recognition, pp. 5620–5631 (2023)
11. Mohammadi, H., Nazerfard, E.: Video violence recognition and localization using a semi-supervised hard attention model. Expert Syst. Appl. **212** (2022)

Language Processing and Recognition

A Two-Stage Textual Preprocessing Pipeline for Medical Image Captioning

Sebastián Rascón-Cervantes[1], Graciela Ramirez-Alonso[1(✉)],
Adrián Pastor López-Monroy[2], Roberto Lopez-Santillan[1]
and Norman A. Rendón Mejía[3]

[1] Computer Vision and Data Science Lab, Universidad Autónoma de Chihuahua,
Facultad de Ingeniería, 31125 Chihuahua, Mexico
{p281831,galonso,jrlopez}@uach.mx
[2] Centro de Investigación en Matemáticas (CIMAT), A.C., Jalisco S/N, Col.
Valenciana, 36023 Guanajuato, Mexico
pastor.lopez@cimat.mx
[3] General Surgery Department, Hospital General "Dr. Salvador Zubirán Anchondo",
31200 Chihuahua, Mexico

Abstract. The training of deep learning models for medical image captioning is highly dependent on the quality and consistency of the associated textual data. In practice, medical captions often include non-visual or context-specific information such as patient metadata, temporal references, or procedural notes that cannot be inferred from the image itself. The presence of such information introduces text-image misalignment and can hinder effective model learning. This study proposes a two-stage textual preprocessing pipeline designed to refine such captions. The first stage removes non-visual elements, and the second applies in-context paraphrasing to restore fluency and increase lexical diversity. This proposed pipeline is evaluated under a text-only training configuration named Med-ToT. Experiments on the ImageCLEFmedical 2024 dataset show improvements of 3.08% in BERTScore, 3.28% in ROUGE-L, 4.38% in BLEU-1, and 1.74% in METEOR when training with the proposed configuration. A stratified BERTScore analysis indicates that 58.6% of the predictions exhibit improved semantic alignment after preprocessing, with gains being more pronounced in samples with low initial scores. In addition, Med-ToT achieves a 44% reduction in sentence-level repetition and completely suppresses the generation of non-visual hallucinations.

Keywords: Medical Image Captioning · Textual Preprocessing · Non-Visual Context Removal · Text-Only Training

1 Introduction

Recent advances in foundation models, particularly Large Language Models (LLMs) and Vision–Language Models (VLMs), have broadened the research frontier of medical image captioning, the task of generating textual descriptions

V. G. Cruz-Sánchez et al. (Eds.): MCPR 2026, LNCS 16623, pp. 273–282, 2026.
https://doi.org/10.1007/978-3-032-23393-1_24

of medical images [12]. These capabilities create opportunities to support clinical workflows and diagnostic reasoning [8]. Despite this progress, current captioning systems still depend heavily on large paired datasets that link images to coherent, clinically meaningful textual descriptions. Nevertheless, not all information contained in these captions is visually grounded, giving rise to a key challenge: text–image misalignment, where captions may include information that cannot be inferred from the visual input, such as patient metadata, temporal references, or procedural details. These elements introduce biases during training and are associated with recurrent error patterns in medical captioning, such as *non-visual hallucination*, where the model generates details not grounded in the image [10], and *sentence-level repetition*, characterized by unintended repetition due to noisy or inconsistent captions [13].

Several datasets have supported progress in this area, including IU X-Ray [3] and MIMIC-CXR [7]. However, both collections focus exclusively on chest radiography, resulting in relatively homogeneous captions. In contrast, the Image-CLEFmedical Captioning dataset [11] covers multiple imaging modalities and anatomical regions, making it a suitable benchmark to study this problem under more heterogeneous and realistic clinical conditions.

Prior work on the ImageCLEFmedical task has focused predominantly on improving the visual component through image augmentation, enhancement techniques, and, more recently, large multimodal architectures and LLM-based frameworks for visual–language integration [6]. While these approaches have advanced architectural design, relatively limited attention has been given to the preprocessing of the textual modality, which is often restricted to basic normalization or simple augmentation schemes. As a result, text–image misalignment is typically left to be handled implicitly by the model, rather than being explicitly addressed at the data level.

Recent NLP-based strategies have explored LLM-driven text augmentation to increase linguistic diversity in medical captioning [2,5,9]. However, these methods typically rely on single-step prompting, offering limited control over the rewriting process and often introducing inconsistencies or hallucinated content [1]. As a result, the problem of text–image misalignment, particularly due to the presence of non-visual information, is still not fully resolved.

This work addresses these limitations through a two-stage textual preprocessing pipeline. The first stage performs targeted removal of non-visual context, while the second applies in-context paraphrasing to restore fluency and increase linguistic diversity. The proposed pipeline is evaluated under a medical text-only training configuration (Med-ToT), where the visual encoder remains fixed and training focuses exclusively on the language component, enabling a controlled analysis of the impact of textual refinement.

Within this context, the present work makes three key contributions:

- Identification and analysis of text – image misalignment in the Image-CLEFmedical caption dataset caused by non-visual information present in the captions.
- A two-stage textual preprocessing framework that reduces this issue by removing non-visual content and applying structured in-context paraphrasing.

– A medical text-only training setup (Med-ToT) that allows a controlled evaluation of caption quality improvements.

2 Methodology

2.1 Dataset

The ImageCLEFmedical 2024 dataset [11], released as part of the ImageCLEF Medical Captioning Challenge, constitutes the starting point of this research and was selected as the most recent available benchmark with standardized training, validation, and test splits at the time of this study. The challenge comprises two subtasks (caption prediction and concept detection), of which only the captioning task is addressed in this work. Nevertheless, the concept vocabulary used for the detection subtask is employed during the inference stage to support the generation process. The dataset includes medical images from six imaging modalities: X-ray, computed tomography (CT), magnetic resonance imaging (MRI), ultrasound, positron emission tomography (PET), and hybrid modalities such as PET/CT. It also spans eight anatomical regions: skull, spine, upper limb/arm, chest, breast, abdomen, pelvis, and lower limb/leg.

2.2 Two-Stage Textual Preprocessing Pipeline

A two-stage LLM-based textual preprocessing pipeline was designed to refine the medical captions from the ImageCLEFmedical corpus by removing non-visual information and improving linguistic quality. The pipeline consists of: (i) pruning of non-visual context and (ii) in-context paraphrasing. The outputs of both stages are combined to form the Cleaned & Paraphrased (C&P) dataset (see Fig. 1). Both stages use a lightweight LLM (DeepSeek-R1 Distill Llama-8B) with instruction-based prompting.

Pruning of Non-visual Context. This stage removes information that cannot be inferred from the image, such as demographic data, temporal references, and procedural notes, retaining only visually grounded clinical content. After validation, 65,754 cleaned captions were obtained. The pruning process is guided by an instruction-based prompt that explicitly enforces filtering rules. Specifically, the prompt includes directives such as: *"Imagine you are an expert radiologist Your task is to ensure that reports contain only information derived from the medical image. Remove any non-visual data, including dates, ages, gender, patient references, temporal expressions (e.g., postoperative, follow-up), and citation or figure references."* These rules are complemented with in-context examples to ensure consistent transformations from raw to cleaned captions. The output is constrained to return only the refined caption, discarding inputs without visually grounded content. This design enables systematic filtering while preserving clinically relevant findings.

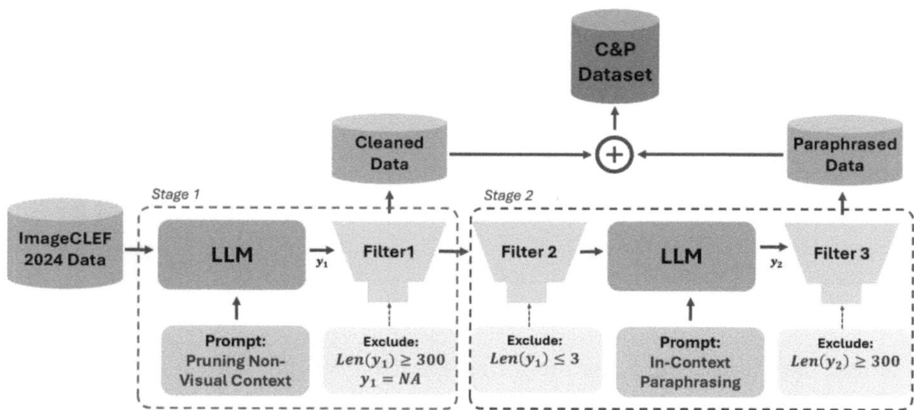

Fig. 1. Overview of the two-stage textual preprocessing pipeline.

In-Context Paraphrasing. This stage reformulates cleaned captions to increase lexical diversity while preserving clinical meaning, yielding 62,468 validated paraphrases. The process is guided by an instruction-based prompt that enforces structured rewriting. The prompt includes directives such as *"Analyze key clinical findings, identify precise medical terminology, and ensure clarity and conciseness without losing meaning."* In-context examples (e.g., *"Heart is enlarged with basal opacities"* → *"Cardiomegaly and lower lung opacities"*) are used to ensure consistent transformations. The output is constrained to avoid introducing new findings and to return only the final paraphrased sentence, or the original input when paraphrasing is not applicable.

Finally, the cleaned and paraphrased repositories were merged to form the Cleaned & Paraphrased (C&P) dataset. This design balances two complementary properties: semantic precision and linguistic diversity. While cleaned captions ensure strict visual grounding by removing non-visual information, paraphrased captions introduce variability that improves generalization. Using only paraphrased captions was also considered; however, retaining both sources provides a more stable training signal by combining high-fidelity descriptions with increased linguistic richness. Additionally, merging cleaned and paraphrased captions effectively acts as a form of data augmentation, increasing the number of training samples while preserving semantic consistency.

2.3 Model Architecture

The model architecture adopted in this study builds upon the framework proposed in [4], which combines a CLIP-based encoder with a GPT-2 decoder for image captioning. The framework is reconfigured for a medical text-only training setup (Med-ToT), allowing the impact of textual preprocessing to be isolated from visual features. To adapt the model to the medical domain, the standard CLIP encoder is replaced with MedCLIP ViT-B/32. The resulting architecture follows a dual-phase design, consisting of a text-only training stage and an inference stage that integrates visual information (see Fig. 2).

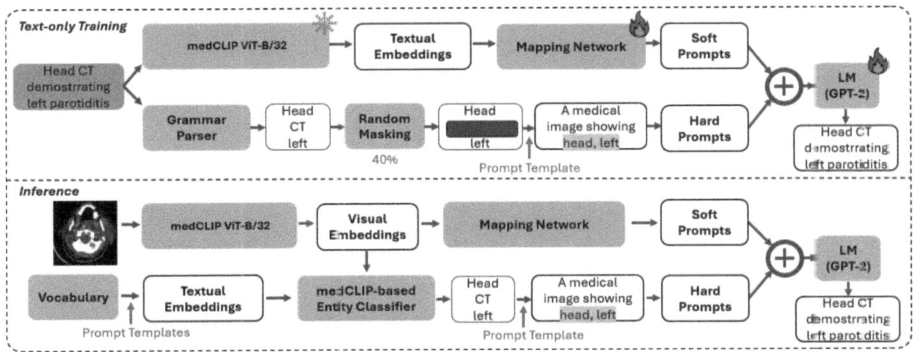

Fig. 2. Overview of the neural architecture adapted for medical image captioning in a text-only training framework, Med-ToT.

During training, textual embeddings obtained from MedCLIP are processed by a compact Transformer-based mapping network to generate a fixed set of soft prompt vectors. In parallel, medical entities extracted from the captions are used to construct hard prompts following a predefined medical template. Both prompt types are concatenated and fed into a GPT-2 decoder, enabling text-only training without requiring paired visual inputs. At inference time, input images are encoded by MedCLIP and projected through the same mapping network to generate soft prompts, while hard prompts are formed based on concept-level similarities with a predefined medical vocabulary. The resulting prompts are fused and passed to the GPT-2 decoder to generate the final medical description. For clarity, both soft and hard prompts are represented as embedding vectors. Soft prompts are directly generated by the mapping network, while hard prompts are constructed from medical templates and subsequently embedded into the same latent space. These representations are then concatenated and used as conditioning inputs to the language model.

3   Results

Model performance was assessed using the official metrics of the Image-CLEFmedical 2024 challenge [11]. All experimental configurations were trained and evaluated three times under identical conditions to account for variability due to random initialization and stochastic optimization. For each metric, the mean and standard deviation across runs were reported.

3.1   Ablation Study

An ablation study was conducted to assess the individual and combined contributions of the two proposed preprocessing stages: pruning of non-visual context (referred to as cleaned) and in-context paraphrasing (referred to as paraphrased)(see Table 1). A paraphrased-only configuration was not evaluated, as paraphrasing only reformulates the cleaned captions. Instead, both cleaned and

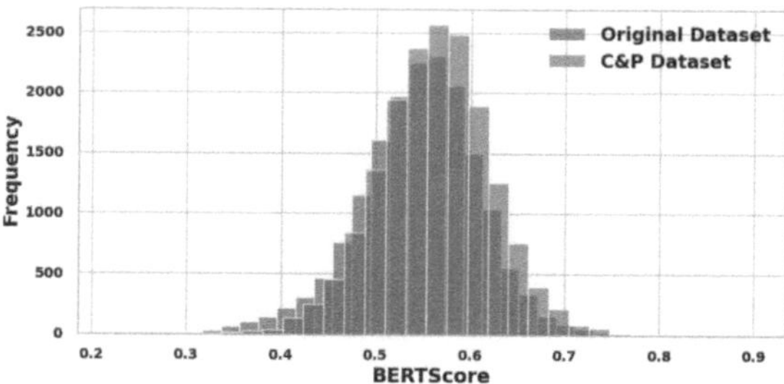

Fig. 3. Histogram of BERTScore distributions for the original and cleaned & paraphrased (C&P) datasets.

paraphrased captions are retained as a form of data augmentation to increase diversity while preserving semantic consistency.

Compared with the model trained on the original dataset, training with the cleaned configuration leads to an average reduction of 13.80% across all four evaluation metrics. The original + paraphrased configuration shows mixed behavior, with BERTScore and ROUGE-L increasing by an average of 2.5%, while BLEU-1 and METEOR decrease by approximately 4.8%. In contrast, training with the combined cleaned + paraphrased configuration produces an average improvement of 3.12% across all evaluated metrics. A Wilcoxon signed-rank test using paired results across runs was conducted by comparing the Cleaned + Paraphrased configuration against each alternative setting (Original, Cleaned, and Original + Paraphrased). The results show that the Cleaned + Paraphrased configuration achieves statistically significant improvements over all other settings ($p < 0.001$), supporting the complementary effect of the two preprocessing stages.

3.2 BERTScore Distribution Analysis

A global analysis of BERTScore distributions was conducted to compare the behavior of the original dataset with the Cleaned & Paraphrased (C&P) dataset. As shown in Fig. 3, the C&P configuration reduces the concentration of predictions with low BERTScore values while increasing the proportion of samples above the 0.50 threshold, indicating an overall improvement in semantic alignment between generated captions and ground-truth descriptions.

Table 1. Ablation results across four evaluation metrics, comparing different preprocessing configurations. Values are reported as mean ± standard deviation.

Configuration	BERTScore	ROUGE-L	BLEU-1	METEOR
Original	0.5456 ± 0.012	0.0916 ± 0.005	0.0548 ± 0.004	0.0576 ± 0.003
Cleaned	0.5402 ± 0.010	0.0784 ± 0.006	0.0427 ± 0.003	0.0474 ± 0.004
Original + Paraphrased	0.5609 ± 0.011	0.0936 ± 0.004	0.0521 ± 0.005	0.0549 ± 0.004
Cleaned + Paraphrased	**0.5624 ± 0.009**	**0.0946 ± 0.003**	**0.0572 ± 0.004**	**0.0586 ± 0.002**

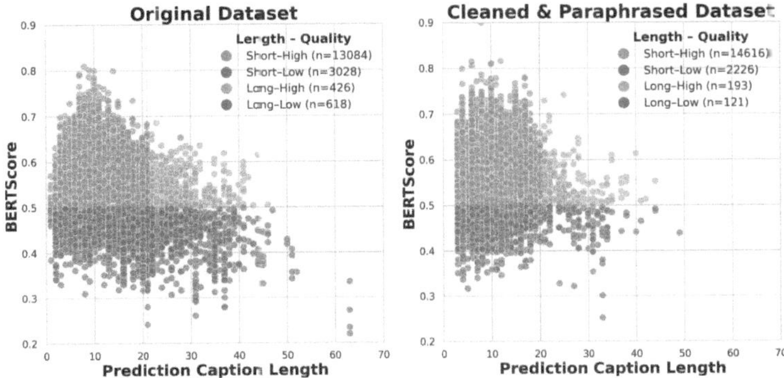

Fig. 4. Relationship between BERTScore and prediction caption length for the original and C&P datasets.

Table 2. Stratified BERTScore improvements by initial score range. Total predictions correspond to samples within each interval, and improved predictions indicate those with increased BERTScore under the C&P configuration. Δ denotes mean $\pm$ standard deviation.

Initial range	Total predictions	Improved predictions	Δ (%)
$x > 0.5$	13,521	7,096 (52.5%)	7.08 ± 5.94
$0.4 < x \leqslant 0.5$	3,324	2,632 (79.18%)	16.15 ± 12.23
$0.3 < x \leqslant 0.4$	381	362 (95%)	46.66 ± 22.29
Overall	17,236	10,101 (58.60%)	10.98 ± 12.49

To further examine generation behavior at the sample level, BERTScore values were analyzed as a function of prediction length (Fig. 4). The model trained with the C&P dataset produces shorter and more stable captions, while the original configuration tends to generate longer predictions. This shift suggests that the proposed preprocessing mitigates verbosity and reduces the tendency toward repetitive or loosely grounded descriptions.

A stratified analysis was also performed by grouping predictions according to their initial BERTScore values. This analysis aimed to assess whether the observed improvements were uniform across samples or more pronounced in challenging cases. The results, summarized in Table 2, show that the largest gains occur for predictions with lower initial BERTScore values, while consistent but smaller improvements are observed for samples with higher initial semantic alignment. Overall, 58.6% of the predictions exhibit improved BERTScore under the C&P configuration, confirming that the proposed preprocessing is particularly effective in difficult cases.

3.3   Qualitative Analysis

A qualitative analysis was conducted to assess the impact of the proposed preprocessing on caption quality. Representative examples (Table 3) highlight common

Table 3. Representative qualitative examples comparing predictions generated with the original and the C&P datasets. Modality terms are highlighted in yellow, clinical findings that match the ground-truth caption are highlighted in blue, and non-matching or incorrect terms are highlighted in orange.

Ground-truth Caption	Predictions
ID: 016000 **GT:** Chest X-ray . Orange arrow indicates a slight increase in cardiothoracic index; green arrow represents a small pleural effusion on the left thorax.	**Orig:** Axial CT image of the thoracic aortic aneurysm . (0.6027) **C&P:** Lateral chest X-ray demonstrates a right-sided pleural effusion . (0.7314)
ID: 013967 **GT:** Chest X-ray demonstrating left-sided pleural effusion .	**Orig:** CT of the thorax showing a large pneumomediastinum (arrow). (0.4685) **C&P:** CT scan of the thorax demonstrates a left-sided pleural effusion . (0.8142)

error patterns in the original configuration, including modality inconsistencies, sentence-level repetition, and non-visual hallucinations. Compared to the original dataset, predictions generated with the Cleaned & Paraphrased (C&P) configuration show improved semantic alignment with the ground truth, more accurate modality references, and better identification of relevant clinical findings. Additionally, modality detection improves by 9.39%, sentence repetition decreases by 44%, and non-visual hallucinations are effectively removed. These results indicate that the proposed preprocessing produces more coherent, visually grounded, and clinically meaningful captions, supporting the improvements observed in the quantitative evaluation.

4   Discussion

The ablation study shows that neither stage is effective in isolation: pruning alone degrades structure, while paraphrasing without filtering retains non-visual noise. In contrast, the combined pipeline consistently improves all metrics, confirming their complementary roles. At the sample level, the C&P configuration produces shorter, more stable captions with reduced repetition and improved semantic alignment, particularly in low-quality cases. Limitations include the lack of explicit modeling of negation and clinical polarity, as well as restriction to English captions. Future work will explore integrating visual information and explicit modality cues.

State-of-the-art approaches in ImageCLEFmedical 2024 achieve BERTScore values up to 0.629 [6], relying on large-scale multimodal architectures. While these models outperform the proposed approach, they depend on complex designs and joint visual–language training. In contrast, the proposed method isolates the textual component under a text-only training, enabling a controlled analysis of preprocessing. Despite its simplicity, the proposed pipeline demonstrates that refining the textual modality alone can improve caption quality, positioning text preprocessing as a lightweight and complementary strategy for multimodal systems. As future work, visual information will be integrated into the training process to further enhance performance. The current text-only setting was intentionally designed to isolate and validate the impact of textual preprocessing, confirming that the observed improvements are primarily driven by the refined textual inputs.

5   Conclusion

This study presents a two-step text preprocessing approach to enhance the quality of medical image captions in a text-only training setting. The findings suggest that removing non-visual context and applying in-context paraphrasing serve complementary purposes: the first step filters out details that can't be inferred from the image, while the second step improves fluency and introduces controlled linguistic variation. When used together, these processes consistently improve performance across all evaluation metrics, reduce repetitive phrasing, and eliminate hallucinated content not grounded in the image.

The findings highlight domain-aware preprocessing as an influential yet often overlooked component in medical image captioning. By removing non-visual artifacts, the proposed framework improves semantic coherence and strengthens the linguistic signal. This supports the role of textual quality in multimodal tasks, even without visual input, while the use of a lightweight local LLM ensures suitability for privacy-sensitive medical settings.

Building on these observations, several directions for future work emerge. Incorporating visual information during training may help to address challenging cases where text alone is insufficient. Additional improvements may derive from explicitly modeling negation and clinical polarity, given their relevance for medical meaning. Extending the pipeline to other datasets will also clarify its generality across different annotation styles and levels of complexity. Although the in-context paraphrasing stage is likely to generalize with minimal adjustments, the pruning of non-visual context will require adaptation to the specific characteristics of each corpus.

Overall, the study positions textual preprocessing as a practical and adaptable component within broader pipelines for medical image understanding, with implications that extend to clinical NLP tasks involving heterogeneous or non-inferable textual content.

References

1. Banerjee, S., Agarwal, A., Singla, S.: LLMs will always hallucinate, and we need to live with this. In: Intelligent Systems Conference, pp. 624–648. Springer (2025). https://doi.org/10.1007/978-3-031-99965-939

2. Dai, H., Liu, Z., Liao, W., Huang, X., Cao, Y., Wu, Z., Zhao, L., Xu, S., Zeng, F., Liu, W., et al.: AugGPT: Leveraging ChatGPT for text data augmentation. IEEE Transactions on Big Data (2025). https://doi.org/10.1109/TBDATA.2025.3536934

3. Demner-Fushman, D., Kohli, M.D., Rosenman, M.B., Shooshan, S.E., Rodriguez, L., Antani, S., Thoma, G.R., McDonald, C.J.: Preparing a collection of radiology examinations for distribution and retrieval. J. Am. Med. Inform. Assoc. **23**(2), 304–310 (2016). https://doi.org/10.1093/jamia/ocv080

4. Fei, J., Wang, T., Zhang, J., He, Z., Wang, C., Zheng, F.: Transferable decoding with visual entities for zero-shot image captioning. In: Proceedings of the IEEE/CVF International Conference on Computer Vision. pp. 3136–3146 (2023)

5. Guo, B., Zhao, D., Dong, X., Meng, J., Lin, H.: Few-shot biomedical relation extraction using data augmentation and domain information. Neurocomputing **595**, 127881 (2024). https://doi.org/10.1016/j.neucom.2024.127881

6. Ionescu, B., Müller, H., Dragulinescu, A.M., Rückert, J., Abacha, A.B., de Herrera, A.G.S., Bloch, L., Brüngel, R., Idrissi-Yaghir, A., Schäfer, H., Schmidt, C.S., Pakull, T.M.G., Damm, H., Bracke, B., Friedrich, C.M., Andrei, A.G., Prokopchuk, Y., Karpenka, D., Radzhabov, A., Kovalev, V., Macaire, C., Schwab, D., Lecouteux, B., Esperanca-Rodier, E., wai Yim, W., Fu, Y., Sun, Z., Yetisgen, M., Xia, F., Hicks, S.A., Riegler, M.A., Thambawita, V., Storas, A., Halvorsen, P., Heinrich, M., Kiesel, J., Potthast, M., Stein, B.: Overview of imageclef 2024: Multimedia retrieval in medical applications. In: Experimental IR Meets Multilinguality, Multimodality, and Interaction. Proceedings of the 15th International Conference of the CLEF Association (CLEF 2024), Springer Lecture Notes in Computer Science LNCS, Grenoble, France (September 9-12 2024)

7. Johnson, A.E., et al.: MIMIC-CXR, a de-identified publicly available database of chest radiographs with free-text reports. Scientific data 6, 317 (2019). https://doi.org/10.1038/s41597-019-0322-0

8. Nie, P., Liu, X.: MedNet: a dual-copy mechanism for medical report generation from images. In: International Conference on Artificial Neural Networks, pp. 469–481. Springer (2023). https://doi.org/10.1007/978-3-031-44210-038

9. Prieto-Ordaz, O., Ramirez-Alonso, G., y Gomez, M.M., Lopez-Santillan, R.: Toward an enhanced automatic medical report generator based on large transformer models. Neural Comput. Appl. **37**, 43–62 (2024). https://doi.org/10.1007/s00521-024-10382-0

10. Qu, Y., et al.: Enhancing LLMs with smart preprocessing for EHR analysis. arXiv preprint (2024). https://doi.org/10.48550/arXiv.2412.02868

11. Rückert, J.: Overview of ImageCLEFmedical 2024-caption prediction and concept detection. In: CLEF 2024 Working Notes. CEUR Workshop Proceedings, vol. 3740, pp. 1437–1455. (2024)

12. Varol Arısoy, M., Arısoy, A., Uysal, İ: A vision attention driven language framework for medical report generation. Sci. Rep. **15**, 10704 (2025). https://doi.org/10.1038/s41598-025-95666-8

13. Xu, J., Liu, X., Yan, J., Cai, D., Li, H., Li, J.: Learning to break the loop: analyzing and mitigating repetitions for neural text generation. In: Proceedings of the 36th International Conference on Neural Information Processing Systems. NIPS '2022, Curran Associates Inc., Red Hook, NY, USA (2022)

Semantic Pattern Recognition in Scientific Literature Using Hybrid Topic Modeling and SciBERT with LoRA-Based Validation

Yessenia Díaz-Álvarez[✉], Raúl Pinto-Elías, Andrea Magadán-Salazar, Noé-Alejandro Castro-Sánchez, and Jorge Fuentes-Pacheco

Tecnológico Nacional de México/Centro Nacional de Investigación y Desarrollo Tecnológico, 62420 Cuernavaca, Morelos, Mexico
{d24ce109,raul.pe,andrea.ms,noe.cs,jorge.fp}@cenidet.tecnm.mx

Abstract. The rapid growth of scientific repositories has made large-scale semantic analysis increasingly dependent on automated methods for discovering latent knowledge structures. This work proposes a scalable hybrid framework that integrates probabilistic topic modeling with contextual embeddings and efficient neural adaptation. The approach combines Latent Dirichlet Allocation (LDA) with BERTopic and SciBERT embeddings. Experiments on arXiv subsets (2,000–10,000 documents) show that BERTopic + SciBERT achieves the best performance ($c_v = 0.65$, Macro-F1 = 0.85), outperforming Top2Vec and CTM. Bootstrap validation confirms statistical significance ($p = 0.001$). Additionally, LoRA-based summarization improves ROUGE and BERTScore, supporting semantic consistency. Scalability analysis shows near-linear runtime growth and stable performance.

Keywords: Semantic Pattern Discovery · Topic Modeling · SciBERT · LoRA · Natural Language Processing

1 Introduction

Pattern recognition is a core area of artificial intelligence that is concerned with identifying regularities, structures, and latent relationships within data [1,2]. In the context of scientific literature, this task involves discovering semantically coherent groups of documents that share conceptual and contextual similarities, referred to in this work as *semantic patterns*.

Open-access repositories such as arXiv contain millions of scientific documents spanning multiple disciplines, making them valuable resources for large-scale semantic analysis. However, their volume and heterogeneity make manual exploration impractical, highlighting the need for automated methods capable of extracting meaningful knowledge structures.

V. G. Cruz-Sánchez et al. (Eds.): MCPR 2026, LNCS 16623, pp. 283–293, 2026.
https://doi.org/10.1007/978-3-032-28393-1_25

Classical topic modeling approaches, such as Latent Dirichlet Allocation (LDA), have been widely used to identify latent thematic structures in document collections [3]. These models rely on lexical co-occurrence patterns and represent documents as mixtures of topics. Although effective in capturing global thematic distributions, they are limited in their ability to model contextual semantics, particularly in specialized scientific domains where terminology and meaning are strongly dependent on context [4].

Recent advances in Natural Language Processing (NLP), particularly those based on Transformer architectures, have enabled the learning of contextualized semantic representations. Models such as BERT generate embeddings that capture syntactic and semantic dependencies across text [5,6]. Domain-specific variants, such as SciBERT, further improve performance by incorporating vocabulary and discourse patterns derived from scientific corpora [7]. In parallel, BERTopic has demonstrated improved topic coherence and interpretability by combining dense embeddings with clustering and class-based term weighting strategies [4,8].

In addition, Parameter-Efficient Fine-Tuning (PEFT) methods, such as Low-Rank Adaptation (LoRA), have emerged as efficient alternatives to full model retraining. LoRA enables the adaptation of large pre-trained models to specific domains by introducing low-rank updates, significantly reducing computational cost while preserving model performance [13].

Despite these advances, the automatic identification of stable and semantically coherent patterns in large-scale scientific corpora remains a challenging task. In particular, there is a need for approaches that simultaneously capture global thematic structure and fine-grained contextual semantics, while also providing mechanisms to validate the semantic consistency of the discovered patterns.

To address this challenge, this work proposes a hybrid framework that integrates probabilistic topic modeling with contextual semantic clustering and abstractive summarization. The main contributions of this work are as follows:

- A hybrid semantic pattern discovery framework that combines LDA with BERTopic and SciBERT embeddings to capture both global and contextual structures.
- A comprehensive experimental evaluation including coherence, Macro-F1, and statistical validation across multiple corpus sizes.
- A semantic validation mechanism based on abstractive summarization using a Transformer model adapted with Low-Rank Adaptation (LoRA).

The remainder of this paper is organized as follows. Section 2 reviews related work. Section 3 describes the methodology. Section 4 presents experimental results. Section 5 discusses the findings and limitations. Section 6 concludes the paper and outlines future research directions.

2   Related Work

Early research in pattern recognition applied to text relied primarily on statistical models designed to identify latent thematic structures within document collections. Among these, Latent Dirichlet Allocation (LDA) became one of the most influential approaches by modeling documents as mixtures of topics based on word co-occurrence patterns [3]. While effective for capturing global thematic distributions, LDA and similar methods are limited by their reliance on the bag-of-words assumption, which restricts their ability to represent contextual semantics.

The introduction of Transformer-based architectures marked a significant shift in semantic representation learning. Models such as BERT generate contextualized embeddings that capture syntactic and semantic dependencies across text, substantially improving performance in a wide range of Natural Language Processing (NLP) tasks [5,6]. Domain-specific adaptations, such as SciBERT, further enhance these representations by incorporating vocabulary and discourse patterns derived from scientific corpora, leading to improved performance in classification, clustering, and semantic similarity tasks within academic texts [7].

Building on these advances, neural topic modeling approaches have emerged that integrate contextual embeddings with clustering techniques. BERTopic, for example, combines dense semantic representations with clustering algorithms and class-based term weighting, resulting in improved topic coherence and interpretability [4,8]. Similarly, models such as Top2Vec and Contextualized Topic Models (CTM) leverage embedding-based representations to jointly learn document and topic structures, often outperforming traditional methods in terms of semantic coherence and topic separability.

Comparative studies, such as Egger and Yu [14], have demonstrated that embedding-based topic modeling approaches, including BERTopic and Top2Vec, consistently outperform classical models such as LDA and NMF. These improvements are primarily attributed to the ability of contextual embeddings to preserve semantic relationships beyond lexical co-occurrence.

More recently, the application of Large Language Models (LLMs) in the scientific domain has expanded significantly. Models such as Galactica [16] have been pretrained on large-scale scientific corpora, demonstrating that domain-specific pretraining improves reasoning and knowledge retrieval capabilities. However, the computational cost associated with full fine-tuning of large models remains a major limitation.

To address this issue, Parameter-Efficient Fine-Tuning (PEFT) methods have been proposed. In particular, Low-Rank Adaptation (LoRA) enables efficient model adaptation by introducing low-rank updates to pre-trained weights, significantly reducing memory and computational requirements while maintaining performance [13]. Extensions such as QLoRA further improve efficiency by incorporating quantization techniques, enabling large-scale models to be adapted on resource-constrained hardware [15].

Despite these advances, several challenges remain. First, many existing approaches focus either on global thematic structure (e.g., LDA) or contextual semantic clustering (e.g., BERTopic), but do not explicitly integrate both perspectives into a unified framework. Second, comparative evaluations often lack statistical validation, making it difficult to assess the robustness of reported improvements. Third, the semantic validity of discovered patterns is rarely evaluated beyond clustering metrics.

In contrast, the approach proposed in this work integrates probabilistic and contextual modeling within a hybrid framework and incorporates statistical validation through bootstrap resampling. Furthermore, it introduces an abstractive summarization component adapted with LoRA as a complementary mechanism to assess semantic consistency. Experimental results demonstrate that the proposed BERTopic + SciBERT configuration achieves superior performance compared to Top2Vec and CTM, confirming the effectiveness of domain-specific contextual representations for large-scale scientific text analysis.

3 Methodology

This section describes the experimental framework used to evaluate the proposed hybrid approach for semantic pattern discovery in scientific literature.

3.1 Dataset and Sampling

The dataset was obtained from the Cornell University arXiv metadata release, which provides structured scientific records including titles, abstracts, and category labels.

To ensure thematic diversity, documents were selected using stratified sampling based on primary arXiv categories. Five dataset sizes were evaluated: 2,000, 4,000, 6,000, 8,000, and 10,000 documents.

Only documents containing both title and abstract were retained. Duplicate entries and incomplete records were removed.

3.2 Preprocessing

Text preprocessing included normalization, stopword removal, and token filtering. Tokens with document frequency lower than 5 and higher than 80% were removed. Stemming and aggressive lemmatization were avoided to preserve domain-specific terminology.

3.3 Probabilistic Topic Modeling (LDA)

Latent Dirichlet Allocation (LDA) is used to capture global thematic structures [3]. Each document d is modeled as a mixture of K topics:

$$p(\theta, z, w \mid \alpha, \beta) = \prod_{d=1}^{M} p(\theta_d \mid \alpha) \prod_{n=1}^{N_d} p(z_{d,n} \mid \theta_d)\, p(w_{d,n} \mid z_{d,n}, \beta) \tag{1}$$

where θ_d represents the topic distribution for document d, and $z_{d,n}$ is the topic assigned to word $w_{d,n}$.

3.4   Contextual Semantic Clustering

To capture fine-grained semantics, BERTopic was applied using SciBERT embeddings [7]. Given a document d_i, its representation is obtained as:

$$\mathbf{e}_i = f_{\text{SciBERT}}(d_i) \tag{2}$$

where $\mathbf{e}_i \in \mathbb{R}^d$ is the contextual embedding.

Clustering was performed using HDBSCAN, and topics were represented using class-based TF-IDF.

3.5   Hybrid Integration

Unlike pipeline-based approaches, the proposed hybrid integration does not merge LDA and BERTopic outputs directly. Instead, both models operate at complementary semantic levels. LDA captures global topic distributions, providing a coarse-grained thematic prior over the corpus. In contrast, BERTopic with SciBERT embeddings captures fine-grained contextual clusters based on semantic similarity. The alignment between both representations is performed at the interpretive level: LDA topics are used to contextualize and explain BERTopic clusters, enabling a hierarchical interpretation of semantic patterns without enforcing strict topic-cluster correspondence. LDA provides global thematic priors. BERTopic + SciBERT provides fine-grained semantic clusters. LDA topics are used as an interpretive layer, while BERTopic clusters are used for evaluation (Fig. 1).

3.6   Abstractive Summarization with LoRA

To validate semantic consistency, an abstractive summarization model was adapted using Low-Rank Adaptation (LoRA) [13]. Instead of updating the full weight matrix W_0, LoRA decomposes the update as:

$$h = W_0 x + BAx \tag{3}$$

where $A \in \mathbb{R}^{r \times k}$ and $B \in \mathbb{R}^{d \times r}$ are low-rank matrices.

3.7   Evaluation Metrics

The following metrics were used:

- Topic coherence (c_v)
- Macro-F1 (using arXiv categories as pseudo-labels)
- ROUGE-1, ROUGE-L, BERTScore

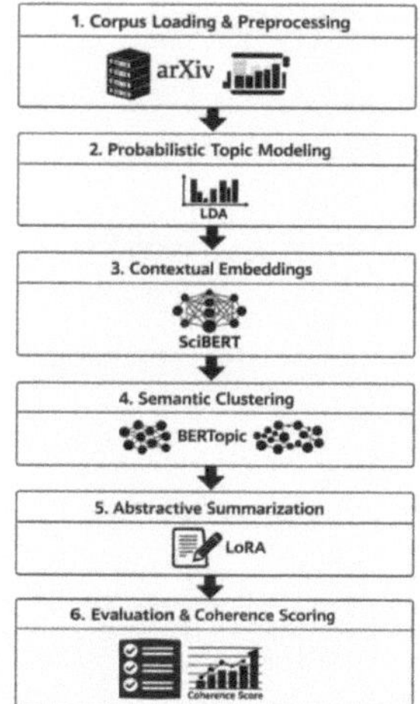

Fig. 1. Hybrid semantic pattern discovery framework. The diagram illustrates the proposed hybrid framework for semantic pattern recognition in scientific literature. Scientific documents are preprocessed and analyzed through two complementary components: Latent Dirichlet Allocation (LDA), which captures global thematic structures, and BERTopic with SciBERT embeddings, which identifies fine-grained semantic clusters. The outputs are interpreted jointly to discover semantic patterns. A LoRA-adapted abstractive summarization model is then used to validate the semantic consistency of the identified patterns.

3.8 Statistical Validation

Bootstrap resampling was applied with 1,000 iterations:

$$\Delta = \frac{1}{n} \sum_{i=1}^{n} (x_i - y_i) \tag{4}$$

Confidence intervals were computed at 95%, and statistical significance was assessed using two-sided p-values.

3.9 Experimental Configuration

Table 1 summarizes the main components and hyperparameters used in the experimental setup. The configuration was designed to ensure a balance between performance, scalability, and computational efficiency.

4 Results and Analysis

This section presents the experimental results obtained from evaluating the proposed hybrid framework for semantic pattern discovery.

Table 1. Experimental configuration

Component	Configuration
Embedding Model	SciBERT
Clustering	HDBSCAN
Topic Model	BERTopic
LDA Parameters	$\alpha = 0.1$, $\beta = 0.01$
LoRA Rank	$r \in \{4, 8, 16\}$
Bootstrap Iterations	1000

4.1   Comparison of Pattern Recognition Methods

Table 2 presents a comparative evaluation of different topic modeling approaches on the 10,000-document subset. Embedding-based approaches consistently outperform lexical and probabilistic baselines. BERTopic combined with SciBERT achieves the highest coherence ($c_v = 0.65$) and Macro-F1 (0.85), indicating superior semantic separability and interpretability.

Table 2. Comparison of semantic pattern recognition methods (10,000 documents)

Method	Representation	c_v	Macro-F1
TF-IDF + K-means	Lexical	0.41	0.68
LDA	Probabilistic	0.46	0.71
Top2Vec	Joint embedding	0.55	0.76
CTM	Contextual topic model	0.59	0.80
BERTopic + MiniLM	Semantic embedding	0.61	0.81
BERTopic + SciBERT	Scientific contextual	0.65	0.85

Figure 2 compares different methods, showing that embedding-based approaches outperform lexical and probabilistic ones. BERTopic with SciBERT achieves the best results, indicating improved semantic separability.

These results indicate that domain-specific embeddings better capture semantic relationships and scientific terminology. The improvement of +0.04 in coherence over MiniLM suggests stronger contextual representation.

4.2   Scalability and Stability Analysis

To evaluate robustness, experiments were conducted across datasets ranging from 2,000 to 10,000 documents. Table 3 show that coherence and Macro-F1 improve as dataset size increases, while variance decreases.

Figure 3 indicates increasing stability of semantic patterns as dataset size grows. Runtime scales approximately linearly, and GPU memory remains below 6 GB, supporting efficient scalability.

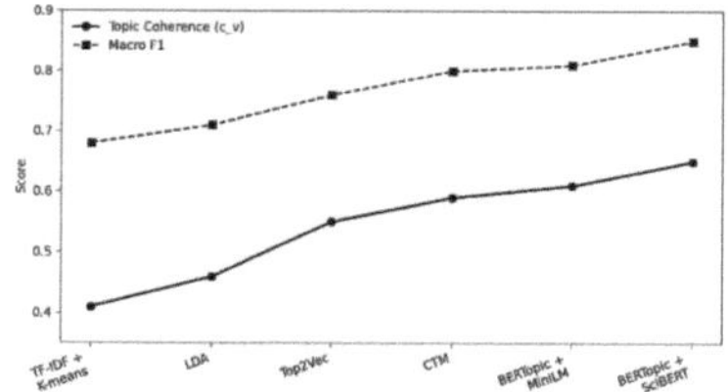

Fig. 2. Performance comparison of topic modeling methods. The chart compares Topic Coherence (Cv) and Macro-F1 scores across TF-IDF + K-means, LDA, Top2Vec, CTM, BERTopic + MiniLM, and BERTopic + SciBERT. Both metrics improve progressively across methods, with BERTopic + SciBERT achieving the highest coherence (0.65) and Macro-F1 score (0.85), indicating superior semantic separability and topic interpretability.

Table 3. Scalability and stability results

Docs	c_v	Macro-F1	Runtime (min)	GPU (GB)
2000	0.60 ± 0.03	0.79 ± 0.02	8.4	3.1
4000	0.62 ± 0.02	0.81 ± 0.02	15.9	3.8
6000	0.63 ± 0.02	0.83 ± 0.01	24.1	4.5
8000	0.64 ± 0.01	0.84 ± 0.01	33.8	5.2
10000	0.65 ± 0.01	0.85 ± 0.01	44.7	5.9

Table 4 shows that LoRA improves summarization performance (ROUGE-L: 0.34 → 0.39, BERTScore: 0.856 → 0.882), indicating better semantic preservation. The LoRA-adapted model consistently improves all evaluation metrics, indicating better semantic preservation and terminological consistency.

Table 4. Abstractive summarization performance

Model	ROUGE-1	ROUGE-L	BERTScore
Base Model	0.39	0.34	0.856
LoRA Model	0.44	0.39	0.882

Table 5 intermediate ranks ($r = 8$) provide the best trade-off between performance and computational cost, while higher ranks yield diminishing returns.

4.3 Statistical Validation

To assess robustness, paired bootstrap resampling was performed. Table 6 confirm that improvements are statistically significant, supporting the robustness of the proposed approach.

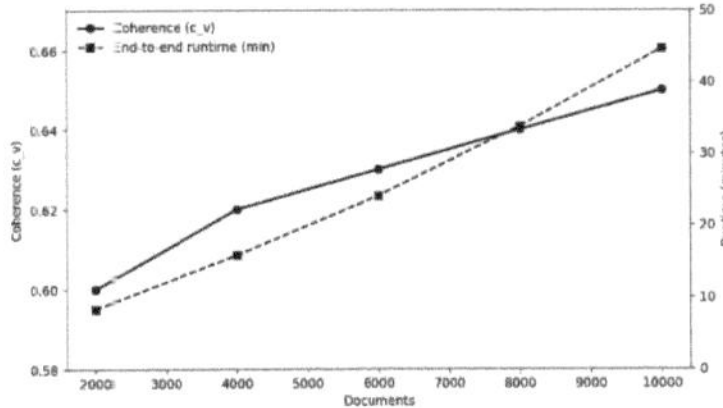

Fig. 3. Scalability analysis across dataset sizes. The chart shows the effect of increasing corpus size from 2,000 to 10,000 documents on topic coherence and computational cost. Topic coherence increases steadily from approximately 0.60 to 0.65, indicating more stable semantic patterns with larger datasets. Runtime also grows nearly linearly, from about 8 to 45 minutes, demonstrating the scalability of the proposed framework while maintaining stable performance.

Table 5. Effect of LoRA rank

Rank	ROUGE-1	ROUGE-L	BERTScore
4	0.42	0.37	0.874
8	0.44	0.39	0.882
16	0.45	0.39	0.884

5   Discussion

The results show that the proposed hybrid framework improves semantic pattern discovery in scientific literature. BERTopic with SciBERT achieves the best performance ($c_v = 0.65$, Macro-F1 $= 0.85$), showing that domain-specific embeddings better represent scientific terminology than other contextual baselines such as Top2Vec and CTM.

A main contribution of this work is the integration of contextual topic modeling with LoRA-based abstractive summarization as a complementary validation mechanism. The improvements in ROUGE-L ($+0.05$) and BERTScore ($+0.026$) suggest better semantic preservation, although this evidence remains indirect.

Scalability analysis shows that performance improves and variance decreases as corpus size increases, while runtime grows approximately linearly and memory usage remains feasible. Bootstrap resampling further confirms that the improvements are statistically significant ($\Delta c_v = 0.04$, $p = 0.001$). Despite these results,

Table 6. Bootstrap significance analysis

Comparison	Metric	Δ	p-value
SciBERT vs MiniLM	c_v	$+0.04$	0.001
SciBERT vs CTM	c_v	$+0.06$	<0.001
LoRA vs Base	ROUGE-L	$+0.05$	0.002

the study is limited to titles and abstracts, and Macro-F1 is based on coarse-grained arXiv categories.

6   Conclusions

This work presents a scalable hybrid framework for semantic pattern discovery by combining LDA, BERTopic, and SciBERT embeddings. The approach captures both global themes and fine-grained semantic structures, outperforming TF-IDF, LDA, Top2Vec, and CTM in coherence, separability, and stability.

LoRA-based abstractive summarization enables efficient domain adaptation, improving semantic preservation with low computational cost, supporting the use of parameter-efficient fine-tuning.

Scalability results show stable performance as corpus size increases, with feasible computational requirements, making the framework suitable for large-scale scientific repositories.

Future work will include full-text analysis, human-centered evaluation, and extension to multilingual and low-resource settings, as well as exploring more advanced Transformer-based models for improved semantic alignment and summarization.

References

1. Duda, R.O., Hart, P.E., Stork, D.G.: Pattern Recognition, 2nd edn. Wiley, New York (2001)
2. Pattern Recognition and Machine Learning. ISS, Springer, New York (2006). https://doi.org/10.1007/978-0-387-45528-0_9
3. Blei, D.M., Ng, A.Y., Jordan, M.I.: Latent Dirichlet allocation. J. Mach. Learn. Res. **3**, 993–1022 (2003)
4. Grootendorst, M.: BERTopic: neural topic modeling with a class-based TF-IDF procedure. arXiv:2203.05794 (2022)
5. Vaswani, A., et al.: Attention is all you need. In: NeurIPS, p. 59986008 (2017)
6. Devlin, J., Chang, M.-W., Lee, K., Toutanova, K.: BERT: pre-training of deep bidirectional transformers. In: NAACL, p. 41714186 (2019)
7. Beltagy, I., Lo, K., Cohan, A.: SciBERT: a pretrained language model for scientic text. In: EMNLP, p. 36153620 (2019)
8. Angelov, D.: Top2Vec: distributed representations of topics (2020). arXiv:2008.09470
9. Bianchi, F., Terragni, S., Hovy, D.: Pre-training is a hot topic: contextualized document embeddings improve topic coherence. In: ACL, p. 759766 (2021)
10. Lewis, M., et al.: BART: denoising sequence-to-sequence pre-training. In: ACL, p. 78717880 (2020)
11. Maynez, J., Narayan, S., Bohnet, B., McDonald, R.: On faithfulness and factuality in abstractive summarization. In: ACL, pp. 1906–1919 (2020)
12. Kryscinski, W., et al.: Evaluating the factual consistency of abstractive summarization. In: EMNLP, p. 93329346 (2020)
13. Hu, E.J., et al.: LoRA: low-rank adaptation of large language models. In: ICLR (2022)

14. Egger, R., Yu, J.: A topic modeling comparison between LDA, NMF, Top2Vec, and BERTopic. Front. Sociol. **7**, 886498 (2022)
15. Dettmers, T., et al.: QLoRA: efficient finetuning of quantized LLMs. Adv. Neural Inf. Process. Syst. (NeurIPS) **36** (2024)
16. Taylor, R., Kardas, M. et al.: Galactica: A Large Language Model for Science. arXiv preprint arXiv:2211.09085 (2022)

Automatic Depressive Symptom Detection on Social Media Using the BDI-II

Cielo Aholiva Higuera-Gutiérrez[1(✉)], Irvin Hussein López-Nava[1],
Manuel Montes-y-Gómez[2], Mario Ezra Aragón[3], and David E. Losada[3]

[1] Centro de Investigación Científica y de Educación Superior de Ensenada
(CICESE), Ensenada, Mexico
`{aholiva,hussein}@cicese.edu.mx`
[2] Instituto Nacional de Astrofísica, Óptica y Electrónica (INAOE), Ensenada, Mexico
`mmontesg@inaoep.mx`
[3] Centro Singular de Investigación en Tecnoloxías Intelixentes (CiTIUS),
Universidade de Santiago de Compostela (USC), Santiago, Spain
`{ezra.aragon,david.losada}@usc.es`

Abstract. Automatic depression detection from social media has been
widely explored as a complementary approach to mental health assessment; however, most existing work has focused on binary user-level classification, paying limited attention to how individual depressive symptoms
are linguistically manifested in online discourse. This study addresses
this limitation through symptom-level depression detection grounded in
the 21 items of the BDI-II. The evaluation considers general-purpose
transformer models, architectures adapted to the mental health domain,
and approaches based on embeddings leveraging large language models
across multiple editions of the eRisk benchmark. Results indicate that
embedding-based approaches such as GPT-4+SVM and LLaMA+SVM,
provide competitive performance with lower computational cost, while
domain-adapted models consistently outperform general-purpose transformers. Symptom-level analysis reveals that affective symptoms are
more reliably detected, whereas cognitively complex, behavioral, or sensitive symptoms remain underrepresented in social media text.

Keywords: Depression detection · Symptom-level analysis · Social
media · Beck Depression Inventory

1 Introduction

Mental disorders represent a critical challenge to global public health, affecting
the quality of life of millions and imposing a significant socioeconomic burden.
According to the World Health Organization (WHO), approximately 332 million
people worldwide suffer from depression, affecting an estimated 5.7% of the adult
population [23]. Despite its high prevalence, a considerable proportion of those
affected do not receive a timely diagnosis or adequate treatment. This gap in

V. G. Cruz-Sánchez et al. (Eds.): MCPR 2026, LNCS 16623, pp. 294–304, 2026.
https://doi.org/10.1007/978-3-032-28393-1_26

care exacerbates morbidity rates and increases the risk of self-harm, with suicide ranking as the third leading cause of death among individuals aged 15–29 years.

Major depressive disorder is a complex and debilitating psychiatric condition arising from a multifaceted interaction of genetic, biological, psychological, and environmental factors [14]. Clinically, it involves a persistent depressed mood or a loss of interest and pleasure in daily activities. The clinical profile encompasses a broad spectrum of cognitive, affective, and behavioral symptoms This symptomatic heterogeneity, coupled with medical comorbidities and social factors that impair functional outcomes, complicates early detection and continuous monitoring outside of controlled clinical environments [8].

To standardize diagnosis and severity assessment, clinical practice relies on standardized instruments such as the Beck Depression Inventory-II (BDI-II), the Center for Epidemiologic Studies Depression Scale (CES-D), and the Patient Health Questionnaire-9 (PHQ-9). Although widely used for screening, BDI-II enables a more fine-grained assessment of symptom-level [3]. Despite their psychometric validity, these instruments depend on periodic clinical consultations, limiting continuous monitoring of disease progression.

In this context, the analysis of digital footprints on social networks has emerged as a source of information [4,21,22]. Platforms such as Reddit and online forums offer a naturalistic environment in which users express emotional states and personal experiences, enabling longitudinal observation of symptom manifestation beyond what is accessible through clinical interviews [4].

However, the transition from massive data to reliable clinical inferences faces technical obstacles, including noisy and informal digital language, semantic mismatches with clinical constructs, and temporal irregularity in posts. This hinders feature extraction with generic models, motivating the need for domain-specific representations and architectures to capture symptom evolution over time.

This study aims to contribute in two main directions. First, it systematically examines the automatic detection of depressive symptoms in social media by comparing general-purpose transformer models, mental health-adapted models, and embedding-based approaches leveraging large language models (LLMs). Second, it analyzes how different depressive symptoms are reflected in online discourse, providing insights into users' linguistic expression of depressive experiences. The analysis is grounded on the 21 symptoms defined in the BDI-II, enabling a fine-grained evaluation aligned with established clinical criteria.

2   Related Work

Automatic depression detection from social media has been widely studied using user-generated text from platforms such as Reddit, X (former Twitter), and online forums [4,20]. Early approaches based on surface-level linguistic features and traditional machine learning classifiers have shown limited ability to capture complex semantics and contextual information [5,7].

Recent work has adopted deep learning and transformer-based models to obtain semantic representations of mental health-related language Ji et al.

[9] introduced MentalBERT, a variant of BERT pre-trained on mental health forums to capture domain-specific expressions of depressive symptoms. Similarly, Aragón et al. [1] proposed DisorBERT, which applies double domain adaptation to social media and mental health data. These approaches mitigate the limitations of feature-based methods and improve modeling in social media text.

However, most studies addressed depression as a binary classification problem at the user level, offering limited clinical interpretability [20]. To move beyond binary detection, clinical instruments such as the CES-D, PHQ-9, and BDI-II have been used to support symptom-level modeling from social media text [7,10,15]. Despite these efforts, symptom-level detection remains challenging due to linguistic ambiguity, symptom overlap, and data imbalance.

CLEF eRisk (Conference and Labs of Evaluation Forum for Early Risk Prediction) has been a long-standing benchmark for clinically grounded research on mental health risk analysis, including depression, with annual editions since its introduction in 2017 [6,11–13,15–18]. Within this framework, work has explored symptom-oriented modeling approaches, focusing on the incidence and expression of depressive symptoms in social media language. Ríssola et al. [19] analyzed the prevalence of BDI-II items in posts authored by users with self-reported depression, showing that certain symptoms are expressed across platforms, whereas others present low incidence despite their relevance. Similarly, Aragón et al. [2] proposed a symptom-level analysis emphasizing interpretability and the distribution of depressive symptoms across users and platforms.

Despite these advances, research on depression and mental health detection, including work with benchmarks such as eRisk, has largely emphasized detection accuracy and leaderboard-oriented comparisons. Consequently, broad evaluations spanning different modeling paradigms remain limited, and little attention has been devoted to understanding why certain depressive symptoms are consistently more difficult to detect. This study addresses this gap through a symptom-level analysis across diverse modeling approaches, examining factors such as limited textual evidence, ambiguity in symptom expression, and a comprehensive analysis of symptom frequency and co-occurrence in social media.

3   Methods

3.1   Symptom-Level Detection

Problem Formulation. Let $S = \{s_1, \ldots, s_{21}\}$ denote the set of depressive symptoms defined in the Beck Depression Inventory-II (BDI-II) [3], and let $\mathcal{X}$ be the space of textual sentences extracted from users' writings. The task is formulated as 21 independent binary classification problems, where each classifier determines whether a given sentence $x_i \in \mathcal{X}$ is relevant to a specific symptom $s_j \in S$. For each symptom s_j, a probabilistic classifier is defined as:

$$f_j : \mathcal{X} \rightarrow [0,1], \qquad j = 1, \ldots, 21. \tag{1}$$

where $p_{i,j} = f_j(x_i)$ represents the estimated probability that text x_i expresses symptom s_j. A binary prediction $\hat{y}_{i,j} \in \{0,1\}$ is obtained by applying a decision rule to the probabilistic output $p_{i,j}$.

Models. Two modeling strategies are considered. First, transformer-based classifiers are fine-tuned for each depressive symptom. Pre-trained language models were obtained from the HuggingFace model hub[1] . Models trained on general-domain text include BERT, RoBERTa, and DistilBERT. To assess the impact of domain adaptation, models pre-trained on mental health data are also evaluated, including MentalBERT, MentalRoBERTa, DisorBERT, and DisorRoBERTa.

Second, embedding-based approaches using LLMs are employed. In this setting, each text is represented as a dense semantic embedding obtained directly from pre-trained LLMs without task-specific fine-tuning. Specifically, sentence embeddings are extracted using GPT-4 via the OpenAI API[2] and LLaMA-3.1 via the Ollama framework[3]. These representations are subsequently classified using a linear Support Vector Machine (SVM).

3.2   Ensemble Strategies

To examine whether combining models improves the detection of depressive symptoms, decision-level ensemble strategies are used. The motivation is that models trained on different data and design choices may capture complementary signals, and aggregating their predictions can improve robustness.

Based on this idea, ensembles are constructed by grouping models into different categories: (i) general-purpose transformer models pre-trained on generic language (e.g., BERT, RoBERTa, and DistilBERT), (ii) specialized models adapted to the mental health domain (e.g., MentalBERT, MentalRoBERTa, DisorBERT, and DisorRoBERTa), and (iii) a global ensemble from all evaluated models.

A Top-k ensemble strategy combines predictions from the k best-performing models on a validation set to evaluate whether a reduced ensemble can achieve competitive performance.

Hard voting aggregates binary predictions from M models as:

$$\hat{y}_{i,j} = \begin{cases} 1, & \text{if } \sum_{m=1}^{M} \hat{y}_{i,j}^{(m)} \geq \lceil \frac{M}{2} \rceil, \\ 0, & \text{otherwise.} \end{cases} \tag{2}$$

Soft voting combines probabilistic predictions from multiple models by averaging their outputs:

$$\hat{p}_{i,j} = \frac{1}{M} \sum_{m=1}^{M} p_{i,j}^{(m)}. \tag{3}$$

A binary prediction is then obtained by applying a decision rule to $\hat{p}_{\text{soft}}$.

4   Symptom-Level Detection

Depressive symptoms differ substantially in how they are expressed in social media text. Some symptoms are explicitly verbalized and frequently reflected in

---

[1] https://huggingface.co/.
[2] https://platform.openai.com/docs.
[3] https://ollama.com.

Table 1. Distribution of depressive symptoms in the corpus (2023–2025). For each BDI-II symptom, #sen denotes the number of labeled sentences, %sen their percentage, avg. len the average length in words, and vocab the number of unique words.

#	Label	#sen	%sen	avg. len	vocab
1	Sadness	2474	5.21	22.64	3040
2	Pessimism	2449	5.16	29.70	4024
3	Past Failure	2224	4.69	26.74	3864
4	Loss of Pleasure	2187	4.61	25.13	4767
5	Guilty Feelings	1966	4.14	24.12	3211
6	Punishment Feelings	2243	4.73	30.06	4694
7	Self-Dislike	2209	4.66	21.22	3126
8	Self-Criticalness	2306	4.86	23.32	4570
9	Suicidal Thoughts	2180	4.59	18.80	3279
10	Crying	2285	4.82	22.04	3701
11	Agitation	2431	5.12	27.17	4730
12	Loss of Interest	2287	4.82	23.92	4217
13	Indecisiveness	2478	5.22	21.22	4219
14	Worthlessness	2058	4.34	23.81	3598
15	Loss of Energy	2182	4.60	22.12	4027
16	Changes in Sleeping Pattern	2284	4.81	22.81	3769
17	Irritability	2314	4.88	20.74	4318
18	Changes in Appetite	2226	4.69	23.58	3987
19	Concentration Difficulty	2033	4.28	23.06	4000
20	Tiredness or Fatigue	2281	4.81	22.94	4223
21	Loss of Interest in Sex	2348	4.95	24.32	4057

users' language, whereas others remain implicit, indirect, or sparsely expressed. This section investigates symptom-level depression detection using independent sentence-level classifiers aligned with the 21 BDI-II items.

4.1   Experimental Settings

Datasets. The "Search for Symptoms of Depression" datasets released as part of the eRisk 2023–2025 evaluation campaigns are used for symptom-level classification. They are designed to identify sentence-level evidence for the 21 depressive symptoms defined in the BDI-II, with sentences annotated as providing positive or negative evidence for each symptom. Table 1 summarizes basic statistics for each depressive symptom.

Table 2. Performance comparison of individual models and ensemble strategies. Results are reported as mean ± standard deviation across the 21 BDI-II symptoms.

Category	Method	Accuracy	Precision	Recall	F1-score
Individual Models	GPT-4 + SVM	**0.877 ± 0.025**	**0.857 ± 0.039**	0.877 ± 0.026	**0.364 ± 0.034**
	LLaMA + SVM	0.876 ± 0.024	0.856 ± 0.039	0.881 ± 0.022	**0.364 ± 0.033**
	MentalRoBERTa	0.860 ± 0.025	0.844 ± 0.041	0.875 ± 0.022	0.349 ± 0.034
	MentalBERT	0.859 ± 0.030	0.842 ± 0.044	0.871 ± 0.026	0.348 ± 0.038
	RoBERTa-base	0.844 ± 0.034	0.833 ± 0.049	0.865 ± 0.027	0.334 ± 0.045
	DisorRoBERTa	0.843 ± 0.033	0.831 ± 0.050	0.863 ± 0.026	0.333 ± 0.046
	DisorBERT	0.840 ± 0.032	0.826 ± 0.043	0.856 ± 0.027	0.329 ± 0.040
	BERT-base	0.834 ± 0.030	0.818 ± 0.043	0.845 ± 0.028	0.322 ± 0.038
	DistilBERT-base	0.831 ± 0.037	0.817 ± 0.048	0.847 ± 0.030	0.320 ± 0.045
Group Ensembles	All models ensemble (soft)	0.872 ± 0.026	0.854 ± 0.040	**0.883 ± 0.023**	0.361 ± 0.034
	All models ensemble (hard)	0.868 ± 0.028	0.851 ± 0.043	0.880 ± 0.025	0.357 ± 0.036
	Specialized ensemble (hard)	0.868 ± 0.027	0.850 ± 0.042	0.878 ± 0.025	0.357 ± 0.036
	Specialized ensemble (soft)	0.861 ± 0.028	0.846 ± 0.043	0.877 ± 0.024	0.351 ± 0.037
	General ensemble (soft)	0.849 ± 0.033	0.835 ± 0.048	0.867 ± 0.027	0.339 ± 0.043
	General ensemble (hard)	0.845 ± 0.033	0.831 ± 0.047	0.861 ± 0.027	0.334 ± 0.042
Top-k Ensemble	Top-3 ensemble (soft)	0.873 ± 0.026	0.854 ± 0.037	0.869 ± 0.029	0.359 ± 0.034

Training and Evaluation. For each symptom, the dataset is split into training (80%) and test (20%) subsets using stratified sampling. The training set supports model selection and validation through five-fold stratified cross-validation.

Transformer-based models are fine-tuned using binary cross-entropy loss with logits, a maximum sequence length of 70 tokens, and a batch size of 32. Training is performed for 5 epochs using the AdamW optimizer with a learning rate of 1×10^{-5} and a weight decay of 1. To address class imbalance, a positive class weight proportional to the ratio of negative to positive samples is applied during training. For embedding-based approaches, sentence embeddings are L_2-normalized prior to classification. SVM classifiers with a linear kernel and balanced class weights are used.

After model selection, final models are retrained on the full training set and evaluated once on the held-out test set.

4.2 Results

The performance of the symptom-level classifiers is summarized in Table 2 across the 21 depressive symptoms defined in the BDI-II. In terms of accuracy, precision, recall, and F1-score, embedding-based approaches achieve the strongest performance, with GPT-4+SVM and LLaMA+SVM showing similar results. Ensemble strategies yield only marginal improvements, with differences across metrics largely falling within the standard deviation.

These findings highlight a trade-off between predictive performance and computational efficiency. While ensembles increase inference complexity, embedding-based approaches achieve comparable performance with a single representation and a lightweight classifier, offering a more favorable accuracy-cost balance.

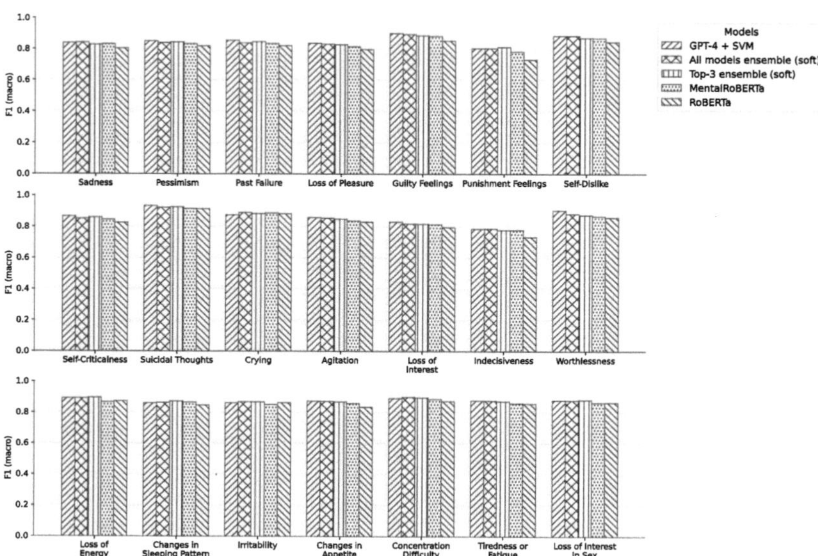

Fig. 1. Symptom-level F1 performance across the 21 BDI-II depressive symptoms for representative models and a soft ensemble.

At the symptom level (Fig. 1), affective dimensions such as Sadness, Guilty Feelings, Worthlessness, and Suicidal Thoughts consistently achieve high performance, likely due to their explicit emotional and self-referential linguistic patterns. In contrast, symptoms related to cognitive and behavioral processes – such as Indecisiveness, Loss of Pleasure, and changes in sleep or appetite– exhibit lower performance and greater variability, reflecting their indirect and context-dependent expression. For these challenging symptoms, performance varies substantially across modeling approaches.

5   User-Level Analysis of Depressive Symptoms

Depressive symptoms may differ in how they are linguistically expressed on social media. While some symptoms are frequently verbalized, others may remain implicit or absent from textual content, despite being clinically relevant. This section analyzes the relationship between clinically self-reported depressive symptoms and their manifestation in social media language at the user level. In particular, it identifies which symptoms are consistently reflected in users' posts and which are underrepresented, helping characterize the limitations of text-based symptom detection systems.

5.1   Dataset

This analysis considers data from the "Measuring the Severity of the Signs of Depression" task released as part of the eRisk 2019–2021 evaluation campaigns.

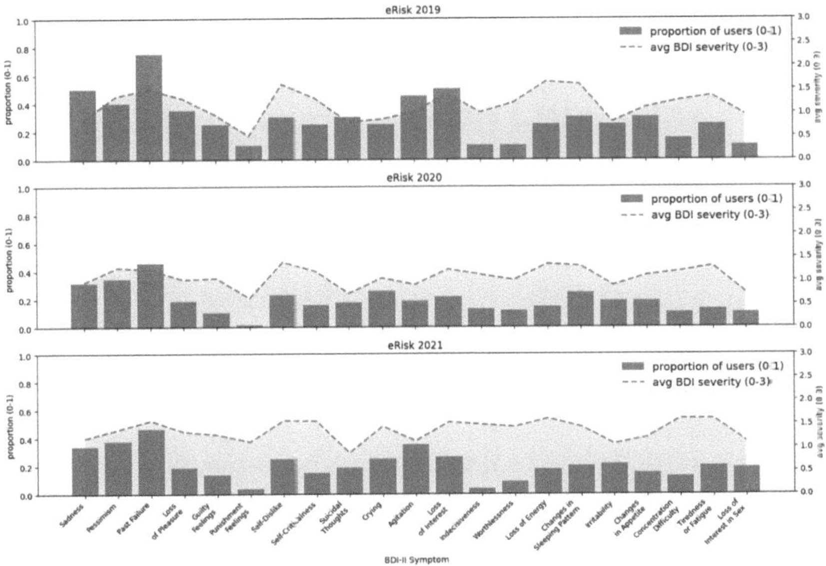

Fig. 2. Alignment between clinical BDI-II symptom severity and linguistic evidence on social media (eRisk 2019–2021).

The dataset consists of Reddit posts authored by users and includes self-reported BDI-II questionnaires providing symptom-level severity scores on a 0–3 scale for the 21 depressive symptoms.

5.2   Extracting Symptoms' Evidence from Posts

Linguistic evidence at the user level is estimated by applying the 21 independently trained symptom-level classifiers to all posts authored by each user.

For a given symptom s_j, user-level linguistic evidence is defined as the presence of at least one post for which the corresponding classifier outputs a positive prediction. Two quantities are computed for each symptom: (i) the average clinical severity score derived from the BDI-II questionnaires, and (ii) the proportion of users exhibiting linguistic evidence of that symptom.

5.3   Results

The analysis includes 170 users with self-reported BDI-II questionnaires. User histories contain an average of 462.8 ± 433.3 posts, but only a small fraction includes depressive symptom evidence. On average, users exhibit 6.9 such posts, indicating a sparse and uneven linguistic manifestation of depressive symptoms.

As illustrated in Fig. 2, several affective and cognitive symptoms—such as sadness, pessimism, past failure, and loss of interest—exhibit relatively high clinical severity and linguistic prevalence. In contrast, other clinically relevant symptoms, including suicidal thoughts, punishment feelings, and loss of energy, are detected in a considerably smaller fraction of users, despite moderate to high severity levels reported in the questionnaires.

Overall, these results indicate that depressive symptoms are unevenly reflected in social media language. Symptoms that are more cognitively accessible or socially acceptable tend to be expressed more frequently, whereas sensitive or stigmatized symptoms remain underrepresented.

6   Conclusions

This work examines symptom-level depression detection using the 21 BDI-II items and compares general-purpose transformers, domain-adapted models, and embedding-based approaches. Results show that embedding-based methods, particularly GPT-4+SVM and LLaMA+SVM, achieve performance comparable to ensemble strategies while remaining computationally efficient. These findings suggest that the additional computational cost of ensemble models may offer limited practical benefit when similar results can be obtained with a single well-performing model.

The analysis also indicates that depressive symptoms are unevenly reflected in social media language: affective and cognitively explicit symptoms are more readily detected, while sensitive or behaviorally oriented symptoms remain underrepresented despite their clinical relevance, highlighting inherent limitations of text-based depression screening systems.

Future work may explore user-level depression detection through temporal representations of BDI-II symptoms, modeling how symptom evidence evolves across longitudinal user histories. Sequential classification models could leverage these temporal patterns to identify depressive cases beyond what is observable from isolated posts.

Acknowledgment. This research was financially supported by the Secretaría de Ciencia, Humanidades, Tecnología e Innovación (SECIHTI) through the scholarship grant 4034491. The last two authors thank the financial support from MICIU/AEI/10.1303 9/501100011033 (PID2022-137061OB-C22), and the Xunta de Galicia - Consellería de Educación, Ciencia, Universidades e Formación Profesional & ERDF (ED431G-2023/04, ED431C 2022/19), and CAMELIA (Cátedras ENIA, TSI-100932-2023-3).

References

1. Aragón, M.E., López-Monroy, A.P., González, L.C., Losada, D.E., Montes, M.: Disorbert: a double domain adaptation model for detecting signs of mental disorders in social media. In: Proceedings of the 61st Annual Meeting of the Association for Computational Linguistics (Volume 1: Long Papers), pp. 15305–15318 (2023)
2. Aragón, M.E., López-Monroy, A.P., Montes-y Gómez, M., Losada, D.E.: Online expressions, offline struggles: using social media to identify depression-related symptoms. Online Soc. Netw. Media **50**, 100338 (2025)

3. Beck, A.T., Steer, R.A., Brown, G.K.: Manual for the Beck Depression Inventory-II. Psychological Corporation, San Antonio, TX (1996)
4. Chancellor, S., De Choudhury, M.: Methods in predictive techniques for mental health status on social media: a critical review. NPJ Digit. Med. **3**(1), 43 (2020)
5. Chiong, R., Budhi, G.S., Dhakal, S., Chiong, F.: A textual-based featuring approach for depression detection using machine learning classifiers and social media texts. Comput. Biol. Med. **135**, 104499 (2021)
6. Crestani, F., Losada, D.E., Parapar, J.: Early detection of mental health disorders by social media monitoring. Stud. Comput. Intell. **1018**, 4 (2022)
7. De Choudhury, M., Gamon, M., Counts, S., Horvitz, E.: Predicting depression via social media. In: Proceedings of the International AAAI Conference on Web and Social Media (2013)
8. Gold, S.M., et al.: Comorbid depression in medical diseases. Nat. Rev. Dis. Primers. **6**(1), 69 (2020)
9. Ji, S., Zhang, T., Ansari, L., Fu, J., Tiwari, P., Cambria, E.: Mentalbert: publicly available pretrained language models for mental healthcare. arXiv preprint arXiv:2110.15621 (2021)
10. Kabir, M., et al.: DEPTWEET: a typology for social media texts to detect depression severities. Comput. Hum. Behav. **139**, 107503 (2023)
11. Losada, D.E., Crestani, F., Parapar, J.: eRISK 2017: CLEF lab on early risk prediction on the internet: experimental foundations. In: Jones, G.J.F., et al. (eds.) CLEF 2017. LNCS, vol. 10456, pp. 346–360. Springer, Cham (2017). https //doi. org/10.1007/978-3-319-65813-1_30
12. Losada, D.E., Crestani, F., Parapar, J.: Overview of eRisk 2018: early risk prediction on the internet (extended lab overview). In: Proceedings of the 9th International Conference of the CLEF Association, CLEF, pp. 1–20 (2018)
13. Losada, D.E., Crestani, F., Parapar, J.: Overview of eRisk at CLEF 2019: early risk prediction on the internet (extended overview). CLEF (Working Notes) **4**, 21(2019)
14. Marx, W., et al.: Major depressive disorder. Nat. Rev. Dis. Primers. **9**(1), 44 (2023). https://doi.org/10.1038/s41572-023-00454-1
15. Parapar, J., Martín-Rodilla, P., Losada, D.E., Crestani, F.: Overview of eRisk at CLEF 2021: early risk prediction on the internet (extended overview). CLEF (Working Notes) **1**, 864–887 (2021)
16. Parapar, J., Martín-Rodilla, P., Losada, D.E., Crestani, F.: Overview of eRisk 2023: early risk prediction on the internet. In: Arampatzis, A., et al. (eds.) Experimental IR Meets Multilinguality, Multimodality, and Interaction. CLEF 2023. LNCS, vol 14163, pp. 294–315. Springer, Cham (2023). https://doi.org/10.1007/978-3-031-42448-9_22
17. Parapar, J., Martín-Rodilla, P., Losada, D.E., Crestani, F.: Overview of eRisk 2024: early risk prediction on the internet. In: Goeuriot, L., et al. (eds.) Experimental IR Meets Multilinguality, Multimodality, and Interaction. LNCS, vol. 14959. Springer, Cham (2024). https://doi.org/10.1007/978-3-031-71908-0_4
18. Parapar, J., Perez, A., Wang, X., Crestani, F.: Overview of eRisk 2025: early risk prediction on the internet. In: Carrillo-de-Albornoz, J., et al. (eds.) Experimental IR Meets Multilinguality, Multimodality, and Interaction. CLEF 2025. LNCS, vol. 16089, pp. 242–265. Springer, Cham (2026). https://doi.org/10.1007/978-3-032-04354-2_15
19. Ríssola, E.A., Aragón, M.E., Losada, D.E., Crestani, F.: On the incidence of depression symptoms on social media. J. Comput. Soc. Sci. **8**(2), 48 (2025)

20. Ríssola, E.A., Losada, D.E., Crestani, F.: A survey of computational methods for online mental state assessment on social media. ACM Trans. Comput. Healthc. **2**(2), 1–31 (2021)
21. Shatte, A.B., Hutchinson, D.M., Teague, S.J.: Machine learning in mental health: a scoping review of methods and applications. Psychol. Med. **49**(9), 1426–1448 (2019)
22. Torous, J., et al.: The growing field of digital psychiatry: current evidence and the future of apps, social media, chatbots, and virtual reality. World Psychiatry **20**(3), 318–335 (2021)
23. World Health Organization: Depressive disorder (depression) (2025). https://www.who.int/news-room/fact-sheets/detail/depression. Accessed 21 Jan 2026

Statistical Analysis of Combined Adversarial Attacks on Spam Detection Models

Samantha Acosta Ruiz[1](✉), Mireya Tovar Vidal[1] , and José A. Reyes-Ortiz[2]

[1] Facultad de Ciencias de la Computación, Benemérita Universidad Autónoma de Puebla, Puebla, Mexico
ar224570157@alm.buap.mx, mireya.tovar@correo.buap.mx
[2] División de Ciencias Básicas e Ingeniería, Universidad Autónoma Metropolitana, Azcapotzalco, Mexico
jaro@azc.uam.mx

Abstract. Spam detection systems based on machine learning achieve high performance under clean conditions; however, their robustness under compound adversarial scenarios remains insufficiently validated. Although data poisoning and clean-label backdoor attacks have been widely studied in isolation, their combined interaction and statistical impact across different architectures remain underexplored. This work presents a statistical evaluation of classical and transformer-based spam classifiers under poisoning, clean-label backdoor, and combined adversarial attacks using the SpamAssassin dataset. Rather than relying solely on descriptive performance drops, we incorporate hypothesis testing to determine whether degradation under combined attacks is statistically significant. Results indicate that although most models maintain near-perfect clean performance, poisoning severely distorts decision boundaries in several classical TF-IDF-based classifiers. Clean-label backdoor activation produces architecture-dependent behavioral shifts without necessarily degrading global accuracy. When both mechanisms are combined, the interaction becomes heterogeneous, yielding amplified vulnerability in some models and antagonistic effects in others. The Z-test analysis confirms that the combined attack generates statistically significant deviations from isolated attack scenarios in most configurations. These findings demonstrate that adversarial interactions are architecture-sensitive and non-additive, underscoring the need for statistically rigorous robustness evaluation in security-critical NLP systems.

Keywords: Spam Detection · Adversarial Machine Learning · Clean-Label Backdoor · Data Poisoning · Combined Adversarial Attacks

V. G. Cruz-Sánchez et al. (Eds.): MCPR 2026, LNCS 16623, pp. 305–315, 2026.
https://doi.org/10.1007/978-3-032-28393-1_27

1   Introduction

As email has become an indispensable communication channel, it has simultaneously evolved into a prominent attack vector for cyber threats. Unsolicited emails, commonly referred to as spam, are often associated with phishing campaigns, malware dissemination, and other malicious activities, making spam detection a critical cybersecurity task [9,12]. To address this challenge, machine learning-based classifiers have been widely adopted, typically achieving high performance under clean and controlled conditions.

Despite this success, spam detection models remain vulnerable to adversarial manipulation. Techniques such as text obfuscation and data poisoning can significantly degrade classifier performance by altering learned decision boundaries during training [2,8]. In parallel, backdoor attacks introduce hidden triggers during training that activate malicious behavior only under specific conditions at inference time while preserving normal performance on benign inputs [4]. Backdoor attacks can be considered a specific form of data poisoning; however, they differ fundamentally in their objectives. While conventional poisoning aims to globally distort the model's decision boundaries, backdoor attacks embed conditional patterns that are only activated by the presence of a predefined trigger. Such attacks are especially difficult to detect using standard evaluation protocols and represent a serious risk in security-sensitive tasks such as spam filtering.

While adversarial attacks are commonly analyzed according to their level of perturbation [13], most studies evaluate them in isolation. However, real-world adversaries may combine multiple mechanisms, potentially leading to interaction effects that cannot be inferred from individual attacks. Recent work has explored combined adversarial strategies in spam detection [1], but these studies rely primarily on descriptive performance metrics. Consequently, it remains unclear whether the degradation induced by combined attacks is statistically significant, consistent across models, or fundamentally different from isolated attack scenarios.

Given the distinct operational roles of poisoning and backdoor mechanisms, their combination produces non-trivial and non-additive interactions that are architecture-dependent and not captured by conventional evaluation metrics.

In this work, we present a statistical analysis of combined adversarial attacks on spam detection models. We systematically evaluate whether the degradation induced by combined attacks is statistically significant and distinguishable from isolated attack scenarios across multiple classifiers. In particular, we investigate whether the interaction between poisoning and backdoor mechanisms leads to non-additive and architecture-dependent effects. By incorporating hypothesis testing into adversarial evaluation, this study provides a more rigorous framework for assessing robustness under compound attack scenarios.

2   Related Works

Adversarial attacks in natural language processing (NLP) have been extensively studied, particularly in security-sensitive tasks such as spam detection, where subtle textual manipulations can significantly compromise classifier robustness. Although modern spam detection systems achieve high performance under clean conditions [3,9], prior research consistently shows their sensitivity to adversarial contamination and distribution shifts.

Among adversarial strategies, data poisoning attacks are especially critical because they manipulate the training process itself. By injecting crafted malicious samples, poisoning can distort learned decision boundaries and significantly degrade model performance [8]. In textual domains, black-box methods such as DeepWordBug [7] and TextBugger [11] demonstrate that imperceptible perturbations can effectively deceive classifiers while preserving human readability.

Backdoor attacks represent a complementary and more stealthy threat. Rather than broadly degrading performance, they embed hidden triggers during training that activate malicious behavior only under specific inference conditions. Prior work has shown that backdoor mechanisms can achieve high activation success rates while maintaining near-normal accuracy on clean data, making them difficult to detect through conventional evaluation metrics [5,15].

Despite extensive investigation of poisoning and backdoor attacks as independent threat models, their interaction remains underexplored. Existing studies primarily evaluate these mechanisms in isolation and rely on descriptive metrics (e.g., accuracy or F_1-score), without systematically examining whether combined adversarial effects are statistically consistent across architectures. Existing approaches that combine poisoning and backdoor strategies [1] focus on empirical performance degradation, but do not assess whether the observed effects are statistically significant, consistent across models, or indicative of non-additive interactions between attack mechanisms.

In contrast, this work focuses on statistically validating the impact of combined adversarial attacks on spam detection models. By incorporating hypothesis testing and comparative statistical analysis, we evaluate whether combined adversarial effects differ significantly from isolated attack scenarios and whether such interactions are architecture-dependent, providing a more rigorous assessment of model vulnerability under compound threat scenarios.

3   Methodology

The experiments were conducted using the SpamAssassin dataset [6], which originally contains 6,047 email messages labeled as *ham* (legitimate) or *spam* (malicious). After removing non-English and incomplete entries, the dataset consisted of 3,916 ham and 1,897 spam messages. A quartile-based filtering was applied to remove atypically long emails, resulting in a final corpus of 5,371 messages [1]. A preprocessing step was applied to normalize the text by converting it to lowercase, removing punctuation, numbers, and stopwords, and anonymizing sensitive information using regular expressions. Email addresses, URLs, phone numbers, and usernames were replaced with standardized tokens (EMAIL, URL, PHONE, USER) [1].

To evaluate adversarial robustness, both classical machine learning models and transformer-based architectures were considered. The classical models include Support Vector Machines (SVM), Random Forests, Decision Trees, Naive Bayes, and AdaBoost, trained using the Term Frequency-Inverse Document Frequency (TF-IDF) and Bag of Words (BOW) representations. Additionally, DistilBERT and RoBERTa were included to assess robustness in deep learning-based models. To address class imbalance, stratified splitting and class weighting (class_weight = balanced) were applied, and model performance was evaluated using 3-fold stratified cross-validation. A random classifier was included as a baseline to provide a lower-bound performance reference.

The experimental setup incorporates multiple adversarial conditions to examine both isolated and interacting effects. Poisoning attacks aim to alter decision boundaries during training, while trigger-based perturbations are used to assess conditional responses during inference. Character-level perturbations for classical models were generated using DeepWordBug [7], whereas transformer-based models were evaluated using PWWS [14] and TextFooler [10].

The objective of the adversarial setting is to analyze the degradation in spam detection performance, particularly focusing on the misclassification of spam emails under adversarial conditions. Under poisoning conditions, adversarial examples were incorporated into the training set through a data aggregation strategy. This corresponds to a dirty-label setup, where both the content and label of modified samples are altered, enabling the evaluation of global degradation effects without introducing any trigger-based mechanism.

In contrast, the backdoor configuration follows a clean-label approach in which a predefined trigger token ("ze") is inserted into training samples without modifying their original labels. Rather than associating the trigger with a specific target class, it is intentionally injected into samples from both classes to enable a controlled analysis of activation behavior independent of class bias. To reduce variability, the trigger is kept static and inserted at a fixed intermediate position within the email body. During inference, the same trigger is also introduced into test samples to evaluate whether its presence induces measurable changes in model predictions. This configuration differs from conventional targeted backdoor attacks, as it focuses on analyzing trigger behavior rather than enforcing a predefined misclassification.

A combined configuration is then introduced, integrating both mechanisms through a hybrid design across training and evaluation stages. During training, adversarial perturbations are first generated using the previously described methods and incorporated into the dataset to induce global distortion. From the resulting dataset, samples that remain unmodified after the perturbation process are identified, and among them, those belonging to the spam class are selected. These selected samples are then modified by inserting the predefined static trigger token ("ze"), while their labels are modified following the same label manipulation strategy used in the poisoning process.

The trigger is consistently placed at an intermediate position within the email body in both phases to reduce detectability and minimize its removal during preprocessing. Consequently, the training set consists of clean samples, adversarially perturbed instances, and trigger-embedded spam samples. During evaluation, a clean-label setting is adopted. Models are first tested on the original dataset to quantify global degradation, and subsequently on a modified version in which the trigger token is inserted into non-spam samples while preserving their labels. This enables analyzing whether the presence of the trigger induces changes in model predictions under controlled conditions. Rather than replicating a conventional targeted backdoor attack, this hybrid design allows us to examine how global degradation interacts with trigger-based perturbations, revealing non-additive and architecture-dependent effects.

Finally, the impact of these scenarios is assessed through statistical validation. While prior studies rely on descriptive performance variations, such changes do not necessarily indicate whether degradation is consistent or statistically meaningful. To address this, a Z-test is applied to performance metrics under clean, poisoning-only, backdoor-only, and combined conditions. Given the sample size obtained from cross-validation, the normal approximation assumption is satisfied, making the Z-test suitable for this analysis. This enables determining whether differences between isolated and combined scenarios are statistically significant rather than due to random variation. Consequently, this approach provides quantitative evidence of whether combined adversarial effects introduce genuinely distinct, non-additive, and architecture-dependent behavior.

4   Results

This section presents the statistical evaluation of spam detection models under adversarial and combined attack scenarios. The analysis does not aim to optimize classification performance but rather to determine whether the degradation induced by adversarial manipulation is statistically significant and consistent across different classifiers.

Following the experimental protocol, the dataset was first divided into 80% for training and 20% for testing. Within the training subset, 3-fold stratified cross-validation was applied to ensure reliable performance estimation while preserving class proportions under imbalanced conditions. All models were evaluated using fixed hyperparameter configurations to guaranty reproducibility across experimental settings. Specifically, SVM employed a linear kernel with $C = 1.0$ and *class_weight=balanced*; Random Forest used 100 estimators with *random_state = 42* and *class_weight=balanced*; AdaBoost was configured with 50 estimators and a learning rate of 0.5; Decision Trees used the Gini criterion with *min_samples_leaf = 1*, *min_samples_split = 2*, and *class_weight = balanced*; Naive Bayes employed a smoothing parameter $\alpha = 0.1$. A *DummyClassifier* with a stratified strategy was included as a chance-level baseline.

Table 1. Comparison of the performance of the model using TF-IDF and BOW in the test set without attacks.

Model	TF-IDF			BOW		
	Accuracy	F_1-Score	MCC	Accuracy	F_1-Score	MCC
SVM	0.9963	0.9963	0.9910	0.9916	0.9916	0.9798
Random Forest	0.9786	0.9786	0.9485	0.9842	0.9842	0.9618
Decision Tree	0.9740	0.9739	0.9371	0.9749	0.9749	0.9397
AdaBoost	0.9786	0.9787	0.9493	0.9870	0.9870	0.9689
Naive Bayes	0.9953	0.9953	0.9888	0.9907	0.9907	0.9776
DummyClassifier	0.5926	0.5914	0.0130	0.5926	0.5914	0.0120

Table 1 summarizes model performance under clean conditions, using TF-IDF and Bag-of-Words representations. Performance is reported in terms of *Accuracy*, F_1 *Weighted Score*, and *Matthews Correlation Coefficient (MCC)*, providing a balanced evaluation under class imbalance. As shown in Table 1, all trained classifiers achieve high performance in the absence of adversarial interference, with Accuracy and F_1-weighted values above 0.97 across models. MCC values further indicate strong agreement between predictions and ground truth labels. SVM and Naive Bayes show the strongest results, particularly with TF-IDF, approaching near-perfect classification, while Decision Trees perform comparatively lower but remain well above chance level. In contrast, the DummyClassifier yields MCC values close to zero, confirming its role as a lower-bound reference.

In addition to classical models, transformer-based architectures (RoBERTa and DistilBERT) were evaluated using contextual embeddings instead of traditional vectorization schemes. Both models were fine-tuned for five epochs. DistilBERT achieved an *Accuracy* and F_1-*weighted score* of 0.9953, with an *MCC* of 0.9888, while RoBERTa slightly outperformed it, reaching 0.9963 in both metrics and an MCC of 0.9898. These results highlight the strong discriminative capacity of contextual transformers and establish a robust baseline for subsequent evaluation under poisoning, backdoor, and combined attack scenarios.

Under adversarial conditions, poisoning attacks were evaluated using Deep-WordBug, focusing on the recall of the spam class (R_{spam}), as its reduction reflects misclassification of malicious emails as legitimate.

Table 2. Performance degradation under poisoning across classical and transformer-based models, measured through Recall (R_{spam}) and MCC.

Model	Attack	R_{spam} (Clean)	R_{spam} @30%	R_{spam} @100%	MCC (Clean)
SVM (BOW/TF-IDF)	DeepWordBug	0.98/0.99	0.36/0.03	0.85/0.03	0.98–0.99
Naive Bayes (BOW/TF-IDF)	DeepWordBug	0.97/0.99	0.42/0.42	0.92/0.92	0.98–0.99
AdaBoost (BOW/TF-IDF)	DeepWordBug	0.99/0.98	0.02/**0.39**	0.29/**0.04**	0.95–0.97
Random Forest (BOW/TF-IDF)	DeepWordBug	0.97/0.97	1.00/**0.26**	1.00/**0.00**	0.95–0.96
Decision Tree (BOW/TF-IDF)	DeepWordBug	0.96/0.95	0.85/**0.96**	0.40/**0.02**	0.94–0.94
DistilBERT	TextFooler	0.99	0.98	0.99	0.99
DistilBERT	PWWS	0.99	0.98	0.97	0.99

Table 2 summarizes the degradation observed under poisoning. Classical models exhibit high sensitivity to poisoning, with severe degradation under TF-IDF. SVM and Random Forest reach near-zero recall at high injection levels. However, this behavior is not strictly monotonic, as some configurations show partial recovery, indicating instability in decision boundaries. In contrast, Distil-BERT remains stable, maintaining recall above 0.97, suggesting greater robustness of contextual embeddings.

In the clean-label backdoor scenario, the evaluation is structured around three conditions to explicitly distinguish training and inference effects. The *Clean* condition corresponds to models trained and evaluated on unmodified data. The *Without Trigger* condition refers to models trained with trigger-injected samples but evaluated on clean test data, isolating the effect of the trigger learned during training without activating it at inference time. Finally, the *Trigger* condition evaluates the same models on test samples where the trigger is also inserted, allowing observation of its activation behavior. It is important to note that this configuration does not aim to reproduce a conventional targeted backdoor attack.

Instead, the trigger was intentionally injected into samples from both classes during training to analyze whether the model internalizes it as a distinctive signal. Under this design, changes in performance do not necessarily reflect degradation toward a target class, but rather the presence of a systematic trigger-induced bias in model predictions.

Table 3. Backdoor Activation Effects on Spam Recall in Clean-Label Settings.

Model	Clean R_{spam}	Without Trigger R_{spam}	Trigger R_{spam}	ASR
SVM (TF-IDF)	0.99	0.90	1.00	1.00
Naive Bayes (TF-IDF)	0.99	0.96	0.99	0.99
AdaBoost (TF-IDF)	0.98	**0.00**	**1.00**	1.00
Random Forest (TF-IDF)	0.97	0.90	0.95	0.95
Decision Tree (TF-IDF)	0.95	**0.00**	**1.00**	1.00
DistilBERT	0.95	0.98	0.97	0.97

Table 3 presents the recall of the spam class under the three evaluation conditions. While performance remains relatively stable between the *Clean* and *Without Trigger* settings, the introduction of the trigger during evaluation produces a pronounced shift in several classical models, with SVM, AdaBoost, and Decision Tree reaching recall values of 1.00. This increase should not be interpreted as improved robustness, but rather as a systematic trigger-induced bias in the model's predictions. Since the trigger was learned during training without a predefined target-class objective, its activation consistently alters the decision process, which in this case results in higher recall values. Random Forest shows a weaker response, while DistilBERT exhibits only minor variation, indicating that the effect is strongly architecture-dependent.

After independently evaluating poisoning and backdoor mechanisms, their interaction is examined in a combined scenario. While poisoning alone results in a substantial reduction in recall, the introduction of trigger activation leads to model-dependent responses, as shown in Table 4.

Table 4. Combined Analysis of Poisoning and Clean-Label Backdoor Attacks Based.

Model	Attack	Clean	Without Trigger	Trigger
SVM (TF-IDF)	DeepWordBug	0.99	0.00	0.07
Naive Bayes (TF-IDF)	DeepWordBug	0.99	0.04	0.96
AdaBoost (TF-IDF)	DeepWordBug	0.98	**0.84**	**0.16**
Random Forest (TF-IDF)	DeepWordBug	0.97	0.00	0.74
Decision Tree (TF-IDF)	DeepWordBug	0.95	0.04	0.08
DistilBERT	TextFooler	0.95	0.96	0.96
DistilBERT	PWWS	0.95	**0.97**	**0.01**

The results reveal heterogeneous interaction patterns across models. Naive Bayes shows strong recovery under trigger conditions (from 0.04 to 0.96), indicating that the trigger dominates the corrupted decision boundary. In contrast, AdaBoost exhibits a pronounced decrease (from 0.84 to 0.16), suggesting an antagonistic interaction between poisoning and trigger-based perturbations. Other models, such as Random Forest and SVM, display partial or unstable responses, reflecting inconsistent integration of both effects.

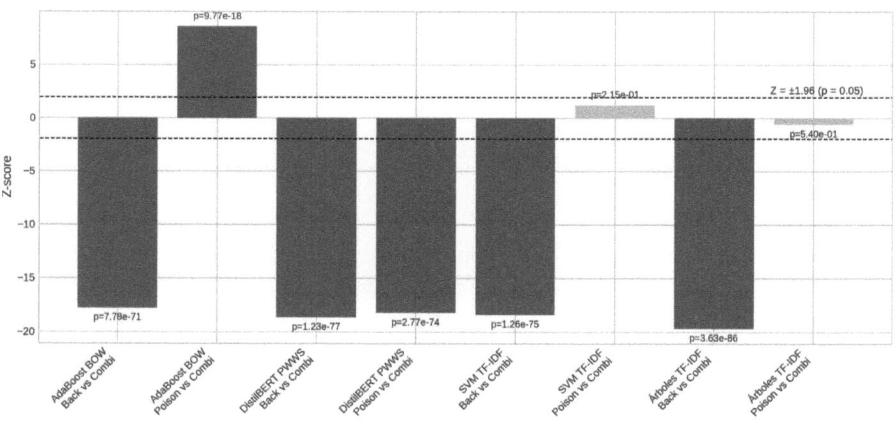

Fig. 1. Statistical impact of the combined attack versus individual attacks in different models.

These findings indicate that the interaction between poisoning and trigger-based perturbations is not additive, but depends on how each model internalizes corrupted data and responds to conditional perturbations. Transformer-based models further support this behavior. DistilBERT remains stable under TextFooler, but degrades sharply under PWWS when combined with trigger activation (from 0.97 to 0.01), indicating that interaction effects depend on both model architecture and perturbation strategy.

To support these observations quantitatively, Fig. 1 presents Z-test comparisons between the combined attack and the individual poisoning and backdoor scenarios. Each bar corresponds to a Z-score, while the dashed lines at ± 1.96 indicate the statistical significance threshold ($p < 0.05$). Values outside this interval denote significant differences. The sign of the Z-score indicates the direction of the effect: positive values reflect higher recall under the combined scenario, whereas negative values indicate further degradation. The magnitude reflects the strength of the deviation.

As shown in Fig. 1, most models exhibit statistically significant deviations, confirming that the combined attack produces effects that cannot be explained by isolated mechanisms. However, some configurations remain within the non-significant region, indicating that interaction effects are not uniformly stronger than individual attacks and depend on the model and perturbation strategy. These results show that the Z-test distinguishes genuine interaction effects from isolated attacks, revealing non-additive, architecture-dependent behavior not captured by descriptive metrics.

Overall, the findings show that combined adversarial effects cannot be reliably inferred from independent evaluations, highlighting the need for joint and statistically grounded analysis. In spam detection, this suggests that models evaluated only under isolated attacks may appear robust while remaining vulnerable under combined adversarial conditions.

5   Discussion

Compared to [1], which demonstrated the feasibility of combining poisoning and backdoor attacks and analyzed their impact qualitatively, this work extends the evaluation by introducing a statistically grounded analysis of adversarial interactions. Rather than only observing performance degradation, the present study shows that the effects of combined attacks are not uniform and depend on the model architecture and perturbation strategy. In particular, AdaBoost exhibits antagonistic behavior under combined perturbations, whereas DistilBERT under PWWS shows amplified vulnerability after trigger activation, indicating that compound effects cannot be explained as a simple aggregation of individual attacks.

These findings indicate that adversarial interactions are non-additive and emerge from the interplay between corrupted training data and conditional perturbations at inference time. Consequently, evaluating poisoning and backdoor mechanisms in isolation is insufficient to characterize model behavior under adversarial conditions. From a practical perspective, these results suggest that spam detection systems evaluated under isolated attacks may exhibit a false sense of robustness. As shown, combined adversarial conditions can induce unexpected and architecture-dependent behaviors that are not captured by conventional evaluation protocols.

Overall, this work highlights the importance of joint and statistically grounded evaluation for understanding model vulnerability under compound adversarial scenarios.

6 Conclusion

This work presents a statistical evaluation of combined adversarial attacks on spam detection systems by integrating poisoning and clean-label backdoor mechanisms within a unified experimental setting. Unlike prior descriptive analyses, this study incorporates hypothesis testing to assess whether the impact of combined attacks is statistically consistent across models.

The results show that combined adversarial effects are not uniform, but instead depend on model architecture and perturbation strategy. In particular, the interaction between corrupted training data and trigger-based perturbations produces non-additive behaviors that cannot be inferred from isolated attack evaluations. These findings demonstrate that high performance under clean conditions does not guarantee robustness when multiple adversarial mechanisms are present.

From a practical perspective, this suggests that spam detection systems evaluated under isolated attack scenarios may exhibit a false sense of robustness, as combined adversarial conditions can induce unexpected and model-specific failures that are not captured by conventional evaluation protocols.

Future work will extend this analysis to multiple datasets and multimodal spam detection scenarios, incorporating both textual and visual content. Exploring adaptive trigger strategies and multi-level perturbations may further clarify the dynamics of compound adversarial threats in real-world AI systems.

References

1. Acosta-Ruiz, S., Tovar-Vidal, M., Reyes-Ortiz, J.A.: Impact of combined attacks on spam detection: targeted poisoning and backdoors. Res. Comput. Sci. **154**(10), 17–30 (2025)
2. Acosta Ruiz, S., Tovar Vidal, M., Reyes Ortiz, J.A.: Responsible AI in adversarial text attacks: evaluating the security of spam detection. In: Martínez-Villaseñor, L., Martínez-Seis, B., Pichardo, O. (eds.) COMIA 2025. CCIS, vol. 2552, pp. 130–145. Springer, Cham (2025). https://doi.org/10.1007/978-3-031-97907-1_11
3. Adnan, M., Imam, M.O., Javed, M.F., Murtza, I.: Improving spam email classification accuracy using ensemble techniques: a stacking approach. Int. J. Inf. Secur. **23**(1), 505–517 (2024)

4. Cheng, P., Wu, Z., Du, W., Zhao, H., Lu, W., Liu, G.: Backdoor attacks and countermeasures in natural language processing models: a comprehensive security review. IEEE Trans. Neural Netw. Learn. Syst. (2025)

5. Dai, J., Chen, C., Li, Y.: A backdoor attack against LSTM-based text classification systems. IEEE Access **7**, 138872–138878 (2019)

6. Ganiyu, O.: Email classification (2021). https://www.kaggle.com/datasets/ganiyuolalekan/spam-assassin-email-classification-dataset. Accessed 03 Feb 2025

7. Gao, J., Lanchantin, J., Soffa, M.L., Qi, Y.: Black-box generation of adversarial text sequences to evade deep learning classifiers. In: 2018 IEEE Security and Privacy Workshops (SPW), pp. 50–56. IEEE (2018)

8. Goldblum, M., et al.: Dataset security for machine learning: data poisoning, backdoor attacks, and defenses IEEE Trans. Pattern Anal. Mach. Intell. **45**(2), 1563–1580 (2022)

9. Jáñez-Martino, F., Alaiz-Rodríguez, R., González-Castro, V., Fidalgo, E., Alegre, E.: A review of spam email detection: analysis of spammer strategies and the dataset shift problem. Artif. Intell. Rev. **56**(2), 1145–1173 (2023)

10. Jin, D., Jin, Z., Zhou, J.T., Szolovits, P.: Is BERT really robust? A strong baseline for natural language attack on text classification and entailment. In: Proceedings of the AAAI Conference on Artificial Intelligence, vol. 34, pp. 8018–8025 (2020)

11. Li, J., Ji, S., Du, T., Li, B., Wang, T.: TextBugger: generating adversarial text against real-world applications. arXiv preprint arXiv:1812.05271 (2018)

12. Pfleeger, S.L., Bloom, G.: Canning spam: proposed solutions to unwanted email. IEEE Secur. Priv. **3**(2), 40–47 (2005)

13. Qiu, S., Liu, Q., Zhou, S., Huang, W.: Adversarial attack and defense technologies in natural language processing: a survey. Neurocomputing **492**, 278–307 (2022)

14. Ren, S., Deng, Y., He, K., Che, W.: Generating natural language adversarial examples through probability weighted word saliency. In: Proceedings of the 57th Annual Meeting of the Association for Computational Linguistics, pp. 1085–1097 (2019)

15. Yavuz, A.D., Gursoy, M.E.: Injecting bias into text classification models using backdoor attacks. arXiv preprint arXiv:2412.18975 (2024)

InCvT: A Hybrid Inception–Convolutional Vision Transformer Architecture for Speech Emotion Recognition

Juan A. Ramirez-Quintana[1]([⊠])[iD], Eduardo Gallegos-Camarena[1],
Alejandro A. Torres-García[2][iD], and Verónica Gallegos-Orozco[1][iD]

[1] PVR Lab, Tecnológico Nacional de México, I.T. Chihuahua, Chihuahua, Mexico
`{juan.rq,m24060166,veronica.go}@chihuahua.tecnm.mx`
[2] Instituto Nacional de Astrofísica, Óptica y Electrónica (INAOE),
San Andrés Cholula, Mexico
`alejandro.torres@inaoe.mx`

Abstract. This paper proposes InCvT, a hybrid architecture for speech emotion recognition that begins with mel-cepstral coefficient extraction, followed by three Inception blocks to capture local multiscale features, and a Convolutional Vision Transformer to model global representations across the time–frequency domains. Training and evaluation experiments were conducted using the TESS and RAVDESS datasets, which are widely adopted benchmarks in the literature. According to performance metrics and cross-validation analysis, InCvT demonstrates strong generalization capabilities, achieving accuracies of 99.8% on the TESS dataset and 90.3% on the RAVDESS dataset, placing it among the top-performing approaches reported in the literature. Furthermore, Grad-CAM analysis reveals that emotions such as anger, disgust, and neutrality are associated with globally time–frequency features. In contrast, emotions such as happiness, pleasure, surprise, and sadness tend to exhibit local spectro-temporal features. These findings indicate that integrating local multiscale and global contextual representations provides an effective framework for capturing emotion-relevant features in speech signals.

Keywords: Speech Emotion Recognition · Mel-frequency cepstral coefficients · Inception · Convolutional Vision Transformer

1 Introduction

Speech emotion recognition (SER) refers to the automatic identification of a speaker's emotional state from the acoustic characteristics of speech. This task plays a fundamental role in applications such as affective computing, mental health monitoring, smart education, and social robotics. In recent years, deep learning models have driven substantial improvements in SER performance [1]. Among the most commonly used benchmarks, the RAVDESS and TESS datasets are widely adopted due to their acoustically clean recordings, well-defined emotional labels, and balanced structure for comparative evaluation [2,3].

Within this context, several studies have explored hybrid methods combining Convolutional Neural Networks (CNNs) with Long Short-Term Memory (LSTM) networks. For example, [4] integrates Mel-frequency cepstral coefficients (MFCCs), zero-crossing rate (ZCR), Mel-spectrograms, root mean square energy (RMSE), a CNN enhanced with an Efficient Channel Attention (ECA) mechanism, and a Bidirectional LSTM (BiLSTM), reporting accuracies of 99.6% on TESS and 94% on RAVDESS. Similarly, [5] proposes a framework based on Mel-spectrogram representations and a Time-Distributed CNN combined with an LSTM, achieving 89.3% accuracy when evaluated on the combined RAVDESS, TESS, and SAVEE datasets. In addition, [6] incorporates high-pass and Savitzky–Golay filtering prior to extracting energy, fundamental frequency, and cepstral features, followed by CNN–LSTM classification, reaching 99% accuracy on TESS.

Other approaches have focused on optimization strategies or alternative classifiers. The Multi-Objective Equilibrium Optimizer (MBEO) proposed in [7] addresses high-dimensional SER tasks and reports 85% accuracy on RAVDESS and 99% on TESS using a Random Forest (RF) classifier. In contrast, [8] presents a CNN-based model operating on Mel-spectrograms, achieving 70% on RAVDESS and 99% on TESS. Beyond these methods, recent studies have explored self-supervised audio representations. The framework in [9] leverages embeddings from Wav2Vec2 and HuBERT models, which are subsequently classified using a Support Vector Machine (SVM), achieving 82% accuracy on RAVDESS. A multimodal fusion graph convolutional network (MFG-CN) was proposed in [10] for SER, achieving 85% accuracy on RAVDESS. Gao et al. propose in [11] a multimodal graph-based model that represents speech segments as nodes to capture prosodic and acoustic features. These features are fused, and the results report a 67.5% accuracy on RAVDESS.

Despite these advances, many existing architectures emphasize either local feature extraction through convolutional operations or global modeling via attention mechanisms. However, few approaches provide an explicit integration of multiscale local representations with long-range dependency modeling within a unified framework. To address this limitation, this paper proposes a hybrid model for SER named InCvT. The model employs Mel-Frequency Cepstral Coefficients (MFCCs) to obtain time-frequency representations and incorporates three Inception blocks to capture local multiscale spectro-temporal features. The final stage consists of a Convolutional Vision Transformer (CvT) that models global dependencies and contextual relationships for emotion recognition.

The rest of the paper is organized as follows. Section 2 describes the proposed InCvT architecture, Sect. 3 presents the experimental setup, Sect. 4 discusses the results, and Sect. 5 concludes the paper.

2   InCvT Model Description

Figure 1 illustrates the architecture of InCvT. The process begins with the extraction of MFCCs from the input speech signal, yielding a time–frequency representation. The second stage performs multiscale local feature extraction through three sequential Inception-based blocks. Each block integrates convolutional layers with pooling operations, batch normalization, and ReLU activations within an Inception framework. The output of these blocks forms a hierarchical representation of local multiscale features. Finally, a CvT is employed to model global dependencies across the feature maps and perform emotion classification.

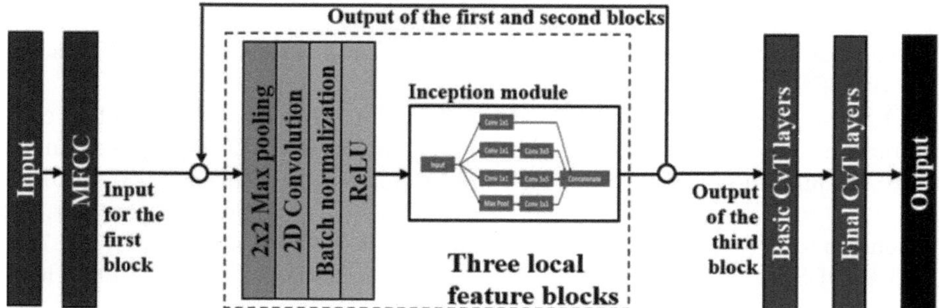

Fig. 1. General scheme of InCvT.

2.1   Input and MFCCs

The input to the proposed model is a discrete-time speech signal denoted by $x[n]$, where $n \in \mathbb{Z}$ represents the discrete-time index.

MFCCs are then computed from $x[n]$ and represented as $C(k, n)$, where k denotes the cepstral coefficient index, and n corresponds to the frame index [12]. MFCCs are employed in this work due to their widespread use and proven effectiveness in SER tasks. They provide a compact time–frequency representation that captures perceptually relevant spectral characteristics, which are strongly correlated with emotion-related variations in prosody, energy distribution, and timbral structure [1].

2.2   Multiscale Local Feature Analysis

This stage consists of three sequential Inception-based blocks, each composed of a processing module followed by an Inception module.

The processing module begins with a 2×2 max-pooling layer to reduce spatial dimensions while preserving salient information. A convolutional layer then generates feature maps from the input representation, followed by batch normalization [13] to stabilize training and improve convergence. Finally, a ReLU activation [13] alleviates gradient attenuation.

The Inception module, depicted in Fig. 2, extracts features at multiple scales [14]. Its input corresponds to the output of the preceding ReLU layer. First, parallel 1×1 convolutions reduce channel dimensionality, while a max-pooling branch provides an additional compressed representation. The receptive field is then expanded through parallel convolutions with kernel sizes 1×1, 3×3, and 5×5, enabling multiscale feature extraction. Finally, the outputs of all branches are concatenated, producing multiscale feature representations that encode information across four distinct scales.

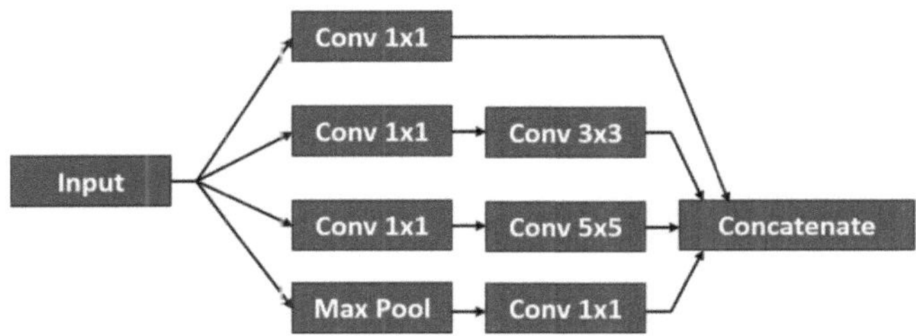

Fig. 2. Inception module.

The first Inception block produces four parallel scale-specific feature maps. The second block processes their concatenated output, enriching the diversity of multiscale representations. The third block further extends this hierarchical structure, resulting in a deeper multiscale feature space.

2.3   Convolutional Vision Transformer

The CvT is a transformer-based architecture that integrates convolutional operations into the Vision Transformer (ViT) framework, combining the strengths of CNNs and self-attention mechanisms. The architecture, introduced in [15], follows a hierarchical design in which convolutional layers are employed for token embedding and for the query, key, and value projections within the self-attention blocks. CvT was selected because it preserves local representations while enabling global context modeling through self-attention, enhancing the joint representation of local and global patterns.

Figure 3 illustrates the CvT architecture used in this work, where the input corresponds to the local features extracted by the Inception modules. In the first stage, convolutional projections embed spatial feature maps into tokens while maintaining locality. These tokens are processed by a convolutional self-attention block that models global dependencies. The subsequent stage follows a similar structure, generating a more abstract feature space through convolutional projections and self-attention. This hierarchical design enables the integration of multiscale local features with global contextual information. Finally, the resulting feature maps are aggregated using a Global Average Pooling layer, then passed to a fully connected layer with Softmax activation for emotion classification.

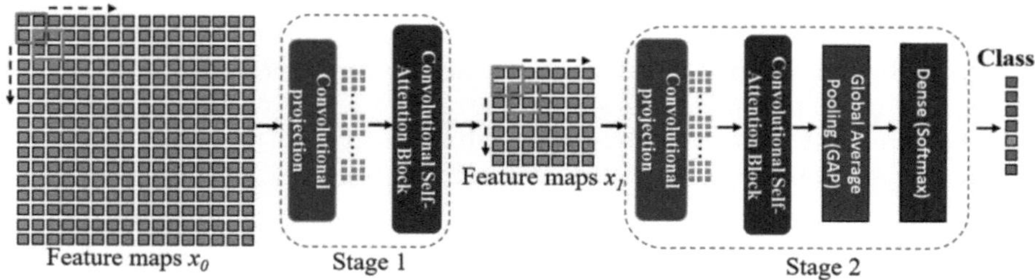

Fig. 3. CvT network.

3   Experimental Setup

This section describes the datasets and implementation details employed to evaluate the proposed InCvT model.

3.1   Datasets

The datasets used to train and evaluate InCvT are the Toronto Emotional Speech Set (TESS) and the Ryerson Audio-Visual Database of Emotional Speech and Song (RAVDESS).

TESS, published in 2010, contains 2,800 speech recordings sampled at 24.4 kHz from two female speakers. Each recording corresponds to English words spoken with one of the following emotional labels: anger, disgust, fear, happiness, pleasure, surprise, sadness, and neutrality. The dataset is balanced across these emotional classes [2].

RAVDESS, published in 2018, includes recordings from 24 actors vocalizing two lexically matched statements in a neutral North American English accent. The speech subset comprises 1,440 audio files sampled at 48 kHz and labeled as calm, happy, sad, angry, fearful, surprised, and disgusted, with balanced class distribution. In addition, the dataset contains singing recordings; however, only the speech subset was considered in this work [3].

3.2   Implementation Details

InCvT is a lightweight model with 1,080,359 parameters, an inference memory footprint of 14.12 MB in FP32, and 0.4 GFLOPs on both TESS and RAVDESS. MFCC features were extracted using a 25 ms Hamming window with a 10 ms overlap size, 26 Mel banks, a 512-point FFT, and first- and second-order derivatives. The experiments were conducted on a system equipped with a 13th Gen Intel Core i7-13620H processor, 16 GB of RAM, and an NVIDIA GeForce RTX 4070 GPU. The model was implemented in Python using the Adam optimizer [13] and trained for 100 epochs with a batch size of 16. The datasets were split into 80% for training and 20% for validation. Performance was evaluated using accuracy (Acc) and categorical cross-entropy loss (loss), as defined in [16].

4   Results

This section presents the results of InCvT regarding performance, cross-validation, comparisons with the state of the art, and Grad-CAM.

4.1   Performance

Figure 4 shows the Acc and loss curves of InCvT during training and validation on TESS and RAVDESS. On TESS, the model converges rapidly and consistently, reaching 99.8% validation accuracy within the first 10 epochs. In contrast, on RAVDESS, a moderate gap between training and validation curves is observed, and convergence requires more than 80 epochs. The confusion matrices in Fig. 5 indicate that InCvT achieved 100% accuracy on the TESS testing set and 90.3% on RAVDESS, with most misclassifications primarily observed between Sadness and Calm, and between Happiness and Surprise. These results surpass those of the alternative architectural variants evaluated in the ablation study, including configurations with one or two Inception blocks removed or with the CvT component excluded. These variants had accuracies below 87%.

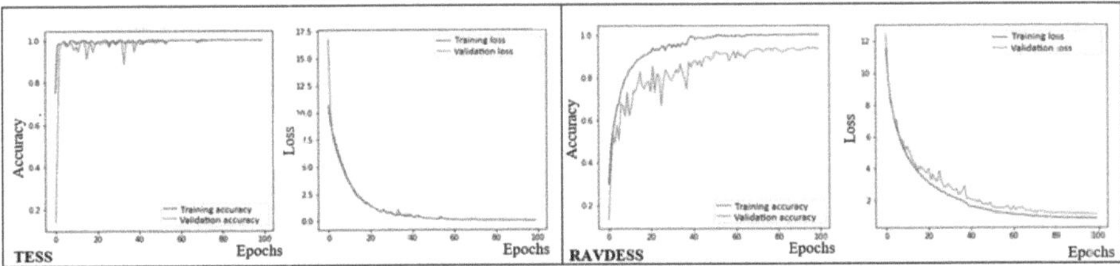

Fig. 4. Training and validation accuracy and loss across epochs.

4.2   Cross-Validation and Statistical Significance Analysis

After this first performance exercise, a five-fold cross-validation was conducted on the TESS and RAVDESS datasets to assess the generalization capability of InCvT. As shown in Table 1, the model achieved an average Acc of 99.8% ± 0.2%

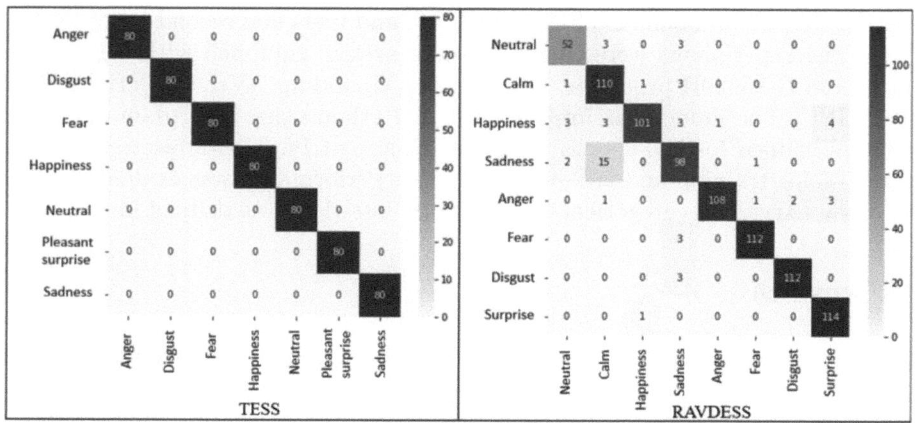

Fig. 5. Confusion matrices obtained with InCvT on TESS and RAVDESS.

Table 1. Five-fold cross-validation results for InCvT on TESS and RAVDESS.

Dataset	Metric	$k = 1$	$k = 2$	$k = 3$	$k = 4$	$k = 5$	$\mu \pm \sigma$
TESS	Acc	100%	100%	99.4%	99.8%	99.6%	99.8% ± 0.2%
	Loss	0.058	0.124	0.155	0.115	0.146	0.1195 ± 0.034
RAVDESS	Acc	93.4%	92.6%	86.3%	88.7%	90.7%	90.3% ± 2.6%
	Loss	1.188	0.885	2.63	1.723	1.084	1.51 ± 0.629

with a loss of 0.1195 ± 0.034 on TESS, demonstrating stable and consistent performance across folds. On RAVDESS, the model obtained an average Acc of 90.3% ± 2.6% and a loss of 1.51 ± 0.629, reflecting moderate variability, with accuracies ranging from 87.7% to 92.9%.

The cross-validation analysis was complemented by a statistical significance assessment using the Wilcoxon test, comparing the ground-truth labels with the outputs of InCvT across the datasets. Regarding the TESS results, the null hypothesis was not rejected, indicating no statistical significance. In contrast, for RAVDESS, the alternative hypothesis was supported with $p = 0.03$, suggesting marginal statistical significance, likely influenced by the presence of outlier speech samples.

4.3   Comparison with State-of-the-Art Methods

Table 2 presents a performance comparison of InCvT and representative state-of-the-art methods evaluated on TESS and RAVDESS. According to the table, InCvT achieves the best performance on TESS and the second-best result on RAVDESS. The method proposed in [4] achieves the highest accuracy on the RAVDESS dataset. However, this approach relies on a computationally complex architecture that integrates several acoustic features (MFCC, Mel-spectrogram,

Table 2. Comparison of InCvT with state-of-the-art methods on TESS and RAVDESS.

Reference	Model	Acc on TESS	Acc on RAVDESS
[4]	CNN + BiLSTM	99.6%	94.8%
[5]	CNN + LSTM	89.3%	89.3%
[7]	MBEO + RF	99%	85%
[8]	CNN	99%	70%
[6]	CNN + LSTM	99%	–
[10]	MFGCN	–	85%
[9]	embeddeds + SVM	–	82%
[11]	graph-based method	–	67.5%
InCvT	Inception + CvT	99.8%	90%

RMSE, and ZCR) alongside a hybrid CNN-BiLSTM classifier. The remaining approaches report lower performance than InCvT on TESS and RAVDESS. These approaches are based on model families such as CNN, LSTM, RF, fusion graph CNN, graph-based method, and SVM architectures, as well as optimization techniques and pretrained embeddings from Wav2Vec 2.0 and HuBERT.

4.4   Grad-CAM Analysis

Figure 6 presents examples of activation maps obtained with TESS. These maps are defined as $M(k, n) = C(k, n) + G(k, n)$, where $C(k, n)$ denotes the MFCCs and $G(k, n)$ corresponds to the Grad-CAM [17] obtained from the last convolutional layer of CvT. The map $M(k, n)$ highlights the relevance of each cepstral coefficient at position (k, n), revealing the most discriminative time–frequency patterns for emotion classification. Following the interpretative framework in [18], the observed activation patterns suggest the following:

- **Anger:** Activation spans low and high cepstral coefficients, consistent with increased energy and vocal tension.
- **Neutrality:** Predominant activation in low cepstral coefficients, reflecting relative spectral stability.
- **Disgust:** Broad activation across coefficients, suggesting diverse spectral involvement.
- **Happiness and Pleasure.** Activation is concentrated in a limited set of mid-range coefficients, indicating more localized spectral emphasis
- **Fear and Sadness:** Sparse activation primarily in lower-magnitude coefficients, which may be associated with reduced vocal tension and prosodic variation.

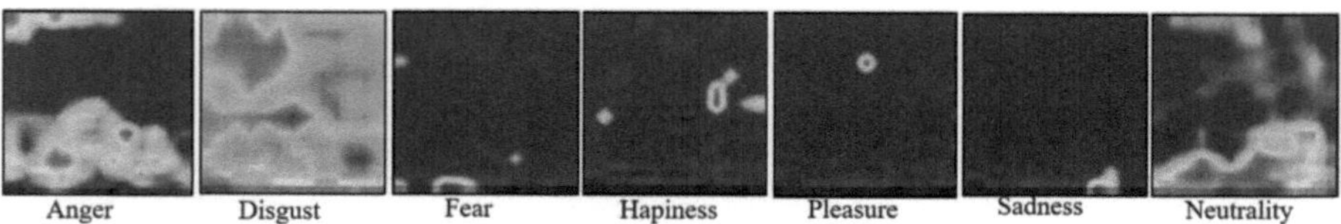

Fig. 6. Grad-CAM activation maps generated by InCvT for representative emotional classes in TESS.

5   Conclusions

This work presented InCvT, a hybrid architecture that integrates three Inception blocks with a Convolutional Vision Transformer to capture multiscale local and global representations from MFCC features for speech emotion recognition. The model was trained and evaluated on the TESS dataset, which includes 2,800 recordings from 2 speakers, and on the RAVDESS dataset, which contains speech samples from 24 speakers across 60 sentences.

Cross-validation results indicate strong generalization performance, achieving accuracies of $99.8\% \pm 0.24\%$ on TESS and $90.3\% \pm 2.6\%$ on RAVDESS. Analysis of the confusion matrices shows that most misclassifications occur between Sadness and Calm, and between Happiness and Surprise. Although performance on RAVDESS is comparatively lower due to greater speaker diversity and sentence variability, InCvT remains a lightweight architecture that achieves the highest accuracy on TESS and the second-highest on RAVDESS among the compared methods. Grad-CAM analysis suggests that InCvT learns discriminative spectral patterns that align with the characteristic properties of emotional speech. Anger and Disgust exhibit broader activation across cepstral coefficients, whereas Neutrality emphasizes lower-order coefficients, consistent with spectral stability. In contrast, Happiness, Pleasure, Sadness, and Fear show more localized cepstral activation, indicating a stronger reliance on specific spectro-temporal regions.

Overall, the proposed architecture effectively integrates local and global feature representations, providing competitive performance together with interpretability. Future work will focus on deploying InCvT in real-time SER systems to evaluate its robustness under practical and acoustically diverse conditions.

Acknowledgments. This research was funded by Tecnológico Nacional de México (TecNM) under grant 24452.26-P and supported by the agreement INAOE-2024-CECN/09.

Disclosure of Interests. The authors have no competing interests to declare that are relevant to the content of this article.

References

1. Ülgen Sönmez, Y., Varol, A.: In-depth investigation of speech emotion recognition studies from past to present – the importance of emotion recognition from speech signal for AI. Intell. Syst. Appl. **22**, art. no. 200351 (2024). https://doi.org/10.1016/j.iswa.2024.200351

2. Pichora-Fuller, M.K., Dupuis, K.: Toronto emotional speech set (TESS). Borealis Data, V1 (2020). https://doi.org/10.5683/SP2/E8H2MF

3. Livingstone, S.R., Russo, F.A.: The Ryerson audio-visual database of emotional speech and song (RAVDESS): a dynamic, multimodal set of facial and vocal expressions in North American English. PLoS ONE **13**(5), e0196391 (2018). https://doi.org/10.1371/journal.pone.0196391

4. Kundu, N.K., Kobir, S., Ahmed, M.R., Aktar, T., Roy, N.: Enhanced speech emotion recognition with efficient channel attention guided deep CNN-BiLSTM framework. arXiv preprint arXiv:2412.10011 (2024)

5. Salian, B., Narvade, O., Tambewagh, R., Bharne, S.: Speech emotion recognition using time distributed CNN and LSTM. In: Proceedings of the International Conference on Advanced Computing and Communication (ICACC), EDP Sciences, pp. 1–6 (2021). https://doi.org/10.1051/itmconf/20214003006

6. Uddin, M.A., Uddin Chowdury, M.S., Khandaker, M.U., Tamam, N., Sulieman, A.: The efficacy of deep learning-based mixed model for speech emotion recognition. Comput. Mater. Continua **74**(1), 1710–1729 (2022). https://doi.org/10.32604/cmc.2023.031177

7. Yue, L., Hu, P., Chu, S.-C., Pan, J.-S.: Multi-objective equilibrium optimizer for feature selection in high-dimensional English speech emotion recognition. Comput. Mater. Continua **78**(2), 1957–1975 (2024). https://doi.org/10.32604/cmc.2024.046962

8. Sareen, V., Seeja, K.R.: Speech emotion recognition using Mel spectrogram and convolutional neural networks (CNN). Procedia Comput. Sci. **258** (2025). https://doi.org/10.1016/j.procs.2025.04.624

9. Chakhtouna, A., Sekkate, S., Adib, A.: Unveiling embedded features in Wav2vec2 and HuBERT models for speech emotion recognition. Procedia Comput. Sci. **232**, 2560–2569 (2024). https://doi.org/10.1016/j.procs.2024.02.074

10. Qi, X., Wen, Y., Zhang, P., Huang, H.: MFGCN: multimodal fusion graph convolutional network for speech emotion recognition. Neurocomputing **611**, art. 128646 (2025). https://doi.org/10.1016/j.neucom.2024.128646

11. Gao, Y., Zhao, H., Zhang, Z.: Adaptive speech emotion representation learning based on dynamic graph. arXiv preprint arXiv:2405.03956 (2024)

12. Davis, S.B., Mermelstein, P.: Comparison of parametric representations for monosyllabic word recognition in continuously spoken sentences. IEEE Trans. Acoust. Speech Signal Process. **28**(4), 357–366 (1980). https://doi.org/10.1109/TASSP.1980.1163420

13. Goodfellow, I., Bengio, Y., Courville, A.: Deep Learning. MIT Press (2016)

14. Yusufoğlu, E., Çobankaya, U., Katip, M.: Integrating inception modules, SE Blocks, and ConvMixer for improved diagnostic feature extraction. Diagnostics **14**(24), 2836 (2024). https://doi.org/10.3390/diagnostics14242836

15. Wu, H., et al.: CvT: introducing convolutions to vision transformers. In: Proceedings of the IEEE/CVF International Conference on Computer Vision (ICCV), pp. 22–31 (2021). https://doi.org/10.48550/arXiv.2103.15808

16. Terven, J., Cordova-Esparza, D.-M., Romero-Gonzalez, J.-A., Ramirez-Pedraza, A., Chavez-Urbiola, E.A.: A comprehensive survey of loss functions and metrics in deep learning. Artif. Intell. Rev. **58**, 195 (2025). https://doi.org/10.1007/s10462-025-11198-7
17. Wang, S., Zhang, Y.: Grad-CAM: understanding AI models. Comput. Mater. Continua **76**(3), 3155–3174 (2023). https://doi.org/10.32604/cmc.2023.041419
18. Majeed, S.A., Husain, H., Salina, S.A., Idbeaa, T.F.: Mel frequency cepstral coefficients (MFCC) feature extraction enhancement in the application of speech recognition: a comparison study. J. Theor. Appl. Inf. Technol. **79**(1), 38–56 (2015). ISSN 1992-8645, E-ISSN 1817-3195

Comparative Statistical Analysis of Sentiment Models in Spanish Political Discourse on YouTube

Guillermo David Barrera Ortega[(✉)][iD], Maria Beatriz Bernabe Loranca[iD], David Pinto Avendaño[iD], and Alberto Carrillo Canán[iD]

Facultad de Ciencias de la Computación, Benemérita Universidad Autónoma de Puebla (BUAP), 72000 Puebla, Mexico
guillebarrera2@gmail.com

Abstract. The NLP literature for Spanish political discourse lacks structural benchmarks that characterise sentiment model *behaviour* independently of ground-truth annotation. This paper fills that gap with a large-scale comparison of four models—AFINN, NRC, TextBlob, and the Transformer-based BETO—applied to 819,051 YouTube comments collected from nine presidential candidates across Mexico, Venezuela, Uruguay, and Ecuador during the 2024–2025 electoral cycle. Rather than evaluating supervised classification performance, we compare polarity distributions through descriptive statistics (mean, median, standard deviation, skewness, kurtosis, neutrality bias) and quantify inter-model agreement via both Pearson and Spearman rank-correlation coefficients. Results reveal systematic, architecture-dependent divergence: lexicon-based models produce conservative, neutral-biased scores, whereas BETO yields bimodal, high-kurtosis distributions with pronounced positive-class outlier rates of 20–22%. These findings establish a reproducible structural benchmark for Spanish-language electoral NLP research.

Keywords: Sentiment Analysis · Statistical Comparison · BETO · Political Discourse · Spanish NLP · YouTube

1 Introduction

Comparative evaluation of Sentiment Analysis (SA) models in Spanish is predominantly framed as supervised classification, requiring manually annotated corpora that are scarce in electoral contexts. This framing obscures an equally important question: how do different architectures *structurally* interpret the same political text? We address this by assembling the first multi-country Spanish YouTube corpus covering nine presidential candidates (Mexico, Venezuela, Uruguay, Ecuador) and conducting a model-agnostic distributional comparison.

Original Contributions. *(i)* A 819,051-comment multi-national corpus with full engagement metadata. *(ii)* Multi-metric distributional profiling (mean,

V. G. Cruz-Sánchez et al. (Eds.): MCPR 2026, LNCS 16623, pp. 327–335, 2026.
https://doi.org/10.1007/978-3-032-28393-1_29

skewness, kurtosis, neutrality bias, outlier rates) for AFINN, NRC, TextBlob, and BETO across all candidates. *(iii)* Dual Pearson/Spearman inter-model agreement analysis, addressing the non-normality of polarity distributions—a methodological gap absent from existing Spanish NLP benchmarks.

2   Related Work

Pang and Lee [1] established the foundations of polarity classification. For Spanish, Cañete et al. [2] introduced BETO (Bidirectional Encoder Representations from Transformers in Spanish), a BERT-base model pre-trained on large Spanish corpora, which González et al. [3] confirmed outperforms multilingual baselines on Twitter emotion classification. Hipólito et al. [4] extended BETO to financial news, also demonstrating that static lexicons such as TextBlob under-estimate cultural nuances in noisy Spanish domains. Méndez et al. [5] documented the high linguistic noise of Latin-American YouTube political comments, where a small user fraction generates a disproportionate share of problematic content. None of these works provides a cross-architecture structural comparison on multi-country electoral YouTube data without ground-truth annotation.

3   Methodology

3.1   Data Acquisition and Preprocessing

Data were retrieved via the YouTube Data API v3 using a custom `YouTubeScraper` (Python). Comments, engagement metrics (likes, replies), video metadata (title, description, tags, category, views, likes, comment count), and channel metadata (country, subscribers) were collected monthly over the 12-month window preceding each election to ensure temporal homogeneity. Preprocessing applied: *LanguageTool* v6 orthographic correction, noise removal (URLs, HTML tags, duplicates, emoji-only entries), NLTK tokenisation, and lemmatisation.

3.2   Sentiment Models

Table 1 summarises the four architectures.

Lexicon Scoring. For AFINN, comment polarity is $S(c) = \sum_{i=1}^{n} v(w_i)$, where $v(w_i) \in [-5, +5]$ is the token valence (0 if absent). For NRC, emotion j is counted as $e_j(c) = \sum_{i=1}^{n} \mathbf{1}[w_i \in \mathcal{L}_j]$. Both Spanish lexicons were produced by Mendoza [6] via automatic translation of the `tidytext` English word lists, with partial manual corrections; residual translation errors are acknowledged by the source repository.

TextBlob Scoring. Polarity and subjectivity are pattern-matched averages over token-level lexicon values: $p(c) = \frac{1}{k} \sum_{i=1}^{k} p_i$, $s(c) = \frac{1}{k} \sum_{i=1}^{k} s_i$, with modifier rules (negation, intensifiers) applied.

Table 1. Model architectures compared in this study.

Model	Type	Output	Spanish adaptation
AFINN [7]	Lexicon	Integer score $\in [-5n, +5n]$	Machine-translated from `tidytext` R package; manual corrections [6]
NRC [8]	Lexicon	Binary emotion counts (8 emotions + pos/neg)	Same translation pipeline as AFINN [6]
TextBlob	Probabilistic	Polarity $p \in [-1, +1]$; Subjectivity $s \in [0, 1]$	Pre-translation to EN via `googletrans`
BETO [2]	Transformer	$[\hat{p}_{POS}, \hat{p}_{NEG}, \hat{p}_{NEU}]$	`finiteautomata/beto-sentiment -analysis`; inference-only

BETO Scoring. The [CLS] representation $\mathbf{h} \in \mathbb{R}^{768}$ is projected through a dense layer and Softmax:

$$[\hat{p}_{POS}, \hat{p}_{NEG}, \hat{p}_{NEU}] = \mathrm{softmax}(W^{\top}\mathbf{h} + \mathbf{b}), \tag{1}$$

using 12-head self-attention [9] over WordPiece embeddings (max 512 tokens, truncation enabled), batches of 500, no fine-tuning on the electoral corpus.

3.3 Statistical Analysis Protocol

For each model and candidate, we compute: mean, median, standard deviation, inter-quartile range (IQR), skewness (γ_1), excess kurtosis (γ_2), neutrality proportion, and outlier rate ($> Q_3 + 1.5 \times IQR$). Inter-model agreement is characterised by both Pearson r (linear association) and Spearman ρ_s (monotonic, non-parametric), since the heavy-tailed bimodal outputs of BETO violate normality assumptions required for r alone to be interpretable.

4 Dataset

Table 2 consolidates the corpus statistics for all nine candidates. The total of 819,051 comments spans Mexico (54.7%), Ecuador (22.5%), Venezuela (18.8%), and Uruguay (3.9%), providing substantial cross-regional coverage.

Table 2. Corpus statistics and engagement metrics by candidate.

Candidate	Country	Comments	Videos	Unique Authors	Avg. Likes/Comm.	Max Likes/Comm.	Max Views/Video
Claudia Sheinbaum	Mexico	128,501	579	76,526	6.1	4,772	1,691,487
Xóchitl Gálvez	Mexico	287,993	594	138,405	8.7	6,487	1,947,562
Jorge Álvarez Máynez	Mexico	31,924	324	24,184	4.6	3,169	2,168,460
Nicolás Maduro	Venezuela	123,184	551	85,260	4.3	2,348	1,475,321
Edmundo González	Venezuela	30,942	265	18,636	3.0	756	459 206
Daniel Noboa	Ecuador	76,290	573	35,903	4.7	3,091	710 131
Luisa González	Ecuador	107,783	573	37,861	4.5	3,116	413 674
Álvaro Delgado	Uruguay	5,318	225	3,400	4.1	240	43,260
Yamandú Orsi	Uruguay	27,116	484	10,384	4.0	931	157 698
Total		819,051	4,168				

The corpus exhibits high engagement variability characteristic of polarised electoral discourse. The primary language is Spanish, encompassing Mexican, Venezuelan, Ecuadorian, and Uruguayan regional varieties. Xóchitl Gálvez yields the highest per-comment engagement density (avg. 8.7 likes/comment, max 6,487), while Edmundo González shows the lowest (avg. 3.0 likes/comment), consistent with the asymmetric visibility dynamics of incumbent vs. opposition political actors.

5   Results and Discussion

5.1   BETO Probability Distributions

Table 3 reports BETO distributional statistics for all nine candidates.

Table 3. BETO probability distribution statistics by candidate (n = comment count per corpus).

Candidate	Prob_POS		Prob_NEG		Prob_NEU		Skew POS	Kurt POS
	Mean	*Median*	*Mean*	*Median*	*Mean*	*Median*		
Claudia Sheinbaum	0.310	0.005	0.232	0.001	0.458	0.228	0.826	−1.241
Xóchitl Gálvez Ruiz	0.124	0.001	0.394	0.015	0.481	0.371	2.310	3.532
Jorge Álvarez Máynez	0.124	0.001	0.381	0.013	0.495	0.488	2.310	3.532
Nicolás Maduro	0.144	0.002	0.413	0.042	0.443	0.194	2.049	2.385
Edmundo González U.	0.257	0.004	0.265	0.003	0.478	0.372	1.116	−0.647
Daniel Noboa	0.140	0.001	0.453	0.122	0.408	0.076	2.101	2.579
Luisa González	0.163	0.002	0.404	0.024	0.433	0.149	1.841	1.538
Álvaro Delgado	0.154	0.002	0.345	0.008	0.501	0.545	1.946	1.946
Yamandú Orsi	0.149	0.002	0.380	0.013	0.472	0.410	2.002	2.164

Across all candidates, the median Prob_POS $\ll$ mean confirms strong right-skewness in the positive channel: BETO assigns high positive probability to a small subset of comments and near-zero to the majority (bimodal distribution). Prob_NEU achieves the highest mean of all three classes (up to 0.501 for Álvaro Delgado), reflecting the model's neutral-default behaviour on ambiguous text. Daniel Noboa shows the highest Prob_NEG mean (0.453), exceeding even the Maduro corpus (0.413), consistent with Ecuador's high-conflict electoral environment. Prob_POS outlier rates range from 20.2% (Xóchitl Gálvez) to 22% (Claudia Sheinbaum), while Prob_NEG and Prob_NEU produce zero outliers under $Q_3 + 1.5 \times$ IQR—a structural asymmetry indicating that positive sentiment is a rare, high-intensity signal in this domain.

Table 4. TextBlob polarity and subjectivity statistics by candidate.

Candidate	Mean Pol.	Med. Pol.	SD Pol.	Skew Pol.	Mean Subj.	SD Subj.
Claudia Sheinbaum	0.103	0.000	0.299	0.594	0.308	0.329
Xóchitl Gálvez	0.020	0.000	0.280	0.187	0.296	0.334
Jorge Álvarez Máynez	0.032	0.000	0.278	0.352	0.300	0.330
Nicolás Maduro	0.044	0.000	0.273	0.263	0.291	0.325
Edmundo González U.	0.096	0.000	0.288	0.582	0.318	0.341
Daniel Noboa	0.021	0.000	0.295	0.210	0.320	0.341
Luisa González	0.037	0.000	0.296	0.276	0.317	0.337
Álvaro Delgado	0.042	0.000	0.279	0.307	0.310	0.323
Yamandú Orsi	0.037	0.000	0.298	0.365	0.327	0.331

5.2   TextBlob Polarity and Subjectivity

All candidates show median polarity = 0 with means slightly positive (range 0.020–0.103). TextBlob's SD (≈ 0.28–0.30) is substantially lower than BETO's (≈ 0.41–0.47), confirming that the translation-plus-lexicon pipeline generates conservative, compressed polarity estimates. Claudia Sheinbaum and Edmundo González show the highest means and skewness (0.103/0.594 and 0.096/0.582 respectively), suggesting a greater fraction of explicitly positive comments in their corpora. Subjectivity is stable across candidates (0.291–0.327), indicating consistent opinion-register usage regardless of political context

5.3   NRC Emotion Distribution

Table 5 shows NRC counts for the Maduro corpus, used here as a representative high-volume, high-polarisation case.

Table 5. NRC aggregate emotion counts—Nicolás Maduro corpus (123,184 comments).

Emotion	Count	Emotion	Count
Positive	204,251	Sadness	82,491
Negative	193,783	Disgust	72,381
Trust	134,303	Joy	72,037
Fear	120,098	Anticipation	71,812
Anger	86,377	Surprise	41,539

The near-parity between Positive (204,251) and Negative (193,783) totals reflects a polarised corpus where pro-government and opposition voices coexist. Trust (>134K) and Fear (>120K) dominate the secondary emotion layer, consistent with the trust-vs.-fear rhetorical frame typical of institutional-crisis discourse. The AFINN lexicon matched $\approx$1,200 distinct Spanish tokens across $\approx$120K comments; the most frequent negative terms include *guerra* (34,920), *corrupción* (27,073), and *fraude* (25,849), while positive terms are anchored in *libertad* (16,807), *dios* (16,209), and *gracias* (15,952). The low token-match ratio confirms known coverage limitations of machine-translated lexicons for colloquial political Spanish [5].

5.4   Polarity vs Subjectivity

Figure 1 shows the TextBlob polarity-subjectivity scatter for the Claudia Sheinbaum corpus. The high concentration of subjective ($s > 0.5$) near-zero-polarity comments is consistent with opinion-based political commentary expressed in a subjective register without strongly valenced lexical items—a pattern reproduced across all nine candidate sub-corpora.

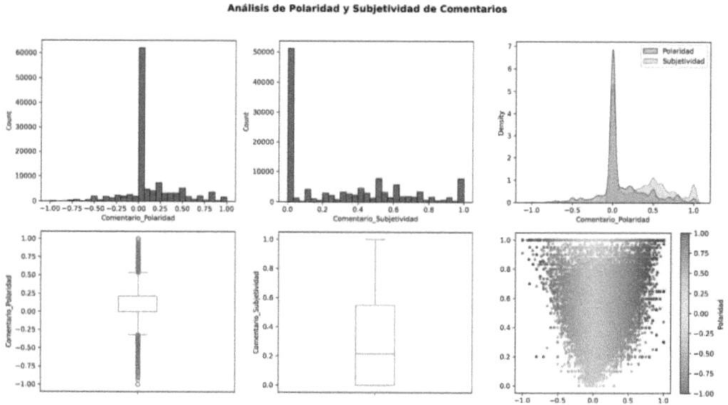

Fig. 1. TextBlob Polarity vs. Subjectivity—Claudia Sheinbaum corpus.

5.5   Inter-model Correlation Analysis

The heavy-tailed, bimodal distributions in Tables 3 and 4 invalidate normality for Pearson r alone. Table 6 summarises both coefficients for the principal model pairs (Claudia Sheinbaum corpus, $n = 128{,}501$).

Table 6. Pearson (r) and Spearman (ρ_s) inter-model correlation (Claudia Sheinbaum corpus; comparable patterns hold across all candidates).

Model A	Model B	Pearson r	Spearman ρ_s
AFINN	NRC polarity	>0.75	>0.75
TextBlob	AFINN	0.35–0.55	lower than r
TextBlob	NRC polarity	0.35–0.55	lower than r
BETO Prob_NEG	AFINN	<0.30	<0.20
BETO Prob_NEG	NRC polarity	<0.30	<0.20
TextBlob pol.	BETO (POS−NEG)	≈0.45	≈0.00

Three patterns emerge. First, AFINN and NRC are highly concordant ($r, \rho_s > 0.75$) across all candidates, expected given their shared translation pipeline [6]. Second, TextBlob agrees moderately with both lexicons on r but shows lower ρ_s, indicating that the EN-translation and modifier rules introduce systematic mid-range reorderings. Third, and most critically, BETO diverges strongly from all lexicon-based models: $r < 0.3$ and $\rho_s < 0.2$ for the BETO–lexicon pairs. The TextBlob–BETO pair ($r \approx 0.45$ but $\rho_s \approx 0$) exposes a case where linear correlation—driven by extreme-sentiment comments—would over-state agreement, validating the need for Spearman alongside Pearson in non-normal sentiment distributions.

6   Qualitative Error Analysis and Model Discrepancies

To address the specific challenges of political discourse in Spanish, such as sarcasm and regionalisms, we conducted a qualitative review of comments where the models showed significant divergence. Table 7 presents a selection of representative cases from the electoral corpus, contrasting the lexicon-based scores (Polarity and Subjectivity) with the contextual classification of the Transformer-based model (BETO).

Table 7. Qualitative analysis of model discrepancies and sentiment metrics.

Comment Fragment	Pol.	Subj.	AFINN	BETO	Linguistic Insight
"¡Viva el frente amplio, delgado segundón!"	0.50	0.45	Positive	**Negative**	Sarcasm: Lexicon is biased by the anchor word "viva"
"Buen artículo no necesita propaganda..."	0.30	0.35	Positive	**Negative**	Irony: "Buen" (Good) is used to criticize disinformation
"Confiamos en el nuevo capitán..."	0.65	0.90	Positive	**Positive**	Agreement in high-subjectivity explicit support
"Delgado es más de lo mismo..."	−0.20	0.50	Negative	**Negative**	BETO captures idiomatic political rejection patterns

The analysis reveals that lexicon-based models (AFINN/NRC) often suffer from "anchor word bias", where a single positive token like *"viva"* or *"buen"* offsets the negative intent of the rest of the sentence. Interestingly, inter-model agreement tends to increase in comments with high subjectivity scores (> 0.80), whereas discrepancies are most frequent in moderately subjective comments (0.30–0.60) where political irony is prevalent. These findings validate the necessity of using Transformer architectures like BETO to capture the nuanced "toxic" or "sarcastic" polarity that simple dictionaries fail to decode.

7   Conclusions

This study provides a structural benchmark for sentiment analysis in Spanish political discourse, analyzing a massive corpus of 819,051 comments. Our results demonstrate that while lexicon-based models offer a computationally efficient baseline, they exhibit a significant 'neutrality bias' and are highly susceptible to linguistic noise, such as sarcasm and irony. The qualitative error analysis further confirms that Transformer-based models, specifically BETO, outperform traditional methods by identifying contextual nuances that dictionaries miss. The statistical comparison showed that BETO provides a more polarized and potentially more accurate representation of the electoral climate. We observed that model discrepancies are closely tied to subjectivity levels: high subjectivity leads to greater agreement, while moderate subjectivity often hides ironical political attacks that only contextual models can detect. These findings suggest that for real-time electoral monitoring, a hybrid approach—combining the speed of lexicons for initial filtering with the contextual depth of BETO for nuanced discourse—is the most robust strategy. Future work will expand this benchmark to include more candidates and real-time monitoring.

References

1. Pang, B., Lee, L.: Opinion mining and sentiment analysis. Found. Trends Inf. Retr. **2**(1–2), 1–135 (2008)
2. Cañete, J., Chaperon, G., Fuentes, R., Pérez, J.: Spanish pre-trained BERT model and evaluation data. In: PMC Workshop on Practical ML for Developing Countries (2020)
3. González, J.A., et al.: Applying sentiment analysis on Spanish tweets using BETO. In: CEUR Workshop Proceedings 2943 (2022)
4. Hipólito, J., et al.: Evaluation of transformer models for financial targeted sentiment analysis on news and tweets in Spanish. PeerJ Comput. Sci. **9**, e1377 (2023)
5. Méndez, A., et al.: Problematic content in Spanish-language comments on YouTube videos about Venezuela's crisis. J. Commun. Disord. **15**(2), 45–67 (2025)
6. Mendoza Vega, J.B.: Traducción al español de los léxicos Afinn y NRC para uso en Procesamiento Natural del Lenguaje (2019). https://github.com/jboscomendoza/lexicos-nrc-afinn

7. Nielsen, F.Å.: A new ANEW: evaluation of a word list for sentiment analysis in microblogs. In: Proceedings of the ESWC Workshop on Making Sense of Microposts, pp. 93–98 (2011)
8. Mohammad, S.M., Turney, P.D.: Crowdsourcing a word–emotion association lexicon. Comput. Intell. **29**(3), 436–465 (2013)
9. Vaswani, A., et al.: Attention is all you need. In: Advances in Neural Information Processing Systems (NeurIPS), vol. 30 (2017)

Medical Applications of Pattern Recognition

Machine Learning Algorithms for Identifying Attention-Deficit/Hyperactivity Disorder Processing Electroencephalographic Signals

Erika Altair Castro-Verazas[1]([✉]) [iD], Saúl Brandon Lima-Portillo[2] [iD], Delia Irazú Hernández-Farías[1] [iD], and Carlos Alberto Reyes-García[1] [iD]

[1] Instituto Nacional de Astrofísica Óptica y Electrónica (INAOE), Puebla, Mexico
erikacv@inaoe.mx, {dirazuhf,kargaxxi}@inaoep.mx
[2] Benemérita Universidad Autónoma de Puebla (BUAP), Puebla, Mexico

Abstract. Attention-Deficit/Hyperactivity Disorder (ADHD) is a neuro-developmental condition characterized by impairments in attention regulation and executive functioning. Electroencephalography (EEG) has been widely investigated as a non-invasive technique to identify neurophysiological alterations associated with ADHD; however, classification performance strongly depends on the cognitive context in which EEG signals are acquired. This study investigates task-dependent EEG patterns for ADHD classification in a Mexican university population using a supervised learning framework. EEG recordings were obtained from 29 adult participants (11 diagnosed with ADHD and 18 control subjects) while performing some activities targeting different cognitive domains: the *Stroop test*, *Digit Span Test* (forward and backward conditions), *Towers of Hanoi*, and *Wisconsin Card Sorting Test*. Spectral features were computed for distinct cortical regions based on 14 EEG channels, including relative power in the *Delta*, *Theta*, *Alpha*, *Beta*, and *Gamma* bands, as well as the *Theta/Beta Ratio* using the Welch's method. Results demonstrate a clear task and region-dependent discriminative behavior. Top-performing models achieved moderate but consistent performance across tasks. Distinct cortical regions emerged as dominant depending on task demands, supporting the hypothesis that EEG discriminability in ADHD is context sensitive rather than globally uniform. These findings highlight the importance of cognitive task design and regional spectral representations for EEG-based ADHD classification and provide a structured framework for future multimodal and larger cohort studies.

Keywords: Attention-Deficit/Hyperactivity Disorder (ADHD) · Electroencephalography (EEG) · Executive functions · Supervised learning · Cortical activity

V. G. Cruz-Sánchez et al. (Eds.): MCPR 2026, LNCS 16623, pp. 339–348, 2026.
https://doi.org/10.1007/978-3-032-28393-1_30

1   Introduction

Attention-Deficit/Hyperactivity Disorder (ADHD) is one of the most prevalent neurodevelopmental disorders affecting both children and adults and is commonly associated with impairments in sustained attention, behavioral inhibition, and executive control. Theoretical models emphasize deficits in inhibitory regulation and executive functioning as central mechanisms underlying ADHD [3]. Neurophysiological studies using electroencephalography (EEG) have reported atypical patterns of brain activity in individuals with ADHD, particularly in frequency-domain characteristics. However, these findings remain highly variable across studies, reflecting both the heterogeneous nature of the disorder and the influence of cognitive context on neural dynamics [2,4].

Previous research suggests that EEG abnormalities in ADHD may depend on task engagement rather than representing stable biomarkers. Differences in cortical activity have been reported across tasks, with region-specific alterations particularly involving frontal and parietal networks [12,14]. Despite this, many EEG studies rely on global feature aggregation or channel averaging, which reduces spatial interpretability and limits the identification of cortical regions contributing to observed differences [2]. Considering that ADHD involves dysfunction across distributed neural systems, regional EEG analysis provides a useful framework for linking spectral alterations to functional brain networks.

Machine learning approaches applied to EEG signals have shown promising results for ADHD classification using spectral features [1]. Nevertheless, many existing studies rely on single-task paradigms or lack rigorous validation strategies, which limits generalization and clinical interpretability [12]. These limitations motivate analytical frameworks that integrate task-based evaluation together with regional EEG analysis.

From a spectral perspective, ADHD has often been associated with increased theta activity and elevated Theta/Beta Ratio (TBR), as well as reductions in higher frequency bands related to attentional and executive processing. Reductions in *Beta* activity have also been associated with deficits in attentional control and executive processing, while *Alpha*-band abnormalities have been linked to atypical inhibitory and attentional mechanisms. Investigating these neurophysiological patterns in Mexican populations is particularly relevant due to the reported prevalence of ADHD symptoms in university students. According to [16], ADHD symptoms have a prevalence of approximately 16.2% among Mexican college students, highlighting the potential impact of attentional disorders in higher education contexts.

In this work, spectral EEG features extracted from multiple cortical regions are analyzed using supervised machine learning techniques to identify neural patterns associated with ADHD. The proposed framework evaluates EEG responses across several cognitive paradigms in order to investigate how discriminative neural patterns vary depending on task demands and brain regions. The rest of the document is organized as follows. Section 2 describes the participants, cognitive tasks, and EEG acquisition procedure. Section 3 presents the machine learning framework used for ADHD classification. Section 4 reports the obtained results, while Sect. 5 discusses the main findings. Finally, Sect. 6 summarizes the conclusions and outlines directions for future work.

2   Methods

We used a dataset[1] comprising multiple physiological modalities, including electroencephalography, galvanic skin response, heart rate, and eye tracking, to investigate ADHD in the Mexican population. The dataset is composed of 59 Mexican college and graduate students.

2.1   Participants

Participants were screened using the *Adult ADHD Self-Report Scale (ASRS)* [9] to evaluate the presence of symptoms related to ADHD. Individuals exhibiting elevated ASRS scores without a prior clinical diagnosis were excluded to avoid potential label ambiguity and ensure a well-defined learning scenario. Following this criterion, the final analyzed sub-sample comprises 29 participants of which 11 had a documented clinical diagnosis of ADHD (7 women and 4 men), while the remaining 18 formed the *control group* (13 men and 5 women). The mean age of the participants was 28.46 years ($SD = 5.66$). Inclusion criteria comprised adults aged 18 to 50 years who enrolled in higher education programs. Exclusion criteria included neurological disorders, severe psychiatric conditions, sensory impairments, and motor limitations that could interfere with task performance or physiological recordings. All participants provided informed written consent before participation. Participants who underwent methylphenidate treatment were instructed to stop the medication at least 24 hours before the experimental session to minimize possible pharmacological effects on EEG activity.

2.2   Cognitive Tasks for Data Collection

The experimental protocol included a set of standardized cognitive tasks widely used in the assessment of attentional and executive functioning in ADHD. These tasks were presented in the following order:

1. *Stroop Test* assessing inhibitory control through ink color naming of incongruent words.
2. *Digit Span Forward (DSF)* requiring forward repetition of progressively longer digit sequences to evaluate attention and working memory.
3. *Digit Span Backward (DSB)* requiring backward repetition of progressively longer digit sequences to evaluate attention and working memory.

---

[1] The EEG dataset collected in this study is expected to be publicly released once the necessary data preparation and institutional procedures have been completed. In the meantime, the anonymized dataset can be shared with researchers for academic purposes upon reasonable request to the corresponding author, with appropriate acknowledgment of the dataset source.

4. *Towers of Hanoi (ToH)* involving rule-based disc transfer to measure planning and executive control.
5. *Wisconsin Card Sorting Test (WCST)*, in which participants inferred and adapted to changing sorting rules, assessing cognitive flexibility.

All tasks were administered in separate blocks, with short rest intervals between them to minimize fatigue and maintain physiological stability.

2.3   EEG Signal Preprocessing and Feature Extraction

Although several signals were recorded during the experimental sessions for developing the dataset we used, the analyses presented in this study focus exclusively on electroencephalography acquired using the *Emotiv EPOC+*, a wireless 14-channel headset. EEG data were processed offline using the EEGLAB toolbox implemented in MATLAB[2] Continuous EEG recordings were downsampled from 256 to 128 Hz and band-pass filtered between 0.5 and 50 Hz. A 60 Hz notch filter was applied to attenuate power line interference. Artifact removal was performed using Independent Component Analysis. Components associated with ocular activity, muscle artifacts, and noise were identified using automated criteria. Event markers corresponding to each cognitive task were integrated into the EEG data to enable task-specific segmentation during subsequent analysis.

EEG features were extracted from 14 scalp channels using 30 second signal segments corresponding to the five cognitive tasks aforementioned. To characterize the spectral content, Power Spectral Density (PSD) was estimated using Welch's method, implemented with 2 second Hamming windows and 50% overlap. Although a 30 s EEG segment represented each cognitive task, Welch's method internally divides this segment into multiple windows of 2 s, computes the spectrum of each window, and averages them to obtain a low variance and robust estimate of the PSD for the entire cognitive condition. From the resulting PSD, total power in the 0.5–50 Hz range was computed, and relative band power was then derived for five canonical frequency bands: *Delta* (0.5–4 Hz), *Theta* (4–8 Hz), *Alpha* (8–13 Hz), *Beta* (13–30 Hz), and *Gamma* (30–50 Hz). In addition, the *Theta/Beta Ratio* was computed to characterize attentional regulation. To reduce inter-subject variability, all numerical features were normalized using z-score normalization before classification. In summary, each subject is characterized by an 84 dimensional feature vector derived from the spectral EEG features.

2.4   Effect Size Analysis of Spectral EEG Features

An effect size analysis was performed before classification to quantify the magnitude and direction of spectral differences between the *ADHD* and *control* groups. Group separability was assessed using *Cohen's d*, a standardized effect size measure widely recommended for quantifying mean differences independent of sample size [6]. While machine learning models provide predictive performance estimates, effect size analysis offers complementary information about the strength

---

[2] (Delorme & Makeig, 2004, http://sccn.ucsd.edu/eeglab).

and direction of neurophysiological differences between groups. This approach allows the interpretation of EEG spectral alterations associated with ADHD beyond purely predictive modeling.

This approach is particularly appropriate for EEG studies, where statistically significant differences may not necessarily reflect physiologically meaningful effects. *Cohen's d* values were calculated from spectral features of the EEG to characterize the strength of band-specific alterations.

The features were averaged over electrodes within each *cortical region* for every subject according to the EEG scalp location. The defined regions were: *frontal* (*AF*3, *AF*4, *F*3, *F*4, *F*7, *F*8), *fronto-central* (*FC*5 and *FC*6), *temporal* (*T*7 and *T*8), *parietal* (*P*7 and *P*8), and *occipital* (*O*1 and *O*2).

The resulting regional measures per subject were subsequently averaged between participants within each group to obtain group estimates for each frequency band and cortical region.

3   Machine Learning for Identifying ADHD

Supervised learning analysis was formulated as a binary classification problem aimed at discriminating between healthy control participants and individuals clinically diagnosed with ADHD. To examine the spatial contribution of EEG activity, electrodes were grouped into cortical regions following the same regional configuration defined in Sect. 2.4. Electrodes were assigned to *frontal*, *fronto-central*, *temporal*, *parietal*, and *occipital* regions. This regional strategy enabled the assessment of spatially localized EEG patterns while preserving interpretability. Five supervised classification algorithms were evaluated: Support Vector Machine with linear kernel (SVM), Logistic Regression (LR), Decision Tree (DT), Random Forest (RF), and Gaussian Naive Bayes (NB). The evaluation was performed using a participant-independent cross-validation strategy, ensuring that data from the same participant were not shared between training and testing sets. Two validation schemes were explored, including 5-fold cross-validation and leave-one-out cross-validation, to assess robustness and stability. Classification models were trained independently for each cognitive task and each regional feature subset, resulting in a comprehensive evaluation across tasks, brain regions, and classifier types. The final classification performance was evaluated using Accuracy (Acc), F1-score (F1), True Positive Rate (TPR), True Negative Rate (TNR), and the Area Under the Receiver Operating Characteristic Curve (ROC-AUC). Overall, the proposed supervised learning framework enabled a systematic investigation of EEG patterns associated with ADHD across tasks and brain regions, providing insight into the neurophysiological variability underlying different cognitive tasks.

4   Results

To characterize spectral differences between the ADHD group and the control group, an effect analysis was conducted using Cohen's d, computed from EEG spectral features averaged across electrodes within each cortical region for each subject and cognitive task.

In Fig. 1, positive values (warm tones) point out higher spectral power in the ADHD group, whereas negative values (cold tones) indicate higher power in the controls. Cohens'd values are visualized using band-by-region heatmaps, facilitating comparisons over tasks and enabling the identification of consistent spectral patterns before the application of machine learning methods.

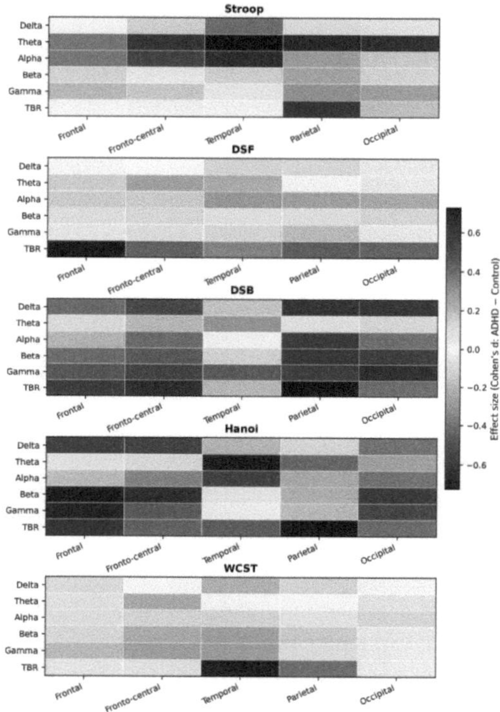

Fig. 1. Effect size maps of task-dependent spectral differences between ADHD and control groups.

Across tasks, *Theta* activity tends to show positive effect sizes, indicating higher power in the ADHD group, particularly during *Stroop* and *Tower of Hanoi*, with effects extending beyond *frontal* regions into *temporal, parietal,* and *occipital* areas. In contrast, the *Beta* and *Gamma* bands frequently displayed negative effect sizes, especially during *Tower of Hanoi* and *Digit Span Backward,* reflecting lower high-frequency activity in the ADHD group in *frontal, fronto-central, parietal,* and *occipital* regions.

TBR emerged as one of the most robust features, showing widespread positive effect sizes across multiple regions in *Stroop, Tower of Hanoi, Digit Span Forward,* and *Digit Span Backward.* In particular, an inversion of this pattern

Table 1. Classification performance obtained for each cognitive task using 5-fold cross-validation. Abbreviations: Stroop = Stroop Test; DSF = Digit Span Forward; DSB = Digit Span Backward; ToH = Towers of Hanoi; WCST = Wisconsin Card Sorting Test.

Task	Region	Model	Acc	F1	AUROC	TPR	TNR
Stroop	Temp	SVM	0.69 ± 0.21	0.58 ± 0.35	0.51 ± 0.39	0.63 ± 0.42	0.73 ± 0.18
DSB	Parietal	NB	0.67 ± 0.20	0.68 ± 0.22	0.75 ± 0.18	0.90 ± 0.22	0.52 ± 0.29
DSF	Frontal	LR	0.75 ± 0.11	0.56 ± 0.34	0.72 ± 0.16	0.60 ± 0.42	0.82 ± 0.17
ToH	Fronto-central	SVM	0.69 ± 0.15	0.61 ± 0.13	0.39 ± 0.28	0.63 ± 0.22	0.70 ± 0.24
WCST	Fronto-central	RF	0.72 ± 0.14	0.58 ± 0.12	0.78 ± 0.22	0.50	0.85 ± 0.22

was observed in the *temporal* (and partially *parietal*) regions during *WCST*, where TBR exhibited negative effect sizes, indicating higher values in the control group. Overall, the effect size maps demonstrate that spectral differences between groups are not uniform across tasks or brain regions but instead become more pronounced and spatially extended under increased cognitive demands.

Table 1 summarizes the best-performing region model combination obtained for each cognitive task. Classification performance was first evaluated using 5-fold cross-validation and subsequently validated under the more stringent leave-one-out scheme to assess generalization across subjects. The highest accuracy was observed during the *Digit Span Forward* task, where *frontal* features combined with Logistic Regression achieved an accuracy of 0.75. *Parietal* features provided the best performance for *Digit Span Backward* (accuracy of 0.67). Notably, this task exhibited a markedly high true positive rate (TPR = 0.90), indicating strong sensitivity for detecting ADHD despite moderate overall accuracy. *Temporal* features yielded competitive discrimination during *Stroop* (accuracy of 0.69). While *fronto-central* regions showed consistent performance on executive tasks, achieving comparable accuracies in the *Tower of Hanoi* and *WCST* (accuracies of 0.69 and 0.72, respectively).

Under LOOCV (see Table 2), classification performance showed increased variability, reflecting the inherent differences between subjects in EEG patterns. Nevertheless, consistent associations between task regions were preserved, and the *parietal, frontal, central,* and *temporal* regions remained dominant depending on the demands of the task. Accuracy ranged from 0.66 to 0.76, and linear classifiers, particularly SVM, exhibited greater robustness. For each task, the results correspond to the best-performing combination of brain region and model and are reported as mean $\pm$ standard deviation across subjects.

5   Discussion

The main contribution of this study is the systematic evaluation of EEG based ADHD classification across multiple cognitive paradigms using a subject wise learning framework. Rather than identifying a single optimal classifier, the results indicate that discriminative EEG patterns depend on the cognitive task

Table 2. Classification performance obtained using Leave-One-Out-Cross-Validation (LOOCV) for each cognitive task.

Task	Region	Model	Acc	F1	TPR	TNR
Stroop	Temporal	SVM	0.66 ± 0.45	0.24 ± 0.44	0.64 ± 0.51	0.78 ± 0.43
DSB	Frontal	SVM	0.69 ± 0.47	0.24 ± 0.44	0.64 ± 0.51	0.72 ± 0.46
DSB	Parietal	DT	0.66 ± 0.48	0.21 ± 0.41	0.55 ± 0.52	0.72 ± 0.46
ToH	Fronto-central	SVM	0.76 ± 0.44	0.28 ± 0.46	0.73 ± 0.47	0.78 ± 0.43
WCST	Fronto-central	RF	0.71 ± 0.46	0.18 ± 0.39	0.50 ± 0.53	0.83 ± 0.38

and on the brain regions involved. Working memory paradigms, particularly the *Digit Span* tasks, produced clearer regional patterns and slightly higher classification performance than other tasks, whereas paradigms that emphasize cognitive flexibility, such as the *WCST*, showed more moderate discriminative capability. These tendencies suggest that neural alterations associated with ADHD may become more detectable when cognitive processes such as sustained attention and working memory are strongly engaged.

The larger standard deviations observed under the LOOCV scheme reflect the high variability across subjects that is characteristic of EEG signals. Since LOOCV evaluates generalization to a single unseen subject at each iteration, performance becomes more sensitive to individual neurophysiological differences and task strategies. This behavior highlights the rigor of subject wise validation but also suggests that the relatively small cohort size of 29 participants may influence performance estimates. Future studies including larger participant samples would help stabilize the patterns observed in this work.

The regional patterns identified across tasks are consistent with known neurocognitive mechanisms. Parietal predominance during *DSB* aligns with the role of the inferior parietal lobule in phonological and semantic processing, while frontal involvement during *DSF* reflects the contribution of frontal regions to executive functions and working memory [5, 13]. Temporal activity during the *Stroop* task may be related to the interaction between language comprehension and production systems, whereas the predominance of pre-central regions in the *Tower of Hanoi* and *WCST* tasks is consistent with executive and motor planning processes [7, 15].

Model comparison further suggests that the discriminative information captured by the extracted EEG descriptors is mainly reflected in broad spectral shifts rather than in complex nonlinear interactions. Because the features represent average spectral activity computed over fixed time windows, linear models showed more stable performance across tasks and validation schemes. In contrast, nonlinear or ensemble approaches exhibited greater variability, possibly due to their sensitivity to differences between subjects when the dataset is relatively small.

These findings are consistent with previous studies that reported moderate to high classification performance in EEG based ADHD detection. For example,

[11] achieved approximately 81% accuracy using mismatch negativity responses obtained during an auditory oddball paradigm together with a linear support vector machine classifier. Similarly, [8] reported about 88% accuracy using spectral EEG representations extracted during the Eriksen Flanker Task and convolutional neural networks. Studies based on resting state EEG have also explored spectral biomarkers. For instance, [10] showed that the theta beta ratio did not reliably discriminate ADHD from control groups, whereas broader spectral power measures presented modest predictive capability.

In contrast, the present study analyzes EEG responses obtained during multiple cognitive paradigms. The results suggest that the discriminative capability of EEG features may depend on the experimental paradigm, since neural patterns associated with ADHD vary according to the cognitive demands of the task and the cortical regions involved.

6   Conclusion

This study presented a subject wise supervised learning framework for analyzing EEG based ADHD classification across multiple cognitive tasks. The results indicate that evaluating EEG signals during cognitively demanding conditions is important for revealing neural patterns associated with ADHD. The analysis also highlights the relevance of regional EEG evaluation and rigorous validation strategies for improving the reliability of EEG based ADHD assessment.

Effect size analysis revealed consistent spectral tendencies, including increased Theta activity and elevated Theta Beta ratio in the ADHD group, together with reductions in higher frequency bands. These differences were not spatially uniform, which reinforces the importance of regional EEG analysis for capturing meaningful neural variability.

From a modeling perspective, linear classifiers exhibited greater stability across validation schemes. This observation suggests that the discriminative information contained in the analyzed EEG descriptors is mainly reflected in broad spectral shifts rather than in complex nonlinear interactions.

Future work should consider larger participant samples in order to improve the robustness of the findings. Additionally, exploring richer EEG representations such as time frequency features, functional connectivity measures, or nonlinear descriptors may reveal complementary discriminative information. Finally, integrating EEG with additional physiological signals such as GSR and heart rate represents a promising direction for developing multimodal approaches for ADHD assessment.

Acknowledgments. This work was supported by SECIHTI. The authors thank the participants who took part in the experimental sessions and the personnel who contributed to the acquisition of the physiological recordings. The authors also acknowledge the support provided by INAOE for facilitating the dissemination of the study and participant recruitment.

Disclosure of Interests. The authors have no competing interests to declare.

References

1. Al Zoubi, O., Mayeli, A., Tsuchiya, N.: EEG-based classification of attention-deficit/hyperactivity disorder using spectral features and machine learning. Biomed. Signal Process. Control **45**, 132–142 (2018). https://doi.org/10.1016/j.bspc.2018.05.015
2. Banaschewski, T., Brandeis, D.: Annotation: what electrical brain activity tells us about attention-deficit/hyperactivity disorder. J. Child Psychol. Psychiatry **48**(9), 846–859 (2007)
3. Barkley, R.A.: Behavioral inhibition, sustained attention, and executive functions: constructing a unifying theory of ADHD. Psychol. Bull. **121**(1), 65–94 (1997)
4. Barry, R.J., Clarke, A.R., Johnstone, S.J.: A review of electrophysiology in attention-deficit/hyperactivity disorder: I. Qualitative and quantitative electroencephalography. Clin. Neurophysiol. **114**(2), 171–183 (2003)
5. Basharpoor, S., Heidari, F., Molavi, P.: EEG coherence in theta, alpha, and beta bands in frontal regions and executive functions. Appl. Neuropsychol. Adult **28**(3), 310–317 (2019). https://doi.org/10.1080/23279095.2019.1632860
6. Cohen, J.: Statistical Power Analysis for the Behavioral Sciences, 2nd edn. Lawrence Erlbaum Associates, Hillsdale (1988)
7. D'Alessandro, M., Radev, S., Voss, A.: A Bayesian brain model of adaptive behavior: an application to the wisconsin card sorting task. PeerJ **8**, e10316 (2020). https://doi.org/10.7717/peerj.10316
8. Dubreuil-Vall, L., Ruffini, G., Camprodon, J.A.: Deep learning convolutional neural networks discriminate adult ADHD from healthy individuals on the basis of event related spectral eeg. Front. Neurosci. **14**, 251 (2020). https://doi.org/10.3389/fnins.2020.00251
9. Kessler, R.C., Adler, L., Ames, M.: The world health organization adult ADHD self-report scale (ASRS): a short screening scale for use in the general population. Psychol. Med. **35**(2), 245–256 (2005)
10. Kiiski, H., et al.: EEG spectral power, but not theta/beta ratio, is a neuromarker for adult ADHD. Eur. J. Neurosci. **51**, 2095–2109 (2020). https://doi.org/10.1111/ejn.14645
11. Kim, S., et al.: Machine learning based diagnosis of drug naive adult patients with ADHD using mismatch negativity. Transl. Psychiatry **11**, 484 (2021)
12. Lenartowicz, A., Loo, S.K.: Use of EEG to diagnose ADHD. Curr. Psychiatry Rep. **16**(11), 498 (2014)
13. Lin, Y., Dadario, N., Hormovas, J.: Anatomy and white matter connections of the superior parietal lobule. Oper. Neurosurg. **21**(3), E199–E214 (2021)
14. Loo, S.K., et al.: Cortical activity patterns in attention-deficit/hyperactivity disorder during arousal, activation and sustained attention. Neuropsychologia **47**(10), 2114–2122 (2009). https://doi.org/10.1016/j.neuropsychologia.2009.04.013
15. Mitani, K., Rathnayake, N., Rathnayake, U.: Brain activity associated with the planning process during the long-time learning of the tower of Hanoi task: a pilot study. Sensors **22**(21), 8283 (2022). https://doi.org/10.3390/s22218283
16. Yáñez Téllez, M.G., Villaseñor Valadez, V.D., Prieto Corona, B., Seubert Ravelo, A.N.: Prevalence of attention deficit/hyperactivity disorder in Mexican university students. Archivos Neurociencias **26**(3), 10–16 (2021)

Graph-Based Modeling of Disfluent Speech for Alzheimer's Detection

Carlos A. Olachea-Hernández[1,2]([⊠]), Luis Villaseñor-Pineda[1], Manuel Montes-y-Gómez[1], and Fernando J. Martínez-Santiago[2]

[1] Instituto Nacional de Astrofísica, Óptica y Electrónica, Cholula, Mexico
ca_olachea@inaoep.mx
[2] Universidad de Jaén, Jaén, Spain

Abstract. Alzheimer's disease (AD) affects speech, producing disfluencies that can serve as early, non-invasive biomarkers of cognitive decline. This work proposes a graph-based approach that models impaired speech as token-level co-occurrence graphs enriched with special nodes capturing filled pauses, repetitions, and self-corrections. Transcripts are obtained automatically, encoded with fine-tuned BERT embeddings, and transformed into graphs that explicitly highlight disfluent patterns. Experiments on the ADReSSo 2021 dataset demonstrate that GNN models outperform a fine-tuned BERT as well as other unimodal baselines, with a GCN achieving the best performance. Explainability analysis using Integrated Gradients confirms that the model successfully leverages disfluent nodes and specific lexical patterns for classification, allowing us to conclude that explicitly encoding local disfluency structures within graph representations provides a more effective and interpretable approach for AD detection than using sequential models.

Keywords: GNN · Alzheimer's Disease · Explainability

1 Introduction

Alzheimer's disease is a major global public health challenge, affecting about 55 million people and expected to nearly triple by 2050 [20]. As the most common dementia, it involves progressive neurodegeneration, with symptoms like cognitive decline and memory loss. With no current cure, early detection is vital for interventions that may slow progression and enhance quality of life. One opportunity for improving its detection arises from the impact of Alzheimer's disease on speech production, leading to *disfluencies* such as filled pauses, repetitions, word-finding difficulties, and incomplete sentences, which serve as observable markers of underlying cognitive strain [6]. Natural language processing (NLP) techniques can transform these disfluency observations into measurable data, providing an early and non-invasive method to identify cognitive decline, in contrast to costly and invasive traditional approaches such as MRI, PET, fluid biomarkers, and neuropsychological tests [14].

V. G. Cruz-Sánchez et al. (Eds.): MCPR 2026, LNCS 16623, pp. 349–358, 2026.
https://doi.org/10.1007/978-3-032-28393-1_31

However, capturing language impairments at a preclinical stage poses challenges, as vocabulary degradation and semantic formulation of utterances are just beginning to change with respect to those from the cognitively healthy population. These changes must be analyzed within the linguistic context in which they arise; that is, it is not enough to focus solely on quantifying the different disfluencies that may appear in speech. In this regard, pretrained transformer-based models can capture these linguistic context thanks to their global attention mechanism, which allows them to weight relevant utterances with disfluencies; however, this same attention might not be the most efficient way to attend to these disfluent parts, given that attention is split evenly from one token to the rest by design, diluting the focus on impaired speech patterns. To address this issue, we propose not to consider the global speech context, but rather to focus on analyzing the context surrounding the disfluencies, which will allow us to highlight some more specific patterns about them.

Recently, Graph neural networks (GNNs) have emerged as an approach to AD detection from text, motivated by the hypothesis that representing language as graphs could capture structural, syntactic, and semantic relationships beyond those captured by sequential models. Unlike RNNs and Transformers, which process text as token sequences, GNNs encode documents as graphs, where nodes represent linguistic units (words, phrases, or documents) and edges represent relationships (co-occurrence, syntactic dependencies, or semantic similarity), enabling explicit modeling of linguistic structure. In this paper, we investigate the potential benefits of explicitly modeling impaired speech within graph representations for use in GNNs, aiming to enhance their focus on disfluent segments and improve both classification accuracy and model explainability. To achieve this goal, and as a first step, we analyze the benefits of GNNs in a unimodal setting, using only interview transcripts from healthy participants and those with Alzheimer's disease, reserving their application with multimodal information for future research.

2   Related Work

Earlier approaches have concentrated on extracting a range of features to identify linguistic deficits in the speech of individuals with Alzheimer's disease. These features encompass lexical, syntactic, and phonetic aspects, derived from both transcripts and audio recordings [15]. The advent of deep learning models has facilitated the development of representations that approximate the semantic content of dialogues and have achieved state-of-the-art results. Notably, several studies have proposed using transformer-based models pre-trained on large general text corpora to generate contextual word representations. These representations can be fine-tuned for specific clinical tasks using relatively small datasets, thereby addressing the challenge of data scarcity. Researchers have investigated multiple fine-tuning strategies to adapt pre-trained transformers for AD detection. We have identified multiple strategies involving: 1) full fine-tuning with AD-labeled transcripts [1]; 2) feature extraction using a frozen BERT, employing pre-trained embeddings as fixed representations, which are then input into classifiers on top [11]. For example, Bang, Han, and Kang [3] proposed attaching a smaller transformer-based classifier with linear layers; 3) hybrid architectures integrating transformer embeddings with a sequential model to capture spatial patterns [16]; 4) the combination of learned representations with handcrafted linguistic features [2]. Nevertheless, transformer-based methods face challenges in AD detection. For instance, explainability techniques have been applied to reveal which words or phrases influence AD predictions, but these post-hoc methods sometimes yield inconsistent or clinically implausible attributions [12]. Also, domain adaptation challenges arise because transformers are pre-trained on formal written text, whereas AD datasets are not only small compared to other text datasets but also consist of spontaneous, disfluent spoken language with grammatical errors and incomplete sentences, leading to instability during fine-tuning.

Graph Neural Networks emerged as a novel method for AD detection. As far as we know, although multimodal approaches have been proposed, the use of GNNs for unimodal textual analysis of Alzheimer's speech transcripts remains largely unexplored. In Cai et al. [4], despite the primary focus being on multi-modal approaches, results for the textual modality are also reported. That study proposes constructing a token-level graph representation of speech, where nodes are based on textual embeddings and are connected by syntactic dependencies. However, no explanation beyond an observation regarding the limited impact of their graph constructions is provided. Other studies report mixed results or results influenced by additional modalities. Lee et al. [8] proposed the use of a vision-language model (VLM) in conjunction with a GNN to measure image-text coherence for dementia detection. In a subsequent work [9], their methodology was extended to implement late fusion, incorporating textual embeddings. However, the primary emphasis remained on the VLM, and no detailed analysis of the textual component was provided.

These previous works have demonstrated the utility of GNNs; however, further research is still required. Specifically, no focused analysis has been conducted on which speech components are most relevant from a graph-based perspective, nor on how these elements influence the final representation. We believe that such analysis could contribute to the development of improved graph construction methodologies, which motivates this work.

3   Proposed Approach

Our proposed solution is implemented in three stages. In the following paragraphs, we provide more details on each stage:

i) **Making the Graph Representation:** To construct the graph representation, we start from the transcripts of the participants' recordings. The transcripts were automatically generated using an automatic speech recognition (ASR) model. A co-occurrence graph–based approach is adopted, in which each token in the transcript is represented as a graph node, whose embedding is obtained using a text encoder (e.g., BERT).[1] Edges are established between two tokens when they appear consecutively, and a weight is assigned based on the frequency with which the tokens co-occur in the same order.

To represent disfluencies —approximated from the ASR outputs— the graph is enriched with special nodes associated with the words involved in these disfluencies, which we refer to as disfluent nodes. These nodes correspond to: (i) *filler words*, which are identified by a list of tokens corresponding to the Interjection category of the Penn Treebak tag set. They are represented by a node labeled as *FLP*; (ii) *pauses*, which are inferred from ASR annotations indicating turn endings or interruptions. These markers are collapsed into a single node labeled as *PAU*; (iii) *repetitions* that are marked when two identical adjacent tokens are identified, and then indicated by a *REP* node; and *self-corrections*, which are indicated by a Large Language Model via simple prompting, and then labeled as *SCR*, respectively.

Figure 1 presents a brief example of the graph construction process, following the steps described above.

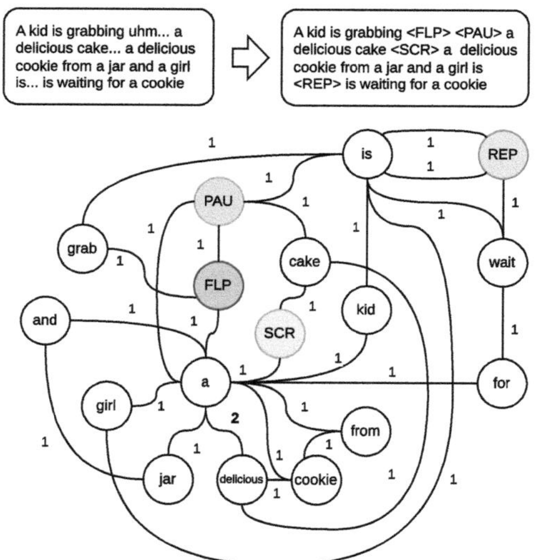

Fig. 1. Enriched graph representation with disfluent nodes in color red (filled pauses), yellow (self-corrections), blue (repetitions), and green (pauses). (Color figure online)

ii) **Graph Processing through Graph Neural Networks:** We implemented 3 types of graph neural networks of each learning type: transductive, inductive, and attention-based. All GNNs were implemented with two

---

[1] It is important to note that a given token may have multiple embeddings depending on its position within the transcript, a phenomenon that frequently occurs in certain grammatical categories such as conjunctions (e.g., "and"). In such cases, the last computed embedding is used as the node representation.

aggregation layers with jumping knowledge [19] to transform and enhance the graph representations, followed by a global pooling operator. The implemented GNN were:

- **Graph Convolutional Network (GCN):** A traditional transductive GNN using the graph convolutional operator proposed by Kipf and Welling [7]. This operator employs a normalized Laplacian matrix to propagate the node information through the network and capture local graph structures.
- **k-dimensional Graph Neural Network (KGNN):** Introduced by Morris et al. [13]. Implements an operator that gathers information from a chosen neighborhood of a specific node using a heuristic method and assigns importance according to edge weights, enabling inductive learning. It does not require the full adjacency matrix, which allows for efficient and targeted learning on graph structures:
- **Graph Attention Network (GAT):** Proposed by [18], this GNN weights neighbor nodes based on inferred attention scores, allowing for highlighting relevant nodes in the graph rather than treating all nodes equally as in previous GNNs, potentially improving the representation.

iii) **Graph Classification:** After the message-passing layers of the GNN, node embeddings are processed through a Self-Attention Graph Pooling (SAG-Pool) layer to generate a compact graph-level representation suitable for the final classifier. SAGPool [10] employs graph convolution to assign attention scores to each node, reflecting both their features and position within the graph topology. It then retains only the top-k nodes and their induced subgraph as the pooled result.

4   Experiments

In our experiments, we used transcripts generated automatically from the A-DReSSo dataset using a Whisper large model. This dataset comprises audio recordings of people describing a diagnostic image [5], categorized into two classes: Alzheimer's Disease (AD) with 122 instances and Healthy Control (HC) with 115 instances. The dataset's authors provide a test split equivalent to 30% of the data (71 of 237 samples).

To establish a baseline for our results, the following models were trained: A fine-tuned BERT model and a Convolutional Neural Network (CNN). We tested multiple configuration settings, and the final hyperparameter values are provided in Table 1.

We present our classification results in Table 2. These results show that GNN models outperform both baselines and that our best-performing architecture is GCN, which achieved an F1 score of 0.82. For reference, we also include SOTA results, which are comparable to ours in their unimodal version (text only), but slightly superior when they considered multimodal information, from the transcripts and their audio.

Table 1. Summary of baseline models and their configurations.

Method	Settings
BERT (fine-tuned) *(baseline 1)*	- Epochs: 3 - Optimizer: AdamW - Learning rate: 5×10^{-5} - Other hyperparameters remained at default values
CNN *(baseline 2)*	- Architecture: 3 parallel conv. layers + MLP classifier + SiLU activation - Convolutional filters: (3, 768) and (5, 768) - Feature maps: 256 per kernel - Pooling: Max-pooling - Epochs: 100 (with early stopping if no improvement in 10 epochs, minimum 30)
GNNs (GCN, GAT, KGNN) *(proposed model)*	- Architecture: 2 graph conv. layers + MPL classifier + SiLU activation - Pooling: Self-Attention Graph Pooling - Epochs: 100 (with early stopping if no improvement in 10 epochs, minimum 30)

Table 2. Macro-averaged performance metrics on the test set.

Type	Method	Prec	Rec	F1	Acc
Baseline	BERT	0.79	0.76	0.74	0.75
	CNN	0.77	0.77	0.77	0.77
Ours	GAT	0.81	0.80	0.80	0.80
	KGNN	0.82	0.81	0.81	0.81
	GCN	0.83	0.82	0.82	0.82
[3]	Only Text	0.83	0.83	0.83	0.83
[3]	Text+Audio	0.88	0.87	0.87	0.87

5   Analysis of Results

An initial analysis of these results consists of evaluating the utility of GNNs in this task. To this end, we analyzed the performance of traditional classification methods using a representation based solely on disfluency counts, without modeling the relationships among them or the context in which they occur, in contrast to what a GNN captures. The results shown in Table 3 clearly demonstrate the usefulness of the proposed GNN-based approach.

As a second analysis, we applied the Integrated Gradients [17] method to calculate attribution scores that quantify the contribution of each graph component to the final decision. The results are illustrated in Fig. 2, where highly relevant nodes are colored green and less relevant nodes are colored red. Similarly, the intensity of the edge colors reflects their degree of relevance. In addition, Fig. 3 presents a general statistic of the presence of the different types of disfluencies in the test set, as well as the number of graphs in which these elements were highly discriminating.

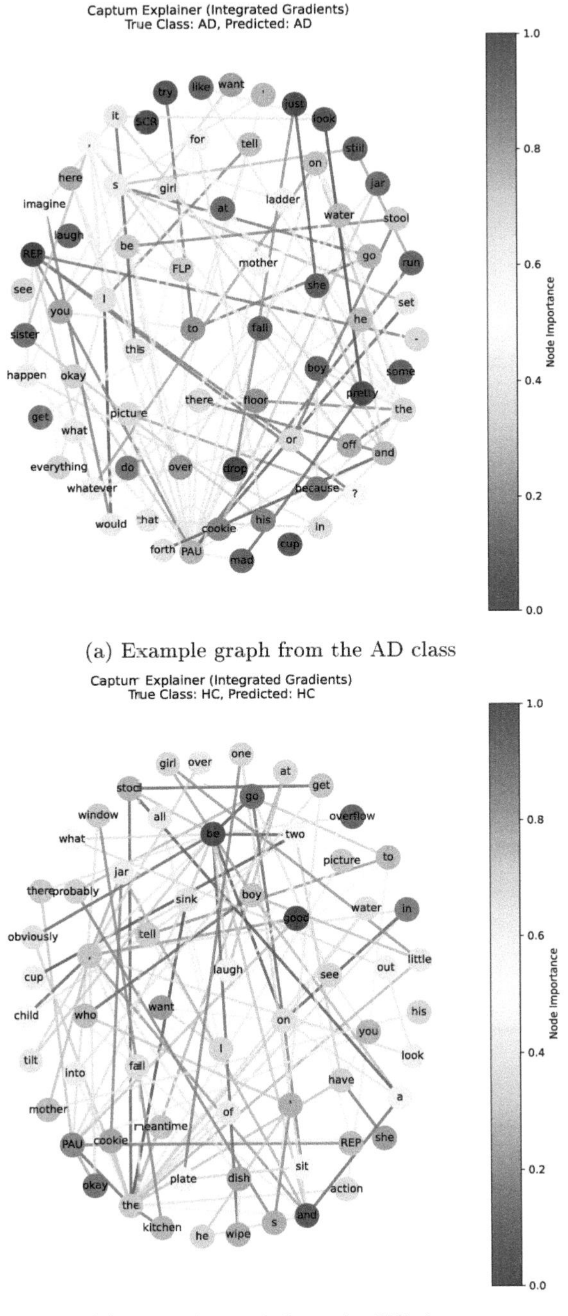

(a) Example graph from the AD class

(b) Example graph from the HC class

Fig. 2. Visual representation of graphs that denote the relevance of all tokens in the transcripts.

Table 3. Results on disfluency-counts classification on Test set.

Method	Prec	Rec	F1	Acc
Naïve Bayes	0.54	0.89	0.67	0.57
MLP	0.59	0.74	0.66	0.61
SVM	0.56	0.69	0.62	0.57

Our analysis of these scores revealed distinct patterns in the words associated with each class. Among Alzheimer's participants (AD class), pauses (PAU) were the most relevant features, followed by filled pauses (FLP), though only a few of these received high attribution scores. Other disfluent features, such as repetitions (REP) and self-corrections (SCR), had lower attribution scores. Pronouns and interrogative pronouns were also frequently relevant in AD attributions. Common relevant words included "okay", "alright", and "well". This pattern likely reflects how AD participants express doubt and may also be influenced by the interviewer, who often encourages AD participants to continue but does not prompt healthy participants (HC class) in the same way. As a result, these words are highly distinctive for the AD group. In contrast, HC attributions included a wider range of token categories. Pauses (PAU) appeared in fewer HC cases and did not receive high attribution values. Filled pauses, repetitions, and self-corrections also received low attribution scores. Nouns, verbs, articles, and other categories were identified as relevant more often than in AD. These results suggest that the model primarily detects the absence of question-related tokens rather than distinguishing specific grammatical categories in HC.

Fig. 3. Distribution of Disfluencies in graphs from the test set.

6 Conclusions

In this work, we introduced a representation that models impaired speech as enriched token-level graphs with explicit disfluency annotations, enabling Graph

Neural Networks to focus on clinically relevant context for Alzheimer's disease detection. Our results indicate that Graph Neural Networks outperform bigger models and similar architectures such as Convolutional Neural Networks. We observed that Graph Convolutional Networks demonstrated a marginal advantage over other tested Graph Neural Network models, likely due to their approach to weight handling.

Despite the theoretical relevance of disfluencies for this task, our proposed representation, even when explicitly incorporating them, yielded only a moderate contribution to overall model performance. A plausible explanation is that disfluency identification relies on automatic transcriptions, which tend to normalize speech and consequently correct or remove part of the disfluent phenomena. This limitation may be attenuating the true impact of disfluencies within the model.

Future work should explore alternative methods to better capture disfluent speech, such as models for self-corrections and phoneme-based transcripts, and investigate the complementarity with acoustic features.

Acknowledgments. I would like to thank SECIHTI for the support provided in the development of this project.

References

1. Balagopalan, A., Eyre, B., Rudzicz, F., Novikova, J.: To BERT or not to BERT: comparing speech and language-based approaches for Alzheimer's disease detection. In: Proceedings of the Annual Conference of the International Speech Communication Association, INTERSPEECH 2020-October (2020)
2. Balagopalan, A., Novikova, J.: Comparing acoustic-based approaches for Alzheimer's disease detection. In: Proceedings of the Annual Conference of the International Speech Communication Association, INTERSPEECH, vol. 6 (2021)
3. Bang, J.U., Han, S.H., Kang, B.O.: Alzheimer's disease recognition from spontaneous speech using large language models. ETRI J. **46**(1) (2024)
4. Cai, H., et al.: Exploring Multimodal Approaches for Alzheimer's Disease Detection Using Patient Speech Transcript and Audio Data (2023)
5. Cummings, L.: Describing the cookie theft picture: sources of breakdown in Alzheimer's dementia. Pragmatics Soc. **10**(2) (2019). https://doi.org/10.1075/PS.17011.CUM
6. López-de Ipiña, K., et al.: On the analysis of speech and disfluencies for automatic detection of Mild cognitive impairment. Neural Comput. Appl. **32**(20) (2020)
7. Kipf, T.N., Welling, M.: Semi-supervised classification with graph convolutional networks. In: 5th International Conference on Learning Representations, ICLR 2017 - Conference Track Proceedings. International Conference on Learning Representations, ICLR (2017)
8. Lee, B., Bang, J.U., Song, H.J., Kang, B.O.: Alzheimer's disease recognition using graph neural network by leveraging image-text similarity from vision language model. Sci. Rep. **15**(1) (2025). https://doi.org/10.1038/s41598-024-82597-z
9. Lee, B., Song, H.J., Park, Y.J., Kang, B.O.: Multimodal Alzheimer's disease recognition from image, text and audio. Sci. Rep. **15**(1) (2025). https://doi.org/10.1038/s41598-025-14998-7

10. Lee, J., Lee, I., Kang, J.: Self-Attention Graph Pooling (2019)
11. Liu, L., Liu, L., Wafa, H.A., Tydeman, F., Xie, W., Wang, Y.: Diagnostic accuracy of deep learning using speech samples in depression: a systematic review and meta-analysis. J. Am. Med. Inform. Assoc. **31**(10) (2024)
12. Liu, Y.L., et al.: Can automated speech recognition errors provide valuable clues for Alzheimer's disease detection? In: ICASSP, IEEE International Conference on Acoustics, Speech and Signal Processing - Proceedings (2025)
13. Morris, C., et al.: Weisfeiler and leman go neural: higher-order graph neural networks. In: 33rd AAAI Conference on Artificial Intelligence (2019). https://doi.org/10.1609/AAAI.V33I01.33014602
14. Mu, Y., Chang, K.X., Chen, Y.F., Yan, K., Wang, C.X., Hua, Q.: Diagnosis of Alzheimer's disease: towards accuracy and accessibility. J. Biol. Methods **11**(1) (2024). https://doi.org/10.14440/JBM.2024.412
15. Petti, U., Baker, S., Korhonen, A.: A systematic literature review of automatic Alzheimer's disease detection from speech and language. J. Am. Med. Inform. Assoc. **27**(11) (2020)
16. Roshanzamir, A., Aghajan, H., Soleymani Baghshah, M.: Transformer-based deep neural network language models for Alzheimer's disease risk assessment from targeted speech. BMC Med. Inform. Decis. Mak. **21**(1) (2021)
17. Sundararajan, M., Taly, A., Yan, Q.: Axiomatic attribution for deep networks. In: 34th International Conference on Machine Learning, ICML 2017, vol. 7 (2017)
18. Veličković, P., Casanova, A., Liò, P., Cucurull, G., Romero, A., Bengio, Y.: Graph attention networks. In: 6th International Conference on Learning Representations, ICLR 2018 - Conference Track Proceedings (2017). https://doi.org/10.1007/978-3-031-01587-8_7
19. Xu, K., Li, C., Tian, Y., Sonobe, T., Kawarabayashi, K.I., Jegelka, S.: Representation Learning on Graphs with Jumping Knowledge Networks (2018)
20. Zeisel, J., Bennett, K., Fleming, R.: World Alzheimer Report 2020 (2020)

Factors Associated with Depression in Mexico: An XAI Comparative Analysis of Tree-Based Classifiers Under Imbalanced Data

Abigail Romero-Trejo[1], Angélica Guzmán-Ponce[2],
Rosa María Valdovinos-Rosas[1(✉)], Laura Cleofas-Sánchez[4(✉)],
and Iván Francisco-Valencia[3]

[1] Facultad de Ingeniería, Universidad Autónoma del Estado de México, Toluca, Mexico
aromerot567@alumno.uaemex.mx, rvaldovinosr@uaemex.mx
[2] Escuela Politécnica Superior, Universidad Católica de Murcia, Murcia, Spain
aguzman@ucam.edu
[3] Centro Universitario Tianguistenco, Universidad Autónoma del Estado de México, Estado de México, Mexico
ifranciscov@uaemex.mx
[4] Tecnológico de Estudios Superiores de Tianguistenco, Tecnológico Nacional de México, Carretera Tenango-La Marquesa, km 22, Santiago Tilapa, C.P 52650 Tianguistenco, Estado de México, Mexico
laura_cs@test.edu.mx

Abstract. Depression is a major public health concern worldwide. Previous studies in Mexico have analyzed its association with sociodemographic factors, but most rely on conventional statistical methods that may not capture complex nonlinear relationships. In this study we compare four tree-based classifiers (Random Forest, XGBoost, LightGBM, and CatBoost) proved on six class balancing strategies, to predict depressive symptoms using data from the 2021–2023 National Health and Nutrition Survey (ENSANUT). LightGBM achieved the highest overall performance, and Shapley Additive Explanations (SHAP) analysis identified age, sex, education, and marital status as the most influential features across balancing scenarios. The results also show that the choice of balancing strategy significantly impacts classifier performance, particularly for the macro F1-score, providing quantitative and transparent evidence to support mental health policies in Mexico.

Keywords: Pattern Recognition · Depression · Tree-Based classifiers · Explainable Artificial Intelligence

1 Introduction

Binary classification in the presence of class imbalance is a recurring challenge in pattern recognition, particularly when it is applied to health-related data [2]. In

V. G. Cruz-Sánchez et al. (Eds.): MCPR 2026, LNCS 16623, pp. 359–368, 2026.
https://doi.org/10.1007/978-3-032-28393-1_32

such environments, the minority class, often the most clinically relevant, is significantly under-represented, leading classifiers to show bias towards the majority class and to produce misleading performance metrics when assessed solely for accuracy. While numerous resampling strategies have been proposed to mitigate this issue, their interaction with different families of classifiers is not fully understood, especially for structured, categorical-heavy datasets common in epidemiological research [2].

Depression is a mental disorder characterized by a persistent low mood and loss of interest in life, affecting approximately 332 million people worldwide. It may result from complex interactions of social, psychological, and biological factors [9]; hence, analyzing these elements simultaneously may reveal patterns and trends that would otherwise remain unnoticed. Detecting such patterns from population surveys is a relevant application of supervised classification, since these surveys exhibit categorical and mixed-type features, inherent class imbalance, and complex nonlinear interactions [13].

Epidemiological studies in Mexico have analyzed the relationship between depression and sociodemographic factors [1,4], but tend to use conventional statistical methods such as logistic regression, which might not capture nonlinear relationships [13]. Machine learning-based studies have applied tree-based classifiers and explainability techniques for depression prediction in other countries [5,8,11,13], but typically focus on a single model or a limited set of resampling strategies without a systematic comparative evaluation.

A frequent issue associated with machine learning models is the "black box" phenomenon, where the model's decision-making process lacks interpretability [6], an important aspect for its application in critical domains such as healthcare. Explainable Artificial Intelligence (XAI) has emerged as a strategy to provide information about how and why a model makes specific decisions [6]. Among XAI methods, SHAP (SHapley Additive exPlanations) has been widely adopted due to its solid theoretical foundation in cooperative game theory and its ability to provide both global and local interpretability [3].

In this context, two important gaps remain. First, there is limited evidence on how the interaction between different tree-based classifiers and class balancing techniques affects recognition performance on Mexican health survey data. Secondly, most existing studies do not provide explainable assessments regarding which sociodemographic characteristics drive predictions under variable imbalance conditions. Although the individual methods employed are well established, to the best of our knowledge, no previous study has systematically evaluated their interaction in this specific setting, nor examined the stability of SHAP-based explanations across multiple balancing scenarios for depression classification in Mexico. This study offers the following contributions:

1. A systematic comparative evaluation of four tree-based classifiers under seven experimental scenarios (original dataset and six resampling strategies), totaling 28 model-strategy combinations evaluated on accuracy, macro F1-score, and ROC-AUC.

2. An explainability analysis using SHAP applied to the best-performing classifier across balancing scenarios, assessing which features are most discriminative and how their importance shifts depending on the resampling approach.
3. Study focused on the Mexican context, which provides specific evidence from each region on the recognition of depression patterns.

2   Related Work

The application of machine learning to mental health classification has grown in recent years. Vu et al. [13] used XGBoost on data from the U.S. NHANES survey, achieving an accuracy and F1 score of 69%, and identified income, sex, and hypertension as key features through SHAP.

Song et al. [11] compared several classifiers on Chinese elderly data (CHARLS); LightGBM achieved the best accuracy (69.6%), with SHAP highlighting health perception, sleep hours, sex, age, and cognitive function. Chen et al. [5] further confirmed age as a relevant predictor using tree-based models with SHAP in Chinese populations. Despite their contributions, these findings vary across countries.

In Mexico, epidemiological studies [1, 4] have examined sociodemographic correlates of depression, but these have predominantly relied on logistic regression. However, we did not identify any studies that perform a systematic comparison of multiple tree-based classifiers that handle the imbalance in Mexican health survey data.

In the medical domain, several studies have investigated the effect of resampling strategies on classifier performance. Welvaars et al. [14] evaluated multiple classifiers trained on seven resampled datasets for predicting hospital readmissions finding that resampling increased AUC and recall but also produced poorly calibrated models. Agyemang et al. [2] compared undersampling, oversampling, and hybrid methods for stroke prediction, concluding that oversampling techniques provided more stable performance. However, these studies focus on clinical datasets; systematic comparisons on population-level survey data with predominantly categorical features remain largely unexplored.

3   Materials and Methods

3.1   Resampling Methods

Class imbalance is a well-documented challenge in pattern recognition that degrades classifier performance, particularly for the minority class. Common resampling strategies include Random UnderSampling (RUS), which reduces the majority class; Random OverSampling (ROS), which duplicates minority instances; and Synthetic Minority Over-sampling Technique (SMOTE), which generates synthetic minority samples via interpolation. Editing-based methods such as Edited Nearest Neighbours (ENN) remove noisy or borderline majority instances. Hybrid approaches combining over- and under-sampling have also been explored to balance the trade-off between information loss and overfitting [14].

3.2 Machine Learning Models

In this study, four tree-based supervised learning models were evaluated:

- Random Forest. Based on decision trees, Random Forest is an ensemble learning method. It can mitigate overfitting as it bases its predictions on a consensus of trees, which are generated using a bagging technique [13].
- XGBoost. It is a variant of the Gradient Boosting (GB) algorithm. It builds a series of decision trees, improving the predictions of the previous ones iteratively [5]. This approach has exhibited outstanding performance in the context of medical research [13].
- LightGBM. Variant of the GB algorithm, however, its operation is based on a histogram learning algorithm [3]. It is well known for its ability to handle categorical variables effectively, as well as for its fast training process [5].
- CatBoost. It is a GB algorithm that employs oblivious (symmetric) trees sequentially. At each level, a single feature is selected to create splitting rules. This model is able to handle categorical features efficiently as well [3].

These models were selected due to their outstanding performance regarding structured data [8] as well as their ability to capture non-linear relationships and complex interactions between variables [13]. Additionally, tree-based models offer native support for categorical features and have been shown to be competitive with or superior to deep learning on medium-sized tabular datasets [2], which makes them particularly suitable for the type of data used in this study.

3.3 Explainability: SHAP

SHAP was employed as XAI technique, based on game theory, it treats features as players and the model outcome as the payoff [3]. SHAP assigns each feature a contribution value by comparing the model output with and without that feature. The Shapley value for feature i is described in Eq. 1:

$$\phi_i = \sum_{S \subseteq M \setminus \{i\}} \frac{|S|!(|M| - |S| - 1)!}{|M|!} \left[f(S \cup \{i\}) - f(S) \right] \tag{1}$$

where M is the set of all features, S is a subset of M without the i-th feature, $f(S \cup \{i\})$ is the prediction made by the model, including the i-th feature, and $f(S)$ is the prediction made by the model excluding this feature [6]. SHAP enables both global interpretation (overall feature importance) and local interpretation (individual prediction explanation).

4 Experimental Results

4.1 Data

The ENSANUT survey follows a probabilistic, stratified, and cluster sampling design and it is nationally representative [4]. ENSANUT collects data about the health status of the population as well as sociodemographic characteristics. Data from 2021, 2022, and 2023 were included in this study, considering only complete information from 32,085 participants aged 20 years or older.

Six sociodemographic variables were selected based on the literature [1,11]: age (discrete), sex (binary), marital status (6 categories), education level (4 categories), region (rural/urban), and employment status. These variables are consistently available across the three ENSANUT editions (2021 to 2023), ensuring comparability. Clinical or psychological variables (e.g., chronic diseases, substance use) were not included because they belong to different ENSANUT questionnaire modules and are not uniformly available for all participants. For non-binary categorical variables, one-hot coding was applied, generating binary columns per category. This allowed the classifiers to capture category-specific effects. As a result, a total of 16 features were obtained.

On the other hand, depressive symptoms were measured using the Center for Epidemiologic Studies Depression scale (CESD-7), validated in the Mexican population [10]. A score ≥ 9 for adults aged 20–59 and ≥ 5 for adults aged 60+ indicates clinically significant depressive symptoms (positive class). The resulting distribution consisted of 6,063 positive cases (Fig. 1) and 26,022 negative cases. which. Figure 1 shows the state-level distribution of positive cases. The highest prevalence of depressive symptoms was found in Aguascalientes (24.12%), Tabasco (23.45%) and Michoacán (21.93%). In contrast, the lowest percentages were observed in Baja California (13.30%), Baja California Sur (14.11%), and San Luis Potosí (14.55%).

Finally, to handling the class imbalance, 7 resampling strategies were applied: RUS, ROS, SMOTE, ENN, RUS+ROS, and SMOTE+ENN. Table 1 shows that the final Imbalance Ratio (IR) depends on the algorithm applied:RUS, ROS, and SMOTE inherently produce a 50/50 distribution, whereas ENN (74/26) and SMOTE+ENN (53/47) yield different ratios depending on the characteristics of the training data.

4.2   Comparative Classifier Performance

The dataset was split using stratified sampling with 70%(22,459) for training and 30% (9626) for testing. The classifiers were trained using the scikit-learn library considering default hyperparameters. Whenever applicable, the random state parameter was set to 42 to ensure reproducibility.

Three metrics were used to evaluate model performance (Table 1): TP, TN, FP, and FN denote true positives, true negatives, false positives, and false negatives, respectively: (1) **Accuracy**, the proportion of correct predictions: $(TP + TN)/(TP + TN + FP + FN)$; (2) **Macro F1-score**, the unweighted mean of per-class F1-scores: $F_{1\text{macro}} = \frac{1}{N} \sum_{i=1}^{N} \frac{2 \cdot \text{precision}_i \cdot \text{recall}_i}{\text{precision}_i + \text{recall}_i}$, where precision $= TP/(TP+FP)$ and recall $= TP/(TP+FN)$, which treats both classes equally regardless of size [6]; and (3) **ROC-AUC**, the area under the receiver operating characteristic curve, commonly used in binary classification [8].

From Table 1, three preliminary conclusions can be drawn. Firstly, on the original imbalanced dataset, all classifiers achieved their highest accuracy val-

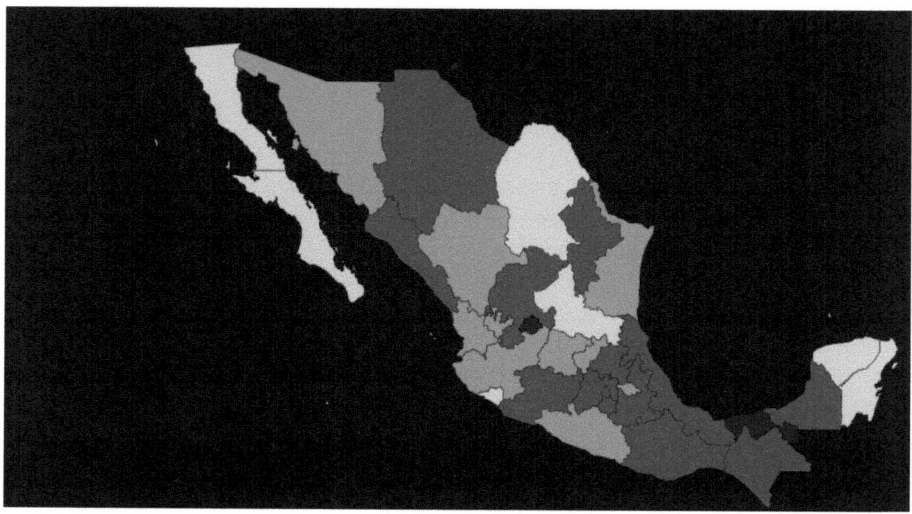

Fig. 1. State-level distribution of clinically significant depressive symptoms (2021–2023). Darker purple tones represent higher proportions. Kepler.gl [12] was used for geospatial visualization and the state-level cartographic boundaries were retrieved from the National Institute of Statistics and Geography [7].

ues (RF: 0.7912, XGB: 0.8096, LGBM: 0.8131, CAT: 0.8126), while their macro F1-scores remained among the lowest, confirming that accuracy alone is insufficient under class imbalance. Notably, Random Forest presents an exception: its F1-score on the original data (0.5827) is the highest among all RF-strategy combinations, suggesting that RF is particularly sensitive to resampling and that balancing does not consistently improve all metrics for all classifiers.

Second, boosting-based models (XGB, LGBM, CAT) consistently outperformed Random Forest across all strategies and metrics. Among them, LGBM achieved the highest accuracy in six out of seven scenarios and the best F1-score in four. Its best configuration (LGBM + ENN) reached an accuracy of 76.26% and a macro F1-score of 63.94%. CatBoost showed competitive results, achieving the best F1-score with RUS (60.58%) and the highest accuracy with SMOTE+ENN (74.11%). Based on overall performance, LGBM was selected for the explainability analysis.

Third, the balancing strategy substantially affects performance. ENN provided the most favorable trade-off, yielding the highest F1-scores for LGBM and CatBoost without severely degrading accuracy. In contrast, RUS reduced accuracy across all models despite improving minority class recognition. Notably, strategies achieving a 50/50 ratio (ROS, SMOTE, RUS+ROS) produced similar results among themselves, suggesting that the resulting class distribution matters more than the specific resampling method used.

Table 1. Performance of the models with the different sampling methods.

Dataset (IR)	RF		XGB		LGBM		CAT	
	Acc	F1	Acc	F1	Acc	F1	Acc	F1
Original (81-19)	79.12	**58.27**	80.96	57.00	**81.31**	56.86	81.26	56.94
RUS (50-50)	62.75	56.04	66.80	59.61	**67.95**	60.52	67.93	**60.58**
ROS (50-50)	67.11	57.94	68.25	60.03	**68.63**	**61.04**	68.40	60.55
SMOTE (50-50)	69.00	58.55	71.09	60.93	**71.97**	**61.95**	71.23	61.09
ENN (74-26)	62.26	54.74	72.75	61.56	**76.26**	**63.94**	75.76	63.52
RUS+ROS (50-50)	67.00	57.78	68.25	60.03	**68.63**	61.04	68.20	60.19
SMOTE+ENN (53-47)	71.89	60.74	73.47	62.31	73.75	**63.05**	**74.11**	62.78

The ROC curve complements these metrics by providing a threshold independent evaluation of classifier discrimination ability [8]. When calculating the
ROC values, a clear separation is observed between Random Forest (AUC: 0.651–
0.673) and the three boosting-based models (AUC: 0.692-0.727), reinforcing the
performance gap reported in Table 1. Among boosting models, LGBM and Cat-
Boost achieved the highest AUC values (up to 0.727), while XGBoost showed
slightly lower discrimination. Within each classifier, the balancing strategy had a
relatively minor effect on AUC, with SMOTE consistently producing the lowest
values. This is expected, since AUC is largely determined by the feature space
and model family rather than the class distribution used during training [14].
This indicates that while resampling substantially affects accuracy and F1-score,
the ranking ability of the models across thresholds remains largely preserved.

4.3 Explainability Analysis

Once LGBM was identified as the best-performing classifier, SHAP summary
plots were generated for all balancing scenarios, however, only two are presented
in this section for clarity to illustrate the impact of class imbalance handling on
interpretability (Fig. 2): the baseline (original dataset), which achieved the highest accuracy, and the ENN strategy, which obtained the best F1-score (Table 1).
A notable finding is that the top three features (age, sex, and elementary education) remained stable across strategies, with minor reordering among mid-ranked
features. However, the magnitude of SHAP values differs notably between scenarios: under ENN, individual contributions reach up to 4, compared to approximately 2 in the original dataset. This suggests that reducing class imbalance
through ENN allows the model to assign stronger individual contributions, likely
due to improved class separability. Older age, female sex, elementary education and widowhood emerged as significant predictors of clinically significant
depressive symptoms. In contrast, younger age, male sex, marriage and higher
education drives the prediction toward the negative class.

Regarding the SHAP importance of sex-related features, since sex is a
binary variable (*male* and *female*). SHAP distributes the marginal contribution

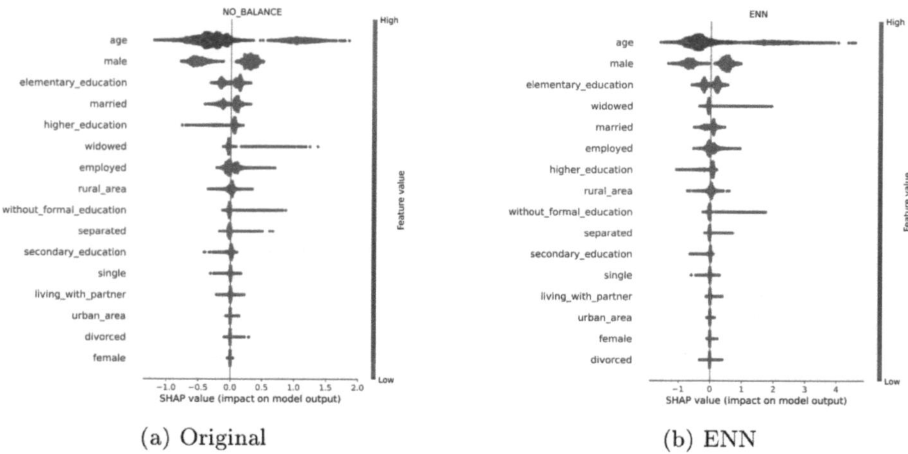

(a) Original   (b) ENN

Fig. 2. SHAP summary plot comparison. Each point represents an individual prediction, x-axis indicates the feature's contribution to the model output. For categorical characteristics, red indicates the presence of the characteristic and blue its absence. For the discrete characteristic *age*, red indicates higher values and blue lower values. (Color figure online)

unevenly between collinear features [3]; in this case, the *male* column absorbs the sex effect: being male pushes predictions toward the negative class, while its absence (i.e., being female) pushes toward the positive class. Therefore, the low SHAP importance of the *female* column does not indicate that sex is irrelevant for depression prediction, but that its contribution is already captured by the *male* column. Accordingly, this apparent asymmetry does not contradict the identified predictors, as the model captures sex information through the *male* feature.

It is important to note that causality cannot be inferred, as the data source is a cross-sectional survey [4], and SHAP may be affected by feature collinearity and nonlinear dependencies [3]. Hence, findings should be interpreted with caution. With that, except for SMOTE, the most important feature pointed out by SHAP was age across balancing techniques. This pattern is also observed in China, as previous studies [5,11] have indicated age as one of the top five features for predicting depressive symptoms, mainly in younger individuals, in contrast to Mexico where it is associated with older people.

Another important characteristic identified was sex. This pattern is consistent with findings in studies conducted in the US, where being female is a significant factor in developing depressive disorder [13]. Finally, in ENSANUT, marital status and educational level stand out as predictors of clinically significant depressive symptoms.

5   Conclusions

This study presents a systematic comparative evaluation of four tree-based classifiers across seven class-balancing scenarios for recognizing patterns of depressive symptoms using Mexican health survey data. The main findings are as follows.

First, LightGBM consistently outperformed Random Forest, XGBoost, and CatBoost, particularly when combined with the ENN balancing strategy, achieving the best macro F1-score (0.6394) while maintaining acceptable accuracy (0.7626) and ROC-AUC (0.7228). Second, the choice of balancing strategy has a significant impact on classifier performance. ENN and SMOTE+ENN provided the most favorable trade-off between accuracy and minority class recognition. Third, SHAP analysis showed that the most discriminative features (age, sex, education, and marital status) remain stable across all balancing scenarios.

Overall, the results indicate that Mexico, in part, exhibits patterns similar to those reported in other countries. However, notable variations were observed that highlight the importance of analyzing the data to better understand the social determinants in each country.

The results contribute to the state of the art in data science by providing empirical evidence on the interaction between tree-based classifiers and class imbalance strategies in a health classification task in Mexico. Future work will explore hyperparameter optimization, feature engineering, cost-sensitive learning approaches, and the inclusion of clinical variables to improve minority class recognition. Additionally, expanding the feature set beyond the six sociodemographic variables available across the three ENSANUT editions by incorporating clinical or psychological variables could provide a more comprehensive understanding of depression factors. Evaluating alternative approaches such as deep learning architectures designed for tabular data would also complement the tree-based classifiers considered in this study [2,8]. To support reproducibility, the code and processed data used in this study will be made available through a public GitHub repository: https://github.com/abigail-rt/XAI_ENSANUT.

Acknowledgments. This research was supported by a national scholarship (CVU: 2159142) granted by the SECIHTI, Mexico.

Disclosure of Interests. The authors have no competing interests to declare that are relevant to the content of this article.

References

1. Agudelo-Botero, M., Giraldo-Rodríguez, L., Dávila-Cervantes, C.A.: Type 2 diabetes and depressive symptoms in the adult population in Mexico: a syndemic approach based on National Health and Nutrition Survey. BMC Public Health **22**(1), 1–10 (2022). https://doi.org/10.1186/s12889-022-14405-0
2. Agyemang, E.F., et al.: Addressing class imbalance problem in health data classification: practical application from an oversampling viewpoint. Appl. Comput. Intell. Soft Comput. **2025**(1), 1013769 (2025). https://doi.org/10.1155/acis/1013769. https://onlinelibrary.wiley.com/doi/abs/10.1155/acis/1013769

3. Ahmed, U., Mahmood, A., Tunio, M.A., Hafeez, G., Khan, A.R., Razzaq, S.: Investigating boosting techniques efficacy in feature selection: a comparative analysis. Energy Rep. **11**, 3521–3532 (2024). https://doi.org/10.1016/j.egyr.2024.03.020. https://www.sciencedirect.com/science/article/pii/S2352484724001653

4. Bose, I., et al.: Mental health, water, and food: relationships between water and food insecurity and probable depression amongst adults in Mexico. J. Affect. Disord. **370**, 348–355 (2025). https://doi.org/10.1016/j.jad.2024.10.116

5. Chen, J.M., Wei, Y.T., Zhou, Q.G., Tao, J.L., Bi, B., Health, P.: Machine learning-based nomogram for predicting depressive symptoms in women: a cross-sectional study in Guangdong Province, China. World J. Psychiatry **15**(8), 1–21 (2025). https://doi.org/10.5498/wjp.v15.i8.106622

6. Guzman-Ponce, A., Valdovinos-Rosas, R.M., Gonzalez-Ruiz, J.L., Franciso-Valencia, I., Raymundo Marcial-Romero, J.: Exploring COVID-19 trends in Mexico during the winter season with explainable artificial intelligence (XAI). IEEE Lat. Am. Trans. **22**(7), 539–547 (2024). https://doi.org/10.1109/TLA.2024.10562257

7. Instituto Nacional de Estadística y Geografía (INEGI): State political division - vintage/millésimé - Mexico (2020). https://hub.huwise.com/explore/assets/georef-mexico-state-millesime/, last updated in 2023. Accessed 25 Mar 2025

8. Kasani, P.H., Lee, J.E., Park, C., Yun, C.H., Jang, J.W., Lee, S.A.: Evaluation of nutritional status and clinical depression classification using an explainable machine learning method. Front. Nutr. (2023). https://doi.org/10.3389/fnut.2023.1165854

9. Organización Mundial de la Salud: Trastorno depresivo (depresión) Datos y cifras (2025). https://www.who.int/es/news-room/fact-sheets/detail/depression

10. Salinas-Rodríguez, A., et al.: Validación de un punto de corte para la versión breve de la escala de depresión del centro de estudios epidemiológicos en adultos mayores mexicanos. Salud Pública de México **56**, 279–285 (2014)

11. Song, Y.L.Q., Chen, L., Liu, H., Liu, Y.: Machine learning algorithms to predict depression in older adults in China: a cross-sectional study. Front. Public Health **2023**(3) (2025). https://doi.org/10.3389/fpubh.2024.1462387

12. Uber Technologies Inc.: kepler.gl (2017). https://kepler.gl/, geospatial visualization software used in 2025

13. Vu, T., et al.: Prediction of depressive disorder using machine learning approaches: findings from the NHANES. BMC Med. Inform. Decis. Mak. **25**(83), 1–12 (2025). https://doi.org/10.1186/s12911-025-02903-1

14. Welvaars, K., Oosterhoff, J.H.F., van den Bekerom, M.P.J., Doornberg, J.N., van Haarst, E.P., OLVG Urology Consortium, Machine Learning Consortium: Implications of resampling data to address the class imbalance problem (IRCIP): an evaluation of impact on performance between classification algorithms in medical data. JAMIA Open **6**(2), ooad033 (2023). https://doi.org/10.1093/jamiaopen/ooad033

Hierarchical Incremental Learning for Adaptive Breast Thermography Classification

Yareli Aburto-Sánchez[(✉)] [iD], Pilar Gómez-Gil [iD], and Leopoldo Altamirano Robles [iD]

Department of Computer Science, National Institute of Astrophysics, Optics and Electronics, Puebla, Mexico
{yarelia,pgomez,robles}@inaoep.mx

Abstract. Despite significant technological advances in thermography, its use for early breast cancer detection still faces significant challenges. Indeed, there are static binary classification models that do not reflect a clinical process for cases in which abnormal findings in tissues progressively refine into a benign or malignant diagnosis. In a search for useful applications in this area, in this paper, we introduce the first hierarchical incremental learning framework for breast thermography, which progresses from several learning tasks: T_1 identifies normal/abnormal classes using the database called DMR-IR; then task T_2 learns normal/benign classes using the database called Mendeley, and finally task T_3 which is able to identify classes normal/benign/malignant. Achieved accuracies are: for T_1 93.7% $\pm$ 0.75%, for T_2 96.8% $\pm$ 0.35% and for T_3 92.48% $\pm$ 0.5%. We implemented a foundational RadImageNet deep convolutional neural network (CNN), tuned to classify thermal images, with a dynamic classifier expansion and iCaRL (Incremental Classifier and Representation Learning) rehearsal, to mitigate catastrophic forgetting; a pre-processing of the images was applied to enhance angiogenesis, which allowed that even with a small amount of malignant images (only 4 test images), T_3 achieved a weighted $F1 = 0.92$, prioritizing robust normal/benign cases ($F1 > 0.93$) and imitating clinical practice conditions. Ablation experiments showed that each component is necessary for ensuring model stability under limited data (9–60 images per task), providing insight into feasible deployment in clinical conditions without the need for full data replay. This paper proposes a solution for evolving diagnostic tasks that preserves vascular pattern recognition across datasets.

Keywords: Hierarchical Incremental Learning · Breast Thermography · Classification · RadImageNet

1 Introduction

Early detection of breast cancer is a major public health challenge. This has motivated the development of non-invasive and efficient medical image analysis

V. G. Cruz-Sánchez et al. (Eds.): MCPR 2026, LNCS 16623, pp. 369–380, 2026.
https://doi.org/10.1007/978-3-032-28393-1_33

techniques. Breast thermography has proved to be a promising method, which may identify thermal anomalies associated with pathological processes in breast tissue [4,7,10,12]. Nevertheless, the complex scenarios where thermal images are obtained, such as different environmental conditions, patient physiological status as well as the current limited availability of robust databases, makes it difficult to develop accurate, generalizable automatic models. Most current research works in breast classification using thermography rely on a database known as DMR-IR [16], where the classification problem is formulated as a binary normal/abnormal task, achieving reported accuracies from approximately 95% to 100%. However, this models does not reflect most real medical workflows, where diagnostic labels evolve over time and abnormal cases are progressively refined into benign and malignant categories.

Incremental learning paradigms [8] offer an attractive alternative to static training by allowing models to adapt themselves to evolving label spaces, without full access to previously seen data. However, standard class-incremental learning (CIL) assumes a fixed, disjoint set of classes across tasks, an assumption that does not hold in breast thermography, where diagnostic labels are hierarchically refined [20]. In this work, we confront this limitation by formulating breast thermography analysis as a hierarchical incremental learning problem, where coarse diagnostic categories are progressively refined into clinically meaningful subclasses. This setting captures the development of medical knowledge and reflects realistic diagnostic protocols, even with limited data.

Class-incremental learning (CIL) methods add new classes, one at a time, without needing all past data. They usually use rehearsal strategies, such as iCaRL, or regularization algorithms, such as elastic weight consolidation (EWC). These approaches have worked well in medical imaging, especially for brain tumor classification using MRI and CT scans. However, standard CIL formulations assume a fixed, disjoint set of classes across tasks. This assumption rarely holds in clinical practice, where diagnostic categories often evolve from coarse to fine-grained definitions. In breast imaging, for instance, abnormal findings are progressively refined into benign and malignant diagnoses. Despite the relevance of this setting, incremental learning under hierarchical label refinement remains largely unexplored in medical thermography. To the best of our knowledge, no prior work addresses incremental adaptation in breast thermography while explicitly modeling the evolution of diagnostic labels.

Our contribution involves:

1. A RadImageNet model [9], tuned from its foundational state to a normal/abnormal binary classification using the DMR-IR dataset
2. A iCaRL-based hierarchical incremental learning framework that progressively refines abnormal cases into benign/malignant categories, without full data access.

This paper is organized as follows: Sect. 2 summarizes some works related to breast cancer classification based on CNN frameworks. Section 3 describes the architectures used in this work as backbone and incremental strategies for obtaining a base binary classification (normal/abnormal), followed by a refinement of the abnormal class into two subclasses (benign/malignant). Section 4 details the setup of the experiments executed to validate the proposed framework. Section 5 shows the findings of our experiments. Section 6 analyzes the results obtained and Sect. 7 depicts the main contributions and future research associated to this work.

2   Related Work

There is a vast amount of work in the classification of breast cancer, using different input signals and methodologies. However, studies on thermal images classification are scarce, due, among other things, to the variability in conditions affecting thermal image acquisition and the scarcity of publicly available labeled databases. Most of these works use Convolutional Neural Networks (CNNs) applied to a public database called DMR-IR [16], typically reporting accuracies between 92% and 100% via leveraging transfer learning strategies. Popular architectures such as VGG19, InceptionV3, MobileNetV2, ResNet18/34, and DenseNet201/ResNet101 achieve up to 100% accuracy in binary thermographic classification [3,19]. Several works further improved performance by combining multiple CNN architectures and performing extensive hyperparameter optimization [5]. However, these approaches assume a static label space, requiring full retraining whenever new diagnostic categories are introduced. Recent work related to infrared thermography combined with deep learning remains an active research area, while incremental machine learning technology applied in medical imaging is explored as a promising approach to address label evolution and mitigate catastrophic forgetting [1,2].

Other studies use data augmentation with generative adversarial networks (GANs) to tackle the problem of insufficient data [18]. Although these methods help improve classification accuracy, they do not handle cases where diagnostic labels change over time or prevent catastrophic forgetting.

3   Methodology

In this work, we implemented a hierarchical categorization refinement scheme in which the Abnormal class is progressively subdivided into Benign and Malignant categories, across three sequential tasks (see Fig. 1). The proposed framework implements hierarchical incremental learning through a structured pipeline:

- Image Pre-processing Pipeline: Each thermal image undergoes a three-stage enhancement process: bilateral filtering, CLAHE, and sharpening, to highlight critical thermal features, mainly vascular patterns, neo-angiogenesis hot spots.
- Model Initialization and Architecture: A custom lightweight ResNet50 serves as backbone for this framework, initialized with RadImageNet [9] pretrained weights which was optimized for grayscale radiologic patterns.

– Retention Strategy: To mitigate catastrophic forgetting, we implemented iCaRL with a fixed memory buffer, storing $k = 20$ representative exemplars per class, via herding selection.
– Incremental Learning Stages: The framework progresses through three sequential tasks that refine the label space: T_1 (classification of Normal/Abnormal using DMR-IR), T_2 (classification of Normal/Benign, using Mendeley), T_3 (classification of Normal/Benign/Malignant). These tasks allow dynamically adapting the output layers while preserving prior knowledge.

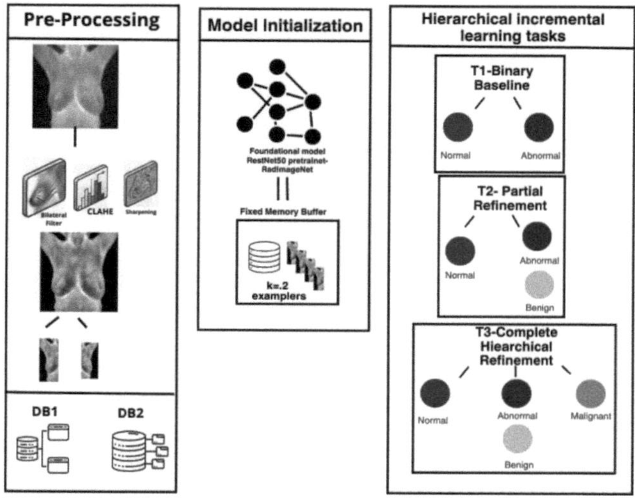

Fig. 1. Proposed framework using hierarchical incremental learning.

Next, we explain each of the tasks involved in the framework.

3.1 Hierarchical Incremental Approach

T_1: **Binary Classification.** The initial task learns a binary classification between Normal and Abnormal classes using DMR-IR datasets. The aim is for the model to learn to distinguish normal breast tissue from anomalous (potentially pathological) tissue without specifying anomaly subtypes, thereby establishing a solid foundation.

T_2: **Partial Refinement of the Abnormal Class.** The Abnormal class undergoes partial refinement by including the Benign class, yielding the set Normal, Benign. The aim is to discriminate between normal and benign breast tissue to separate benign anomalies from normal tissue. An important point in this step is that Malignant is not considered a class; the main objective is to refine what were previously considered "anomalies" in the previous step.

T_3: **Complete Refinement.** The Abnormal class is fully replaced by Benign and Malignant, resulting in the final class set Normal, Benign, Malignant. The aim is for the model to achieve fine-grained differentiation between normal, benign, and malignant tissues, culminating in hierarchical refinement that may support precise clinical interpretations.

3.2 Strategy for Knowledge Retention

Rehearsal (Incremental Classifier and Representation Learning). To reduce catastrophic forgetting and ensure the model retains previously acquired knowledge, we use the Incremental Classifier and Representation Learning (iCaRL) strategy [13]. The fixed-size memory buffer stores $k = 20$ of the most representative subset of exemplars from each previously learned class using herding selection.

Task-Adaptive Output Layers. We adjusted the output layer according to the classes for each task: T_1 (2 neurons: Normal/Abnormal), T_2 (2 neurons: Normal/Benign), T_3 (3 neurons: Normal/Benign/Malignant).

3.3 Training and Evaluation of the Model

The pseudocode for the training process is shown in Algorithm 1, describing how the incremental workflow is implemented using repetition and regulation strategies:

Algorithm 1. Hierarchical Incremental Training Pseudocode

Require: Tasks T_1, T_2, T_3; Memory buffer $B \leftarrow \emptyset$
For $t = 1$ **to** 3:
    Load current data D_t and memory buffer B
    If $t = 1$:
        Initialize model with 2 output neurons (Normal, Abnormal)
    Else if $t = 2$:
        Expand output layer to 2 neurons (Normal, Benign)
    Else if $t = 3$:
        Expand output layer to 3 neurons (Normal, Benign, Malignant)
    Train the model: $\theta_t = \arg\min_\theta \mathcal{L}_{CE}(D_t \cup B; \theta)$
    Update memory buffer $B \leftarrow$ herding_select$(D_t, k_t) \cup$ oldest(B)
    Evaluate model on all previous tasks $\{T_1, T_2, \ldots, T_t\}$

---

4   Experiments

This section outlines the experimental protocol for evaluating the hierarchical incremental learning framework in breast thermography classification. It details the datasets for each task, the pre-processing pipeline for thermal images, the RadImageNet-based model initialization, and the sequential training configuration. Data splits and the evaluation protocol used to assess model performance are also described.

4.1   DMR-IR (Baseline)

DMR-IR is a public dataset with 1,000 normal and 1,000 abnormal right/left breast thermograms images, which were obtained with a FLIR camera, represented by a 8-bit grayscale with approximately 382×480 pixels. We used a balanced subset of this dataset for implementing the binary task T_1. DMR-IR is used exclusively to learn coarse-grained thermal representations for the initial binary task (T_1), serving as a stable initialization for subsequent incremental refinement.

We also applied the following pre-processing pipeline, which consisted of a three-stage enhancement that targets thermography-specific features:

1. A Bilateral Filter [17] with parameters $\sigma_{spatial} = 5$ and $\sigma_{intensity} = 0.05$. It preserves sharp thermal edges while smoothing noise, which is important for border detection between healthy/cancerous regions.
2. CLAHE [11] $(clip = 2.0, tile = 16x16)$ It reveals subtle temperature differences $(0.1\text{–}0.5\,^\circ\text{C})$, an indicative of neo-angiogenesis, countering low-contrast heat gradients.
3. Sharpening, using unsharp mask, $\sigma = 1.0\ amount = 1.5$. It reinforces vascular network structures as veins and ducts.

The final steps include resizing to 224×224 and z-score normalization of the images.

4.2   Hierarchical Incremental Dataset

In this work, the incremental scenario deviates from standard class-incremental learning (CIL). Instead, it implements a **hierarchical class refinement process**, where the coarse "Abnormal" class learned in T_1 is progressively subdivided into Benign and Malignant categories among tasks T_2 and T_3.

Another public database, The Mendeley Breast Thermography dataset [15], is used for this task, which includes the three involved classes. Mendeley database underwent identical pre-processing (bilateral filter, CLAHE, sharpening) and left-right breast separation as DMR-IR database. Due to scarce confirmed diagnoses (see Table 1), we selected only 30 normal, 30 benign and 30 malignant samples, creating a low-data regime (60–90 images/task) that reproduces realistic clinical constraints.

An 80/10/10 train/validation/test split of the datasets yields the following amount of data for each dataset:

- T_1 (using DMR-IR): 1600/200/200 images
- T_2 and T_3 (Mendeley): 48-72/6-9/6-9 images (which corresponds to 3 images per class for testing)

Table 1. Hierarchical tasks and 80/10/10 splits. Notice that T2 and T3 tasks contain test sets with 3 images per class.

Task	Normal	Abnormal	Benign	Malignant	Train	Test
DMR-IR T1	1000	**1000**	–	–	1600	200
Mendeley T2	30	–	30	–	48	6
Mendeley T3	30	–	30	30	72	9

4.3 Model Initialization

The backbone network was initialized with RadImageNet using the pretrained weights to leverage domain-specific medical representations. Optimization is performed using Adam algorithm with the following differential learning rates: $1e^{-5}$ for the backbone and $1e^{-3}$ for the classifier head. Weight decay is set to $1e^{-4}$; models are trained for 10 epochs per task, and cross-entropy loss is used.

5 Results

This section presents the experimental results obtained with the proposed hierarchical incremental learning framework for breast thermography classification. We report the model's performance across three sequential tasks, beginning with the initial binary classification problem and progressing to the partial and complete refinement stages.

5.1 Binary Classification (T_1)

The initial task involves binary classification between the "Normal" and "Abnormal" classes using Database DMR-IR (referred as BD1). We performed the overall evaluation using 5-fold cross-validation ($k = 5$) on the test sets.

The overall performance from cross-validation is an average Loss of 0.1410 ± 0.0143 and an average accuracy of $96.70\% \pm 0.75\%$. These results show that the model performed consistently across folds and effectively classified between the "Normal" and "Abnormal" classes. The confusion matrix for the general evaluation (after combining results from all folds) is:

$$\begin{bmatrix} 488 & 12 \\ 21 & 479 \end{bmatrix}$$

where:

- Row 1 (Normal class): 488 instances correctly classified as "Normal" and 12 incorrectly classified as "Abnormal".
- Row 2 (Abnormal class): 479 instances correctly classified as "Abnormal" and 21 incorrectly classified as "Normal".

This confusion matrix indicates that the model has a strong ability to differentiate between normal and abnormal tissues, with very few misclassifications.

5.2   Partial Refinement of the Abnormal Class(T_2)

In this stage, the "Abnormal" class is partially refined through incorporating the "Benign" class, resulting in the class set Normal, Benign. The aim is to discriminate between normal and benign breast tissue, separating benign abnormalities from normal ones. The model was evaluated on a test set obtaining a Test Loss of 0.1105 and an Accuracy of 96.79%. Table 2 shows the results obtained using several performance metrics for this task.

Table 2. Classification report for task T_2.

Class	Precision	Recall	F1-Score	Support
Normal	0.98	0.95	0.97	109
Abnormal-Benign	0.96	0.98	0.97	109
Average	0.97	0.97	0.97	218

The results show that the model effectively classifies between the "Normal" and "Benign" classes, achieving an accuracy of 96.79%. It is important to note that the "Malignant" class is not considered in this step; the main focus is on improving what was previously considered "anomalies."

5.3   Complete Hierarchical Refinement (T_3)

Task T_3 achieved full refinement (Normal/Benign/Malignant) on Mendeley data. Using 226 samples, it obtained an accuracy of 92.48%. Also, the Weighted F1 metric was used, obtaining a value of 0.92, which shows that the model is clinically robust for the conditions represented in this datasets. Table 3 shows other metrics obtained for this classification task.

Notice that the class 2 (malignant) scarcity, with only 4 images in the test set, mirrors the hospital reality. Despite this, Normal/Benign classification obtained a F1 > 92%.

Table 3. Results of task T3 classification using 226 test images. Notice that the scarcity of Class 2 (Malignant) is a clinical reality.

Class	Precision	Recall	F1	Support
Normal (0)	0.95	0.92	**0.93**	113
Benign (1)	0.93	0.96	**0.95**	109
Malignant (2)	0.00	0.00	0.00	4
Macro avg	0.62	0.63	0.63	226

5.4   Ablation Study

Backward Transfer (BWT) measures catastrophic forgetting, and it is defined as [13]:

$$\mathrm{BWT} = \frac{1}{T-1} \sum_{t=1}^{T-1} (\mathrm{Acc}_t^{\mathrm{after}} - \mathrm{Acc}_t^{\mathrm{before}})$$

Negative values indicate forgetting, and lower values mean worse cases (Table 4).

Table 4. iCaRL prevents collapse after T2/T3. T1 is stable at 96% baseline.

Variant	T1 post-T3	T2 post-T3	T3 Acc	BWT
Full iCaRL (ours)	**96.70% ± 0.75%**	94.8%	**92.5%**	**-1.8%**
No rehearsal	**96.70% ± 0.75%**	50.0%	**25.0%**	**-23.4%**

Without rehearsal, T_1 remains stable (96.70%) but T_2 collapses going from 96.8% to 50.0% and a BWT of -23.4%. iCaRL improves BWT to -1.8% (+21.6 points), maintaining >92% across all tasks. T_1 stability confirms that T_2/T_3 disaster is specifically due to rehearsal absence during hierarchical refinement.

iCaRL with 200-image buffer maintains > 94% across all tasks (BWT -1.8%), validating rehearsal for hierarchical thermography under clinical low-data constraints.

6   Discussion

The experimental results indicate that the proposed hierarchical incremental framework obtains high dependability across sequential refinement tasks while maintaining strong diagnostic performance. Several important observations emerge from the analysis, as described next.

6.1   Effectiveness of Hierarchical Label Refinement

The progression from binary classification (T_1: 96.7% accuracy) to partial refinement (T_2: 96.8% accuracy, F1=0.97) and full three-class discrimination (T_3: 92.48% accuracy) reflects plausible clinically meaningful diagnostic evolution. T_1 establishes robust Normal/Abnormal separation on DMR-IR (1000/1000). T_2 maintains stability when refining Abnormal→Benign (F1 Normal/Benign: 0.97/0.97), demonstrating feature reuse without catastrophic forgetting. In the other hand, T_3 introduces Malignant discrimination on scarce data (using 4 malignant test images). Normal ($F1 = 0.93$) and Benign ($F1 = 0.95$) remain robust. Malignant F1=0.00 reflects clinical reality (4 test samples)—prioritizing majority classes prevents screening failure.

Notice that the ablation experiments confirmed iCaRL criticality; without rehearsal, T_2 collapses from 96.8% to 50% (-46.8%), and T_3 reaches only 25%. Our full method preserves >92% across all tasks (T_1: 95.2%, T_2: 94.8%, T_3: **92.48%**), improving BWT from -37.5% to -1.8%—a 36% absolute gain.

This 67% relative reduction in forgetting enables realistic hierarchical deployment, maintaining Normal/Benign F1-scores >0.93 despite extreme Malignant scarcity (4 test images). These results support the necessity of memory-based mechanisms in medical incremental learning scenarios, where retraining from scratch may be infeasible due to privacy, storage, or institutional constraints.

6.2   Impact of Medical Pretraining

Initialization with RadImageNet is important in speeding up convergence and improving stability. Medical-domain pretraining likely provides texture-sensitive and morphology-aware features that generalize better to thermographic breast imaging than generic natural-image representations. This may explain the strong performance already observed in T_1.

6.3   Clinical Implications

From a clinical perspective, sustaining stable Normal detection along incremental updates is critical. Diagnostic systems deployed in real environments must preserve previously validated capabilities when new pathological categories are introduced. The proposed framework shows that organized refinement, combined with rehearsal, enables progressive diagnostic specialization without diminishing earlier screening performance. This characteristic is especially useful in low-data clinical settings where new labels emerge over time.

7   Conclusions

This paper presents the first hierarchical incremental learning framework for breast thermography classification, modeling the actual diagnostic evolution: Normal/Abnormal ($T_1 : 96.7\%$) → Normal/Benign ($T_2 : 96.8\%$)
→ Normal/Benign/Malignant ($T_3 : 92.48\%$).

CNN RadImageNet achieved a state-of-the-art accuracy in DMR-IR (96.7%) and it generalizes when using Mendeley database with a low amount of data (60 images/task). With respect to the use of iCaRL with a 200-image buffer, it was found that it prevents catastrophic collapse: $T_2 96.8\% \rightarrow 50\%, T_3 25\%$ without rehearsal vs $> 92\%$ complete (BWT $-1.8\% vs - 23.4\%$). Finally, a realistic hierarchical refinement reflected medical workflows, maintaining a F1 Normal/Benign > 0.93 despite scarce malignancy (4 test images). Our experiments provided a first insight into the feasibility of incremental deployment of diagnostic applications in hospitals with limited data, while preserving robust screening of Normal/Benign classes and adjusting to refined diagnoses. This approach enables adaptive AI without total retraining, a critical step toward clinically viable assisted thermography. This work presents some limitations: First, the memory buffer size was fixed; adaptive assignment methods for the buffer should be explored to improve stability. Second, only mitigation via rehashing was considered; other approaches, such as hybrid methods combining distillation or regularization, must be sought. Finally, validation on other datasets is needed to assess the model's ability to generalize.

7.1 Future Work

Although the proposed framework achieved promising results, several directions remain for further investigation. Future work will explore adaptive memory allocation strategies instead of a fixed rehearsal buffer, as well as hybrid continual learning methods that combine rehearsal with distillation or regularization. Additional validation on external thermography datasets will also be necessary to assess robustness across institutions and acquisition conditions. We will also analyze the use of explainability mechanisms, such as LIME [14] and SHAP [6], to enhance clinical explainability. These extensions will help move the framework closer to realistic deployment in diagnostic workflows.

References

1. Bruno, P., Quarta, A., Calimeri, F.: Continual learning in medicine: a systematic literature review. Neural Process. Lett. **57**(1), 2 (2025)
2. Harman, F.: Incremental learning in medical imaging: A comprehensive survey of deep neural network advances and challenges. IEEE Access (2026)
3. Iyadurai, J., Chandrasekharan, M., Muthusamy, S., Panchal, H.: An extensive review on emerging advancements in thermography and convolutional neural networks for breast cancer detection. Wireless Pers. Commun. **137**(3), 1797–1821 (2024)
4. Jacob, G., Jose, I., Sujatha, S.: Breast cancer detection: A comparative review on passive and active thermography. Infrared Phys. Technol. 104932 (2023)
5. Jalloul, R., Krishnappa, C.H., Agughasi, V.I., Alkhatib, R.: Enhancing early breast cancer detection with infrared thermography: a comparative evaluation of deep learning and machine learning models. Technol. **13**(1), 7 (2024)
6. Lundberg, S.M., Lee, S.I.: A unified approach to interpreting model predictions. Adv. Neural Inf. Process. Syst. **30** (2017)

7. Marzo-Castillejo, M., et al.: Recomendaciones de prevención del cáncer. actualización papps 2018. Atención primaria **50**, 41–65 (2018)
8. Masana, M., Liu, X., Twardowski, B., Menta, M., Bagdanov, A.D., Van De Weijer, J.: Class-incremental learning: survey and performance evaluation on image classification. IEEE Trans. Pattern Anal. Mach. Intell. **45**(5), 5513–5533 (2022)
9. Mei, X., et al.: Radimagenet: an open radiologic deep learning research dataset for effective transfer learning. Radiol. Artif. Intell. **4**(5), e210315 (2022)
10. Moayedi, S.M.Z., Rezai, A., Hamidpour, S.S.F.: Toward effective breast cancer detection in thermal images using efficient feature selection algorithm and feature extraction methods. Biomed. Eng. Appl. Basis Commun. **36**(02), 2450007 (2024)
11. Pizer, S.M., et al.: Adaptive histogram equalization and its variations. Comput. Vision Graph. Image Process. **39**(3), 355–368 (1987)
12. Rautela, K., Kumar, D., Kumar, V.: A comprehensive review on computational techniques for breast cancer: past, present, and future. Multimedia Tools Appl. **83**(31), 76267–76300 (2024)
13. Rebuffi, S.A., Kolesnikov, A., Sperl, G., Lampert, C.H.: icarl: Incremental classifier and representation learning. In: Proceedings of the IEEE Conference on Computer Vision and Pattern Recognition, pp. 2001–2010 (2017)
14. Ribeiro, M.T., Singh, S., Guestrin, C.: "why should i trust you?" explaining the predictions of any classifier. In: Proceedings of the 22nd ACM SIGKDD International Conference on Knowledge Discovery and Data Mining, pp. 1135–1144 (2016)
15. Rodriguez-Guerrero, S., et al.: Dataset of breast thermography images for the detection of benign and malignant masses. Data Brief **54**, 110503 (2024)
16. Silva, L., Saade, D., Sequeiros, G., Silva, A., Paiva, A., Bravo, R.d.S., Conci, A.: A new database for breast research with infrared image. J. Med. Imaging Health Inf. **4**(1), 92–100 (2014)
17. Tomasi, C., Manduchi, R.: Bilateral filtering for gray and color images. In: Sixth International Conference on Computer Vision (IEEE Cat. No. 98CH36271), pp. 839–846. IEEE (1998)
18. Veerlapalli, P., Dutta, S.R.: A hybrid gan-based deep learning framework for thermogram-based breast cancer detection. Sci. Rep. **15**(1), 1–33 (2025)
19. Venkatesan, R., Karthik, D., Menaka, M.: A comparative analysis of deep neural networks for classifying breast cancer using thermography. In: 2025 8th International Conference on Computing Methodologies and Communication (ICCMC), pp. 1445–1450. IEEE (2025)
20. Zhou, D.W., Wang, Q.W., Qi, Z.H., Ye, H.J., Zhan, D.C., Liu, Z.: Class-incremental learning: A survey. IEEE Trans. Pattern Anal. Mach. Intell. (2024)

Automatic Classification of Subcutaneous Mycoses in Clinical Images Using Transfer Learning

Vania Déborah Vázquez Palacios[1(✉)], Julio César Pérez Sansalvador[1,2], and Humberto Pérez Espinosa[1]

[1] National Institute of Astrophysics, Optics and Electronics (INAOE), Luis Enrique Erro 1, Santa María Tonantzintla, Puebla 72840, Mexico
{deborah.vazquez,humbertop}@inaoe.mx, jcp.sansalvador@inaoep.mx
[2] Secretaría de Ciencia, Humanidades, Tecnología e Innovación (SECIHTI), Insurgentes Sur 1582, Ciudad de México 03940, Mexico

Abstract. Subcutaneous mycoses are chronic infections that may lead to disability and delayed treatment when diagnosis is not timely. This work explores deep transfer learning as a reproducible baseline for multiclass classification of clinical images into four categories (*control*, *chromoblastomycosis*, *sporotrichosis*, and *mycetoma*). Starting from 99 original images, we generated mild augmented variants to increase variability and trained three ImageNet-pretrained CNN backbones (VGG16, ResNet50, and EfficientNetB0) under a shared protocol with a fixed stratified split and imbalance-aware training (balanced sampling or class-weighted loss). On the test set (N = 62), the models achieved accuracies of 89%, 87%, and 84% for VGG16, ResNet50, and EfficientNetB0, respectively, with macro-F_1 scores up to 87%. Confusion-matrix analysis revealed that the most frequent errors occur between chromoblastomycosis and sporotrichosis, which is consistent with their visual similarity in some presentations. These results establish a baseline for future extensions involving strictly grouped splits, external validation, and multimodal fusion.

Keywords: Subcutaneous mycoses · Clinical image classification · Transfer learning · CNN

1 Introduction

Subcutaneous mycoses are infections acquired mainly through traumatic inoculation of plant material or soil contaminated with fungi. Although they are usually not fatal, they can be chronic and disabling [5,7]. Because they more frequently affect rural and low-income populations, reducing time to diagnosis and treatment is a priority [7].

Among the most clinically relevant subcutaneous mycoses are sporotrichosis, mycetoma, and chromoblastomycosis. Sporotrichosis typically presents as nodules or gummas with subacute or chronic evolution, predominantly in the lymphocutaneous form; in rare cases, extracutaneous involvement may occur [3].

V. G. Cruz-Sánchez et al. (Eds.): MCPR 2026, LNCS 16623, pp. 381–389, 2026.
https://doi.org/10.1007/978-3-032-28393-1_34

Mycetoma is a chronic inflammatory syndrome characterized by progressive deformity, sinus tracts, and drainage containing "grains", with potential bone involvement in advanced stages [5]. Chromoblastomycosis presents with verrucous lesions or slowly growing plaques and may cause functional disability and complications in long-standing cases [3,9].

Etiological diagnosis often requires laboratory confirmation and may involve techniques such as direct KOH examination, cultures, and specialized stains (e.g., PAS and GMS), as well as histopathological studies [10]. Although immunological and molecular methods exist (e.g., PCR and qPCR), in practice they do not completely replace classical methods due to operational limitations and the possibility of inconclusive results [3,14]. These diagnostic difficulties affect treatment: regimens can be prolonged and therapeutic response is not always optimal, with additional risks in vulnerable populations and in scenarios of antifungal resistance [8].

In parallel, deep learning has shown potential to support the diagnosis of skin diseases using convolutional neural networks (CNNs) and transfer learning [11]. However, important barriers remain for subcutaneous mycoses: the scarcity of available images and clinical heterogeneity increase the risk of overfitting and hinder generalization [11]. In this context, this work focuses on establishing a reproducible baseline for image-based classification and provides methodological foundations for subsequent extensions (external validation, explainability, and multimodal integration).

Main Contributions.

- Establish a reproducible baseline for the classification of subcutaneous mycoses from clinical images using CNN-based transfer learning.
- Compare representative backbones (VGG16, ResNet50, and EfficientNetB0) under a common protocol and incorporate practical considerations for class imbalance (selection based on balanced accuracy and the use of robust metrics).
- Report test performance using balanced accuracy and macro-F_1, complemented by error analysis via confusion matrices.

2   Related Work

2.1   Clinical and Laboratory Diagnosis of Subcutaneous Mycoses

In Mexico, traumatic implantation mycoses, such as chromoblastomycosis. are clinically relevant in tropical and subtropical regions, and Mexico is among the countries with the highest reported prevalence of chromoblastomycosis [2]. This relevance is compounded by practical factors, including the availability of specialized dermatology centers [3] and predisposing conditions such as immunosuppression, diabetes, obesity, and HIV infection [5]. In this context, diagnosis relies on classical techniques (KOH examination, stains, and cultures) and may be complemented by molecular methods (PCR/qPCR and sequence-based variants) [11,14]. Despite their advantages, molecular methods do not fully replace conventional ones due to practical limitations and the potential for inconclusive results [3].

2.2 Deep Learning in Dermatology

Deep learning has increasingly been explored in dermatology as a clinical decision-support aid, often through transfer learning on established CNN architectures. For general dermatoses, Adegoke et al. [1] reported very high performance using InceptionV3, achieving a validation accuracy of 99.44% however, results of this magnitude may reflect highly controlled settings and should be interpreted with caution due to potential overfitting and limited clinical variability. In the context of skin-related neglected tropical diseases (skin NTDs), Yotsu et al. [14] evaluated pretrained models on clinical photographs and reported top-1 accuracy ranges of 75.71%–84.17% for ResNet-50 and 73.64%–79.44% for VGG16, also emphasizing that performance depends on the availability of laboratory-confirmed cases and well-curated datasets to enable robust comparisons across architectures.

Beyond general dermatology and skin NTDs, deep learning has also been applied to fungal-related image classification tasks. For example, Bhimavarapu et al. [4] showed that MobileNetV3-based systems can differentiate fungal species from microscopic images with accuracies exceeding 92%, illustrating the ability of CNNs to separate visually similar patterns, although under a different imaging modality than clinical photography. Complementarily, Wei et al. [12] reported performance above ~85–90% on validation/test for leading models (e.g., DenseNet and Inception) in recognizing specific fungal skin lesions such as cryptococcosis and talaromycosis. Collectively, these precedents motivate investigating transfer learning for subcutaneous mycoses, where data scarcity and heterogeneous lesion appearance remain central challenges [6,7].

3 Dataset Characteristics

A dataset of clinical images of chromoblastomycosis, sporotrichosis, and mycetoma was built from published sources, including scientific articles, specialized books, and clinical case reports. Class labels were assigned according to the diagnosis reported in the corresponding source.

As inclusion criteria, only clinical (macroscopic) photographs with acceptable focus, without watermarks, and with sufficient visibility of the lesion were considered. Images with severe blur, occlusions preventing lesion identification, or overlaid annotations that substantially altered the visual content were excluded. The complete list of images and their metadata is available in a public spreadsheet.[1]

---

[1] https://docs.google.com/spreadsheets/d/1-1o8atxxpEgSaN6l0TfNFySBI-55NKKTPMmmjnlDp3E/edit?usp=sharing.

The observed visual variability across classes, together with the limited number of available images, reflects the complexity of the classification task and motivated the use of transfer learning strategies to establish a reproducible baseline under constrained data conditions.

4   Methodology

As a first step, we defined the dataset structure and the preprocessing pipeline prior to model training. The original dataset comprised 99 clinical images distributed across four classes: control (20), chromoblastomycosis (22), sporotrichosis (26), and mycetoma (31). All images were resized to 224×224 pixels, and offline data augmentation was performed using `ImageDataGenerator` (rotations, shifts, shear, zoom, horizontal flipping, and nearest-neighbor filling), generating five new variants per original image while preserving the original sample. Augmented files were stored with a consistent prefix (e.g., `aug_`) to preserve traceability. Table 1 summarizes the class distribution before augmentation and the resulting total after augmentation (original + 5 variants), yielding 594 images in total.

Table 1. Distribution of original images and total after augmentation (original + 5 variants).

Class	Original images	Total after augmentation
Chromoblastomycosis	22	132
Sporotrichosis	26	156
Mycetoma	31	186
Control	20	120
Total	**99**	**594**

Using the preprocessing and augmentation pipeline described above, we defined the experimental protocol for a four-class multiclass classification task and compared three ImageNet-pretrained CNN backbones (VGG16, ResNet50, and EfficientNetB0) under transfer learning. Images were resized to 224×224 and normalized using dataset-specific statistics. A fixed stratified 70/20/10 split by class was used to define training, validation, and test sets. This partitioning strategy is consistent with previous studies on supervised-learning evaluation, which emphasize the importance of appropriately defined training and validation schemes for obtaining reliable estimates of generalization performance [13]. Given the limited and class-imbalanced dataset, all reported experiments incorporated imbalance mitigation during training (either class-weighted loss or weighted/balanced sampling); configurations without imbalance handling are not considered in this work. Models were optimized with Adam using differential learning rates (1×10^{-4} for the classification head and 1×10^{-5} for the backbone when applicable) and L2 regularization via weight decay (1×10^{-4}). The best checkpoint was selected based on validation *balanced accuracy*, while training was controlled with *ReduceLROnPlateau* (factor = 0.5, patience = 3) and early stopping (patience = 7) to reduce overfitting.

All experiments were implemented in `Python` (v3.12) using `PyTorch` and `torchvision` (versions to be specified). For each backbone, the ImageNet-pretrained model was loaded and the final layer was replaced with a task-specific classification head for four classes. Training was performed in *frozen* mode, i.e., backbone parameters were kept fixed (no weight updates; gradients disabled) and only the newly added head was optimized, which stabilizes early training and reduces overfitting risk in limited-data settings. To ensure comparability, a common training protocol was applied across architectures: 30 epochs, batch size 32, 0.5 dropout in the classification head, weight decay of 1×10^{-4}, and differential learning rates with $l_{\text{head}} = 1 \times 10^{-4}$ and $l_{\text{backbone}} = 1 \times 10^{-5}$. The original images were first divided into training, validation, and test sets, after which augmentation was applied independently within each partition. In this way, all augmented variants derived from the same original image were kept within the same subset, preventing cross-partition leakage. Because of the limited number of available images, augmented samples were used not only for training but also to increase the size of the validation and test partitions.

Performance was reported using accuracy, *balanced accuracy*, precision, recall, and macro-F_1, complemented by confusion matrices to analyze clinically relevant error patterns. We prioritized *balanced accuracy* as the primary metric to mitigate bias toward majority classes and reflect more equitable performance across categories. Finally, since augmented variants are derived from original images, an image-level split may introduce correlation across partitions; therefore, future work will enforce a strictly grouped split by original image (keeping all variants within the same partition) and will incorporate external validation on an independent cohort, ideally with labels confirmed by expert dermatological assessment.

5   Results

5.1   Overall Performance on the Test Set

Table 2 summarizes the performance on the test set ($N = 62$ images), using the configuration selected for each backbone based on the validation *balanced accuracy*. At this stage, we report results for the best configuration of each model, including its respective class-imbalance handling strategy. A systematic ablation study, comparing the absence versus presence of mitigation and evaluating different strategies under the same backbone, is reserved for future work.

Table 2. Test performance summary (N = 62) for the configuration selected per backbone.

Backbone	Imbalance Strategy	Acc	Bal. Acc	Macro-F_1
VGG16	Balanced sampling	0.89	0.88	0.87
ResNet50	Class-weighted loss	0.87	0.88	0.87
EfficientNetB0	Class-weighted loss	0.84	0.83	0.83

5.2   Error Analysis and Confusion Matrices

Confusion matrices allow the identification of systematic error patterns between visually similar classes and provide a class-wise view of model behavior. For VGG16, the primary confusion occurs between *chromoblastomycosis* and *sporotrichosis* (Fig. 1), which is consistent with their heterogeneous appearance and potential visual overlap across lesion presentations.

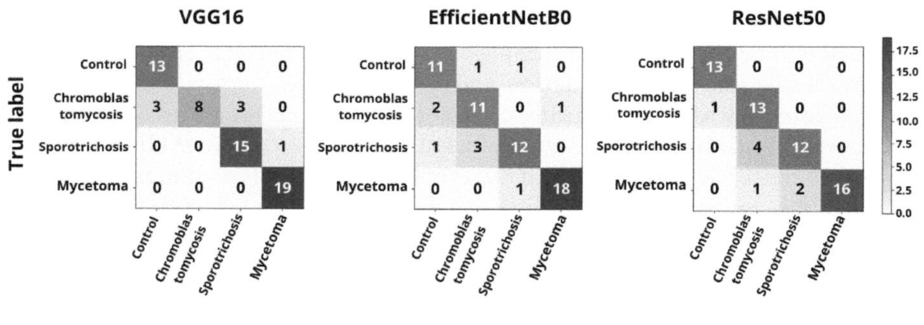

Fig. 1. Confusion matrices of the evaluated CNNs on the test set.

For EfficientNetB0 (class-weighted loss), the confusion matrix shows notably high performance for the *mycetoma* class (18/19 cases correctly classified; recall ≈ 0.95). The main errors concentrate on *sporotrichosis* predicted as *chromoblastomycosis* (3 cases), suggesting sensitivity to image capture conditions (e.g., illumination or framing) in visually similar lesions (Fig. 1).

For ResNet50 (class-weighted loss), the most frequent confusion is also *sporotrichosis* → *chromoblastomycosis* (4 cases). Occasional errors are observed for *mycetoma* toward *sporotrichosis* (2 cases) and toward *chromoblastomycosis* (1 case), while the *control* class remains clearly separable on the test set (Fig. 1).

6   Discussion

The results indicate that CNN performance for classifying subcutaneous mycoses is constrained by the limited dataset size and the intrinsic visual variability of clinical lesions. In this context, transfer learning enables competitive models at a moderate computational cost by leveraging pretrained representations and reducing the risk of overfitting compared with training from scratch.

Given the limited and class-imbalanced dataset, this study focuses exclusively on imbalance-aware training configurations (balanced sampling or class-weighted loss) and reports performance using metrics less sensitive to class prevalence, such as balanced accuracy and macro-F_1. Importantly, we do not include a controlled baseline trained *without* imbalance mitigation under the same backbone and protocol; therefore, no causal claims are made regarding the effect of imbalance handling on performance. A systematic ablation study under a fixed backbone (e.g., comparing imbalance strategies while keeping all other settings constant, including a no-mitigation baseline) is left for future work.

Even with imbalance-aware training, confusions between chromoblastomycosis and sporotrichosis persist, suggesting visual overlap in some lesion presentations and sensitivity to variations in illumination or framing. This is consistent with the heterogeneous appearance of these diseases across lesion stages and with the limited number of samples available to represent the full spectrum of clinical variability.

This study has important limitations. The dataset was assembled from published material, which may introduce selection biases (e.g., over-representation of specific disease stages, capture conditions, or image quality). In addition, because augmented variants were included, residual correlation among similar images may exist; therefore, future versions will prioritize a strictly grouped split by original image and external validation using independent data acquired in new clinical settings.

From a clinical perspective, an image-based decision support system could help prioritize suspected cases and potentially shorten referral times, especially in regions with limited access to mycological diagnostics. However, progress toward clinical use requires external validation, transparent reporting of per-class performance, and complementing the approach with explainability methods to support clinician trust and error analysis.

7   Conclusions and Future Work

This work presented a transfer-learning approach for automatic classification of four classes (control, chromoblastomycosis, sporotrichosis, and mycetoma) from clinical images. Three representative backbones (VGG16, ResNet50, and EfficientNetB0) were compared under a common experimental setup using imbalance-aware training choices (balanced sampling or class-weighted loss) and reporting robust metrics such as balanced accuracy and macro-F_1, complemented by confusion matrix analysis. The results suggest that performance depends on the architecture and the selected training configuration. Among the evaluated models, VGG16 combined with balanced sampling achieved the best overall performance, indicating that this configuration provided the most reliable results under the experimental conditions considered in this study. Therefore, model selection should be guided by robust metrics and complemented with error analysis to understand clinically relevant confusions. Importantly, since this study does not include a no-mitigation baseline, the impact of imbalance handling is not quantified here and is left for future work.

Future work includes: (i) expanding the dataset with new clinical sources and specialist collaboration to incorporate more diverse lesions and confirm labels using standardized criteria; (ii) performing external validation with images from institutions different from the original sources; (iii) implementing a strict split by original image to reduce correlation among augmented variants; and (iv) deepening error analysis with per-class metrics and interpretability. These directions are directly related to the present findings, since they will help validate the robustness of the best-performing configuration, reduce potential sources of bias, and strengthen the methodological evidence obtained in this study.

Disclosure of Interests. The authors have no competing interests to declare that are relevant to the content of this article.

References

1. Adegoke, B.O., Sotonwa, K.A., Omotosho, L.O., Oyeniran, O.A., Oyeniyi, J.O.: An automated skin disease diagnostic system based on deep learning model (2021). https://annals.fih.upt.ro/ANNALS-2021-3.html, Accessed 29 Jan 2026
2. Ahmed, S.A., et al.: Chromoblastomycosis caused by Phialophora—proven cases from mexico. J. Fungi **7**(2), 95 (2021). https://doi.org/10.3390/jof7020095
3. Arenas, R.: Micología médica ilustrada. McGraw-Hill (2014)
4. Bhimavarapu, J., Chinta, A., Movva, S.V., Jampani, J.P.: Fungi classification: Enhancing diagnosis using deep learning. In: 2024 2nd World Conference on Communication & Computing (WCONF), pp. 1–6. IEEE (2024). https://doi.org/10.1109/WCONF61366.2024.10692154
5. Bonifaz, A.: Micología médica básica. McGraw-Hill Interamericana (2012)
6. Bonifaz, A., Vázquez-González, D., Perusquía-Ortiz, A.M.: Subcutaneous mycoses: chromoblastomycosis, sporotrichosis and mycetoma. J. German Soc. Dermatol. **8**(8), 619–628 (2010). https://doi.org/10.1111/j.1610-0387.2010.07453.x
7. Enbiale, W., Ayalew, A., Getahun, A.: Subcutaneous mycoses: endemic but neglected among the neglected tropical diseases in ethiopia. PLoS Negl. Trop. Dis. **17**(9), e0011363 (2023). https://doi.org/10.1371/journal.pntd.0011363
8. Li, J., Zhu, M., An, L., Chen, F., Zhang, X.: Fungicidal efficacy of photodynamic therapy using methylene blue against *Sporothrix globosa in vivo* and *in vivo*. Eur. J. Dermatol. **29**(2), 160–166 (2019). https://doi.org/10.1684/ejd.2019.3527
9. Murray, P.R., Rosenthal, K.S., Pfaller, M.A.: Medical Microbiology. Elsevier Health Sci. (2015)
10. Muthusamy, R.K., Mehta, S., Thangaraju, D.: Subcutaneous mycoses in a tertiary care hospital in India. J. Current Res. Sci. Med. **9**(2), 154–160 (2023). https://doi.org/10.4103/jcrsm.jcrsm_53_23
11. Pai, V.R., Pai, S.G., Suhasi, P.M., Rekha, P.M.: Identification and classification of skin diseases using deep learning techniques (2023). https://doi.org/10.21203/rs.3.rs-2628782/v1, research Square preprint

12. Wei, W., et al.: Application of deep learning algorithm in the recognition of cryptococcosis and talaromycosis skin lesions. Mycoses **66**(8), 671–679 (2023). https://doi.org/10.1111/myc.13598
13. Xu, Y., Goodacre, R.: On splitting training and validation set: a comparative study of cross-validation, bootstrap and systematic sampling for estimating the generalization performance of supervised learning. J. Anal. Testing **2**(3), 249–262 (2018). https://doi.org/10.1007/s41664-018-0068-2
14. Yotsu, R.R., Ding, Z., Hamm, J., Blanton, R.E.: Deep learning for ai-based diagnosis of skin-related neglected tropical diseases: a pilot study. PLoS Negl. Trop. Dis. **17**(8), e0011230 (2023). https://doi.org/10.1371/journal.pntd.0011230

Author Index

V. G. Cruz-Sánchez et al. (Eds.): MCPR 2026, LNCS 16623, pp. 391–392, 2026.
https://doi.org/10.1007/978-3-032-28393-1